Business and Professional Communication:

Principles and Skills
for Leadership

Steven A. Beebe
Texas State University—San Marcos

Timothy P. Mottet
The University of Texas—Pan American

Allyn & Bacon

Boston   New York   San Francisco
Mexico City   Montreal   Toronto   London   Madrid   Munich   Paris
Hong Kong   Singapore   Tokyo   Cape Town   Sydney

Acquisitions Editor: Jeanne Zalesky
Assistant Editor: Megan Lentz
Marketing Manager: Blair Tuckman
Production Supervisor: Beth Houston
Editorial Production Service: Lifland et al., Bookmakers
Manufacturing Buyer: JoAnne Sweeney
Electronic Composition: Nesbitt Graphics, Inc.
Interior Design: Gina Hagen
Photo Researcher: Poyee Oster
Cover Administrator: Joel Gendron

Library of Congress Cataloging-in-Publication Data
Beebe, Steven A., 1950-
  Business and professional communication : principles and skills for leadership / Steven A. Beebe, Timothy P. Mottet.
    p. cm.
  Includes bibliographical references and index.
  ISBN 978-0-205-48591-8
  1. Communication in management. 2. Business communication. 3. Leadership. 4. Communication. I. Mottet, Timothy P. II. Title.
  HD30.3.B42 2010
  658.4'5--dc22
                    2009019695

10 9 8 7 6 5 4 3 2 1 WEB 13 12 11 10 09

Allyn & Bacon
is an imprint of

www.pearsonhighered.com

ISBN-10: 0-205-48591-X

ISBN-13: 978-0-205-48591-8

Dedicated to

Sue Beebe
　　　—SAB

Rick Gonzalez
　　　—TPM

Brief Contents

Contents

Chapter 3 | *Using Verbal and Nonverbal Messages* 46

Chapter 4	*Listening and Responding*	69

Chapter 7 | *Interviewing Principles and Skills*   *142*

Chapter 8 | *Interview Types*   *166*

PART III   **COLLABORATION SKILLS**

Chapter 9 | *Collaborating in Teams*   *191*

Chapter 12 | *Supporting and Organizing Professional Presentations*　　274

Appendix A | *Writing for Business*   *361*

Appendix B | *Managing Time: Managing Communication*   *379*

Preface

We agree with James Humes, who said, "The art of communication is effective leadership." Consequently, this book is about two things: communication and leadership. Communication and work go hand in hand; it's hard to talk about the workplace without also talking about the communication that makes work happen. Closely linked to any discussion of workplace communication is the art and science of leading others. To be effective in the twenty-first-century workplace, you need to be able to communicate and influence others in positive and ethical ways. The purpose of this book is to prepare readers for the communication and leadership demands of the modern workplace by presenting key communication principles and skills that will allow them to be successful in business and professional settings.

A Focus on Communication Principles

As students begin their study of business and professional communication and glance at this book's table of contents, the number of terms, ideas about leadership and communication, and skills that are covered may seem overwhelming. To help them make sense out of the information that we present, we've organized our study of business and professional communication around five fundamental communication principles, as shown below, that can enhance their communication skill and leadership abilities. Together, these five principles provide readers with a framework for understanding how communication works at work. Following are the five principles that form the basis of this book:

   Principle One: Be aware of your communication with yourself and others.

   Principle Two: Effectively use and interpret verbal messages.

   Principle Three: Effectively use and interpret nonverbal messages.

   Principle Four: Listen and respond thoughtfully to others.

   Principle Five: Appropriately adapt messages to others.

   The communication principles we emphasize should look familiar—they are included in most introductory communication courses as well as in most business and professional communication textbooks. They are also the principles that are presented

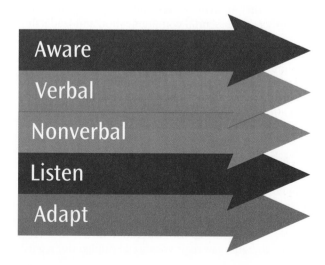

Aware

Verbal

Nonverbal

Listen

Adapt

in our companion book, *Communication: Principles for a Lifetime*, by Steven A. Beebe, Susan J. Beebe, and Diana K. Ivy.

In most business and professional communication texts, communication principles are introduced early and then are rarely explicitly mentioned. In contrast, we clearly integrate core communication principles into our discussion of business and professional communication skills. We introduce the five principles in Chapter 1 and make explicit references to them throughout the book. We also include a margin icon, like the one included in the margin here, to highlight discussions of the principles as we apply them to business and professional communication skills. In addition, we summarize chapter content from the perspective of these principles at the end of each skill development chapter.

These five principles showcase decades of research as well as the wisdom of those who have taught communication and corollary leadership skills during the past century. We don't claim that they represent *everything* you need to know about communication and leadership. They do, however, summarize considerable knowledge about the communication process and what constitutes effective communication and about how to ethically influence others in business and professional settings.

A Focus on Communication Skills

We believe a course in business and professional communication should develop students' communication competence. To be effective in business and professional settings is to be a skilled communicator. That's why we've linked the five fundamental principles of human communication to three communication skill sets that are vital to effective performance in the workplace.

First, we connect the five communication principles to the skill of relating to others. Relationship skills are essential in working with others in a variety of business and professional arenas. In addition to helping students understand how professional relationships are established and maintained, we focus on specific skills they can use to relate to others, such as how to interview others, how to be interviewed, and how to manage interpersonal conflict.

Collaborating with others is a second skill set that we focus on in Chapters 9 and 10. Working in groups and teams and attending and leading meetings occupy a considerable amount of time in the contemporary work environment. Whether collaborating face to face or in electronically mediated situations, today's workers must not only understand the goals of working collaboratively, they must have the skills to work together effectively. We focus on skills that help provide necessary structure to accomplish tasks and help manage the interaction that occurs as workers collaborate and relate to others. Solving problems and making decisions as a team and unleashing the creative potential of groups are key skills that are emphasized in Chapters 9 and 10.

Finally, in addition to relating and collaborating, contemporary workers are frequently called on to present their ideas to others. Whether in one-on-one conversations, during meetings, or in presentations to larger audiences, being able to present information to others as well as to persuade others are essential communication and leadership competencies.

Rather than presenting communication skills as an array of unrelated behaviors, we show how the five fundamental communication principles, developed in the early chapters, inform the three skill sets of relating, collaborating, and presenting. As shown in the model on the facing page, we link each of the five fundamental communication principles to the skills that are needed to be an effective communicator.

A Focus on Leadership

Leadership and communication skill go hand in hand. As suggested by the book's subtitle, *Principles and Skills for Leadership*, the communication principles and skills we discuss are presented to enhance students' leadership talent. Although some students may aspire to an influential leadership role, such as being chief executive officer at a large company, many others are simply trying to figure out their vocational calling. But regard-

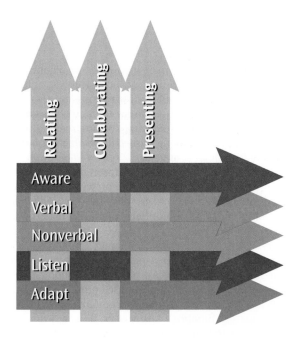

less of how lofty students' professional goals are, in the contemporary workplace they *will* influence others through the way they communicate with people. A person need not be officially appointed in order to be a leader. That's why we've infused our discussion of business and professional communication with principles and skills for leadership.

Beginning in Chapter 1, we introduce students to key leadership approaches and then explicitly discuss how communication principles and skills are integral to being an effective and ethical leader. Although most business and professional communication textbooks include a discussion of leadership, we believe that being an effective leader depends on being an effective communicator in the workplace. So every chapter includes discussion and references to leadership principles and skills. And because we believe an effective leader is also an ethical leader, we include a feature called Communication Ethics @ Work that emphasizes the importance of acting in ethical ways.

Overview of the Book

The opening chapter provides a prelude to the study of business and professional communication by presenting an explication of communication models and concepts. We then introduce the five communication principles and show how those principles are linked to the critical skills of relating, collaborating, and presenting. We also introduce students to an overview of the study of leadership during the past century.

Chapters 2 through 5 present each of the five communication principles in more detail. Chapter 2 discusses the principle of being aware of self and others (Principle 1), noting how a person's social style reflects his or her self-concept as well as his or her perceptions of others. Getting students to understand their approach to leadership and the role of organizational culture also helps enhance their awareness of themselves and others. Chapter 3 presents the key principles of using and interpreting verbal messages (Principle 2) and nonverbal messages (Principle 3). Chapter 4 identifies the core process of listening and responding to others (Principle 4). Chapter 5 helps students adapt to others (Principle 5) by understanding how personality, culture, and gender influence how we send and interpret messages.

Having given readers a firm understanding of the fundamental principles of human communication, in the remaining chapters of the book we apply the principles of communication to the three most important skill sets used in business and professional contexts: relating, collaborating, and presenting. We begin with the skill of relating to others: Chapter 6 describes different types of workplace relationships and emphasizes how to understand and manage conflict at work. Chapters 7 and 8 cover essential information to help students relate to others during interviews. Chapter 7 emphasizes core principles and skills of interviewing. Chapter 8 identifies the classic types of interviews that are most often encountered in business and professional settings: information gathering interviews, job interviews, and appraisal interviews.

Building on the skill of relating to others in interpersonal contexts, we next turn our attention to collaborating with others. Chapter 9 helps students apply the five communication principles to a variety of group and team situations and also helps students understand how teams work. Chapter 10 focuses on the ubiquitous business meeting and how to make meetings effective. Skills for enhancing decision making, problem solving, and creativity in meetings are presented, along with skills for facilitating meeting discussion, avoiding groupthink, and reaching consensus.

The final section of the book presents four chapters that discuss the vital professional skill of presenting messages to others. Chapter 11 prescribes how to develop a message, including how to focus on the audience and establish speaker credibility. Chapter 12 helps students find and use interesting and appropriate supporting material and organize a message for maximum clarity and impact. How to deliver a presentation and use a wide array of visual and auditory support is the focus of Chapter 13. The last chapter, Chapter 14, offers tips and strategies for informing, persuading, and presenting special kinds of speeches in professional settings. Particular emphasis is placed on developing business briefings and reports as well as on using persuasive strategies to sell products and services to others.

Two appendixes apply the five principles of communication to special business and professional communication functions. Appendix A is a primer on writing skills. Appendix B offers strategies to help students manage their time and improve their work productivity using key time-management and communication-management strategies.

Special Features to Help Students Learn: Our Partnership with Students and Instructors

It is our hope that rather than viewing this textbook as an inert compilation of words, students will see interactive connections between the principles and skills we discuss and their business and professional careers. To that end, we've incorporated several pedagogical features to connect the book's content to students' professional lives. Our special features help turn information into a responsive communication message that applies communication principles and skills to their careers in meaningful ways.

Principles Model

We illustrate the importance of the five fundamental communication principles with a model introduced in Chapter 1 that provides the overarching structure for the book. The colorful model, which reappears in several chapters to reinforce the five principles, gives students a clear visual referent to help the principles stick in their minds and inform their practice.

Principles Icons

To ensure that students never lose sight of how the information they are learning relates to the five fundamental principles, we've included margin icons to highlight information that embodies one or more of the communication principles that anchor our discussion.

Chapter-End Principles Summary

Beginning with Chapter 6, our first chapter to emphasize communication skills, we conclude each chapter with a cogent summary of how the chapter content reflects each of the five communication principles. Thus, students not only have margin icons to help them see connections between the principles and the text we present, they have a crisply presented summary to help them clinch their understanding of the chapter content as it relates to each of the five communication principles.

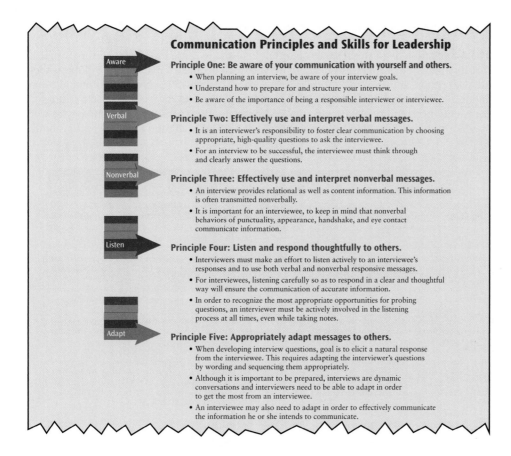

Communication Principles and Skills for Leadership

Principle One: Be aware of your communication with yourself and others.
- When planning an interview, be aware of your interview goals.
- Understand how to prepare for and structure your interview.
- Be aware of the importance of being a responsible interviewer or interviewee.

Principle Two: Effectively use and interpret verbal messages.
- It is an interviewer's responsibility to foster clear communication by choosing appropriate, high-quality questions to ask the interviewee.
- For an interview to be successful, the interviewee must think through and clearly answer the questions.

Principle Three: Effectively use and interpret nonverbal messages.
- An interview provides relational as well as content information. This information is often transmitted nonverbally.
- It is important for an interviewee, to keep in mind that nonverbal behaviors of punctuality, appearance, handshake, and eye contact communicate information.

Principle Four: Listen and respond thoughtfully to others.
- Interviewers must make an effort to listen actively to an interviewee's responses and to use both verbal and nonverbal responsive messages.
- For interviewees, listening carefully so as to respond in a clear and thoughtful way will ensure the communication of accurate information.
- In order to recognize the most appropriate opportunities for probing questions, an interviewer must be actively involved in the listening process at all times, even while taking notes.

Principle Five: Appropriately adapt messages to others.
- When developing interview questions, goal is to elicit a natural response from the interviewee. This requires adapting the interviewer's questions by wording and sequencing them appropriately.
- Although it is important to be prepared, interviews are dynamic conversations and interviewers need to be able to adapt in order to get the most from an interviewee.
- An interviewee may also need to adapt in order to effectively communicate the information he or she intends to communicate.

Communication Ethics @ Work Feature

A text on communication and leadership that fails to emphasize ethics could lead students to conclude that the goal of one's professional career is to win at all costs using any method that achieves results. We disagree with that conclusion. Effective communicators are ethical communicators. That's why we've included a special feature that relates chapter content to an ethical issue or question. These boxes can be used for student reflection, class discussion, or assignments to help students see relationships between doing well and doing good.

>>> **COMMUNICATION ETHICS** @ WORK

Evaluating your own ethical business practices is one way for you to become aware of your communication with yourself and others. Use the following self-assessment guide to identify your ethical strengths and weaknesses.[34] Answering "Yes" to any of the questions below can suggest some areas where you may be ethically weak.

- Have I conducted personal business on company time?
- Have I used or taken company resources for personal purposes?
- Have I called in sick when I really wasn't?
- Have I used a derogatory term when referring to another person?
- Have I told or passed along an ethnic joke or sexually oriented joke?
- Have I engaged in negative gossip or spread rumors about someone?
- Have I "bad mouthed" the company or management to co-workers?
- Have I pried into a co-worker's conversations or private affairs?

- Have I passed along information that was shared with me in confidence?
- Have I knowingly ignored or violated an organizational rule or procedure?
- Have I failed to follow through on something I said I would do?
- Have I withheld information that others needed?
- Have I "fudged" on a time sheet, billing sheet, estimate, or report?
- Have I knowingly delivered a poor quality or defective good or service?
- Have I lied or manipulated the truth to make a sale?
- Have I accepted an inappropriate gift or gratuity?
- Have I taken credit for something that someone else did?
- Have I failed to admit to or correct a mistake I made?
- Have I knowingly let someone make an error and get into trouble?

Communication and Globalization @ Work Feature

The combination of greater reliance on technology and increased workplace diversity means that today's workers are just as likely to interact with people from around the globe as they are with people in their own workplaces. We want students to see how the communication and leadership principles and skills they are learning apply to diverse workplace settings in the twenty-first century. We provide tips and strategies for working with technology as well as adapting to colleagues and customers who have different cultural or ethnic backgrounds.

>>> **COMMUNICATION AND GLOBALIZATION** @ W O R K

Founded in 1991 by Stanford professor and designer David Kelley of David Kelley Designs, IDEO was recently featured on the popular innovative business website FastCompany.com as among the fifty most innovative companies in the world. IDEO helps organizations innovate through design, and the company focuses on three things: the design, the service, and the human element. David Kelley is a human resources leader. His leadership style is grounded in the assumption that employees are assets that can be developed. In addition to helping companies design new products and solve problems, IDEO also helps companies re-engineer their corporate cultures to focus on the development of human resources. According to Kelley, its focus on the consumer and worker experience has made IDEO one of the most successful and effective international design firms. Among IDEO's clients are AT&T, Nestle, Intel, Lufthansa, and Samsung.

Although there are many facets about IDEO that set it apart as a different kind of organization, the company's commitment to the human experience has helped catapult it to international success. The company is innovative not only in terms of new product designs, but also in terms of new experiences. In a project with Kaiser Permanente, a health maintenance organization, IDEO researchers determined that business was declining in Kaiser hospitals because patients and families were unhappy with the overall aesthetic experience of the hospitals and waiting rooms. After revamping waiting rooms and expanding emergency rooms to accommodate both patients and family, Kaiser found that the answer to increasing business was not building expensive new facilities. Rather, overhauling the patient experience was all that was needed to make people choose a Kaiser hospital.

The corporate atmosphere at IDEO also reflects a human resources approach to leadership in which innovation and creativity are guiding norms. IDEO executives believe in letting the people lead. IDEO employs over 350 people, including scientists, engineers, designers, and researchers who work together in teams. The employees decorate their respective work areas any way they wish, and collaboration is the key to innovation at IDEO. As IDEO has shown, when you take innovative design ideas and integrate them into the human experience, the results are not only effective, but also profitable.[19]

Communication Skills @ Work Feature

A business and professional communication course should be grounded on principles and theory but should also help students apply their knowledge to real-world situations. In the workplace, communication is an *applied* art. We therefore emphasize how to translate the principles we present to enhance students' communication skills. To augment our practical application of communication principles, we present special features to help students enhance their skill in communicating with others on the job.

>>> **COMMUNICATION SKILLS** @ W O R K

Because physical appearance influences ability to lead in the workplace, it's important that you pay attention to this important source of nonverbal communication. Here are a few suggestions for how to communicate a professional physical appearance at work:

- *Monitor physical appearance standards.* Observe how a number of your co-workers dress in your office, unit, or division. What type of clothing are they wearing (suits, sport coats and slacks)? How are they wearing their clothing (shirts tucked in, hanging out)? What type of shoes are they wearing (open-toed or closed, wingtips, sneakers)? How much jewelry do they wear (earrings, nose studs)? What about their hairstyles (pulled back or down, facial hair)?
- *Match the formality of your manager's appearance.* Observe your manager: If you're uncertain of appearance standards, it's always a good thing to match your manager's appearance in terms of formality. Your manager ultimately sets the standards for appearance in your work unit. Is your boss's appearance formal, or is it more relaxed?
- *Dress for the occupation.* Another appearance suggestion is to dress for the job or the occupation. Most occupations have an established standard for dress and grooming. For example, most bankers dress in dark suits, construction foremen wear jeans and steel-toed boots, and school principals wear khakis, white shirts, and blazers.
- *When in doubt, dress for the job you want.* Whenever you're in doubt about how you should dress and appear in the workplace, it's best to dress for the job you would like to have one day. In other words, appear more formal than informal. A more formal appearance gives the impression that you care about your work and your organization. Appearing too informal can give the opposite impression.
- *Appear neat and well groomed.* It is assumed that we will appear neat and well groomed when we go to work. Appearing neat means wearing clothing that is clean and pressed, shoes that are clean and polished, and appropriate artifacts (for example, a belt, a briefcase). Appearing well-groomed means being bathed, making sure your hair is styled, and having fresh breath and clean fingernails.

Chapter-End Activities and Applications

Each chapter concludes with additional material to help students apply the chapter content to their lives. The chapter-end material also helps instructors augment class discussion with activities, assignments, and resources to extend chapter content. Specifically, we provide discussion questions to help prompt class discussion or to be used by students as a study aid. To complement the in-text Communication Skills @ Work feature, we provide even more skill-building activities at the end of each chapter.

Discussion Questions

1. Describe the five stages in the listening process. How are these stages interrelated?

2. Identify listening barriers that can be encountered at work. Give a personal example of an experience of each.

3. Choose one of the listening barriers mentioned in the chapter, and explain a strategy for overcoming this barrier.

4. Explain three steps for listening effectively to others.

5. What are the three skills for effectively responding to others? Give examples.

6. List five strategies we can use to help others listen to us. Why is it important to help others listen?

Building Your Skills

1. Assess your receiver apprehension by completing the following assessment measure.[69] Respond to each item by indicating the extent to which it describes you using the following scale: 5 = Strongly agree, 4 = Agree, 3 = Sometimes, 2 = Disagree, 1 = Disagree

____ 1. When I am listening I feel nervous about missing information.

____ 2. I worry about being able to keep up with the material being presented in class.

____ 3. Sometimes I miss information in class because I am writing notes.

____ 4. I feel tense and anxious when I am listening to important information.

____ 5. I am concerned that I won't be able to remember information I've heard in lectures and discussions.

____ 6. Although I try to concentrate, my thoughts sometimes become confused when I'm listening.

____ 7. I worry that my listening skill is not very good.

Recap Boxes and Chapter Summaries

Educational theorists confirm that students learn through repetition. To make sure the key content is reinforced, we insert clear, cogent Recap boxes throughout the text to distill essential chapter content. We also provide a narrative summary of key information at the end of the early chapters to help students review and master the material.

Comprehensive Pedagogical Learning Resources

In addition to the Recap boxes and chapter summaries, we provide chapter-opening learning objectives and a brief outline of chapter content at the beginning of each chapter. We also define all boldfaced key terms in the margins and provide a Glossary at the end of the text.

Special Resources for Students

MyCommunicationKit is an online supplement that offers book-specific learning objectives, chapter summaries, flashcards, and practice tests as well as video clips and activities to aid student learning and comprehension. Also included in MyCommunicationKit are Research Navigator and weblinks, both of which provide assistance with and access to powerful and reliable research material. Available at www.mycommunicationkit.com (access code required).

In addition to MyCommunicationKit, the Pearson Business and Professional Communication Study Site is another great resource for students. This open-access website at www.abbpcomm.com includes practice tests (featuring essay and multiple-choice questions) and weblinks.

Special Resources for Instructors

The Instructor's Manual/Test Bank was prepared by Valerie Manno Giroux, University of Miami, and Charles Francis. The Instructor's Manual portion includes a sample syllabus, learning objectives, lecture outlines, and sample class discussion questions. The Test Bank contains multiple-choice, true/false, and essay questions for each chapter. Each question includes a reference to a page number and is rated by skill level.

The test questions are also available electronically through our new, web-based, computerized testing system, MyTest. The user-friendly interface enables instructors to view, edit, and add questions, transfer questions to tests, and print tests from any computer with Internet access. Available at http://www.pearsonmytest.com (access code required).

A PowerPoint Presentation Package, prepared by San Bolkan, California State University, Long Beach, is available for download at the Pearson Instructor's Resource Center, www.pearsonhighered.com/irc (access code required). This text-specific package provides PowerPoint slides for each chapter of the book, containing lecture outlines as well as figures and photos from the text. In addition, the Business and Professional Communication DVD includes video clips that emphasize the communication skills relevant to the professional world, such as interviewing and presenting. Available to adopters on request to a Pearson sales representative.

Acknowledgments

Although our two names appear on the cover, creating a book is a team project involving many people. We are grateful to the many individuals who helped us make this book a reality. We are indebted to the scholars and practitioners whose research and ideas inform the principles and skills that constitute the content of this book. We also are thankful for our students, past and present, who have helped us shape our approach to teaching. A textbook reflects our roles as both scholars and educators; our students continue to enrich our lives, and their questions, feedback (both encouraging and constructive), and very presence in our classrooms make us better authors.

We are especially thankful for the outstanding editorial support we have received from our colleagues and friends at Pearson/Allyn & Bacon. Karon Bowers, Pearson Editor-in-Chief, continues to be an important friend and mentor who is always there with needed support, information, and inspiration. Jeanne Zalesky, Acquisitions Editor for Communication, has provided exceptional encouragement and insight that has shaped our approach to this project. Our development editor, Hilary Jackson, has infused this book with intelligent creativity, a wealth of ideas, and considerable knowledge about writing and editing; she has been the perfect development editor to help us transform our vision into the words you are holding in your hand. Karen Black, a trusted friend and skilled researcher, has provided outstanding support in acquiring permissions for our book; her gift for attention to detail and her administrative talents enhanced our productivity. We also are indebted to Diana Ivy, a cherished friend, whose work informs this project, as we drew on the five communication principles that also appear in the book she co-authored.

We appreciate the many excellent educators and teachers who read the manuscript and helped us polish our prose and our ideas. We thank the following individuals for sharing their teaching skill, subject-matter expertise, and vast experience to make this a better book:

Shae Adkins, Lone Star College; Michele S. Foss-Snowden, California State University–Sacramento; Edwin Ray Fowler, El Paso Community College; Kim Gatz, Northern Illinois University; Valerie Manno Giroux, University of Miami; Stacey D. Gish, Western Kentucky University; Bob Harrison, Gallaudet University; Jacqueline Irwin, California State University–Sacramento; Amy Tilton Jones, Del Mar College; Brendan B. Kelly, University of West Florida; Jacqueline Layng, University of Toledo; Kelly Petkus, Austin Community College;

Jessica Samens, Minnesota State University–Mankato; Brian Sheridan, Mercyhurst College; Timothy Steffensmeier, Kansas State University; Amy Veuleman, McNeese State University; Elizabeth J. Vick, Northern Virginia Community College; Shirley J. Washburn, Roosevelt University; and Mark Zampino, University of Hartford.

We each have been influenced by colleagues, friends, teachers, and family members who have offered their support and inspiration for this project. Timothy is grateful for his former colleagues at Texas State University–San Marcos and for current colleagues at The University of Texas–Pan American (UTPA). Tim would like to give special thanks to Richard Cheatham, Sue Hall, Mary Hoffman, Sondra Howe, Marian Houser, and Phil Salem at Texas State, who were particularly supportive of this project. He would also like to thank his new colleagues at The University of Texas–Pan American—Yanrong Chang, Jeff McQuillen, Trey Mikolasky, Marian Monta, Liz Parker-Garcia, Jessica Parker-Raley, Marisa Saavedra, Kimberly Selber, Jack Stanley, and Sharon Valdes—who were extremely supportive during his transition to UTPA. Tim is especially grateful to Dora Saavedra for introducing him to a wonderful opportunity at UTPA, the Henry W. and Margaret Hauser Endowed Chair in Communication, and to the UTPA leadership team: Chair Salma Ghanem, Dean Dahlia Guerra, and Provost Paul Sale.

Another group of individuals who have supported Tim in the writing of this textbook are his former graduate students at Texas State's Teaching and Learning Academy and his graduate students at UTPA: Gil Castillo, Andrea Fuentes, Claudia Martinez, Rebekah Sepulveda, and Stephanie Shimotsu. Tim is particularly grateful to Katrina Newell, a very gifted graduate student from UTPA, who served as his research assistant on this book project. Tim's friendship with Steve and Sue Beebe, Jim McCroskey, Virginia Richmond, and Marilyn and Robert Root is a constant source of encouragement and guidance. He is grateful for the love of his family, including his parents Carol and Joe Mottet, as well as Julie and Rob Johnson, Dan and Barb Mottet, Doug and Jane Mottet, Maria and Alfredo Gonzalez, and Prieto and Anita Gonzalez. Finally, Tim would like to extend a very special thanks to Rick Gonzalez for his love, patience, understanding, and support. Tim is most appreciative of the inspiration he receives from Rick and for the education he has received from him. Halikalani.

Steve, too, is grateful for many friends and colleagues who have offered support and encouragement for this project. His colleagues in the Department of Communication Studies at Texas State University–San Marcos continue to be supportive of his research and writing endeavors. Steve is especially grateful for co-authors on other book projects, John Masterson, Mark Redmond, Diana Ivy, David Roach, and Sue Beebe, for influencing his ideas on this project. Steve is especially thankful for Tim Mottet's friendship and his collaboration on this project. He is also thankful to his friend and research colleague Kosta Tovstiadi for providing research support for this book. Consulting partners and friends Laurie Romig, Dennis Romig, and Jim Bell have significantly influenced this project through their skill in transforming research conclusions into practical applications. Jill Collett and Peter Collett, valued friends from Oxford, England, have provided helpful feedback and much-appreciated support. Sue Hall, Senior Administrative Assistant in the Department of Communication Studies and Steve's "right hand," Meredith Clayton, Administrative Assistant II, Sondra Howe, former graphic designer, and current graphic designer Malinda Murry have each provided outstanding support and skilled, professional assistance that has made this project a reality. Finally, Steve is grateful for the enduring support and love of his family. His sons, Mark and Matthew Beebe, have made the business of being a dad the most important life profession a person could have. Steve's in-laws, Herb and Jane Dye, continue to be a source of gentle graciousness and generous support. And his parents, Russell and Muriel Beebe, have offered a lifetime of ethical lessons and love and have demonstrated the power of a loving partnership through seven decades of marriage. Finally, this book (and every other book Steve has written) would not have been possible without the support, editorial expertise, encouragement, and thoughtful commentary provided by his life companion, best friend, and loving wife, Sue Beebe.

Steven A. Beebe
San Marcos, Texas

Timothy P. Mottet
Edinburg, Texas

Business and Professional Communication

Chapter 1
Communicating and Leading at Work

chapter outline

After reading this chapter, you should be able to

- Define communication and describe why communication is important.

- Identify and describe each of the five major communication principles.

- Explain the three major communication skill sets: relationship skills, collaboration skills, and presentation skills.

- Define leadership and explain the relationship between leadership and communication.

- Compare and contrast leading, managing, and following.

- Identify and describe six approaches to leadership.

Although you're probably not familiar with the name Howard Schultz, you are familiar with Starbucks. The company Schultz leads is the world's largest coffee retailer.[1] Schultz attributes his leadership success to his communication skills, which he developed as a communication major at Northern Michigan University.[2] Rather than communicating to employees, shareholders, and customers through advertising and mediated messages, Schultz prefers face-to-face communication. His ability to influence others has made him one of the world's most innovative leaders. According to Schultz, Starbucks is successful not because of high-gloss and expensive Madison Avenue advertising campaigns, but because of its grass-roots, word-of-mouth advertising based on the relationships that Starbucks employees form with customers. He even states, "Word of mouth, we discovered, is far more powerful than advertising."[3] Although Starbucks has had its ups and downs as a company, it has a leader who knows the importance of communication in helping Starbucks remain competitive.

This book is about two things: communication and leadership. Specifically, it's about how you can apply communication skills to lead in the workplace. Communication and work go hand in hand; it's hard to talk about the workplace without also talking about the communication that makes work happen. And closely linked to any discussion of workplace communication is the art and science of leading others. Leaders develop relationships, build teams, and make presentations before groups of people. To be effective in the workplace, you need to be able to use communication to influence others in positive and ethical ways.

> *The art of communication is the language of leadership."*
>
> —JAMES HUMES

You may think that you're not really interested in being a leader; you may just want to get a job and enjoy a productive life. Or, you may aspire to a major leadership role, such as chief executive officer at a large company. Regardless of your professional goals, and even if you don't aspire to be the next Donald Trump or Oprah Winfrey, you *will* influence others through the way you communicate with people. There is a difference between being a leader and exerting leadership influence. You don't have to be anointed "the leader" to use leadership skills. Whether or not you perceive yourself as a leader, regardless of your job title, you will influence others through the way you communicate with them.

People who communicate effectively do well on the job. Others find the communication demands of their jobs challenging.[4] The purpose of this book is to prepare you for the communication and leadership demands of the modern workplace by introducing you to key communication principles and skills to help you be successful at work.

As you begin your study of business and professional communication and glance at this book's table of contents, the number of leadership and communication terms, ideas, and skills that we'll discuss may seem overwhelming. To help you make sense out of the many ideas and the vast amount of information that we present, we will organize our study of business and professional communication around five fundamental principles that can enhance your communication skill and leadership abilities.[5] Together, these five principles provide you with a framework for understanding how communication works in the workplace:

> Principle One: Be aware of your communication with yourself and others.
>
> Principle Two: Effectively use and interpret verbal messages.
>
> Principle Three: Effectively use and interpret nonverbal messages.
>
> Principle Four: Listen and respond thoughtfully to others.
>
> Principle Five: Appropriately adapt messages to others.

These five principles indicate how to enhance not only your communication abilities but your leadership talents as well. You may be taking a course in business and professional communication with the hope of just getting a good job and keeping it. Or, perhaps you already have a job and you have visions of someday climbing a bit higher on the corporate ladder. Either way, we encourage you to consider your career not just in terms of your job but also in terms of your potential to lead others.

The five fundamental principles of communication operate together rather than independently and constitute a model of the key elements that enhance communication effectiveness. At the top of the model (Figure 1.1) is the principle of being aware of your communication with yourself and others. One of the first things you learned about yourself, when you were just an infant, is that you are a separate individual apart from others. You next learned that you could use verbal and nonverbal messages to influence others.

Figure 1.1 | Communication Principles for Leadership

Infants learn that expressing their displeasure (by crying) or pleasure (by smiling) results in reactions and responses from others. The fourth principle, listening and responding, develops after we've learned to express our thoughts and emotions verbally and nonverbally. Listening and responding to others helps you implement the fifth principle. The principle of adapting to others is a more sophisticated principle that assumes that you are aware of your messages and others' messages, that you have learned to use and interpret verbal and nonverbal messages, and that you listen and respond and then appropriately adapt your communication to accomplish your communication goals. Together these five principles help explain how we influence others through communication.

The five principles reflect decades of research as well as the wisdom of those who have taught communication and corollary leadership skills during the past century. We don't claim that everything you need to know about communication and leadership is covered by these five principles. They do, however, summarize considerable knowledge about the communication process and what constitutes effective communication and about how to ethically influence others in business and professional settings.

To lead is to influence others. You influence others through your communication. Thus, you lead by the way you communicate with others—so leadership and communication are inextricably linked. When you learn communication skills you are also learning leadership skills. Your very presence in an organization, regardless of your job title or level within the organization, will have an influence on others. By enhancing your communication competence you will also enhance your leadership abilities. To help you accomplish your professional goals, whether you work in a large corporation, a small business, or in a profession such as law, medicine, or education, this book will help you enhance what you'll spend most of your time doing at your job: communicating with others. And because of the link between communication and leadership, the five communication principles that serve as the basis for the many ideas, concepts, and skills that we present are also leadership principles.

Before elaborating on these five communication principles for leadership, we'll first discuss the nature of communication, as well as why it's important to develop effective communication skills. Then we provide an overview of the three sets of business and professional communication skills: relating, collaborating, and presenting.

Communication: Making Sense and Sharing Sense

JetBlue Airlines, a low-cost airline based in New York, apologized to its customers after it mismanaged its response to an ice storm and forced customers to remain on a JetBlue aircraft for 11 hours. JetBlue used its website as well as YouTube to offer an apology to the traveling public.[6] However, many of the company's customers never saw the apology. What JetBlue learned was that just placing a message on a website doesn't mean that communication has occurred. Communication happens not when a message is crafted and sent, but when the message has helped create meaning for someone. Let's explore the nature and definition of communication in more detail and also emphasize why being an effective communicator is a vital twenty-first-century workplace skill.

The Nature of Communication

Reduced to its essence, **communication** is the process of acting on information.[7] Someone does something or says something, and there is a response from someone else in the form of an action, a word, or a thought. As JetBlue Airlines learned, information is not communication. "I put it in the memo. Why didn't you do what I asked?" "It's in the company policy statement!" "It's on the website." These expressions of exasperation assume that if you send a message, someone will receive it. Communication does not operate, however, as a linear, input-output process. What you send is rarely what others understand. Human communication is more sophisticated than simply sending and receiving messages.

Human communication is the process of making sense out of the world and sharing that sense with others by creating meaning through the use of verbal and nonverbal messages.[8] Let's examine the key elements of this definition.

- *Communication is about making sense.* We make sense out of what we experience when we interpret what we see, hear, touch, smell, and taste. To make sense out of a message we look for patterns or structure and we relate what happens to us at any given moment to something we've experienced in the past. An effective communicator attempts to learn as much as possible about his or her listeners so that the message crafted makes sense to the listeners.

- *Communication is about sharing sense.* We share what we experience by expressing it to others and to ourselves. We use words as well as nonverbal cues (such as gestures, facial expressions, clothing, music) to convey our thoughts and feelings to others.

- *Communication is about creating meaning.* Meaning is created in the hearts and minds of both the message source and the message receiver. We don't send meaning, we *create* it, based on our experiences, background, and culture.

- *Communication is about verbal and nonverbal messages.* We use both words and nonwords (nonverbal behaviors) to create meaning. Words and nonverbal behaviors are symbols that you use to derive meaning that makes sense to you. A **symbol** is something—a word, sound, visual image, gesture, object—that represents a thought, a concept, another object, or an experience. The words on this page are symbols that you use to derive meaning that makes sense to you. Some symbols are nonverbal, such as your use of gestures, posture, tone of voice, clothing, and jewelry. Nonverbal messages primarily communicate emotions and attitudes—our feelings of joy or sadness, our likes and dislikes, or whether we're interested or uninterested in others.

Our definition of human communication suggests that the message we express is not always the message that is interpreted. Making sense and sharing sense with others is a fragile process. It's also a transactional process that occurs both in person and via mediated channels such as via text message or email.

Human communication is transactional. When we communicate with another person who is physically present, the communication is **transactional**, meaning that messages are sent and received simultaneously. As you talk to someone, you also respond to that person's verbal and nonverbal messages, even while you speak.[9] Whether in a brief visit in someone's office or in a meeting, and even if you remain silent (or embarrassingly, nod off to sleep), your nonverbal behavior provides information to others about your emotions and interest or lack of interest. The transactive nature of communication suggests that you cannot *not* communicate. Ultimately, people judge you by your behavior, not by your intent. And since you always behave in some way (even when you are asleep), there is the potential for someone to make sense out of your behavior.

Communication the process of acting on information.

Human communication the process of making sense out of the world and sharing that sense with others by creating meaning through the use of verbal and nonverbal messages.

Symbol a word, sound, visual image, gesture, or object that represents a thought, a concept, another object, or an experience.

Transactional occurring simultaneously.

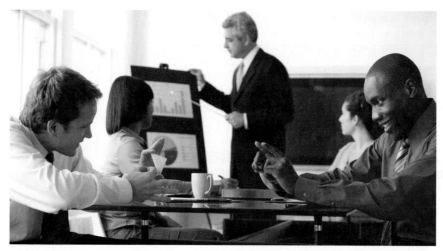

The behavior of these employees communicates their lack of interest in the presentation being given. Communication doesn't have to be verbal.

Source the originator of a thought or emotion, who puts it into a code that can be understood by a receiver.

Encoding the process of translating ideas, feelings, and thoughts into a code.

Decoding the process of interpreting ideas, feelings, and thoughts that have been translated into a code.

Message written, spoken, and unspoken elements of communication to which people assign meaning.

Receiver the person who interprets a message.

Channel the means by which a message is expressed to the receiver.

Noise interference, either literal or psychological, that hinders the accurate encoding or decoding of a message.

Feedback the response to a message.

Context the physical, historical, and psychological environment in which communication occurs.

Content the new information, ideas, or suggested actions that a speaker wishes to express.

Leaders typically communicate using transactive communication assumptions. When a team member is going through a difficult time, leaders stop what they're doing and spend time listening and talking to the team member. Leaders who are paying close attention to the team members' nonverbal messages and are carefully listening to them can adapt their communication accordingly to meet team members' communication needs without team members having to ask for help. Leaders and team members together create messages and meanings by closely paying attention to each other's verbal and nonverbal messages and by adapting their communication accordingly.

The components of human communication. Key elements of communication include source, message, channel, and receiver. The **source** of a message is the originator of the ideas and feelings expressed. The source puts a message into a *code* that can be understood by a receiver. Putting ideas, feelings, and thoughts into a code is called **encoding**. Just the opposite of encoding is the process of **decoding**; this occurs when the receiver interprets the words or nonverbal cues generated by the source. The **message** is the information being communicated. The **receiver** of the message is the person or persons who interpret the message. The **channel** is the means by which the message is expressed to the receiver. If you're typical, you receive messages through a variety of channels—through face-to-face conversation as well as through your phone or your computer.

As we've emphasized, what we express isn't always interpreted as we intend. Noise happens. **Noise** is anything that interferes with a message being interpreted as it was intended. If there were no noise, then all of our messages would be interpreted accurately. But noise is always present. Noise can be literal and physical—blaring music coming from a stereo as you're trying to hold a conversation with someone—or it can be psychological, such as competing thoughts, worries, and feelings that capture our attention and distract us from other communication.

Another element that is integral to communication is feedback. **Feedback** is the response to a message. Without feedback, communication is less likely to be effective. When your boss says, "Would you please give me a copy of the Williamson proposal?" you may say, "Is that the Bob Williamson proposal or the Kyra Williamson proposal?" Your quest for clarification in response to the request is feedback. Feedback can seek additional information or simply confirm that the message has been interpreted: "OK, I'll have the Williamson proposal on your desk by this afternoon."

One final component of communication is **context**—the physical, historical, and psychological environment of the communication. All communication takes place in some context. A meeting held in an executive boardroom is likely to raise different communication expectations than a brief conversation held around the water cooler. The context of the designer-decorated executive boardroom will likely result in more formal communication exchanges than you'd find in conversations among people standing around a workroom water cooler. The physical environment has an effect on how people communicate.

The communication-as-transaction perspective acknowledges that when we communicate with another, we are constantly reacting to what our partner is saying and expressing. Figure 1.2 illustrates the process we've been describing: We send and receive messages at the same time. Even as we talk, we are also interpreting our partner's nonverbal and verbal responses. Transactive communication also occurs within a context, and noise can interfere with the quality of communication and the accuracy of interpretations of messages. As we send messages, we monitor the degree to which the other person understands our message using feedback.

As you transactively communicate with others, it's important to understand two key dimensions of every instance of human communication—the content dimension and the relational dimension. The **content** of communication messages is the new information, ideas, or suggested actions that a speaker wishes to express. Another name for the content dimension

Figure 1.2 | Communication as Transaction

that may be more appropriate for the workplace is *task dimension*. Leaders communicate content messages with others in order to accomplish certain tasks—to get work completed.

The **relational dimension** of a communication message is usually more implied; it offers cues about the emotions, attitudes, and amount of power and control the speaker feels toward the listener.[10] The relational dimension is conveyed more by nonverbal messages than by words. Another way of distinguishing between the content and relational dimensions of communication is to consider that the content of a message refers to *what* is said, whereas the relational cues are provided in *how* the message is communicated. Although someone may say, "It was a pleasure to meet you," you know that the person didn't necessarily mean it if he or she does not make eye contact with you or shake your hand.

The Importance of Communication

A number of recent studies underscore the need for and importance of communication skills for the twenty-first-century workplace. How you communicate has an impact on the quality of your work and your potential for successfully leading others.

- In a recent survey of recruiters from companies with more than 50,000 employees, communication skills were cited as the single most important factor in choosing managers.[11] The survey, conducted by the University of Pittsburgh's Katz Business School, points out that skill in both written and oral communication, as well as an ability to work with others, are the main factors contributing to job success.[12]

- A national survey of employers revealed that the lack of basic and effective oral and written business communication skills appeared to be a major stumbling block for new entrants into the job market.[13] Employers also ranked the leadership skills of four-year college graduates as deficient, noting their inability to collaborate, work in teams or groups, and solve problems.[14]

- A study conducted by the research firm Robert Half Technology reports that information technology (IT) workers need more than technical abilities—they also need to be well-rounded business professionals. Nearly 45 percent of respondents said their IT staff members needed to improve their project management skills and could improve verbal and written communication abilities. Organizational and interpersonal skills also were listed as underdeveloped skill sets needed by information technology workers.[15]

- Temporary job service agencies, such as Kelly and Manpower, report that they are having more success placing job candidates with good communication or interpersonal skills than candidates with higher degrees.[16]

Relational dimension the dimension of communication that offers cues about the emotions, attitudes, and amount of power and control a speaker feels in relation to listeners.

Why is there so much evidence that communication skills are important to your business and professional work success? It's because regardless of what your job title is, you'll spend most of your time communicating with others. Research has found that you'll spend up to 90 percent of your work day communicating with others.[17] These research conclusions, about both the prevalence and the importance of communication, should reassure you that you're investing your time and money wisely by studying business and professional communication. When you complete your studies, you'll have a set of communication skills on your resume that can enhance your career success. Communication skills are leadership skills. These essential skills will immediately make you competitive in a global marketplace. Specifically, you will be able to demonstrate the following skills:

- Relationship skills: Manage conflict, negotiate solutions, and interview others
- Collaboration skills: Conduct meetings, facilitate discussions, make decisions, and collaboratively solve problems
- Presentation skills: Develop and deliver informative briefings, public relations presentations, training sessions, and sales presentations

In addition to putting these skills on your resume and demonstrating your communication competence during a job interview, you will also be able to talk more intelligently about how and why these communication skills are important in the twenty-first-century workplace.

Leading Others: Communication Principles at Work

Underlying our description of human communication are five principles that provide the foundation for leadership. These fundamental principles apply when communicating with others one on one, in groups or teams, or when making a professional presentation to an audience. We will briefly introduce each of the principles and discuss them in greater detail in the chapters that follow.

We will use these five communication principles as the foundation of the book. *To help you make a connection between these five core principles and the material we present about communication and leadership, a small version of the model presented in Figure 1.1, like the one that appears in the margin here, will appear in the margin to label the principle or principles we are discussing.*

Principle One: Be Aware of Your Communication with Yourself and Others

The first principle is to be aware of your interactions with others while at work. Effective communicators are conscious, or "present," when communicating. Ineffective communicators mindlessly or thoughtlessly say and do things they may later regret. Being aware of your own (and others') communication involves two important processes. First, it's important to be aware of what motivates or drives a person to communicate. For example, some people are motivated to communicate with others in order to avoid being lonely; they want to be included. Others are driven to communicate in order to control others.[18] Becoming aware of what motivates you and others to communicate will help you adapt your communication to make it more effective, which is the focus of our fifth communication principle.

Second, it's important to be aware that people perceive situations differently. No two people perceive in the same way. You may see a situation one way and your manager may see it another way. These perceptual differences result in a number of communication problems at work. In the next chapter we present skills to help you become more aware of why you and others communicate the way you do, as well as skills to help you check your perceptions, which can improve communication accuracy and understanding. To be an effective leader or follower, regardless of the type of work involved, it's important to be aware of your own thoughts, assumptions, and communication behavior and the behavior of others as well.

Principle Two: Effectively Use and Interpret Verbal Messages

The second principle we introduce here and elaborate on in Chapter 3 is to effectively use and interpret verbal messages. We communicate through a **language**, which consists of symbols and a system of rules that make it possible for people to understand one another. The effective communicator both encodes and decodes messages accurately; he or she selects appropriate symbols to form a message and interprets carefully the messages of others. As we noted earlier, symbols are words, sounds, visual images, gestures, or even objects that represent thoughts, concepts, other objects, or experiences. The words on this page are symbols that you use to derive meaning that makes sense to you.

Since a number of today's organizations are global, with offices located throughout the world, it's becoming more important for employees to be bilingual—to be able to read and write using at least two language systems. As a leader you will have ample opportunity to instruct others in how to complete a particular task. It's essential that your followers understand your verbal messages and that you understand theirs. Mastering the principle of effectively using and interpreting verbal messages will enhance your role as a VIP—a *verbally* important person—who understands the power of words to influence others.

Principle Three: Effectively Use and Interpret Nonverbal Messages

Nonverbal communication is communication other than written or spoken language that creates meaning for someone. Unspoken messages can communicate powerful ideas or express emotions with greater impact than mere words alone. A leader patting an employee on the back or an employee slamming shut an office door not only conveys a message but communicates emotion. Our emotions are communicated primarily through our use of nonverbal messages. If you have ever said, "It's not what he said that bothered me, it's how he said it," then you already understand the power of nonverbal communication. You may have a potential customer telling you that she will call you next week (the verbal message). However, you know that she will not call you because you sensed a lack of sincerity in her voice (the nonverbal message). Again, it's not *what* she said ("I will call you next week"), but *how* she said it (insincere tone of voice, lack of eye contact, or fidgeting) that created and conveyed the meaning to you. We will continue our discussion of nonverbal messages in Chapter 3 and provide you with skills to help you put into practice this communication principle for leadership.

Principle Four: Listen and Respond Thoughtfully to Others

Although effective leadership requires being able to develop and send messages to others that are meaningful, it is equally important, if not more important, for leaders to listen and receive messages from others. Listening involves being **other-oriented**, which is what we are being when we consider the needs, motives, desires, and goals of others. A crucial part of leadership is your being able to meet the needs of the people you lead. The only way you know what people need is to listen to them. What are they telling you? What are they not telling you? Listening is so important to leadership that Steven Covey, a well-known leadership expert, features listening as one of his seven habits of highly effective people. Covey notes, seek first to understand, then to be understood.[19]

Listening is a process. It not only involves receiving messages, it also includes responding thoughtfully to what others are saying. Sending responsive messages involves asking questions that are related to what the person is talking about, restating in your own words what you hear the other person saying, and being nonverbally responsive by leaning forward, making eye contact, and nodding your head. Responsive messages are affirming. They

Language a system of symbols and rules for their use that make it possible for people to understand and communicate with one another.

Nonverbal communication any communication, other than written or spoken language, that creates meaning for someone.

Other-oriented focused on the needs, motives, desires, and goals of others in one's communication.

communicate to other people that they have been listened to and that you understand them. Chapter 3 will discuss in greater detail how you can enhance your leadership effectiveness by developing your listening skills.

Principle Five: Appropriately Adapt Messages to Others

Leading others requires you to develop and use communication that is appropriately adapted to the people you lead. When you adapt a message to others, you make choices about how to best develop that message in order to achieve your communication goal. The workplace is full of diversity; chances are that you will be working with people from all over the globe and with both men and women. A one-size-fits-all approach to communication doesn't work in the twenty-first century. In order for messages to have an impact, they must be tailored to the people receiving them.

Adapting to others does not mean that you tell others what they want to hear. That would be unethical. Instead, you tell others what you want them to hear, but in ways that will make sense to them and that they will accept. Another way to tailor your communication is to adapt to another person's personality. Some people are talkative, others are quiet. Some people enjoy a good argument, others find arguing annoying. Your ability to adapt and adjust your communication makes others more comfortable and enhances understanding. In Chapter 5 we will discuss this principle in greater detail and point out how you can lead more effectively by adapting to personality, culture, and gender differences.

RECAP: Communication Principles

Communication Principle	Description
Principle One: Be aware of your communication with yourself and others.	Be mindful of your communication and conscious of what motivates you and others to communicate.
Principle Two: Effectively use and interpret verbal messages.	Select appropriate symbols in order to clearly communicate messages to others, and decode others' messages carefully.
Principle Three: Effectively use and interpret nonverbal messages.	Use unspoken symbols to communicate the emotional and relational aspects of your message.
Principle Four: Listen and respond thoughtfully to others.	Actively listen to others, using responses to ensure and demonstrate you have understood the message correctly.
Principle Five: Appropriately adapt messages to others.	Customize messages to enhance message clarity; consider the personal, social, and cultural characteristics of listeners.

Leading Others: Communication Skills at Work

In the workplace you communicate—make sense and share sense with others—to achieve specific work objectives. You achieve those objectives through three sets of communication skills: you relate, you collaborate, and you present messages to others. Communication in the interpersonal context helps develop and manage workplace relationships. Communication in teams allows people to collaborate with others. Finally, communication in the public context takes place through effective business and professional presentations.

Figure 1.3 | Communication Principles and Skills for Leadership

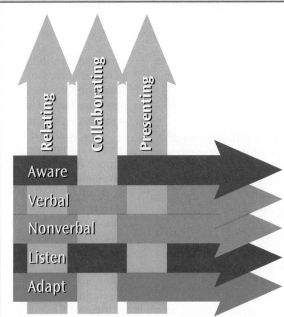

Although each context is different, the communication principles remain the same. You use the same five principles to develop and manage relationships as you do to make effective sales presentations to potential customers. What's different is how the communication principles are applied. You will see how the five communication principles are woven throughout the three contexts (interpersonal, team, and public) and how the context determines how the principles are applied to achieve communication goals as you assume leadership roles. In the model in Figure 1.3 you'll note that the same five principles are present regardless of whether the skill is relating, collaborating, or presenting. In each context, you draw on all five fundamental principles.

Relating to Others: Interpersonal Communication

A **relationship** is an ongoing connection we make with others through interpersonal communication.[20] To relate to someone is to give and take, listen and respond, act and react. When we talk about a good or positive relationship with someone, we often mean that we are together, or "in synch." You will develop and manage relationships with your manager, your co-workers, with the people you lead, and with your customers and clients. Communication allows the relationships to develop. Without communication, there are no relationships. To effectively relate to others, you should be aware of your communication, effectively use verbal and nonverbal messages, listen and respond, and appropriately adapt your messages to others in interpersonal situations.

Interpersonal communication occurs when at least two people interact with each other to mutually influence each other, usually for the purpose of developing and managing their relationship. You engage in interpersonal communication when you interview for a job or visit with a colleague. You communicate so as to develop a relationship with an interviewer with the hope of influencing the person—convincing him or her that you're the most qualified for the position. When talking with a colleague, you may be swapping office stories or just talking about the weather.

Yet true interpersonal communication occurs not simply when you interact with someone, but when you treat the other person as a unique human being. Think of all human communication as occurring on a continuum ranging from impersonal communication to interpersonal communication. **Impersonal communication** occurs when you treat people as objects, or when you respond to their roles, as when responding impersonally to a sales clerk or waiter, rather than to the unique person.

Two characteristics distinguish interpersonal communication from other forms of communication. First, interpersonal communication is mutually influential. When two people are

Relationship an ongoing connection developed with another person through interpersonal communication.

Interpersonal communication communication that occurs when two people interact to mutually influence each other, usually for the purpose of managing relationships.

Impersonal communication communication that occurs when people are treated as objects, or when others respond to people's roles rather than to who they are as unique people.

Communication allows interpersonal relationships to develop, as individuals engage in a simultaneous process of creating meaning and influencing each other.

interpersonally communicating, whether face to face, by phone, or even via a video connection, the process is simultaneous—both persons are communicating (sending and receiving messages) at the same time, and their influence is mutual. Interpersonal communication is not a one-sided monologue; it's a dialogue in the sense that both individuals are influenced and creating meaning simultaneously.[21]

The second distinguishing characteristic is that interpersonal communication is a fundamental means of developing and managing relationships. In effective relationships, all individuals feel that their verbal and nonverbal messages are understood and that there is a relational harmony based on a common understanding between the communicators. We will apply the five communication principles for leadership to the interpersonal context when we discuss relating to others in Chapter 6, and developing and conducting interviews, which is the focus of Chapters 7 and 8.

Collaborating with Others: Team Communication

Another set of skills comes to the fore in collaborating with others. To collaborate is to work with other people to achieve a specific outcome. In business and professional settings you will typically collaborate with others when working in groups and teams. **Group communication** is the verbal and nonverbal message transaction that occurs among from three to about fifteen people who share a common purpose or goal, who feel a sense of belonging to the group, and who exert influence on others.[22] A group must have at least three people. What's the upper limit on the number of people for meaningful group discussion? Some scholars say fifteen, others say more. The bigger the group, the less influence each person has on the group and the greater the chance that sub-groups or splinter factions will emerge. You experience group communication when you facilitate a meeting with the people you lead or when you attend a staff meeting with your co-workers.

Two attributes, in addition to the size of the group, distinguish group communication. First, members of a group have a common goal—something that members all would agree is the reason for the group's existence. Members of a small group need to be able to identify with the group and its purpose; they should sense that it is *their* group. Second, group members exert influence on each other. Each person potentially influences the actions and responses of others. Even if a group member sits silently, his or her silence has the ability to influence others and is a powerful form of nonverbal communication. Each group member, by virtue of being a member of the group, has the potential to exert influence on—and thus, to lead—the group.

A **team** is a coordinated group of individuals who collaborate to achieve a specific, common goal. A team is more highly structured and organized than a group. Teams are groups that have evolved to have clearly defined roles, duties, and responsibilities for team members. We will elaborate on the distinction between a group and a team in Chapter 9.

Since you'll spend so much of your work time collaborating with others on the job, Chapter 9 will allow you to see how groups and teams work. Chapter 10 will provide you with specific strategies for improving team meetings. As we examine group communication and discuss how to build teams, we will apply each of the five communication principles for leadership.

Presenting to Others: Public Communication

Public communication occurs when a speaker addresses a gathering of people to inform or persuade and even sometimes entertain them. This type of communication tends to cause anxiety for some because it requires developing, organizing, and delivering a presentation

Group communication verbal and nonverbal message transaction that occurs among from three to about fifteen people who share a common purpose or goal.

Team a coordinated group of individuals who collaborate to achieve a specific common goal; usually more structured and organized than a group.

Public communication communication that occurs when a speaker addresses a gathering of people with the intent to inform, persuade, or entertain them.

to an audience. Public communication tends to be more formal and more structured than interpersonal or team communication. As a leader you will have ample opportunities to make presentations before business and professional colleagues. In this book we will help you apply the five principles of communication when making a number of different types of business presentations: informative briefings, reports, public relations presentations, sales presentations, introductions, and ceremonial presentations (presenting an award, making a toast).

Of the three communication contexts (interpersonal, group, public), public communication has the distinction of being the one that has been formally studied the longest. In 333 B.C. Aristotle wrote his famous work called *The Rhetoric*, which was the first fully developed treatment of the use of speech to convince an audience. He defined **rhetoric** as the process of discovering the available means of persuasion in a given situation. Today, many communication departments have several courses that focus exclusively on how to persuade others, design and deliver both informative and persuasive messages, and evaluate the messages of others. Although we have certainly advanced in our understanding of informing and persuading others in the past two millennia, much of what Aristotle taught has withstood the test of both time and scholarly research.

Our focus in Chapters 11, 12, 13, and 14 is to present strategies and skills to use as you develop, support, and deliver professional business presentations. As with interpersonal and team communication, we will discuss public communication through the perspective of the five principles that anchor our study.

Leadership: Influencing Others Through Communication

Postcards were all the rage in the early twentieth century in David City, Nebraska, yet J. C. Hall knew he needed a bigger market than a small Nebraska town in which to sell his imported postcards. So in 1910 he hopped on a train to Kansas City with a couple of boxes of postcards under his arm and a vision for making money. He started a mail order postcard business from his Kansas City YMCA room. After some initial success, however, he found that people weren't buying postcards like they used to. He needed to change the focus of his business. His brother Rollie joined him in 1915, and together they started making their own greeting cards. Things were going well until a fire destroyed their entire greeting card stock. Having listened to his customers' needs, J. C. decided to hire an illustrator to make Christmas cards. Good move: Business boomed. J. C.'s other brother, William, joined the business and under J. C.'s leadership, the brothers continued their success. In 1928 they started printing the word "Hallmark" on the backs of the cards. When J. C. died in 1982, he left $100 million to charity. Today Hallmark Cards has annual sales of more than $4 billion.[23]

J. C. was successful for three reasons. He was aware—he knew what his customers wanted; he listened to them (he led by listening—our fourth communication principle). He was a master communicator, and he used his communication and leadership skills to adapt to a changing marketplace. Can you learn the same principles and skills of leading others that J. C. Hall used to establish a multimillion-dollar company? We believe the answer is an unequivocal yes. As the chapter-opening quote from James Humes proclaims, "The art of communication is the language of leadership."

Whether it's who comes out on top on *American Idol* or who becomes the next president of the United States, we're often fascinated with who emerges as number one. More specifically, we're interested in who becomes a leader, what a leader does, and how a leader maintains his or her leadership position. Typically it's the leader who both sets the tone of an organization or a team and establishes the work agenda.

A key question we explore in this book is what are the underlying communication principles that enhance leadership? Reduced to its essence, to lead is to influence. **Leadership** *is the process of influencing others to achieve goals through verbal and nonverbal messages*. We especially like Alan Keith's definition of leadership: "Leadership is ultimately about creating a way for people to contribute to making something extraordinary happen."[24] Leaders can make something happen by influencing others through either ethical or unethical means. An ethical leader doesn't try to coerce others through brute force or by knowingly using inaccurate or inappropriate appeals to fear. It's not only what a leader says but often what a leader does that provides influence and direction. Some view a leader as someone

Rhetoric the process of discovering the available means of persuasion in a given communication situation.

Leadership the process of influencing others to achieve goals through verbal and nonverbal messages.

An effective leader influences others through both verbal and nonverbal communication.

who delegates and directs the team. Others see a leader as someone who is primarily responsible for ensuring that whatever task is assigned or designed by the group is completed. In most teams, groups, and organizations there are many leaders, not just one person who influences others. In fact, each team member undoubtedly influences what the group does or does not achieve.[25] So it's likely that you will provide leadership even though you may not be formally designated "the leader." In an effectively led team, team members feel greater satisfaction, are more productive, and are less likely to be absent.[26] The quality of leadership influences virtually every aspect of what it feels like to be in any organization.

If you want to make sure you *don't* end up as a leader when working collaboratively, follow these prescriptions suggested by communication researchers Aubrey Fisher and Don Ellis:[27]

1. Be absent frequently.
2. Don't contribute to the conversation; just passively listen and don't volunteer information.
3. Keep the meeting notes and don't offer substantive comments.
4. Do what others ask, but don't ask others to do things.
5. Forcefully and frequently suggest that your ideas are the best ideas.
6. Make people laugh and tell jokes that don't relate to the topic at hand, suggesting that you don't take the group seriously.
7. Suggest that you have the answers to most questions.
8. Let team members know you don't like anyone who serves as a leader.

As we've noted, in most groups and teams there are usually several people who assume a leadership role of some kind. Who serves as a leader and who becomes a follower often changes as the topic, situation, and team members change from meeting to meeting. Leadership roles can also morph and change during the same meeting.

Leading Versus Managing

There are differences between being a leader and being a manager. A **manager** is someone who has been appointed to coordinate and facilitate, whereas a leader influences others even if he or she has not been designated to assume a specific leadership role. Metaphorically speaking, a manager's job is to keep the trains running on time, while the leader's job is to design the trains. Managers keep things organized and emphasize accomplishing the task. Leaders are focused not just on short-term accomplishments, but also on how the team, group, or organization will accomplish its goals over the long term. For example, a sales *manager* is a person who coordinates his or her sales staff's schedules, determines what products will be promoted, and makes recommendations about how to format sales reports. A sales *leader* is someone at the executive level who works with the sales staff to develop new and innovative sales strategies, influences which sales techniques are used most frequently, and is a major influence in deciding who gets hired and promoted. A manager coordinates the work; a leader influences the major changes in designing and implementing the work. Leaders also typically seek to change the present situation, whereas managers are usually interested in simply making the current situation operate effectively. To lead is to be responsible for "influencing, guiding in direction, course, action, opinion."[28]

Although a boss may have legitimate power to be the leader, even those not in a leadership role can influence team or organizational behavior. A leader is someone who has an ability to influence others regardless of whether she or he has been given the title "leader."

Manager someone who has been appointed to coordinate and facilitate, to keep things organized and accomplish a task.

Leading Versus Following

The relationship between leaders and followers is symbiotic: A leader can't lead unless there are those who follow her or him; you can't have one without the other. If the key role of a leader is to influence others through communication, the prime task of a follower is to ethically and appropriately respond to the influence of a leader.

The word *follower* sometimes connotes a person who may wait to be told what to do rather than move forward on his or her own initiative. Without effective followers, however, little would get accomplished. So followers have more power and influence in organizations than they may perceive that they have. The labor movement in the United States is based on the inherent power of those who are asked to follow the lead of those in charge. Labor unions and collective efforts to organize followers are a well-established element of contemporary organizations.

An effective follower does more than respond to a micromanaging leader; good followers use their own ideas and strategies to achieve their work goals. Precisely what do effective followers do? One researcher found that skilled followers engage in two activities: (1) They are independent and critical thinkers rather than passive and noncritical thinkers, and (2) they actively engage in the work, rather than waiting to be told what to do.[29] In most situations, the best followers are those who rate highly on both of these important attributes.

Although we've suggested that the best follower is someone who is both an independent and critical thinker and actively engaged in the task, the best follower style ultimately depends on the nature of the task; the trustworthiness, credibility, and ethics of the leader; and the specific situation. If the task is routine, doesn't violate sound ethical principles, and is well conceived, it may be best to simply do the work assigned. It may be a job that doesn't call for much independent thought, such as taking customer orders at a fast-food restaurant—the work simply needs to be done. Yet for more complicated tasks—such as helping a customer design a new computer system, independent, critical thinking may be what is needed. If the assigned task is unethical (involves lying, concealing information, harming others), simply conforming to the wishes of the leader is not appropriate.

Leadership Approaches

Are people born with traits that make them leaders, or can anyone be taught to lead? What are the key functions and styles of leadership? Scholars who study how to develop leaders approach the study of leadership in several different ways. Although you may now have a clearer sense of what leadership is and how leaders are different from managers and followers, at the beginning of our study of communication and leadership, it is useful to understand how the study of leadership has been approached. Knowing different approaches to studying and developing leaders can help you identify and enhance your own leadership skills. We'll identify six approaches for classifying and developing leaders: (1) trait, (2) functional, (3) styles, (4) situational, (5) transformational, and (6) servant leadership.

Trait approach. The question of whether leaders are born to lead is the focus of the trait approach to leadership. The **trait approach** to leadership suggests that there are certain psychological and physical attributes or traits that make leaders effective. According to this approach, if you are born with these traits, or if you cultivate specific leadership skills, then you will be a good leader. So those who subscribe to a trait approach to leadership will select someone to be a leader who possesses those traits. Over the course of several years of study, leadership researchers have identified intelligence, confidence, social skills (including communication skills), administrative skills, and enthusiasm as some of the traits effective leaders typically possess. One research study found that across several cultures, the most admired qualities of a leader are honesty, being forward-looking, competence, and being inspirational.[30] Another study found that leaders who had good argumentation skills and were not afraid to speak up were more likely to be effective than those who were not as skilled in asserting their ideas and who were apprehensive about speaking up.[31]

Peter Ueberroth knows what leaders should be able to do. He was the founder of the second largest travel company in the United States, a former commissioner of Major

Trait approach an approach to leadership that focuses on the psychological and physical attributes or traits that make leaders effective.

League Baseball and former chair of the U. S. Olympic Committee, and a current director of Coca Cola. When he was asked what traits he looks for in a leader, he said that, in addition to integrity, he looks for curiosity, and added, "The smartest people are the ones who continue to drive for information,"[32]

Historian Doris Kearns Goodwin identified a list of traits she believes are attributes of great American presidents. Her list of top leadership traits includes the courage to stay strong, self-confidence, an ability to learn from errors, a willingness to change, and emotional intelligence.[33]

But are we saying that if a person possesses these specific traits she or he will be a good leader? Additional research suggests that although many leaders do seem to have traits or special skills that can enhance their ability to influence others, *just having these traits does not necessarily mean that a person will be an effective leader.* Many of the attributes that researchers have identified may be important but are not sufficient to make a leader effective. One pair of classic research studies critically examined dozens of research investigations that claimed to identify specific leadership traits. The results of these studies were inconclusive.[34] The researchers concluded that there is no single set of traits or characteristics that predicts who will be a leader. Leadership is more complicated than that. The situation, the motivation and talents of the group or team members, and other factors determine which leadership approach is best.

The functional approach. The **functional approach** to leadership suggests that leaders exist to perform essential functions or behaviors that help an organization or team achieve its goals. Rather than identifying personality characteristics or other traits, the functional approach to leadership divides the essential leadership behaviors or functions that enhance the workings of a group into two categories: (1) task functions and (2) process functions.

Task functions are those behaviors that help the team or organization get the work done. Whether the leader is appointed or elected, one of his or her responsibilities is to ensure that the task the group is undertaking is completed. But don't get the idea that only one person performs these specific functions. Several different people can perform task functions. Sometimes the functions are explicitly assigned to people, and at other times the functions are accomplished as sensitive and skilled people become aware that these task functions need to be performed.

One of the key task functions of a leader is to organize the work; groups and organizations need procedural leaders to help get the job done. What leaders say, how effectively they listen, and how they adapt messages to others help them effectively ensure that the following common procedural tasks get done:

- Setting the agenda
- Recording what is accomplished
- Determining when a meeting begins and ends
- Distributing information before a meeting

Besides organizing the work, leaders also help get the work done by carrying out some of the following tasks:

- Initiating or proposing new ideas
- Seeking information and opinions
- Giving information
- Elaborating on the ideas of others
- Evaluating ideas

In most organizations and teams, many if not most people assume task roles. A team member who rarely helps with any of these tasks often earns the undesirable title of "slacker."

The second major kind of function leaders assume in groups, in addition to task functions (both procedural and work), is **process functions**. Process leaders help maintain a harmonious climate by encouraging amiable relationships among people. To attend to process functions, leaders listen and respond to others. They seek to maintain a friendly

Functional approach an approach to leadership that suggests that leaders perform essential functions, tasks, and processes that help an organization or team achieve goals.

Task functions behaviors that help a team or organization get work done.

Process functions functions performed by leaders that help maintain a harmonious climate by encouraging amiable relationships among others.

environment that also promotes honest, frank discussion. Conflict is a normal and expected part of working with others. It would be unusual if there were no conflict among people in groups. Process leaders focus on managing relationships. Specific process roles include the following:

- Encouraging reticent members to talk
- Mediating conflict
- Compromising or helping other to compromise
- Gatekeeping: monitoring and acting to ensure some members don't talk too much and others don't talk too little

It is possible for one person to perform both task and process functions. But just as with task leadership, several people will likely help maintain a group or team's process. Some colleagues may be good encouragers but let someone else perform the gatekeeping function, for example. In most organizations these process roles are not formally assigned, whereas some of the task functions may be assigned ("Daria, would you make copies of this report?") It is unlikely that you will start a team meeting by saying, "OK. Mamie, you're in charge of making sure that Jack and Linda talk more during this meeting." Process roles are assumed when needed. Skilled leaders remain alert to when these process functions need to be performed and adapt accordingly. These roles usually emerge, based on the needs of the group or organization and the personalities, skills, sensitivity, and past experiences of the people who are present.

The styles approach. A leadership style is a preferred way of behaving to influence others. The styles approach to leadership suggests that leaders use one of three primary styles when attempting to accomplish the work of the team or the organization: (1) authoritarian, (2) democratic, or (3) laissez faire. The strategies used to influence people usually fall into one of these broad categories.[35]

Authoritarian leaders influence by giving orders and seeking to control others. Military officers assume this leadership style, so do dictators like Hitler. But you don't have to be in the military or in a dictator-ruled country to experience an authoritarian leadership style. Perhaps you've been in a group and wondered "Who put her in charge?" Or, maybe you noted that action needed to be taken, so you asked someone to do what you thought needed to be done.

Democratic leaders, as you might suspect from the name, consult with others before issuing edicts. This type of leader seeks to join in the process of influencing without bulldozing the group into action it may resent. Sometimes formal votes are taken, but the leader or leaders will gauge the reaction of the group through dialogue and by reading nonverbal cues. Democratic leaders are aware of the needs of the team or organization rather than focused on achieving their own personal agenda. In addition to just being aware of what is needed, they adapt their behavior to respond to the needs of the team. They are more likely than the authoritarian leader to listen and thoughtfully respond to the wishes of the team. Their verbal and nonverbal messages are based on awareness of both the task at hand and the feelings of team members.

Most North Americans are usually more satisfied with their participation in a team if it is led by a democratic leader than if it is led by an authoritarian leader. There is evidence that people led by an authoritarian leader will spend more time on task getting the work done, but this occurs only when the leader is present. When the authoritarian leader is absent, the workers work less.

Authoritarian leaders leaders who influence by giving orders and seeking to control others.

Democratic leaders leaders who consult with the group before issuing edicts.

Laissez-faire leaders take a hands-off, laid-back approach to influencing others. *Laissez faire* is a French phrase that implies noninterference. This leadership approach is based on the assumption that the less direction provided by the leader, the better. In many ways this type of leader shies away from actively influencing the group. He or she influences only when pushed to lead.

This type of leadership is easiest to spot in an elected or appointed leader who won't lead. In some cases a laissez-faire leader fears making a mistake. In other cases this type of leader just wants to be liked and doesn't want to ruffle anyone's feathers. But as the slogan goes, not to decide is to decide. The laissez-faire leader is influencing the group by his or her silence or inactivity. The group may be bewildered and have high uncertainty, but the laissez-faire leader is reluctant to act. Although there are times when teams and organizations like the freedom that comes with a laissez-faire leader, over time such a hands-off approach can result in chaos. In general people seem to prefer democratic leaders more than laissez-faire nonleaders.

RECAP: Leadership Styles

Authoritarian Leaders

- Make all policy decisions.
- Determine what will happen one step at a time; future steps are not made clear to the group.
- Tell people what to do.

Democratic Leaders

- Discuss all policy decisions with group members. The group makes decisions by consensus.
- The group discusses what steps need to be taken. Group members work together to develop both short-term and long-term action steps.
- Serve as facilitators to develop a collaborative approach to accomplish the group's work.

Laissez-Faire Leaders

- Give minimal direction to discussions of policy decisions. Group members must initiate discussions about policy and procedures.
- May supply information about what steps are to be taken, if asked. The leader does not volunteer information.
- Do not participate in making work assignments.

Adapt

Laissez-faire leaders leaders who take a hands-off, laid-back approach to influencing others.

Situational leadership an approach that views leadership as an interactive process that links a particular style of leadership with such factors as culture, time limitations, group member personalities, and the work the group needs to do.

After learning about the different styles of leadership the question many people ask is, "Which style works best?" The answer: *It depends.* The effective leader adapts his or her style to fit the needs of the organization and the task at hand. This is why the principle of adapting to others is so important. Because teams and organizations are open systems, and because things change, a skilled leader takes many things into consideration when enacting his or her leadership style, which gives rise to the situational approach to leadership.

The situational approach. During a crisis, people need a quick-thinking, decisive leader who can orchestrate what needs to be done. During more routine situations, the leader may just need to back off and let others "do their thing." And at still other times a leader needs to play a more active role in gathering ideas and information from people. Because leadership style is not a one-size-fits-all concept, a skilled leader adapts to the situation. The **situational leadership** approach views leadership as an interactive process that links a particular style of leadership with such factors as culture, time limitations, group member personalities, and the work the group needs to do. Sometimes a group needs a strong, authoritarian leader to make decisions quickly so that the group can achieve its goal. After the September 11, 2001 attacks on the World Trade Center in New York city, mayor Rudolf Giuliani received high praise for his quick, decisive action to cope with the devastation and the city's emotionally battered population. The city needed a strong leader to help restore order in the chaos. Although most groups prefer a democratic leadership style, leaders sometimes need to be more assertive.

Groups with clear, highly structured goals and a high level of stress may work best with a more authoritarian leadership style. For example, for workers on an assembly line making microwave ovens, the task is to produce as many ovens as possible in a short amount of time; in this high-stress situation, more directive, authoritative leadership may be needed. But if a team of advertising executives is trying to develop ideas for new ways to sell microwave ovens, a less authoritarian, more nondirective democratic or even laissez-faire leadership style may be best. The less structured nature of the task calls for a less structured, less strict leadership approach. So, according to the situational leadership approach, the answer to the question "What's the best leadership style?" is "It depends."

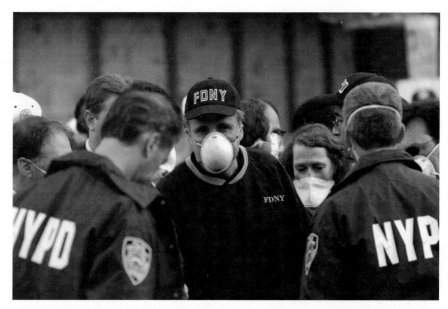

The situational leadership approach was exemplified by Mayor Rudy Giuliani, who adapted quickly to respond to the dire situation in New York City following the 9/11 attacks in 2001.

One simple rule for determining the appropriate leadership style is this: When the leader emerges naturally from the group or is leading a group that exists to carry out a single task, the group will permit him or her to be more directive. If the group will be together for some time and the quality of group relations is important to the functioning of the team, a more participative democratic leadership style is in order.[36]

Transformational leadership approach. To transform something is to change it from what it is now to something new and different. **Transformational leadership** is the process of influencing people to see the future in new ways. The transformational leader influences the team or organization by giving the team a glimpse of the future, energizing or realigning the culture, or giving the organization a new structure.[37] The leader influences by helping team members see all of the possibilities within the team, including those that may not yet be visible.[38] President Barack Obama's oratorical skill in encouraging a shared political vision has inspired many people to unite around a specific cause. Microsoft founder Bill Gates challenged existing ways of thinking and developed the world's largest software development company. Michael Dell transformed the way computers were marketed in the late twentieth and early twenty-first centuries. Entrepreneur Mark Zuckerberg, founder of Facebook, transformed the way people make social connections using the Internet. Each of these leaders helped to transform the people they lead by building a shared vision, challenging existing ways of thinking, and thinking holistically, from a systems perspective.

Three fundamental skills of transformational leadership have been identified by author Peter Senge:

1. *Build a shared vision.* Don't impose a vision, but listen to team members and then help them shape the future together, rather than just announcing what the future will be.

2. *Challenge existing ways of thinking.* A transformational leader pushes and prods the team or organization to think in new ways.

3. *Be a systems thinker.* Transformational leaders are aware of the interconnectedness of people, plans, resources, inputs, and outputs.[39]

Communicating a vision that people can support is one of the most important functions of a transformational leader. An authoritarian leader would just announce "Here's your vision: now get it done." The democratic leader would ask, "What vision do you want?" The laissez-faire leader would do nothing about developing a vision unless asked to create a vision by someone else. The situational leader would say, "Let's see what type of team I'm leading and then I'll determine how to articulate and share a vision." The transformational leader paints a vivid picture of the future based on an understanding of both individual members

Transformational leadership the process of influencing people to see the future in new ways.

and the culture of the entire organization. The transformational leader understands the needs, goals, hopes, and fears of individuals and is able to develop a collective vision that draws on this knowledge of the people whom he or she leads. Listening skills, interpersonal skills, conflict management skills, and feedback skills are essential competencies for transformational leaders. Such leaders also provide inspiration, motivation, and intellectual stimulation for the team. In addition, they consider the cultural backgrounds of those whom they lead. Research supports the important role of culture in determining the best way to transform a team or organization.[40]

Servant leadership approach. To be a servant is to support, nurture, and assist others. Several researchers have identified a leadership style, known as **servant leadership**, in which the leader explicitly views himself or herself as being of service to the group or team.[41] Robert Greenleaf, one of the first researchers to develop the concept of servant leadership, described it this way:

Servant leadership a style of leadership in which the leader explicitly views himself or herself as being of service to the group or team.

> It begins with the natural feeling that one wants to serve, to serve first. Then conscious choice brings one to aspire to lead. The difference manifests itself in the care taken by the servant—first to make sure that other people's highest priority needs are being served. The best test is: Do those served grow as persons; do they, while being served, become healthier, wiser, freer, more autonomous, more likely themselves to become servants?[42]

>>> COMMUNICATION SKILLS @ WORK

Most sports teams have a coach to support the team. A good coach provides the right mix of motivation, encouragement, information, and skill-development tips to help the team function at top form.[43] Team coaching, according to management consulting experts J. Richard Hackman and Ruth Wageman, is "direct interaction with a team intended to help members make coordinated and task-appropriate use of their collective resources in accomplishing the team's work."[44] An effective coach should have a knowledge of team performance and process improvement methods and the communication skill to support team members and leaders.[45] Many teams in businesses and professional settings use a coach to provide external support and expertise to help the team enhance its performance.[46] One of the key elements of a high-performing team is external support and recognition. A skilled team coach can provide that recognition and support.[47] Sometimes the coach may be a supervisor or a boss at the next-higher level of the organization. Or a coach could be someone hired by the organization or team to serve as a consultant or guide to help the team do its work.

What specific coaching strategies work best to help a team accomplish its work? Here's a list, developed by Hackman and Wageman, of the most powerful research-based coaching strategies that make a difference in team performance.

- Team coaching suggestions should focus more on team effort, strategy, knowledge, and skill than on general issues related to interpersonal relationships; a good coach should focus more on the work that needs to be done and less on personalities and team member relationships.

- A team needs motivational support when it is just beginning its work; early in the team's history it's especially important for the team members to receive personal encouragement and support to energize the team.

- A team needs help with the nuts and bolts of the work it's doing at the mid-point of a team's development. When the team is most heavily involved in accomplishing its task, the team needs a coach who can provide ideas, resources, and strategies directly related to accomplishing its work.

- Team coaching is most effective if it focuses on specific team member performance outcomes and processes directly related to achieving the clear, elevating goal of the team; observations about team member behaviors that are not related to achieving the team's goal are less helpful.

- Effective coaching messages that are supported with evidence, are well-organized, and are presented clearly are more helpful than unsupported, disorganized, and unclear messages.

- A team can benefit by reviewing its processes and procedures after it has accomplished its goals; post-project coaching helps the team perform better on its next task.

- A team can receive fresh insights, new perspectives, and new ideas from a skilled and well-qualified team coach. The best coaches consider what the team needs at various stages of its development and provide thoughtful, encouraging, and work-relevant advice.

To be a servant leader is to actively work to meet the needs of others while keeping an eye on the needs of the entire group, team, or organization that the leader is influencing.

Listen

What do servant leaders do? Leadership researcher Larry Spears, building on the initial idea of servant leadership, suggested that among the key actions of a servant leader were listening, empathy, and healing.[48] Underlying these behaviors is the notion that a servant leader has a high concern for people, relationships, and team member satisfaction—servant leaders desire to serve others; they wisely think about the future, are purposive, and strive to leave the organization better than they found it.

As you read through the description of a servant leader, you may be thinking "This person sounds too good to be true." We're not suggesting that a servant leader always makes the best choices or is indeed a perfect leader. But a servant leader is one who is motivated to both *do good* and *do well*. For a servant leader, the ends do not justify the means. What matters is not only the outcome that is achieved but also the manner in which the team acts to achieve the outcome. A servant leader may not even be thinking consciously about the list of attributes we've identified as hallmarks of a servant leader; the servant leader is comfortable being in the background and working to achieve the goals of the team rather than drawing attention to his or her own efforts.

RECAP: Leadership Approaches

Approach	Description
Trait	Effective leaders possess certain traits or characteristics that contribute to their effectiveness.
Functional	Leaders influence others by performing two primary functions:
	• Task functions, which help accomplish the work.
	• Process functions, which help establish a positive climate.
Styles	Leadership is enacted in three primary styles:
	• Authoritarian leaders direct and control others.
	• Democratic leaders solicit input from others and seek to lead by involving others in the decisions.
	• Laissez-faire leaders intentionally influence others only when asked or directed by others to lead.
Situational	Leadership is an interactive process in which a leader adapts his or her approach based on the needs of the group.
	• More structured tasks in high-stress situations call for more directive leadership.
	• Less structured tasks in situations in which positive interpersonal relationships are important call for more democratic, collaborative approaches to leadership.
Transformational	A leader influences others by
	• Developing a shared vision.
	• Using listening and relationship-building skills to create a climate of trust.
Servant	A leader influences others by
	• Being altruistic: sacrificing for others.
	• Being an emotional healer: listening, supporting, empathizing.
	• Being wise: thinking about the future as well as the present.
	• Being persuasive: using arguments, reasoning, logic, and information to convince others rather than demanding change.
	• Being an organizational steward: striving to leave the organization better than he or she found it.

Summary

Communication is essential for leadership. At its most basic level, human communication is the process of making sense out of the world and sharing that sense with others by creating meaning through verbal and nonverbal messages. Leaders influence others through communication. One's ability to be an effective leader is in many ways dependent on communication skills. Although numerous studies link communication competence with success on the job, many new professionals and leaders enter the job market lacking communication skills.

Five principles are fundamental to leadership and business and professional communication. First, be aware of your communication with yourself and others. Being mindful of your communication is important to help you improve your communication. Second, effectively use and interpret verbal messages. Words are powerful, and they influence our thoughts, our actions, and our relationships with others. Third, effectively use and interpret nonverbal messages. Unspoken cues provide important information about our emotions and attitudes. Fourth, listen and respond thoughtfully to others. Being able to accurately interpret the messages of others enhances comprehension and relational empathy. Fifth, appropriately adapt messages to others. It is important to adapt messages to others to enhance both understanding and empathy.

The five principles are applied to three different business and professional communication contexts in which different skill sets are emphasized: interpersonal communication emphasizes relationship skills, team communication emphasizes collaboration skills, and public communication emphasizes presenting messages to audiences. Interpersonal communication is a special form of communication that occurs when two people interact simultaneously and mutually influence each other, usually for the purpose of developing and managing relationships. Team communication occurs in a group in which individuals collaborate with each other to achieve a specific, common goal. Public communication occurs when a speaker addresses a gathering of other people to inform, persuade, or entertain them.

The chapter presented six leadership approaches. The trait leadership approach is based on the idea that effective leaders possess certain traits or characteristics that make them effective. Second, the functional leadership approach considers two elements of leadership: task functions, which help accomplish the group's work, and process functions, which help establish an overall positive climate. Third, the styles approach to leadership identifies three primary leadership styles: authoritarian (which emphasizes directing and controlling others), democratic (which is a participative leadership style), and laissez faire (in which a leader only leads when asked or when absolutely needed). Fourth, the situational leadership approach views leadership as an interactive process in which a leader adapts his or her leadership style to the needs of the group. A leader using the fifth approach, the transformational approach, influences others by developing a shared vision while listening and relating to those whom he or she leads. Finally, according to the servant leader perspective, a leader's key function is to serve, facilitate, and help the organization or group achieve its full potential.

Discussion Questions

1. Define communication and describe the components of the communication process.

2. Explain what it means to say that communication is transactional.

3. Identify and describe each of the five major communication principles.

4. Differentiate among the three contexts of communication: interpersonal, team, and public communication.

5. What is the difference between leading and managing others? What is the difference between leading and following?

6. Describe, compare, and contrast the trait, functional, styles, situational, transformational, and servant leadership approaches.

Building Your Skills

1. Keep a "conversation journal" for one week. Note times when someone's message is not received in its intended form. Where did the miscommunication originate in each case? At the source? With the receiver? Why do you think the miscommunication occurred?

2. In pairs or groups of three, brainstorm about situations in which you have either given or received messages whose relational portion was different from the content of the message. (Think of times when the words used in a message didn't exactly match the tone of the message.)

3. Comparing Leadership Styles. Your instructor will divide the class into several groups. One person in each group should be appointed to lead a group discussion to answer the following question: What can or should be done to lower the cost of college textbooks? The instructor will have each group leader use a different leadership style. One group leader will be instructed to use the democratic leadership style, another to use a laissez-faire leadership style, and another to use an authoritarian style. Following the group discussion, each group should discuss the pros and cons of the specific leadership style that was enacted in their group.

4. What are your best leadership attributes? What leadership skills should you work to enhance? Make a list of your best leadership attributes. Make a second list of the leadership skills and competencies that you'd like to enhance. Note the role and function of communication in your list of leadership skills.

5. Followership Questionnaire.[49] Complete the following questionnaire to assess your followership style—your approach to being led by others. For each question, choose a number from 0 to 6 to indicate the extent to which the statement describes you. 0 indicates that the statement rarely applies to you, and 6 indicates that it almost always applies to you.

_____ 1. Does your work help you fulfill some societal goal or personal dream that is important to you?

_____ 2. Are your personal work goals aligned with the organization's priority goals?

_____ 3. Are you highly committed to and energized by your work and organization, giving them your best ideas and performance?

_____ 4. Does your enthusiasm also spread to and energize your co-workers?

_____ 5. Instead of waiting for or merely accepting what the leader tells you, do you personally identify which organizational activities are most critical for achieving the organization's priority goals?

_____ 6. Do you actively develop a distinctive competence in those critical activities so that you become more valuable to the leader and the organization?

_____ 7. When starting a new job or assignment, do you promptly build a record of successes in tasks that are important to the leader?

_____ 8. Can the leader give you a difficult assignment without the benefit of much supervision, knowing that you will meet your deadline with highest quality work and that you will "fill in the cracks" if need be?

_____ 9. Do you take the initiative to seek out and successfully complete assignments that go above and beyond your job?

_____10. When you are not the leader of a group project, do you still contribute at a high level, often doing more than your share?

_____11. Do you Independently think up and champion new ideas that will contribute significantly to the leader's or the organization's goals?

_____12. Do you try to solve the tough problems (technical or organizational), rather than look to the leader to do it for you?

_____13. Do you help out other co-workers, making them look good, even when you don't get any credit?

_____14. Do you help the leader or group see both the upside potential and downside risks of ideas or plans, playing the devil's advocate if need be?

_____15. Do you understand the leader's needs, goals, and constraints, and work hard to help meet them?

_____16. Do you actively and honestly own up to your strengths and weaknesses rather than put off evaluation?

_____17. Do you make a habit of internally questioning the wisdom of the leader's decision rather than just doing what you are told?

_____18. When the leader asks you to do something that runs contrary to your professional or personal preferences, do you say "no" rather than "yes"?

_____19. Do you act on your own ethical standards rather than the leader's or the group's standards?

_____20. Do you assert your views on important issues, even though it might mean conflict with your group or reprisals from the leader?

Finding Your Followership Style: Add your ratings for the statements as shown below, and calculate the total score for each set of items.

Independent Thinking Items: $1 + 5 + 11 + 12 + 14 + 16 + 17 + 18 + 19 + 20 =$ _____

Active Engagement Items: $2 + 3 + 4 + 6 + 7 + 8 + 9 + 10 + 13 + 15 =$ _____

Now, record the total for each set of items on the graph below. Mark your total Independent Thinking score as a point on the vertical axis; mark your total Active Engagement score as a point on the horizontal axis. Now, connect the two scores with horizontal and vertical lines. The point where these two lines intersect will fall in one of the quadrants of the graph and will indicate your followership style:

Exemplary Follower

Alienated Follower

Passive Follower

Conformist Follower

Pragmatist Follower

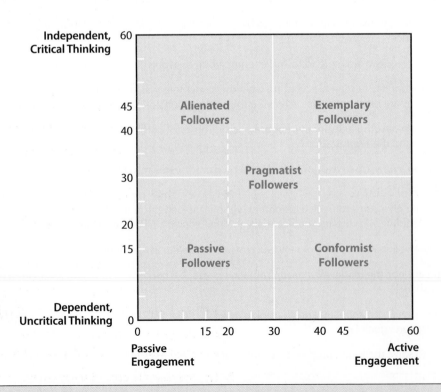

Chapter 2
Being Aware of Self and Others: Enhancing Communication and Leadership

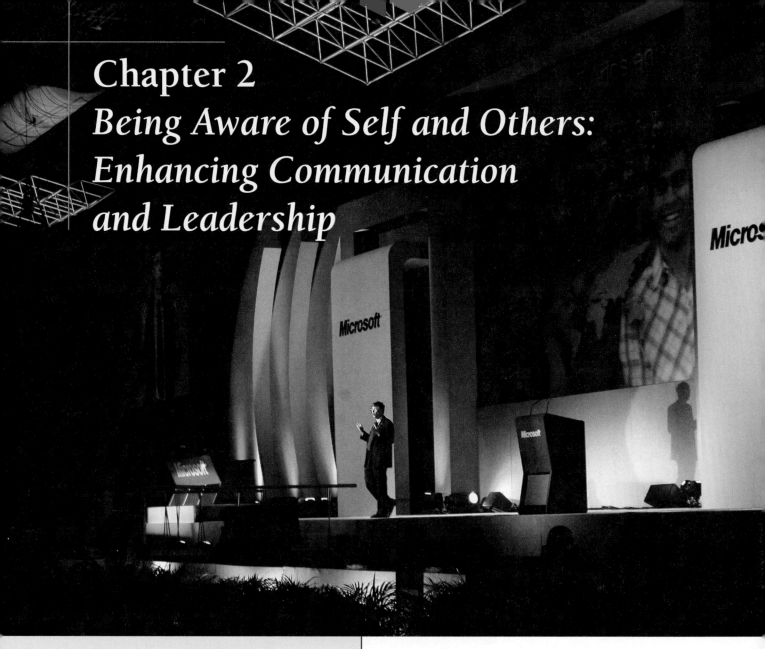

chapter outline

After reading this chapter, you should be able to

■ Describe what it means to be self-aware in communication with others, and explain why self-awareness is important.

■ Define social style and discuss the effects of social style on communication behaviors.

■ List and describe each of the four social styles.

■ Discuss some ways of adapting your communication to others' social styles.

■ List and define each of the four main approaches to leadership.

■ Evaluate a real-life working environment in terms of the organization's or a supervisor's leadership style and basic assumptions.

■ Explain how written rules, stories, metaphors, ceremonies, and artifacts contribute to the culture of an organization.

■ List and describe each of the three types of ethical challenges, and give examples.

Aware

What do Bill Gates, Chair of the Bill and Melinda Gates Foundation; Michael Dell, CEO of Dell Computers; Ann Mulcahy, Chair and CEO of Xerox; Angela Merkel, Chancellor of Germany; and Patricia Woerts, CEO of Archer Daniels Midland all have in common? To reach the pinnacle of their professions, they all had to be aware of others as well as to be aware of their own thoughts, feelings, and inner messages to themselves. Each of these leaders became a leader because he or she had an internal motivation to succeed. They responded to their inner voices, which motivated them even in the face of challenges and obstacles. They were also cognizant of how others reacted to their ideas and leadership influence. Although you may not aspire to the top leadership job in your chosen profession, your level of awareness of the communication around you is a strong predictor of your ability to achieve your personal and professional goals.

As we noted in Chapter 1, the first principle that guides the communication and leadership skills in the workplace is to *become aware of your communication with yourself and others.* Figure 2.1 illustrates where Principle One fits into our model of Communication Principles and Skills for Leadership. You will notice that becoming self-aware is at the top of the model, suggesting that effective workplace communication begins with self-awareness. Being self-aware typically occurs in two steps. First, you become aware of how you and others communicate. Second, you determine if the way in which you communicate with yourself and others is effective. By being self-aware you can answer the question, Am I meeting my goals? You can also determine if the people with whom you interact are achieving their goals. If not, what's going wrong? Adhering to our first principle of communication is central to monitoring your own accomplishments and how you communicate with other people.

> "Don't bother just to be better than your contemporaries or predecessors. Try to be better than yourself."
>
> —WILLIAM FAULKNER

Mindfulness is awareness of your own and others' thoughts, actions, and motivations.[1] It is your ability to get out of your own head and into others' heads. Being mindful is the process of actively paying attention not only to how you communicate and relate to your customers, employees, colleagues, or superiors, but also to how they communicate with you. If the saying "open mouth, insert foot" immediately comes to mind after you said something you wish you hadn't, then you already understand the importance of being mindful in your communication with others and how difficult mindfulness is to achieve.

One framework, attributed to Abraham Maslow, helps explain the process of becoming self-aware. This framework has also been used to explain the attainment of communication skills and suggests that people operate at one of four levels:

1. *Unconscious incompetence*: We are unaware of our own incompetence. We don't know what it is that we don't know.

Mindfulness awareness of your own and others' thoughts, actions, and motivations.

Figure 2.1 | Communication Principles and Skills for Leadership

Aware

Verbal

Nonverbal

Listen

Adapt

2. *Conscious incompetence*: At this level, we become aware or conscious that we are not competent. We know that there is something we don't know.

3. *Conscious competence*: We are aware that we know or can do something, but it has not yet become an integrated skill or habit.

4. *Unconscious competence*: At this level, skills become second nature. We know or can do something, and we don't have to concentrate to be able to act on that knowledge or draw on that skill.

1. awkward
2. mechanical
3. natural

To better understand how this framework operates, consider Lizette, who is a sales manager for a new condominium complex. Her job is to sell condo units. Lizette has been on the job for one month. She is an ineffective sales manager—she is pushy and aggressive, and potential customers are turned off by her approach. Unfortunately, Lizette is unaware of her own ineffective communication and how she is perceived by her potential clients. Lizette typifies Level 1 awareness—she doesn't know what it is that she doesn't know.

After a few months on the job, Lizette begins to realize that her approach to selling is not working. She begins to notice how her clients are reacting to her communication and that her clients are not happy with her service. She is now at Level 2 awareness—she knows that there is something she doesn't know. To enhance her communication skills and, in particular, her selling skills, Lizette takes a course in persuasive communication and sales. On completing the course, Lizette begins to apply what she learned in class to her selling. She pays careful attention not only to her communication, but also to her clients' communication. Lizette begins to adapt to the needs of her clients and her sales increase dramatically. Lizette is now at Level 3 awareness. She knows what she needs to do. However, she still has to think about doing it. Communicating effectively has not yet become a habit.

After one year on the job, Lizette has become the top salesperson and has been promoted to manage sales at a new property. She is now a natural salesperson and she makes selling appear effortless. Lizette has finally reached Level 4 awareness. She is selling without having to think about selling. Effective communication skills and selling techniques now come naturally.

This chapter explains how to become more aware of your own communication and the communication of others. Like Lizette, you can work through the four levels of awareness and become a more mindful communicator and leader at work. This awareness will allow you to more effectively adapt your communication to others. Some leaders have a way of making their communication fit with others' communication styles. For example, if your client is task oriented and driven to reach goals, then he's probably not interested in small talk and discussing weekend plans. So, you adapt your communication style to fit your client's style. You become task oriented as well, and you keep your communication focused on helping your client reach his goals.

Mindful communicators are also aware of three other important aspects of leadership—leadership assumptions, organizational culture, and ethics. If you assume a leadership role, you may be guided by a set of beliefs about what motivates people to behave. Some leaders believe that followers are motivated by rewards and punishments. Other leaders believe that followers are motivated by becoming active participants in the leadership process. What about you? What assumptions do you have about followers—and are they accurate?

Leaders are mindful of organizational culture and how it's created through communication. Organizational culture is always changing and evolving and includes multiple factors such as traditions, stories, metaphors, ceremonies, and artifacts. Effective leaders are plugged into the culture of their organization and know how to use their communication to influence that culture.

Finally, are you aware of the role that ethics play in leadership and communication? Your ethics are revealed through your communication, and your communication ultimately reinforces your ethics. Being aware of ethical issues will begin to prepare you for the ethical challenges that you will face as a leader.

Be Aware of Your Own and Others' Social Styles

Awareness begins with an understanding of how you communicate with others and how others communicate with you. Your **social style** is a pattern of communication behaviors

Social style a pattern of communication behaviors that others observe when you interact with them.

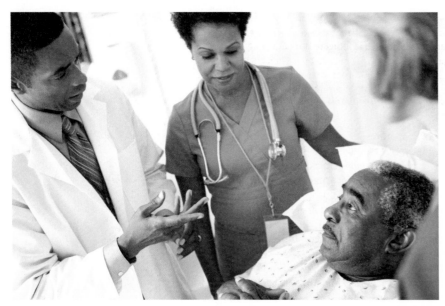

Those in service professions, like this doctor and nurse, tend to be amiables. Their social style is characterized by responsiveness to others.

that others observe when you interact with them.[2] A manager who immediately gets up from her desk and greets you with a warm smile and a handshake, compliments you on your appearance, and asks you about your family has a social style that is noticeably different from that of a manager who greets you without eye contact while completing an email, then asks you numerous questions about the status of the project you're leading (and grumbles about the answers you give). Your social style is similar to your signature—your handwritten signature is unique. Similarly, your social style is unique; no one has a social style that perfectly matches your own. Becoming a mindful communicator and leader involves becoming aware of your own social style and others' social styles. This awareness allows you to more effectively adapt your communication to others.

Identifying Your Social Style

Your social style is a combination of two primary dimensions—assertiveness and responsiveness. **Assertiveness** is the capacity to make requests; to actively disagree; to express positive or negative personal feelings; to initiate, maintain, or disengage from conversations; and to stand up for oneself without attacking another.[3] **Responsiveness** is the capacity to be sensitive to the communication of others, to be seen as a good listener, to make others comfortable in communicating, and to recognize the needs and desires of others.[4] To assist you in becoming more self-aware of your own social style, we encourage you to complete the self-report measure in Rating Scale 2.1. Depending on your self-reported levels of assertiveness and responsiveness, your social style will fall into one of the following four quadrants: amiable, analytical, driver, or expressive.[5]

Amiable. If you're an **amiable**, you are a relationship specialist and are high on responsiveness and low on assertiveness. Adjectives used to describe amiables include *conforming, unsure, pliable, dependent, awkward, supportive, respectful, willing, dependable*, and *agreeable*. Amiables seem to be most comfortable working in environments where they can provide services and be supportive and helpful in their relationships with others. Such people are often drawn to careers in teaching, human resources, social work, psychology, and other helping professions.

Analytical. If you're an **analytical**, you are a technical specialist and are low on both responsiveness and assertiveness. The adjectives used to describe analyticals include *critical, indecisive, stuffy, picky, moralistic, industrious, persistent, serious, exacting*, and *orderly*. Professions such as science, engineering, construction work, accounting, and certain aspects of law often have a high proportion of people with this style. Some research suggests that analyticals are more likely to be apprehensive about communication and thus more withdrawn and quiet.[6] As a result, analyticals may be less effective communicators than others and more resistant to interacting with others.

Driver. If you're a **driver**, you are a control specialist and are low on responsiveness and high on assertiveness. Among the adjectives used to describe drivers are *pushy, severe, tough, dominating, harsh, strong-willed, independent, practical, decisive*, and *efficient*. These people might be small-business owners, top managers, production managers, administrative personnel, politicians, or in other decision-making positions. Because of their ability to take responsibility and direct others, top management often puts these individuals into positions of control.

Expressive. If you're an **expressive**, you are a social specialist and are high on both responsiveness and assertiveness. The adjectives used to describe expressives include

Assertiveness an individual's capacity to make requests, actively disagree, express positive and negative personal feelings, and stand up for himself or herself without attacking another.

Responsiveness an individual's capacity to be sensitive to the communication of others, be seen as a good listener, and to make others comfortable in communicating.

Amiable a social style characterized by high responsiveness and low assertiveness. People with this style are considered relationship specialists; they enjoy working in supportive and helpful roles.

Analytical a social style characterized by low responsiveness and assertiveness. Individuals with this social style are considered technical specialists; they enjoy working in technical positions.

Rating Scale 2.1   Identifying Your Social Style[7]

Following is a list of twenty personality characteristics. Please indicate the degree to which you believe you display each characteristic while interacting with others by marking whether you (5) *strongly agree* that you exhibit the characteristic, (4) *agree* that you exhibit it, (3) are *undecided*, (2) *disagree* that you exhibit the characteristic, or (1) *strongly disagree* that it applies. There are no right or wrong answers. Work quickly; record your first impression.

_____ 1. Helpful
_____ 2. Defend my own beliefs
_____ 3. Independent
_____ 4. Responsive to others
_____ 5. Forceful
_____ 6. Have strong personality
_____ 7. Sympathetic
_____ 8. Compassionate
_____ 9. Assertive
_____ 10. Sensitive to the needs of others

_____ 11. Dominant
_____ 12. Sincere
_____ 13. Gentle
_____ 14. Willing to take a stand
_____ 15. Warm
_____ 16. Tender
_____ 17. Friendly
_____ 18. Act as a leader
_____ 19. Aggressive
_____ 20. Competitive

Scoring instructions:

Add your ratings for these characteristics to determine your Assertiveness score:
$2 + 3 + 5 + 6 + 9 + 11 + 14 + 18 + 19 + 20$

Add your ratings of these characteristics to determine your Responsiveness score:
$1 + 4 + 7 + 8 + 10 + 12 + 13 + 15 + 16 + 17$

Scores above 34 indicate high assertiveness or responsiveness. Scores below 26 indicate low assertiveness or responsiveness. Scores between 26 and 34 indicate moderate levels of assertiveness or responsiveness.

Now map your assertiveness and responsiveness scores on the graph below to determine your social style. First, find the point on the vertical axis that corresponds to your assertiveness score, and draw a horizontal dotted line in from that point on the axis. Then find the point on the horizontal axis that corresponds to your responsiveness score, and draw a vertical dotted line up from that point on the axis. Place a dot at the point where these two lines intersect; the quadrant in which the dot falls indicates your social style. For example, if you scored 35 on assertiveness and 46 on responsiveness, you would fall within the "Expressive" quadrant.

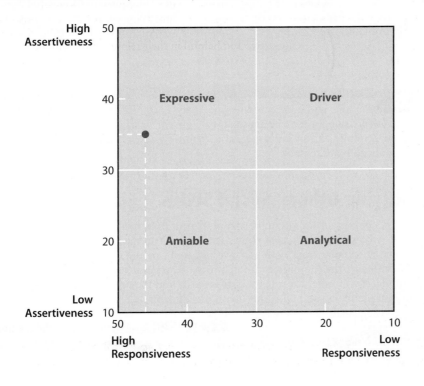

Driver a social style characterized by high assertiveness and low responsiveness. Persons with this social style are considered control specialists; they often enjoy working in leadership and management positions.

Expressive a social style characterized by high assertiveness and responsiveness. Individuals with this social style are considered social specialists; they are able to use their communication skills to gain recognition and attention, and enjoy being noticed by others.

>>> **COMMUNICATION SKILLS** @ WORK

One of the ways you can make your awareness of social styles work for you is to style flex.[8] To style flex, follow three steps: (1) identify your social style, (2) identify the other person's social style, (3) use the following style-flexing strategies and communication skills.

If You Have an Amiable Social Style

When communicating with an **Analytical** person	When communicating with an **Expressive** person	When communicating with a **Driver**
• Be punctual, focus on the task, use a formal tone • De-emphasize feelings: minimize eye contact, avoid touch • Be systematic: develop a plan, follow the rules • Be organized: prepare in advance, use specific details in presentations	• Increase your speed, respond and decide promptly, minimize paperwork • Increase your energy: stand up straight, use expressive gestures and eye contact, talk louder, faster, and with more intensity than you might normally • Focus on the big picture: prioritize topics and focus on those of highest priority; avoid specific details • Initiate conversations, avoid tentative language, disagree tactfully	• Set realistic goals and develop a plan • Prioritize topics and focus on those of highest priority; avoid the details • Be organized: present options, anticipate questions and prepare answers, focus on results • Avoid tentative language • Identify problems; disagree tactfully

If You Are a Driver

When communicating with an **Analytical** person	When communicating with an **Expressive** person	When communicating with an **Amiable** person
• Slow down: analyticals react negatively to pressure to be speedy; avoid pushing • Listen more: drivers tend to want to talk; invite the person to speak, and paraphrase what she or he says • Minimize expressive gestures and monitor your speech; speak more slowly and with less intensity than you might normally	• Be aware of and acknowledge the other person's feelings; be warm and enthusiastic • Allow for fun and joking; pay attention to and comment on the other person's physical space (office decorations, photos) • Be confirming: recognize the other's contributions; be supportive; provide incentives	• Be genuine: engage in personal conversation and offer appropriate self-disclosure • Be supportive: be a good listener, paraphrase what the other person says and respond appropriately; be appreciative and helpful • Focus on feelings: pay attention to the other person's nonverbal cues; amiables will not always voice their unhappiness

competent, excitable, versatile, reacting, ambitious, stimulating, enthusiastic, dramatic, and *friendly.* Persons with an expressive social style are often found in sales, entertainment, and advertising, or may be artists, musicians, or writers. These people know how to use their communication skills to gain recognition and attention and they like being seen and noticed by others.

Identifying Others' Social Styles

Although it's important for you to be aware of your own social style, what may be more important is how others perceive your social style. You may consider yourself to be a driver when others you work with perceive you to be an amiable. This perceptual difference may influence the communication that occurs between you and the people you lead. For example, if you supervise a team of lifeguards and they perceive you to be very laid back and easygoing (an amiable), they may consider you to be a "pushover." Rather than you supervising them, they may supervise you and you may become frustrated at your inability to take control and direct them. It's important to remember that others communicate not with the person *you* perceive yourself to be, but with who *they* perceive you to

• Prepare thoroughly; gather all necessary details and information to build credibility	• Be flexible with your time; listen and respond; practice patience	• Slow down: as a driver, you often speak fast because you like to get things done; relax deadlines and avoid rushing

If You Have an Expressive Social Style

When communicating with an **Analytical** person	When communicating with a **Driver**	When communicating with an **Amiable** person
• Be task-focused, punctual, formal • Be systematic: follow the rules, have a plan • Prepare thoroughly, focus on facts and specific details, provide evidence • Minimize expressiveness; avoid dramatic gestures and vocal intensity	• Be task-focused, punctual, formal • Plan your work: determine specific goals and objectives • Be organized: prepare thoroughly and know what you intend to say; use facts and be results-oriented • Avoid power struggles: both Expressives and Drivers are assertive; make an effort to listen more; slow down and be willing to negotiate	• Allow the other person to speak more; paraphrase what you hear • Be supportive: make the other person feel understood; listen with empathy • Minimize expressiveness, use tentative or provisional language ("possibly," "maybe," and "could") • Slow your speech, relax deadlines, avoid rushing; amiables tend to take longer to make decisions

If You Have an Analytical Social Style

When communicating with an **Expressive** person	When communicating with a **Driver**	When communicating with an **Amiable** person
• Be warm, build rapport, offer appropriate self-disclosure • Speak more rapidly than you might normally; react quickly • Say what you think: speak up, disagree tactfully, identify problems rather than ignoring them • Be flexible; improvise, relax the rules, be encouraging	• Prioritize your information and share the most important points; avoid subpoints or details unless asked • Be results oriented and practical • Say what you think • Present options, but allow the person to determine his or her own objectives and goals; relax the rules	• Be genuine; build rapport; offer appropriate self-disclosure; be loyal • Provide structure: define the job, assist in planning • Avoid logical appeals; focus on main points and leave out details • Be supportive and helpful; make the other person feel understood; recognize his or her contributions

be. If the lifeguards perceive you to be an amiable, even though you perceive yourself to be a driver, the lifeguards will communicate with you as though you were an amiable. Effective leadership begins with understanding this important perceptual difference.

To become more aware of how others perceive you as well as of how you perceive others' social styles, we encourage you to again complete Rating Scale 2.1. This time, however, we suggest using the measure in a couple of different ways. First, you may want to ask a classmate or someone you work with to use the measure to evaluate you. This way, you can become more aware of how others perceive your social style and you can compare your self-perception with how another person perceives you. You may also want to complete the measure while focusing on a real-life workplace relationship that is important to you.

The information you obtain by having a co-worker use the measure of social style to evaluate you will help you better understand why others communicate with you in a particular manner. For example, maybe you have always wondered why some people seem to be scared of you or appear threatened by you. It may be because they perceive you to be a driver—but what they may not know is that you're really an analytical. Although having this self-awareness is important, what you do with it is even more important. The next section of this chapter provides you with some practical skills to help you put your new self-awareness of social styles to work for you.

Adapt

Adapting to Social Styles

Being aware of your social style and the social styles of others allows you to adapt your communication, which enhances your ability to be effective. **Style flexing** is a process of adapting your communication to how others communicate. For example, if you're an analytical leader who is working with a team of drivers, you will enhance your leadership effectiveness if you communicate more like a driver. This would include being direct with members of the team, focusing on outcomes, and allowing them the freedom to determine goals and objectives. Again, this is not your preferred way of communicating with others, but it's how drivers communicate. The Communication Skills @ Work feature suggests ways to help you style flex to others' social styles.

According to management communication consultants Robert and Dorothy Bolton, style flexing is a way of tailoring communication to another person's processes.[9] When you style flex, you maximize the fit between you and another person. Most men have their suits tailored to ensure that they fit perfectly. When your suit fits you perfectly, you look and feel better. When workplace relationships fit, you're more productive and effective.

Becoming aware of your own and others' social styles gives you important information that you can use to more effectively lead others. Another source of information that will enhance your ability to lead others is awareness of the beliefs and assumptions that you hold about leadership.

Style flexing the process of adapting your communication to how others communicate.

Classical leadership a leadership style that assumes that there is one best way to perform a specific task within an organization with maximum efficiency, and that a leader's job is to influence workers to behave in this way.

Be Aware of Your Own and Others' Leadership Assumptions

Becoming a mindful communicator and leader involves becoming aware of the beliefs you have about what motivates people to follow leaders. Why do you believe people would follow you, and how do these beliefs ultimately influence your leadership style and ability to lead? Researchers have identified four different categories of assumptions about leadership that may help answer this question: classical, human relations, human resource, and systems assumptions.

Classical Leadership

The **classical leadership** assumptions are based on the principle that there is one best way for a team or organization to perform a given task. The leader's job is to influence the workers to behave in ways that help them produce goods or services in the most efficient and effective way possible. The work is organized to be performed with no wasted motions. Time is money, and the more quickly the work can be accomplished, the better. Most fast-food restaurants organize their teamwork using classical assumptions of leadership. The manager assumes that she is in charge and that her team will perform and follow her. When you place your order for a hamburger, the people who make your meal don't typically huddle and say, "Well, what's the best way to make this hamburger?" The manager or the organization has already decided this for them. The procedure has been established and the team members' job is to produce the hamburger as fast as possible, following this procedure. An organization or team that operates with a classical assumption about leadership has identified a clear leader who is expected to keep things running like clockwork, and team members have accepted that they're fulfilling the role that is needed. Work is organized like an assembly line in which each person has been

Communication between manager and employees at a fast-food restaurant chain is focused on completing specific tasks in an efficient manner.

trained to do his or her part in producing whatever it is that the team is creating.

The classical approach to leadership and work was developed by a management theorist who lived and worked over one hundred years ago. Fredrick Taylor's 1911 book *The Principles of Scientific Management* was influential in helping leaders structure work so

Figure 2.2 | Tall and Flat Organizations

that it could be done in effective and efficient ways.[10] Max Weber is another author who wrote about classical approaches to looking at bureaucracies or formal organizations.[11] Weber noted that organizations are structured by rules and regulations and driven by people who have legitimate authority to control and direct people's behaviors. The classical leadership approach assumes that workers are motivated to work hard if they are rewarded when they do a good job and not rewarded if they are not working hard.

From a classical point of view, organizations can be described as being either tall or flat. Figure 2.2 illustrates the differences between tall and flat organizations. A tall organization is one that has many layers of managers or leaders between the person at the head of the organization (president or chief executive officer) and workers on the lowest level. A flat organization is one in which most employees are at the same level. A small family-run restaurant is an example of a flat organization.

Communication in organizations that operate using classical leadership assumptions is typically downward; the leader is a person with the power and authority to tell the others in the organization or team what to do. Team members are not expected to spend much time collaborating with others to figure out how to do their jobs. They have been trained to do their work with little variation. Communication is usually about the task at hand; there is little attention focused on relationships. "Just do it" might be the slogan that summarizes a classical leadership approach. Tacked onto that slogan would be the charge to "do it quickly" and "do it efficiently."

Human Relations Leadership

Management research conducted in the 1920s and 1930s found that human beings are complicated. People are influenced not just by power and position but have their own motivations for working hard or not. You can't just tell people what to do and expect that they will do it. Humans are, in fact, influenced by their working conditions and how they are treated in the workplace.

Abraham Maslow's well-known theory of human needs being organized into a hierarchy of five levels also helped management and leadership theorists understand how to enhance productivity. Maslow's five needs, arranged from most basic to higher-level needs, are (1) physiological needs (for food, water); (2) safety needs (to feel secure and safe); (3) affiliation needs (to belong to a group and have friendships with others); (4) self-esteem needs (to feel positive about oneself); and (5) self-actualization needs (to become the best possible person you can be).[12] Although management researchers have not found consistent support for the precise theory Maslow described (the needs may not operate as a hierarchy; we sometimes need several things at the same time), his research continues to have intuitive appeal and has served as a framework for basic assumptions about how people behave in relationships as well as the workplace.

One breakthrough, large-scale research project had a major impact on our understanding of the importance of focusing on human relationships in the workplace. Research conducted by Elton Mayo and Friz Roethlisberger at the Hawthorne plant of the Western Electric Company revealed what became known simply as the *Hawthorne effect*.[13] These studies found evidence that the way people are treated has an impact on their work. When trying to test whether changes in working conditions (such as improvements in the workroom lighting) had an effect on work productivity, the Hawthorne researchers found that just paying attention to workers and asking for their input on the working conditions influenced work output and work climate. In other words, its not just directing people to do a job that influences the amount and quality of work that gets accomplished—people are influenced by their own desire for recognition and their need to feel positive about what they are doing. The research also documented the important role of communication in establishing a positive work climate, such as leaders listening to employees' concerns and asking for their input.

Another influential management researcher, Fredrick Herzberg, suggested that there are two levels of motivators that influence how people respond to their work, their working conditions, and leadership from others.[14] Herzberg called the first level of motivators **hygiene factors**. These are basic aspects of one's job that simply have to be there for a worker to feel satisfied. Hygiene factors include such things as salary, working conditions, and the quality of supervision workers receive. If the hygiene factors are present, that's good—but these factors alone won't necessarily motivate a worker to work harder, faster, or better. The second level of motivators, which Herzberg called motivation factors, will, if present, actually motivate a worker to do a better job. **Motivation factors** include how interesting the work is, whether a worker receives recognition for a job well done and opportunities for promotion, and the amount of job responsibility a person has. As with Maslow's research, there has not been consistent research support for Herzberg's model. But leaders and managers continue to use Herzberg's assumptions to attempt to motivate and lead others.

In addition to Maslow, Mayo and Roethlisberger, and Herzberg, Douglas McGregor provided a clear and easy-to-understand model to help leaders lead.[15] According to McGregor, **Theory X** leaders are those who adhere to the classical approach to work—leaders should tell people what to do and reward them when they produce good work and punish them if they don't. Theory X also assumes that people are lazy and don't like to work and only work when they are pushed and controlled.

Theory Y assumptions are in stark contrast to Theory X assumptions. Theory Y suggests that for most people, work is like play—we enjoy working just for the fun of it. We work not in response to rewards and punishment but simply because we inherently want to do a good job. A job well done is satisfying in and of itself. McGregor believed Theory Y was the best approach to leading others. Theory Y captures the essence of the human relations approach to leadership: Treat people well, have good relationships with them, and they will work hard and do a good job.

Communication based on the human relations approach to leadership concerns both task and relationship issues. Communication is not always directed downward, telling people what to do; it can take the form of conversations with colleagues about how to best do whatever job confronts the team. And communication based on the human relations approach is more informal than that based on the classical approach, which emphasizes doing things according to company policy and standard operating procedures. With the human relations approach, it's OK to allow exceptions to policy and procedures if they keep people happy. People will work harder if they have some influence over how the job is done. People have influence through communication. So, rather than limiting communication among workers, the human relations approach encourages communication.

Human Resources Leadership

As the name suggests, the **human resources** leadership approach views people as resources who can be full partners in enhancing a team or organization. As noted

Hygiene factors basic aspects of a job that have to be there for a worker to feel satisfied about the work, including salary, working conditions, and supervision.

Motivation factors aspects of a person's job that motivate the person to do better.

Theory X a view of leadership that assumes that workers are generally lazy and that a leader's job is to reward good work and punish bad work.

Theory Y a view of leadership that assumes that workers are self-motivated and inherently want to do a good job. If a leader treats people well and builds good relationships with them, they will work hard.

Human resources an approach to leadership that views workers as resources who can be full partners in enhancing a team or organization.

earlier, the human relations leadership approach views people as needing positive encouragement rather than just direction; however, some people view the human relations approach as a way to manipulate people by being nice to them so that they work harder. This third approach, the human resources leadership approach, seeks to empower people to participate in the work of the organization or team. The human resources approach to leadership might provide such perks as free ice cream in the company cafeteria or introduce casual-dress Fridays to induce a more positive work climate. In contrast to the human relations approach, a human resources approach asks workers and team members what they like or dislike and gives them more control over work processes, rather than just trying to manipulate them with pleasantries. One best-selling leadership book, *Side-by-Side Leadership*, by leadership expert Dennis Romig, advocates a human resources approach to leadership.[16] According to this well-written book, the best leaders do not merely lead from "on high" but are partners who work side by side with their teams and are involved in the day-to-day operations of the organization.

The human resources approach to leadership views all people in the team or organization as individuals who have feelings and emotions and also have intellectual resources to accomplish the task. The approach emphasizes both the task at hand and the people who do the work. The classical approach focuses more on the work, whereas the human relations approach has a heavy emphasis on people's motivation for work. The human resources leadership approach emphasizes both people and work.

Leadership researchers Robert Blake and Jane Mouton's book *The New Managerial Grid* describes various management styles that draw on the various leadership assumptions we've discussed.[17] The grid, shown in Figure 2.3, has two dimensions: (1) a concern for people and (2) a concern for production. These two dimensions are similar to the task and relationship roles that we discussed in the last chapter, and they combine to produce five different management or leadership styles. First is the impoverished leader (1, 1 on the grid), who has little concern for people or work productivity. Second is the country club leader (1, 9 on the grid); this leader influences by emphasizing comfort and a positive

Figure 2.3 | The Managerial Grid

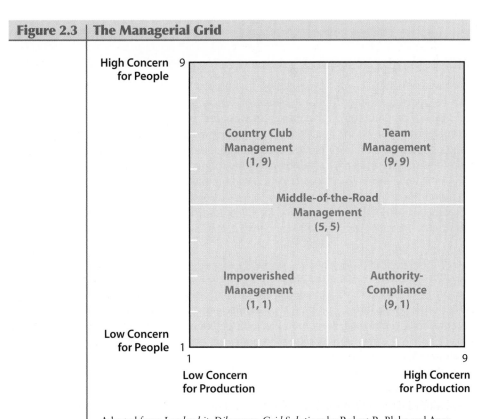

Adapted from *Leadership Dilemmas–Grid Solutions* by Robert R. Blake and Anne Adams McCanse (formerly *The Managerial Grid* by Robert R. Blake and Jane S. Mouton). Houston: Gulf Publishing Company. Copyright 1991 by Grid International, Inc.

climate but does little to focus on work productivity. Third is the middle-of-the-road leader (5, 5), who leads by compromise. In the upper right-hand corner of the grid is the team management leader (9, 9), who has a high concern for both people and the task. This leader views people as resources to work with rather than colleagues who should be manipulated with pleasantries or forced to do the work with threats and punishments. Last is the authoritative leader (9, 1), the leader who says "It's my way or the highway. Do what I say or you're gone."

Another human resources advocate was management consultant William Ouchi, who suggested that neither Theory X nor Theory Y, proposed by Douglas McGregor, was the best leadership assumption. Ouchi proposed Theory Z.[18] **Theory Z** emphasizes treating people as resources to empower rather than as objects to manipulate with either threats (Theory X) or rewards (Theory Y). Theory Z assumes that people have a long-term relationship with the organization or team and that the ongoing relationship is based on trust, collaboration, and leadership practices that will benefit everyone in the organization or team, not just those in leadership positions.

The communication in a group, team, or organization that uses a human resources paradigm flows not just from the top down or horizontally, but from all directions, with a special emphasis on upward communication. Information is shared in many channels, including face to face. As suggested by Blake and Mouton's managerial grid, the content of the communication stems from concerns about both people and productivity.

Systems Leadership

A **systems approach** to leadership views organizations and teams as complex interconnected sets of elements that are not easily influenced by simple techniques or tools. A systems approach acknowledges the messiness and interrelatedness of teams and organizations. A **system** is any entity (such as an organization, a group, or a team) that is made up of many interconnected and interdependent pieces. Each part of the system has an impact on every other part of the system; none really functions without the other pieces of the system.

Theory Z an approach to leadership that assumes that people have a long-term relationship with an organization and that the relationship is based on trust, collaboration, and a common organizational goal.

Systems approach an approach to leadership that views organizations and teams as complex interconnected sets of elements that are not easily influenced by simple techniques and tools.

System any entity (such as an organization, a group, or a team) that is made up of many interconnected and interdependent pieces.

>>> COMMUNICATION AND GLOBALIZATION @ WORK

Founded in 1991 by Stanford professor and designer David Kelley of David Kelley Designs, IDEO was recently featured on the popular innovative business website FastCompany.com as among the fifty most innovative companies in the world. IDEO helps organizations innovate through design, and the company focuses on three things: the design, the service, and the human element. David Kelley is a human resources leader. His leadership style is grounded in the assumption that employees are assets that can be developed. In addition to helping companies design new products and solve problems, IDEO also helps companies re-engineer their corporate cultures to focus on the development of human resources. According to Kelley, its focus on the consumer and worker experience has made IDEO one of the most successful and effective international design firms. Among IDEO's clients are AT&T, Nestle, Intel, Lufthansa, and Samsung.

Although there are many facets about IDEO that set it apart as a different kind of organization, the company's commitment to the human experience has helped catapult it to international success. The company is innovative not only in terms of new product designs, but also in terms of new experiences. In a project with Kaiser Permanente, a health maintenance organization, IDEO researchers determined that business was declining in Kaiser hospitals because patients and families were unhappy with the overall aesthetic experience of the hospitals and waiting rooms. After revamping waiting rooms and expanding emergency rooms to accommodate both patients and family, Kaiser found that the answer to increasing business was not building expensive new facilities. Rather, overhauling the patient experience was all that was needed to make people choose a Kaiser hospital.

The corporate atmosphere at IDEO also reflects a human resources approach to leadership in which innovation and creativity are guiding norms. IDEO executives believe in letting the people lead. IDEO employs over 350 people, including scientists, engineers, designers, and researchers who work together in teams. The employees decorate their respective work areas any way they wish, and collaboration is the key to innovation at IDEO. As IDEO has shown, when you take innovative design ideas and integrate them into the human experience, the results are not only effective, but also profitable.[19]

Systems approaches use the term *synergy* to describe how the whole is greater than the sum of its parts. A team or organization has synergy because it is more than just the individual elements in those entities. Something new is created when the pieces of the system come together. Your body is a synergistic system; it is more than just a collection of individual organs and appendages. *You* are greater than just the sum of your various parts. And each part affects the other parts. If you stub your toe, every other part of your body (your entire system) is affected by your injury. Your brain registers pain, you say "Ow!" and you might limp when you walk. Your body is an open system in that it is influenced not only by what happens inside it but also by what happens outside it. Like your body, organizations are open systems, influenced by both internal and external forces.

A fundamental principle of systems theory is that because every part of the system is connected to all of the other parts, if one part of the system is affected, then the entire system will feel the effects. Think of a child's mobile that has different dangling pieces suspended by strings: Touch one part of the mobile and all of the other parts move. That's what happens in any interconnected system—what happens to one element affects all elements of the system. Decisions a leader makes have far-reaching consequences and touch the lives of many people. For example, when a leader decides to cancel the roll-out of a new product or service, this decision has a ripple effect, affecting other aspects of the business including sales, accounting, purchasing, and engineering.

A systems approach to leadership suggests that the leader or leaders in a team or organization should be mindful of the total picture or the entire system when attempting to influence how work is to be accomplished. From a systems perspective, communication is vital to keep the elements of the system connected. A leader's job is to help different elements of the system (the organization or team) stay connected. But it's not just the leader who facilitates communication. Everyone in the system has a responsibility to help

RECAP: Leadership Assumptions

Assumption	Description	Implications for Communication
Classical Leadership	• Workers are motivated by rewards and punishment. • There is one best way to efficiently accomplish the task; work should be structured by someone in authority.	Communication is typically directed from the top down.
Human Relations Leadership	• People are motivated by their individual needs. • Rewards are better than punishment in motivating others; it is important to have a positive, pleasant work climate to achieve maximum worker productivity.	Communication between individual workers is encouraged. Some upward communication is encouraged. Downward communication is intended to maximize worker productivity.
Human Resources Leadership	• Workers want to be involved in determining how the work should be accomplished. • Rather than manipulating workers with only positive messages, leaders share information with workers and involve them in both the work procedures and work outcomes.	Upward communication is emphasized as well as horizontal communication. Worker involvement in decisions is fostered. Downward communication reflects the point of view of workers.
Systems Leadership	• Teams and organizations are interconnected, interrelated entities. • Each element in a system affects all other elements.	Communication (in all directions at all times) is encouraged and is viewed as a transactive process.

the system function effectively. So communication is a key resource for leaders and followers when viewing an organization as a system. For example, when Juan Ocha, mayor of South Padre Island, Texas, was preparing for a hurricane, he was responsible for coordinating communication among various local, state, and federal agencies. He made sure agency leaders had the names and contact numbers of local leaders. He also encouraged local leaders to openly share information with numerous agencies who were helping the island prepare for the pending hurricane. Teams that are connected to other parts of the organization (or to local government, as in the case of South Padre Island) tend to be higher-functioning teams. Team members, and especially team leaders, help the team tap the information, ideas, and resources available throughout the organization.[20] Communication flows in all directions all of the time.

Be Aware of Organizational Culture

We've emphasized that there are many things to be aware of as you communicate with others in business and professional settings—your own perceptions of yourself as well as how you are perceived by others, your social style and the social styles of others, and underlying assumptions about leadership. A key factor that has a pervasive influence on each of these elements is the culture of an organization.[21] Culture is a concept used by anthropologists to describe the distinctive beliefs, values, assumptions, and rules that distinguish one group of people from another group. To paraphrase anthropologist Clifford Geertz, "People are animals suspended in webs of significance they have spun. I take culture to be those webs".[22] Like the webs of significance that connect disparate elements in a system, culture is a pervasive element that touches all of our communication with others.

Organizational culture is the learned pattern of beliefs, values, assumptions, rules, and norms that are shared by the people in an organization. Organizational culture includes what it feels like to be in an organization—whether the organization maintains a rigid, do-it-by-the-book approach or is a more relaxed, informal place to work. The culture of an organization also affects all aspects of how the work is accomplished. Your shopping experience at Wal-Mart, for example, is probably different from your shopping experience at an upscale department store like Nordstrom. Both sell shirts, socks, and shoes, but what it feels like to shop at each place is distinctive and different from the experience at the other retail establishment. The stores have a different organizational culture in terms of how employees interact with customers. You are met at Wal-Mart by a greeter who shoves a shopping cart your way; at Nordstrom you receive more individual attention (and pay higher prices.)

Why is it important to be aware of organizational culture? Because it influences how you communicate with others. If you're not aware of the organizational culture and so fail to adapt to either implicit or explicit cultural expectations, you may create conflict and stress. Imagine that your first job was at Google, where you enjoyed an open and flexible organizational culture, and then you changed jobs and worked for another software company that had a more traditional and rigid organizational culture. If you couldn't adapt to the change in culture you'd likely experience anxiety and uncertainty. Or, if you're working in an organization that has a strict dress code, you clearly need to be aware of those rules. But other rules and assumptions may be less obvious and less formal, such as whether you address your boss as Ms. Hall or Sue.

The culture of an organization influences more than just such superficial things as what style of clothes you wear or what you call your boss. The culture influences the way you do your work. How closely you adhere to deadlines, how quickly you respond to email messages, and how you observe unwritten rules (such as whether it's acceptable to hang out in the coffee room when the supervisor is there) may influence whether you get a pay raise or not, or even whether you'll keep your job. To be aware of more than just surface features of organizational culture, it's important to understand how organizational culture is developed and evolves.

The Nature of Organizational Culture

Organizational culture experts Tom Peters and Robert Waterman identified sixty-two "excellent" organizations during the 1980s and discussed these organizations in their

Organizational culture the learned pattern of beliefs, values, assumptions, rules, and norms that are shared by the people in an organization.

book *In Search of Excellence*.[23] Peters and Waterman identified the cultural factors that they believed made these companies outstanding. They noted that the companies focused on such things as emphasizing good customer relations, taking quick and decisive action to solve problems, encouraging positive and supportive co-worker relationships, and focusing on what the company did best (whether it was making Post-It notes or hamburgers). Many people bought this book because they thought that if excellent companies had these management and cultural assumptions, then *every* organization that strove to be excellent should adopt the same culture. It was ultimately discovered, however, that not every successful organizational culture has the same elements. As time went on, not all of the excellent companies featured in Peters and Waterman's book endured. Some struggled financially and others went bankrupt. What the *In Search of Excellence* authors documented with the passage of time is that there is no one perfect organizational culture. Organizational cultures are complicated and complex, for several reasons: Organizational cultures emerge through communication, are expressed both explicitly and implicitly, include many factors that shape the culture, are multilayered, and change over time.

Organizational culture is created through communication. What it feels like to be in an organization, as well as the way things get done there, are ultimately rooted in how people communicate with other people. The rules (explicit requirements), roles (who does what), assumptions (underlying beliefs about the nature of work and human relationships), and values (what is good and what is bad) don't just happen—the forces that contribute to organizational culture are created through interaction among the people there. Some aspects of the culture may be explicitly spelled out in writing. But most cultural aspects are not; instead, people learn them by observing as well as by talking with other people. You learned the organizational culture at your school not just by reading the student handbook, but also by observing other students and talking with them.

There is considerable research about how we are socialized to a particular job or organization. To be "socialized" means to understand what is expected of us when we work in an organization.[24] It is through our communication with others—whether it's our boss, our colleagues, or our customers—that we truly understand the culture of an organization.

Organizational culture is communicated both explicitly and implicitly. Sometimes organizational culture is explicitly spelled out in written policies and verbal directives, and in other instances, the culture is conveyed indirectly through the example set by others. Maybe you've worked in an organization that had explicit rules prescribing when you should arrive at work and take breaks; perhaps you had to punch a time clock. Yet in another organization, rules were more relaxed—you didn't have to report in at a precise time and you could come and go as you liked as long as the work got done. There were no written rules about work time; new workers just followed the example set by others. Employees at Google, for example, have a relaxed culture that includes free gourmet meals, exercise rooms, and even laundry and dry cleaning services. These perks are not included in a contract. However, they are an aspect of the corporate culture at Google that was explicitly established by Google's founders—and they are part of what people who work at Google have implicitly come to expect from the organization.

Organizational culture includes multiple factors. There is not just one factor that contributes to what it feels like to be in an organization, but many factors. The forces that contribute to the organizational culture include what you see, what you read, and what you hear when you visit an organization. What should you observe to get a sense of organizational culture? Here are a few of the factors that simultaneously shape and reflect organizational culture:

- *Written rules and policies:* As we've noted, sometimes organizational culture is explicitly expressed in written polices. These rules and policies may be found on a website or in a handbook or presented during orientation sessions. But if you only looked at the written policies, you'd miss a lot of the forces that shape the culture. It's often more informal communication channels that give you the most important clues about organizational culture.

- *Stories:* "Hey, did you hear what happened to Marciale last night?" Not only will such an opening line get your attention, but the story itself can offer clues to the culture of an organization. The stories and gossip that circulate in an organization reveal information about the values and expectations of the organization. Are supervisors valued or made fun of? Are staff members respected? Do people express genuine warmth for others, or are suspicion and mistrust embedded in the tales that are told? Listening to the stories and how they are expressed (whether with playful humor or mean spirits) can help you identify organizational culture.

- *Metaphors:* Noting the metaphors—the comparisons or analogies that are used to describe the organization—can provide clues about organizational culture. "We're all like family here," says your new co-worker. That metaphor sends a different message than someone saying, "Welcome to the crazy house."

- *Ceremonies:* Noting organizational rituals and what gets celebrated and rewarded can give you insights into what is valued. If employees get awards for perfect attendance or for achieving high work output, then those achievements are clearly valued by the organization. If people get recognition for working 10, 20, or 30 years at the organization, then you know that longevity is valued and rewarded. Do colleagues frequently go out to lunch together to celebrate birthdays? What gets celebrated and the behaviors that are spotlighted provide significant clues about organizational culture.

- *Artifacts and decor:* Do people have cubicles or private offices? Is there matching furniture, or do people have a hodgepodge of chairs and desks in their workspace? The attention given to what the physical space in the organization looks like is another clue that helps decode the organizational culture. Fine art on the office walls rather than tattered and torn posters suggests that top management wants to create an inviting work experience. The appearance of an organization can give you insight into whether it's an austere, serious work environment or a place where people are encouraged to have fun.

Organizational culture is multilayered and multifaceted. When we talk about the culture of an organization, don't get the idea that there is only one culture per organization—there are many layers and pockets of organizational culture within a single organization. People in upper management may operate in a formal, structured organizational culture but the custodial staff may have a more relaxed, joking, and informal culture. Employees may go out for drinks after work or socialize after hours with each others' families. Middle managers, however, may never socialize outside of work. Even at the same level of an organization there may be different cultural expectations. For example, perhaps in a company's Software Development department, everyone jokes with their colleagues and tells silly stories, and people laugh a lot. But in the Information Technology department, there is a more serious, get-down-to-business approach to work. Although both departments are at the same level in the organization, there are organizational cultural differences that are due to tradition and the personalities and social styles of the workers. As organizational culture expert Judith Martin has noted, "Some aspects of the culture will be shared by most members . . . other aspects . . . will be interpreted differently by different groups, creating subcultures that overlap and nest within each other."[25]

There is no one single culture that defines a single organization. Subcultures—cultures that emerge within a more dominant culture—add to the complexity of the

Organizational cultures often reflect the social styles of employees and may include such traditions as celebrating co-workers' birthdays.

fabric of the overall culture. Even in a small organization such as a fast-food restaurant, there can be different cultures within the larger culture. One work crew may be somber and approach their work with dread while another crew may playfully enjoy the work of serving customers and making sandwiches.

Organizational culture changes. The culture of an organization today may not be the culture of the organization next month. Organizational cultures morph and evolve based on a number of factors, including the people who join or leave the organization, the adoption of new policies or the discarding of old policies, new technology, new leadership, and a host of other factors. Because organizational culture is fluid, it's sometimes hard to pin down the organizational culture once and for all. It was Greek philosopher Heraclitus who said, "You can never step in the same river twice." One constant element in our lives, as well as in our work, is change. The pace of life and the development of new technological tools that are being introduced into the workplace support Heraclitus's notion that, because of change, the "river" that was here yesterday is different than the "river" here today. The organizational culture of yesterday is not the organizational culture of today or tomorrow.

Organizational Culture and Leadership

We've noted why it's important to be aware of organizational culture as a general concept, but it's especially important to understand the culture of an organization as you develop leadership experience. Such awareness can help you understand your role as both a leader and a follower. "Why is she doing this now?" asks an exasperated team member. Or, "What is the reason for this new policy? Don't we have enough to do without filling out new forms on the web?" asks a frazzled co-worker. Understanding the role of organizational culture can give you insight into the "Why" questions that you and others may ask when working in business and professional settings, especially when a leader proposes a new idea. A new policy, procedure, or ritual may be instituted not because of the whim of the leader (although that certainly may be the case), but as a result of the leader's understanding of the organizational culture. Rather than trying to interpret the action of a specific leader microscopically, in isolation from the larger culture of the organization, viewing leadership behavior from the broader perspective of organizational culture may provide new insights as to why new initiatives are suggested.

Leaders influence the culture of an organization by the symbols they use, both verbal symbols (what leaders say) as well as nonverbal symbols (what leaders do). Organizational culture expert Edgar Schein has identified five ways leaders communicate organizational culture through the symbols they use: (1) what they focus on and pay attention to; (2) how they react to major events and crises; (3) their actions as role models, coaches, or teachers; (4) the criteria they use to reward others; and (5) the criteria used to recruit, promote, and "excommunicate" others from the group.[26] Each of these ways of transmitting culture to an organization involves using symbols to communicate which behaviors in an organization should increase or decrease. As business expert Stanley Davis has noted, "Caring for the culture cannot be delegated. It can be shared but not left for someone else to do. The leader is the fountainhead. . . . If the leader is a great person then inspiring ideas will permeate the corporation's culture."[27] As we've emphasized, leadership is not always embodied in one person—many people influence others through communication. So, many people within an organization who influence or lead have the potential to influence the organizational culture. And with the power of influencing the culture of an organization comes certain ethical obligations and responsibilities.

Be Aware of How Ethics Influence Effective Leadership

Mindful leaders are aware that ethics play an important role in the leadership process. **Ethics** are the beliefs, values, and moral principles by which we determine what is right and wrong. Being sensitized to ethical communication and becoming aware of how to lead in an ethical manner will, we hope, prevent you from being seduced into unethical leadership practices.

off the mark   by Mark Parisi

offthemark.com

THE NEXT CORPORATE TREND: FLAMBOYANT FRIDAYS

Cartoon © Mark Parisi, Printed with Permission, www.offthemark.com

Ethics the beliefs, values, and moral principles by which we determine what is right and wrong.

A recent survey by the Ethics Resource Center found that 43 percent of employees surveyed believed their leaders were not good models of ethical leadership.[28] A number of headlines in the country's leading business periodicals and newspapers reporting unethical leadership practices support this survey finding.[29] Enron Corporation, which was the country's leading energy trading company, collapsed because of unethical communication and leadership practices; 31,000 people who worked for the company lost their jobs.[30] Another highly publicized example of unethical leadership involved Dennis Kozlowski, former CEO for Tyco International, who was charged with stealing $170 million in compensation and bonuses from the company he ran for 10 years, and an additional $430 million from its investors.[31]

For most people, being ethical means being sensitive to others' needs, giving people choices rather than forcing them to behave in a certain way, keeping sensitive information private, not intentionally decreasing others' feelings of self-worth, and being honest in presenting information. Unethical communication does just the opposite.

Being honest is a key element of ethical communication. If you knowingly withhold key information, lie, or distort the truth, then you are not communicating in an ethical manner. In addition to losing their jobs, many Enron employees also lost their retirement savings.[32] Enron executives were notorious for encouraging and influencing employees to invest in the organization, when these very executives at the same time were divesting or pulling out their stock and reinvesting it elsewhere, knowing that Enron was in financial trouble.[33]

Leaders are confronted with a number of ethical challenges. It's important for you to be aware of these challenges and prepared to manage them, including challenges of deceit, responsibility, and consistency.[34]

Challenge of Deceit

Leaders usually have access to information that gives them power. Depending on how they decide to use the information, they may deceive people. If they decide to disclose the information, they must decide when to release it and to whom. If leaders decide to reveal the information, they may run the risk of violating someone's trust. If they

>>> COMMUNICATION ETHICS @ WORK

Evaluating your own ethical business practices is one way for you to become aware of your communication with yourself and others. Use the following self-assessment guide to identify your ethical strengths and weaknesses.[35] Answering "Yes" to any of the questions below can suggest some areas where you may be ethically weak.

- Have I conducted personal business on company time?
- Have I used or taken company resources for personal purposes?
- Have I called in sick when I really wasn't?
- Have I used a derogatory term when referring to another person?
- Have I told or passed along an ethnic joke or sexually oriented joke?
- Have I engaged in negative gossip or spread rumors about someone?
- Have I "bad mouthed" the company or management to co-workers?
- Have I pried into a co-worker's conversations or private affairs?

- Have I passed along information that was shared with me in confidence?
- Have I knowingly ignored or violated an organizational rule or procedure?
- Have I failed to follow through on something I said I would do?
- Have I withheld information that others needed?
- Have I "fudged" on a time sheet, billing sheet, estimate, or report?
- Have I knowingly delivered a poor quality or defective good or service?
- Have I lied or manipulated the truth to make a sale?
- Have I accepted an inappropriate gift or gratuity?
- Have I taken credit for something that someone else did?
- Have I failed to admit to or correct a mistake I made?
- Have I knowingly let someone make an error and get into trouble?

decide to keep the information to themselves, they may mislead others who may need the information. This type of misleading occurred at Enron. The executive team had access to information that informed them that their company and their financial investments in the company were in trouble. Rather than sharing the information with others, they decided to keep the information to themselves so they could protect their own assets.[36] Ethical leaders manage the challenge of deceit by avoiding the following behaviors:

- Lying, especially when the lies will lead to personal benefit.
- Using information solely for personal benefit.
- Withholding knowledge that may benefit others.
- Collecting information that violates others' privacy rights.
- Disclosing information to people who do not have a need for or right to the information.

Challenge of Responsibility

As a leader, you're not only responsible for your own ethical behavior, you're also responsible for the ethical behavior of your team members. How your followers behave ultimately reflects on you. Although you don't have direct control over how your team members behave, you do have indirect control, in that you set the ethical tone for how your team is to conduct business. For example, if your followers see you taking office supplies home for personal use, processing time cards inaccurately, or treating administrative assistants and custodians in a disrespectful manner, then chances are they, too, will behave in a similar way. Ethical leaders manage the challenge of responsibility by

- Modeling ethical conduct at all times.
- Acknowledging and trying to correct ethical problems.
- Taking responsibility for the consequences of their orders and actions.
- Taking reasonable steps to prevent the unethical treatment of others.
- Holding themselves to the same standards as their team members.

Challenge of Consistency

Leaders interact with a variety of different team members and in different situations, making it difficult to behave in a consistent manner. Not all team members have the same needs, and effective leaders are aware of these individual differences and try to meet the needs of each team member. The challenge of consistency occurs when team members perceive leaders treating team members differently. If a leader treats all followers in a consistent manner, then some team members' needs will go unmet. If the leader treats team members differently, then some team members may perceive the leader as having favorites. Ethical leaders manage the challenge of consistency by

- Being proactive and informing team members that in order to lead in an ethical manner, it's important to treat team members as individuals with individual needs.
- Informing team members of the criteria they use for making decisions.
- Sharing with team members, when appropriate, how they went about making a decision.

Your awareness of these ethical challenges will influence the communication you use to manage them. Although working through such challenges is never easy, the five principles of communication will help you begin this process of leading in an ethical manner.

Summary

This chapter introduced you to the first of five communication principles: *Be aware of your communication with yourself and others.* In this chapter, we discussed ways to become a more mindful communicator at work. This process begins by becoming aware of social styles and why they're important. Your social style is a pattern of communication behaviors that others observe when you interact with them. It is your social signature. Your social style is a combination of two primary dimensions—assertiveness and responsiveness. Assertiveness is the capacity to make requests, whereas responsiveness is the capacity to be sensitive to the communication of others. When these two dimensions are combined, they yield four different social styles: expressive, amiable, driver, and analytical. The chapter also discussed style-flexing skills, which are strategies for adapting your social style to others' social styles to ensure effective and productive communication.

Second, becoming a mindful communicator involves being aware of the leadership assumptions that ultimately influence your approach to leadership. Leadership is the process of influencing others to achieve goals through verbal and nonverbal messages. How you influence others depends on some of the assumptions you have about what motivates people to behave. Four leadership assumptions were detailed: classical, human relations, human resources, and systems approaches. The classical approach assumes that there is one best way to perform a specific task. The human relations approach assumes that people are motivated by their individual needs. The human resources approach assumes that workers want to be involved in determining how work should be accomplished. The systems approach assumes that teams and organizations are systems and that each element in the system affects all other elements.

Third, you need to be aware of how the communication symbols we use at work, such as written policies, stories, metaphors, ceremonies, and artifacts, create the organizational culture. In addition to creating the culture, these symbols also influence workplace communication. Put another way, communication creates the culture and the culture influences the communication. It's a reciprocal process.

Fourth, the need to be aware of how ethics influence leadership is a growing concern for leaders, followers, and organizations. Leaders are confronted with a number of ethical challenges that must be managed well if the leader is to remain effective. The challenge of deceit focuses on how leaders should manage and use information. At times leaders must withhold important information, thereby deceiving a person. At other times, a leader must distribute information that may violate a person's privacy. The challenge of responsibility arises because leaders are responsible not only for their own behaviors, over which they have direct control, but also for the behaviors of others, which they control only indirectly. The challenge of consistency occurs when leaders are perceived as treating followers in an inconsistent manner. Although leaders strive for consistency, at times they must be inconsistent.

Discussion Questions

1. Describe what it means to be self-aware in communication with others, and explain why self-awareness is important.

2. Define social style. Discuss the effects of social style on communication behaviors.

3. List and describe each of the four social styles.

4. Discuss some ways of adapting to other social styles in your communication with others.

5. List and define each of the four main approaches to leadership (classical, human relations, human resources, and systems theory).

6. Evaluate the workplace at a current or previous job by identifying the leadership assumptions that appear to be operating there and describing the organizational culture.

7. List and describe each of the three ethical challenges, and give examples.

Building Your Skills

1. Think of a time at work that you or someone you know was faced with an ethical challenge. What do you think you did right? What, if anything, do you wish you had done differently?

2. Compare your own results on Rating Scale 2.1 with those of a few classmates. Create a skit to demonstrate the styles represented in your group.

3. Describe in your journal an instance when you had to use style flexing to communicate effectively with someone at work.

4. Reflecting on your current job or a previous job, evaluate the organization in terms of the basic assumptions about leadership that guide the organization. Does your supervisor have a classical approach to leadership? Do you have a boss who consistently uses rewards and punishments? Or is the organization more aligned with the human resources approach? Give examples to support your ideas.

5. Discuss with another classmate one of the three ethical challenges leaders can face. Now, find a real-life example in current events of a leader struggling with an ethical challenge. What would you do if you were that leader? What could he or she have done better?

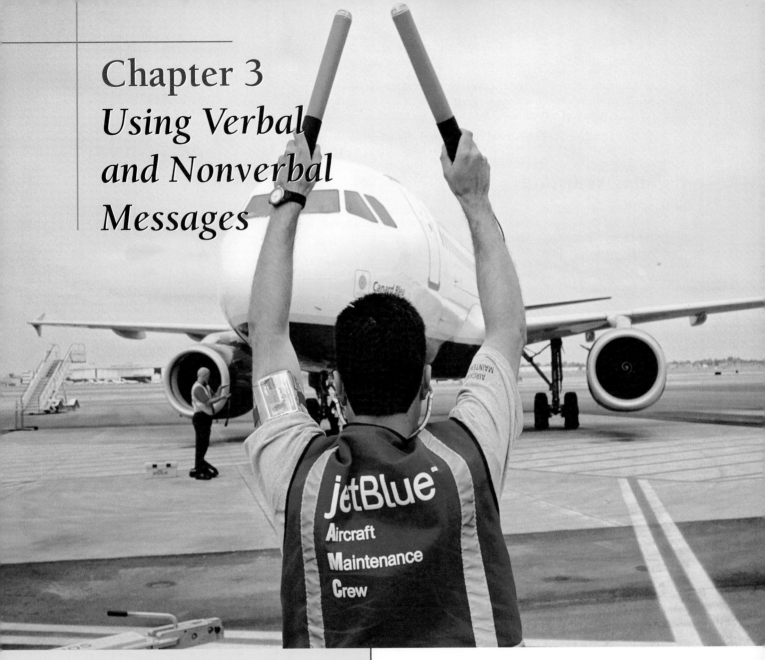

Chapter 3
Using Verbal and Nonverbal Messages

chapter outline

After reading this chapter, you should be able to

- Explain the difference between the denotative and connotative meanings of a word.

- Differentiate the three aspects of communicating clear verbal messages: being concrete, being concise, and being relevant. Give an example of each.

- Give examples of both descriptive "I" language and evaluative "you" language.

- Implement the six strategies for supportive communication.

- List and describe the six functions of nonverbal communication.

- Explain and give examples of eight strategies for using nonverbal messages to enhance leadership.

- Describe several ways to avoid or respond to sexual harassment in the workplace.

Leaders influence others by using verbal and nonverbal messages. In many ways, verbal and nonverbal messages are the tools of leadership. As a new leader, your first job will be to understand how to use and interpret messages that are appropriate for the workplace. For example, Starbucks puts its new baristas through an extensive training program so that they will develop proficiency in the "coffee" vocabulary, which is a must before they ever hit the Starbucks' sales floor.[1] The same is true of airline service managers who lead teams of ground service employees. These professionals must master a number of hand gestures that are used to help pilots steer their jets into specific locations on the tarmac. Since the noise from jet engines makes verbal messages impossible, ground service employees communicate with each other using elaborate systems of hand gestures and body movements. Whether leading baristas at Starbucks or ground service employees at an airport, leaders use verbal and nonverbal messages to get the job done.

To help enhance your leadership effectiveness, we're going to emphasize two more communication principles for leadership.

Principle Two: Effectively use and interpret verbal messages. Figure 3.1 illustrates where this second principle fits into our model of communication principles and skills for leadership. **Verbal messages** are messages that use words to create meaning. A **language** is a system of symbols (words or vocabulary) common to a community of people and structured by grammar (rules and standards) and syntax (patterns in the arrangement of words). Every business and professional setting has a language that is unique. Your ability to lead will depend on your ability to use and interpret verbal messages unique to your workplace. Using and interpreting verbal messages effectively will allow you to get the work done by making messages clear, supportive, and assertive.

Principle Three: Effectively use and interpret nonverbal messages. Principle Three is also highlighted in Figure 3.1. **Nonverbal messages** are visual and audible symbols that do rely on words or language to create meaning. Nonverbal messages are not only visual messages, such as hand gestures and posture, but also messages that we can hear. People sigh when they're bored; they use a vocal interrupter when they want to signal to others that they would like to add something to the conversation. Using and interpreting nonverbal messages effectively will allow you to get work done by focusing on the relational aspects of messages, those communicated by such means as physical appearance, posture and movement, facial expressions and eye contact, and touch.

> *Don't use words too big for the subject. Don't say "infinitely" when you mean "very"; otherwise you'll have no word left when you want to talk about something really infinite."*
>
> —C. S. LEWIS

How To Communicate Clear Verbal Messages

In order to communicate clear messages, it's important to understand how people interpret verbal messages. People interpret verbal messages in a couple of ways—denotatively

---

Figure 3.1 | Communication Principles and Skills for Leadership

Aware

Verbal

Nonverbal

Listen

Adapt

Verbal messages messages that use words to create meaning.

Language a system of symbols (words) common to a community of people and structured by grammar (rules and standards) and syntax (patterns in the arrangement of words).

Nonverbal messages visual and audible symbols that do not rely on words but create meaning for the receiver.

and connotatively. When we interpret the **denotative meaning** of verbal messages, we interpret the words literally; we use the dictionary's definition. When we interpret the **connotative meaning** of verbal messages, we interpret the words based on our personal experiences. To illustrate the difference between denotative and connotative interpretations, let's take a look at the word *merger*. Some people interpret *merger* literally, to mean the joining together of two or more companies or organizations. However, some people who have survived a corporate merger interpret the word based on their personal experiences; to them the word stimulates feelings of fear, anxiety, and anger and has connotations of disruption and stress brought on by layoffs or unfamiliar new routines.

To make messages clear, it's important to consider how others will interpret your verbal messages. If people receiving your verbal messages have experience with the topic you're communicating about, chances are they will interpret your message on a connotative level. If the information you're conveying is unfamiliar to others, they are more likely to interpret the message on a denotative level.

Learning how to make your verbal messages concrete, concise, and relevant are three skills that will help you make verbal messages clear.

Be Concrete

A word is **concrete** if you can experience what the word refers to (the referent) with one of your senses. If you can see it, touch it, smell it, taste it, or hear it, then it's concrete. If you cannot do these things with the referent, then the word is an abstract word. As illustrated in Figure 3.2, all words fall on a continuum from concrete to abstract.

For example, "interoffice communication" is abstract, a "memo" is a concrete example of the process. "Professional development" is an abstract concept, whereas a "conflict-management training program" would be a concrete example of the concept. Using concrete words and phrases in the workplace helps avoid miscommunication. Being clear by using concrete words is especially important as workplaces become more diverse and international.

There are times, however, when more abstract words may be preferred. **Strategically ambiguous messages** are unclear messages that you use in a careful manner to reach specific goals.[2] There are times when being too concrete and honest may have consequences. For example, suppose your manager asks you for some feedback on her management style and you find her style defensive and combative. Even though your manager is

---

Denotative meaning the literal or dictionary definition of a word.

Connotative meaning the interpretation of a word based on personal experiences.

Concrete referring to something you can experience with your senses.

Strategically ambiguous messages messages that may not convey all available information or may be unclear and are used purposely by the source to reach some goal.

Figure 3.2 | Abstract-Concrete Word Continuum

ABSTRACT ←————————————————————————→ CONCRETE

Justice	Legal system	Attorney	Jonathan Butterfield, Attorney at Law
Money management	Financial plan		Budget
Human resource	Employee		Jane Smith, second-shift supervisor
Software	Operating system		MAC OS 10.4.11
Creature	Mammal	Dog	Mickey, a Border Collie
Employment	Blue-collar job		Second-shift production supervisor
Mobility	Vehicle	Compact car	2008 MINI Cooper S
Sweetness	Dessert		Crème brulée

asking for your feedback, this is probably a situation in which using an abstract message may be advantageous. Rather than saying that her management style is too "defensive," you say "I notice that you're not afraid to say what you think." This response is ambiguous in that it doesn't clearly communicate an evaluation; it's neither positive nor negative but open to interpretation.

In the following sections we'll discuss ways of communicating concrete verbal messages at work.

Use specific words. Specific words clarify meaning by narrowing down the discussion from a general category to a particular group within that category. For example, a district manager mentions in a meeting that she is concerned about employees' performance, when in reality she is only concerned about sales representatives' job performance. The "sales representative" employee group is a specific category within the larger employee group. The sales group may unfortunately miss the fact that the district manager's message is aimed at them, and thus take it less seriously. By narrowing the topic, we make our verbal messages more specific and thus more concrete and clear, reducing miscommunication.

Use precise words. Precise words are those that most accurately express meaning; they capture shades of difference. For example, when discussing a co-worker's communication in a meeting, Armando mentioned that the co-worker was too "aggressive." To some people, aggressive communication means communication that is hostile, demanding, attacks another person personally, or pushes a sale too hard. To others, an aggressive communicator is someone who is assertive and competitive. Because there are different types of aggressive communication, it is best to be as specific as possible. In this case, Armando might do better to describe the specific aggressive behaviors that were inappropriate. For example, Armando might point out that the person in question demanded that his co-workers work around his schedule, called his co-workers "a group of slackers," and threatened his potential clients by indicating that if they didn't purchase a particular product from him he would drop them from the preferred customer program.

Use jargon carefully. **Jargon** is language that is used by a particular group, profession, or culture and may not be understood or used by other people. Most professional workplaces are full of jargon. When we're new on the job, it usually takes us a while to learn the new language. Part of any new employee orientation program is to teach new trainees the language of the workplace. New employees at Walt Disney World, for example, attend the Disney University where they are introduced to a new vocabulary: the language of the theater. Rather than being an employee, you're a "cast member." Uniforms are referred to as "costumes" and customers are "guests." Use of jargon helps us fit in, makes our communication faster and easier, and makes us more likeable to our co-workers.

Jargon a word or phrase used by a particular group that may not be understood by members outside that group.

>>> COMMUNICATION ETHICS @ WORK

When Merck introduced a prescription painkiller, Vioxx, to the market, it instantly became a popular money-making drug for the pharmaceutical giant. The popularity of this drug stemmed from its manufacturer's claim that the drug had no gastrointestinal side effects, making it superior to other available pain relievers.

However, a number of external clinical trials showed that use of Vioxx increased cardiovascular risk. Investigations showed that even before the drug was introduced, there was awareness at Merck that Vioxx might carry significant cardiovascular risk. Although Merck's advertising mentioned the lack of gastrointestinal side effects, it did not include any mention of the heart-related risk. The U.S. Food and Drug Administration required Merck to send letters to physicians to correct "false or misleading impressions and information." Ultimately the company withdrew its money-making drug from the market. Merck's stock price fell by 40 percent and the company faced a loss of billions of dollars.[3]

This episode revealed a practice that many consider unethical: omitting information. Are there times at work, however, when telling every detail of what you know may not be the best thing to do? Does this depend on the nature of the situation? What do you think? When considering whether to omit information, what factors should you take into consideration? Do you think a purposeful omission is a lie? Is lying ever justified?

Although jargon serves a useful purpose, it can be confusing to those who are not familiar with it. Who is receiving your verbal messages? Will they understand your jargon? Many working professionals quickly internalize new jargon and vocabulary; they forget that not long ago this jargon didn't make any sense. Just as jargon can create positive identity and affiliation among those who share it, it can also create negative identity and a lack of affiliation or a feeling of exclusion among those who are not familiar with the jargon.

Be Concise

A concise verbal message is brief and one from which unnecessary words and phrases have been removed. For example, assume you're an employee listening to a human resource representative explain company policy regarding the use of the Internet while on the job. He says the following in his presentation: "Although it is our policy to provide Internet access to enable employees to conduct the on-line communications necessary to enact their job responsibilities, the Internet should not be utilized for personal communications or nonbusiness-related activities." You lose interest in the message because it's too wordy. Here's a concise message that conveys the same meaning: "Use the Internet only for company business." This message is targeted, concise, and efficient. It clearly articulates the company's policy on the Internet using as few words as possible. In fact, communication researchers have identified communication efficiency or conciseness as one of the criteria used to differentiate competent from incompetent communicators.[4] In the U.S. workplace, where "time is money" and productivity is highly valued, concise communicators are considered more competent than long-winded and verbose communicators.[5]

Following are some ways you can make your verbal messages more concise:

- *Use simple words and phrases.* Rather than talking about the Health Maintenance Organization, you discuss the health plan. Instead of talking about the World Wide Web, you refer to it as the Internet or the web.

- *Reduce unnecessary contextual information.* Don't discuss detailed background information leading up to the point. Instead, get to the point.

>>> COMMUNICATION AND GLOBALIZATION @WORK

The South American country of Ecuador has the United States beat when it comes to a critical wireless technology. Americans may be ten times as wealthy, but Ecuadorians send four times as many text messages.[6] Text messaging—or SMS (short messaging service), as it's more commonly known overseas—is evolving beyond simple communication into a delivery mechanism for vital content and a mobile interface to the wired world. But if you want to get a taste for this revolution, you'll have to head abroad.

Cell phone users in other countries such as Ecuador and the Philippines average more than 200 SMS messages a month. The Danes and Irish average 100 a month. Americans manage to tap out fewer than 50. Why the difference? In part, it's simply a matter of critical mass, with people adopting SMS because their friends are using it.

If U.S. businesses want to continue to compete in the global marketplace, they will need to bring successful SMS services into businesses here at home. Internet search engine giant Google understands this, which is why it's basing much of its wireless development in London, not Mountain View, California.

What kinds of businesses succeed using SMS overseas? In cell-phone–saturated Finland, there are popular TV programs where you can send texts that scroll onto the screen in a live chat, and others where you direct a character with SMS. Exponentia, a startup business in Vancouver, British Columbia, has a service that allows Canadians to predict the next play by SMS in everything from golf to hockey. And in Britain, retailer HMV is launching a service that lets customers buy CDs and DVDs by texting a message to a number found in a newspaper ad. In Thailand, Pepsi ran a World Cup promotion with text-message codes found under soda bottle caps.

The growth of text messaging in a global marketplace requires us to open our minds to a new technology that could untether commerce, social networks, and other applications originally tied to PCs. As innovators begin to translate services originated abroad to U.S. cell phones, we'll start really "getting the message."

- *Communicate solutions.* The workplace is about finding and implementing solutions to problems. Many professionals don't need to know all of the people and situations that contributed to a particular problem. They're not interested in learning about the problem. They are interested in solutions to problems.

Be Relevant

Relevant messages are messages that satisfy others' personal needs and goals.[7] Much of your communication in the workplace will be instructional: Your goal will be to help others learn. Informing a co-worker about a new procedure or training a group of new employees in a skill are examples of when you would want to use relevant messages. When you make messages relevant to others, you put yourself in the other person's shoes for a while and you answer the question "How does this information benefit me?" For example, effective teachers find ways of making course content immediately useful for students. Teachers' ability to use relevant messages in their teaching has been associated with a number of important instructional outcomes, such as student motivation and learning.[8]

Although text messaging is already quite popular as a means of social communication in the United States, its use is becoming increasingly necessary for U.S. businesses that want to compete globally.

Here are a few strategies for making your verbal messages more relevant to those receiving them, whether they are your superiors, subordinates, co-workers, or customers.

Explain the usefulness of information. Instead of making the message about you and your needs, make the message about the other person's needs. For example, if your manager is reluctant to upgrade the software on your computer because of cost, use messages that inform your manager of how the upgraded software will ultimately help her reach her monthly performance goals.

Use other-focused rather than self-focused messages. Other-focused messages are receiver-centered, whereas self-focused messages are source-centered. Table 3.1 illustrates

Table 3.1   Other-Focused Versus Self-Focused Messages

Self-Focused Messages	Other-Focused Messages
I'm Ricardo Gonzalez from Progresso Corporation. My presentation will cover the following four points: Progresso product line, our partnering criteria, our point-of-sale promotional plans, and what we need from you.	I'm Ricardo Gonzalez from Progresso Corporation. Let me make sure I understand your priorities for our time together. Based on our previous conversations, here's what I think you're after.
I'd like to cover the material I have in about 25 minutes and then open it up for questions.	You'd like to open up the Hispanic youth market, and you see an opportunity with Progresso's products to do that.
I'm very proud of the new Muzika2, which builds on the massive feature set of the Muzika product line. Although physical dimensions are somewhat larger, the Muzika2 includes Tortis and WAV playback support and a dedicated Optical Line-in i-Socket.	You've said that durable MP3 players are priced out of reach for most of your market. Our durable new Muzika2 has many features of the much more expensive MP3, but at half the cost. The only real sacrifice is that the Muzika2 is a fraction larger.

Relevant messages messages that others perceive to satisfy their own needs and goals.

the two types of messages with excerpts from a sales presentation.[9] Although the content of the two types of messages in Table 3.1 is essentially the same, the messages are framed from two different perspectives. A potential customer will perceive the other-focused messages to be more relevant and may perceive a sales representative using the self-focused messages as self-absorbed and more interested in meeting his or her own personal needs than the needs of the customer.

Use familiar examples. If you're pitching a new product to a customer, make the new product relevant and familiar to the customer by comparing and contrasting the new product to an old product that the customer is currently using and is familiar with.

RECAP: Communicating Clear Verbal Messages

Goals	Tools	Definitions	Example
Be concrete	Use specific words	Specific words clarify meaning by narrowing down the discussion from a general category to a particular group within that category.	Rather than referring to all customers, refer to the specific group of customers (for example, preferred customers, repeat customers)
	Use precise words	Precise words are those that most accurately express meaning; they capture shades of difference.	Rather than referring to your co-worker as "lazy," point out that she consistently fails to help you with the quarterly report.
	Use jargon carefully	Jargon is language that is used by a particular group, profession, or culture and may not be understood or used by other people.	Instead of directing a new employee to the CCA building, tell her the name of the building (Corporate Communication and Advertising).
Be concise	Use simple words and phrases		Instead of saying, "We're going to work on the logistics," you simply say, "We're going to plan."
	Reduce unnecessary contextual information	State the point of a message and avoid detailed background information.	At a job interview, don't tell a potential employer unnecessary details about your recent termination.
	Communicate solutions		Report the committee's findings at the meeting; avoid discussing the problem-solving methods.
Be relevant	Explain the usefulness of information	Make a message about the other person's needs.	Explain to a supervisor the financial benefits of an upgraded computer system.
	Use other-focused rather than self-focused messages		Rather than saying, "Here's what I would like to talk about," ask "What would you like to know about?"
	Use examples familiar to your intended audience.		Rather than refering to a successful leader from the past, you refer to a contemporary leader.

How To Communicate
Supportive Verbal Messages

Like a state or a region of the country, every workplace has a climate. Some workplace environments are supportive, meaning that there is a climate of trust, caring, and acceptance. Other workplace environments are competitive, meaning that there is a climate of hostility and mistrust. Hostile climates develop when employees are disgruntled, which often happens when two companies merge and form one larger company. This was the case when computer maker Hewlett-Packard purchased Compaq computer in 2002. Although the combined company was financially stronger and had a larger share of the computer market, the two employee groups did not trust each other, because of layoffs that followed the merger and different ways of doing business.[10] What makes the difference in the climate of a workplace is the communication that is used in it.[11] Communication scholar Jack Gibb suggests the following verbal communication strategies for creating a supportive workplace environment.[12]

Use Descriptive "I" Language Rather Than Evaluative "You" Language

Most people don't like to be judged or evaluated. Criticizing and name-calling obviously can create relational problems at work, but so can attempts to diagnose others' problems or win their affection with insincere praise. In fact, any form of evaluation creates a climate of defensiveness. One way to avoid evaluating others is to eliminate the accusatory *you* from your language. Statements such as "Your work is always late" or "You're not a team player" attack a person's sense of self-worth and usually lead to a defensive reaction.

Instead, use the word *I* to describe the other person's behavior.[13] For example, suppose you are working with someone you perceive to have an attitude problem. Rather than saying, "You have an attitude problem," which will only provoke defensiveness, try describing what you see and hear the other person doing and saying. In other words, what does a "bad attitude" *look* and *sound* like? Try saying, "I see you rolling your eyes, sighing, looking away from me, and crossing your arms, which leads me to believe that you're unhappy with me." This type of message opens the door for conversation. "You" language is evaluative and judgmental; "I" language remains descriptive and detailed, which helps the other person see how his or her behavior is affecting you and your goals.

Although we've discussed the importance of using "I" messages versus "you" messages, interpersonal communication researchers Amy Bippus and Stacy Young found that simply prefacing messages with the word *I* instead of *you* doesn't always eliminate conflict.[14] Sometimes simply using an "I" message may be too subtle to take the sting out of a more negative message you want to express to another person. You may need to first use an affirming message followed by an "I" message when communicating negative information to another person. An **affirming message** is one that reveals that you value another person; it communicates support. Saying something like "I don't want you to misinterpret what I'm about to say, because I really do care about you," or "I appreciate all that you do; however, I need to let you know what I see going on at work" may have a better chance of enhancing communication in conflict situations than simply using descriptive "I" language versus evaluative "you" language.

Affirming message a message that reveals that you value and support another person.

Using "I" language when evaluating another's work contributes to a supportive workplace environment.

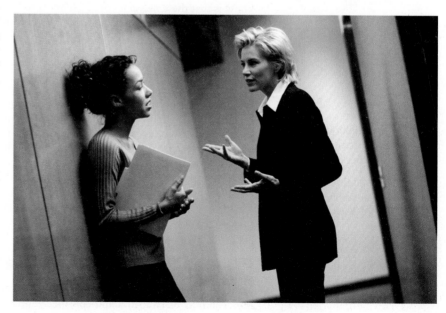

Solve Problems Rather Than Control Others

Most of us don't like others' attempts to control us. Someone who presumes to tell us what's good for us is likely to cause us to feel defensive and not supported. We suggest you communicate from a problem orientation rather than from a controlling orientation. A *problem orientation* is an approach that views a situation as a problem that can be solved together. Leaders who use this kind of approach make requests of others; in other words, they ask others for their help and support in solving a problem, hoping that they will "buy into" the solution. A *controlling orientation* is an approach that views a situation as a problem that one person solves by telling another person what to do. Leaders who use this kind of approach make demands on others. A problem orientation would sound like this: "We have a problem and I need your help solving it." A controlling orientation would sound like this: "There's a problem and I need you to do this to fix it." Again, the goal is to manage the situation without provoking defensiveness. Most people don't like being told what to do. Instead, people prefer being a part of the solution by being asked to help.

Be Genuine Rather Than Manipulative

To be genuine means that you seek to be yourself rather than someone you're not. It also means taking an honest interest in others and considering the uniqueness of each individual and situation. Try managing a difficult situation at work by being honest with the other person. For example, has your manager ever influenced you to work an extra shift by making you feel guilty? Have you ever been in a meeting where another person got his or her way by distracting the other group members from the real problem? Manipulation usually increases defensiveness and suspicion in others.[15] When they feel as though they've been manipulated, people usually say, "Why didn't he just come out and say what the problem was?" or "Why did she have to go behind our backs?" To be genuine is to be honest and upfront about problems and issues that affect the workplace.

Empathize Rather Than Detach from Others

The word **empathy** comes from the Greek word for "passion" and from a translation of the German word *Einfuhlung*, meaning "to feel with." To empathize with someone is to try to feel what he or she is feeling, rather than to simply think about or acknowledge the feelings of another person. Empathy occurs when we try putting ourselves into the other person's shoes or try seeing a problem as he or she sees it. Rather than remaining detached, try saying, "Help me to understand the problem from your perspective." When working through a difficult situation at work, some people say, "I don't care. I'm not going to deal with this." Although they may believe that this is the best way to manage the situation, what they don't know is that these messages of detachment only cause more anger, ill feelings, and distrust. Even if what another person is saying to you feels like a personal attack, try empathizing.

Be Flexible Rather Than Rigid

Flexible people qualify their language by using **conditional statements**, which qualify what is being said and leave room for interpretations. For example, a manager for a pharmaceutical sales company says, "*In my opinion*, one of the reasons sales are down is because the sales representative lacks communication skills." **Declarative statements** are expressed as truths and leave no room for interpretation. For example, a manager might say, "Sales are down because the sales representative lacks communication skills." Rigid people have a tendency to use declarative statements rather than conditional statements. Do you know anyone who always has the answer to every question and the solution to every problem? This type of "always right" attitude, which is perceived as rigid and unbending, usually increases defensiveness in workplace settings.

Present Yourself as Equal Rather Than as Superior

You can anger others by letting them know that you view yourself as better than they are. You may be educated and consider yourself intelligent. However, you don't need to

Empathy the emotion experienced by someone who feels what another is feeling.

Conditional statements statements that qualify what is being said; they leave room for interpretation.

Declarative statements statements expressed as truths that leave no room for interpretation.

announce it. In many ways, being a humble leader and presenting yourself as equal and similar rather than as superior and different will enhance your leadership effectiveness. Some people manage difficult situations at work by "pulling rank" with others; they might say, "I'm the leader and you're not," or "I have been here longer than you." We feel certain that you've already experienced these types of messages at school and work. Superior messages showcase differences rather than similarities. To enhance supportiveness, we encourage you to present yourself as an equal to others. For example, a message that reflects equality might be "Since we are colleagues and work together every day, it's important that we work out our differences."

RECAP: Communicating Supportive Verbal Messages

Verbal Communication Strategies	Examples
Use Descriptive "I" Language Rather Than Evaluative "You" Language	Instead of telling a co-worker, "You're not a team player," say something like "I didn't see you participating in the meeting today."
Solve Problems Rather Than Control Others	Instead of telling an employee whom you supervise "Don't do that," say, "Maybe this will work better."
Be Genuine Rather Than Manipulative	Rather than making up an excuse about why you missed an important deadline, to get your manager to feel sorry for you, be honest with her about your mistake.
Empathize Rather Than Detaching from Others	Don't ignore or quickly end a conversation with a member of your team if you know she needs someone to listen to her.
Be Flexible Rather Than Rigid	Rather than telling someone "I'm right, you are wrong," use more conditional language: "I may be wrong, but . . ."
Present Yourself as Equal Rather Than as Superior	Ask an employee, "Can we get this done today?" rather than telling him, "I am the manager and I need you to do this now."

How To Understand Nonverbal Messages

It's your first day on the job and you're being introduced as the new leader of the team. You walk into a crowded room and notice that the only empty chair is at the front of the room. The person introducing you invites you to sit down in this chair. Although where people sit in a meeting may seem trivial, it's quite important. The positions of chairs in a room or around a conference table send nonverbal messages that communicate power and status. Understanding the significance and power of nonverbal messages will enhance your ability to lead effectively.

Researchers have found that people form impressions of strangers within as few as two seconds of meeting them by observing their nonverbal messages. What's interesting is that these instant impressions rarely change, even after the two people have become better acquainted.[16] If you are to interpret others' nonverbal messages accurately, it's important to understand what makes nonverbal communication unique, including its characteristics and functions.

Understanding Characteristics of Nonverbal Communication

There are a number of characteristics that make nonverbal messages unique from verbal messages, including their ability to convey feelings, form relationships, express truth, and reveal a culture.

Nonverbal messages convey feelings. Social psychologist Albert Mehrabian concluded that as little as 7 percent of the emotional meaning in messages is communicated through verbal channels.[17] The most significant source of emotional communication is our face—according to Mehrabian's study, it carries as much as 55 percent of the emotional meaning in messages. Vocal cues such as volume, pitch, and intensity communicate another 38 percent of the meaning. In all, 93 percent of the emotional meaning in our messages is communicated through nonverbal channels. Although these percentages do not apply to every communication situation, the results of Mehrabian's study do illustrate the potential power of nonverbal messages in communicating emotion.[18] Researchers continue to find new ways to measure the impact of nonverbal messages in the communication of emotions.[19]

Nonverbal messages form relationships. Nonverbal messages allow us to connect with others. Whereas verbal messages convey the content of a message (*what* is being said), nonverbal messages (*how* it is said) convey or establish the nature of the relationship. Nonverbal messages tend to convey meaning about the quality of the interaction that is taking place.[20] For example, upon leaving a job interview, the applicant hears the interviewer saying, "Thanks for coming to the interview. I will be giving you a call." The verbal message (*what* is said) sounds promising, and the nonverbal messages (*how* it was said) suggests that the interviewer is sincere and will probably be calling soon to extend the job offer: The interviewer makes direct eye contact and shakes the applicant's hand firmly and vigorously. If the interviewer had avoided eye contact and seemed awkward or rushed, the applicant would have been right to feel doubtful that the interviewer would call.

Nonverbal messages express truth. If you want to know how people really feel or what they think about a particular topic, pay attention to their nonverbal messages. Although people try to hide their true feelings, especially at work when others may be evaluating them, feelings have a tendency to "leak out" through nonverbal messages. Nonverbal leakage cues

>>> COMMUNICATION AND GLOBALIZATION @ WORK

With the advent of new technologies, our world is becoming increasingly smaller.[21] The workplace at home is more diverse, leading to a need for increased cultural sensitivity. As well, many companies no longer operate solely on American soil. This has led to an increased need for more cultural awareness when communicating at work. Even the most well-intentioned ideas can be misunderstood in cross-cultural communication.

For example, the Shanghai World Financial Center is a skyscraper that has been intermittently under construction in Shanghai, China, since 1997. Work was temporarily interrupted by the Asian financial crisis in the late 1990s and later to accommodate design changes by the developer. The most distinctive feature in the design of the building is an aperture (an opening) at the peak. The aperture, a structural element intended to relieve wind pressure on the immensely tall building, originally was designed in the form of a circular "moon gate." After the American architecture and development firm Kohn Peterson Fox (KPF) submitted the intended design, they began facing protests from the Chinese, including the mayor of Shanghai, who considered the circle design to be too similar to the rising sun design of the flag of Japan, China's historical enemy.

Facing potential protests because of the design, in 2005 KPF submitted an alternative design for the building and used a trapezoidal hole instead of the circle at the top of the tower, changing the controversial circular design. This example illustrates what can happen when someone (or in this case, an American company) with good intentions simply misunderstands what a symbol might represent to those from another culture.

Being culturally sensitive is now a marketable skill in the workplace. Although not all cross-cultural nonverbal communication problems are of the magnitude described in the example above, smaller nonverbal faux pas can be problematic when working and doing business in a global marketplace. The following websites suggest ways to help you develop cross-cultural business etiquette skills.

www.businesstravelogue.com
This site has reports and general information on international business etiquette. Among other things, there are sections on gestures, taboos, and manners.

www.worldbiz.com
This site provides a series of country-specific reports on international business travel. The topics covered include dining etiquette and protocol.

reveal how you really feel or think about a topic or a problem. For example, a man may say, "Her comment didn't bother me," but you know the comment did bother this person: You saw his face drop and his posture slump when his co-worker made the comment. When someone's verbal and nonverbal messages don't match, we have a tendency to trust the nonverbal messages.

Why do we have a tendency to believe nonverbal more than verbal messages? Research suggests that people are not always consciously aware of their nonverbal messages. When you speak, you have a tendency to think about what you're going to say; even if it's just a brief statement, you encode your verbal message consciously. With nonverbal messages, there is very little, if any, conscious encoding. Nonverbal

messages are more spontaneous and are conveyed by means outside of your conscious awareness. Your nonverbal messages "leak" from your body. You can slow down the leaking by becoming more aware of how you use nonverbal messages. [22]

Cross-cultural communication requires cultural sensitivity. The designers of the Shanghai World Financial Center learned this the hard way.

Nonverbal messages are culture bound. The nonverbal messages that work in one culture may not work in another culture. Every culture has its own rules and standards for what is appropriate nonverbal behavior. Although in the United States the thumbs-up sign usually conveys a positive meaning, in the Middle East, the thumbs-up sign is an obscene gesture.[23] Every workplace also has a culture or a way of behaving that is unique to the specific organization. This workplace culture is revealed in the kinds of nonverbal communication that people use in that organization.

Understanding Functions of Nonverbal Communication

Nonverbal messages serve six functions in the communication process: substituting, complementing, repeating, regulating, accenting, and contradicting.

Substituting. Substituting occurs when we use a nonverbal message to replace a verbal message. Rather than verbally telling you to be quiet while she takes a phone call during a meeting, your manager puts her index finger to her lips in a vertical position, which most people understand to mean "be quiet."

Complementing. Complementing occurs when the verbal and the nonverbal messages are expressed *at the same time*, enriching the meaning that is created. A person saying, "It was nice meeting you," while at the same time shaking the other person's hand is using the handshake to complement the verbal message.

Repeating. Repeating occurs when we use a verbal message and then follow up the verbal message with a nonverbal message that means the same thing. When we say "Time out" and then follow up the verbal message with the time-out hand gesture used by football referees, we are using a nonverbal message to repeat the verbal message.

Regulating. Regulating occurs when we use nonverbal messages to control the interaction patterns in a conversation. If we want to make a comment during a meeting, we might raise a hand or at least a finger. This signals to others that we want to add something to the conversation.

Accenting. As you'll see later in the chapter, certain aspects of the voice (including the emphasis given to words) are considered nonverbal communication. Accenting occurs when we emphasize only part of a verbal message. Consider all the different ways you can change the meaning in the following statement by emphasizing a different word.

"*I* didn't say you had an attitude problem."

"I *didn't* say you had an attitude problem."

"I didn't *say* you had an attitude problem."

"I didn't say *you* had an attitude problem."

"I didn't say you *had* an attitude problem."

"I didn't say you had an *attitude* problem."

"I didn't say you had an attitude *problem*."

Contradicting. When the nonverbal message is incongruent with the verbal message, we have a contradiction. For example, you say with a smile how disappointed you are in your employee's job performance. We usually expect nonverbal and verbal messages to create or stimulate the same meaning in others. Whenever the messages are incongruent, it takes most of us a little time to figure out the intended message. Many comedians use the contradiction function of nonverbal communication very effectively. People find sarcasm and irony funny because of the mixed meanings.

We encourage you to not only observe these six functions of nonverbal communication at work but identify how you use the six functions in your own nonverbal communication with others. You will begin to see and appreciate the multifaceted nature of this important message system.

RECAP: Nonverbal Characteristics and Functions

Nonverbal Characteristics	Example
Nonverbal messages convey feelings.	A manager bounces his leg when he is nervous.
Nonverbal messages form relationships.	An interviewer offers you a strong handshake as you are leaving a job interview.
Nonverbal messages are believable.	Your co-worker shouts "I'M NOT ANGRY WITH YOU!!"
Nonverbal messages are culture bound.	In some corporate cultures, employees are expected to wear only tailored business suits.

Nonverbal Functions	Example
Substituting	A leader gives her team members the "thumbs-up" following a sales presentation to an important client.
Complementing	Your boss nods while saying "yes."
Repeating	When giving directions, a pedestrian tells you to turn north on the highway, then points to the north.
Regulating	A team leader uses hand gestures to control who talks during a meeting.
Accenting	When he arrives at the last minute before your presentation, you ask your co-worker "*Where* have you *been?*"
Contradicting	When asked how things are at home, a co-worker lowers her head and avoids eye contact while answering, "Fine."

How To Interpret Nonverbal Messages

Your ability to use and interpret nonverbal messages effectively at work depends on your ability to recognize various sources of nonverbal messages, including physical appearance, vocal qualities, gestures, eye contact, space, use of time, touch, and the environment.

Physical Appearance

Leaders in most organizations must project a professional image through their physical appearance. Enhancing your physical appearance, so that others in the workplace perceive you as a leader, is important.

Physical attraction. Our attraction to others because of their appearance—their bone structure, weight, stylishness, and grooming—is referred to as **physical attraction**. Although many people don't want to believe that physically attractive people do better on the job than physically unattractive people, research suggests otherwise. For example, over a ten-year period, attractive MBA graduates earned more than unattractive MBA graduates.[24] (Individuals were deemed "attractive" based on a set of criteria established by the research, such as symmetrical facial features, among other characteristics.) Somewhat surprisingly, in the MBA study, good looks were more of a factor in men's salaries than in women's salaries.[25] In another study examining tipping behavior in restaurants, researchers concluded that female (and not male) servers earned more tips on average if they were physically attractive.[26]

Another important aspect of physical attraction, especially for men, is height. According to Henry Biller, a professor at the University of Rhode Island, "men of average or above-average height are seen as more mature, uninhibited, positive, secure, masculine, active, complete, successful, optimistic, dominant, capable, successful, and outgoing."[27] Other research studies concluded that graduating college seniors who were 6 feet 2 inches tall or taller enjoyed starting salaries $4,000 higher than seniors 5 feet 5 inches tall or under.[28] Although some people may be disappointed in these research findings, they allow us to become more aware of how physical appearance affects communication. The following section details some of the ways you can enhance your physical appearance and, in turn, others' perceptions of your leadership effectiveness.

Clothing. Dressing for success has been the subject of many books, and for good reason.[29] How we dress on the job not only conveys our personal sense of style, it also creates meaning in the minds of others.[30] In other words, people notice our clothing and they form impressions of us based on what we're wearing. This is one of the reasons some companies invest huge sums of money developing and designing company uniforms that communicate the appropriate image to customers.[31] It's important to dress not only in a manner appropriate for our workplace but in a manner that will lead other people to take us seriously and perceive us to be credible.

Most workplaces require employees to dress in a professional manner. Professional dress is associated with a number of important variables that benefit employees, such as perceptions of increased status, competence or knowledge, trustworthiness, and the ability to influence others.[32] Some organizations spell out professional dress. For example, flight attendants have to follow a rigid dress code that is detailed in a comprehensive employee handbook. There is different appropriate dress for walking through airports, boarding and deplaning passengers, and serving passengers while in flight.[33] Other organizations leave it up to the employees to figure out what professional dress entails.

As organizational cultures change and as employers seek ways to attract a new generation of employees, many workplaces in the United States have allowed dress codes to slowly evolve away from the traditional professional dress toward a "business-casual"

Physical attraction the attraction we have toward others because of their appearance

F MINUS: © Tony Carrillo / Dist. by United Feature Syndicate, Inc.

>>> **COMMUNICATION SKILLS** @ WORK

Because physical appearance influences ability to lead in the workplace, it's important that you pay attention to this important source of nonverbal communication. Here are a few suggestions for how to communicate a professional physical appearance at work:

- *Monitor physical appearance standards.* Observe how a number of your co-workers dress in your office, unit, or division. What type of clothing are they wearing (suits, sport coats and slacks)? How are they wearing their clothing (shirts tucked in, hanging out)? What type of shoes are they wearing (open-toed or closed, wingtips, sneakers)? How much jewelry do they wear (earrings, nose studs)? What about their hairstyles (pulled back or down, facial hair)?
- *Match the formality of your manager's appearance.* Observe your manager: If you're uncertain of appearance standards, it's always a good thing to match your manager's appearance in terms of formality. Your manager ultimately sets the standards for appearance in your work unit. Is your boss's appearance formal, or is it more relaxed?
- *Dress for the occasion.* Another appearance suggestion is to dress for the job or the

occupation. Most occupations have an established standard for dress and grooming. For example, most bankers dress in dark suits, construction foremen wear jeans and steel-toed boots, and school principals wear khakis, white shirts, and blazers.

- *When in doubt, dress for the job you want.* Whenever you're in doubt about how you should dress and appear in the workplace, it's best to dress for the job you would like to have one day. In other words, appear more formal than informal. A more formal appearance gives the impression that you care about your work and your organization. Appearing too informal can give the opposite impression.
- *Appear neat and well groomed.* It is assumed that we will appear neat and well groomed when we go to work. Appearing neat means wearing clothing that is clean and pressed, shoes that are clean and polished, and appropriate artifacts (for example, a belt, a briefcase). Appearing well-groomed means being bathed, making sure your hair is styled, and having fresh breath and clean fingernails.

style, which is a toned-down version of traditional professional dress.[34] According to a 2005 benefits survey conducted by the Society for Human Resource Management, out of 386 human resource professionals questioned, 41 percent of organizations in 2005 had a casual dress code policy in place every day.[35] In organizations that had a business-casual dress policy, employees reported greater morale, productivity, and camaraderie among co-workers.[36]

Artifacts. An **artifact** is a personal object we use to convey our identity; it's an accessory. Examples of artifacts include jewelry, eyeglasses, sunglasses, scarves, hairpieces, handbags, briefcases, and hats, to name a few. In many ways, we use artifacts to decorate the body. If used in moderation, artifacts signal to others our style and our unique sense of self.

When researchers asked recruiters to determine the appropriateness of jewelry for men and women on the job, their findings were very stereotypical and sex-typed. Recruiters found three items of jewelry acceptable for women: button earrings, chain chokers, and necklaces. And although necklaces, rings, and earrings were considered acceptable for women, they were less acceptable for men.[37]

Communication researchers John Seiter and Andrea Sandry found that job candidates with either a nose piercing or an ear piercing were perceived by interviewers as significantly less trustworthy, less sociable, and less knowledgeable than candidates not wearing any jewelry. Although a nose or an ear piercing did not significantly affect how attractive the interviewer perceived the candidate to be, a single body piercing lessened the perceived hirability of the candidate—candidates with a single body piercing were less likely to be hired.[38] Another researcher examining the effect of eyebrow piercing on employer perceptions of job candidates' hirability found a similar result, and found that neither the type of business nor the size of the organization made a difference in perceptions of hirability.[39]

Artifact a personal object used to communicate some part of one's identity

Voice

How many times have you heard "It's not what you said, but how you said it that bothered me"? This common expression reveals the importance of **vocalics** (also referred to as *paralanguage*), which are the nonverbal aspects of our voice, including pitch (how high or low a speaker's voice is), rate (how fast the person speaks), and volume (how loudly the person speaks). Verbal messages help us to "say what we mean" whereas nonverbal messages, and especially vocalics, help us to "mean what we say."

Researchers have documented how our use of vocalic cues influences how others perceive us. In general, Americans who speak faster and louder than average are usually perceived as more powerful, knowledgeable, confident, trustworthy, and socially attractive by other Americans.[40] Of course, there are situations when speaking fast and loud would be entirely inappropriate. We are expected to adapt our vocalics based on the situation. For example, if you were to make a sales presentation to Japanese clients whose English comprehension was limited, it would be wise to speak more slowly and perhaps more quietly.

One study found that managers who were perceived by their employees as varying their vocalic cues were more well liked than those who did not vary the pitch, volume, and rate of their voices and were perceived as being more credible and influential than managers whose vocalic cues were more monotonous or flat.[41] People who alter their vocalic cues are perceived as expressive and sociable, two perceptions that serve leaders well.[42]

Body Movement, Posture, and Gestures

The study of gestures, posture, and body movement is referred to as **kinesics**. In one of their most comprehensive contributions to nonverbal research, Paul Ekman and Wallace Friesen classified movement and gestures according to their functions. They identified three categories of gestures that are important for leaders: emblems, illustrators, and regulators.

Emblems. An **emblem** is a gesture that has a direct verbal translation and may substitute for a word or phrase. If you walk into your manager's office and he holds up an open palm without looking at you, you immediately know that your manager doesn't want to be interrupted. If you're giving a presentation and your supervisor holds up two fingers, you know you have two minutes to wrap up the presentation. Other common emblems that substitute for verbal messages include the time-out sign (a referee using two extended hands to form a T) and the quiet sign (placing an index finger up to the lips). Emblems are shortcuts that allow you to communicate with others, especially in situations when you cannot use verbal messages.

Illustrators. We frequently accompany a verbal message with an **illustrator** that illustrates (draws a picture) or complements the verbal message. Illustrators allow you to clarify or intensify the meaning of the message. For example, when we are giving directions to another person, most of us use our hands to draw a picture in the air of where the other person should go. Not only does your use of illustrators help others decode and interpret your message, but illustrators also help you in encoding or developing a message.[43] Research has also suggested that our use of illustrators helps us to remember our messages. People who illustrated their verbal messages remembered 20 percent more of what they said than those who didn't illustrate, or use gestures, when communicating.[44]

Regulators. A **regulator** is a nonverbal cue that helps control the interaction and flow of communication between people. Regulators help you manage turn taking in a conversation. When someone tries to cut you off in a conversation, you hold up a hand or give the person a raised eyebrow, which signals "wait, I'm not finished." When you're finished and you want the other person to speak, you give the other person a head nod, which signals his or her turn.

Vocalics the nonverbal aspects of the voice, including pitch, rate, and volume.

Kinesics the study of gestures, posture, and body movement.

Emblem a gesture that has a direct verbal translation and may substitute for a word or phrase.

Illustrator a gesture that illustrates or complements a verbal message.

Regulator a nonverbal cue that helps control the interaction and flow of communication between two people.

One type of regulator that is important in the development of quality relationships is a back channel cue. **Back channel cues** are nonverbal behaviors that signal to the other person that we are listening to them and we wish for them to continue talking. When listening to a friend, many of us will interject sounds such as "um," "uh-huh," and "hmm" to signal that we are listening and that we are interested in the conversation.[45]

Facial Expression and Eye Contact

Although there's a saying that some people "wear their emotions on their sleeves," they actually wear their emotions on their faces and in their eyes. In business and professional settings, it's important to monitor what your face and eyes reveal about who you are and how you're feeling.

Researchers have found that although our faces provide a great deal of information about emotions, we quickly learn to control our facial expressions.[46] In fact, some jobs require people to mask or hide their feelings.[47] These employees have learned to control the facial muscles that ultimately convey their feelings. Others try to mask their feelings and are less successful; their emotions leak from their faces and eyes.

In addition to conveying your emotions, your facial expressions and eye contact also influence how others perceive you. Researchers have concluded that people who smile more often are perceived to be more intelligent than those who smile less often.[48] Also, smiling behavior has been shown to enhance sales.[49] The research examining eye contact is equally powerful. Direct eye contact has been associated with a number of positive relational qualities that are valued and rewarded in the workplace. For example, researchers have concluded that direct eye contact enhances others' perceptions of your credibility, self-esteem, and emotional control or calmness, all perceptions that enhance leadership effectiveness.[50] Use of direct eye contact allows you to be more persuasive in getting others to comply with your wishes than someone who uses evasive or indirect glances.[51] Also, increased eye contact enhances your chances of being hired for a job and perceptions of your leadership potential.[52]

Space

Have you ever had a conversation with someone who stood too close to you? You slowly edged backward to add some distance, and the other person took a step forward to maintain the close distance. Rather than focusing on the conversation and what the other person was saying, you were distracted and uncomfortable. This scenario, which many people have experienced, reflects the importance of **proximity**, or the space and distance we maintain from others in our communication with them.

In his study of *proxemics*, Edward T. Hall identified four spatial zones that we unconsciously define for ourselves.[53]

- *Intimate space.* Intimate space is the zone extending from 0 to 1½ feet from someone; it is reserved for only those with whom we are well acquainted, unless we're forced to stand close to another person, such as in a crowded elevator. Someone who wanted to intimidate another person might make a point to stand in that person's zone of intimate space.

- *Personal space.* Personal space is the zone that extends from 1½ to 4 feet from a person; it is our "comfort zone," where most of our conversations with family and friends occur.

- *Social space.* The zone of social space ranges from 4 to 12 feet from a person; it is reserved for most formal group interactions as well for as our professional relationships.

- *Public space.* Public space begins at 12 feet from us; it is the distance from the audience used by most speakers making public presentations.

It's important to respect others' personal space when communicating with them at work. Although you probably don't consciously recognize how you use space to communicate, chances are you do notice when others violate your personal space or when they penetrate your intimate space (also known as your *body-buffer* zone).[54] Research clearly suggests that when you invade another person's personal space, the

Back channel cues nonverbal cues that signal to the other person that we are listening and wish for them to continue talking.

Proximity the physical space and distance that we maintain in our communication with others.

other person notices that you're too close, and this usually causes the person to perceive you less favorably.[55]

Culture also determines how we use space in our communication with others. For example, South Americans, Southern and Eastern Europeans, and Arabs communicate at closer distances than Asians, Northern Europeans, and North Americans, who require more conversational distance when communicating.[56] For these reasons, remaining respectful of others' use of space is important. Here are some behaviors to help you effectively interpret nonverbal proxemic cues in a diverse workplace environment:

- Increase distance. You will want to increase the distance between you and another person if you see the person stepping away from you, leaning back, crossing his or her arms, turning to the side, or failing to make direct eye contact.

- Decrease distance. You will want to decrease the distance between you and another person if you see the person stepping toward you, leaning forward, turning his or her body so that it directly faces yours, or making direct eye contact.

Time

Chronemics is the study of how people use and structure time. In U.S. workplaces, "time is money," and most working professionals take time seriously. Researchers have concluded that people pay attention to how co-workers use time on the job. In a study of administrative assistants, researchers found that people who arrived on time for appointments were perceived more positively than people who were late and even people who were early. On-time arrivers were perceived as being more knowledgeable, composed, and friendly than late or early arrivers.[57] Researchers have also found that leaving work before the boss does conveys the message that a person is not dedicated to work, and such people are often overlooked for promotions.[58]

At times, we are in control of our time. We sit down and plan our work; we develop a work schedule. At other times, time is in control of us—as when we have to drop everything to meet a deadline at work. Put simply, we use time and are used by time differently. Anthropologist Edward Hall studied how people use time.[59] For example, a manager who schedules a staff meeting for 1:00 and begins the staff meeting exactly at 1:00 is a manager who has a *displaced point pattern*. This type of person uses time in a precise manner. Other people have a *diffused point pattern* and use and structure time in an approximate manner. A manager who schedules a staff meeting for 1:00 and begins the staff meeting at 1:15 is someone who has a diffused point pattern. Working professionals quickly learn about their co-workers' patterns in use of time. This knowledge then guides them in how they work.

Touch

The study of how human touch communicates is referred to as **haptics**. Touch is the most misunderstood source of nonverbal behavior.[60] You can probably remember a situation when someone touched you and you walked away confused, wondering what the touch meant. There are a variety of reasons why people use and interpret touch differently. Some of these reasons are based in personalities.[61] Some people simply have a tendency to communicate using a lot of touching—it's a part of who they are, their personalities. They hug when saying hello or goodbye and they put their arm around others while communicating. Other people are more **touch avoidant**, which is the tendency to generally avoid touch in interpersonal interactions.[62] People with high touch avoidance have a tendency not to touch others when communicating and prefer not to be touched by others.

Culture also affects how touch is used to communicate with others. For example, certain cultures are **high-contact cultures**, which means that touching is quite commonplace.[63] In European and Middle Eastern cultures, men kiss each other on the cheek as a greeting. Other cultures are **low-contact cultures**, in which touching is uncommon. In some Asian cultures, touching as a way to show affection is rare and is considered inappropriate.[64]

Because touch is often misunderstood, we recommend that leaders limit their touching to what is referred to as *social/polite touch*. This type of touch is used

Chronemics the study of how people use and structure time.

Haptics the study of how we communicate through touch.

Touch avoidant the tendency to avoid touch in interpersonal interactions.

High-contact culture a culture in which touching is seen as commonplace and appropriate.

Low-contact culture a culture in which touching is uncommon.

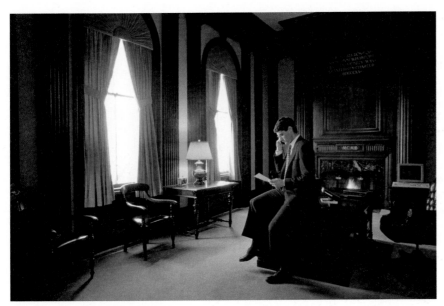

Effective professional communication requires acknowledgment of an individual's power. Observing status symbols, such as this office, can help you determine who in an organization has power.

to acknowledge the presence of another person. An example would be a handshake when greeting someone.

Physical Environment

Your physical environment—the actual space that you work in—influences not only how others perceive you but also how you interact with others. In many organizations, physical environment is used to convey status. **Status** is an individual's importance and prestige. To communicate effectively and appropriately in professional settings, it's important to acknowledge status symbols. People in power assume you know that they have status. If you remain uncertain of who has status and power in your organizations, you can begin by observing offices.

In some large corporations, men and women with the most power usually occupy the largest offices with the most windows.[65] These offices often have floor-to-ceiling walls and a door. To gain access to the offices, you usually have to enter through an adjoining office, which is where the administrative assistant works and serves as a gatekeeper. A **gatekeeper** is a person who controls the flow of communication within an organization. The gatekeeper controls who gets in and who doesn't. In other words, the gatekeeper controls the level of privacy that the high-status person has earned. Those with the least amount of status usually occupy what has been referred to as a "cube." A **cube** is a small modular office unit that lacks floor-to-ceiling walls and a door. It includes no gatekeeper and offers minimal privacy. Cubes are usually spaced closely together to maximize office space. Some refer to these multiple modular office units as "cube farms."

How To Communicate Nonverbal Messages To Enhance Leadership

One way to enhance your leadership effectiveness using nonverbal messages is to use nonverbal immediacy behaviors. According to nonverbal communication researcher Albert Mehrabian, **immediacy** is a perception of physical and psychological closeness that is created by using certain nonverbal behaviors.[66] According to Mehrabian, the principle underlying immediacy is simple: We like and respond positively to people who tend to display immediacy cues and avoid or respond negatively to those who don't. Among the nonverbal immediacy cues that show liking and interest are the following:[67]

Status an individual's importance and prestige.

Gatekeeper a person who controls the flow of communication within an organization.

Cube a small, modular office unit with no door and no floor-to-ceiling walls.

Immediacy a perception of psychological and physical closeness.

- Proximity: Closeness, reduced distance between people
- Body orientation: Face-to-face or side-by-side, forward body angle
- Eye contact
- Facial expression: Smiling, open eyes
- Gestures: Head nods, use of hands and arms
- Posture: Open and relaxed, arms oriented toward the other person
- Haptics: Touch appropriate for the situation
- Vocalics: Higher pitch

Following are some nonverbal behaviors that will enhance immediacy and therefore your leadership effectiveness:

- *Use a firm handshake.* A firm handshake is one that is strong (but not so strong as to cut off the other person's blood supply), vigorous (meaning it has an appropriate amount of energy), adequate in duration (not too brief or too long), and complete (meaning that you grip the other person's hand fully so that your palms are touching).[68]

- *Use direct eye contact.* Maintain direct eye contact while talking to others and while listening. Most people associate direct eye contact with honesty and trustworthiness.[69]

- *Use a confident voice.* A confident voice has energy and volume, a quick tempo, only a few short pauses, high and varied pitch, expressiveness, and fluency.[70]

- *Dress professionally.* As noted earlier, professional dress includes not only clean, neat clothing but also good grooming.

- *Adopt an upright and relaxed posture.* Maintain an open body orientation (arms uncrossed, exposing the front of the body toward the other person), stand up straight, square your shoulders, place your hands down at your sides with open palms, and relax your body.

- *Use expressive gestures.* Dale Leathers, who studied nonverbal communication extensively, recommends the following five ways to make effective use of gestures: (1) Gestures should be used to add emphasis to the points being made; (2) gestures should be spontaneous, relaxed, and unrehearsed; (3) gestures should be used to signal that we wish to speak or that we want someone else to speak; (4) gestures with the hands and arms should be kept away from the body, thus increasing their persuasive impact; and (5) gestures should indicate our feelings and emotions.[71]

- *Use space to lead.* Leaders typically sit at the end of a rectangular or oval table during meetings.[72] At round tables, the person who is most visible to others usually emerges as the group leader.[73]

- *Use responsive cues.* Nonverbally responsive behaviors signal that you're paying attention to another person; they're validating: nodding the head affirmatively, maintaining eye contact, displaying an expressive face, showing interest by taking notes, sitting up and leaning forward, and using back channel cues that suggest that you understand what the other person is saying.[74]

How To Manage Sexually Harassing Messages at Work

It is important to effectively use and interpret verbal and nonverbal messages at work, but it is equally important to know what verbal and nonverbal messages are inappropriate at work. As a leader, you need to be aware of (1) how verbal and nonverbal messages can be used to sexually harass others, and (2) how verbal and nonverbal messages can be interpreted as sexual harassment. According to Susan Webb, who runs a consulting firm that specializes in human relations issues and is editor of the *Webb Report*, a national newsletter on sexual harassment, **sexual harassment** is "deliberate and/or repeated sexual or sex-based behavior that is not welcome, not asked for, and not returned" (p. 12).[75] Sex-based behavior is expressed through both verbal and nonverbal messages. To lead others more effectively, you need to know how sexual harassment is experienced and how to avoid sexual harassment.

Experiencing Sexual Harassment

To better understand how others experience sexual harassment, we will examine three components of Webb's definition of sexual harassment.

The first step is to be able to recognize when the verbal and nonverbal messages and behaviors in question are sexual or sex-based in nature. This type of communication can be placed on a continuum from least to most severe. Examples of least severe include telling sexual jokes or making sexual innuendos, flirting, or asking someone out on a date. Examples of most severe include forced fondling, attempted or actual rape, and sexual assault.

The second step is observing that the verbal and nonverbal messages are deliberate

Sexual harassment deliberate and/or repeated sexual or sex-based behavior that is not welcome, not asked for, and not returned.

and/or repeated. Some messages are so graphic that the first time they are conveyed, they are considered sexual harassment. Other messages are more subtle and can be considered sexual harassment only if they are repeated—for example, brushing up against someone in the break room. According to Webb, "the more severe the behavior is, the fewer times it needs to be repeated before reasonable people define it as harassment; the less severe it is, the more times it needs to be repeated" (p. 13).[76]

Third, sexual harassment is not welcome, not asked for, and not returned. Webb mentions that "the less severe the behavior is, the more responsibility the receiver has to speak up; the more severe it is, the less responsibility the receiver has to speak up" (p. 14).[77] In other words, if an employee is being harassed with sexual jokes or innuendoes or is in the room when others are viewing pornography on the Internet, then it's the employee's responsibility to inform the others of the sexually harassing behavior. If the behavior is severe, such as fondling or sexual assault, then the employee should immediately discuss the situation with a supervisor, whose responsibility it is to manage the situation.

Also, there are two major classifications of sexual harassment—quid pro quo harassment and hostile environment harassment. **Quid pro quo sexual harassment** is actual or threatened use of rewards or punishment to gain sexual compliance from a subordinate.[78] (*Quid pro quo* is a Latin phrase that roughly translates as "something for something else.") An example of quid pro quo sexual harassment in the workplace would be a manager threatening not to promote an employee unless the employee has sex with the manager. It's sex or no promotion—something for something else. **Hostile environment sexual harassment** is unwelcome conduct of a sexual nature that interferes with a person's ability to perform a job or gain an education and that creates a hostile, intimidating, or offensive working environment.[79] Examples of hostile environment sexual harassment in the workplace include constant use of lewd remarks and offensive language that demeans a person's sex.

Avoiding Sexual Harassment

Once you know what sexual harassment is, it's important to avoid it. Although the majority of working professionals are aware of the more severe forms of sexual harassment, many are probably less aware of the more subtle forms of sexually harassing messages and behavior. Research suggests that men and women perceive sexual harassment differently. Kim Lane Scheppele, a political science and law professor at Princeton University, summarizes the male-female differences this way: "Men see the sex first and miss the coercion. Women see the coercion and miss the sex" (p. 26).[80] She points out that if sexual harassment were to occur in front of a mixed group, many of the women would call it sexual harassment and many of the men would probably call it a joke.

Debbie Dougherty, a communication researcher who studies sexual harassment, reported that

> Men perceive fewer behaviors as harassing than women . . . and men perceive most harassing behavior as normal. For the most part, men do not experience as many sexual overtures as harassment as do women . . . . When males do recognize that the behavior is harassing, they may feel complimented by the experience. (p. 445)[81]

The following sections present a few communication strategies for avoiding sexually harassing another person at work.

Avoid sexual messages and behaviors. Sexual jokes, inappropriate touching, and sexual teasing are to be avoided. We often assume that others are like us and that they share our attitudes, beliefs, values—and our sense of humor. In the diverse workplace, this assumption is inaccurate. What one person takes as joking another may find offensive and degrading.

Avoid sex-based messages. Sex-based messages are not necessarily sexual in nature but are based on the person's sex. Here are a few examples:

"This is man's work. What are you doing here?"

"You should be home having more babies."

Quid pro quo sexual harassment actual or threatened use of rewards or punishments to gain sexual compliance from a subordinate.

Hostile environment sexual harassment unwelcome conduct of a sexual nature that interferes with a person's ability to perform a job or gain an education and that creates a hostile or intimidating environment at the workplace.

[To a stay-at-home dad] "Why aren't you out working like other guys? You need to bring home the bacon, not raise kids."

"You're here only because of the affirmative action program."

Stop communicating harassing messages once informed. Suppose that although you do not perceive your behavior as harassment, another person clearly does, and the individual takes responsibility and informs you of how he or she feels. To ignore this information is a clear violation of sexual harassment policy. Also, remember that jokes at first may not be bothersome, but over time, jokes cease to be funny and people become uncomfortable when they have to listen to them repeatedly.

Monitor others' nonverbal messages and behaviors. Although people should be upfront and inform you when they find your messages sexually harassing, not everyone can be as assertive as they need to be in certain situations. Some may feel threatened; others may not want to be pegged as being "uptight" or "not a team player." Because of peer pressure, they may not express their discomfort. Some may even say "it doesn't bother me." But their nonverbal behavior reveals that they are bothered. (For example, their arms may be crossed, or they may be using an adaptor, such as tapping a foot.)

Summary

Verbal and nonverbal messages are the tools of effective leadership. People in business and professional settings who use and interpret verbal and nonverbal messages effectively become leaders. Their leadership gives them the ability to influence others and to effect change in the workplace. Put simply, they make work happen. *Principle Two: Effectively use and interpret verbal messages* focuses on your ability to understand and use language. *Principle Three: Effectively use and interpret nonverbal messages* examines how you use visual and audible symbols that do not contain words or language to create meaning.

The chapter discussed three sets of verbal communication skills that will help you use and interpret verbal messages effectively. The first skill set focuses on making messages concrete, concise, and relevant. The second verbal communication skill set involves communicating supportive messages that enhance the communication climate. The third verbal communication skill set is aimed at communicating assertive messages—that is, making requests rather than demands.

To effectively use and interpret nonverbal messages, it is important to understand the unique characteristics, functions, and sources of nonverbal messages. Nonverbal messages are unique in that they convey our feelings and emotions, they convey relational cues, which help us form relationships, they tend to be authentic and believable, and they are culture-bound. Nonverbal messages function on a variety of levels, which means they serve a number of purposes. For example, nonverbal messages can be used to substitute, complement, repeat, regulate, accent, or contradict. In many ways, these functions are tools that leaders can use to enhance their verbal messages and their ability to influence others. Finally, there are eight sources of nonverbal messages, including physical appearance; vocalics; body movement, posture, and gestures; facial expressions and eye contact; use of space; use of time; touch; and physical environment.

It is essential to understand how verbal and nonverbal messages can be used in a destructive manner to sexually harass others in the workplace. The chapter defined and described sexual harassment and introduced some communication strategies for avoiding sexually harassing messages.

Discussion Questions

1. What are the three aspects of clear verbal messages? Describe and give an example of each.

2. Give an example of both descriptive "I" language and evaluative "you" language.

3. What are six strategies for creating supportive communication?

4. What are four ways to use nonverbal communication to enhance leadership in the workplace?

5. What are some appropriate ways to respond to sexual harassment at work?

6. Identify six functions of nonverbal communication and provide an example of each.

Building Your Skills

1. For each of the following terms, provide both a denotative and connotative definition.

Word	Connotative Meaning	Denotative Meaning
Justice		
Foreign		
Environment		
Leadership		
Home		
War		
Value		
Language		

2. In this chapter, you learned that the words you use can enhance or detract from the quality of your relationships. More specifically, using descriptive "I" language rather than evaluative "you" language is helpful to prevent a defensive reaction when addressing a conflict. Think of a specific conflict in your life and re-create the conversation you had at the time using "you" language. Then re-create the same conversation using descriptive "I" language.

3. Get together with some friends at a local mall or another public location. Watch the nonverbal behavior of those around you; observe the cultural norms. Take notes and compare yours with those of your friends, identifying any similarities and differences.

4. Start a nonverbal behavior journal, and take some time every week to reflect on the nonverbal communication you use during your daily routine. Jot down some behaviors you use and what they communicate.

   Now try an experiment: Choose some behaviors that you do regularly, and stop doing them for one day. For example, if you meet a friend at the same place for lunch every day, sit in a different seat or at a different table. Or, when you talk with your supervisor, make a point to shake his hand (if you don't normally do that) or avoid looking him in the eye. Do people notice the change in your behavior? How do they react? Are they confused? Defensive? Annoyed? What accounts for the reactions?

5. Think of a leader who has been very influential in your life. This can be someone you know personally or a more widely known leader. Now, list some of the verbal and nonverbal communication behaviors this leader uses. What are the messages that are effective? How does this person communicate his or her leadership using verbal and nonverbal messages?

Chapter 4
Listening and Responding

chapter outline

After reading this chapter, you should be able to

- Understand how people listen and describe each of the five listening steps: selecting, attending, understanding, remembering, and responding.

- Discuss how the five listening steps are interrelated.

- Identify listening barriers at work, and give examples of each.

- Discuss strategies for overcoming listening barriers at work.

- Describe strategies for effectively listening to others. Be able to explain the stop, look, and listen steps and why they are important.

- Describe three skills for effectively responding to others.

- List five strategies to use to help others understand your messages.

Leading others begins by understanding others. We understand others by listening to them. According to Steven Covey, an internationally respected leadership authority and organizational consultant, effective leaders are also effective listeners. In fact, listening is so critical to effective leadership that Covey considers it one of his seven habits of highly effective people.[1]

Unfortunately, listening is a communication leadership skill that most people struggle with on the job, and one of the main reasons for this struggle is that people have not been taught how to listen.[2] Most of our communication training has focused on developing reading and writing competencies, and little if any attention has focused on developing listening and speaking competencies. This is unfortunate, since research suggests that people who work in business and professional settings spend on average 32 percent of their communication time listening and 26 percent speaking, compared to 23 percent writing, and 19 percent reading.[3] While it's incredibly important to learn how to read and write, the majority of our communication time is spent listening to others—a skill in which we have the least amount of formal training and education.[4]

> *Most of the successful people I've known are the ones who do more listening than talking."*
>
> — BERNARD M. BARUCH

Business and professional organizations have noticed the listening skill deficiency and are beginning to voice their unhappiness. Corporations and various business organizations are putting pressure on colleges and universities to fix the problem. Here's what they're saying:

- The *Wall Street Journal* reported that faculty members in business schools across the country believe that communication leadership and interpersonal skills are lacking in today's MBA graduates. Historically, neither conflict management nor listening training has received significant attention, leaving individuals to master critical communication skills on their own.[5]

- The American Institute of Public Accountants listed listening as one of the top skills employers seek in entry-level employees as well as those being considered for promotion.[6]

- Executives of Fortune 500 companies as well as those who conduct several management-training programs across the United States identified listening as one of the most important communication skills needed in today's workplace.[7]

- The National Board of Engineering Education and the Accreditation Board for Engineering and Technology (ABET) have developed new standards for accreditation to evaluate departments and colleges of engineering around the country. One of their recommendations is for all future engineers to develop listening skills.[8]

- Employers believe that job satisfaction, individual performance, and organizational outcomes are enhanced by working professionals who listen well. Institutions of higher education must ensure that students develop listening competencies before graduating from college.[9]

To address these concerns and enhance your listening and responding skills, this chapter will introduce you to our communication Principle Four: *Listen and respond thoughtfully to others.* Figure 4.1 illustrates where this principle fits into our communication principles for leadership model. Effective leaders do more than just listen to others, they also respond to what others are saying. Responding thoughtfully means that we let others know that we're listening to them. We might ask a follow-up question or nod our head to show that we're actively listening.

Some people confuse hearing with listening. Although listening requires hearing, not all hearing is listening. Have you ever heard someone speaking to you, but seconds later found yourself saying, "I'm sorry, what did you say?" You *heard* the person, but you were not *listening* to the person. **Hearing** is the physiological process of decoding sounds. We hear when the sound waves captured by our ears cause the eardrum to vibrate. The vibrating eardrum then causes the middle ear bones (the hammer, anvil, and stirrup) to vibrate. Eventually, the sound vibrations are translated into electrical impulses that signal the brain. In contrast, **listening** is the process of receiving, constructing meaning from, and responding to verbal and nonverbal messages.[10] When we listen, not only do we hear the messages, but we also decode, or

Listen

Hearing the physiological process of decoding sounds.

Listening the process of receiving, constructing meaning from, and responding to verbal and nonverbal messages.

| Figure 4.1 | Communication Principles and Skills for Leadership |

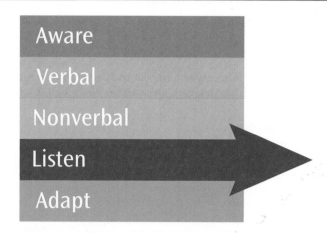

assign meaning to them, and then respond to the other person to let him or her know that the message was received. Listening is a process that involves five stages: selecting, attending, understanding, remembering, and responding.

1. To **select** a message is to focus on one sound as you sort through the numerous noises competing for your attention.

2. To **attend** to a message is to focus on a specific message. Just because you select a message doesn't mean you pay attention to it.

3. To **understand** a message is to assign meaning to (that is, to decode) the verbal and nonverbal messages that you're receiving.

4. To **remember** a message is to be able to retrieve the message from your memory.

5. To **respond** to a message is to let people know whether you understood their message and to validate or acknowledge them personally.

Listening and responding thoughtfully to others is a critical leadership communication skill because it helps us develop and maintain relationships with others in the three different workplace communication contexts that we will be reviewing in this book: interpersonal, small group, and presentational speaking. In business and professional settings, good interpersonal relationships allow us to get the work done; they allow us to reach our goals. In small groups and teams, our ability to listen and respond thoughtfully to others allows us to provide vision and direction for the group, while also facilitating group discussions and making sure that all group members have a voice in the problem solving or decision making process. Finally, when making presentations, our ability to listen and respond thoughtfully to others' questions before, during, and after the presentation allows us to continue clarifying our messages and persuading and influencing others.

This chapter is divided into four sections in which we will discuss (1) overcoming listening barriers, (2) listening effectively to others, (3) responding effectively to others, and (4) helping others listen effectively to you.

Overcoming Listening Barriers

Although we spend one-third of our communication time on the job listening, some say we don't use that time well. One day after hearing something, most people remember only about half of what was said. It gets worse. Two days later, our listening comprehension drops by another 50 percent. The result: Two days after hearing an informal discussion or a formal presentation, we remember only about 25 percent of what we heard.[11]

Select to focus on one sound among all the sounds competing for attention.

Attend to focus on a specific message.

Understand to assign meaning to the verbal and nonverbal messages received.

Remember to recall information from memory.

Respond to let another person know whether you understood a message or to validate the other person.

What keeps you from listening well? The most critical listening barriers are information-processing barriers and context barriers.

Overcoming Information-Processing Barriers at Work

How you process information can be a barrier to effective listening. Four information-processing barriers are processing rate, information overload, receiver apprehension, and shifting attention.

Processing rate. One of the barriers to listening that has been well documented is the difference between our ability to process information and the rate at which information comes to us. Research suggests that we can listen and process information faster than most people speak. While attending a meeting, have you ever said to yourself, "I wish he would speak faster. I'm getting bored." Most people speak on average between 150 and 175 words per minute; however, we process language at a rate of between 600 and 800 words per minute.[12] This difference in our capacity to speak and our capacity to listen or process information leaves most of us with extra time on our hands. Our attention begins to wander and we quickly become bored and distracted. Processing speed becomes a listening barrier. If this occurs, you might want to use one of the following strategies:

- *Summarize the information.* Take advantage of the extra time by mentally summarizing what the speaker is saying.
- *Provide the speaker with feedback.* Use nonverbal regulatory cues such as hand gestures that encourage the speaker to speak more rapidly.

Although we have the ability to listen and process language faster than most people can speak it, in instructional settings (when we are being trained or instructed in

>>> COMMUNICATION AND GLOBALIZATION @ WORK

Think about how many times you have had problems understanding someone from a different culture—or even from a different subculture. For example, if you're a parent of a young teen, you may not always understand your son or daughter's language or ways of thinking. Now think about how many times someone from a different cultural background may have had problems understanding you. For many of us, cross-cultural encounters are an increasingly important part of everyday life. Much of the misunderstanding between people of different cultures can be traced to problems in listening.

What's interesting is that we don't have to travel far to have a cross-cultural experience. In fact, sociolinguist Deborah Tannen argues that men and women are socialized into two different cultural groupings that make it difficult for them to listen to and understand each other at work.[13] For example, during a break from a videoconference, a woman commented to her male colleague how wonderful it was for her to see, hear, and interact with her friends and colleagues from all over the world. The man agreed and then launched into a lengthy and detailed description of how the videoconferencing technology worked. The woman became a bit irritated by the technical detail and ended the conversation.

As this example suggests, people sometimes have different views of the purpose of a conversation. The woman made her comment about seeing her friends from across the globe as a way of expressing her emotional connection to her international colleagues. She wanted her male colleague to listen and respond to her relational message. The male colleague took this opening as a chance to reveal his knowledge of videoconferencing technology and to teach his female colleague some of the things he knew. While both people probably had good intentions and may have thought they were listening and responding appropriately in a friendly conversation, they had differing expectations about the direction such a conversation should take. The male colleague may have believed that a "good conversation" was one with interesting, factual content; the female colleague may have believed a good conversation to be one with personal content, which disclosed her feelings. The man may have also been more interested in hearing himself talk than he was in listening.

What this implies for listening is that when we hear someone speak, we are not only hearing the words he or she says. We are also activating our own expectations and are evaluating the speaker in terms of our expectations. An important listening skill that we all need to develop is empathy: listening for the *purpose* of the conversation from the speaker's perspective. This is particularly important in intercultural communication, including the communication that occurs between men and women.

>>> COMMUNICATION SKILLS @ WORK

As a working professional in the information age, you will need to overcome information overload. Although there is no immediate solution to this particular problem, there are a number of "band-aids" that will temporarily relieve some of the information overload symptoms:

- *Identify your listening goal.* Although we are usually unaware of it, most of us listen for a purpose; we have a goal for listening. These goals include listening for enjoyment, to learn, to evaluate, and to empathize. When our goal is enjoyment, we listen to relax and to be entertained. When our goal is to learn, we listen to increase understanding so that we can apply new information. When our goal is to evaluate, we listen critically, meaning that we listen to discern fact from fiction, to analyze evidence, and to identify fallacies in the reasoning process. When our goal is to empathize, we listen so we can feel what the other person is feeling. To prevent information overload from being a barrier, listen selfishly. Be aware of what you want and need; listen in order to meet your listening goal. For example, listening to learn and to evaluate requires a different process than listening to empathize.

Listening to evaluate requires careful attention to details and specific factual information. When listening to empathize, we listen for feelings and for nonverbal cues that express or reveal emotions.

- *Ask for help with prioritizing and filtering messages.* We need to recognize that our information processing capabilities are limited—our brains are capable of only so much information processing at once. When we become overloaded with information at a meeting or while listening to instructions, we need to ask others to help us prioritize or filter the information. We need to ask, "Which information is most important at this time? Which information can I put aside for now and act on later? Can I ignore any of this information?" The answers to these questions allow you to prioritize the information; they allow you to know which information is most urgent and important.

- *Record or take notes on the information.* If you become overloaded with information while attending a meeting or a presentation, ask if it would be acceptable to record the meeting or presentation. If an audio recorder is unavailable, be sure take notes highlighting important information and deadlines.

---

how to perform an unfamiliar job or given new product information), our listening comprehension has a tendency to decrease if the trainer or sales representative is speaking too quickly.[14] When trainers or instructors speak too quickly (that is, faster than the average 150 to 175 words per minute), we have a problem processing the new and important information, and our listening comprehension decreases significantly.[15] If this occurs, you might want to use one of the following strategies:

- *Provide the speaker with verbal feedback.* Most trainers and instructors are receptive when students ask them to slow down or to repeat information.

- *Provide the speaker with nonverbal feedback.* Slow the speaker down by using nonverbal regulators that signal that a slower speaking rate is needed.

Information overload.   Another processing barrier similar to processing rate is **information overload,** which is an inability to effectively process information because there's too much of it. At work, a number of people will want you to listen to them. Your boss will be texting and emailing you with information you need to make important decisions. Your employees will be leaving you voice mails indicating that they cannot make it to work. Suppliers and sales reps will be knocking at your door wanting you to act quickly on the latest sales incentive that could possibly save your office money. At some point, you reach saturation, or information overload. You get to a point where it becomes difficult to select, attend to, understand, remember, and respond to new information.

Without question, information overload (or what some communication consultants refer to as "message meltdown") is a problem for many of today's organizational communication professionals. This issue is becoming even more important with the emergence of communication technologies that increase the quantity of interaction and response times (i-Phone, BlackBerry).[16] For example, the amount of email that is forwarded daily is one of the reasons for message meltdown. Consider some of the following research findings:

- The Radicati Group, a technology market research firm, estimated that there were 1.2 billion email users worldwide in 2007 and that this number is

Information overload the inability to effectively process information because there is too much of it.

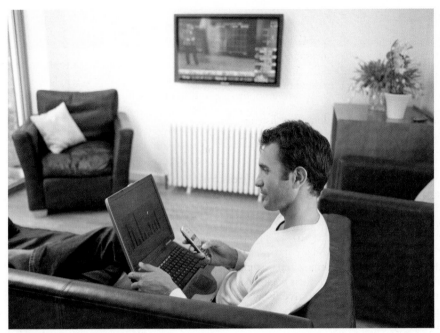

For many, information overload isn't limited to the workplace. A message meltdown is even more likely to occur when someone brings work home.

expected to rise to 1.6 billion by 2011. Furthermore, approximately 183 billion emails were sent each day in 2006, and the number of wireless email users will grow from 14 million in 2006 to 228 million in 2010.[17]

- A study conducted by Ferris Research, an information technology consulting company, estimated the number of business email users worldwide in 2009 at around 800 million.[18]

Receiver apprehension. Another barrier to listening is receiver apprehension, which is the fear of misinterpreting, inadequately processing, and/or not being able to adjust psychologically to messages sent by others.[19] If you have ever experienced anxiety when listening to one of your professors or while taking notes during class, you understand how this information-processing barrier prevents you from listening well. It's frustrating. You want to listen, but your anxiety about selecting, attending to, understanding, remembering, and responding to the information prevents you from doing what you want to do: to listen and learn. This type of apprehension also occurs in the workplace.[20] For example, you might be on the phone with a customer service employee who is providing you with a lot of account numbers you need to do your job. Because you need this information to do your job, you experience anxiety, which is distracting and lessens your ability to listen and process information.

Research suggests that people with high levels of receiver apprehension not only have trouble listening and remembering what they've heard, they also make less money and learn less.[21] It's also important to know that receiver apprehension is partly biologically based, meaning that it's partially genetically determined.[22] Put simply, it's a natural part of who we are and unlikely to change. It's important to find ways to cope with receiver apprehension.

Shifting attention. The second stage in the listening process is attending, or paying attention to messages. If we're to understand, remember, and respond to messages appropriately, we first have to select and attend to them. As noted earlier, in the workplace, there are numerous messages competing for our attention. Many professionals are expected to "multi-task" (the workplace catchphrase for the new millennium). Although this is the expectation in the workplace, research suggests that our brains are not built for multi-tasking and that there are mental health risks to continued multi-tasking, such as depression and burnout.[23] The research also suggests that the quality of work decreases, especially for difficult tasks, as multi-tasking demands increase.[24] Even though we think we're getting more work done, listening comprehension—and therefore the quality of our work and our relationships—is likely less than ideal.

Another factor that influences attention in the listening process is that men and women attend to information differently. Emerging research evidence suggests that men are more likely to have difficulty attending to multiple messages: When they are focused on a message, they may have more difficulty than women in carrying on a conversation with another person.[25] Men have a tendency to "lock on" to a message, whereas women seem more adept at shifting between two or more simultaneous messages. For example, when men listen to a sales pitch or a marketing plan, they seem lost in thought—unaware of the other voices around them. Women, on the other hand, are more likely to be paying attention to the presentation while also paying attention to the other chatter that is going on in the room. What are the implications? It may be especially important for women to stop and focus on the messages of others, rather than on either internal or external competing messages. And men may need to be sensitive to others who may want to speak to them, rather than becoming fixated on their own internal messages or on a single external message.

Overcoming Context Barriers at Work

In addition to barriers related to how we process information and self-barriers that occur when our emotions and thoughts distract us from important messages, listening barriers can arise from the communication context or situation. Specifically, time, place, and external noise can interfere with our ability to select, attend to, understand, remember, and respond to messages.

Barriers of time and place.   The time of day as well as our location affect listening comprehension. Are you a morning or an evening person? (Most people are one or the other.) If you're a morning person, chances are listening is a chore during the evening hours. And if you're an evening person, you struggle with listening in the morning. Researchers have long documented the fact that people have an internal biological clock, or what is referred to as a *circadian rhythm* (from two Latin words meaning "about a day").[26] Researchers have recently located the gene that is partially responsible for our biological clocks. This gene influences brain activity and mental alertness, which obviously play important roles in how we listen to others.[27] The 9-to-5 workplace favors morning people, according to *Wall Street Journal* reporter Jared Sandberg. According to Sandberg, of all the possible conflicts and irritants in the office, among the most difficult to bridge is that between morning and evening people.[28] It's important to understand that not all of your co-workers will be at their peak when you are.

Another obvious time barrier is simply the *lack* of time. Effective listening requires time. With our propensity to multi-task and over-schedule our workdays, time is a limited resource, and its lack hinders effective listening. To overcome these time barriers, we recommend the following listening strategies:

- *Be aware of your biological clock.* If you know that you have to attend an important early morning sales meeting and you're an evening person—or if, as a morning person, you've been up since 5 a.m. and the meeting starts late in the day—be prepared to compensate. Go into the meeting prepared to listen. Know your listening goals. Take plenty of notes. Ask for handouts and outlines. Record the meeting if possible or make sure that someone is recording the minutes of the meeting.

- *Be appropriately assertive.* Let others know when it's not a good time for you to listen. If you're busy doing other work or meeting a deadline, politely let the other person know this, and offer to talk to him or her at another time. Most people in the workplace are quite sensitive to important deadlines and last-minute requests.

In addition to the barrier of time, place or location can be a barrier to effective listening. For example, maybe a co-worker begins sharing very private and sensitive information with you in the lunch room. It might be easier to listen to this type of information at a restaurant over dinner rather than in the office. Or perhaps one of your employees approaches you in the supermarket on a Saturday morning and wants to "talk shop." Listening in these situations becomes a struggle, and being appropriately assertive is always a good suggestion. Many people simply don't realize the inappropriateness of the place and need to be politely reminded: "I'm interested in what you have to say, but let's discuss this somewhere else."

External noise.   *Noise* is anything that interferes with or distorts the listening process. Although you may think of noise as external sounds, noise can be processed by any of your five senses. Not just sounds, but sights, something touching us, and even tastes and smells can act as noise and affect listening ability.

For most people, the best listening environment is one that offers as few distractions as possible. In the workplace, the best listening environment is usually the quietest one. Trying to listen to others while attending a crowded trade convention or a loud reception or on the job site can hamper effective listening and responding. If you encounter noise barriers when trying to listen to someone, we suggest that you be appropriately assertive: Let the other person know that you're distracted and you need to find another place to have the conversation. Most people you talk to will appreciate such a request.

Listening barriers such as self-barriers, information-processing barriers, and context barriers distort or interfere with the process of listening. Listening barriers prevent us from interpreting messages accurately; the messages that were encoded and sent are not necessarily the messages that are received and decoded. Learning to listen effectively in the workplace depends on our ability to overcome these listening barriers.

RECAP: Skills for Overcoming Listening Barriers

Listening Barrier Category	Listening Barrier	Description	Strategies
Information-Processing Barriers	Processing Rate	People can take in messages faster than others talk, so your mind may wander while trying to actively listen.	• Mentally summarize the information • Provide the speaker with verbal and nonverbal feedback
	Information Overload	Sometimes there are too many messages coming at you, making it difficult to process any of them.	• Identify your listening goal • Ask for help with prioritizing and filtering messages • Record or take notes on the information
	Receiver Apprehension	You may be anxious about your ability to accurately understand and respond to the messages you are hearing.	• Seek clarity from others • Ask for agendas, outlines, or organizing information • Record information and/or take notes
	Shifting Attention	Multi-tasking allows people to attend to several messages at once, but it can cause them to fail to actively listen to any of them. Men and women attend differently.	• Women may need to stop and focus on individual messages • Men may need to learn to be sensitive to others who want to talk • Avoid multi-tasking while trying to listen
Context Barriers	Barriers of Time and Place	Trying to listen when you are not mentally alert, when time is limited, or when the location is inappropriate	• Be aware of your biological clock—know when your best times of the day are for actively listening • Be appropriately assertive—let others know when the time or the place is not appropriate for the conversation
	External Noise	External factors may affect your ability to listen effectively, including sights, sounds, smells.	• Change location—try to find a quiet place • Be appropriately assertive—let the other person know if you are unable to listen because of external noise

Listening Effectively to Others

Learning to listen effectively on the job involves developing a new set of skills. Although these skills appear simple, they're quite complex. As you know from Chapter 3, communication occurs on two levels—the content level and the relational level.[29] When you listen to someone talk, you usually focus on the content—on *what* the person is saying. For example, your new manager is informing you of her new priorities. The content of the communication are her new priorities: to increase customer satisfaction levels, to decrease workers' compensation claims, to decrease use of sick leave, and to increase customer commitment to products and services offered by the company.

Effective listeners also pay close attention to the relational messages that are embedded in the communication—that is, *how* the person conveys messages. The relational aspects of a message convey feelings, emotions, and attitudes; they allow us insight into how the person feels about what she or he is saying. For example, when your new manager informs you of the new priorities, you see her grim facial expression and hear sternness and a tone of seriousness in her voice. You quickly decode this to mean that she is not happy with the performance of the department. Although she does not directly say that she is unhappy and disappointed, she clearly communicates this message through her nonverbal behavior which conveys her feelings, emotions, and attitudes. Effective listening requires you to listen on both levels; you must listen to what the other person is saying and to how the other person is saying it.

Another reason why listening requires a complex set of skills is because we live in an age of information, but not necessarily an age of knowledge. Many people in the workplace automatically assume that information and knowledge are the same thing.[30] They're not. Information is a nugget of data that lacks meaning. It's useless. Knowledge is information that is made useful. Listening allows us to transform information into knowledge by understanding and using the information. When we comprehend and apply the information to solve problems, we are working with knowledge and not information.[31]

A simple rule for crossing a street that many of us learned in kindergarten will help you listen for content and relational meanings and convert information into knowledge: Stop, Look, and Listen.

Stop: Turn Off Competing Messages

If you're serious about listening, then you need to be serious about turning off messages that compete for selection and attention, the first two stages in the listening process. It's not always easy to turn off competing messages in the workplace. A lot of literal and psychological noise distorts or interferes with the process of listening, such as cell phones ringing and vibrating or worries you may have about meeting a deadline. Many of these can become listening barriers, as we've seen.

Another barrier to effective listening is the desire to talk rather than to listen. An example would be a boss who says, "I want to listen to you" but ends up talking for an entire meeting. How can we listen when we're too busy talking? Listening occurs when we're silent. One team of researchers wanted to know the impact of a training program that developed listening skills, including the effects of being silent for 12 hours.[32] The researchers studied three groups of people. One group heard a lecture about how to be better listeners. A second group promised not to talk to anyone for 12 hours; rather than talking, they listened. A third group both heard the lecture on listening and were silent for 12 hours. Following the various activities, all groups took a listening comprehension test. The results: There were no differences among the three groups in listening test scores; all groups seemed to listen equally well. But those who were silent for 12 hours reported that they thought they were more attentive to others and more conscious of being good listeners. This research supports the saying that "You have been given two ears and one mouth so that you will listen more and talk less."

When you commit to listening, you must become other-oriented rather than self-centered. Listening is not about you. It's about the other person. Becoming other-oriented requires a process called **social decentering**, which is stepping away from your own thoughts and attempting to experience the feelings of another person.[33] Social decentering allows you to have empathy with another person. To experience *empathy* is to feel what another person is feeling. In essence, you're asking yourself this question: "If I were the other person, how would I be feeling?" The process of social decentering requires mindfulness, or a conscious awareness, that is often difficult to achieve in a fast-paced and deadline-driven workplace. Social decentering occurs when you commit to turning off competing messages and to listening on both the content and the relational levels. Pay attention while listening to others. If your attention drifts, your self-awareness will help you redirect your attention back to the speaker.

Other strategies that may help you stop and turn off competing messages include the following:

- *Prepare yourself physically.* One way to physically prepare yourself to listen is to use the SOLER process.[34]

   S = Squarely face the person. Orient your body toward the person.

   O = Open the body position. Unfold arms and remove obstacles or barriers between you and the other person.

   L = Lean toward the person.

   E = Eye contact. Look directly at the person.

   R = Relax. Anxiety interferes with information processing. Try to be calm, and focus on the speaker or the interaction between people.

Social decentering the process of stepping away from your own thoughts and attempting to experience the feelings of another person.

- *Prepare yourself by setting the scene for attentive listening.*[35] Avoid having serious conversations in locations that offer too many distractions. An overflowing desk, the instant messaging tone informing you of an on-going conversation, or a ringing phone compete for your attention. As an alternative, use a conference room or go outside for a brief walk to talk and listen.
- *Prepare yourself by arriving early to meetings.*[36] A few extra minutes will give you the time you need to make a transition mentally and physically from one activity to the next. According to Richard Bierck, a communication consultant and writer for the *Harvard Management Communication Letter*, people need time to compose themselves by asking themselves the following questions: Am I ready to listen? What is the purpose for listening? What outcome do I want?

Look: Listen with Your Eyes

Is it easier for you to listen to someone when you can see the person? Have you ever been in a conversation with someone on the phone or while texting and felt that you had to meet with the person face to face instead? Do you get annoyed when you are attending a lecture and someone sits down in the seat immediately in front of you, blocking your view of the speaker? If you're like most people, you prefer to look at the person you're listening to. Research suggests that we listen more effectively when we can see the other person.[37] Specifically, there is a significant increase in our listening comprehension when we can see *and* hear, rather than only hearing the other person speak.[38]

Nonverbal

Learning to listen with the eyes requires paying particular attention to others' non-verbal messages, which is *Principle Three: Effectively use and interpret nonverbal messages.* Although listening with the ears allows you to capture the content of another person's message, the eyes allow you to more accurately decode and interpret the relational aspects of the message.[39] Nonverbal communication researcher Albert Mehrabian has pointed out that verbal messages convey the *explicit* meanings (the content) of our communication, whereas nonverbal messages convey the *implicit* (relational) meanings. According to Mehrabian, implicit messages are nonverbal behaviors that express feelings and attitudes about the content conveyed by speech."[40] For example, we may not detect the urgency (implicit) in someone's request to complete a task until we actually see the person's face. Once we see the person's face we have a visual nonverbal message to couple with the verbal message, allowing us to decode and interpret the message more accurately.

>>> COMMUNICATION ETHICS @ WORK

Have you ever been put in a tight spot simply because you were a good listener? There are times when the information you hear creates a moral dilemma. As a long-time employee of a local business, I listened to frequent discussions of certain pay policies and ways to change them to increase profits. Sometimes I would question the ethics of making these changes, as they affected employees who were not being informed of the changes. After leaving the organization, I was relieved to be free of that ethical dilemma—until one day a friend called with a problem. A supervisor was asking her to change some financial policies so as to take pay from employees to benefit the business. She felt it was unethical, but she was new in the position and worried about losing her job. I realized it was the same ethical dilemma I had had at my old position, and was again confronted with a crisis of conscience.

Sometimes, when others know you are a good listener, they may share sensitive information with you. What do you do with that information? I could have called my friend's company's headquarters, speaking on condition of anonymity, and shared what I suspected was going on. But I also felt responsible in some way to protect my friend's employment. The information she had shared with me was known by only two people. I did not want to jeopardize her job, nor did I want the employees to be taken advantage of.

What do you think? What would have been the best course of action? Has there ever been a time when listening to someone made you privy to sensitive information? What did you do with the information?

How effective are you in reading other people's nonverbal messages? In the workplace, people don't always speak their minds for a variety of reasons. It's frustrating, but true. You'll be expected to hear what others are "really" saying, even when they don't say a word—you'll be expected to read between the lines. Although you may believe this to be a difficult process, Malcolm Gladwell, author of the best-seller *Blink: The Power of Thinking Without Thinking*, argues that humans have an uncanny ability to read people and to automatically and instantaneously detect their attitudes and feelings even without talking to them.[41] Gladwell refers to this ability as *rapid cognition*, which is our ability to know and understand something without being able to explain why or how we know it. If you have ever had a hunch about a person and later found out that this hunch was true or accurate, you've experienced rapid cognition.

There are a number of biological explanations for rapid cognition,[42] but we can improve our innate ability to listen with our eyes by improving our ability to interpret others' nonverbal behaviors. Mehrabian found that we synthesize and interpret nonverbal cues along three primary dimensions: pleasure (liking), arousal (interest), and dominance (status).[43]

- *Look for liking cues.* People who like what they're talking about and find the topic pleasurable will probably use some of the following observable behaviors: forward body lean, head nods, direct eye contact, smiling, open body orientation, and expressive gestures and voice.[44]

- *Look for interest cues.* People who have a genuine interest in and passion for what they're talking about will probably use some of the following observable behaviors: vibrant voice, dynamic gestures, excited facial expressions, and energetic body movements.[45]

- *Look for status cues.* People who consider themselves to be important (high status) will probably use some of the following observable behaviors when communicating with a person of lower status: relaxed body posture, less direct body orientation, a downward head tilt, and less smiling, head nodding, and facial animation.[46] People who perceive themselves to have less status than their communication partner will often display a tense body posture and a direct body orientation and are likely to break eye contact before the other person does.

When you attempt to interpret others' nonverbal communication, you must realize that there is a good deal of room for error. Humans are complex, and they don't always send clear messages. But the more you learn about nonverbal communication, especially the liking, interest, and status cues, the more likely you are to select, attend to, understand, remember, and respond to others effectively and appropriately.

Listen: Understand Both Major Ideas and Details

Here's a question to think about: Do you learn best when a teacher gives you the big picture first and then the details, or do you prefer to hear details first and then get the big picture? If you prefer the big picture first, you would have trouble listening to a customer who goes into detail about a complicated problem that she is having with a product that you sold her last week. In fact, after she finished speaking you might still be confused about the actual problem. You would need to ask the customer, "So what exactly is the problem?" If you prefer to hear details first, you would have trouble listening to a customer who explains in general terms a problem that she is having with the product. You would need to ask a number of detail-oriented questions in order to fully understand the problem. In many ways, learning and listening are very similar. Both processes require us to convert information into knowledge or to make sense out of what we're hearing from another person.

If you prefer getting the big picture first and then the small details, you're considered to have a **whole-part learning style**.[47] If you prefer learning the details first and then getting the big picture, you have what is considered a **part-whole learning style**.[48] Although we may have preferences for learning and listening, others don't always accommodate our particular preferences. To listen well, we have to be able to do three listening activities simultaneously: (1) listen for the major ideas in a message, (2) listen for the details in a message, and (3) link the details with the main ideas of the message.

Whole-part learning style the style of a learner who prefers learning the big picture first, then the details.

Part-whole learning style the style of a learner who prefers learning details first, before the big picture.

Listen for major ideas in the message. Some of us get bogged down in the details and we miss the major idea of a message. In fact, studies suggests that poor listeners are more likely to focus on only facts and data, rather than the overall point of the message.[49] For example, you listen to a customer who is not happy with the service he has been receiving from your company. Rather than hearing the general idea that the customer is unhappy with the overall service, you're busy listening for the details of this customer's unhappiness: You want to pinpoint the cause of the unhappiness. Rather than listening on the relational level (recognizing that the customer is unhappy and wants you to acknowledge the unhappiness), you're listening on the content level (focusing on what's the problem and how to fix it). When this type of "micro listening" occurs, we unfortunately fail to hear the larger idea.

Asking "pre-questions" is a strategy that has been shown to enhance macro-level listening, or listening for the larger ideas in someone's message.[50] A pre-question is a question that one formulates mentally prior to listening to another person speak. Prior to listening to a manager, co-worker, subordinate, or a customer, mentally formulate some questions that you want to find answers to while listening:

- How is this person feeling about the situation?
- What does this person want or need from me?
- Why does this person have this want or need?

Pre-questions serve to filter incoming information, preparing the brain to decode or process relevant information, which in this case are the "big ideas."[51] Research suggests that this type of listening strategy enhances the listening process.[52]

Listen for the details in the message. Some of us listen for only the big ideas and we miss all the important details. This tendency can be a hindrance when you are trying to solve problems. How can you solve problems if you miss the important details? If you listen only on the relational level, you're going to miss important details you need to solve the problem. In many workplace situations, your job is to select, attend to, understand, and remember details. You can take notes or record the details in some other way, and develop ways of jogging your memory. If details are not forthcoming, then you need to become more active in the listening process by probing and asking the other person the standard questions: Who? What? Where? When? How? and Why? Answers to these questions can provide you with the details you need.

Link the details with the main ideas. Listening is a complex skill that requires us to be able to link information together. When we link information together, we organize it, making it understandable and useful; we convert information into knowledge. Our ability to link and organize information allows us to listen on both the content level (the details) and the relational level (the main ideas). We must be able to listen to and recognize a customer's dissatisfaction and frustration with our product or service while simultaneously listening for the Who? What? Where? When? How? and Why? Linking the customer's frustration with information about who is involved, what occurred, when it occurred, why it occurred, and how it occurred will allow us to address not only the customer's frustration (relational level), but also the customer's problem (content level).

One way to link information is to use **elaboration strategies**, which are mental processing strategies that give information new meaning by organizing the information.

Elaboration strategies mental processing strategies that give information new meaning by organizing the information.

DILBERT: © Scott Adams / Dist. by United Feature Syndicate, Inc.

Elaboration strategies have been shown to enhance listening effectiveness.[53] Here are a few suggestions for linking details and main ideas:

- *Create interrelationships between the details and main ideas.* How are they related? Is there a direct relationship or is it an indirect relationship? Is there a cause-and-effect relationship?
- *Create a mental map of the details and main ideas.* Now mentally draw arrows to show the various relationships.
- *Connect the information (details and main ideas) to what you already know.* How is the information similar? How is it different?
- *Reframe the details and main ideas in a new context.* Think about the information differently by putting it in a different situation or context. Would the details and main ideas still be related as you believe they are, or would there be different relationships?
- *Reorganize or rearrange the details and main ideas.* Mentally put the details and main ideas into different categories or put them in chronological order. How are the details and main ideas affected by this reorganization?

Listen actively. Another way to link details with main ideas is to listen actively, which is a distillation of the other recommendations we've offered thus far. Today's professional workplace requires active listeners who are engaged with both their minds and their hearts to capture both the content and the relational dimensions of others' messages.[54] Active listeners are engaged both physically and mentally in the listening process.[55] The following behaviors reflect an active listener:[56]

- Gives full attention to the other person.
- Focuses on what is being said.
- Asks questions for clarification.
- Withholds judgment until the full message is received.
- Has an alert and upright posture.
- Responds with forward body lean, head nods, and direct eye contact.

The best listeners are mentally alert, physically focused on the other person, and actively involved in seeking understanding. They stop what they're doing and consciously focus on the other person. They look for the nonverbal behaviors that convey the relational meanings in the message. And they listen actively by linking the details of the message to the main ideas.

We mentioned that listening is very similar to learning. Just as you have a dominant style for learning, listening researchers argue that you have a dominant listening style.[57] To learn more about your listening style, take a few minutes to complete and score the Listening Styles Inventory in Rating Scale 4.1, developed by listening researchers Glenn Pearce, Iris Johnson, and Randolph Barker.[58]

Responding Effectively to Others

The title of this chapter, "Listening and Responding," reflects the active listening process that we introduced in the preceding section. Active listeners not only stop, look, and listen, they also respond to the speaker. As you'll recall, listening is a process that includes *responding*. Thoughtfully responding to others serves several purposes. First, it tells a speaker how well we understand his or her message. Second, it lets a speaker know how the message affects us; whether we agree or disagree with a message. Third, in many situations our response to a speaker validates the speaker; it lets the speaker know that we're "with" him or her. Ultimately, all of these responsive messages allow the speaker to adapt his or her communication more appropriately to ensure that listeners understand the messages.

In this section of the chapter, we'll review three sets of skills for responding to others while listening to them: responding with verbal messages, responding with nonverbal messages, and responding with empathic messages.

Rating Scale 4.1 Listening Styles Inventory

The following items relate to your listening style. Circle the number of the response that best reflects your behavior. Please be candid.

Items	Almost Always	Often	Sometimes	Seldom	Almost Never
1. I want to listen to what others have to say when they are talking.	5	4	3	2	1
2. I do not listen at my capacity when others are talking.	5	4	3	2	1
3. By listening, I can guess a speaker's intent or purpose without being told.	5	4	3	2	1
4. I have a purpose for listening when others are talking.	5	4	3	2	1
5. I keep control of my biases and attitudes when listening to others speak so that these factors won't affect my interpretation of the message.	5	4	3	2	1
6. I analyze my listening errors so as not to make them again.	5	4	3	2	1
7. I listen to the complete message before making judgments about what the speaker has said.	5	4	3	2	1
8. I cannot tell when a speaker's biases or attitudes are affecting his or her message.	5	4	3	2	1
9. I ask questions when I don't fully understand a speaker's message.	5	4	3	2	1
10. I am aware of whether a speaker's meaning for words and concepts is the same as mine.	5	4	3	2	1

Grand total = ____ + ____ + ____ + ____ + ____

Now consult the Interpretation Scale.

Place an X on the part of the scale below that corresponds to your grand total score. Your listening style is described below.

50	45	38	28	10
Active	Involved	Passive	Detached	

The **active listener** gives full attention to listening when others are talking and focuses on what is being said. This person expends a lot of energy participating in the speaking-listening exchange, which is usually evidenced by an alert posture or stance and much direct eye contact.

The **involved listener** gives most of his or her attention to the speaker's words and intentions. This person reflects on the message to a degree and participates in the speaking-listening exchange. The involved listener practices some direct eye contact and may have alert posture or stance, although this may be intermittent.

The **passive listener** receives information at though being talked to rather than participating as an equal partner in the speaking-listening exchange. While the passive listener assumes that the responsibility for the success of the communication is the speaker's, he or she is usually attentive, although attention may be faked at times. The passive listener seldom expends any noticeable energy in receiving and interpreting messages.

The **detached listener** withdraws from the speaking-listening exchange and becomes the object of the speaker's message rather than its receiver. The detached listener is usually inattentive, uninterested, and may be restless, bored, or easily distracted. This person's noticeable lack of enthusiasm may be marked by slumped or very relaxed posture and avoidance of direct eye contact.

Note: The listening inventory gives you a general idea of your preferred listening style, based on how you view yourself. The scores indicating styles are approximations and should be regarded as such. Your listening style may change, depending on the given situation or your interests, intentions, or objectives.

RECAP: Skills for Listening Effectively to Others

Listening Skill	Listening Strategies	Examples
Stop: Turn Off Competing Messages	Prepare yourself physically.	Turn toward the person, look the person in the eye, and relax.
	Prepare yourself by setting the scene.	If necessary, move to another room away from distractions.
	Prepare yourself by getting to meetings early.	Arriving a few minutes early is best, but even being a few seconds early will help you to refocus on the new task.
Look: Listen with Your Eyes	Look for liking cues.	Look for forward body lean, head nods, direct eye contact, smiling, open body orientation, and expressive gestures and voice.
	Look for interest cues.	Observe for vibrant voice, dynamic gestures, excited facial expressions, and energetic body movements.
	Look for status cues.	Observe body posture, body orientation, head position, and amount of smiling, nodding, eye contact, and facial animation.
Listen: Understand Both Major Ideas and Details	Listen for the major ideas in the message.	Ask questions to get at the major point of the message, which may be the relational message.
	Listen for the details in the message.	Ask questions about the specific details in the message.
	Link the details with the main ideas.	Use elaboration strategies for organizing the information in order to fully understand the message.
	Listen actively.	Give the other person your full attention, focus, ask questions, paraphrase, and withhold judgment.

Responding with Verbal Messages

There are a number of verbal responses that allow us to provide a speaker with important feedback. Here are a few of them:

- *Communicate messages that let the speaker know that you understand the message*; for example, "I understand. I see what you're saying."
- *Communicate messages that let the speaker know that you need clarification*; for example, "I'm confused. Can you give me another example?"
- *Communicate messages that let the speaker know that you're interested and need more information*; for example, "I find what you're saying fascinating. Do you mind going into more detail?"
- *Communicate messages that let the speaker know that you'd like him or her to continue speaking*; for example, "OK, then what happened?"
- *Communicate messages that let the speaker know that you'd like to say something*; for example, "May I add something to what you're saying?"

What all of these verbal responses have in common is that they all convey that we've been paying attention to what the speaker is saying. Again, it's important that speakers use these messages as feedback and adapt their communication appropriately.

Responding with Nonverbal Messages

In some business situations, such as at a formal board meeting, it may not be appropriate to respond to a speaker with verbal messages. In these situations, we can respond with nonverbal messages, which are as important as (if not more important than) verbal messages. Nonverbal responsive messages include visual (sight) and aural (sound) cues. We've already noted a few visual nonverbal responsive cues: forward body lean, head nods, taking notes, and making eye contact with the speaker. A few of the aural cues include back channel cues, which were discussed in Chapter 3, including vocal assurances that signal understanding and "vocal starters" or utterances that signal that the listener would like to add something to the conversation. To get an idea of how nonverbally responsive you are in conversations, complete the assessment measure in Rating Scale 4.2.

You might be asking yourself, "Does a smile, head nod, or forward body lean really make that much of a difference when listening to others?" It does! Not only does using nonverbally responsive behaviors enhance listening comprehension, but speakers who see others responding using the above behaviors feel motivated, satisfied, and effective in their communication.[59] It's a win-win situation. How important is it to you that others be nonverbally responsive when they're listening to you? How do you feel when you're speaking to someone and you get a blank stare from them? Most people become distracted and begin to feel frustrated or insecure when this happens. Remember, nonverbal messages convey relational cues; when others don't respond to us nonverbally, we feel somewhat rejected and unsupported. We feel "unheard."

Responding with Empathic Messages

Empathy, as we noted earlier in this chapter, is the process of feeling what another person is feeling. Empathizing is more than just acknowledging how another person feels; it is making an effort to feel what the other person is feeling. Responding with empathy is especially important when we want to support and encourage others. Although most people don't think of the workplace as a place where feelings are openly

---

Rating Scale 4.2   Measure of Nonverbal Responsiveness

How responsive are you when listening to others? Take a few minutes to complete this self-report measure of nonverbal responsiveness.[60] The items comprising this measure will also make you aware of various nonverbal responsive behaviors.

Rate each behavior in the list using the following scale: Never = 0, Rarely = 1, Occasionally = 2, Often = 3, Very Often = 4

When listening to others, how often do you . . .

_____   display facial expressions that reflect your positive attitude.

_____   show interest by taking notes on what the other person is saying.

_____   smile at the person who is talking to you.

_____   nod your head while the other person is talking to you.

_____   look at the other person who is talking to you.

_____   smile while you're asking the other person questions.

_____   sit up and lean forward while listening.

_____   gesture with your hands and arms while the other person is talking to you.

_____   use vocal inflections that convey your positive attitude toward the person talking.

_____   use vocal starters that suggest that you want to say something.

_____   respond quickly to the other person's questions or comments.

_____   use vocal variety in tone, pitch, rate, and volume to indicate that you're interested in what the other person is saying.

_____   use vocal assurances that let the other person know that you understand his or her message.

Scoring Instructions: Sum your scores for the 13 items. Scores above 26 indicate high nonverbal responsiveness. Scores below 26 indicate low nonverbal responsiveness.

shared and people support and encourage each other by listening and responding with empathic messages, the role of emotions in the workplace is becoming more important and is a focus of study for organizational communication researchers.[61]

Empathy is a communication tool that can be used to accomplish a number of communication goals, such as building important workplace relationships, repairing workplace relationships, defusing workplace conflict, and even influencing clients and customers to purchase your products and services. Here are three strategies that will enhance your ability to respond to others with empathic messages.

Ask appropriate questions. As we listen for information and attempt to understand how another person is feeling, we may need to ask a number of questions. Most of our questions serve one of four purposes: (1) to obtain additional information ("Can you tell me more about the problem?"); (2) to check how the other person feels ("Are you frustrated because you didn't meet your deadline?"); (3) to ask for clarification ("What did you mean when you said we need to outsource?"); or (4) to verify that you have reached an accurate conclusion about the other person's intent or feeling ("So are you saying you'd rather work at home than at the office?").

Verbal

Paraphrase message content. After we have listened and asked appropriate questions, we need to check whether our interpretations are accurate by paraphrasing the content of a speaker's message. **Paraphrasing** is restating in our own words what we think the other person is saying. Paraphrasing is different from repeating what someone has said; that would be parroting, not paraphrasing. When we paraphrase content, we summarize the details and the main ideas. Here are some common scripts, or ways to begin paraphrasing:

> "So here is what seems to have happened . . ."
>
> "Let me see if I got this right. You're saying that . . ."
>
> "Here's what I understand you to mean . . ."
>
> "So the point you seem to be making is . . ."
>
> "You seem to be saying . . ."

Paraphrasing restating in your own words what you think another person is saying.

When a listener paraphrases the content and feelings of a speaker's message, the speaker is not only more likely to know that the message was understood but also more likely to trust and value the listener.

Paraphrase emotions. The most important goal of empathic responding is to make sure that we understand the speaker's feelings and let him or her know that we understand. How do we do this? Paraphrasing emotions is similar to paraphrasing content. Here are some common scripts to use to begin paraphrasing emotions:

> "So you feel . . . ."
>
> "Emotionally, you're feeling . . ."
>
> "I get a sense that you're feeling . . ."
>
> "Is this how you're feeling: you're feeling . . ."

Listening and responding to others with empathy can accomplish many communication goals, including enhancing the quality of your workplace relationships.

Paraphrasing emotions or content can be especially useful in the following workplace situations:

- Before you take an important action.
- Before you argue with or criticize your business partner or associate.
- When your business partner or associate has strong feelings.
- When your business partner or associate just wants to talk.
- When your business partner or associate is using jargon that you don't understand.
- When you encounter new ideas.[62]

Although many people don't associate responding with the process of listening, it's an integral component of effective listening. Developing skills for responding with verbal messages, nonverbal messages, and empathic messages not only enhances our listening comprehension, but it also enhances the quality of our workplace relationships.

RECAP: **Skills for Effectively Responding to Others**

Responding Skills	Examples
Responding with Verbal Messages	Let the speaker know you understand: "Yes, I see what you mean."
	Let the speaker know you need clarification: "I don't understand. Could you explain that another way?"
	Let the speaker know you are interested but need more information: "That is exciting! What did you do next?"
	Let the speaker know you'd like to say something: "That sounds interesting. May I add something?"
Responding with Nonverbal Messages	Lean forward, nod your head, take notes, make eye contact with the speaker.
	Use vocal assurances: "Uh huh . . ."
Responding with Empathic Messages	Ask appropriate questions: "Then what happened?"
	Paraphrase message content: "This is what I hear you saying . . ."
	Paraphrase emotions: "So, it sounds as though you feel . . ."

Helping Others Listen Effectively to You

Have you ever thought about how others listen to you? Do you often have to repeat what you say to others because they quickly forget what you said to them? When others don't listen to you, whom do you blame? Do you blame them for not listening? Or do you blame yourself for not making it easy for others to listen to you? If you're like most people, you probably tend to blame the other person for not listening to you. Have you ever thought that maybe you're the problem? Consider the following questions when diagnosing why others may not be listening to you as carefully as you would prefer:

- Do you bore others when you communicate with them? Do you leave a positive impression on others? Are you memorable?
- Do you convey information in a confusing manner?
- Do you communicate too much information to others?
- Do you give those listening to you an opportunity to ask questions, take notes?

In the following pages we'll focus on the five stages of the listening process—selecting, attending, understanding, remembering, and responding—and suggest ways you can help others listen to you in each stage.[63]

Helping Others Select Your Messages

Before someone can listen to your message, he or she must select it from other competing messages. How can you help other people select your messages? Here are a few suggestions:

Move closer to the other person. As discussed in Chapter 3, proxemics is the study of space. We can help others select our messages by moving closer to them or by making ourselves available to them. Have you ever had a manager who claimed to have an open door policy, but every time you dropped by her office, she gave you "that look" that clearly said "Don't interrupt"? If you want people to listen to you, you have to help them select your messages by physically moving closer to them or by communicating that it's OK to approach you, such as by making direct eye contact, using open body position, and gesturing (for example, waving someone into your office).

Make the information useful. People tend to select information that is immediately useful to them. You can enhance selection by increasing the utility or usefulness of your message.

If you want people to listen to you, you have to give them a reason to listen. Show how the information will benefit them on the job: "Here's how what I'm about to say will benefit you"

Adapt messages to others' beliefs. People have a tendency to select messages that are consistent with their attitudes, beliefs, and values. Give some consideration to how well your messages will fit your listeners' belief systems. If what you're about to say will go against their beliefs, find ways to make your messages more palatable or convincing. For example, if you're discussing sexual harassment with a group of guys who don't believe that sexual harassment occurs that often on the job, be prepared to share statistics with them.

Adapt

Helping Others Attend to Your Messages

How can you help other people attend to your messages? They may have selected your message, but that doesn't mean they will necessarily pay attention to it. Try some of the following suggestions for getting people to pay attention to your messages.

Make messages novel. People pay attention to messages that are unusual and unique. If we want others to pay attention to our messages, we need to make the messages stand out from all the others. Flight attendants who work for Southwest Airlines are known for making their routine and very boring safety demonstrations novel and humorous.[64] They make people want to listen to their safety instructions.

Make messages concrete. Use words in your messages that are vivid and clear; whenever possible, refer to things that listeners can see, smell, feel, taste, or touch. Avoid using words that are abstract. For example, Monica, a division leader for a large clothing retailer, is encouraging her store managers to be transformational leaders. She loses many of them because they don't understand what a transformational leader is. The leadership jargon is abstract to them. To make her message concrete so her store managers pay attention to her, Monica needs to explain that transformational leaders (1) develop clear sales goals, (2) invent new sales techniques, and (3) reward employees for reaching goals.

Make messages moderate in length. People pay attention to messages that are moderate in length. Staci, who is a wedding planner, tries to pitch her services to a prospective customer. But the bride-to-be loses interest in the sales pitch because it's too long. At an initial meeting, Staci doesn't need to go into detail about every possible service she can provide. Brief messages are equally problematic; a message that is too brief doesn't contain any relevant information and can be missed altogether. So what's moderate? It depends on the person who is receiving our message. Staci should use her prospective customer's nonverbal cues as a gauge. If the bride-to-be is engaged and asking questions, then Staci should continue. If the bride's attention is waning, then it's time to wrap up the sales pitch. Staci can also stop and ask a question to probe her customer's level of interest and engagement.

Helping Others Understand Your Messages

Assuming that others have selected and paid attention to your message, how can you help them understand, decode, or assign appropriate meanings to the message? Here's what we do to get others to understand our messages. You too might find these strategies helpful.

Fit messages into existing schema. A **schema** is a mental representation of knowledge. Think of a schema as a mental "box" or "filing cabinet" where you classify, categorize, and file concepts. For example, suppose you're training employees to use a new presentation software program. Chances are the employees have used PowerPoint—so they have a schema for presentation software, and that schema is PowerPoint. To enhance their understanding of your messages, show them how the new presentation software program is similar to and different from PowerPoint. Tapping into an existing schema helps others understand your message and makes listening easier.

Develop a new schema. Sometimes others don't understand us because they don't have an existing schema, or filing cabinet, for the new information. Using the above example, imagine that you were teaching employees how to use a new software presentation program, but they were unfamiliar with PowerPoint. Chances are they would be totally lost. To enhance their listening—and more importantly, their understanding—you would need to give them a new schema. You might begin by first telling the employees that developing a slide presentation is like being an artist who paints beautiful pictures. They begin with a blank slide, which is the canvas. Then, you could introduce the toolbox, which is like the painter's

Schema a mental representation of knowledge.

palette. Next, teach them how to create a background for all of the slides, which is like adding a first coat of paint. If people don't have a schema for understanding new information, it's important to develop one for them.

Use listeners' frame of reference.   Another way to enhance understanding and listening is to tap into the experiences of those who are listening. What is their frame of reference? In other words, rather than explaining something using your own experiences, use the experiences of those who are listening. For example, if new employees don't understand the sick leave policy that you're trying to explain to them during orientation, ask them how the sick leave policy worked at their last company. Use their experiences with sick leave as a starting point, and then make the necessary adjustments in the conversation to ensure that the employees understand how your company's sick leave policy works.

Helping Others Remember Your Messages

How can you help other people remember your message? If you've been successful up to this point, your listeners have selected your message, are paying attention to your message, and understand your message. Now, how do you help them remember it? Here are a few suggestions:

Use redundancy.   For most of us, the more we hear something, the more important we think it is, and the more likely we are to remember the information. Making a message redundant is repeating the information or reiterating the information. **Repeating** is simply restating the information using the same words in the same order. **Reiterating** information is restating the information using different words. Saying, "Our number-one priority is your safety. Our number-one priority is your safety" is an example of repeating. Saying, "Our number-one priority is your safety. Your safety is immensely important to us" is an example of reiteration. Making messages redundant enhances others' ability to remember and recall information when needed.

Use memory joggers.   A **mnemonic device** is a short rhyme, phrase, story, joke, or other mental technique (such as a mental picture) for making information easier to memorize. A mnemonic is useful when trying to remember a list of terms or instructions. For example, if you're certified in CPR, you learned a mnemonic device for remembering how to save a person's life using ABC: A is for *airway*, B is for *breathing*, and C is for *circulation*. Memory joggers are shortcuts that enhance memory and recall of information.

Use the principle of primacy and recency.   This principle states that people are more likely to remember information that is presented first (primacy) and/or last (recency) during a conversation or a presentation.[65] Research suggests that messages in the middle of a conversation or a presentation are often forgotten. To enhance others' abilities to remember our messages, it's important to position the important messages toward the beginning and toward the end of our communication with them. Students preparing for the ministry are often instructed in how to prepare and deliver an effective sermon that people will remember: Begin by telling parishioners what you're going to tell them. Next, tell them. Finally, tell them what you just told them. This sage piece of advice recognizes the importance of the primacy and recency effect. If parishioners are going to remember any part of the sermon, they're most likely to remember what the minister said to begin the sermon and what he or she said to end it.

Helping Others Respond to Your Messages

How can you help other people respond to your messages? While the selecting, attending, understanding, and remembering stages of the listening process are focused on the person who is listening and receiving the messages, responding aids the source of the messages—the person who is talking. When receivers respond to a source, the source uses this information as feedback and adapts his or her messages accordingly. If messages are adapted appropriately, then the people receiving the messages will understand the information better and are more likely to remember the information. For example, if you're talking to a group of co-workers and they all look confused (raised eyebrows, wrinkled foreheads, sighs of frustration), it's important that you use this feedback and adapt your messages to clarify the confusion.

But sometimes people don't know how to respond, especially in more formal presentations. Because feedback cues are so important to a speaker, we encourage you to consider some of the following ideas:

Repeating restating information using the same words in the same order.

Reiterating restating information using different words.

Mnemonic device a short rhyme, phrase, or other mental technique that makes information easier to memorize.

RECAP: Skills and Strategies for Helping Others Listen Effectively to You

Skills	Strategies	Examples
Helping Others Select Your Messages	Move closer to the person.	Move toward your listener in order to more effectively communicate the message.
	Make the information useful.	Show that the information has utility: "Here's something that you will find helpful . . ."
	Adapt messages to others' beliefs.	Share information in a way that makes it easier for others to pay attention: "I know you've been frustrated that work is piling up and it seems that nothing is being done to hire more staff. Here's where we stand on the staffing problem."
Helping Others Attend to Your Messages	Make messages novel.	Include humor in a monotonous message or tell a story from a different perspective.
	Make messages concrete.	Avoid jargon and abstract language. Rather than discussing the "interoffice communication problem," refer to the specific issue at hand: people aren't responding to their email.
	Make messages moderate in length.	Watch the nonverbal cues of the listener to gauge whether your message is too long; and if so, wrap things up.
Helping Others Understand Your Messages	Fit messages into existing schema.	When discussing a work situation with co-workers who are big sports fans, use a football analogy to help them understand.
	Develop a new schema.	When training co-workers to analyze workplace problems, have them consider the following questions about a particular situation: "What are the strengths? What are the weaknesses? What are the opportunities? What are the threats?"
	Use listeners' frame of reference.	When training new employees, refer to some of their experiences at their former employers to help them make sense of the policies and procedures at the your organization.
Helping Others Remember Your Messages	Use redundancy.	Repeating: "We care about the customer, we care about the customer."
		Reiterating: "We care about the customer. The customer is the reason we're in business."
	Use memory joggers.	During CPR training, the trainer encourages participants to remember the ABCs of CPR: A for Airway, B for Breathing, and C for Circulation.
		When trying to resolve a conflict, use the PUGSS model: P for Problem, U for Understanding, G for Goals, S for possible Solutions, and S for agreed-on Solution.
	Use the principle of primacy and recency.	Put the most important information at the beginning and end of the message.
Helping Others Respond to Your Messages	Encourage questions.	Let listeners know that it is ok to interrupt with questions, or set aside a time when they can ask questions.
	Encourage note taking.	Let the listeners know they can take notes while you talk. This can also help them to ask questions.
	Encourage nonverbal responsiveness.	Head nods, forward body lean, and other nonverbal responses allow listeners to develop a better understanding of the message.

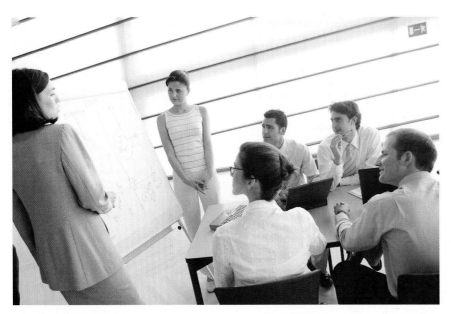

Encourage your audience to respond to your message. Their responses will help you appropriately adapt information so that the audience can better understand and remember it.

Encourage questions. If the situation allows for this, encourage the receivers of your messages to interrupt you at any point with their questions. (If you would prefer not to be interrupted, assure listeners that you will answer their questions, and then have them hold their questions until a designated point in the conversation or presentation.) People need to be encouraged to ask questions. Many times, people don't ask questions out of fear that they will appear stupid. Give people permission to ask "stupid" questions.

Encourage note taking. Give people permission to take notes during your conversation or presentation. When people take notes, it lets the source know that the receivers consider the information important. In many ways note taking is validating to the speaker; it's a form of encouragement. Also, note taking encourages questions, which enables a speaker to know if he or she is making any sense to the audience.

Encourage nonverbal responsiveness. Because many listeners would prefer not to ask questions, encourage them to use nonverbal messages to convey *both* their understanding and their confusion. When people are engaged and understanding, they usually use direct eye contact, forward body lean, head nods, and vocal assurances that express their understanding. When people are disengaged and confused, they usually fail to make eye contact, lean back in their chairs, slouch, or sigh to express their frustration and lack of understanding. To a speaker, these nonverbal responsive messages are an invaluable source of information.[66] If the nonverbal responses convey understanding, then we can continue our conversation or presentation. If the nonverbal responses convey confusion, then we need to slow down, repeat and reiterate, and answer listeners' questions to clarify the confusion.[67]

Research also suggests that when receivers of messages are engaged in the physical act of responding to and elaborating on messages (that is, asking questions, taking notes, responding nonverbally), they are more likely to have a better understanding of the information and be better able to recall and use it.[68] Put simply, the physical act of responding to messages enhances listening.

It's important to remember that when others don't listen to us, we might be part of the listening problem. Rather than blaming others for not listening to us, there is much that we can do to help others select, attend to, understand, remember, and respond to our messages.

Summary

Leading others begins by understanding others. To understand others, you must begin by first listening and responding to them. The purpose of this chapter was to help you develop your listening and responding skills, which is the fourth communication principle for leadership. Effective leaders do more than just listen to others; they also respond to what others are saying. Responding thoughtfully means letting others know that we're listening to them.

The listening process includes five important steps: selecting, attending to, understanding, remembering, and responding to others' verbal and nonverbal messages. To select a message is to focus on one sound as you sort through the myriad of noises competing for your attention. Once you select the sound or message, you attend to, or focus on, it. To understand a message is to assign meaning to the verbal and nonverbal messages that you're receiving. To remember is to recall the information. To respond is to let others know that you understand their message.

Many people struggle with listening. They have a difficult time overcoming listening barriers: both information-processing barriers and context barriers. Although doing so is challenging, you can develop a number of important skills to overcome these listening barriers.

To become a better listener, consider three simple steps: Stop, Look, and Listen. To stop means to be mindful of what you are listening to. To look is to listen with your eyes—to focus on nonverbal messages that provide an abundance of information about the emotional meanings in messages. To listen involves the skill of simultaneously capturing the details in messages and the main ideas of messages, and then linking the two together.

What makes listening a communication process is that the person listening (the receiver) is also an active participant (a source), because he or she responds to the other person and the other person's messages. We respond to speakers by using verbal, nonverbal, and empathic messages.

The chapter concluded by presenting skills you can use to help others listen more effectively to you. Although most people put the responsibility for listening on the other person or the audience, you're also responsible for helping others listen to you. You can help others select, attend to, understand, remember, and respond to your messages in an effective and appropriate manner.

Discussion Questions

1. Describe the five stages in the listening process. How are these stages interrelated?

2. Identify listening barriers that can be encountered at work. Give a personal example of an experience of each.

3. Choose one of the listening barriers mentioned in the chapter, and explain a strategy for overcoming this barrier.

4. Explain three steps for listening effectively to others.

5. What are the three skills for effectively responding to others? Give examples.

6. List five strategies we can use to help others listen to us. Why is it important to help others listen?

Building Your Skills

1. Assess your receiver apprehension by completing the following assessment measure.[69] Respond to each item by indicating the extent to which it describes you using the following scale: 5 = Strongly agree, 4 = Agree, 3 = Sometimes, 2 = Disagree, 1 = Disagree

   _____ 1. When I am listening I feel nervous about missing information.

   _____ 2. I worry about being able to keep up with the material being presented in class.

   _____ 3. Sometimes I miss information in class because I am writing notes.

   _____ 4. I feel tense and anxious when I am listening to important information.

   _____ 5. I am concerned that I won't be able to remember information I've heard in lectures and discussions.

   _____ 6. Although I try to concentrate, my thoughts sometimes become confused when I'm listening.

   _____ 7. I worry that my listening skill is not very good.

_____ 8. I regularly cannot remember things I have just been told.

_____ 9. I feel anxious or nervous when I am listening in class.

_____ 10. I prefer reading class material rather than listening to it, so I don't have to feel stressed about catching all the information the first time.

Scores can range from 50 down to 10. The higher your score, the more likely you are to experience some anxiety when you listen to others and the harder you may have to work at developing strategies to improve listening comprehension.

2. Rank the barriers to listening discussed in this chapter from most to least problematic for you. Then discuss strategies for overcoming your top three barriers.

3. Think of a time when you felt your message was not understood by the receiver. In particular, have you experienced a situation at work when a supervisor or co-worker didn't understand a concern you had? Discuss what you could have done differently, focusing on the strategies listed in this chapter for helping others understand you. How will you remember to use these strategies in your future communication?

4. Think back on a difficult conversation you have had. Then think about each of the five stages of listening in the conversation—at what point did you select, attend, understand, remember, and respond to the other person's message? Did you fail to adequately carry out any of the five stages? If so, try to identify any problems that may have prevented you from completing the stage.

5. In a small group of three or four, discuss the importance of learning to listen effectively. What are some areas where you need work? What do you think society says about the importance of actively listening?

6. Imagine you are training a group of new employees at a customer service firm. How would you teach them to listen actively? Could you explain the skill effectively?

Chapter 5
Adapting to Differences: Personality, Culture, and Gender

chapter outline

After reading this chapter, you should be able to

■ Explain how biology and culture influence our communication and how an awareness of these influences can help you better adapt your communication to others.

■ Define and explain the communication behaviors of people who differ in terms of the communication traits of willingness to communicate, communication apprehension, and argumentativeness.

■ Suggest communication strategies to use with people who differ on the various communication traits.

■ Explain the differences between high-context and low-context cultures and how culture influences message directness, time orientation, and conflict communication.

■ Explain three ways to adapt to cultural contexts.

■ Differentiate between the cultural dimensions of individualism/collectivism, decentralized and centralized power distribution, and tolerance for uncertainty versus need for certainty.

■ Differentiate between sex and gender.

■ Explain the significance of men's status lenses and women's connection lenses. Describe how these are exemplified in the use of the four conversation rituals: ritual apology, ritual opposition, compliments, and small talk.

Adapt

One characteristic of the workplace that is both a strength and a challenge for leaders is that no two people are alike. We're different in terms of our personalities, cultural backgrounds, and our genders. Although this diversity adds a richness of ideas and perspectives to the business and professional setting, it also challenges leaders to adapt their communication. A communication style that works for one individual doesn't necessarily work for another. Effective leaders have the ability to assess how people are different and then adapt their communication to fit the unique needs of the individual.

Principle Five: Appropriately adapt messages to others reminds us that a "one-size-fits-all" communication style doesn't work in the twenty-first-century workplace. Figure 5.1 presents our now-familiar model, which completes the discussion we started in Chapter 1. Although you might be thinking that this fifth communication principle is a byproduct of a contemporary "me-centered" culture, it's an ancient communication principle. In 333 B.C., Aristotle was among the first to observe that effective communicators are those who analyze their audience and then create messages adapted to that particular audience. In the workplace, effective leaders are those who adapt messages to others rather than expecting others to adapt to the leader's messages.

We introduce this principle last because often people learn how to adapt only after they have learned the other four communication principles. Being able to adapt to others is based on an ability to be aware—mindful of others and other-oriented, the focus of Principle One. Adapting requires effectively using and interpreting verbal and nonverbal messages, which are the skills referred to in Principle Two and Principle Three. Finally, listening and responding thoughtfully to others—Principle Four—allows us to understand others better. Once we understand how others are thinking and feeling we can better adapt our message to them.

The purpose of this chapter is to help you understand what makes people different from one another and to suggest ways you can adapt your messages to communicate more effectively with people on the job. The chapter is divided into four sections. The first section discusses two key factors that have been shown to influence our communication behaviors: our biology and our culture. The second section examines how personality influences communication at work. The third section focuses on how culture affects communication behavior on the job. The fourth section reviews how gender influences communication in the business and professional workplace. Each section discusses the communication skills and strategies that will help you lead others by adapting to their personalities, cultural differences, and genders.

> *Adaptability is not imitation. It means power of resistance and assimilation."*
>
> — MAHATMA GANDHI

Understanding Biological and Cultural Influences on Communication at Work

Have you ever wondered why you communicate the way you do? You may be very talkative and outgoing; you have a way of relating to and connecting with people. Others are attracted to you because they feel comfortable when they're talking with you. On the other hand, you might be a person who is reserved and shy; you have a difficult time relating to others. People have a tendency to avoid you because they have a difficult time communicating with you.

Communication researchers have been studying why some people are more effective than others in using their natural ability to speak and listen.[1] Two key factors that influence and shape how we communicate with others are biology and culture. Researchers refer to the biological influence as "nature" and the cultural influence as "nurture."[2] Some communication researchers argue that we're *born* with the ability to communicate effectively, which is the nature perspective. Others argue that we can *learn* how to communicate effectively, which is the nurture perspective. Although some researchers argue that biology (nature) plays a larger role than culture (nurture) in our communication behaviors, most communication researchers take an interactionist position, which means that they assume that communication behaviors are influenced by both nature and nurture.[3] Communication is not an "either/or" proposition, but a dualism.

Biological Influences

Communication researchers Michael Beatty and Jim McCroskey and their colleagues are beginning to better understand how the genes you inherited from your parents influence

| Figure 5.1 | **Communication Principles and Skills for Leadership** |

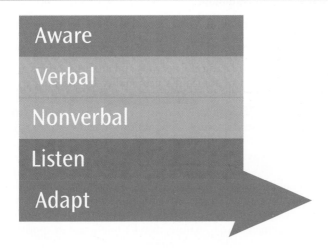

your communication behaviors.[4] When you hear people say that your voice or mannerisms are just like your mother's or your father's, they're referring to the impact that your biology has on your communication.

Researchers are beginning to make interdisciplinary connections between the fields of neurology (brain functioning), psychology (personality), and communication (talk behavior, nonverbal expressiveness). This interdisciplinary approach to the study of human communication is referred to as the **communibiological perspective**.[5] Your brain functioning, which is in large part inherited from your parents, affects your personality and your communication behaviors. Put simply, what makes you unique and different from others in the workplace are the genes you inherited from your parents.

A large percentage of your communication behaviors is heavily influenced by how your brain functions.[6] Perhaps you've wondered why you're shy or why you experience anxiety when communicating with others. Researchers now know that you did not necessarily *learn* to become shy or anxious when communicating with others. Instead, you were *born* shy and anxious; it's a natural process that is a result of your brain functioning.[7]

Cultural Influences

Culture is a learned system of knowledge, behavior, attitudes, beliefs, values, and norms that is shared by a group of people.[8] Through the nurturing you received from your parents and other family members who raised you, you learned your culture. Communication is a large part of the cultural system at home and work. Many communication researchers argue that communication behaviors are learned primarily by watching and modeling others' communication behaviors.[9] People have a tendency to imitate behavior. You learn how to communicate by interacting within cultural and social systems, including your family, friends, school, church, workplace, and community.

For example, the organizational culture of a Fortune 500 company headquartered in New York is probably quite different from that of a family-run sports bar in a small Midwestern city. A Fortune 500 company is most likely a tall organization where employees learn to make decisions only after formally communicating up the chain of command with their supervisors. A family-run business, on the other hand, is probably a flat organization, where employees learn to make their own decisions (refer to Figure 2.2 in Chapter 2). Also, New York is known as a city where people learn to communicate in an assertive manner regardless of where they are from originally. To be effective in New York city, people learn the culture of assertive communication. However, when conducting business in a small Midwestern city, people learn to communicate in a less assertive manner. The communication culture is more reserved and quiet.

Knowing that a part of your communication is influenced by your biology and your culture is the first step in becoming aware of how these factors influence communication and how you may need to adapt your communication to accommodate others' biological and cultural differences.

Communibiological perspective an interdisciplinary approach to the study of human communication that makes connections between the fields of neurology, psychology, and communication.

Culture a learned system of knowledge, behavior, attitudes, beliefs, values, and norms that is shared by a group of people.

Adapting to Personality Differences

The genetic code you inherited from your parents plays an instrumental role in the formation of your personality and your social style, discussed in Chapter 2. A **personality trait** is "any distinguishable, relatively enduring way in which one individual differs from another."[10] Some people are naturally nervous and anxious; others are more relaxed and easygoing. We get an idea of someone's personality by listening to the person and by watching him or her communicate. A **communication trait** is a label used to describe a person's communication behaviors.[11] When asked to describe others, you usually describe their personalities by describing their communication traits. For example, you might say, "He's very outgoing, talkative, funny, and animated" or "She's very assertive and argumentative." In many ways, your communication is an expression of your personality.

Having an awareness of your own communication traits and the traits of others will give you additional insight into what motivates a person to communicate in a particular manner. This understanding will also enable you to more effectively adapt your communication to the other person. For example, if you're going to be communicating with someone you know is argumentative by nature, then it's important to approach the conversation with enough reasons and evidence to argue your case successfully.

Three traits that have been shown to influence how you communicate with others and how others communicate with you in the workplace include willingness to communicate, communication apprehension, and argumentativeness. The following sections provide a brief description of each of the traits, invite you to assess your communication traits by completing a series of self-report measures, and make recommendations for adapting your communication as a leader to accommodate these differences in communication traits.

Willingness to Communicate

The most basic communication trait is **willingness to communicate (WTC)**, which is an individual's natural tendency to initiate communication with others.[12] Before reading any further, we recommend that you complete the WTC measure in Rating Scale 5.1 to become aware of your willingness to communicate with others.

High WTC individuals enjoy talking and look for opportunities to initiate communication with others. Low WTC individuals, on the other hand, don't find communication as enjoyable and prefer to avoid communication with others. These individuals are usually labeled as shy because they don't readily engage in communication behavior. In the workplace, "high talkers" (high WTC people) tend to be the individuals who roam the hallways looking for people to engage in conversation. Low talkers (low WTC people), however, tend to leave their offices rarely, and when they do, it's for a specific purpose. If others engage them in conversation, they keep it short and return to their offices.

Because communication is valued in the United States and in the workplace, high talkers are usually rewarded for their willingness to communicate, and low talkers suffer some consequences for preferring not to communicate.[13] Research suggests that people who are willing to communicate are generally perceived more positively than those who are less willing to communicate.[14] "Low talkers" are perceived to be[15]

- Less likely to be hired.
- Less likely to be promoted.
- Less qualified to do their jobs.
- Less motivated to do their jobs.
- Less cooperative in the workplace.

It's important to understand that this list of descriptions is based on people's *perceptions*. Low talkers and high talkers may be equally qualified, motivated, and cooperative on the job; however, working professionals tend to perceive low WTC individuals as less so compared to high WTC individuals.[16]

You can adapt to those with a low willingness to communicate so as to enhance workplace communication:

- *Refrain from forming premature judgments.* Sometimes we evaluate others simply based on their communication behaviors or lack of communication behaviors. Instead, we need to form perceptions based on the quality of people's work and other job performance factors that are important to the organization.

Personality trait any distinguishable, relatively enduring way in which one individual differs from another.

Communication trait a label used to describe a person's communication behaviors.

Willingness to communicate (WTC) an individual's natural tendency to initiate communication with others.

Rating Scale 5.1   Willingness to Communicate Measure

Below are twenty situations in which a person might choose to communicate or not to communicate.[17] Assume that you have *completely free choice*. Indicate to the left of each statement what percentage of the time you would choose to communicate in each situation: 0 = never, 100 = always.

_____ 1. Talk with a service station attendant
_____ 2. Talk with a physician
_____ 3. Present a talk to a group of strangers
_____ 4. Talk with an acquaintance while standing in line
_____ 5. Talk with a salesperson in a store
_____ 6. Talk in a large meeting of friends
_____ 7. Talk to a police officer
_____ 8. Talk in a small group of strangers
_____ 9. Talk with a friend while standing in line
_____ 10. Talk with a waiter or waitress in a restaurant
_____ 11. Talk in a large meeting of acquaintances
_____ 12. Talk with a stranger while standing in line
_____ 13. Talk with a secretary
_____ 14. Present a talk to a group of friends
_____ 15. Talk in a small group of acquaintances
_____ 16. Talk with a garbage collector
_____ 17. Talk in a large meeting of strangers
_____ 18. Talk with a spouse, partner, girlfriend, or boyfriend
_____ 19. Talk in a small group of friends
_____ 20. Present a talk to a group of acquaintances

Scoring Instructions: The WTC measure is designed to indicate how willing you are to communicate in a variety of contexts with different types of receivers. The higher your total WTC score, the more willing you are to communicate in general. Similarly, the higher your given subscore for a type of context or audience, the more willing you are to communicate in that context, or with that type of audience.

The WTC permits computation of one total score and seven subscores. The subscores relate to willingness to communicate in each of four common communication contexts and with three types of audiences.

Subscore	Scoring Formula
Group discussion	Add your scores for items 8, 15, and 19; then divide by 3.
Meetings	Add your scores for items 6, 11, and 17; then divide by 3.
Interpersonal conversations	Add your scores for items 4, 9, and 12; then divide by 3.
Public speaking	Add your scores for items 3, 14, and 20; then divide by 3.
Stranger	Add your scores for items 3, 8, 12, and 17; then divide by 4.
Acquaintance	Add your scores for items 4, 11, 15, and 20; then divide by 4.
Friend	Add your scores for items 6, 9, 14, and 19; then divide by 4.

To compute your total WTC score, add the subscores for Stranger, Acquaintance, and Friend. Then divide by 3.

Norms for WTC Scores

Group discussion	More than 89: High WTC;	Less than 57: Low WTC
Meetings	More than 80: High WTC;	Less than 39: Low WTC
Interpersonal Conversations	More than 94: High WTC;	Less than 64: Low WTC
Public Speaking	More than 78: High WTC;	Less than 33: Low WTC
Stranger	More than 63: High WTC;	Less than 18: Low WTC
Acquaintance	More than 92: High WTC;	Less than 57: Low WTC
Friend	More than 99: High WTC;	Less than 71: Low WTC
Total WTC	More than 82: High Overall WTC;	Less than 52: Low Overall WTC

- *Do not take another person's quietness personally.* Some people are bothered or even offended when others don't communicate with them. You need to understand that someone's being quiet is a part of his or her personality; it's just the way the person is and it usually has nothing to do with you.

You can also adapt to and lead others who have high willingness to communicate:

- *Give them opportunities to communicate or place them in positions that are a fit for their communication trait.* Place high WTC individuals in positions where they represent the organization as spokespeople or representatives. For example, high WTC individuals are a natural fit for sales and marketing positions. Make their communication trait benefit the organization.

- *Monitor their communication behavior.* Too much communicating may prevent people from getting their work done or may prevent others from getting their work done.

Communication Apprehension

If you have ever experienced a bit of stage fright, then you've experienced **communication apprehension (CA),** which is fear or anxiety associated with either ongoing or anticipated communication with another person or persons.[18] To become aware of your level of communication apprehension, complete the communication apprehension measure in Rating Scale 5.2.

People who score high in communication apprehension experience fear when communicating with others in a variety of contexts, including in meetings, in small groups, one on one, or when giving a speech. People low in communication apprehension rarely experience fear when communicating with others. One situation in which most people have a degree of fear and anxiety, even those low in communication apprehension, is when speaking in front of others in more formal situations such as giving a business presentation.

Research suggests that one in five Americans experiences an abnormally high level of communication apprehension in all contexts.[19] For these individuals, communication apprehension is a disorder that prevents them from doing their best in the workplace. Highly apprehensive individuals have a tendency to behave in one of the following three ways.[20] First, they avoid communication. Rather than informally socializing with colleagues outside of work, for example, apprehensive individuals make excuses for not attending these social situations. Unfortunately, these informal situations are often opportunities for professionals to network with and influence each other. Second, when apprehensive individuals cannot actually avoid communication, they tend to withdraw from it. Rather than speaking up at a meeting and presenting their ideas, they tend to remain silent. Unfortunately, this reduces their ability to implement their ideas and influence others. Because of their communication withdrawal, individuals who are high in communication apprehension are often overlooked for promotions. Third, they experience communication disruptions. Apprehensive individuals have a tendency to communicate using improper articulation and pronunciation as well as too many vocal disfluencies or interrupters, such as "uhh," "ahh," "um," or "like." Because of these communication disruptions, apprehensive individuals tend not to be taken seriously.

You can adapt to and lead those who are low in communication apprehension by following these guidelines:

- *Place them in positions with high communication demands.* Many leadership positions require professionals who can make presentations and facilitate meetings with ease and comfort.

- *Monitor the quality and quantity of their communication.* Although nearly everyone experiences some degree of communication apprehension, it's important to monitor those who are low in this trait. These individuals are less guarded about their communication and may talk too much or say things they later wish they hadn't said. So, a simple reminder of the possible consequences of phrasing statements carelessly or of not being discreet can help a person avoid "putting his foot in his mouth."

Communication apprehension (CA) fear or anxiety associated with ongoing or anticipated communication with another person or persons.

Rating Scale 5.2	Personal Report of Communication Apprehension (PRCA-24)

From James C. McCroskey, An Introduction to Rhetorical Communication: A Western Rhetorical Perspective, 9e. Published by Allyn and Bacon/ Merrill Education, Boston, MA. Copyright © 2006 by Pearson Education. Reprinted by permission of the publisher.

This instrument is composed of twenty-four statements concerning your feelings about communicating with other people.[21] Indicate in the space provided the degree to which each statement applies to you by marking whether you (1) strongly agree, (2) agree, (3) are undecided, (4) disagree, or (5) strongly disagree with each statement. There are no right or wrong answers. Many of the statements are intentionally similar. Work quickly and record your first impression.

_____ 1. I dislike participating in group discussions.

_____ 2. Generally, I am comfortable while participating in a group discussion.

_____ 3. I am tense and nervous while participating in group discussions.

_____ 4. I like to get involved in group discussions.

_____ 5. Engaging in a group discussion with new people makes me tense and nervous.

_____ 6. I am calm and relaxed while participating in group discussions.

_____ 7. Generally, I am nervous when I have to participate in a meeting.

_____ 8. Usually I am calm and relaxed while participating in meetings.

_____ 9. I am very calm and relaxed when I am called on to express an opinion at a meeting.

_____ 10. I am afraid to express myself at meetings.

_____ 11. Communicating at meetings usually makes me uncomfortable.

_____ 12. I am very relaxed when answering questions at a meeting.

_____ 13. While participating in a conversation with a new acquaintance, I feel very nervous.

_____ 14. I have no fear of speaking up in conversations.

_____ 15. Ordinarily I am very tense and nervous in conversations.

_____ 16. Ordinarily I am very calm and relaxed in conversations.

_____ 17. While conversing with a new acquaintance, I feel very relaxed.

_____ 18. I'm afraid to speak up in conversations.

_____ 19. I have no fear of giving a speech.

_____ 20. Certain parts of my body feel very tense and rigid while I am giving a speech.

_____ 21. I feel relaxed while giving a speech.

_____ 22. My thoughts become confused and jumbled when I am giving a speech.

_____ 23. I face the prospect of giving a speech with confidence.

_____ 24. While giving a speech I get so nervous I forget facts I really know.

Scoring Instructions: The PRCA permits computation of one total score and four subscores. The subscores are related to communication apprehension in each of four common communication contexts: group discussions, meetings, interpersonal conversations, and public speaking. To compute your scores, merely add or subtract the scores for each item as indicated below.

Subscore Desired	Scoring Formula
Group discussion	Add 18 to the total of your scores for items 2, 4, and 6; then subtract your scores for items 1, 3, and 5 from this total.
Meetings	Add 18 to the total of your scores for items 8, 9, and 12; then subtract your scores for items 7, 10, and 11 from this total.
Interpersonal conversations	Add 18 to the total of your scores for items 14, 16, and 17; then subtract your scores for items 13, 15, and 18 from this total.
Public speaking	Add 18 to the total of your scores for items 19, 21, and 23; then subtract your scores for items 20, 22, and 24 from this total.

To obtain your total score on the PRCA, simply add your four subscores together. Your total score should range between 24 and 120. If your score is below 24, or above 120, you have made a mistake in computing it.

Scores on the four contexts (group discussion, meetings, interpersonal conversations, and public speaking) can range from a low of 6 to a high of 30. Any score above 18 indicates some degree of apprehension. If your score for the public speaking context is above 18, you are like the overwhelming majority of Americans.

Average scores on the PRCA-24 are as follows:

Total Score:	66
Group discussion	15
Meetings	16
Interpersonal conversations	14
Public speaking	19

Below are a few recommendations for adapting to those high in communication apprehension so as to enhance workplace communication:

- *Monitor how you perceive quiet people.* Understand that a person's apprehensiveness is to a large extent outside his or her control. Check your perceptions of others by focusing on their work performance rather than their talk or lack of talk.

- *Refrain from putting highly apprehensive individuals in situations or positions requiring a high level of communication.* Goodness-of-fit is achieved when the communication demands of a position fit a person's personality and communication traits. For example, staffing a receptionist's position with a person high in communication apprehension would not be considered a good fit.

- *Provide alternative channels for communication.* For example, rather than requiring all staff members to make oral presentations at work, allow individuals options such as communicating through memos, email, or voice mail.

- *Inform highly apprehensive individuals of options for interventions.* There are a number of instructional, treatment, and medical interventions for managing communication apprehension.[22] These are discussed in more detail in Chapter 12.

Argumentativeness

Argumentativeness is a communication trait of people who have a tendency to advocate strongly for their own position on an issue and criticize the positions of other people.[23] A person who is argumentative enjoys a good debate. To determine your own argumentativeness, complete the self-assessment instrument in Rating Scale 5.3. This will help you become more aware of this communication trait and how it may affect others' perceptions of you as well as how you perceive others.

Do you know people who like to argue? Although many people perceive arguing to be a destructive form of communication, if it's done well, it's quite constructive, and an ability to argue clearly is valued in business and professional settings.[24] People who are argumentative can think critically and argue for or against a particular proposal using reasons and evidence. Research clearly indicates that professionals who can argue well are also considered more effective in their jobs.[25] Specifically, highly argumentative individuals, when compared to less argumentative individuals, tend to be better at taking perspective or understanding another person's position on an issue. For example, when deciding how to operate the registration desk of a medical facility, a supervisor and her staff have different ideas. In a constructive argument, they each present their reason for operating the registration desk in a particular manner. Because the supervisor is high in argumentativeness, she values looking at an issue critically, from all perspectives, in order to make an informed decision. She is persuaded by the good reasoning staff members use, and she takes their perspective even though she had her own ideas of how the registration area should be arranged and organized. Individuals high in argumentativeness are naturally curious and thus tend to learn more about others, including their customers or their competitors' products and services. Another quality of people high in argumentativeness is that they tend to be better leaders and have followers who are more satisfied and committed to their jobs.[26] For example, when there is disagreement on a policy or procedure, argumentative leaders have a way of managing the emotions while helping others critically examine the issues by focusing on the evidence or the facts rather than on what a few people might say.

Although there are a number of benefits to being argumentative, people who are low in argumentativeness tend to perceive highly argumentative individuals as verbally

Argumentativeness a tendency to advocate strongly for one's own position on an issue and criticize the positions of other people.

Rating Scale 5.3   Measure of Argumentativeness

This questionnaire contains statements about arguing controversial issues.[27] Indicate in the space provided the degree to which each statement applies to you by marking whether it is (1) almost never true, (2) rarely true, (3) occasionally true, (4) often true, or (5) almost always true. (Remember, consider each item in terms of *arguing or debating controversial issues;* the scale is not focusing on personal, emotional arguments.)

_____ 1. While in an argument, I worry that the person I am arguing with will form a negative impression of me.

_____ 2. Arguing over controversial issues improves my intelligence.

_____ 3. I enjoy avoiding arguments.

_____ 4. I am energetic and enthusiastic when I argue.

_____ 5. Once I finish an argument I promise myself that I will not get into another.

_____ 6. Arguing with a person creates more problems for me than it solves.

_____ 7. I have a pleasant, good feeling when I win a point in an argument.

_____ 8. When I finish arguing with someone I feel nervous and upset.

_____ 9. I enjoy a good argument over a controversial issue.

_____ 10. I get an unpleasant feeling when I realize I am about to get into an argument.

_____ 11. I enjoy defending my point of view on an issue.

_____ 12. I am happy when I keep an argument from happening.

_____ 13. I do not like to miss the opportunity to argue a controversial issue.

_____ 14. I prefer being with people who rarely disagree with me.

_____ 15. I consider an argument an exciting intellectual challenge.

_____ 16. I find myself unable to think of effective points during an argument.

_____ 17. I feel refreshed and satisfied after an argument on a controversial issue.

_____ 18. I have the ability to do well in an argument.

_____ 19. I try to avoid getting into arguments.

_____ 20. I feel excitement when I expect that a conversation I am in is leading to an argument.

Scoring Instructions: To compute your argumentativeness score, do the following:

>   Step 1: Add your scores on items 2, 4, 7, 9, 11, 13, 15, 17, 18, and 20.
>
>   Step 2: Add 60 to the sum you obtained in step 1.
>
>   Step 3: Add your scores for items 1, 3, 5, 6, 8, 10, 12, 14, 16, and 19.
>
>   Step 4: Subtract the total you obtained in step 3 from the total obtained in step 2.

If the number you obtain in step 4 is between 73 and 100, you tend to be high in argumentativeness. If the number is between 56 and 72, you tend to be moderately argumentative. If the number is between 20 and 55, you tend to be low in argumentativeness.

To determine your tendency to approach argumentative situations, add your scores on items 2, 4, 7, 9, 11, 13, 15, 17, 18, and 20.

To determine your tendency to avoid argumentative situations, add your scores on items 1, 3, 5, 6, 8, 10, 12, 14, 16, and 19.

Argumentativeness trait: subtract the total of the ten tendency-to-avoid items from the total of the ten tendency-to-approach items. Positive scores indicate a tendency to approach arguments. A higher positive score (between 20 and 40) indicates high argumentativeness. Negative scores reflect a tendency to avoid arguments. A higher negative score (between −20 and −40) reflects low argumentativeness.

aggressive and overbearing at times. You can adapt to less argumentative individuals in the following ways to enhance workplace communication:

> • *Be aware that individuals who are not argumentative tend to perceive highly argumentative individuals as being verbally aggressive.* If you get a defensive reaction from the other person when you begin to argue, know that they're probably interpreting your messages as an attack.

Aware

- *Use **feed-forward messages**, which are messages that inform others of how to process information.* For example, "What I am about to say is not intended to be verbally aggressive, but I would like to challenge your ideas."
- *Use nonverbally immediate behaviors when arguing.* Monitor your tone of voice for warmth, keep an open body orientation, and lean forward rather than away from the other person (which can signal defensiveness). These nonverbal behaviors add warmth and communicate approachability rather than aggressiveness.
- *Use nonverbally responsive behaviors when listening to others argue.* Leaning forward, using direct eye contact, nodding your head, and using back channel cues are examples of nonverbally responsive behaviors. These nonverbal behaviors signal to others that you're actively listening to them and their arguments.

To adapt to highly argumentative individuals, try these guidelines:

- *Engage them in debates.* Make sure you have logical claims and evidence to support your claims. For example, when meeting with your supervisor to request more space for your retail business, make sure you go into the meeting prepared with sales figures that indicate how you are growing your business.
- *Play the devil's advocate.* A **devil's advocate** is someone who criticizes or opposes something purely in order to provoke a discussion or an argument. A devil's advocate is in many ways an ally whose goal is to help strengthen another's case by pointing out weaknesses. For example, if you own a restaurant and one highly argumentative waiter suggests that the restaurant is losing business because the menu doesn't include healthier food items, challenge his ideas rather than simply agreeing with him.
- *Learn how to argue.* Although argumentativeness is to some extent biologically based,[28] people can learn how to argue. It just may come more naturally for some than for others. Chapter 14 will provide more detail on how to organize, develop, and present arguments.

RECAP: Communication Traits

Trait	Definition
Willingness to Communicate	An individual's natural tendency to initiate communication with others.
Communication Apprehension	Fear or anxiety associated with either ongoing or anticipated communication with another person or persons.
Argumentativeness	A tendency to advocate strongly for one's position on an issue and criticize the positions of other people.

Understanding the relationships between personality and communication traits reveals how and why individuals differ in their workplace communication. Understanding how and why people differ in their workplace communication will allow you to adapt your communication to them more effectively. Some of your communication behaviors are natural, meaning that they are influenced by your biology or the genes you inherited. However, you can learn to modify and adapt your communication in order to interact more effectively with others and become a leader in the workplace.

Feed-forward messages messages that inform others of how to process information from you.

Devil's advocate someone who criticizes or opposes something in order to provoke a discussion or an argument.

Adapting to Cultural Differences

We learn about our culture by interacting with others. As we mentioned earlier, culture is a learned system of knowledge, behavior, attitudes, beliefs, values, and norms that is shared by a group of people.[29] Culture and communication, says anthropologist Edward T. Hall, are inseparable—you can't talk about one without discussing the other.[30] There is ample evidence to document the influence of culture on how you work and live.[31] According to researcher Geert Hofstede, your culture is like "mental software" that helps you understand the world.[32] Like the software and operating system in a computer, your culture provides a framework that shapes the messages you send and receive every day.

If you're like most people, you're unaware of your computer's software until a glitch occurs and your computer fails to work properly. Your cultural software is very similar. It remains invisible until there's a problem. Problems occur when you work with others whose "cultural software systems" are different from your own. For example, some cultures are less time-sensitive than others. Rather than meeting an important deadline for a particular project or arriving early for a meeting, you might find people from some cultures not being worried about punctuality and deadlines. To them, deadlines and start times for meetings are fluid and can always be changed. Such problems occur with regularity in business and professional settings, particularly as the workplace becomes more diverse and as we interact more often with people from different or unfamiliar cultures.[33] For example, by 2050, whites will make up 46 percent of the population and blacks will make up 15 percent. Hispanics, who make up about 15 percent of the population today, will account for 30 percent in 2050. Asians, who make up about 5 percent of the population currently, are projected to increase to 9 percent by 2050.[34]

Two frameworks that can help you become aware of how culture influences communication in business and professional settings are cultural contexts and cultural values.

Cultural Contexts

The **cultural context** of any communication consists of the nonverbal cues that surround and give meaning to the messages. In this sense, *all* nonverbal cues are part of the cultural context. In some cultures, people give more weight to the surrounding nonverbal context than to the explicit verbal message when interpreting the overall meaning of a message. Other cultures place less emphasis on the nonverbal context and greater emphasis on what someone says.

For example, when you interview for a job, you may be scanning the face of your interviewer and looking for nonverbal clues about the impression you're making on the interviewer. These contextual cues give meaning to help you interpret the interviewer's message. Edward T. Hall helped us understand the importance of cultural context when he categorized cultures as either high-context or low-context.[35]

In **high-context cultures**, nonverbal cues are extremely important in interpreting messages. Communicators rely heavily on context—they gather subtle information from facial expression, vocal cues, and even silence in interpreting messages. People from Asian, Arab, and Southern European countries are more likely to draw on context to help them interpret messages.

People in **low-context cultures** rely more explicitly on language and on the meanings of words and use fewer contextual cues to send and interpret information. Individuals from low-context cultures, such as North Americans, Germans, and Scandinavians, may perceive people from high-context cultures as less attractive, knowledgeable, and trust-worthy, because they violate unspoken low-context cultural rules of conduct and communication. For example, people from high-context cultures may be perceived to be "beating around the bush" rather than getting to the point, and indirectness may sometimes be perceived as manipulation. Individuals from low-context cultures often are less skilled in interpreting unspoken contextual messages.[36] Figure 5.2 summarizes differences in communication style between high-context and low-context cultures.

Message directness, time orientation, and conflict communication are three characteristics of culture that vary depending on whether a culture is a high-context or a low-context one and that affect communication in the business and professional workplace.

Cultural context the nonverbal cues related to culture that surround and give meaning to messages.

High-context cultures cultures in which nonverbal cues are extremely important in interpreting messages.

Low-context cultures cultures in which people rely more on explicit language and words and use fewer contextual cues to send and interpret information.

To understand the cultural context of communication, it helps to attend to all nonverbal cues, including the attire of your communication partner.

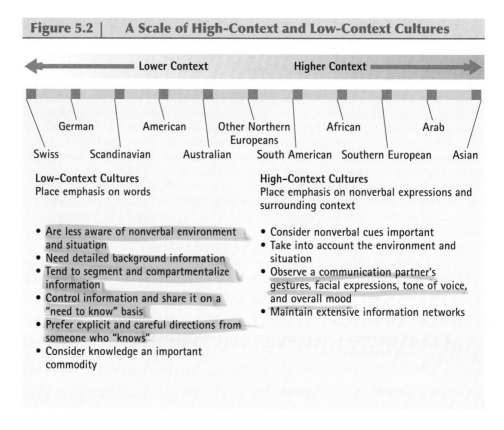

Figure 5.2 | A Scale of High-Context and Low-Context Cultures

Lower Context ← → Higher Context

German   American   Other Northern Europeans   African   Arab

Swiss   Scandinavian   Australian   South American   Southern European   Asian

Low-Context Cultures
Place emphasis on words

- Are less aware of nonverbal environment and situation
- Need detailed background information
- Tend to segment and compartmentalize information
- Control information and share it on a "need to know" basis
- Prefer explicit and careful directions from someone who "knows"
- Consider knowledge an important commodity

High-Context Cultures
Place emphasis on nonverbal expressions and surrounding context

- Consider nonverbal cues important
- Take into account the environment and situation
- Observe a communication partner's gestures, facial expressions, tone of voice, and overall mood
- Maintain extensive information networks

Message directness. As we've noted, some messages are direct or explicit, whereas others are indirect or implicit. **Message directness** indicates the extent to which a message expresses details clearly and leaves no doubt as to the intended meaning. In high-context cultures, people use more indirect messages, whereas in low-context cultures, people use more direct messages. Suppose that you supervise Rebecca, who was born and reared in the United States, a low-context culture. She sits next to you in your office suite. One morning Rebecca is chilly and she asks you to turn up the heat in the office suite. Because Rebecca is from a low-context culture, she has learned that direct messages are appropriate. Her message is explicit and you both consider her request a reasonable one. Because you want Rebecca to be comfortable, you turn up the heat, and the temperature issue is resolved.

Assume that you also supervise and share the suite with Keiko, who was born and reared in Japan, a high-context culture. Keiko, too, is chilly; however, rather than asking you to turn up the heat, she shivers, puts on her jacket, and when she talks to you, her voice quivers. Rather than directly asking you to turn up the heat, she simply conveys the same message implicitly by using nonverbal messages. To a person from Japan, asking a supervisor to turn up the heat would be considered inappropriate. Instead, high-context messages (shivering, putting on more layers of clothing) are used with the hope that the supervisor will recognize and decode the contextual cues and adjust the thermostat.

Time orientation. **Time orientation** refers to how members of a culture structure, organize, and use time. High-context cultures tend to be *polychronic*, whereas low-context cultures tend to be *monochronic*. In **polychronic cultures**, human relationships and interactions are valued over arbitrary schedules and appointments. Many things occur at once (since people manage multiple relationships and conversations at the same time) and interruptions are frequent. Monochronic cultures are just the opposite: **Monochronic cultures** stress a high degree of scheduling, concentration on one thing at a time, and an elaborate code of behavior built around promptness in meeting obligations and appointments.[37]

Polychronic cultures, which include those in Latin America and the Middle East, to name two regions, consider time an intangible resource, meaning that it can't be quantified. Working professionals in these cultures consider time to be in abundance; there's enough time to get everything done. Work activities tend to be event-based, meaning that an event may take priority over other tasks. For example, if a team succeeded in meeting a goal, team members would take time to celebrate the accomplishment and would worry

Message directness an indication of the extent to which a message expresses details clearly and leaves no doubt as to the intended meaning.

Time orientation how members of a culture structure, organize, and use time.

Polychronic cultures cultures in which human relations and interactions are valued over arbitrary schedules or appointments.

Monochronic cultures cultures that stress a high degree of scheduling, concentration on one thing at a time, and promptness.

less about getting back to work on the next task. Professionals in polychronic cultures tend to be more flexible with their use of time. Monochronic cultures, which include Germany, Scandinavia, and Switzerland, to name a few, consider time a tangible resource that *can* be quantified. Working professionals in these cultures consider time to be scarce; there's not enough time to get everything done. Work activities tend to be time-based, and professionals tend to be inflexible when it comes to their time.[38]

According to Hall, North American culture tends to be high in both monochronism and polychronism. North Americans tend to multi-task, or to engage in a number of activities at once (which is a polychronic characteristic), because they consider time to be a scarce resource (which is a monochronic view).[39] Knowing that two cultural time orientations are operating in the U.S. workplace, it is important for professionals to consider how their approach to time may affect workplace communication when doing business with men and women from different cultures.

Conflict communication. Cultural values influence how conflict is communicated and managed. Researchers have found that people in low-context cultures give greater importance to task, or *instrumental*, issues than do people in high-context cultures.[40] The priority is getting the job done, and sometimes this task-oriented priority is pursued at the expense of workplace relationships. It's not uncommon to hear someone from a low-context culture say, "I'm sorry if what I said hurt you, but it's the price of doing business."

In high-context cultures, the relational, or expressive, aspects of managing conflict take on special importance.[41] Keeping workplace relationships in balance, maintaining friendships, and managing the emotional climate often are given a higher priority in a high-context culture than is achieving a particular outcome. In high-context cultures, workplace conflict is carefully managed so as to not embarrass the other person. The goal is to help the other person "save face." As a result of conflict a task may remain unfinished; however, relationships are preserved.

Cultural Values

By paying attention to what a culture values, you can learn important clues about how to adapt your communication so that you respond appropriately to others' communication, establish quality relationships, and avoid making embarrassing errors. Although there are considerable differences among the world's cultures, it's important to remember that people from other cultures may have more in common with you and your communication style than you think initially. Researchers have identified *pan-cultural values*, which are common to all cultures. For example, regardless of where they are from, people from around the world tend to value truth and respect for another person's dignity and to assume that innocent people should not suffer harm.[42] Rather than assuming that cultures are completely different, it may be equally important to acknowledge our similarities when communicating with people from different cultures.

To clarify the differences between cultures, Geert Hofstede has identified five dimensions of cultural values: individualism versus collectivism, distribution of power (either centralized or decentralized), avoidance of uncertainty versus tolerance for uncertainty, short-term versus long-term orientation, and masculine versus feminine cultural perspectives.[43] An overview of Hofstede's research conclusions, based on studies of several countries, is included in Table 5.1.

Individualism versus collectivism. People from **individualistic cultures**, like that of the United States, have learned to value their own interests more than those of the overall group. Individualistic cultures offer their members a great deal of freedom, the belief being that freedom makes it possible for each person to achieve personal success. The U.S. workplace reflects the individualistic culture, with, for example, performance reviews that determine whether individuals are rewarded, based on whether they met their goals and objectives, and salary bonuses that reward individual effort. Workplaces in individualistic cultures tolerate and encourage organizational "stars" (otherwise known as "golden boys" or "golden girls").

People from **collectivistic cultures**, like that of Japan and other East Asian cultures, learn to value the interests of their group or community more than their individual interests. Collectivistic cultures offer their members a close-knit social network whose members have a primary loyalty toward one another and the group to which they belong. Collectivistic cultures value what people do together and reward group achievement.

Individualistic cultures cultures whose members value individual interests over group interests.

Collectivistic cultures cultures whose members value group or community interests over individual interests.

Table 5.1	Hofstede's Five Cultural Dimensions		
Value Dimension	**Description**	**High Score**	**Low Score**
Individualism (IDV)	Degree to which a society reinforces individual or collective achievement and interpersonal relationships	Indicates that individuality and individual rights are paramount within the society. Individuals may tend to form a larger number of looser relationships.	Typifies societies of a more collectivist nature with close ties between individuals. Reinforces extended families and collectives where everyone takes responsibility for fellow group members.
Distribution of Power (Power Distance Index, PDI)	The degree of equality or inequality between the people in a country's society	Indicates that inequalities of power and wealth have been allowed to grow in the society. These societies are likely to follow a caste system that does not allow significant upward mobility.	Indicates the society de-emphasizes the differences between the citizens' power and wealth. In these societies, equality and opportunity for everyone is stressed.
Uncertainty Avoidance Index (UAI)	The level of tolerance for uncertainty or ambiguity within the society (that is, tolerance for unstructured situations)	Indicates that the country has a low tolerance for uncertainty or ambiguity. Creates a rule-oriented society that institutes laws, regulations, and controls in order to reduce the amount of uncertainty.	Indicates that the country has less concern about ambiguity and uncertainty and has more tolerance for a variety of opinions. Reflected in a society that is less rule-oriented and more gladly accepts change.
Long-Term Orientation (LTO)	Degree to which a society embraces or does not embrace long-term devotion to traditional values.	Indicates that the country subscribes to the values of long-term commitment and tradition. This is thought to support a strong work ethic in which long-term rewards are expected as a result of today's hard work.	Indicates that the country does not reinforce a long-term, traditional orientation. In such cultures change can occur more rapidly, as long-term commitments and traditions do not become impediments to change.
Masculinity (MAS)	The degree to which a society reinforces or does not reinforce the traditional masculine work role model of male achievement, control, and power.	Indicates that the country experiences a high degree of gender differentiation. Males dominate a significant portion of the society and power structure, with females being controlled by males.	Indicates that the country has a low level of differentiation and discrimination between genders. Females are treated equally with males in all aspects of society.

In collectivistic cultures, to receive individual recognition would be considered dishonorable, since it elevates the individual above the group. One of this book's authors, who used to work in the airline industry, remembers a flight to Tokyo on which one of the employees of a Japanese company refused his first-class seat so as to not dishonor the other members of the group he was traveling with.

In business and professional settings, this cultural value affects how people approach and manage conflict. Stella Ting-Toomey, a leading intercultural communication researcher, suggests that people from individualistic cultures are more likely to use direct, confrontational methods of managing disagreements than are people who value a collective or team approach to group work.[44] She also points out that people from collectivistic cultures, especially cultures that place considerable emphasis on nonverbal messages, are more comfortable with nonconfrontational and indirect methods of resolving differences. Ting-Toomey finds that people from individualistic cultures are more likely to use facts or principles as the basis for approaching conflict, negotiation, or persuasion. People from collectivistic cultures adopt more relationship-based messages to manage differences.[45]

Decentralized versus centralized power. Some cultures, referred to as **decentralized power cultures,** value a broad distribution of power. The power is in the people, or the many, not in any one single person or group. In the workplace, this cultural value is reflected in how decisions are made. For example, it's not unusual for a leader to conduct a meeting at which employees examine and discuss problems together and then each employee has a vote on how the problem should be solved or what decision is going to be made. The power is in the individual votes or voices of the employees rather than in a single leader. Research suggests that people from Australia, Israel, Denmark, New Zealand, and Ireland typically prefer minimal power differences between members of the culture; they strive for more equal distribution of authority and control.[46]

Other cultures, referred to as **centralized power cultures,** value a more concentrated or narrow distribution of power. The power is in one person or a select few. The general assumption is that some people will have more power, control, and influence than others. Professionals from cultures that value centralized power are probably more comfortable with managerial styles in which clear lines of authority are followed. Rather than calling a meeting and asking employees to vote on how a problem should be solved or how a decision should be made, leaders are more likely to make the decision without consulting with group members and without group members objecting to the leader having most of the power.

Acceptance of uncertainty versus preference for certainty. The contemporary workplace is full of uncertainty and change.[47] We live in a global economy in which a small amount of change in, say, the Tokyo stock market has a ripple effect on the markets everywhere else in the world. **Uncertainty avoidance** is a measure of how accepting a culture is of a lack of predictability. Cultures that are low in uncertainty avoidance are those in which people tolerate uncertainty; they have learned to live with the fact that their ability to predict the future is limited. Many professionals from these cultures are more comfortable taking risks, and they tend to be more tolerant of others who engage in behavior that goes against what is considered normal. Verbal messages such as "It will work itself out" or "Let's go with the flow" are indicative of cultures in which uncertainty avoidance is low. People from Singapore, Hong Kong, Jamaica, and Denmark are more comfortable with uncertainty.[48]

Cultures that are high in uncertainty avoidance are those in which people don't like uncertainty; thus, they learn ways to structure their lives to provide as much certainty and predictability as possible. Cultures in which people need certainty to feel secure are more likely to develop and enforce rigid rules for behavior and to establish elaborate codes of conduct. Verbal messages such as "Let's develop an action plan that includes the tasks that need to be completed, who is responsible for the task, and the deadlines" or "What does company policy say about that issue?" are indicative of cultures where uncertainty avoidance is high. People from Greece, Portugal, and Guatemala generally do not like uncertainty.[49]

Short-term versus long-term orientation. Given the pressure they are under to make money and turn an instant profit, it's difficult for some leaders and professionals from Western industrialized cultures to understand that not all of the world's organizations are interested in short-term results. Cultures that have a long-term orientation value long-term commitment, thriftiness, and perseverance. People in these cultures value delayed gratification and are willing to work hard knowing that the profits and rewards of their hard work may not materialize for a number of years. Countries that tend to have a long-term orientation include Japan, South Korea, Taiwan, and China. People in cultures that have a short-term orientation value fulfilling immediate social obligations and protecting oneself from embarrassment. These cultures tend to be focused on short-term results. Countries that tend to have a more short-term orientation include Norway, Pakistan, Canada, East Africa, and the United States.[50]

Masculine versus feminine values.   Some cultures emphasize traditional male values, such as getting things done and being more assertive; other cultures place greater emphasis on traditional female values: building relationships and seeking peace and harmony with others. These values are not only about biological differences; they are general approaches to interacting with other individuals. People from **masculine cultures** tend to value more traditional roles for men and women. People (both men and women) from masculine cultures value achievement, heroism, material wealth, and making things happen. They tend to have more of a task orientation. People from Japan, Australia, Venezuela, Italy, Mexico, and Great Britain tend to have a cultural value that is more masculine than feminine.[51]

Men and women from **feminine cultures** tend to value such things as caring for the less fortunate, being sensitive to others, and enhancing the overall quality of life.[52] They

Decentralized power cultures cultures in which people value a broad distribution of power; the power belongs to the people, or the many, not to one person or group.

Centralized power cultures cultures that value a more concentrated or narrow distribution of power; power is held by one person or a select few.

Uncertainty avoidance a measure of how accepting a culture is of a lack of predictability.

Masculine cultures cultures in which people have a task orientation and tend to value achievement, heroism, material wealth, and more traditional roles for men and women.

Feminine cultures cultures in which people have more of a social orientation and tend to value caring, sensitivity, and enhancing quality of life.

tend to have more of a social orientation and to focus more on collective concerns, such as cooperative problem solving and maintaining a friendly atmosphere. People from Sweden, the Netherlands, Denmark, Finland, Chile, and Thailand tend to have a cultural orientation that is more feminine than masculine.[53]

Despite the distinctions discussed above, we caution you to avoid making sweeping generalizations about every person in any cultural group. Just as there are differences between and among cultures, there are differences *within* cultural groups. For example, for centuries, most countries had "masculine" cultures. Men and their conquests were featured in history books and men had more influence in all aspects of any society than women. But today's cultural anthropologists see some shift in these values. This is reflected in a very slowly growing number of women who serve in leadership roles in some of the world's major organizations and institutions.[54]

RECAP: Cultural Values

Cultural Values	Description
Individualism	Individualistic cultures value personal interests above group interests.
Collectivism	Collectivistic cultures value group or community interests above individual interests.
Decentralized Power Distribution	Decentralized cultures value putting power in the hands of the population, rather than one person or group.
Centralized Power Distribution	Centralized cultures value putting the power in the hands of one leader or a select few.
Tolerance of Uncertainty	Cultures that accept uncertainty tolerate "not knowing" and understand that their ability to predict the future is limited.
Need for Certainty	Cultures that value certainty learn ways to structure life to provide as much certainty and predictability as possible.
Short-Term Orientation	Short-term orientation cultures value change and are more interested in and focused on short-term results.
Long-Term Orientation	Long-term orientation cultures value long-term commitment and respect for tradition.
Masculine Values	Masculine cultures value a task orientation and being more assertive.
Feminine Values	Feminine cultures value caring for others and enhancing the overall quality of life.

Adapting to Cultural Contexts and Values

Becoming aware of cultural contexts and values and how they influence the business and professional workplace is the first step a leader should take to develop a leadership style that will be effective in a global and diverse environment. The second step is to learn how to adapt communication to the various cultural contexts and values. Below are a few strategies that may help you adapt your communication.

Adapt

Study other cultures. If you already experience cultural differences at work or if you will be working in different cultures, it's wise to prepare yourself by doing your homework. If you're going to another country, start by reading a reputable travel guide and by talking to colleagues who have worked in that culture. The Internet is also a useful tool for learning more about different cultures.

Identify other people's cultural backgrounds. If you're about to work with people from a different culture, it's beneficial to identify their cultural background. Are they from a traditionally low-context or high-context culture? Will they respond better to a direct

>>> COMMUNICATION AND GLOBALIZATION @ WORK

In their book *Globality: Competing with Everyone from Everywhere for Everything,* consultants Harold Sirkin, James Hemerling, and Arindam Bhattacharya examine how globalization is causing organizations to rethink how they do business.[55] The authors urge U.S. companies to "adapt, adopt, and synthesize ideas from everyone and everywhere" in order to compete in a global marketplace.[56] Put another way, our ability to survive in a global marketplace will depend on our abilities to cross cultures and to work with people who don't think, believe, or act as we do.

Intercultural communication can be a dynamic experience but occasionally, due to the inability to interpret people correctly, it can be a challenge. Building an understanding of other people's cultures, their communication styles, and their behaviors can go a long way in improving relationships and being more successful in an intercultural work environment.

If your business will involve a variety of intercultural experiences, specific training and education in the field of intercultural communication is wise. But even without trawling through lots of books and articles or even taking part in an intercultural communication workshop, it is possible to implement some basic principles to help improve one's intercultural communication skills. The following tips offer insight into dealing more effectively with people and not letting culture become a divisive issue when working in international and multicultural environments.

1. Be Patient: Keep in mind that working in an intercultural setting may be just as frustrating for the people you are trying to communicate with as it is for you. It is important to understand that being patient will communicate openness and tolerance.
2. Establish Rules: Since cultures place different values on things such as meeting deadlines and punctuality, some rules for business should be established. Rather than having the ground rules imposed from someone who is not directly involved in the exchange, try developing some rules by soliciting ideas and discussing these with team members.
3. Ask Questions: Do not be afraid to find out the answers to some confusing messages the old fashioned way: by asking. A simple explanation may be all you require to move ahead with agreement. Often, such directness is what is missing from an intercultural exchange.

4. Respect Others: You cannot earn respect without first demonstrating it to others. This is the basis for all intercultural communication and will go a long way in enhancing your experience.
5. Write Things Down: It has been shown that people who do not yet speak another language proficiently can generally better understand the written word. Writing things down is another way to ensure you have the most accurate communication possible.
6. Be Aware of Time: Not everyone in the world thinks "time is money." Fostering an understanding about time and how it is viewed in another culture will help to build quality business relationships. Keep that in mind when making decisions about deadlines and meetings.
7. Exercise Caution with Humor: Be very careful about using humor in an intercultural environment. What you may find funny could be quite offensive to another. In some cultures, such as in Russian culture, humorous banter is not appropriate in a business environment.
8. Double-Check Solutions: In any business setting, double checking is important to ensure that all parties are in agreement. This means repeating solutions, conclusions, meeting dates and times, and deadlines. Having everything in written form also helps with double checking.
9. Be Positive: When faced with problems, steer clear of blame and conflict. Stay positive, analyze the problem, and work as a team to build strategies and solutions to ensure the problem never occurs again.
10. Engage in Self-Reflection: A good intercultural communicator not only looks outward but also looks inward. Take time to reflect on your own communication and management style and see where you can improve as an individual.

Research on intercultural communication and work in multicultural environments continue to show that the culturally diverse team is usually the most inventive and vibrant. In order for true synergy to occur—for the blending of energies to produce something bigger than the sum of the parts—careful consideration must be given to the cross-cultural communication competencies at work.

---

verbal message or to an indirect nonverbal message? Figure 5.2 may give you a general idea of what to expect in a particular culture.

Develop messages appropriate for a person's cultural background.   Suppose you and a new colleague are planning to meet together over lunch. It would be appropriate to say to the other person. "I don't care for the food at that restaurant. Can we eat at this one?" if he or she was from a low-context culture—but the statement would be inappropriate if the person was from a high-context culture; the message is too direct. In high-context cultures, it's important to remain less direct and use the context and the nonverbal cues to convey your message. Rather than saying, "I don't care for the food at that restaurant. Can we eat at this one?" you would simply pause for a few seconds after the other person suggested it, hesitate to respond, and perhaps raise your eyebrow. These nonverbal contextual cues would signal to the other person that you would rather not eat at the restaurant.

Interpret messages based on the sender's cultural background. Pay attention to what the other person is trying to communicate both verbally and nonverbally. Read between the lines: What is he or she not telling you? Do the verbal and nonverbal messages match? For example, if you suggest a restaurant, is your colleague verbally communicating that the restaurant choice is fine, while the nonverbal message is that he or she would rather eat someplace else? If the person is from a high-context culture, it's important to trust and decode the nonverbal message and give it more weight than the verbal message.

Understanding the relationships between culture and communication traits allows us to better understand how people communicate and interact with each other. Next, we examine the relationships between gender and communication.

Adapting to Gender Differences

Men and women communicate differently at work.[57] Becoming aware of these differences and adapting communication accordingly is just another way you can enhance your leadership effectiveness in the workplace. Although sex and gender are related, and although the terms often are used interchangeably, there are some distinctions that we would like to make. **Sex** refers to biological characteristics that are present from the time of birth. Different pairs of chromosomes—XX for females, XY for males—provide clear genetic coding for how the body will develop. We use the terms *male* and *female* to describe biological sex.

Gender refers to the cultural and psychological characteristics that are associated with our biological sex; gender is a cultural construction of what it means to be a man or women. The terms *masculine* and *feminine* are used most often when referring to gender. In many ways, your gender is an implicit rulebook that informs you of how you are to behave and communicate. Unlike sex, which is biological, gender is learned or developed through the nurturing process and through your interactions in your culture.

Although not all biological males (people of a particular sex) communicate in a masculine manner (that is, in a way considered typical or appropriate for their gender) nor all females in a feminine manner, your sex and gender are highly correlated. Research reveals that men in many cultures tend to approach communication by focusing on the content dimension of communication, whereas women tend to approach communication by focusing on the relational dimension.[58] As we first noted in Chapter 1, the **content dimension** of human communication focuses on *what* is said, or the verbal message. The **relational dimension** involves *how* the verbal message is said, based on tone of voice, facial expressions, and other nonverbal behaviors. The latter dimension often tells us how to interpret the former. We will discuss how gender affects communication at work by examining powerful and powerless language and conversational rituals.

Sex biological characteristics present from birth that identify an individual as male or female.

Gender the cultural and psychological characteristics that are associated with biological sex.

Content dimension the communication dimension that focuses on what is said; the verbal message.

Relational dimension the communication dimension that focuses on how a message is said; the nonverbal message.

Gender differences in language use and conversational rituals affect communication in the workplace.

Powerful and Powerless Language

Linguist Robin Lakoff was one of the first researchers to identify a power difference between men and women's use of language. She described these different types as powerful and powerless language.[59] **Powerful language** is stereotypically masculine and is characterized by assertiveness. It tends to be task oriented—oriented toward getting things done—and it focuses more on the information being exchanged (the *what*) than on relational elements (the *how*) in the message. **Powerless language** is stereotypically feminine and is characterized by an emphasis on connecting with others and fostering harmonious relationships. Powerless language focuses more on the quality of the relationships between individuals than on the information being exchanged. More emphasis is placed on the nonverbal elements of communication (*how* something is communicated) than on content (*what* is communicated).[60]

"Must you precede everything you say with 'This is your captain speaking'?"

Here are a few examples of powerful and powerless verbal messages and how men and women use them differently.[61]

- *Women use more hedges than men.* A *hedge* is a statement that limits the speaker's responsibility. It softens or weakens the meaning of the idea. Examples of hedge words include *somewhat*, *perhaps*, *possible*, or *maybe*. Here are examples to illustrate the difference:

  Powerful Verbal Message: "They are entering our market. We need to develop a strategy that will prevent them from taking our customers."

  Powerless Verbal Message: "It seems *possible* that they are entering our market. *Perhaps* we should develop a strategy that will prevent them from taking our customers."

- *Women use more tag questions than men.* A *tag question* is a combination of a sentence and a question, treated as a single unit. Here are examples of the difference:

  Powerful Verbal Message: "That's an interesting idea."

  Powerless Verbal Message: "That's an interesting idea, isn't it?"

- *Women use more intensifiers than men.* An *intensifier* is a word that is evaluative and that conveys emotions. Examples of intensifiers include *extremely*, *tremendously*, and *incredibly*. Here are examples to illustrate the difference:

  Powerful Verbal Message: "I'm happy for you and proud of your accomplishment."

  Powerless Verbal Message: "I'm *incredibly* happy for you and *so* proud of your *tremendous* accomplishment."

Research has shown that people who use powerless messages are perceived as having a lower social status and as being less knowledgeable, trustworthy, and dynamic than people who use powerful messages.[62] In one workplace study, both male and female employees perceived female leaders as less effective if they communicated using powerless verbal messages.[63] In another study, researchers found that people who used powerful language were perceived as being more credible or more believable than those who used powerless language.[64]

Conversational Rituals

Linguist Deborah Tannen examines how men and women communicate differently on the job.[65] Tannen argues that men and women use different **conversational rituals**, which are routine scripts that we have learned to use when talking and responding to others. According to Tannen, men learn to send and receive messages through a *status lens* (see Figure 5.3). A status lens is a perception process that leads men to focus on who has more

Powerful language language that is stereotypically masculine: direct, assertive, task-oriented, and focused more on the content of a message.

Powerless language language that is stereotypically feminine: indirect and focused more on the quality of a relationship than on the information being exchanged.

Conversational rituals learned, routine scripts that people use when talking and responding to others.

Figure 5.3 | Gender Lenses

**Women's
Connection Lens**

High
Status

Closeness   Distance

Low
Status

**Men's
Status Lens**

prestige and power in the conversation. The language men use puts them in a "one-up" or "one-down" position in conversation and determines their status level. The stereotypical example of men one-upping each other with the size of fish they caught on their fishing trip illustrates how men use communication to assert status. According to Tannen, when men want to put someone down, they use direct statements, such as "Your fish is smaller than the one I caught."

Many women, according to Tannen, communicate using a *connection lens* (see Figure 5.3). A connection lens is a perception process that leads women to focus on who is closer or further away from them psychologically or emotionally. Many women use communication to bring others closer or to keep others at a distance. For example, a woman may fail to invite another women to an after-work social function. According to Tannen, women punish others by pushing them away and keeping them at a distance.

The problem with conversational rituals is that they can sometimes misfire. Put simply, the message sent doesn't equal the message received. Tannen mentions that when someone in the United States greets you, they often use the conversation-opening ritual, "Hi, how you're doing?" They expect the other person to interpret the question ritually rather than literally. They expect, "I'm fine. How are you?" If they get a complete health report, the ritual has misfired.

Here are a few of the conversational rituals that Tannen has identified in her research:[66]

Verbal

Ritual apology. Women often say, "I'm sorry" and mean it not as an apology, but as a *conversational smoother* or as a way of expressing concern. Like a drop of oil added to a squeaky hinge, a conversational smoother allows a person to communicate more smoothly and with less friction. For example, during a meeting Angelica states, "Oh, I'm sorry, I have one more item that I would like to add to the agenda." With this statement, Angelica is not actually apologizing but rather using ritual apology to appear less abrupt and possibly to express concern for other people's time. In terms of the female connection lens, Angelica uses ritual apology as a way to bring others closer. Ritual apology may misfire when men interpret the ritual as an actual apology. From the point of view of male status lens, Angelica may be undermining her authority by appearing less organized and therefore weak.

>>> COMMUNICATION SKILLS @ WORK

Here are a few recommendations for using your awareness of conversational rituals to adapt your workplace communication.

- *Be aware that men and women have different conversational rituals.* If you're male, understand that a woman's use of ritual apology is a way to express concern. If you're female, understand that a man's use of ritual opposition is a way to explore ideas.
- *Monitor others' nonverbal behaviors to confirm that they interpreted your ritual correctly.* Nonverbal expressions such as a raised eyebrow may signal misunderstanding.
- *If you're male and receive a compliment from a female, offer a compliment in return.* If a compliment is unwarranted, try sharing at least one positive comment about her job performance.

- *If you're female and don't receive a compliment from a man in response to one you offer, understand that it's probably that he doesn't understand the conversational ritual.* Let him know how much you value and occasionally need compliments.
- *If you're male, try using ritual apology and rapport talk when communicating with a female.* A woman will likely appreciate it if you temporarily suspend ritual opposition and report talk rituals when communicating with her.
- *If you're female, try using ritual opposition and report talk when communicating with a male.* A man will likely appreciate it if you temporarily suspend ritual apology and rapport talk when communicating with him.

Ritual opposition. Men often play the role of devil's advocate in conversations with others, and this conversational ritual has been known to misfire when it is used with women. Consider the following conversation between Dean, who is editor of a men's fitness magazine, and Sarah, who is a writer for the magazine. Sarah pitches the following idea for a feature article:

Sarah: How about a story about men who are compulsive about fitness to the point that it's dangerous and unhealthy?

Dean: How does your idea fulfill the mission of the magazine, which is to promote health and fitness?

Sarah: Well, the article would conclude with a list of ways that men can be fit and healthy in a balanced manner.

Dean: But, isn't compulsive fitness an issue that women face more than men?

A woman may interpret this conversation ritual as a challenge or a rejection of her idea, whereas a man might use the ritual to tease out ideas and explore them more critically. Based on this exchange, Sarah may decide the idea is not a good one and drop it. However, Dean may not be opposed to the idea but wants to probe Sarah's thinking and her angle for the feature article.

Compliments. Exchanging compliments is a conversational ritual, especially for women. According to Tannen, when a woman compliments another woman, she also expects to receive a compliment.[67] Exchanging compliments is a way to relate to and connect with another person. The ritual misfire can occur when men don't reciprocate compliments. Consider Dahlia and Tomas, who are colleagues. Following a meeting, Dahlia compliments Tomas on his presentation. Because Tomas doesn't reciprocate the compliment, Dahlia is forced to ask, "What did you think of my presentation?" Then, rather than following the ritual and complimenting Dahlia, Tomas provides a detailed critique of what he thought of her presentation. This is clearly a ritual misfire. At times, men interpret messages literally rather than ritually. Dahlia was not expecting a critique of her presentation. Instead, she expected her ritual compliment to be reciprocated with a compliment.

Small talk rituals. Men and women often use small talk to relate to others. Small talk is a type of social lubrication that allows conversations to run more smoothly. Men and women have different small talk rituals, which can be misinterpreted. As noted earlier, according to Tannen, many women use rapport talk and many men use report talk.[68] **Rapport talk** focuses on sharing information about relationships, whereas **report talk** focuses on sharing factual or statistical information. Both forms of small talk are used to relate and connect with others. However, men and women go about it quite differently in their conversation rituals. Women tend to interpret men's report talk as too impersonal and men tend to interpret women's report talk as too personal.[69]

Rapport talk talk focused on sharing information about relationships.

Report talk talk focused on sharing practical or statistical information.

RECAP: Conversational Rituals

Rituals	Description
Ritual Apology	Refers to the common use of the phrase "I'm sorry" as a conversational smoother or to express concern; most often used by women.
Ritual Opposition	Typically a masculine behavior, this refers to the use of disagreement to get to the bottom of an idea; this is also called playing "devil's advocate."
Compliments	The ritual compliment is offered to build relationships, and a reciprocated compliment is usually expected; women typically display this behavior.
Rapport Talk	Involves sharing information about relationships; this is typically a feminine behavior.
Report Talk	Involves sharing factual or statistical information; typically a masculine behavior.

Using Both Masculine and Feminine Communication Styles

Adapt

Rather than communicating in a strictly masculine or a strictly feminine manner, research is beginning to suggest that flexibility is needed in the twenty-first-century workplace. Although the contemporary workplace is still influenced by masculine models of management, communication researchers argue that there is increasingly a place for feminine speech styles at work.[70] The professional workplace will benefit if women adopt more masculine (powerful) ways of speaking and men adopt more feminine (powerless) ways of speaking. Tannen argues that both communication styles have benefits. Her claims have been supported by research indicating that employees who perceive their managers and supervisors using mixed or blended speech styles consider them to be more effective than supervisors who use the speech style associated with their sex (a man using powerful verbal messages, a woman using powerless verbal messages).[71] Being appropriate and effective in today's diverse workplace requires the ability to adapt and use both powerful and powerless messages.[72]

Understanding the relationships between gender and communication traits increases your understanding of how men and women communicate and interact with each other differently. This understanding will allow you to adapt your communication so that you can lead men and women more effectively.

Summary

The contemporary workplace is diverse, which is both a strength and a challenge for leaders. Diversity can promote a type of creative synergy or energy that enables business and professional workplaces to survive in a very competitive global society. The challenge is that leaders have to learn how to communicate with different types and groups of people in order to be effective. A "one-size-fits-all" communication model no longer works in the twenty-first-century workplace.

Our fifth and final communication principle for leadership is *appropriately adapt messages to others*. We introduced this principle last because you have to learn the preceding four communication principles for leadership in order to effectively adapt your messages to others. You must be aware of how you communicate with others and how others communicate with you, which is the focus of Principle One. Adapting also requires effectively using and interpreting verbal and nonverbal messages, which are the skills highlighted by Principle Two and Principle Three. Finally, listening and responding thoughtfully to others—Principle Four—allows you to understand others better. When you understand how others are thinking and feeling, you can adapt your communication accordingly. The purposes of this chapter were to help you understand what makes people different from one another, and to suggest ways you can adapt your messages to communicate more effectively with people on the job.

People differ for two major reasons—biology and culture. Your biology influences your communication because it determines your personality, which is partially inherited from your parents and grandparents. Your culture influences your communication through interaction within your cultural and social systems, including family, friends, schools, churches, and communities.

To explore more closely how biology and culture influence your communication, the chapter examined a number of communication traits, including willingness to communicate, communication apprehension, and argumentativeness. Willingness to communicate is an individual's natural tendency to initiate communication with others. Communication apprehension is fear or anxiety associated with either ongoing or anticipated communication with another person or persons. Argumentativeness is a person's tendency to advocate strongly for his or her own position on an issue and criticize the positions of other people. These traits influence not only your communication behaviors but also how you perceive others and how others perceive you.

To examine how culture influences your communication, the chapter explored cultural contexts and cultural values. High-context and low-context cultures differ in terms of how nonverbal messages are used and interpreted. Three characteristics of culture that illustrate how cultural contexts influence communication include message directness, time orientation, and conflict communication. Cultural dimensions include individualism/collectivism, power distribution (decentralized/centralized), degree of avoidance of uncertainty, short-term/long-term orientation, and masculine/feminine perspective. Adapting to these cultural values includes studying other cultures, identifying the other person's cultural background, developing messages that are appropriate for the cultural background, and interpreting messages based on a person's cultural background.

Finally, the chapter explored how to adapt to gender differences by first discussing the differences between sex and gender and then examining how men and women use the content and relational dimensions of communication differently. Specifically, men and women have been shown to differ in their communication in terms of how they use powerful/powerless language, conversational rituals, and nonverbal communication. Powerful language is stereotypically masculine and is characterized by assertiveness. Powerless language is stereotypically feminine and is characterized by an emphasis on connecting with others and fostering harmonious relationships. Conversational rituals are the routine scripts that people learn to use when talking and responding to others, including ritual apology, opposition, compliments, and small talk. Both men and women would do well to adapt their communication by using a combination of masculine and feminine communication styles.

Discussion Questions

1. How do biology and culture influence communication? Why is it important to be aware of these influences in a business and professional setting?

2. Define and explain the communication behaviors of people who differ with regard to the traits of willingness to communicate, communication apprehension, and argumentativeness.

3. Describe the difference between high-context and low-context cultures, and give some examples of how these differences might affect communication in the workplace.

4. Discuss three ways to appropriately adapt to cultural contexts and values.

5. Differentiate between sex and gender.

6. Identify and define each of the four conversational rituals discussed in the chapter.

Building Your Skills

1. As an exercise to help you understand gender-based communication, ask both men and women the following questions and pay particular attention to the major differences.

- What is the basic reason for communicating?
- Which of the following statements most accurately reflects your general attitude toward communication: (a) When asking for information or making requests of someone, it is best to get to the point. (b) It is better to take some time to talk and get to the background of a situation before getting to the bottom line of what you are trying to say.
- What bothers you most when you talk to someone of the opposite sex?
- Do you think men and women know how to really listen to each other? Why or why not?

Compare your results to those of your classmates. Are there any general similarities?

2. State whether your own culture is a low-context or high-context culture, and why you believe that to be true. Discuss with a classmate the characteristics of your culture that indicate that it is either high-context or low-context, and give examples to support your position.

3. Role play with a member of the opposite sex a first conversation or conflict disagreement between dating partners. First enact the conversation from the perspective of your own sex. Then, enact the conversation again but with the roles reversed. Note any differences that emerge in how the conversation plays out. Do you detect any stereotypical behaviors that emerge when you swap roles? Does this help you better understand the opposite sex and their communication patterns?

4. In a small group, identify an example of a culture that exhibits each of the different cultural values discussed in the chapter. Use one of your examples as the basis for a skit to perform for the class. See if the class can identify the cultural value you are demonstrating.

5. Take the time to complete each Rating Scale in this chapter (willingness to communicate, communication apprehension, and argumentativeness). Next, write up a report of the results and analyze them. What do they reveal about your communication style? How can you use this information to adapt your own communication?

6. Give personal examples from your own life of each of the conversational rituals mentioned in this chapter.

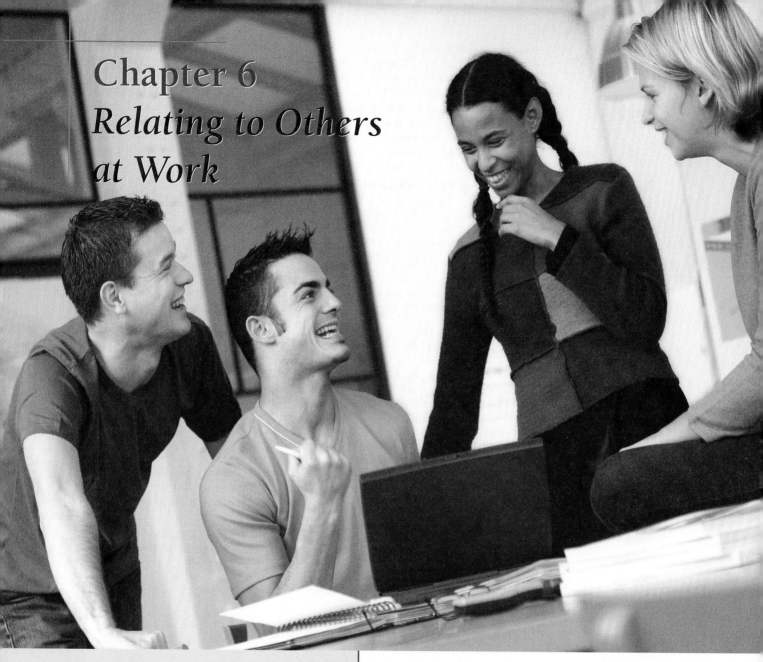

Chapter 6
Relating to Others at Work

chapter outline

After reading this chapter, you should be able to

■ Understand different types of workplace relationships, such as those with managers, co-workers, subordinates, clients, and customers.

■ List skills for relating to others with whom you have workplace relationships.

■ Understand what relational conflict in the workplace is.

■ Describe skills and strategies for dealing with conflict in the workplace.

■ List skills for managing emotions during a conflict in the workplace.

■ Define and give an example of each of the workplace negotiation strategies.

■ Understand how to effectively negotiate a win-win solution.

A person's ability to lead is dependent on his or her ability to develop and maintain constructive relationships. A **relationship** is an ongoing connection made with another person through interpersonal communication. Have you ever worked for a leader who took a genuine interest in you, listened to your needs, gave you work assignments that showcased your strengths, and recognized your efforts when you met performance goals? Chances are you have also worked for a leader who was only interested in getting the job done. Although this person may have said he or she was genuinely interested in you as a person, he or she rarely listened to your needs, had a tendency to take credit for the work you and your team members completed, and assigned more work rather than taking time to recognize you for what you had just accomplished.

> *Leadership is communicating people's worth and potential so clearly that they come to see it in themselves."*
>
> — STEPHEN R. COVEY

The first leader described above is a **person-focused leader:** someone who understands the importance and value of getting to know people on a personal level. For this type of leader, the person takes priority over the work. When a leader gets to know an employee, the employee is more likely to be motivated to do the work and do it well. The second leader described above is a **task-focused leader:** someone who believes that work takes priority over the person, who might be overheard saying, "Who's got time to get to know the employees on a personal level? There's too much work to get done in a short amount of time."

The two leaders we've described reflect opposites ends of the task-person continuum of workplace relationships, but most leaders know that the workplace requires leaders who can balance both the tasks and the personal dimensions of the workplace. Figure 6.1 illustrates this relationship continuum.

At the left end of the continuum is the task dimension. At the right end of the continuum is the person dimension. Effective leaders develop workplace relationships that balance both of these extremes. Leaders know that if they are too task-oriented, they forget about the person doing the work. If leaders are too person-oriented, they forget about the work that needs to get completed. Effective leaders have learned how to manage both the task and the person dimensions of workplace relationships—that is, they operate in the middle zone of the continuum.[1]

The purpose of this chapter is to help you relate to others in a professional manner by helping you balance the task and person dimensions of workplace relationships. In Chapters 7 and 8, we will continue our discussion of how to relate to others in a professional manner by examining the interview process. In Chapter 7 we will discuss principles for effective interviews, and in Chapter 8 we will examine a number

Relationship an ongoing connection made with another person through interpersonal communication.

Person-focused leader a leader who places value on and makes a priority of getting to know people on a personal level.

Task-focused leader a leader who believes that work takes priority over personal relationships.

| Figure 6.1 | **Workplace Relationship Continuum** |

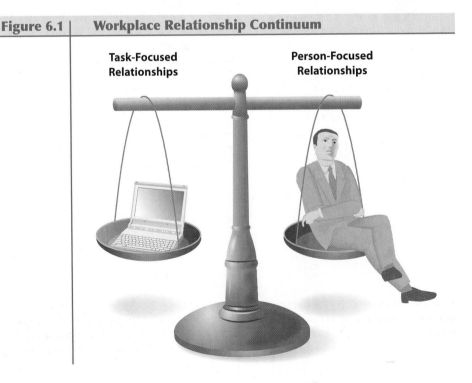

Task-Focused Relationships   Person-Focused Relationships

| Figure 6.2 | **Communication Principles and Skills for Leadership** |

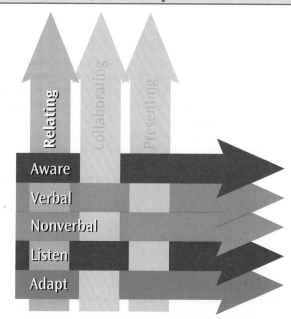

of different types of interviews including information-gathering, job, and appraisal interviews. Relating to others requires using the five communication principles for leadership we discussed in Chapters 1 through 5. These principles are illustrated in Figure 6.2 and reviewed below.

Principle One: Be aware of your communication with yourself and others. Being aware that work gets done through relationships is a fundamental leadership principle that many leaders fail to understand. The workplace is full of different types of relationships. Being aware of how these various types of relationships are similar and different will enhance your leadership communication.

Principle Two: Effectively use and interpret verbal messages. Leaders are required to delegate, manage conflict, and negotiate. All of these communication acts require effectively using and interpreting verbal messages.

Principle Three: Effectively use and interpret nonverbal messages: Nonverbal messages play an important part in developing and managing relationships. In fact, the majority of our feelings are communicated through nonverbal messages. Being nonverbally responsive to others enhances your ability to develop quality relationships at work, which will also allow you to lead more effectively.

Principle Four: Listen and respond thoughtfully to others. Managing conflict constructively and negotiating win-win solutions requires you to listen and respond thoughtfully to others. Learning how to use the Stop, Look, and Listen principles of effective listening will boost your leadership effectiveness.

Principle Five: Appropriately adapt messages to others. Since the workplace is a network of relationships, leaders must be able to adapt their communication to a variety of different types of relationships.

Understanding Types of Workplace Relationships

Effective leaders understand how the various types of workplace relationships differ and how to adapt communication accordingly to remain influential in these various types of relationships. This section reviews four different types of workplace relationships, including relationships with managers, co-workers, those you lead, and your customers.

Skills for Relating to Your Manager

One of the more important relationships that you have at work is the one you have with your manager or supervisor. The ability to relate to your manager is a major factor in determining your success at work.[2] Research suggests that your performance and job satisfaction improve as you communicate more effectively with your manager.[3] Because of the power difference between you and your manager, the relationship usually begins with a task focus. As your relationship develops, it usually becomes more balanced, focusing equally on task and the person. Unfortunately, some managers and employees lack the relational communication skills needed, and this limitation has a negative effect on employees' job performance and satisfaction. This communication skill deficiency prevents relational development and the relationship remains unbalanced—more task-focused, less person-focused.

To ensure that your relationship with your supervisor is balanced, it's important to develop skill in the use of **upward communication,** which is the communication that flows from subordinates (employees) to superiors (managers). Managers who are receptive to their employees' upward communication have employees who are more productive, motivated, satisfied with their work, and more likely to adopt change and to perceive their manager to be more open and approachable.[4]

"Managing up" is a communication concept that continues to receive attention in the academic literature and the popular press.[5] Managing up occurs when subordinates first identify their managers' goals, strengths and weaknesses, and preferred working style and then adapt their communication to meet the needs of their managers. For example, if your manager has a tendency to conduct disorganized meetings, you may be able to manage up by asking if you can help plan meetings. If your manager agrees, you might recommend some things that would ensure a productive meeting, such as seeking input from others as to what should be discussed at the meeting and developing an outline or an agenda that will help your manager process the meeting. It's important to understand that according to the "managing up" concept, subordinates are partially responsible for the effectiveness of their managers. Just as managers are supposed to support and bring out the best in their employees, subordinates, too, can support and bring out the best in their superiors. Put simply, it's a relationship. Managers influence employees and employees influence managers.

Unfortunately, not all managers are receptive to upward communication. Sometimes your manager's resistance to your upward communication is outside of your control. For example, a manager with a high need for control or one who is stubborn and resistant to change may not be receptive to upward communication. What you can do to help your manager be less resistant is to carefully develop the messages you use in your upward communication. There are five guidelines that you should follow when developing messages: Upward communication should be positive, timely, supportive of current policy, and sent directly to the person who can act on it; it should also have intuitive appeal (that is, it should make sense).[6] Although it is easier to communicate successes than failures, unfortunately, part of the relationship that you have with your manager is to communicate failures and negative information. Thad Green and Jay Knippen, management professors and consultants, have outlined eight communication procedures for communicating up negative information or communicating failures to a boss:[7]

Verbal

1. Introduce the problem.
2. Provide background information.
3. Tell about the failure.
4. Discuss resolving the failure.
5. Acknowledge responsibility.
6. Note positive results of failure.
7. Summarize key points.
8. Thank the manager.

Upward communication communication that flows from subordinate to superior.

Offshoring sending work to be done in other countries with lower labor costs.

Telecommuting working from somewhere other than an office using mobile technology.

According to Green and Knippen, these eight steps will help ensure that the negative communication flows upward and will help enrich the relationship that you have with your manager.

>>> COMMUNICATION AND GLOBALIZATION @ WORK

Offshoring and *telecommuting* are terms that you're no doubt familiar with, but you're going to be hearing more about both in the years to come. **Offshoring** occurs when companies send work to other countries. Companies send work overseas for a variety of reasons, but the main reason is that it's financially beneficial. IBM, Intel Corporation, and General Electric are just a few of the American companies that are engaged in offshoring. In addition to blue-collar or factory work, white-collar or professional work is also being offshored. Offshoring has created a demand for people who can telecommute and manage international teams from all over the globe, according to Frank Levy, an economist at MIT.[8]

Telecommuting occurs when people accomplish their work using laptop computers, cell phones, personal digital assistants, fax machines, and other technology, rather than commuting via automobile or plane to another country to conduct one's job. Telecommuting used to refer to employees' working from home rather than going into an office. Today, telecommuting has a more global connotation; people work from hotel rooms, airport lounges, international conference facilities, and extended stay residences, which house executives for long periods of time. At IBM, 40 percent of the workforce has no official office; at AT&T, a third of leaders are working in the field with no office.[9]

Although telecommuting is required in order to work for some global companies, more organizations are developing telecommuting policies to attract and retain people who might prefer not to work from 9:00 to 5:00 or in a traditional office. For example, the Best Buy corporation is learning that there are a number of benefits to telecommuting, such as increased performance, satisfaction, retention, and morale, to name a few.[10]

However, even in this day of growing technology and open-mindedness toward flexible work arrangements, telecommuting still comes with a cost: diminished *face time*. This may not affect you early in your career. As long as you're an individual contributor with enough talent, you can do almost any job from home. But what you can't do very well from home is lead. This brings us to face time. Jack Welch, former CEO of General Electric, states that "companies rarely promote people into leadership roles who haven't been consistently seen and measured. It's a familiarity thing, and it's a trust thing. People who get promoted are not necessarily stars during every 'crucible' moment at the office, but at least they're present and accounted for. And their presence says: Work is my top priority. I'm committed to this company. I want to lead."[11]

Telecommuting also sends a message: that you value lifestyle flexibility over career growth. This can be fine if it is the message you intend to send. A survey released by the online benefits company Life Care found that flexible work arrangements were the most coveted employee benefit, beating out even health care. Everyone must weigh the options when considering telecommuting.[12]

If you are interested in telecommuting, the following websites may be helpful in providing more information about skills and strategies to make telecommuting work for you.

www.todaysengineer.org
This site features an article outlining some skills and strategies for making telecommuting work and describing how telecommuting can affect your career goals.

www.networkworld.com/net.worker/research/telecommuting.html
This site features some up-to-date research as well as resources for those considering switching to telecommuting.

www.gilgordon.com/telecommutesafe
An interesting perspective on the benefits of telecommuting, including increasing efforts to "go green" by encouraging businesses to offer the telecommuting alternative.

www.forbes.com/execpics/2003/07/14/telecommute.htm
This site includes many excerpts reflecting some disadvantages of telecommuting, particularly for employers.

www.businessweek.com
This website features current articles on telecommuting in the modern business world.

Skills for Relating to Your Co-Workers

Developing quality relationships with your co-workers is important for several reasons.[13] First, you spend more time on the job with your co-workers than you do at home with your loved ones.[14] According to a Harris Interactive poll, the 9-to-5 work day is becoming a thing of the past. Americans are spending more time working than they did 30 years ago: In 1973, Americans spent 41 hours per week on the job; in

2008, they spent approximately 48 hours per week on the job, and the number of hours is expected to increase in the years ahead.[15] Although not a substitute for our families, quality workplace relationships make our working lives more meaningful. Another reason that quality relationships with co-workers are important is that your co-workers are instrumental in showing you the ins and outs of a new job—your co-workers teach you how to survive in the organization and provide you with information you need to do your job well. Finally, having quality co-worker relationships is positively related to job satisfaction, job productivity, and job involvement.[16]

Because co-workers usually have equal power (meaning that they don't have any authority over each other), their relationships tend to be more person-focused than task-focused. This equality in power promotes **horizontal communication,** which is the communication that occurs between peers working at the same level within an organization. According to one study, which examined horizontal communication over an extended period of time, people devoted anywhere from one-fifth to two-thirds or more of their daily conversations to this form of communication.[17]

Communication researchers Scott Myers and Aaron Johnson discussed three types of peer relationships that reveal differences between task-focused and person-focused relationships.[18] The first is an *information co-worker*. This peer provides information about the organization and other work-related tasks. The relationship is task-focused. The second is a *collegial co-worker*, who not only provides job-related feedback but also shares mutual work and family concerns. The relationship is both task-focused and person-focused; it's blended. The third is a *special co-worker*. The special peer provides emotional support and personal feedback and serves as a friend. The relationship is person-focused.

Myers and Johnson concluded that these different types of co-workers (information, collegial, special) used different types of communication behaviors. For example, information co-workers used more task-oriented communication ("shop talk") than special co-workers, who used more relation-oriented communication (discussion of non-work and personal topics).[19]

One important aspect of the horizontal communication that occurs between co-workers is their use of the grapevine, or the informal network for workplace information. Co-workers use the grapevine to send and receive information about such things as who got fired and hired, what is happening in the various units within an organization, and what job openings are available that would advance their careers.[20] Research suggests that information from the grapevine is used to clarify and enforce workplace rules that keep people working well together.[21] In one study, the informal grapevine network circulated information about the poor behavior of others that could not be printed in an office newsletter because of privacy concerns. Co-worker to co-worker communication through the grapevine ultimately helps organizations maintain control.[22]

The results of one survey provide some insight into how employees rate the grapevine compared to other sources of information. The survey was completed by 1,000 employees from organizations in the United States. In response to a question about preferred sources for trustworthy information, employees identified the following preferences:[23]

- 86 percent preferred a supervisor or manager;
- 71 percent preferred the grapevine or co-workers;
- 70 percent preferred face-to-face meetings;
- 47 percent preferred print publications;
- 45 percent preferred the company website;
- 35 percent preferred external media.

There are reasons why co-workers believe the information they get from the grapevine or other co-workers. Management researcher Keith Davis reported that between 75 and 95 percent of all grapevine information is correct.[24] And, Davis noted, in addition to being an accurate source of information, the grapevine is fast.

Skills for Relating to Those You Lead

Horizontal communication
communication between peers.

Many people who work in business and professional settings look forward to the opportunity to lead and manage others. Although some new professionals enter the workforce ready to manage, many do not possess the relational communication skills needed to lead others.[25] In fact, many fail to see management for what it is—a relational communication process. Successful managers understand that "work gets done through relationships." Managers who cultivate high-quality and trusting relationships with their employees have satisfied and committed employees who see to it that the manager and employees succeed together.[26] These employees comply with their managers' requests and directions and remain loyal to them.[27] Many of them go above and beyond the call of duty for their manager. Managers who are unsuccessful in developing nurturing and trusting relationships with their employees are likely to have dissatisfied employees. Dissatisfied employees have a tendency to resist their managers' directions and do only the minimum amount of work.[28] Some dissatisfied employees have even been known to sabotage their managers' careers.[29]

"There's no easy way I can tell you this, so I'm sending you to someone who can."

Because of the power difference that exists between managers and employees, the relationship usually begins with a task focus. Effective managers quickly learn that in order to cultivate nurturing and trusting relationships, they must learn to balance the relationship so that it is equally task-focused and person-focused.

As Figure 6.1 suggests, effective leaders manage from the middle of the workplace relationship continuum. These managers understand that by taking care of their employees (within reason), they will ensure that the employees take care of them. Managing from the middle of the continuum requires **downward communication**, or the communication that flows from superiors (managers) to subordinates (employees). (As noted earlier, managers must at the same time remain receptive to upward communication, or the communication that flows upward from their subordinates).

Daniel Katz and Robert Kahn identified five types of messages that generally flow from managers to employees.[30] The first is job instructions. The second is job rationale, or an explanation of why the job is important and how it relates to the organization as a whole. Information on policy and procedures are the third type of message that flows down from managers to employees. These messages informs employees of work-related practices and regulations as well as company benefits. The fourth type of message is feedback, which informs employees of how they are doing on the job. The fifth type of message is designed to motivate. Managers are responsible for motivating employees by giving them an understanding of the organization's mission (its purpose) and vision (where it's going). For example, Google, a company that many of you are familiar with, has a simple mission statement that serves to motivate and focus employees. Google's mission is *to organize the world's information and make it universally accessible and useful.*[31] A clear mission statement, along with a management style that gives employees a lot of leeway and support to make the mission statement a reality, serves to motivate Google employees. If you're a user of Google, you will probably agree that the employees of Google are fulfilling their mission.

An important part of how managers relate to those they supervise is how they delegate duties and responsibilities. **Delegation** is a manager's assignment of a specific task or project to an employee.[32] Have you ever had a manager who told you to complete a project, but didn't tell you how to do it, give you any additional help, or tell you when the project was due? When this happens, employees can feel "dumped on"; the manager is being too task-focused and not person-focused. To manage from the middle of the task-person continuum, managers must learn to delegate carefully by focusing not only on the task, but also on the person, and must understand what the employee needs to complete the project. DRGRAC is an acronym that will help you delegate effectively to others.[33] Table 6.1 presents the DRGRAC method of delegation.

In many ways, DRGRAC is a quick summary of the five types of downward messages identified by Katz and Kahn. It covers job instructions, job rationale, policy and procedures, feedback, and motivation. The DRGRAC method of delegation and downward communication focuses equally on the task and the person. In each step, there is obvious attention to the task. Each step also protects the manager/employee relationship, since each person in the

Downward communication communication that flows from superiors to subordinates.

Delegation a manager's assignment of a specific task or project to an employee.

Table 6.1	**DRGRAC Method of Delegating**
	Downward Communication for Delegation
Desired **R**esults	• Describe the task or project. • Define its purpose and note how it fits into the big picture. • Detail what the end result should look like. • Describe the intended outcomes.
Guidelines	• Describe guidelines for accomplishing the project. • Detail the rules for completing the project (for example, it must be completed by a particular deadline, with a budget not to exceed a certain amount). • Discuss feasible deadlines for completing the project.
Resources	• Detail resources for completing the project (money, tools, materials, technology, special training). • Identify other personnel who will be involved, if any, and describe their roles.
Accountability	• Detail how the employee will be evaluated. • Establish agreed-on standards of performance and measures of success. • Describe individual responsibilities. • Establish metrics, or measures, for such things as quality (What level of quality is to be achieved? How will it be measured?), time (How will time be measured? Workdays only? Weekends?), and cost (What is over budget? Under budget? What's acceptable?). • Agree on a date to review progress.
Consequences	• Describe the rewards of accomplishing the project with the available resources. • Describe the consequences of not accomplishing the project with the available resources.

relationship has a complete understanding of the desired results, guidelines, resources, accountability, and consequences. DRGRAC promotes a mature relationship based on mutual trust and respect.

Skills for Relating to Your Customers and Clients

Relating to your customers and clients is becoming increasingly important to your success in business and professional settings, especially since we live in a service economy, which is quite different from the farming or industrial economies of the nineteenth and twentieth centuries.[34] A service economy is based on businesses' ability to anticipate the needs of customers and to develop and market products and services that meet these needs. For example, Steve Jobs at Apple Computer identified a consumer need for portable and personalized music systems that utilized computer technologies, and under his leadership, Apple developed and delivered the iPod to millions of people throughout the world.

Researchers are learning that task-focused relationships do not necessary result in satisfied or loyal customers.[35] With minor exceptions, customers who are treated in a depersonalized manner walk away feeling unsatisfied. To enhance the quality of the service provider–customer relationship, **outward communication**, which is the communication that occurs between a service provider and a customer, needs to be focused on meeting the needs of the customer.

Wendy Zabava Ford has conducted a number of research studies examining customer-service communication.[36] Ford's research finds that personalized service, which occurs within a person-focused relationship, is "tailored service, or service that attempts to address the unique needs of the individual customer."[37] Examples of communication behaviors associated with personalized service include asking questions to identify customers' specific needs, offering options and advice to customers, and spontaneously sharing information on topics of interest to customers.

One example of personalized service is consumer credit counseling, which is a lifeline for people who have reached the spending limit on their credit cards. This personalized service is based on a relationship between the holder of the credit card and a financial

Outward communication
communication between a
service provider and a customer.

>>> COMMUNICATION **ETHICS** @ WORK

Gift giving is, in many cultures, a very important form of non-verbal communication. The U.S. business culture generally does not advocate gift giving, but in the Japanese and Russian business cultures, to name two, gift giving is highly important. Cultures also differ with regard to what constitutes an appropriate business gift, and the manner in which gifts should be presented and received. Should one accept gifts offered by a client or a customer? Is it ever morally correct?

A utilitarian—that is, a person who judges the correctness of actions on the basis of the maxim "the greatest good for the greatest number"—would find nothing wrong with gift giving. Both the giver and the person receiving the gift are benefiting from the interchange. But the real world isn't that simple. Is accepting a holiday ham or turkey from the customer service rep for the company that leases copy machines to your business acceptable? Is the gift a gesture intended to express thanks for doing business with the copy machine company, or is there an implied bribe: "If you accept this gift, then you need to continue doing business with us."

What do you think? Does whether or not gift giving is ethical depend on the gift giver's intention? If so, how do you know what those intentions are? For example, because the customer service rep gave the holiday turkey during a season when gift giving is a common traditional practice with some service-providing companies, some would probably consider it ethical to accept the gift. It's important to understand the gift in terms of the context: the relationship between the gift giver and receiver, the tradition of gift giving, and the time of year in which the gift is offered.

Other factors to consider when deciding on the acceptability of gifts is how the gift may influence your decision making and whether there are consequences for not accepting a gift. If you feel the gift will influence your decision making in any way, it is wise not to accept it. Also, if you feel that the gift giver would be insulted if you rejected the gift and this rejection would damage the relationship, then you may want to reconsider. Because there is a cultural dimension to gift giving and receiving, you want to be particularly sensitive to how your reactions to gifts might be interpreted by an international business associate.

counselor. Your counselor helps you pay off your credit card debt by taking over control of your paychecks. The counselor redirects your paychecks from your pocket to your credit card debt, and he or she provides counseling services that help you live on a limited budget for as long as is necessary. The counselor usually begins this personalized service by asking you about your needs and goals—for example, "When do you want to be debt free?" Depending on how you answer this question, the counselor puts together a plan to enable you to reach your personal goals.

Adapt

>>> COMMUNICATION **SKILLS** @ WORK

Much has been written about customer service. It's a popular topic among university as well as non-academic researchers.[38] Although there are varying opinions on which customer service skills are most effective, the following ten communication strategies seem to summarize the findings of academic research and the popular press:[39]

1. *Greet customers in a polite and friendly manner.* Say "Good Morning," "Good Afternoon," or "Good Evening" rather than "Hi," "Hello," or "Howdy."
2. *Identify customers' needs by asking questions and listening actively.* Paraphrase the customer's words to ensure understanding.
3. *Identify products and services related to the customer's needs.*
4. *Provide accurate product or service information.*
5. *Offer explanations that are complete and understandable.* Use precise, concrete, jargon-free language.
6. *Encourage questions from the customer.* Listen for new information rather than making assumptions.
7. *Build rapport by adjusting your communication style to more closely match the customer's communication style.* Adjust your speaking rate, volume, grammar, gestures, and posture to match the customer's style.
8. *Use supportive phrasing* such as "My pleasure" when you can comply with a customer's request; say, "We regret" rather than "We don't" when you are unable to comply with a customer's request.
9. *Demonstrate regard for the customer by using appropriate turn-taking.* Affirm the customer by using nonverbally responsive behaviors such as forward body lean, direct eye contact, and head nods.
10. *Summarize what was agreed on,* what was said, and what action will be taken; confirm when action will be taken and by whom.

In another study by Chaz Koermer and Lynda McCroskey, social courtesies (for example, greeting customers politely, expressing thanks) as well as social pleasantries (small talk about the news, the weather, or sports) predicted customer satisfaction and loyalty.[40] Although one would hope that social courtesies, such as saying hello and goodbye, and social pleasantries such as small talk would be a part of all customer service encounters, these courtesies are becoming more and more rare in American culture. In fact, some people believe that customer service providers in the United States are becoming downright rude.[41]

Learning how to enhance outward communication is becoming more important, since dissatisfied customers have found new channels for communicating their concerns about poor customer service. Marketer and consumer advocate Pete Blackshaw has researched the effects of poor outward communication.[42] He found a number of dissatisfied customers who are tired of not being heard, of having their complaint letters, emails, and voice mails dismissed. To ensure that their complaints are being heard, angry customers are using blogs and YouTube to voice their complaints. According to Blackshaw, this type of communication is forcing companies to improve their customer service. For example, Dell computer was blasted in a number of blogs focusing on poor customer service. Once the blog discussion started, numerous unhappy Dell computer users joined in and posted their own stories and experiences of poor customer service. According to Blackshaw, "A swarm of digital termites ended up eating away at the reputation Dell had spent countless millions of dollars to create."[43]

In summary, when communicating with customers and clients, the research clearly suggests that building a relationship with the customer by using social courtesies and pleasantries and by providing personalized service—finding out the customer's needs and then meeting those needs—will ensure that customers are not only satisfied but prefer to give you their future business and to recommend your business to other potential customers and clients.

RECAP: Types of Workplace Communication

Relationship Type	Communication Direction	Definition
With Manager	Upward Communication	Communication that flows from subordinates to superiors.
With Co-Workers	Horizontal Communication	Communication that occurs between those working at the same level in an organization. This tends to be more person-centered communication.
With Those You Lead	Downward Communication	Communication that flows from superiors to subordinates. This requires a conscious effort to communicate from both a task perspective and a relational perspective.
With Customers	Outward Communication	Communication that occurs between a product provider or a service provider and the customer. This needs to be focused on meeting the needs of the customer.

Understanding Relational Conflict at Work

Relational conflict at work is inevitable. Conflict occurs when someone prevents you from reaching your goals. Workplace conflict is so common that you will experience it almost every day of your professional work life. You will experience conflict with your manager, with your colleagues and co-workers, with those you supervise and lead, and with your customers and clients.

Some workplace conflict is trivial, such as conflict arising from a person playing a radio too loud or an employee consistently arriving late to meetings. Other workplace conflicts are quite serious, such as conflict caused when a manager sexually harasses employees or a colleague bullies co-workers. In many ways, workplace conflict is like a disease.

If it goes untreated, it becomes contagious and infects others. If the disease is properly diagnosed and treated, relationships can eventually heal.

The Nature of Workplace Conflict

We mentioned earlier that relational conflict occurs when others prevent you from reaching your goals. More specifically, **relational conflict** has been defined as an expressed struggle between at least two interdependent individuals, each of whom perceives incompatible goals, scarce rewards and resources, and interference from the other person in achieving his or her goals.[44] Understanding the terms in this definition will help you better diagnose conflict situations you experience in the workplace.

Expressed struggle. It's important that you let others know when there is a problem or when they're blocking your goals. You need to express your frustration and concerns. If your supervisor doesn't give you the money or help you need to do your work, then you need to inform her that you cannot complete all of the assigned projects. You can't expect her to read your mind. Conflict needs to be expressed.

Interdependence. Much of your success in business and professional settings depends on the other people with whom you work. Work life is not a solitary activity. It's a group or team activity, and your ability to be effective depends on how effective others are around you. Because you're dependent on others to complete a task or project or to share feedback about a new design or product, conflicts are likely to arise.

Perceived incompatible goals. Many times you get into conflict with others because you perceive the other person as not wanting the same things you want. Sometimes your goals are indeed different. At other times, however, it only appears that your goals are different. An example of this would be a retail store manager's deciding to resolve a customer complaint by offering the customer a free pair of jeans. The district manager perceives the free pair of jeans as being too generous and decides to block the manager's actions. Both the store manager and the district manager want a satisfied customer; however, they are in conflict about how to reach this goal.

Interpersonal conflict can also occur when another person blocks you or prevents you from reaching your goals. The district manager could block the store manager's goal of providing excellent customer service by not giving her the tools she needs to do her job. When another person blocks you from achieving your goals or pursues goals that are (or appear to be) incompatible with your own, you're likely to find yourself in conflict.

Perceived scarce rewards and resources. Have you ever been in a situation in which you did all the work but got no credit? Have you ever been asked to complete a job without being given enough time, properly trained employees, or the appropriate computer hardware and software? Either situation can lead to relational conflict.

All of the elements of the definition of relational conflict are important, because they allow you to diagnose conflict by identifying some of the possible causes. For example, two people may perceive that their work goals are incompatible, when they're actually not. Perhaps they're frustrated by the lack of rewards that they get for their work or the lack of resources that would enable them to do their work with greater efficiency. When faced with a conflict, understanding why the conflict is occurring is the first step in managing the conflict.

Many working professionals don't like conflict because they don't know how to manage it. Experts argue that managing workplace conflict is one of the most important skills for leaders.[45] Many leaders don't last long in their positions because they don't know how

Relational conflict an expressed struggle between at least two interdependent individuals, each of whom perceives incompatible goals, scarce rewards and resources, and interference from the other person in achieving his or her goals.

Relational conflict is not uncommon in the workplace. The ability to manage such conflict is one of the most important skills a leader can have.

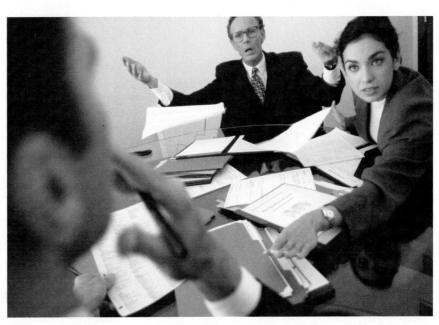

to effectively manage the conflicts they have with their followers or the conflicts that employees have with each other.[46] For these reasons, it's important to understand how people communicate conflict and how to manage relational conflict at work.

Conflict Styles

A useful tool for understanding different people's **conflict styles**, which is the way people are perceived to express and manage conflict, is the managerial grid developed by Ralph Kilmann and Kenneth Thomas, which is illustrated in Figure 6.3.[47] The horizontal axis (the bottom of the grid) reflects your concern for production, or tasks. This dimension focuses on getting the job done. If you have a high concern for task, your focus is on production or output; if you managed a coffee house, your concern would be on the total number of cups of coffee or coffee specialty drinks sold in a single day of operation. If you have a low concern for task, you are less concerned about output.

The vertical axis (the left of the grid) reflects your concern for people. This dimension focuses on the relationships you have with others including your boss, co-workers, subordinates, vendors, and customers. If you have a high concern for people, your focus is on meeting their needs rather than meeting your own needs. Again, if you managed a coffee house, your concern would be on ensuring that your employees were satisfied with their jobs by trying to meet their scheduling, social, and inclusion needs. You would also be concerned with whether your customers were satisfied with their coffee and the overall experience. If you have a low concern for people, you are less concerned about meeting others' needs and more interested in ensuring that your own needs are met. By rating your own or another person's concern for task and concern for people on a scale from 1 (low) to 9 (high), you can identify people's conflict styles, or the way they probably approach communicating conflict. Five conflict styles have been identified. Which style best describes how you communicate conflict? Becoming aware of your own conflict style will not only help you manage relational conflict more effectively, it will also help you adapt to others' conflict styles.

Avoider. An individual with a low concern for task and a low concern for people is an **avoider**. These individuals manage conflict by steering clear of it; if they do get involved in conflict, they quickly remove themselves from the situation. At other times, they deny that problems even exist. An avoider might manage conflict by stating the following:

Conflict style the way people are perceived to express and manage conflict.

Avoider someone who manages conflict by steering clear of it.

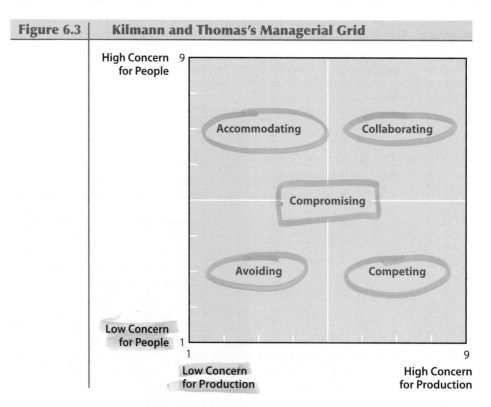

| Figure 6.3 | **Kilmann and Thomas's Managerial Grid** |

High Concern for People 9

Accommodating   Collaborating

Compromising

Avoiding   Competing

Low Concern for People 1

1   9

Low Concern for Production   High Concern for Production

- "This is not a problem for me. I don't have a conflict."
- "I need to run. See you later."
- "I'm going to go and let the two of you work this out."

Accommodator. An individual with a low concern for task and a high concern for people is an **accommodator**. These individuals manage conflict by giving in and surrendering. They have a desire to please others and will often ensure that others' needs are met at the expense of their own needs and at the expense of the tasks or the jobs that need to get accomplished. An accommodator might manage conflict by stating the following:

- "Although this is not going to help us get the job done, I agree with you."
- "This is important to you, so let's do it your way."
- "To manage this conflict, I want what you want."

Competitor. An individual with a high concern for task and a low concern for people is a **competitor**. These individuals manage conflict by being assertive and pushing their ideas or solutions to problems on others regardless of what others think, believe, or feel. A competitor might manage conflict by stating the following:

- "This is the way it's going to be; I don't care what you think."
- "To manage this conflict, there is only one solution."
- "I have experience with this issue and you don't. Let's fix it my way."

Collaborator. An individual with a high concern for task and a high concern for people is a **collaborator**. These individuals manage conflict by working with others to solve problems and make decisions. They take into consideration others' opinions and feelings before making any final decisions. A collaborator might manage conflict by stating the following:

- "What do you think we should do to manage this conflict?"
- "Together, let's look at the various issues on the table."
- "This solution has been proposed. Can you support it?"

Compromiser. An individual with a moderate concern for task and a moderate concern for people is a **compromiser**. These individuals manage conflict by being able to give up part of what they want in exchange for the other person's giving up part of what he or she wants in a particular conflict situation. A compromiser may manage conflict by stating the following:

- "I'm willing to give this up if you're willing to give that up."
- "To manage this conflict, I'm willing to meet you halfway."
- "Let's both go back and revise what it is we need and want."

Although compromising is a realistic conflict management style in today's workplace, you don't always get what you want when you compromise—you've given up something in order to get something. Collaboration, on the other hand, is probably the most preferred conflict style, because rather than giving up something, you and the other person work together until you find a creative alternative solution that allows you both to get what you want.

Regardless of your conflict style, there are times when you need to adapt your style because of the situation. Table 6.2 provides some guidelines on when you might want to adapt your conflict style to fit the situation.[48]

Understanding the nature of relational conflict on the job is the first step in learning how to manage conflict at work. The elements of our definition will guide you in diagnosing the conflict and identifying the causes of the conflict. Also, knowing how relational conflict is communicated (through competing, collaborating, compromising, avoiding, or accommodating) allows you to be prepared to manage conflict, which is the focus of the next section of this chapter.

Accommodator someone who manages conflict by giving in rather than engaging in the conflict.

Competitor someone who manages conflict by being competitive and pushing ideas and solutions on others.

Collaborator someone who manages conflict by being willing to work with others to solve problems and make decisions.

Compromiser someone who manages conflict by giving up part of what he or she wants in exchange for the other person's giving up part of he or she wants.

Adapt

RECAP: Conflict Styles

Conflict Style	Description
Avoider	This style involves a low concern for the task and a low concern for people. This person often removes himself or herself from the conflict or denies that it exists.
Accommodator	This style involves a low concern for task and a high concern for people. This person often desires to solve a conflict by pleasing others.
Competitor	This style involves a high concern for task and a low concern for people. This person can be overly assertive in handling conflict.
Collaborator	This style involves a high concern for both task and people. This person tries to solve conflict by reaching a solution that meets everyone's needs.
Compromiser	This style involves a moderate concern for both task and people. This person manages conflict by encouraging all parties to sacrifice something to reach a common goal.

Table 6.2	Adapting Conflict Style to Situation
Conflict Style	**Situation**
Use an Avoiding Style	• When an issue is trivial, or more important issues are pressing • When you perceive no chance of satisfying your own concerns • When potential disruption outweighs the benefits of resolution • When you need to let people cool down to regain perspective • When gathering information supercedes making an immediate decision • When others can resolve the conflict more effectively • When issues seem tangential or symptomatic of other issues
Use an Accommodating Style	• When you find you are wrong—to allow a better alternative to be presented, to learn, to show your reasonableness • When the issue is more important to others than it is to you—to satisfy others and maintain cooperation • When you need to build social credits for later issues • When you need to minimize the loss when you are outmatched • When harmony and stability are especially important • When you need to allow subordinates to develop by learning from mistakes
Use a Competing Style	• When quick, decisive action is vital • When the conflict is over important issues with unpopular consequences (such as cost cutting, enforcing unpopular rules, discipline) • When the conflict is over issues vital to company welfare and you know you're right • When working with people who take advantage of noncompetitive behavior
Use a Collaborating Style	• When both sets of concerns are too important to be compromised so you need to find an integrative solution • When your objective is to learn • When you need to merge insights from people with different perspectives • When you need to gain commitment by incorporating concerns into a consensus • When you need to address emotional issues that have interfered with a relationship
Use a Compromising Style	• When goals are important, but not worth the effort or potential disruption of more assertive modes • When opponents with equal power are committed to mutually exclusive goals • When you need to achieve temporary settlement on complex issues • When you are under time pressure to arrive at expedient solutions • When you need a backup when collaboration or competition is unsuccessful

Managing Relational Conflict at Work

Three sets of skills can help you manage relational conflict while leading others: skills for managing the workplace climate, skills for managing emotions, and skills for managing conflict conversations.

Skills for Managing Workplace Climate

In Chapter 3, the workplace was described as having a climate or a weather pattern. For example, some workplaces have clear, blue skies: Leaders and employees trust each other and enjoy working together and workplace conflict is minimized. In other workplaces, the climate is stormy: Leaders and employees do not trust each other. Perhaps leaders abuse their power by making demands of others or employees spread false rumors. Both behaviors are the equivalents of bolts of lightening, and they damage workplace relationships. In these climates, conflict is common. What makes the difference in the workplace climate or weather pattern is the communication that is used. Researchers have identified a number of leadership strategies that you can use to make the workplace climate more positive and thus reduce conflict.[49]

Determine the absolutes. When leading others, it's important that you establish some basic workplace rules, such as being punctual, dressing appropriately for the job, and not drinking or using illegal drugs on the job. Inexperienced leaders have a tendency to establish too many workplace rules, which increases workplace conflict because leaders must enforce the rules they make. Rather than establishing too many rules, it is recommended that you determine only the absolutes, the minimum number of rules people need to work in a safe and respectful manner.

Perceive the possible. When leading others, it's important to have realistic expectations of others' performance. When you try to be too controlling, people feel coerced, and they rebel and resist. Followers make mistakes and they don't always work up to their potential. Some latitude must be provided. It's not reasonable to expect people to behave in an ideal manner at all times.

Determine what is worth sacrificing for. When leading others, it's important to pick your battles carefully. Not every employee infraction is worth a reprimand or is even worth addressing. Sometimes, leaders need to look the other way. It's important to ask, "Is this infraction worth damaging an otherwise good workplace relationship?"

Know when to avoid confrontation. When leading others, it's important to manage conflict constructively. One principle for managing conflict constructively is to avoid having a confrontation with another person in public. People lose face when you confront them in public. It's humiliating for them. Also, others notice how inappropriately you managed the situation, which reflects poorly on you.

Win by losing graciously. When leading others, you will make mistakes. It's important to admit your mistakes publicly, take responsibility for them, and apologize for them. Leadership expert Jim Collins, in his book titled *Good to Great*, stresses the importance of what he refers to as leadership humility. According to Collins, great leaders take risks and because of their risk taking, they make mistakes. Taking responsibility for their mistakes and apologizing for them makes leaders humble and in many ways strengthens their ability to lead others more effectively.[50] Additionally, employees will learn to admit mistakes more readily as a result of your modeling a leadership style that is forgiving.

Skills for Managing Emotions

One problem that most people have when trying to manage conflict is controlling their emotions. Most conflicts provoke emotional responses: anger, hurt feelings, frustration, fear, or defensiveness. Although some people want to manage conflict when they're upset to show the other person their level of anger and frustration and to release bottled-up emotions, these emotional outbursts usually ignite the other person's emotions and result in emotional contagion. Like conflict in general, emotions are like a virus that spreads very quickly from one person to another.[51] We have a tendency to mimic each other's behaviors. If you approach a conflict situation in a hostile or defensive manner, the other person, maybe even without knowing it, starts mimicking your behaviors and begins feeling hostile and defensive too.[52] If you're going to be successful at managing a conflict, you must become aware of the contagion effect and try to prevent it from occurring. Although you do not have control over the other person's emotions, you can affect his or her emotions indirectly by managing your own emotions during a conflict conversation. Here are a few suggestions for how you might prevent the contagion effect.

Select a mutually acceptable time and place to discuss the conflict. Let the other person know that you would like to discuss something important and find out when the other person might be available. Make sure this time works for you and your schedule too. If you or the other person is tired, there's a risk of becoming locked in an emotion-charged confrontation. It's best to have a conflict conversation when you're both well rested. Also, make sure you have some privacy for your conversation.

Monitor the emotional temperature. Let the other person know that you expect the conversation to be respectful and that if the conversation becomes too emotional, you will call a "time out" or postpone the conversation until the emotions have subsided. For example, you might say, "I know we both feel strongly about the decision to not promote Leslie to unit manager, but I hope we can calmly discuss other alternatives for her career development." Verbal messages like this acknowledge feelings but also reinforce expectations for being polite to one another.

Be nonverbally responsive to others. Emotions are conveyed primarily through nonverbal messages.[53] And remember that we don't have as much control over our nonverbal messages as we do our verbal messages; emotions have a tendency to "leak" out of us in our nonverbal behavior.[54] Many times these leaked cues convey negative emotions. Although it is natural to have a closed body orientation (to cross arms and pull back) during conflict conversations, try remaining nonverbally responsive to the other person. Make appropriate eye contact. Ensure an open body position by facing the person, uncrossing arms and legs, leaning forward, and using appropriate head nods. Nonverbally responsive messages have a tendency to defuse or neutralize negative emotions.[55]

Avoid personal attacks, name-calling, profanity, and gunny-sacking. Because conflict situations are usually emotionally charged, it is easy to resort to what conflict researchers refer to as "below-the-belt" fighting.[56] This type of conflict is expressed by attacking the individual and making the conflict personal. Profanity, which is usually not acceptable in the workplace, or a personal attack is usually reciprocated by the other person. This cycle of negative emotional expression needs to be broken if there is to be any hope of managing the conflict in a constructive manner. Another way to manage emotions is to avoid engaging in gunny-sacking, or kitchen-sink fighting.[57] Gunny-sacking occurs when a person begins discussing a single conflict situation and then continues to unload or dump on the other person all of the things that have been bothering him or her. Essentially, it's emptying the "gunny-sack" of grievances. This type of conflict management is perceived as unfair by most people and increases negative emotions. To avoid gunny-sacking, limit the scope of your conflict conversation to a single issue rather than multiple issues.

Skills for Managing Conflict Conversations

Imagine you're having a problem with your co-worker Michael. Rather than talking behind his back, you discuss the problem with Michael directly. But while you're talking, something happens almost without your knowing it: Michael "spins" the conversation so that the problem seems to be about you and not him. It happens quite often and it can be frustrating. If we're not careful, people can hijack conflict conversations. When this happens, we walk away from the conflict conversation asking ourselves, "How did that happen? Why did I let him do that?" In reality, the problem is not just the other person's and it's not just yours. Because you and the other person are interdependent, the problem belongs to both of you.

To keep your conflict conversation on track and work toward a solution acceptable to both individuals, consider structuring your conversation using what we refer to as the PUGSS model of conflict management. Each letter of the PUGSS acronym represents a different part of the conversation:[58]

- P = Describe the *Problem*
- U = Achieve *Understanding*
- G = Identify *Goals*
- S = Brainstorm *Solutions*
- S = Select the best *Solution*

The advantage to using the PUGSS model is that it keeps conflict conversations focused and it helps people prepare their conflict messages. Here's how the process works.

Describe the problem. What is the other person saying or doing that is bothering you? Using "I" language, describe the problematic behavior. "This is what I see you doing. This is what I hear you saying. This is how I'm feeling."

Achieve understanding. Make sure the other person understands the problem. Simply ask, "Do you know why this is a problem?" You might want to ask the person to paraphrase what she or he hears you saying to confirm understanding. If the person doesn't understand, which is common, then continue to describe the problem but in a different way. It is important to not continue to the next step in the conversation until you're confident that the other person understands the problem.

Also, make sure the person doesn't hijack or deflect the conversation and make the problem about you. For example, if you're discussing with an employee the fact that the person is frequently late, the employee may change the subject and mention that you need to be less rigid and more understanding. If this occurs, tell the person that you'd be happy to follow up at another time to hear his or her thoughts about your being rigid and not understanding. Then redirect the conversation back to the employee's tardiness problem. In other words, keep the conversation focused on the employee's behaviors, not on yours. That's a different conversation that should be conducted at another time.

Identify goals. Next, let the other person know what you want and need. Find out what the other person wants and needs. Once you have identified individual goals, identify the goals you have in common. Build on your common goals. For example, if you're working with an employee who is constantly late to work, you might mention that the goal you have in common is for this person to remain employed. You might say, "I know you want to keep your job, and I want you to keep your job too. Our goal is the same. Now let's work together to reach this goal." People are usually surprised to find out that they have a number of common or similar goals.

Brainstorm solutions. Now that the problem and goals have been identified, it's time to find a solution. Ask, "What can we do to fix the problem? How can we ensure that both of our goals are met?" Withhold all evaluation and generate as many creative solutions as possible.

Select the best solution. Finally, select the best solution. Evaluate each of the brainstormed solutions and compare each to the goals you've identified. If a solution doesn't meet the goals of both people, then it's not the *best* solution. Continue evaluating each solution until you come up with one that meets all goals identified above.

Figure 6.4 reflects how PUGSS might unfold in a real relational conflict in the workplace. This particular conflict, which actually occurred, involves two employees who work in the same office. One of the employees, Marisa, brings her infant daughter to work, as she has been unable to arrange childcare. The other employee, Rick, is distracted by the child's crying and often ends up doing Marisa's work.

For most people, working through conflict is troublesome and difficult because there's so much uncertainty. We have no idea how the conflict conversation is going to go. This uncertainty produces a lot of anxiety. One of the advantages of using PUGSS to structure your conflict conversations is that it makes managing and resolving conflict like working through a script. To reduce the uncertainty and anxiety, we encourage you to plan your conflict conversations and structure them using the PUGSS model.

There is simply no way to escape relational conflict at work. In order to manage conflict when it occurs, you must first ensure that the workplace climate is conducive to managing conflict. Workplace environments that are supportive, trusting, caring, and accepting ensure that relational conflict is managed well. Second, you must manage your emotions carefully by managing conflict at the appropriate time and place, explaining

Figure 6.4	The PUGSS Approach to Conflict

Describing the Problem

Rick: Do you have a second? I have a problem and I know that you can help me fix it.

Marisa: Sure, come in. What's the problem? How can I help?

Rick: Something has been bothering me.

Marisa: What is it?

Rick: I haven't been able to get much work done lately. I begin a project that requires concentration and then I hear your child crying. The other day she cried from 9:00 a.m. until 11:00. I was feeling very frustrated.

Marisa: Yes, she was not having a good day. I'm so sorry.

Rick: I have also had other employees assign me work that is usually given to you. Yesterday, the Director of Marketing asked me to stuff all of these envelopes and I don't even report to her. I feel like I'm getting dumped on because others don't want to burden you with additional work. I'm feeling a bit abused by this situation, and I'm frustrated and anxious.

Achieving Understanding

Rick: Do you understand why this is a problem for me?

Marisa: I think so. Here's what I hear you saying: My child bothers you and others are dumping my work on you because they perceive me as having too much to do, with my child and everything else.

Rick: Your child is not the distraction, but her crying is.

Marisa: I also didn't know that others perceived me as ineffective.

Rick: I don't think anybody thinks you're ineffective at all—I just think they perceive you as having your hands full with your workload and your child.

Marisa: I understand. Again, I apologize for this and I'm glad you brought this problem to my attention. Let's fix it.

Rick: What do you suggest we do to fix the problem?

Identifying Goals

Marisa: What do you need to get your job done?

Rick: I need a quiet work environment. I also need others to know that you're available so they stop giving me your work. I don't feel our work is equally distributed. What do you need?

Marisa: I need to be able to care for my daughter and work at the same time. Being a single working mother is challenging.

Rick: Well, yes—I can't even imagine how hard it must be.

Marisa: Well, we both need our jobs and we like working here. . . .

Rick: Also, we're good friends and I don't think we want this to damage our friendship.

Marisa: I agree completely. What do you see as being a workable solution?

Brainstorming Solutions

Rick: How about having your parents care for her while you're working?

Marisa: I could see if I could change offices so we wouldn't bother you.

Rick: How about seeing if the company might help you finance daycare?

Marisa: How about you change your work schedule and work nights? Is that a possibility?

Rick: Could you get a babysitter with whom you could exchange babysitting services? For example, you sit with the other person's child on the weekends and this person could sit with your child during the week.

Selecting the Best <u>Solution</u>

Marisa: Why don't I see if I could change my office so that my daughter and I will be out of your way?

Rick: I think that would meet my need for a quiet workplace; however, I still believe people will perceive you as having your hands full and they will come to me. Is it possible for your parents to care for your child during the day?

Marisa: Well, unfortunately my parents aren't capable of caring for my daughter. They're not comfortable around babies. My mother pops Valium every time we step foot in the house and my dad leaves once my daughter begins to cry.

Rick: What about exchanging babysitting services with a neighbor?

Marisa: That idea might work. . . . My neighbor is a firefighter and he works two 24-hour shifts during the weekend. I could watch his kids all weekend, and I believe he would be willing to watch my daughter during the workday.

Rick: That would meet both of my needs and yours. Do you agree?

Marisa: I do agree. All I want is good childcare for my daughter and to keep my job.

---

your expectations for how you will treat each other during the conflict conversation, being nonverbally responsive, and avoiding personal attacks, name-calling, profanity, and gunny-sacking. Third, it's important to plan and structure your conflict conversations to ensure that you reach a solution you both can agree on.

RECAP: Using PUGSS to Manage Conflict Conversations

Describe **Problem**	Use descriptive "I" language to describe what the other person is doing that is bothering you
Achieve **Understanding**	Make sure the other person understands what the problem is
Identify **Goals**	Identify individual needs and common goals
Brainstorm **Solutions**	Offer all solutions that come to mind, without evaluation
Select Best **Solution**	Choose the solution that best meets all parties' needs, or combine solutions to create a new one

Negotiating Solutions at Work

Another important tool that is essential to effective leadership is negotiation, which is a particular type of conflict management. **Negotiation** has been defined as an exchange of proposals and counterproposals as a means of reaching a satisfactory settlement to a conflict.[59] Whereas all negotiation is a form of conflict management, not all conflict management is negotiation. For example, if you supervise an employee who comes to work under the influence of alcohol, you have a conflict that needs to be managed. There is no negotiation. The employee violated one of the workplace rules that usually results in immediate termination. In contrast, negotiation occurs when there is room for bargaining or for "give and take." You give some and the employee gives some until you reach a solution that suits both of you. In short, you exchange proposals and counterproposals until you can agree. During negotiation, your proposals change and evolve. It's rare to leave the negotiation process with your first proposal untouched.

You will use negotiation strategies during the interview process when a company offers you a job. You have an idea of what the position and your skills are worth; however, the company also has an idea of a starting salary for you. That's when you begin the negotiation process. For example, you will take the job for $35,000. The company offers $27,000 and an extra week of vacation. After a strategic conversation, you and the company's representative agree on an annual salary of $31,000 without the extra week of vacation. This illustrates the exchange of proposals and counterproposals.

Negotiation an exchange of proposals and counterproposals as a means of reaching a satisfactory settlement to a conflict.

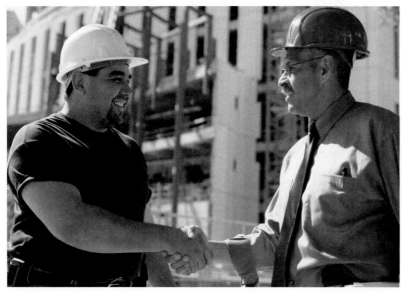

An effective leader successfully uses negotiating skills to strengthen workplace relationships and resolve conflicts.

Another example would be when you're trying to arrange your work schedule. You have certain scheduling needs, and your manager has certain scheduling needs. Ideally, negotiation occurs when you and your manager exchange proposals for your schedule and revise the proposals until you reach a satisfactory settlement. Negotiation can allow you to create a better fit between the requirements of the organization and your needs, abilities, and preferences.[60] Negotiation allows you to tailor a particular job so that it fits you.

In the next section, we examine six negotiation strategies and communication skills for negotiating win-win solutions. Coupling the negotiating strategies with the negotiation communication skills will allow you to be effective in your leadership position by continually enhancing your relationships with your manager, co-workers, those you lead, and your clients and customers.

Negotiating Strategies

A **negotiating strategy** is the overall approach you take when you exchange proposals and counterproposals with another person when negotiating a settlement to a conflict. Stephen Covey, an expert in leadership studies, suggests that your negotiating strategy is influenced by your paradigm.[61] A **paradigm** is a worldview; it's a way of thinking or a set of attitudes that guide your communication and behavior. Six paradigms that may guide people in negotiation include win-win, win-lose, lose-win, lose-lose, win, and win-win or no deal.[62] Which paradigm influences how you approach the negotiating process? Becoming aware of your paradigm and how it influences your negotiating strategies will enhance your ability to negotiate solutions more effectively in the workplace.

Win-win. This negotiating strategy seeks mutual benefit; it uses a cooperative rather than a competitive approach to finding a solution. People with a win-win paradigm are empathic listeners; they try to see and understand the problem from the other person's perspective. Win-win negotiators also are appropriately assertive, which means that they make their needs and their feelings known without attacking the other person; they make requests. For example, "In order for both of us to be successful, I need you to increase your share of the market by the end of next month. In return, I'm willing to give you additional resources to help you make that happen." This message conveys a win-win strategy in that both individuals are getting their needs met.

Win-lose. This negotiating strategy is unfortunately quite common among people in business and professional settings. In fact, in many businesses, this is standard operating procedure. This approach uses competition rather than cooperation in negotiating solutions to problems. People acting on the basis of a win-lose paradigm are more concerned with the self than with the other person and his or her needs. Win-lose negotiators are verbally aggressive—they are more likely to attack the other person's character or make demands in order to get their way. It is important to understand the difference between verbally aggressive people and assertive people. "I'm going to work the Monday through Friday schedule; you're not going to get your selfish way this time" is an example of verbal aggression. On the other hand, "I would like to request a Monday through Friday work schedule so that I may take care of my aging parents on the weekend" is an example of being appropriately assertive.

Lose-win. This negotiating strategy is one typically used by someone who is submissive, which means that the person yields or gives in to the needs of the other person while ignoring his or her own needs and burying his or her own feelings. A person who negotiates on the basis of a lose-win paradigm is a people pleaser but often ends up being dissatisfied.

Lose-lose. This strategy might be best expressed as "If I'm going down, you're going down with me." The lose-lose approach is a destructive attitude rather than a negotiating

Negotiating strategy the overall approach taken in an exchange of proposals and counterproposals during negotiation of a settlement to a conflict.

Paradigm a worldview; a way of thinking or a set of attitudes that guide your communication and behavior.

strategy. This approach is never recommended. Although it may not be your own approach to negotiating a solution, it may well be the other person's, and oftentimes you'll be unable to influence the person's attitude. People who use a lose-lose strategy usually don't have a lot of consideration for the other person and don't have the courage or the assertiveness needed to pursue other alternatives or solutions. People with a lose-lose paradigm envy and criticize others while also putting themselves down. For example, you might hear a team leader say to another team leader, "Your team always meets its goals because they cut corners. My team couldn't meet its goals even if we cut corners. If you're not willing to do the extra work, then we aren't either."

Win. This negotiating strategy might be expressed as "As long as I win, I don't care if you win or lose." People who approach negotiation with this overall strategy or paradigm only think about what *they* want. They forget that effective negotiation involves at least two people. Although they don't actively seek to make others lose, they do whatever it takes to win.

Win-win or no deal. This negotiating strategy might best be expressed as "If we both can't be winners, then let's not play this game." Some leadership experts consider win-win or no deal the highest form of negotiation because it requires that negotiators equally respect their own needs and the needs of others.[63] With a "win-win or no deal" strategy, both parties agree that the only acceptable solution is going to be a win-win. If that kind of solution cannot occur, then both parties agree to disagree and terminate all negotiations until a later time.

   For example, suppose you want to negotiate a printing job with FedEx Office. You need color brochures to market your new business and you want them to do the job because of their quality and reputation. You have a limited budget. FedEx Office wants your business, because they know you will be a loyal and longtime customer. Unfortunately, their price for printing color brochures is too expensive for your operating budget. Because you both want to work together but cannot come to an agreement on the printing price, you simply say, "Let's wait on this. Let's give it some time and see if we can come up with another agreement." After a few days, you return to FedEx Office and propose something different. This time you ask if FedEx Office will agree to increase the number of brochures they print for you at the price they already quoted if you change the brochure from a five-color brochure to a two-color brochure. You get more brochures printed, and they get your business and reduce their printing costs (since color ink is significantly more expensive than paper). The situation is a win-win.

RECAP: Negotiating Strategies

Strategy	Description
Win-Win	This strategy uses a cooperative approach to finding a solution and seeks mutual benefit.
Win-Lose	This strategy uses a competitive approach to finding a solution; each negotiator is most concerned with his or her own needs.
Lose-Win	A negotiator using this strategy submits to the other person and ignores his or her own needs.
Lose-Lose	This strategy uses an "if I go down, you are going down with me" approach.
Win	This strategy occurs when negotiators are only concerned about getting their own needs met and winning.
Win-Win or No Deal	This strategy takes into account everyone's needs. The negotiator is not happy until everyone wins.

Skills for Negotiating Win-Win Solutions

In the preceding section we introduced the PUGSS model, which is a general model for managing conflict. The following skills will supplement the steps of the PUGSS model when you use it during the exchange of proposals and counterproposals that constitutes negotiation.[64]

Adapt

Separate the people from the problem. In many negotiation situations, people have a difficult time separating the issues from the individuals involved. As the negotiator, try separating the people from the problem. When discussing the problem, don't associate a name with it. For example, some people take it personally if they perceive that they are getting assigned too much work. Rather than saying, "Jesse believes that the workload in the department is not equally divided and that he is doing too much of the work," try saying, "*It has come to my attention* that the workload in the department may not be equally divided." Your goal is to depersonalize the issues that need to be negotiated. (In fact, if you're the leader, it might be beneficial for you to take responsibility for the problem. You might say, "I know I've divided up the department workload unfairly lately.")

Focus on interests, not positions. When you negotiate solutions to problems, you usually focus on positions rather than on interests. A **position** is what each person wants to see in the negotiated outcome. An **interest** is a desire, need, concern, or fear. In many situations, interests remain invisible; all you see are people's positions. But the invisible interests are in many ways much more important than people's positions. According to professional negotiators Roger Fisher and William Ury, "Interests motivate people; they are the silent movers behind the hubbub of positions. Your position is something you decided upon. Your interests are what caused you to so decide."[65]

When negotiating, look below the surface at what is motivating a particular person's positions. The motivation is the interest. Rather than meeting the other person's position, see if you can meet the other person's interest. For example, Jesse wants to renegotiate his job description because he feels he is doing too much of the work in his department. His position is to ensure that the workload is equally distributed. His *interest* is to be recognized, appreciated, and possibly compensated for the extra work that he is doing. To enhance the negotiation process, spend time listening to those involved in the negotiating process. Try to understand their motivations—their interests—and to meet these important interests.

Invent proposals that are mutually beneficial. Generate as many options or proposals as possible that will benefit *all* individuals in the negotiating process. If you're going to exchange proposals, you need a number of them. The more proposals you have, the more likely you are to find one that benefits all parties to the negotiation. Also, when inventing proposals, consider the other side's perspective. Would they consider a given option plausible or possible? Would they find it attractive? If not, then eliminate the option from your list of possible proposals. One of the proposals that you might offer to Jesse would be to redistribute the workload, which addresses his position. Other proposals that you might exchange focus on his underlying interest—his concern that he is not being recognized, appreciated, or valued for the extra work that he does. You could write a letter for Jesse's personnel file, commending him for going "above and beyond the call of duty," offer him a financial bonus for the extra work he does, give him "comp time" or a day off with pay, or promote him. Remember, inventing proposals that address the other person's *interest* is sometimes more important than meeting the person's *position*.

Use objective criteria to evaluate proposals. When exchanging proposals and counterproposals, it's important to have criteria, or acceptable standards, that both sides can use to evaluate the proposals. It's important to know what makes a proposal acceptable or unacceptable. If you don't know what you're looking for, you won't recognize it when you see it. When judges make a ruling, they use laws as their criteria. When teachers evaluate student work, they use the standards outlined in the assignment as their criteria. These criteria allow judges and teachers to make decisions that are consistent and understandable to others. Before entering into negotiation, it's best to identify a set of criteria that both sides will consider fair and reasonable. How do you do this? In the workplace some standards for fair and reasonable criteria have already been established. Consider the following:

- *Precedent:* What formal judgments have already been made pertaining to this workplace issue?
- *Tradition:* What's been done in the past in the workplace?
- *Professional Standards:* What do professional organizations advocate as acceptable workplace practices and procedures?

Position in a conflict, what each person wants to see in a negotiated outcome.

Interest a desire, need, concern, or fear that motivates one to take a particular position.

- *Rules of Conduct:* What policies does the company enforce with all employees, regardless of rank, position, or title?
- *Employment Law:* What state and federal standards must a company follow in order to be working within the law?
- *Industry Standards:* What do our competitors do? What guidelines do they follow?

When negotiating Jesse's grievance that the workload in the department is not equally distributed, you could use a number of the above criteria to evaluate the various proposals that both sides are exchanging. For example, you might use tradition, or what's been done in the past, as your criterion for evaluating proposals. To apply this criterion, you could consult Jesse's job description. A **job description** is a written description of the responsibilities and requirements that have been traditionally associated with a specific job. In other words, it describes how the job has been conducted in the past. After reviewing this document, you would both know whether Jesse is doing the work outlined in his job description or work that falls outside his job description. The job description provides you with standards that might enable you to reach a win-win solution.

To summarize: The process of negotiating win-win solutions is similar to managing relational conflict; however, negotiation *always* involves the exchange of proposals and counterproposals. Some relational conflict situations may not require the exchange of proposals; the problem in question may not be subject to negotiation. To negotiate effectively, it's important to understand the paradigm (the overall negotiating strategy) that you're using and the paradigm that the other person is using to negotiate a solution. There are six negotiation paradigms, or overall strategies: win-win, win-lose, lose-win, lose-lose, win, and win-win or no deal. Finally, negotiating win-win solutions requires separating people from the problem, focusing on interests rather than positions, inventing proposals that are mutually beneficial, and using objective criteria to evaluate the proposals.

Job description a written description of the responsibilities and requirements of a specific job.

RECAP: Negotiating Skills for Win-Win Solutions

Skill	Description
Separate the people from the problem.	When discussing a problem, don't associate it with a name. If you are the leader, take responsibility for the problem yourself.
Focus on interests, not positions.	Rather than focus on people's desired solutions, focus on their needs and ultimate goals.
Invent proposals that are mutually beneficial.	Consider the other's perspective when developing proposals, and generate as many as possible, withholding evaluation.
Use objective criteria to evaluate proposals.	Use mutually agreed-on criteria for evaluating proposals.

Communication Principles and Skills for Leadership

Principle One: Be aware of your communication with yourself and others.

Aware

- Be aware of how others perceive you in terms of interpersonal attraction, similarity, and status.
- Be aware of the types of communication you use in your various workplace relationships with supervisors, subordinates, co-workers, customers.
- Be aware of your own and others' conflict styles when relating in the workplace.

Principle Two: Effectively use and interpret verbal messages.

- To delegate effectively, use verbal messages that follow the DRGRAC method: stating desired results, establishing guidelines, providing resources, clarifying accountability, and describing consequences.

- In a conflict conversation, use descriptive "I" language to clearly communicate the problematic behavior.

- When negotiating using a win-win strategy, use objective criteria to evaluate solutions.

Principle Three: Effectively use and interpret nonverbal messages.

- In a conflict conversation, manage emotions before working to resolve the conflict.

- To enhance others' perception of your relational closeness, use nonverbal immediacy behaviors

- To reduce the chances of the other person's becoming defensive during a conflict conversation, use nonverbal responsive behaviors: forward body lean, eye contact, head nods, open body position, and uncrossed arms.

Principle Four: Listen and respond thoughtfully to others.

- Listening involves stopping competing messages, looking for nonverbal behaviors that enhance the meaning, and listening for the big ideas rather than getting bogged down in the details.

- In a conflict conversation, listen carefully to all needs before attempting to reach a solution.

- When negotiating solutions, use strategies designed to incorporate all perspectives, such as using objective criteria and inventing proposals that are mutually beneficial.

Principle Five: Appropriately adapt messages to others.

- Use appropriate communication in the various workplace relationships: upward, downward, horizontal, and outward communication.

- Become aware of others' perceptions of you, and adapt your messages accordingly.

- When using outward communication with your customers, remember to orient it toward their needs.

Discussion Questions

1. What are the different types of workplace relationships?

2. List skills for relating to others within each workplace relationship.

3. What are five factors that contribute to relational conflict in the workplace?

4. Describe at least three strategies for dealing with conflict in the workplace.

5. List skills for managing emotions during a conflict in the workplace.

6. Define and give an example of each of the workplace negotiation strategies discussed in the text.

7. How do you effectively negotiate a win-win solution?

Building Your Skills

1. Review the different types of conflict styles discussed in the chapter and decide what type of conflict style you often use. What makes you think so? What kinds of strategies can you use to be more effective in your conflict conversations? Share your thoughts with a classmate.

2. When facing a conflict in the workplace, we often begin the conversation by accusing another person. This commonly is done using evaluative "you" language. Generate a list of statements that might be used in conflict (such as "You are lazy," "You are not a team player") and then rephrase each one as an "I" statement.

3. Review Figure 6.4. Then, get together with another classmate and decide on a potential workplace conflict. Take sides on the issue, then work together to develop a "conflict conversation" following all the steps of the PUGSS model. Role-play the conversation in front of the class.

4. Develop your own negotiation strategy for a potential workplace issue. This can be either a current issue in your own workplace or a created issue. Discuss your strategy with your classmates. Why do you think it will be effective?

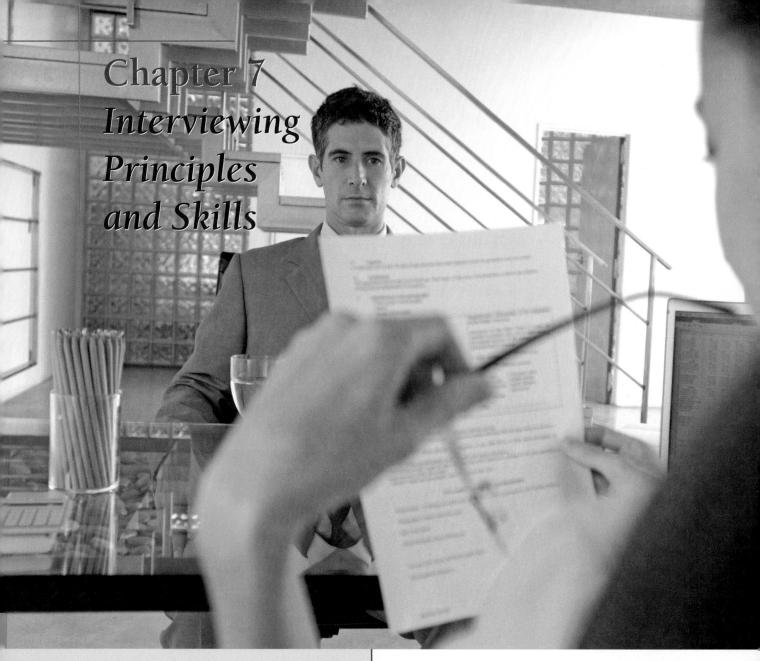

Chapter 7
Interviewing Principles and Skills

chapter outline

After reading this chapter, you should be able to

- ■ Identify and define primary and secondary interview goals.

- ■ Understand how to prepare effectively for an interview, including identifying goals, selecting the appropriate person, and arranging the interview.

- ■ Describe the difference between structured and unstructured interviews, and explain the steps in structuring an interview.

- ■ Discuss the different types of interview questions as well as the appropriate sequence to use.

- ■ Discuss the interviewer's and interviewee's roles during the opening, body, and closing portions of an interview.

- ■ Describe how to listen and respond effectively during an interview.

- ■ Explain what it means to be a responsible interviewer.

- ■ Explain what it means to be a responsible interviewee.

As the chapter opening quote says, interviewing is a dance. When you're interviewing others, you lead the dance. When you're being interviewed, you follow and take your cues from the lead dancer. The interview dance is an important relationship that allows you to network and connect with other professionals. Through the interview process, you're able to obtain information as well as to inform and influence others in important ways. Consider the following everyday workplace examples of interviewing:

- Lisa, a department store manager, conducts an appraisal interview with Brian, a wardrobe consultant, about his job performance during the fourth quarter.

- Alexi conducts an information-gathering interview with Sophie, who is a project leader for a prominent software company. Alexi wants to find out more about Sophie's job duties and the skills needed in this profession.

- Nick, a journalist, interviews a mayor in a gulf-coast city recently devastated by a category-four hurricane about the status of the city and her people.

- Monique is being interviewed by Celeste, her personal trainer at the gym, to identify her personal fitness goals.

An **interview** is a form of oral interaction structured to achieve a goal; it often includes just two people (interviewer and interviewee) but can include more than two people, who take turns speaking and listening. Interviewing is an interpersonal process of asking and answering questions. An effective interview meets three criteria:

> "Interviewing is like ballroom dancing; to keep from stepping on each other's toes, you must lead and follow at the same time without the other person knowing."
>
> — ANONYMOUS

- It's *structured*. The interview is a planned conversation that includes an introduction, a body, and a conclusion.

- It's *goal oriented*. The planned conversation has a purpose. The goal of Nick's interview with the mayor was to obtain information. The goal of Lisa's interview with Brian was to review his job performance.

- It's *role directed*. The interview includes two roles—the interviewer and the interviewee. Usually, the primary role of the interviewer is to lead and facilitate the conversation by asking questions. The primary role of the interviewee is to answer questions. In most informal conversations, the talk time of two individuals is equal. In an interview, the talk time is unequal, with the interviewee usually talking 70 percent of the time and the interviewer talking only 30 percent of the time.[1]

In your professional life you will have an opportunity to be both an interviewer and the interviewee. When looking for a job, you will be the interviewee. When trying to get information for a news story to be published in a local magazine, you will be the interviewer. Many of the principles and skills we will be discussing in this chapter apply to both the interviewer and the interviewee. There are times, however, when a particular set of skills will be required for a particular role; those unique skills will be highlighted.

There are several different types of interviews. For example, an *information-gathering interview* is a focused, structured conversation whose goal is to seek out important information from another person. The goal of the structured conversation in a *job interview* is to assess the qualifications and skills of a person for employment. An *appraisal interview* is a conversation in which a supervisor or employer shares information with an employee about his or her job performance. If your goal is to sell a product or service, then you want to conduct a **persuasive interview**, which is a structured conversation intended to influence a person's attitudes, beliefs, or behaviors. For example, if you're selling wireless telephone services, you would want to ask the potential customer a series of questions in order to identify his or her needs and then demonstrate how your wireless phone services meet these needs. These various types of interviews will be discussed more thoroughly in Chapter 8.

Regardless of the type of interview, the five communication principles for leadership, which are illustrated in Figure 7.1, are important to the interview relationship. Through your use of these five principles, you will be able to effectively interview others as well as be interviewed by others.

Principle One: Be aware of your communication with yourself and others. Being aware of your interview goal and how to prepare and structure the interview enhances your ability to reach the goal. Also, having an awareness of what it means to be ethically responsible to your communication partner influences the communication that occurs during the interview.

Interview a form of oral interaction structured to achieve a goal; it often includes just two people (but can include more) who take turns speaking and listening.

Persuasive interview a structured conversation intended to influence a person's attitudes, beliefs, or behaviors.

Figure 7.1	Communication Principles for Leadership

Principle Two: Effectively use and interpret verbal messages. If you're the interviewer, the success of the interview depends on the type and quality of the questions you ask. If you're the interviewee, the success of the interview depends on how well you respond to questions. Regardless of the role, asking and responding to questions in a thoughtful and clear manner is critical.

Principle Three: Effectively use and interpret nonverbal messages. Since the interview is a relationship, it's important to manage the relational cues that are communicated nonverbally. For example, it's important to be punctual, to dress appropriately, and use firm handshakes and direct eye contact throughout the interview process.

Principle Four: Listen and respond thoughtfully to others. Since the interview is a goal-driven conversation, listening and responding are critical. In the interview process, active listening includes asking questions, paraphrasing, and taking notes. Responding includes letting the other person know you're listening by using nonverbal messages (attentive posture, head nods), as well as verbal ones ("I'm interested. Can you tell me more?")

Principle Five: Appropriately adapt messages to others. The interview process is like a ballroom dance that requires two partners to adapt to each other's moves. When the other person doesn't understand your question, you adapt by rephrasing the question. When the other person is hesitant to offer additional information, you adapt by probing. When the other person is silent, you adapt by paying attention to what the other person is *not* telling you.

Preparing the Interview

Unlike an ordinary conversation between two people, an interview is a planned conversation that needs to be prepared, which is the first stage of interviewing. Preparing an interview involves three skills: identifying the interview goal, identifying the appropriate person, and arranging the interview.

Identify the Interview Goal

Whether you're the interviewer or the interviewee, the interview has a goal. In fact, it has primary and secondary goals. The primary goals are obvious. If you're conducting an information-gathering interview, your goal is to obtain information. If you're interviewing for a job, your goal is to get the job. Although the primary goal is important and unique to the type of interview, the more important goals are the secondary goals, which fall into two types—task goals and relational goals—and are the same regardless of the interview type and whether you're the interviewer or interviewee. **Task goals** include asking and answering questions in a clear, concise, and thoughtful manner in order to acquire and convey appropriate information. **Relational goals** include using interpersonal skills so as to be perceived as interpersonally attractive and believable. Achieving the secondary task and relational goals allows you to reach your primary goal.

For example, if you're going for an employment interview, your primary goal is to get the job. Your secondary goal is to answer all of the interviewer's questions in a clear and concise manner that reveals how your educational background, job skills, and employment experiences meet the needs of the organization. Another task goal is to ask thoughtful questions of the interviewer that reveal your knowledge of the organization and your understanding of the organization's needs. Your relational goal is to demonstrate your interpersonal skills, such as your ability to listen carefully, self-disclose appropriately, and resolve conflict constructively, while also appearing open and approachable.

Identify the Appropriate Person

Much time is wasted when you interview the wrong person or when the wrong person interviews you. It's important to spend time in the preparation stage of the interview process identifying the appropriate person for the interview. Who will allow you to reach your interview goal? If you're preparing to conduct an information-gathering interview, then you need to know who has the information you need. If you're looking for a job, then you need to make sure you interview with the person who makes hiring decisions. If you're conducting a persuasive interview and trying to sell a potential client on a new product, you need to make sure you interview the person in an organization who is approved to make such decisions.

Here are a few suggestions for identifying the appropriate person for an interview:

Consult professional organizations and membership directories. Most organizations have a professional association and a directory of names and contact information that can help you identify the appropriate person. If you're interested in careers in training and development and want to conduct an information interview with a training and development practitioner, you might locate a practitioner through the American Society of Training and Development (ASTD), the professional association for men and women who work in the training and development business. You could consult the ASTD membership directory at http://www.astd.org/ASTD.

Use organizational websites. The Internet makes it much easier to locate appropriate individuals. If you're a sales rep for a pharmaceutical company and you need to identify a specific physician at a local hospital with whom to conduct a persuasive interview, you can use the Internet to find the hospital, the appropriate physician, and additional biographical information about the physician that will help you conduct a more effective persuasive interview.

Use personal contacts, acquaintances, and networks. Most people undervalue their personal networks—they don't think of them when they want to locate the appropriate person for an interview. It's important that you use both your primary and secondary networks. Your primary network is made up of your family and friends. Your secondary network includes your friends' friends. Your family members and your friends can connect you to their own personal and professional networks. This type of networking increases your chances of identifying the appropriate person for an interview.

Use your instructors. Another great way to locate the appropriate person is to ask your instructors. College and university instructors and professors are experts in their fields and have a number of important personal and professional contacts. Your instructors may be able to refer you to the appropriate person.

Call the organization directly. You can always contact the organization or office where you believe the appropriate person works and ask the receptionist for his or her assistance: "Can you put me in touch with the person who would be able to. . . ."

Arrange the Interview

If you're the interviewer, you need to arrange the interview, which includes arranging the time, location, and setting.

Task goals in an interview, asking and answering questions in a clear, concise, and thoughtful manner in order to convey appropriate information.

Relational goals in an interview, using interpersonal skills so as to be perceived as attractive and credible.

>>> **COMMUNICATION AND GLOBALIZATION** @ WORK

At the Switzerland-based international investment banking firm UBS, video conferencing and phone interviews have been used to help screen job candidates for about five years, says Anthony Brown, a managing director and head of human resources for the firm's New York office. If the job is in New York and involves working with the London office, for example, a phone interview or a videoconference with the applicant and those in the London office is much cheaper than flying the job candidate to London and enables UBS to save a considerable amount of money.[2]

Video Conference Interviews

According to Karen Friedman, a media and communication training consultant, although videoconferencing saves employers time and money, job applicants often are at a disadvantage and have a difficult time putting their best foot forward in such an interview.[3] Friedman, a former television reporter and anchor, suggests that companies need to prepare job candidates for a videoconference interview. "Tell the person you realize this isn't the same as a face-to-face interview and [he or she] isn't a media professional," Friedman says. She also suggests coaching applicants on where to look, how wide the video image will be, and what to do with their hands. Possible technical issues also should be discussed beforehand, and candidates should be reassured that it's perfectly acceptable for them to interrupt should they not be able to hear or should some other technical difficulty arise. Because technology-based interviews cannot convey an applicant's personality as well as face-to-face interviews, Friedman also recommends instructing job candidates to be as conversational as possible.

To learn more about the videoconference interview, consult the following website: www.shrm.org/hrmagazine/07March.

Telephone Interviews

Brad Karsh has conducted hundreds of phone interviews. He is the president of JobBound, an international career consulting company. In an article in *Advertising Age*, he discussed the many mistakes job candidates make during phone interviews.[4] According to Karsh, the biggest problem is that "people happen to sound quite boring; you lose a lot of personality when you talk on the phone. And when you add the fact that people tend to be more serious in an interview than in normal situations, the problem is compounded."

The telephone interview is the second step in the process for many recruiters. During a phone interview, interviewers can check out whether you are as good as you sound on paper, if you are articulate, and if you'd be a good person to have join the organization. Most importantly, a phone interview serves as a way to narrow down the pool to finalists and semifinalists. Many employers use telephone interviews when it is not practical to bring an international candidate to the office.

Telephone interviews can be especially challenging because it is difficult to gain rapport with the interviewer when you cannot see each other's body language. Good phone manners, clarity of speech, tone of voice, and the content of your answers increase in importance.

Few people get hired solely on the basis of a phone interview. The phone interview is a way for both the candidate and the interviewer to test the waters.

Here are a few of Karsh's suggestions for handling a telephone interview:

- Dress for the interview. You don't need to be dressed in a suit, but don't be sitting there in your pajamas. Wake up early, take a shower, and dress for the day.

- Warm up your voice. There's nothing worse than picking up the phone, saying "hello," and having your voice crack.

- Talk on a landline rather than a cell phone. Landlines are more dependable. You're less likely to drop a call when using a landline, and the reception tends to be clearer.

- Be animated and expressive. Get excited. Stand up, talk with your hands, and smile. Even though the interviewer cannot see your smile, the interviewer can hear it.

Schedule time. Before beginning the interview, have an idea of how much time will be needed to reach the interview goal and then let the person you will be interviewing know how much time will be needed. It's important to structure and conduct the interview so as to honor this time commitment. It's also important to ensure that the interview time fits into the rhythm of the interviewee's workday. For example, if you're conducting an information-gathering interview with a restaurant manager to assess the manager's needs, it's probably best to schedule the interview after the breakfast rush or during the mid-afternoon lull to avoid the lunch and dinner rush.

Identify location. Finding the appropriate location is another aspect of arranging an interview. Since effective interviewing requires an intense period of listening, it's important to find a location with as few distractions as possible. If you are conducting a performance appraisal interview or a health interview, you will want a location that ensures privacy, as such interviews can include conversations about sensitive and private information. If interviewees don't feel that their conversations are private, they may not divulge important and necessary information, thus preventing interviewers from reaching their goals.

Arrange physical setting. How the furniture is arranged for an interview communicates how the interview is going to take place. When interviewers sit behind their desks, they communicate power, status, and formality. When interviewers sit face to face with interviewees at a small table, they communicate equality, accessibility, and informality. The physical arrangement influences the tone of the interview. Some airport lounges have lavish conference rooms that may at first glance seem quite appropriate for interviews. But closer inspection reveals that these ornate and formal rooms are cold and impersonal. The long and wide conference table puts a physical barrier between interviewer and interviewee. To remedy this physical barrier, the interviewer and interviewee may decide to sit side by side. However, this physical arrangement makes it difficult to see each other. Setting up the room ahead of time while keeping in mind how the physical arrangement will influence the interview is an important aspect of arranging an interview.

RECAP: Preparing the Interview

Identify Interview Goal	Primary Interview Goals
	• Information-Gathering Interview: To seek out information
	• Job Interview: To assess a person's skills for employment or to obtain employment
	• Performance Appraisal Interview: To share information with an employee about job performance
	• Persuasive Interview: To influence a person's attitudes, beliefs, and behaviors
	Secondary Interview Goals
	• Task Goals: To ask and answer questions in a clear, concise, and thoughtful manner in order to acquire and convey appropriate information
	• Relational Goals: To use interpersonal skills to enhance perceptions of credibility and interpersonal attractiveness
Identify Appropriate Person	Identify the person who has the information needed or the person who makes decisions by consulting professional organizations, websites, personal contacts, and networks
Arrange the Interview	Schedule Time: Determine how much time is needed, inform the other person of the time commitment, and honor the time commitment
	Identify Location: Identify an appropriate place for the interview by determining the level of privacy needed
	Arrange Physical Setting: Ensure that the physical arrangement of the interview location communicates the level of power, status, and formality desired for the interview

Structuring the Interview

Having planned the interview, it's time to structure it, which is the second stage of interviewing. Structuring the interview is the responsibility of the interviewer, not the interviewee. Before you begin structuring the interview, it's important to understand the differences between structured and unstructured interviews and how the interview goal determines the amount of structure. Once you determine the amount of structure you need, you begin structuring the interview by identifying interview topics and writing and sequencing interview questions.

Understand Structured Versus Unstructured Interviews

Construction workers use scaffolding when they are working on the outside of a building. Scaffolding is a framework made up of poles and platforms that supports the workers and allows them to do their jobs. Interview structure is the framework, or scaffolding, that supports the interviewer and the interviewee. As illustrated in Figure 7.2, interview structure falls on a continuum from structured to unstructured. **Structured interviews are scripted and include a set of standard questions that are asked of every person who is interviewed. Unstructured interviews** are unscripted conversations that are unique to the individual being interviewed; they do not include a standard set of questions. Unstructured interviews allow an interviewer to probe and follow up on an interviewee's response to a question ("Tell me more about that experience," "Can you elaborate more on that issue?"), whereas structured interviews usually don't allow for this type of detour. Most interviews, however, are moderately structured and fall somewhere between the two polar opposites of this continuum. **Moderately structured interviews include elements of both structured and unstructured interviews.** Interviews with this type of structure include some scripted questions and the flexibility to deviate from the script if necessary.

There are advantages and disadvantages to both structured and unstructured interviews. Structured interviews ensure that all interviewees are treated in a consistent manner. They usually take less time and are easier for the interviewer to control; they require less skill. Another advantage to a structured interview is that because all interviewees are asked the same questions, it is easier to compare interviewee answers. The largest disadvantage of a structured interview is that interviewers have no flexibility to follow up or probe interviewees' comments that may reveal important information.

Although unstructured interviews are usually more difficult to control and take more time to complete, they often reveal valuable information that allows interviewers to reach their goals. For example, Kimberly is interested in managing her family's landscaping business and wants to find out what it's like to work with and manage family members. She conducts an information-gathering interview with Brad, who manages his family's restaurant. Rather than going into the interview with a structured set of questions, Kimberly simply asks, "What's it like to work in a family business?" Kimberly can then follow up with additional questions to explore Brad's responses in detail.

Conducting an unstructured interview requires more skill on the part of the interviewer. Interviewers must listen carefully to the interviewee's answers and then follow up with probing questions that they hope will get the interviewee to reveal important information. This type of listening and probing can be time consuming. Despite this disadvantage, the unstructured interview allows interviewers to take detours that often lead to important information that may never have been uncovered in a structured interview.

Structured interview a scripted interview that uses a set of standard questions that are asked of every person who is interviewed.

Unstructured interview an unscripted interview that is unique to the individual being questioned; it does not include a standard set of questions.

Moderately structured interview an interview that includes some scripted questions but allows the interviewer the flexibility to deviate from the script.

Figure 7.2 | **Continuum of Interview Structure**

STRUCTURED	UNSTRUCTURED
Scripted	Unscripted
Interactive	Transactional or Conversational
Standard Set of Questions	Questions Adapted to Interviewee

Identify Interview Topics

When structuring an interview, interviewers need to identify the interview topics. An **interview topic** is a standard theme that is explored with a particular category of questions that are asked during the interview. Each type of interview has a standard set of topics; for each topic, there is a set of questions that focus on it. For example, when news reporters and journalists conduct information-gathering interviews, they usually structure their interview questions around the five "W" question topics: Who, What, Where, When, and Why. For example, with the "Who" interview topic, an interviewer might ask Who was involved? Who are they? Who do they belong to? Who do they want to influence?

When conducting a job interview with a job applicant, an interviewer usually develops and arranges questions by employment-related topics: Education, Job Skills, Prior Work Experience,

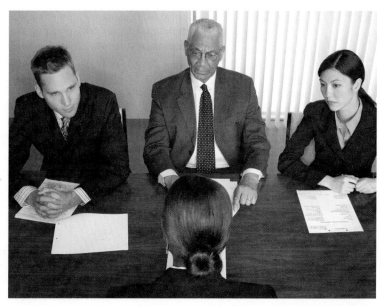

Interviewers must understand the structure of the interview they're conducting and identify topics and questions appropriate for that structure.

Career Path and Goals. For each of these interview topics there is a set of specific questions that relate to the topic. For example, when focusing on the topic of Education, the interviewer might ask interviewees questions about where they went to school, their degree programs, and their major fields of study. Interviewees, too, have a set of questions to ask the interviewer that are structured and arranged to cover such interview topics as Job Requirements, Manager Expectations, Advancement Opportunities, and Salary and Benefits. Such questions help interviewees reach their own interview goal: to appear competent, articulate, and ambitious. For example, an interviewee who asks an interviewer about the opportunities that new employees have for advancement within the organization reveals his or her level of motivation and ambition.

When managers conduct appraisal interviews, they usually structure and arrange questions by the following interview topics: Employee's Self-Appraisal, Performance Gaps, Causes of Performance Gaps, Ways to Reduce Performance Gaps. The manager may begin by asking a set of questions that tap into the topic of Employee's Self-Appraisal, such as "Tell me how you think you're doing in your new position," and "Do you consider yourself to be reaching your performance goals?" Answers to these questions allow the manager to gauge the questions to ask when exploring the other interview topics. If an employee says that she's reaching her performance goals in her new position, the interviewer might use this response to explore a new line of questioning focusing on teamwork. For example, the interviewer might ask, "What role did the team play in helping you reach your performance goals?"

Whether you're structuring an information-gathering interview, job interview, appraisal interview, or persuasive interview, you begin the structuring process by identifying interview topics that will allow you to reach your interview goal. Once you have identified the interview topics, it's time to begin writing the interview questions that will allow you to obtain the information you need about each of the identified topics.

Write Interview Questions

Writing effective interview questions is another communication skill that interviewers are responsible for when structuring an interview. We will examine four major categories of interview questions: open questions, closed questions, probing questions, and hypothetical questions.

Open questions. An **open question** is broad and unstructured and allows the respondent considerable freedom to determine the amount and kind of information she or he will provide. Most open questions are either questions of value, questions of process, or questions of policy. *Questions of value* ask respondents to discuss what they consider to be important. *Questions of process* ask respondents to talk about how they might do something. *Questions of policy* ask respondents to talk about what they might change or propose.

Interview topic a standard theme that is explored with a particular category of questions that are asked during an interview.

Open question an interview question that is broad and unstructured and allows the respondent considerable freedom to determine the amount and kind of information she or he will provide.

For example, suppose you're conducting an information-gathering interview with the new president of the university for an article to appear in the school newspaper. Here are some open questions you might use in this type of interview:

- Question of Value: What makes an *excellent* university?
- Question of Process: *How* do you lead?
- Question of Policy: What changes *should* be made to improve the university?

The italicized word in each of the above questions is a clue to the question type. Questions of value usually include a word that gets at the worth of something (such as *excellent*). Answers to value questions usually reveal what a respondent considers to be important or the respondent's priorities. Questions of process usually begin with *How*, which encourages the respondent to discuss a series of actions. Answers to process questions usually reveal the steps a respondent would take to accomplish a particular goal. Questions of policy usually include the word *should*. Answers to policy questions can reveal the actions the respondent wants to take in the future or changes the respondent would like to make.

Here are some questions that tap into values, processes, and policies and that might be asked of an applicant in a job interview.

- Question of Value: *What* are you looking for in a company?
- Question of Process: *How* do you resolve conflict with co-workers?
- Question of Policy: What *should* employers do to motivate employees?

Because open questions encourage an interviewee to share information almost without restriction, they are useful in determining opinions, values, and perspectives. Open questions are most appropriate in less structured interviews when time is not limited.

Closed questions. A **closed question** is one that limits the range of possible responses and requires a simple, direct, and brief answer. Consider a personal trainer at a gym who is talking to someone who is considering purchasing a gym membership. The trainer conducts an informal persuasive interview to help the potential customer identify his needs and goals and to convince him that the gym can meet those goals. The trainer might ask a number of closed questions:

- What is your weight?
- How many complete meals do you eat daily?
- How many times per week do you exercise?

All of these questions can be answered with direct and brief responses. Some closed questions allow you to select from a range of responses:

How would you classify your physical condition?

A. Very Good

B. Good

C. Average

D. Poor

E. Very Poor

Closed questions enable an interviewer to gather specific information because they restrict interviewees' freedom to express personal views or elaborate on responses. They also allow an interviewer to ask a greater number of questions in a limited amount of time. Closed questions are most appropriate in structured interviews.

Probing questions. A **probing question** is one that encourages the interviewee to clarify or elaborate on partial or superficial responses and that usually directs the discussion in a particular direction. The use of probing questions is one way to tell an experienced from a novice interviewer. The novice interviewer sticks to scripted questions and doesn't deviate from the script regardless of the interviewee's response to a question. The experienced interviewer, however, carefully listens for ways to deviate from the scripted questions to get additional relevant and precise information from an interviewee.

Closed question an interview question that limits the range of possible responses and requires a simple, direct, and brief answer.

Probing question an interview question that encourages the interviewee to clarify or elaborate on partial or superficial responses and that usually directs the discussion in a particular direction.

The following paragraphs describe four of the more popular types of probes and ways to use them.[5]

A *nudging probe* encourages the respondent to continue responding to a question; it nudges the person. Interviewers use the nudging probe when they feel an interviewee's response is incomplete. The nudging probe is usually a single word or a very short phrase, such as

- Go ahead . . .
- Please continue.
- And then . . . ?
- So . . . ?

A *clearinghouse probe* is used when interviewers want to make sure that they have exhausted the questioning on a particular topic. Because interviewers sometimes don't ask important questions, clearinghouse probes encourage interviewees to volunteer information that may provide a more complete answer to an asked or unasked question. Following are examples of clearinghouse probes:

- Is there anything else that you would like to add about this issue?
- Is there anything that we have not covered that you consider important?
- What question have I not asked that you want to answer?

An *informational probe* is used when an interviewer wants the interviewee to elaborate on a response in order to clarify a point. Here are a few examples of information probes:

- To clarify, can you tell me more about that concern?
- What do you mean when you say . . . ?
- How did you respond to that situation?

A *reflective probe* is used when an interviewer wants to ensure that he or she understands the interviewee's response to a question or a series of questions. Reflective probes are a way to resolve uncertainty. Here are a few examples of reflective probes:

- Are you saying that . . . ?
- This is what I hear you saying . . .
- You think, then, that in this situation you would . . .
- Am I correct in assuming that you believe that . . . ?

Hypothetical questions. A **hypothetical question** is one that asks for an interviewee's reaction to an imaginary emotion-arousing or value-laden situation in order to gauge the person's likely reaction in a real situation. For example, Gerri is a member of the human resources team at a large publishing company. She is interviewing people to assess the workplace environment. During her information-gathering interview with Chance, an employee in the information technology department, she asks the following questions:

- Would you want your son or daughter to work for this company? Why or why not?
- If you were the president of this company, what five changes would you make immediately and why?

Hypothetical questions are also used during job interviews to find out how potential new employees might respond to unique circumstances.

- You believe one of your co-workers is stealing from the company, but you're not certain. What would you do?
- Your co-workers continue to look at pornography on the Internet after you've told them that this makes you uncomfortable. If you discuss the problem with your manager, you know that your co-workers will make things uncomfortable for you. How would you handle this situation?

Hypothetical question a question that asks for an interviewee's reaction to an imaginary emotion-arousing or value-laden situation in order to gauge the person's likely response in a real situation.

RECAP: Writing Interview Questions

Question Type	Definition	Sample Questions
Open	A question that is broad and unstructured and that allows the respondent considerable freedom to determine the amount and kind of information she or he will provide.	• What are you looking for in a company? • How do you lead others? • How should managers motivate employees?
Closed	A question that limits the range of possible responses and requires a simple, direct, and brief answer.	• Are you willing to relocate? • How many times have you missed work? • How many meals do you eat daily?
Probing	A question that encourages the interviewee to clarify or elaborate on partial or superficial responses and that usually directs the discussion in a particular direction.	• Tell me more about your concern. • What do you mean when you say . . . ? • And then what happened?
Hypothetical	A question that asks for an interviewee's reaction to an imaginary emotion-arousing or value-laden situation in order to gauge the person's likely reactions in a real situation.	• You believe that one of your co-workers is stealing from the company, but you're not certain. What would you do? • If you were to become the manager of this unit, what five changes would you make and why?

Sequence Interview Questions

Open, closed, probing, and hypothetical questions may be used in any combination, as long as their sequence is thoughtfully planned. An **interview schedule** is a guide that lists all of the questions and follow-up probes to be used in an interview so that the interviewer can sequence interview questions. An interview schedule serves as the interviewer's script. Depending on the goals of the interview, interview questions may be arranged into one of three basic sequences: funnel, inverted funnel, or tunnel.

Funnel sequence. A questioning sequence that begins with broad, open questions and proceeds toward more closed questions is a **funnel sequence**. Using a funnel sequence allows an interviewee to express views and feelings without restrictions, at least early in the interview. For example, Seth, a senior in college, is conducting an information-gathering interview with a corporate event planner, because he thinks he would like to pursue event planning as a career. Seth structures his interview using the funnel sequence of questions shown in Figure 7.3.

Seth's first question is an open-ended one about the rewards of the profession. He becomes a bit more specific in his second question by asking about the two different types of event planning. With his third question, he narrows the focus further by asking about only corporate events. His fourth question asks about specific steps the event planner took to get his job in corporate event planning. Finally, Seth's fifth and final question is a closed question that requires a yes-or-no response. With the funnel sequence, the interview begins with open questions and the increasingly closed questions serve as probes.

Inverted funnel sequence. A questioning sequence that begins with closed questions and proceeds to more open questions is an **inverted funnel sequence**. Using the inverted funnel sequence encourages the interviewee to answer questions quickly. It's an easy way to begin an interview because the questions require only brief responses or descriptions. For example, Jamie manages a temp agency and is responsible for interviewing people to find

Interview schedule a guide that lists all of the questions and follow-up probes to be used in an interview so that the interviewer can sequence questions.

Funnel sequence a questioning sequence that begins with broad, open questions and proceeds toward more closed questions.

Inverted funnel sequence a questioning sequence that begins with closed questions and proceeds to more open questions.

Figure 7.3	Funnel Sequence

1. What is it about event planning that you find rewarding?

2. How does corporate event planning differ from planning nonprofit events?

3. What types of corporate events do you plan?

4. What steps did you take to become a corporate event planner?

5. If you had it to do all over again, would you be an event planner?

out their job skills and work-related experiences so that she can place them in jobs that fit their skills and experiences. Figure 7.4 illustrates how Jamie structures her interview questions using the inverted funnel sequence.

Jamie's first two questions are closed questions that require only brief responses. Jamie's third, fourth, and fifth questions are more open-ended questions that require greater elaboration. These open-ended questions are intended to get interviewees to reveal not only their attitudes and values, but also how they might handle a particular situation at work. With the inverted-funnel sequence, the interview begins with closed questions and the open-ended questions serve as probes.

Tunnel sequence. A questioning sequence that uses a combination of open and closed questions to gather a large amount of information in a short amount of time is a **tunnel sequence,** With this type of questioning sequence, no probing or follow-up questions are asked. The interviewer is interested in breadth rather than depth of responses. Rather than using an information probe ("Tell me more about that") or a hypothetical question to get at more detailed information (more depth), the interviewer simply moves to the next open or closed question to capture more breadth (more topics) during an interview. Again, the reason for using the tunnel sequence is that it allows an interviewer to gather a lot of general information in a limited amount of time. For example, Kole is a wardrobe

Figure 7.4	Inverted Funnel Sequence

1. Are you seeking part-time or full-time employment?

2. Can you relocate?

3. What computer skills do you have?

4. What motivates you to do a good job?

5. How do you go about solving problems?

Tunnel sequence a questioning sequence that uses a combination of open and closed questions to gather a large amount of information in a short amount of time.

RECAP: Sequencing Interview Questions

Sequence Type	Description	Reason for Using
Funnel Sequence	A questioning sequence that begins with broad, open questions and proceeds toward more closed questions.	Allows interviewees to express views and feelings without restrictions early in the interview.
Inverted Funnel Sequence	A questioning sequence that begins with closed questions and proceeds to more open questions.	Encourages interviewees to answer questions quickly so as to "jump start" the interview.
Tunnel Sequence	A questioning sequence that includes a combination of open and closed questions without any probing or follow-up questions.	Allows interviewers to gather a lot of information in a limited amount of time—to "tunnel through" a topic.

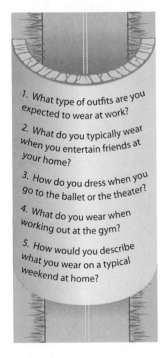

Figure 7.5 | Tunnel Sequence

1. What type of outfits are you expected to wear at work?

2. What do you typically wear when you entertain friends at your home?

3. How do you dress when you go to the ballet or the theater?

4. What do you wear when working out at the gym?

5. How would you describe what you wear on a typical weekend at home?

consultant at an upscale department store. His goal is to persuade Leticia to let him pull together a wardrobe for her. He interviews Leticia to get a better idea of her wardrobe needs by asking the questions in Figure 7.5.

All of Kole's questions focus on a different aspect of Leticia's lifestyle and her wardrobe needs. The questions are a way to "tunnel through" her lifestyle; they allow Kole to assess Leticia's needs quickly so that he can pull together a wardrobe that Leticia will purchase. Kole's interview goal is to capture the breadth of Leticia's fashion needs rather than to learn about them in depth. Again, with the tunnel sequence, the interview consists of a series of open and closed questions that capture as much breadth (the greatest number of topics) as possible. The interview doesn't include probing questions, which usually capture depth or details.

Conducting the Interview

Conducting the interview is the third stage. Although an interview differs from an ordinary conversation in being planned and structured, in one way an interview *is* similar to a conversation with a friend. Most conversations have three parts. First, you greet someone to open the conversation. Second, you conduct the conversation, which communication scholars refer to as "processing the body" of the conversation. Third, you bring the conversation to a close. Interviews have these same three parts. Although it is the interviewer's responsibility to structure and conduct the interview, it's important that interviewees become aware of how interviews are conducted so they know what to expect in the opening segment, the body, and the closing segment of the interview conversation.

Open the Interview

The opening of any interview is crucial, because it sets the stage for the interview. The opening creates a climate that influences how the interview will unfold. Although most openings include both task and relational messages, they're more focused on relational messages. **Task messages** focus on the content of the interview and might include information about how the interview will be structured and how long the interview will take. **Relational messages** focus on building rapport and establishing a relationship; they're more personal. Asking the other person how she or he is doing, commenting on the weather, or discussing plans for the weekend are examples of relational messages.

Task messages messages that focus on the content of an interview.

Relational messages messages that build rapport and are aimed at establishing relationships.

Opening the interview includes three skills: making a positive first impression, establishing rapport, and clarifying the goals of the interview.

Make a positive first impression. First impressions are important, especially in interview situations; interviewers have been shown to treat interviewees more positively during an interview if their first impression of the interviewee is favorable.[6] In addition to being on time and being appropriately dressed for the interview, another way to make a positive first impression is to use a firm handshake: Research on handshaking etiquette and business protocol strongly suggests that a handshake has a meaningful impact on people's first impressions of others and how they evaluate them.[7] Specifically, a firm handshake is associated with positive personality and communication traits, whereas a limp handshake is associated with negative personality and communication traits. A firm handshake is characterized by completeness of grip (palm to palm), moderate strength (not too weak, not too strong), a moderate amount of energy, and moderate length (not too brief, not too long) and is accompanied by direct eye contact.[8]

Establish rapport. Developing a connection or an emotional bond makes the interview process more comfortable and enjoyable for both the interviewee and the interviewer. One way to establish rapport is to initiate conversations about current events, sports, film, or local items of interest. Linguist and communication researcher Deborah Tannen refers to these polite conversational starters as rapport talk. According to Tannen, rapport talk "greases the wheels" of a conversation and enhances liking for each other.[9] Both interviewer and interviewee can establish rapport by listening actively to the other, using nonverbal responsive behaviors, and by asking appropriate follow-up questions.

Clarify interview goals. Finally, it's important to open the interview by clarifying the goals of the interview. To do this, the interviewer needs to explicitly state the purpose of the interview; for example, "The purpose of our interview today is to collect information about your job skills and work experiences." It's also important for the interviewer to clarify for the interviewee how the interview will be structured. An interviewer might say, "I'll begin with a set of questions about your job skills. Then I would like to discuss your accomplishments in your current position. Finally, I would like to answer your questions." Finally, it's considerate for the interviewer to inform the interviewee of how long the interview will take.

Interviewers treat interviewees more positively if they are on time and appropriately dressed for the interview. An interviewee's firm handshake, accompanied by direct eye contact, also contributes to a strong first impression.

Nonverbal

Verbal

>>> COMMUNICATION ETHICS @ WORK

Marilee Jones, former Dean of Admissions at the Massachusetts Institute of Technology, was known as a guru of the movement to tame the college admissions frenzy. In spring 2007 she admitted that she had fabricated her own educational credentials, and she resigned after nearly three decades at M.I.T. Officials of the institution said she did not have even an undergraduate degree.[10]

"I misrepresented my academic degrees when I first applied to M.I.T. 28 years ago and did not have the courage to correct my resume when I applied for my current job or at any time since," Ms. Jones said in a statement posted on the M.I.T. website. The position she was applying for all those years ago did not have a degree requirement, but Ms. Jones explained she was trying to impress her potential employer.

Although researchers agree that making a positive impression is important, they acknowledge that some people manipulate how others perceive them.[11] During the interview, some interviewees become someone they're not in order to reach their interview goal. Can a first impression be managed so carefully that it doesn't accurately reflect a person's true character and identity? How is this a problem?

To summarize, interview openings are usually more focused on relational messages than on task messages. Your goal when opening an interview is to make a positive first impression, establish rapport with the other person, and, if you're the interviewer, to clarify the goals of the interview.

Process the Body of the Interview

Once the interviewer has made efforts to put the interviewee at ease during the opening of the interview, the interviewer begins processing the body of the interview. This part of the interview tends to focus more on task-related messages than on relational messages. The body of the interview is where the interviewer and the interviewee ask each other questions. As noted earlier in the chapter, interviewing experts suggest that participation in most interviews (with the exception of persuasive interviews) ought to be distributed in roughly a 70:30 ratio, with the interviewee doing most of the talking. We'll first discuss the interviewer's role in processing the body of the interview and then the interviewee's role.

Interviewer's role. The interviewer is responsible for processing the body of the interview by accomplishing several communication tasks. The interviewer begins by asking the prepared questions (open, closed, probing, hypothetical) from the interview schedule while following the questioning sequence (funnel, inverted funnel, tunnel).

Since the primary goal of an interview is to obtain information from the interviewee, it's important for the interviewer to listen actively to the interviewee. Listening actively means paying attention not only to what interviewees say but also to how they say it. Inexperienced interviewers sometimes become so distracted by keeping track of how much time they have or by thinking ahead to the next question that they fail to listen to interviewees' responses to questions.

The interviewer is also responsible for keeping the interview focused by controlling the breadth and depth of the questioning. If the goal is to obtain a lot of information on a variety of topics in a limited amount of time, then the interviewer is going for breadth (range of topics) and not depth (details of a single topic). If the goal is to probe one particular idea, event, or episode, then the interviewer will focus on depth by probing the interviewee's responses to questions.

It's important to keep a record of the interview. An interviewer does this either by recording the interview or by taking notes during the interview, or both. If you're going to record the interview, you must get the interviewee's permission before you begin. Note taking must be done carefully. If you spend too much time taking notes, you may miss important information and the interviewee may perceive you as disrespectful.

Another important task for the interviewer is to answer the interviewee's questions. Anticipate what these questions might be and be prepared to answer them clearly and concisely. Finally, it's important for the interviewer to keep the interview on schedule. Being conscious of the interviewee's time is an effective way of communicating respect for the person.

Interviewee's role. The interviewee is responsible for processing the body of the interview by accomplishing three important tasks. The first is to listen actively, which is one way to impress an interviewer. One of the authors of this book used to conduct a number of interviews each year when he worked for a large corporation. He was surprised to learn how ineffective interviewees were at listening—they would answer questions that he hadn't asked! Carefully listen to the question and before responding, make sure you understand by paraphrasing the question: "This is what I hear you asking . . . Is that correct?" This ensures that you're not answering questions that were not asked. It also demonstrates a communication skill that many working professionals value.

Interviewees also need to provide thoughtful and clear responses. Many people are not comfortable with silence, and this discomfort creates a natural tendency to fill the silent void by responding immediately to an interviewer's question rather than taking a few moments to reflect on the question. When you begin responding too quickly, your responses may not be as thoughtful or as clear as you'd like. Thoughtful interview questions require thoughtful responses. Become comfortable with a few seconds of silence and mentally compose your response to an interview question so that your responses are meaningful.

Communication researcher Mary Mino found that interviewers evaluate not only *what* interviewees say but also *how* they say it. Interviewers perceived interviewees to be sincere and intelligent if their responses were thoughtful (the *what*). Also, interviewers perceived interviewees as outgoing, assertive, enthusiastic, emotionally stable, and creative if their responses were delivered clearly (the *how*). Clear responses are those in which the interviewee uses appropriate articulation (no mumbling or slurring), speaks at an appropriate speed (not too fast or slow), and uses appropriate pauses and phrasing.[12] Pauses signal the end of one idea and the beginning of a new idea; clarity is achieved when you use pauses to punctuate your thoughts, just as you use periods and commas when you write.

Finally, although in most interviewing situations it's the interviewer who asks the questions, it's also important for interviewees to ask appropriate questions. At some point most interviewers will ask the interviewee, "Do you have any questions for me?" Appropriate questions are those that reflect positively on the interviewee. For example, Audrey is interviewing for a job as a sales manager for an upscale hotel chain. During her interview she mentions that she is aware that the chain has received numerous prestigious awards for "service excellence" from travel magazines and that the company will be adding hotels on the west coast. Audrey asks, "What makes your hotels different from other hotels?" and "Are there advancement opportunities on the west coast for interested employees?" These questions show the interviewer that Audrey has prepared herself for the job interview by researching the company's background. Questions that demonstrate preparedness reflect positively on job candidates.[13]

Appropriate questions are those that help the interviewee reach his or her interview goal. For example, Jade manages a customer service call center for a large computer manufacturer. Throughout the year, she has reduced the amount of sick leave her employees have taken. Unfortunately, during her performance appraisal interview, Tony, her supervisor, does not ask her about sick time. Since he did not ask her about this important issue, Jade asks, "Tony, according to the vice president of human resources, the company has been paying out too much money in sick time and this hurts the company's productivity and bottom line. Is reducing the number of sick days taken by employees still a priority?" Tony answers, "Yes. How are your sick leave numbers?" Jade then answers the question with a report detailing how she has reduced sick leave. This allows her to bring to her supervisor's attention an important achievement and to demonstrate her responsible approach to her job.

"Your resume states that you've worked with 2 presidents, won the Nobel Prize and climbed Mt. Everest. That's all fine and dandy, but how are you at telemarketing?"

www.cartoonstock.com

Close the Interview

Like opening the interview, closing the interview tends to focus more on relational rather than task-related messages. Closing the interview requires four tasks: review and summarize the interview, encourage continued friendly relations, discuss the next step, and exchange thank yous.

Summarize the interview. A primary function of the conclusion of an interview is to summarize the interview. Both the interviewer and the interviewee should be aware of and agree on what happened during the interview. To ensure understanding and agreement, the interviewer needs to summarize the highlights of the discussion and ask for any clarification. Comments such as "Here is what I believe we accomplished today during our interview . . . . Do you agree?" or "Let me take a few minutes to summarize our interview . . . . What clarifications are needed?" help the interviewer and the interviewee review the highlights of the interview.

Encourage friendly relations. Another function of the conclusion is to encourage friendly relations. The rapport established during the opening of the interview needs to be threaded throughout the interview all the way through the conclusion. Because not all interviews are positive experiences for interviewees (as when a manager conducts a performance appraisal with an employee who is not performing up to expectations), it's important to maintain the relationship. Comments such as "I'm glad we had a chance to talk about this problem" or "Thank you for sharing and listening" enable both parties to feel that they have had a positive and productive interview.

Discuss the next step.   Have you ever left an interview wondering, "Now what?" All interviews, regardless of the type, need to be closed by discussing the next step. For example, if you're conducting an information-gathering interview to find out what someone likes and dislikes about his or her chosen profession because you're interested in a similar career, the next step may be to ask the person to email you names of other individuals whom you may want to interview. If you're conducting an appraisal interview with an employee who is not performing his or her job well, then the next step is to inform the employee of the behaviors that need to be changed or modified and schedule a follow-up meeting. The next step after a job interview is to inform the applicant when decisions will be made and how applicants will be notified.

Exchange thank yous.   The final task in closing an interview is to exchange thank yous. Interviewing requires another person's time, and in the business and professional setting, time is a limited resource. Linda Kaplan Thaler and Robin Koval, authors of *The Power of Nice,* argue that being nice (remembering names, saying thank you) is an undervalued habit.[14] Thaler and Koval attribute the success of their New York ad agency to their being civil to their clients. Although saying thank you is quite easy and is a matter of courtesy and common sense, it is not done enough, according to these authors.

Although closing an interview requires some task-related messages, the bulk of the messages have a relational focus. Without appropriate closure, interview participants leave the interview with questions and uncertainty. To ensure that this doesn't occur, interview participants need to review and summarize the interview, encourage continued friendly relations, discuss the next step, and exchange thank yous.

RECAP: Conducting the Interview

Interview Steps	Communication Skills
Open the Interview	Make a positive impression
	Establish rapport
	Clarify interview goals
Process the Body of the Interview	Interviewer's role
	• Ask questions
	• Listen actively
	• Control breadth and depth of questioning
	• Take notes
	• Answer interviewee questions
	• Monitor time
	Interviewee's role
	• Listen actively
	• Provide thoughtful and clear responses
	• Ask appropriate questions
Close the Interview	Summarize the interview
	Encourage friendly relations
	Discuss the next step
	Exchange thank yous

Listening and Responding During the Interview

Listening and responding during the interview is the fourth stage of interviewing. You can prepare the interview, write and structure the interview questions, and conduct the interview by asking appropriate questions, and still the interview seems clumsy and awkward. Good interviewers know how to take part in the dance that is an interview and, in particular, how to lead the dance. Put simply, they don't always follow a canned script or interview schedule. Remember, an interview is a structured conversation in which both the interviewer and the interviewee ask and answer questions; an interview involves a certain give and take. One communication principle that will make your dancing more elegant is to listen and respond appropriately during the interview. Appropriate listening and responding prevents us from stepping on each other's toes. Although we discussed listening and responding extensively in Chapter 4, it deserves another mention here as a fundamental principle of interviewing.

Listen Effectively

As mentioned in Chapter 4, effective listening requires three steps: Stop, Look, and Listen. The following section discusses these important listening skills as they pertain to interviewing.

Stop. Because interviewing requires a great deal of focused attention on the other person, it's important that both the interviewer and the interviewee eliminate as much literal and psychological noise as possible. Here are a few strategies for turning off competing messages.

- Select an appropriate interview location that will minimize literal noise. The lobby of a busy convention hotel is probably not the most appropriate place for an interview. Instead, find a more secluded and private location.
- Silence cell phones, pagers, and other communication devices.
- Inform others that you don't want to be interrupted during the interview.
- Arrive early for the interview to give yourself time to mentally prepare and to review your notes and questions.

Look. A part of interview dancing is being able to detect where a person is going in a conversation. At times, interviewers and interviewees may wonder: "Am I talking too much?" "Am I talking too little?" "Am I answering the questions in the manner she prefers?" "Am I on the right track?" Many of these questions swirling around our heads while interviewing can be answered by carefully looking at the other person's nonverbal behaviors. As an interviewee, it's important to pay attention to the interviewer's nonverbal regulatory behaviors, the cues that help control the interaction and flow of communication between people. If you're taking too long to answer a question, interviewers may use their hands to signal you to speed up. If you're talking too quickly, they might use their hands to signal you to slow down. If you're not answering the question appropriately, interviewers may use vocalic interrupters, such as "I . . ." or "uh . . ." to signal that they want to clarify the question or ask it in a different way.

It's also important to read between the lines during an interview. Listening with the ears (paying attention to the verbal messages) allows you to capture the content of a message; "listening" with the eyes (paying attention to the nonverbal messages) allows you to capture the relational aspects of a message. Listening with your eyes gives you the opportunity to see the other person's eyes, facial expression, posture, and hand gestures. These nonverbal behaviors may add to or alter the meaning of verbal messages. Listening with the eyes allows us to better regulate the give and take that takes place during an interview.

Listen. During an interview, it's important that both the interviewer and the interviewee listen for the major ideas and for the details. For example, during a job interview, the interviewer might ask job candidates to describe some of their major accomplishments and then follow up with probing questions that get at more detailed information about each accomplishment. In order to get a more complete picture of the candidates' accomplishments, the interviewer must connect the major accomplishments with the details that led

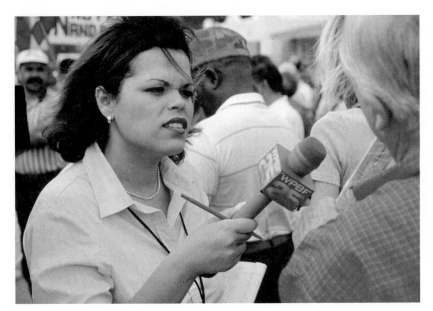

Listening with the eyes, which helps regulate the give and take of an interview, can benefit both the interviewer and the interviewee.

up to the accomplishments. (Chapter 4 listed and explained some of the listening skills that enable people to make these important connections.)

Respond Appropriately

Responding appropriately to the other person is another way to enhance the interview dance. Responding complements the listening process in two ways.[15] First, responsive messages validate and affirm the person who is speaking. Second, verbal and nonverbal responsiveness allows you to gauge whether the other person understands what you're saying. It's important for interviewers to look for and recognize these important feedback cues and then adapt their communication accordingly.

Interviewing Responsibilities

Our fifth and final interviewing stage is understanding the responsibilities of both the interviewer and interviewee. Since interviewing is a structured oral interaction in which important information is exchanged, and since decisions are made based on this information, it's important that you communicate in an ethical manner. Whether you're the interviewer or the interviewee, you have a responsibility to ensure that the interview is conducted in an ethical manner.

As we noted in Chapter 2, ethics are the beliefs, values, and moral principles by which we determine what is right and wrong. One way to better understand ethical communication is to examine unethical communication. Unethical communication manipulates listeners, restricts listeners' choices, and contains false information. In the interview context, both interviewers and interviewees have been known to engage in unethical communication. In fact, one study conducted by Ward Howell International, Inc., an executive headhunting firm, found that more than one in four executives reported that in the previous year, their organizations had hired employees whose job qualifications, educational credentials, or salary histories had been misrepresented during the interview process.[16]

Although some types of interviews are subject to specific ethical guidelines unique to those types of interviews (see Chapter 8), all interviewers and interviewees, regardless of interview type, should adhere to the following basic ethical principles:

- Don't manipulate the other person.
- Don't restrict the other person's choices or answers to questions.
- Don't convey false or misleading information to the other person.

The following section discusses communication strategies that both interviewers and interviewees can use to ensure that interviews are ethical.

Interviewer Responsibilities

There are several things an interviewer needs to do in order to interview another person in an ethical manner.

State your purpose in advance. One way to avoid manipulating the interviewee is to state clearly and in advance what you, as the interviewer, need and want from the interviewee. For example, have you ever answered your door to find someone who wants to interview you about the last time you cleaned your carpets? If you're not careful, this person will end up in your living room cleaning your carpets with a new line of steam cleaners that you can purchase for "a low monthly fee." If you're like most people, you resent this type of persuasive interview and you feel manipulated. A more ethical approach would be for the salesperson to first state his name, the company he represents, and the purpose for his visit.

Allow the interviewee to make uncoerced responses.   Because there is a power differential in many interview situations—the person conducting the interview has more power than the person being interviewed—it is important for the interviewer to avoid coercing or influencing the interviewee to answer a question he or she would prefer not to answer or to respond in a manner that would be against his or her will. For example, during a performance appraisal interview, your interviewer puts you in an awkward position by asking you about another employee's work performance. A more ethical approach would be to ask whether other employees' job performance affects your job performance. This question is more general and doesn't box you into a corner. According to communication researchers Steven Ralston and William Kirkwood, ethical interviewing occurs when interviewers equalize the power by allowing interviewees the freedom to respond without the threat of negative consequences.[17]

Ask unbiased questions.   Another way to make sure your communication is ethical during an interview is to avoid using biased, or **leading, questions**, which suggest (implicitly, and sometimes even explicitly) the expected or desired answer. An interviewer using a leading question leads the interviewee toward a particular answer by making "it easier or more tempting for the respondent to give one answer than another."[18] For example, during an employment interview, an interviewer might ask, "I'm assuming that you're willing to relocate, is that correct?" A more ethical way to ask this important question would be "If this job were to require you to move to a new city, how willing would you be to relocate, on a scale from 1 (completely unwilling to relocate) to 10 (eager to relocate)?" This question doesn't make an assumption about moving or force the interviewee into answering yes or no, but instead allows the interviewee to choose from a range of responses. Put simply, this type of unbiased question gives the interviewee the opportunity to make a free, uncoerced response.

Avoid unlawful questions.   There are a number of questions that it is illegal to ask during interviews, especially job interviews. The following interview questions are considered unlawful and interviewers should not be asking interviewees these questions:[19]

- How old are you?
- What religion do you practice?
- Are you married? Divorced?
- Do you have a family? Do you intend to have a family?
- What is your race?
- What is your sexual orientation?
- What is your national origin/ethnicity/ancestry?
- Are you a citizen of the United States? (Although this information is important for an interviewer to know when seeking an employee to work in the United States, the question cannot be asked in this manner. Instead, the interviewer needs to ask, "Are you legally authorized to work in the United States?")
- Are you disabled or handicapped? (Again, because the answer to this question is important for some job descriptions, interviewers need to get the answer by asking a lawful question: "Are you able to perform the essential functions of this job without accommodation?")
- Have you been arrested? (Unless the interviewee is applying for a security sensitive position, this question is unlawful.)
- Have your wages ever been garnished?

Convey honest, accurate information.   To make sure that interviewees can make decisions that are in their best interests, it's important to be honest about the information you present during the interview and to avoid intentionally withholding information from the interviewee. For example, during a job interview, a candidate asks when the position is going to be filled. Knowing that the new job has not been approved by the vice president of human resources, the interviewer says, "We hope to extend an offer soon." This statement is misleading because the interviewer is intentionally withholding important information. It is the

Leading question a question that suggests either explicitly or implicitly the answer expected.

interviewer's responsibility to explain to the interviewee that she cannot give an exact date when the position will be filled because the job has not yet been approved.

Another important aspect of conveying honest information is keeping promises. If an interviewer says he plans to notify all job candidates on Friday about the status of their interviews, then he must do so—it's an ethical responsibility. At times, interviewers get caught up in the excitement of the interview conversation and make promises they know they cannot keep. For example, a job candidate mentions during an interview that the pay doesn't meet her salary expectations. Because the interviewer wants to hire the candidate, she promises her that the starting salary will be increased prior to her start date. This is an unethical interviewing practice because the interviewer knows that she cannot keep her promise but uses it to manipulate the job candidate into "signing on the dotted line."

Respect confidentiality.   The ethical principle of **confidentiality** requires interviewers to keep information disclosed during an interview private. If an interviewee asks an interviewer to keep something said during the interview confidential, it is unethical for the interviewer to share that information with others. For example, during a job interview, the job candidate mentions that he is interested in transferring to a new position within the company because of poor management in his current department. It would be unethical for the interviewer, who happens to be friends with one of the managers in this interviewee's department, to share this information with the manager. During interview situations, "What's said in the office stays in the office."

Interviewee Responsibilities

Someone who is being interviewed also has a responsibility to communicate in an ethical manner.

Answer questions honestly.   It's the interviewee's responsibility to answer all of the interviewer's questions honestly. By giving honest answers to questions, we adhere to two of the three basic ethical principles: We avoid manipulating the interviewer and we don't limit the interviewer's options and choices. For example, to say during a job interview that you can begin work immediately when you know you can't is dishonest. If the interviewer needs to fill the position immediately and he extends an offer that you know you cannot accept, you have both manipulated the interviewer into giving you a job and limited the interviewer's choices. Had he continued to interview additional job candidates, he might have found a qualified person who could begin the job immediately.

Answering questions honestly also means not misrepresenting the facts about prior positions you've held or your history when being interviewed. For example, a twenty-one-year-old college student who sold advertisements for the school newspaper for four semesters cannot honestly claim to five years' full-time sales and marketing experience. Similarly, you can't say you have international work experience when the only experience you have is one month studying Spanish in a Mexican border town to fulfill your foreign language requirement for graduation. It is unethical to claim to have a skill needed for a particular position when you don't have the skill. Instead, you can say you will do what is necessary to acquire the skill as soon as possible.

Although as noted earlier, businesses have been known to hire people whose job qualifications, educational credentials, or salary histories had been misrepresented during the interview process, research also suggests that both interviewers and work colleagues are able to detect when job applicants are not telling the truth or when they've misrepresented their credentials. One of the ways we detect deception is when verbal and nonverbal messages don't match. For example, while an interviewee is telling the interviewer how confident she is because of her extensive background experience, her nonverbal behavior is communicating a lack of confidence. She is fidgeting in her chair, her voice is soft, and it takes her a while to formulate answers to questions that should be easy to answer for a person with her background experience. Research also indicates that, once a person is hired, his or her colleagues can detect whether the person was dishonest during the interview process.[20]

Keep your word.   Don't make promises that you cannot keep. Interviewers are expected to keep their word, and the interviewee has the same responsibility. If you say that you can begin work in two weeks, you will be expected to begin the new job in exactly two weeks. Sometimes we make promises we know we cannot keep out of fear of the other person's response. Such empty promises will eventually backfire in business and professional contexts, where an individual's credibility is vital to his or her success in the organization.

Confidentiality the ethical principle that requires interviewers to keep information disclosed during an interview private.

>>> COMMUNICATION SKILLS @ WORK

Although it is illegal for an interviewer to ask certain questions, nevertheless you may be presented with an illegal question at some point. Here are a few suggestions for answering such a question in an honest manner:[21]

- *Answer the question directly*. Even though you know that the question is unlawful, you answer it anyway: "Yes, I am gay."

- *Answer the question indirectly*. Rather than answering the question directly, you "tap dance" around the question: "I value diversity and look forward to helping this organization fulfill its mission as a company that values and respects diversity and cultural differences."

- *Seek clarification*. Before answering the question, politely ask the interviewer to explain why the question is important: "I'm having a difficult time understanding how one's sexual orientation may be related to the duties of this job. Can you help me understand?"

- *Redirect the question*. Focus the question on the job requirements. "What you've said so far suggests that sexual orientation is not as much an issue as an applicant's ability to work weekends and travel extensively. Is this correct?"

- *Decline to answer the question*. State politely that you would rather not answer the question: "My sexual orientation has always been a private and personal matter for me and I would prefer to keep it private. I hope you understand."

- *End the interview*. Let the interviewer know that you're uncomfortable with the question(s). "I'm feeling uncomfortable with these questions, and despite my qualifications and five years of work experience, I don't believe I am a good fit for your organization. I would prefer that we end the interview. I hope you understand."

Respect confidentiality. Because some of the information that is exchanged in an interview can be personal or sensitive, it's important to keep the information to oneself and not to share it with others, particularly if the interviewer specifically asks you to keep the information confidential. For example, if you learn through an informational interview that an employee is about to be fired, you should not share this sensitive information with anyone. Violating this type of trust with an interviewer will ultimately backfire on the interviewee. Although the business and professional world appears very large, professionals are highly networked through professional organizations and technology—so their world is actually quite small. If you fail to respect confidentiality, or engage in any other unethical interviewing behavior for that matter, the word travels quickly, eliminating the likelihood of your reaching your interview goal.

RECAP: Interviewing Responsibilities

Interviewer Responsibilities	State your purpose in advance.
	Allow interviewee to make uncoerced responses.
	Avoid unlawful questions.
	Ask unbiased questions.
	Convey honest information.
	Respect confidentiality.
Interviewee Responsibilities	Answer questions honestly.
	Keep your word.
	Respect confidentiality.

Interviewers and interviewees are responsible to each other during an interview. A number of communication skills ensure that interviewers and interviewees conduct the interview in an ethical manner.

Communication Principles and Skills for Leadership

Principle One: Be aware of your communication with yourself and others.

- When planning an interview, be aware of your interview goals.
- Understand how to prepare for and structure your interview.
- Be aware of the importance of being a responsible interviewer or interviewee.

Principle Two: Effectively use and interpret verbal messages.

- It is an interviewer's responsibility to foster clear communication by choosing appropriate, high-quality questions to ask the interviewee.
- For an interview to be successful, the interviewee must think through and clearly answer the questions.

Principle Three: Effectively use and interpret nonverbal messages.

- An interview provides relational as well as content information. This information is often transmitted nonverbally.
- It is important for an interviewee, to keep in mind that nonverbal behaviors of punctuality, appearance, handshake, and eye contact communicate information.

Principle Four: Listen and respond thoughtfully to others.

- Interviewers must make an effort to listen actively to an interviewee's responses and to use both verbal and nonverbal responsive messages.
- For interviewees, listening carefully so as to respond in a clear and thoughtful way will ensure the communication of accurate information.
- In order to recognize the most appropriate opportunities for probing questions, an interviewer must be actively involved in the listening process at all times, even while taking notes.

Principle Five: Appropriately adapt messages to others.

- When developing interview questions, the interviewer's goal is to elicit a natural response from the interviewee. This requires adapting questions by wording and sequencing them appropriately.
- Although it is important to be prepared, interviews are dynamic conversations and interviewers need to be able to adapt in order to get the most from an interviewee.
- An interviewee may also need to adapt in order to effectively communicate the information he or she intends to communicate.

Discussion Questions

1. Describe the primary and secondary interview goals discussed in this chapter.
2. List and explain the three steps in preparing for an interview.
3. List and describe the steps in structuring an interview.
4. Differentiate between open and closed interview questions. Why is it important to consider sequence when writing questions?
5. Describe the difference between structured and unstructured interviews.
6. List ways an interviewer and an interviewee can listen and respond appropriately in an interview.
7. Explain what it means to be a responsible interviewer.
8. Explain what it means to be a responsible interviewee.

Building Your Skills

1. Reflect back on your first job interview. In light of what this chapter had to say about the interviewee's roles, list three things you did incorrectly in that interview, and explain why. Then write down what you would do differently.

2. Think of someone you admire and would like to interview in order to gain information about the person's career path. Write a list of six questions to ask this person, keeping in mind the types of questions discussed in the chapter. Also, pay attention to sequencing. Be prepared to provide justification for the questions and the sequence.

3. Watch an information-gathering interview on a television program such as *60 Minutes* or *20/20*. Identify the different types of interview questions used in the interview. Also, discuss the question sequencing. Analyze how effectively the interviewer and the interviewee performed their particular roles.

4. Work together with a classmate to practice a performance appraisal interview. Assume the employee's performance has been lacking. Write out several questions and role-play the interview, remembering to listen and respond appropriately. Then switch roles.

5. Reflect on the ethical responsibilities mentioned in the chapter. Discuss these responsibilities from the perspective of the interviewer and the interviewee; if possible, refer to a real-world example.

6. Imagine you are a public relations coordinator for a major pharmaceutical company and you need to interview the supervisor of one division about a new program aimed at helping the company "go green." How would you prepare for the interview?

Chapter 8
Interview Types

chapter outline

After reading this chapter, you should be able to

- Differentiate among the three types of interviews discussed in this chapter: information-gathering, job, and appraisal interviews.

- List and describe the different types of information-gathering interviews.

- Define a career-search interview. Explain how to effectively prepare to conduct such an interview.

- List and describe the five steps in preparing a job interview.

- Define the three types of job skills and offer examples of each.

- Discuss impression management in the job interview.

- Define the two types of feedback in an appraisal interview.

- Discuss ways to provide and receive supportive feedback and corrective feedback.

Leaders participate in the interview process on a regular basis. Whether they're interviewers or interviewees, they apply the communication skills discussed in Chapter 7: preparing, structuring, and conducting the interview; listening and responding during the interview; and being responsible and ethical throughout the interview. As a professional, you will use these skills in three primary types of interviews: information-gathering interviews, job interviews, and appraisal interviews.

You take part in an information-gathering interview when you need information from others or when others need information from you. For example, if you're the editor of a company newsletter, you probably conduct information-gathering interviews with employees so you have information to include in the newsletter. You will take part in a job interview when you're looking for a job for yourself or when it's your responsibility to hire other people. An appraisal interview occurs when your manager reviews your work performance with you at the end of the year or when you conduct a performance review with one of the employees you lead.

Although interviews differ depending on whether you're the interviewer or the interviewee, it's important to remember that all interviews are relationships. Whether you're collecting information, trying to get a job, or informing employees about their work performance, an interview is a conversation in which people relate to each other by asking and answering questions in order to achieve a specific goal. To ensure that these interview conversations go well, you need to understand how to prepare, conduct, and follow up on information-gathering, job, and performance appraisal interviews.

> "*Wait for those unguarded moments. Relax the mood and, like the child dropping off to sleep, the subject often reveals his truest self.*"
>
> — BARBARA WALTERS

Information-Gathering Interviews

An **information-gathering interview** is a focused, structured conversation whose goal is to seek out information from another person. Of all the three interview types, it is the most common and is one that leaders use daily.

Preparing an Information-Gathering Interview

Identify the interview goal. To prepare an information-gathering interview, the interviewer needs to first be aware of his or her goal for the interview. What type of information do you need? Here are some possible goals of information-gathering interviews:

- *To investigate an issue or an event.* Newspaper and television reporters are responsible for reporting the news, which includes finding and locating information. Reporters identify appropriate individuals and then ask them questions such as Who? What? Where? When? How? and Why? to uncover a news story.

- *To conduct research to identify patterns and trends.* Some businesses have research units that are responsible for conducting market research. These professionals make phone calls and survey customers to identify their needs and levels of satisfaction with products and services.

- *To diagnose and to solve problems and develop interventions.* For example, nurses and doctors interview patients to diagnose health problems and devise appropriate treatment. Personal trainers, who work in fitness centers, interview new members to identify physical fitness needs and goals in order to recommend appropriate cardiovascular, muscle toning, and resistance workout routines. Financial advisors interview clients to diagnose investing problems and help the clients develop new investing habits.

- *To learn why employees are leaving an organization.* In an **exit interview**, an employer gathers information from an employee about his or her work experiences. Since turnover can be expensive, leaders are interested in understanding why good employees leave an organization. They use this information to enhance the workplace environment and prevent additional turn-over.

One interview goal of many students who are taking a class in business and professional communication is to gather information on the different types of careers and jobs that

Information-gathering interview a focused, structured conversation whose goal is to seek out information from another person.

Exit interview an interview in which an employer gathers information from an employee who is leaving the organization about his or her work experiences.

are available to them after graduation. This type of information-gathering interview is referred to as a **career-search information interview**. Research suggests that 25 percent of the people who get hired at any organization are known to the employer before a job opening actually exists, and half of all jobs are filled by the time they are advertised.[1] Conducting a career-search information interview is a way for those in an organization to get to know you even when a job is not available. When a position does become available, these people may consider you for the position even before they begin the search process. In the following sections we will discuss this particular type of information-gathering interview.

Identify the person to interview. Once you have a clear interview goal, it's time to identify the appropriate person to interview. You want to interview a working professional who holds a position that you find interesting and that you might like to have one day. According to sociologist Mark Granovetter, most people believe that their job contacts will be close friends and relatives, or their "strong ties"—when the reality is just the opposite. According to Granovetter, job contacts usually come from our friends' and relatives' network of friends (or, our "weak ties")."[2] After surveying over 280 residents in a Boston suburb who had taken a new job within the past year, Granovetter learned that only 17 percent of the people surveyed had found their jobs through close friends and relatives. The majority learned about their new positions from people who were only distant associates—old college friends, former colleagues, friends of friends—or weak ties.[3]

The best way to identify a person for a career-search information interview is to use both your strong ties and your weak ties. Ask around. Use your network. Let others know what you're doing and why you're doing it. Let them know what you need. For example, one of the authors of this book decided during his senior year in college, that he wanted to become a buyer for Macy's. Not knowing anyone in the Macy's organization, he started asking his family members for assistance. One of his uncles heard he wanted to talk with a Macy's employee. As it turned out, this uncle worked for a man at the Pepsi Cola Corporation whose best friend's wife was a buyer for Macy's. Through this network of weak ties, your author identified the appropriate person for the interview. The interview went well and resulted in an offer from Macy's of a job as an assistant buyer.

Schedule the interview. Next, you need to schedule the interview. Some sources suggest writing a letter to arrange the information-gathering interview.[4] Others suggest emailing the identified person to make the necessary arrangements. However, according to some career consultants, because postal mail may get lost and email is too easy to dismiss, the phone is the preferred way to arrange a career-search information interview.[5]

Arranging a career-search information interview tends to be quite easy, since most people like talking about themselves and their work. Many professionals are flattered to be asked for an interview and enjoy helping others get started in a career.

Conducting an Information-Gathering Interview

Open the interview. As the interviewer, you open the interview by ensuring that you make a positive first impression, establish rapport, and clarify your interview goals, which are important tasks in any interview situation. All three of these tasks were discussed in detail in Chapter 7. It is important to arrive early to locate the appropriate parking lot and office and to dress appropriately. Although a career-search information interview is not a job interview, it is recommended that you dress as though it were and in a manner that reflects the culture of the organization. To do this, you might want to check with your friends and professional acquaintances who might have insight into the dress standards of the organization.

After a warm greeting, a firm handshake, and an expression of appreciation for the person's taking the time to meet, you need to state your goal or your purpose for the interview: "I am interested in learning more about the work that you do, since I believe it may be something that I would like to do after graduating from college." To remain mindful and respectful of the interviewee's time, it is recommended that you confirm the amount of time the interviewee has for the conversation and let him or her know how you're going to record answers to your questions. For example, if you decide to make an audio recording of the conversation, you need to obtain permission. If you're going to take notes, then you may want to let the person know that you may pause in your questioning from time to time to do that.

Career-search information interview an interview in which you gather information about careers, jobs, and organizations and network with others so that you will have a job when you are ready for one.

Table 8.1	Questions for a Career-Search Information Interview

The following questions have been shown to be helpful for gathering information when interviewing people about jobs and careers that you find interesting.

- How did you get into this line of work? Into this particular job?
- What do you like most about your job? What do you like least?
- If you had to do it all over again, would you choose this line of work?
- Can you walk me through your typical workday?
- What has surprised you about your current position?
- Describe the ideal person for this career or job.
- What questions could I expect to be asked if I were interviewing for this position?
- What should I look for in a company when interviewing for this type of position?
- What trends do you anticipate occurring in this line of work over the next ten years, and how are you going to prepare to meet these changing trends?
- How do you recommend I begin preparing myself to adapt to these changing trends?
- In what ways were you prepared for your job? In what ways were you not prepared for your job?
- What college or university courses do you wish you had taken to prepare you for this position? Do you wish you had concentrated on a different major?
- What professional organizations do you recommend I join to begin building my professional network?
- Who else should I talk to about this type of career, position, or job? Could you provide me with additional names or contacts?

Process the interview. To process the body of the interview, you ask questions, listen to answers, and respond appropriately. Table 8.1 lists some open-ended questions that would be appropriate for your interview schedule—which, as discussed in Chapter 7, is a guide that lists all of the interview questions in a single document and is helpful for sequencing the questions.

Now it's time to begin the interview dance—the give-and-take of the interview conversation. Remember the 70:30 ratio rule, which suggests that, ideally, the interviewee should talk about 70 percent of the time and the interviewer about 30 percent of the time. Following each question, it's important to listen carefully and show that you're listening by making as much eye contact as possible and by using nonverbal responsive behaviors. Another way to enhance listening effectiveness and note-taking accuracy, and to support the interviewee, is to paraphrase what you hear the interviewee saying. Depending on the amount of time you have and whether you're reaching your interview goals, you can continue to ask questions, using the various probes discussed in Chapter 7 to gain additional insight. Or, you can ask the interviewee if there are questions that you have not asked that should be asked.

Close the interview. To close a career-search information interview, it's important to summarize the interview, get the name of another contact if possible, and express your thanks and appreciation to the interviewee. Summarizing the interview may mean restating some of the main ideas or themes that you learned during the interview. Because of the importance of personal and professional networks in getting a job, ideally you'll want to leave the interview with a lead or the name of a contact for another interview. Finally, close the interview by expressing your thanks and appreciation to the interviewee for taking his or her time to meet with you.

Following Up an Information-Gathering Interview

Express thanks. One of the goals when following up on an interview is to leave a positive impression and to thank the interviewee for his or her time. Immediately following the interview, send a note of thanks to the interviewee. The note can be short and simple: *"I wanted to thank you for talking with me yesterday about your job and career path. I very much appreciated your taking time out of your busy schedule to do this. Again, thank you. Best wishes,"* followed by your signature. Make sure you spell the person's name correctly in the note. To ensure that you know the correct spelling and address, take the person's business card.[6] It would also be a good idea to send an email or a note to thank the individual who referred you to your interviewee. This type of personal expression leaves a good impression on many people and reflects a maturity and thoughtfulness that is appreciated.

Process your notes.   Another follow-up activity is to take time to process the interview notes. Review the questions and the interviewee's responses and summarize the key findings. Take a few minutes to write additional notes. What questions remain? What concerns did the interview uncover? What did the interviewee say that clarified your thinking?

Take the next step.   Finally, make sure to follow through on the next step. Make an appointment with your next interviewee, develop additional questions based on your prior interview experiences, and begin the process all over again. The purpose of conducting multiple career-search information interviews is not only to learn more about the career field that you find interesting, but also to develop your professional network.

Job Interviews

The goal of the structured conversation in a **job interview** is for the interviewer to assess the interviewee's qualifications and skills for employment. During the information interview, you played the role of the interviewer. In the job interview, you will be the interviewee.

Preparing a Job Interview

To prepare the job interview, you need to (1) identify your interview goal, (2) develop your resume, (3) identify and research the appropriate organization, position, and contact person, (4) write a cover letter, and (5) arrange the interview.

Aware

Identify the interview goal.   As the interviewee, you need to clarify your interview goal. You do this by conducting a self-assessment and becoming aware of your skills. You begin by asking yourself what you know and what you can do that an employer would consider desirable. Your task is to identify skills that are marketable. According to one survey of employers, more than 90 percent of the people they interviewed could not adequately describe the skills they possessed.[7] To help you identify your skills, we will describe three types: adaptive skills, transferable skills, and job-related skills.

Self-management skills, referred to as **adaptive skills**, are the skills that allow you to be social and to function every day; they allow you to adjust to a variety of situations. Some of these adaptive skills are based in your personality and include such social qualities as being approachable, warm, good-natured, humble, loyal, committed, and flexible. Other adaptive skills are functional and allow you to get things done, including being able to manage time and meet deadlines; being organized, punctual, and motivated; following instructions, taking initiative, and being resourceful. Although many of us take these social and functional skills for granted, a number of people have few or underdeveloped adaptive skills.

Skills that are useful in a variety of jobs and positions are referred to as **transferable skills**. You can begin by identifying the skills that you're learning in this business and professional communication class: You are learning interviewing, conflict management, meeting management, group problem-solving, and sales presentation skills, to name a few. Other important communication-related transferable skills include leading, negotiating, instructing, establishing and maintaining relationships, and counseling. The ability to think critically, to analyze data, and to use technology are other transferable skills that are highly valued in today's organizations.

Many positions require **job-related skills** that are specific to that particular occupation. For example, to be an accountant, you need to understand standard accounting practices, such as double-entry bookkeeping, and the various categories of accounting (such as financial, management, and tax accounting). To be considered for a position as an airline pilot, you need to be able to fly an airplane and to have logged a certain number of flight hours. Most jobs or professional positions have a **job description**, which is a document outlining the specific skills required for that particular position. The following resources will help you learn more about the various types of jobs and career fields that are available:

* *Occupational Outlook Handbook* and the *Dictionary of Occupational Titles,* which are more than likely located in your library

Job interview a structured interview in which an interviewer assesses an interviewee's qualifications and skills for employment.

Adaptive skills self-management skills that allow you to adjust to a variety of social situations.

Transferable skills skills that are useful in a variety of jobs and positions.

Job-related skills skills that are specific to a particular occupation.

Job description a document outlining the specific skills required for and basic duties of a particular position.

- The U.S. Department of Labor's *Occupational Information Network* (O*NET) at www.onetcenter.org
- *JIST* is a publisher devoted to career information. The company's website at www.jist.com contains helpful information on job descriptions, self-assessment tools, sample resumes, and interview tips.

Before applying and interviewing for a position, you need to conduct an inventory of your job-related skills. Since many college students have limited professional work experience, it's important to identify job-related skills you have developed while a student. For example, many students interested in careers in public relations have taken courses focusing on public relations; students interested in journalism may have worked as staff members for the college newspaper. From experiences such as these, you can begin to identify job-related skills that you're developing that fit the job description. Although you may not be as proficient at the skills as you would prefer, such extracurricular activities are an excellent beginning.

It can be frustrating to read job descriptions that require applicants to have professional work experience or skills that come only after working in the profession for a number of years. It may help to know that although job-related skills are important, a study conducted jointly by the U.S. Department of Labor and the American Association of Counseling and Development, titled *Workplace Basics—The Skills Employers Want*, indicates that adaptive and transferable skills appear to be more important than job-related skills.[8]

The ultimate interview goal is to identify a job that is a good fit with your personality type, skills, and abilities. You begin this process by carefully assessing your adaptive, transferable, and job-related skill sets.

RECAP: Assessing Your Skills

Adaptive Skills	Skills that allow you to interact socially and adapt to changing situations	Managing time, taking initiative, being resourceful, loyal, flexible, humble, and committed
Transferable Skills	Skills that are useful in a variety of jobs or positions	Team building, leading, negotiating, managing meetings, giving sales presentations
Job-Related Skills	Skills that are specific to a particular task or occupation	For example, an accountant needs to understand economics; a restaurant manager needs to have business skills; a pharmacy rep needs to have knowledge of trends in the pharmaceutical industry

Develop a resume. A **resume** is a concise, well-organized, written description of your background, training, and qualifications for a job. How long should your resume be? Many employers don't expect a resume to be longer than two pages; some will look only at a one-page resume. (Resumes of experienced career professionals may be longer than two pages, however.) Although your resume is important in helping you land a job, its key function is to help you get an interview—it's how you perform in the interview that determines whether you get the job. Employers rarely hire someone based only on a resume. Most employers spend less than a minute—and some only a few seconds—looking at each resume. Therefore, your resume should be clear and easy to read and should focus on the essential information an employer seeks.

Most employers will be looking for standard information on your resume. Study the sample resume in Figure 8.1.[9] These essential pieces of information should be included on your resume:

- *Personal information*: Employers will look for your name, address, phone numbers, email address, and web page address (if you have one). Provide phone numbers where you can be reached during both the day and the evening.
- *Career objective*: Many employers will want to see your career objective. Make it brief, clear, and focused. You may need to customize your career objective for the different positions you seek.

Resume a concise, well-organized, written description of your background, training, and qualifications for a job.

| **Figure 8.1** | **Sample Resume** |

Jacqueline Vasquez
109 East 4th Avenue
Edinburg, TX 78539
(956) 282-1052
jlvasquez@yahoo.com

Professional Objective:
Seeking a position in human resources as a training specialist.

Education:
Bachelor of Arts degree
Major: Communication Studies; Minor: Business
The University of Texas–Pan American
Graduation date: May 20XX

Professional Experience:
20XX–Present: Intern, Convergys, McAllen, TX
Assisted in creating a leadership training program. Wrote copy for flyers and display ads. Made cold calls to prospective clients.

20XX–August, 20XX: Intern, Target, Edinburg, TX.
Developed sales training seminar. Coordinated initial plan for writing advertising copy for Crest, Inc.'s ad campaign.

20XX–20XX: Supervisor, S&B Associates, Mission, TX.
Supervised three employees and edited training materials.

20XX–20XX: Advertising sales representative and reporter, *The Pan American*, Edinburg, TX. Sold ads for the university paper and worked as student life reporter.

Other Experiences:
20XX–20XX: Summer jobs and part-time work

Skills:
Team Leadership, Photography, Computer Proficiency, Research and Analysis, Public Speaking, Customer Service

Accomplishments and Honors:
Paid for the majority of my college education while maintaining a 3.5 GPA
Presidential Scholarship
Vice-President of the University of Texas–Pan American's Communication Studies Club
Coordinator of *Panorama*, the student yearbook

Professional Organizations:
American Society for Training and Development
Communication Studies Club
National Communication Association

Interests:
Photography, tennis, softball, theatre

References:
Available on request.

- *Education*: Include your major, your degree, your graduation date, and the institution you attended.
- *Experience*: Describe your relevant work experience, listing your most recent job first. Include the names of employers, dates when you worked, and a very brief description of your duties.

DILBERT: © Scott Adams / Dist. by United Feature Syndicate, Inc.

- *Honors and accomplishments*: List any awards, honors, offices held, or other leadership responsibilities.
- *Optional information*: If you have volunteer experience, have traveled, or have computer skills or other pertinent experience, be sure to include this information if it is relevant to your objective and the job.
- *References*: **References** are people who can speak positively about your skills and abilities to an employer. At the bottom of your resume, indicate that your references are available on request. Some job postings may request applicants to provide a list of references' names, phone numbers, and email addresses. If so, you can attach a separate page to your resume.

Identify and research appropriate organization, position, and contact person. Once you have your resume in hand, you identify and research the organization, position, and person whom you will contact to arrange an interview. Some experts suggest that students may want to begin the process of identifying the appropriate position first and the organization second. Others suggest identifying the organization first and the position second. For example, if Seth is interested in a managerial position, he may want to identify as many entry-level management positions as possible and begin the research process. He doesn't care about the type of organization or industry that is offering the job, as long as it's an entry-level management position. He might end up interviewing to be a manager of a waste management company, a local coffee shop, or the accounts receivable department of a large hospital.

Seth could also conduct his job search by first identifying the type of organization or industry that he would like to be associated with, and then focusing on finding the right position within the industry. Many students tend to be more certain of the types of organizations they would like to be associated with and less certain of the types of positions that might be available. For example, some students may want to work in the entertainment industry (film, music, restaurants, nightclubs); some may want to work in the health care field (hospitals, clinics, labs, surgical units, hospice care); others may want to work in the transportation industry (airlines, cruise ships, trains, mass transit). Let's assume that Seth is interested in airline marketing and sales, but there are no positions available. It may be wise for Seth to get his foot in the door of the industry by interviewing for a position as a ticket agent and then searching for jobs within the industry using trade publications, internal job postings, and professional networks.

According to Richard Nelson Bolles, author of *What Color Is Your Parachute?*, a popular job-hunting book, students tend to underestimate the power of their personal networks (friends, family, acquaintances) when researching and locating a job. The three worst ways to look for a job, according to Bolles—which also happen to be the ways most often used by college students—are

1. Using the Internet.
2. Mailing out resumes to employers at random.
3. Answering advertisements in professional or trade journals.

The three best ways to look for a job, according to Bolles—and the least often used by college students—are

1. Asking for job leads from family members, friends, people in the community, and staff at career centers—in other words, utilizing personal networks.

2. Knocking on the door of any employer, factory, or office that interests you, whether the firm currently has a vacancy or not.

3. Using the Yellow Pages to identify subjects or fields of interest to you in the town or city where you want to work, and then calling up the employers listed, to ask if they are hiring for the type of position you can do.[10]

Write a cover letter. Once you have inventoried your skills, developed a resume, identified the organization and position you want to interview for and the person who will conduct the interview, you need to write a cover letter. A **cover letter** accompanies a resume and is a sales pitch that argues why you're the best candidate for the position. Cover letters need to be targeted to a particular job and person. You want your cover letter to result in a job interview, so it needs to be written persuasively and to argue that your educational training, work experience, and career interests are a fit for the position. Figure 8.2 is one example of a cover letter. For additional samples, visit www.jobweb .com/Resources/Library/Samples.

As Figure 8.2 illustrates, a cover letter should include the following parts:

- *Introduction.* In the introduction, you need to let the reader know what position you're applying for and how you learned of the opening. If you're responding to an advertisement, refer to the job title and the publication in which you found the ad. If you're applying for a position that someone referred you to, indicate the name of the person who referred you.

- *Body.* In the body of the letter, you need to sell yourself: You need to make a convincing argument that you have the skills and knowledge that the position requires and that you're a good fit for the position and the organization. Provide enough details to let your reader know that you're familiar with the organization and the skills and knowledge needed in this particular position.

- *Action step.* In this part of the letter, you want to let your reader know the next step you will take—usually, this is a request for an interview. Let your reader know when you will call and your intentions when you call.

- *Conclusion.* End the letter by expressing your appreciation for the reader's time and consideration of your resume.

Schedule the interview. Finally, it's time to schedule the interview, which means communicating with the identified person and asking for an interview. According to career consultant Michael Farr, most jobs are filled before they are advertised, so if you have a choice, don't wait until the job is advertised to ask for an interview.[11] In fact, one study reports that up to 32 percent of all open positions are filled by internal transfers or promotions.[12] According to Farr,

> The best time to search for a job is before anyone else knows about it. Most jobs are filled by someone the employer meets before a job is formally open. So the key is to meet people who can hire you before a job is available. Instead of saying, "Do you have any jobs open?" say "I realize you may not have any openings now, but I would still like to talk to you about the possibility of future openings."[13]

Some career consultants suggest that arranging an interview by phone is preferred to using email, because email is easily ignored. Phone calls get the contact person's attention and provide a more interactive experience, and saying no to a potential interviewee is harder on the phone. It is also recommended that you develop a phone script prior to placing a phone call to ask for an interview. This script should take no more than 30 seconds to communicate. Here are a few pointers for developing your script:[14]

1. *Introduce yourself.* "Hello, my name is _____."

2. *State your interest in a position.* "I am interested in a position as . . . ." Do not ask, "Do you have any jobs?" This question is easily answered with a "No." If you're interested in a hotel management position, then you need to state, "I'm interested in a management position within the hospitality industry."

Cover letter a document that accompanies a resume; a sales pitch that argues why you are the best candidate for a position.

Figure 8.2	Sample Cover Letter

1234 West Avenue
McAllen, TX 78541
April 10, 20XX

Ms. Maria Pulido
Director of Human Resources
University Hospital
1201 West University Drive
McAllen, Texas 78541-4646

Dear Ms. Pulido:

I am applying for the Communication Specialist position that was advertised through the University of Texas–Pan American Career Services Office. I consider this position to be a fit with my educational training, work experience, and career interests.

First, my educational training has prepared me to manage communication to internal and external audiences, two aspects of the position mentioned in the advertisement. I have completed a number of courses related to the position you advertised, including interpersonal communication, organizational communication, health communication, and writing for the media. These courses focused not only on developing messages targeted to specific audiences, but also on developing relationships with members of internal and external audiences.

Second, I have work experience in corporate communication that will allow me to immediately make a contribution to University Hospital. As a communication intern for Memorial Hospital, I was responsible for conducting survey research to assess employees' needs regarding internal communication and then developing communication products and services to meet those needs.

Third, this position is a fit in terms of my career interest, which is to become a communication professional in the health field. I enjoy the hospital environment and working with health professionals. University Hospital has an excellent reputation and I would like to become a part of the team responsible for this reputation.

Please consider my request for a personal interview to discuss further my educational training, work experience, and career interests. I will call next week to see whether a meeting can be arranged. Should you wish to reach me, please feel free to contact me at 956-566-0899 or pthomas@utpa.edu.

Thank you for your consideration.

Sincerely,

Patrick Thomas

Patrick Thomas

3. *Describe your strengths and skills.* Describe your transferable and job-related skills. "I have well-developed communication skills, including speaking clearly, listening actively, and solving customer service problems in a constructive manner. I also have experience using hotel reservation software."

4. *Mention your adaptive traits*: "I am a committed and loyal employee who is dependable, mature, and resourceful. I learn quickly and require minimal direction."

5. *Ask for the interview.* "When can I come in for an interview to discuss employment opportunities with your organization?" This appropriate and assertive question makes it more challenging for a potential employer to reject your request.

>>> COMMUNICATION AND GLOBALIZATION @ WORK

Heather B. Armstrong ignited a fierce debate about privacy issues in 2002 after she was fired from her job as a web designer and graphic artist because she had written satirical accounts of her experiences at a dot-com startup on her weblog, dooce.com. She did not challenge her termination and has refrained from identifying her place of employment in interviews. Armstrong warns her fellow bloggers: "I was naive. I was writing these caricatures of my colleagues . . . I didn't think anyone would be reading it."[15]

Ms. Armstrong is a blog celebrity. Her blog became well known when she was fired from her job. The debate sparked by her termination led to the term *dooced* being used to mean losing one's job because of one's website. Since then a number of people have lost their jobs for a similar reason.

Googling people is also becoming a way for bosses and potential employers to do background checks on employees, with no disclosure required. Googling someone gets around discrimination laws, as employers can find out all manner of information that is legally off limits in interviews: your age, your marital status, the value of your house (along with an aerial photograph of it), the average net worth of your neighbors, fraternity pranks, papers you wrote in college, liens, bankruptcies, political affiliations, and the names and ages of your children.[16]

According to a survey of 102 executive recruiters by ExecuNet, an executive job-search and networking organization, 75 percent of recruiters use search engines and social-networking sites to uncover information about candidates, and 26 percent of recruiters have eliminated candidates because of information found online.[17]

Search engines aren't going away, so here are some tips to help job seekers clean up their "e-dirt."

Google yourself. First, find out what's out there. Go to a popular search engine (Google.com, Yahoo.com, or MSN.com will do) and type your name in quotation marks. If you find something you'd rather the world didn't see, contact the site's owner and ask that it be removed.

Clean up your Facebook or MySpace page. Search engines might not find your risqué profile on a social networking site like Facebook.com or MySpace.com, but that doesn't mean it's hidden from recruiters. Chris Hughes, a spokesman for Facebook, says he's heard that recruiters with alumni email addresses log in to look up job candidates who attended the same school the recruiters did.

Bury your dirt. You may be able to cover up your e-dirt by crowding it out with positive information. Search engines typically rank their results based on the number of sites that link to those pages. The more links, the higher the search ranking. Make sure the pages you want recruiters to see have more links to them than the pages you'd rather keep hidden.

Tune in to your blog buzz. Just because you may be paranoid doesn't mean people aren't talking trash about you online. You can monitor your web presence through sites like Pubsub.com, which will alert you by email when your name is mentioned in Internet newsgroups, blogs, and securities filings.

The following resources may be helpful in cleaning up your e-dirt:

http://abilitiesenhanced.com/digital-dirt.pdf
This great website by online company ExecuNet offers a career guide complete with tips for "cleaning up your dirt," as well as some advice for avoiding problems with your online reputation.

www.careerjournal.com/jobhunting/usingnet
The Executive Career Site for the Wall Street Journal Online features several articles about the development of the problem of online reputations and e-dirt. There are some great tips on how to "hide" or "bury" your e-dirt to keep it from coming back to haunt you.

Conducting a Job Interview

Open the interview. In many ways, a job interview is like a first date. Although the interviewee and the interviewer are vaguely familiar with each other, assuming that both have done their homework, there is still much uncertainty. This uncertainty usually causes you to feel nervous and apprehensive because you don't know the outcome of the interview. Will the interviewer like me? Will the interviewer consider me qualified for the position? Will I get a second interview? Will I get the job? Interestingly, many interviewers also find the process of interviewing nerve-racking. Research suggests that many interviewers have limited experience in interviewing others. Because of this inexperience, they too experience anxiety and fear.[18] The purpose of the interview is to reduce this uncertainty; to determine if there is a good fit between the position and the organization and the interviewee's skills, experiences, and values. Both the interviewee and the interviewer must agree on whether there is a good fit.

To open the job interview, it's important for the interviewee to make a positive first impression. We usually know within the first few minutes of meeting someone how a first date is going to go, and an interview is no different. This ability is the "blink" concept that Malcom Gladwell wrote about in his bestseller *Blink*. Gladwell describes how and why people have the ability to make important decisions in seconds. According to Gladwell, our instantaneous judgments are for the most part accurate and can be trusted.[19]

The following paragraphs review some tools you can use to make a positive first impression. Research suggests that interviewees who manage their first impressions by engaging in appropriate waiting-room behavior, dressing appropriately, using technology strategically, and making a professional introduction are perceived as socially skilled and desirable by interviewers.[20]

Making a good first impression usually begins even before you meet your interviewer, the moment you step foot into the office or waiting area. Never underestimate the power and influence of an administrative assistant or other support staff. Since administrative assistants will be working alongside you if you're hired, some interviewers value their input and their impressions, such as how you treated them while waiting for the interview. Did you greet them in a pleasant manner? Did you establish rapport with them? Did you arrive early, just in time, or late for the job interview? Did you leave the waiting area as you found it when you arrived? Did you wish the person a pleasant day when you left? Although all of these behaviors may appear insignificant and unimportant, they're in fact quite revealing. Many executives have termed these "off-stage" types of behaviors "the Waiter Rule." How people treat waiters (or others who wait on, serve, or support people) is usually how they treat people in general.[21] Take advantage of your waiting room time and begin making a positive first impression by developing relationships with those who work in administrative support positions.

How you dress for the job interview influences how others perceive you. For example, several studies have found that interviewers judged job candidates' credibility and attractiveness on the basis of their interview dress rather than on their interviewing skills.[22] Although job applicants want to dress appropriately for their interview, many applicants don't know what is meant by the word *appropriate*. Some job applicants believe that what might be considered appropriate for one job and interviewer may not be appropriate for the next. Although there is some truth to this, there are standards or principles for appropriate interview dress that cross all types of jobs and industries.[23]

Nonverbal

- Wear clean, pressed clothes that appropriately cover the body (no exposed midriffs); wear polished shoes (no flip-flops, sandals, or open-toed flat shoes).

- Be well groomed: clean and styled hair, clean and appropriate length fingernails, fresh breath, no strong cologne or perfume.

- Wear moderate amounts of jewelry. Do not overdecorate the body. Remove hats, sunglasses, cell phone earpiece devices, MP3 player earphones, and chewing gum prior to the interview.

- Cover or hide tattoos, and remove any jewelry in a nontraditional location, such as nose, tongue, or multiple ear piercings.[24]

In addition to the preceding principles of appropriate interview dress, there are some, standards of appropriate dress specific to women and men. For women, the standard interview outfit is classic: a navy blue skirt suit worn with a single strand of pearls, and matching dress shoes with a heel of moderate height. Interviewers seem to agree that a candidate can't go wrong with a well-tailored suit in a neutral color (black, navy, or gray). Minimal makeup can also help candidates look and feel their best in an interview.

For men, a suit in a dark, neutral color, a white or blue dress shirt, and a tie in a conservative pattern are considered appropriate for most formal job interviews. It is recommended that men wear natural fabrics, like wool or cotton, and black polished shoes with heels that are not worn down. Socks must match the color of the pants and not the color of the shoes and should not sag around the ankles.

Another way to ensure a positive first impression is to monitor how you represent yourself using technology. What would an interviewer learn about you if he or she were to Google your name? What would an interviewer learn about you by viewing your Facebook or MySpace page or searching on YouTube? Also remember that an interviewer may not have access to Facebook, but his or her family members might. This was the case with administrators with the San Antonio school district who were in the process of hiring new teachers for their schools. The children of the administrators were better able to do cyber background checks on future teachers than were the administrators, who were limited to traditional ways of conducting background checks. What the administrators found (through their children) were teacher applicants whose interview personas were inconsistent with how they presented themselves online.[25]

Video resumes and e-portfolios can capture an applicant's personality and showcase his or her presentation skills and abilities.

Some companies are beginning to request video resumes in addition to the traditional paper resume.[26] For many employers, "showing" (video resumes) is becoming more important than "telling" (paper resumes). According to one human resource professional, video captures personality and helps an employer determine whether the individual would be a good fit for the organization.[27] Here are a few pointers on how to prepare a video resume to ensure a positive first impression.[28]

- *Keep it brief.* Managers have limited time. You don't want the interviewer or hiring manager to turn you off before you have showed them who you are and what you can do for them.

- *Dress appropriately.* Your video resume is going to be the first impression. You need to dress like you're going to a job interview.

- *Adapt to the audience.* Adapt your video to the position, organization, and industry. The video you prepare for a position at a bank should not be the same video you prepare for a position at an art gallery.

- *Show your personality.* This is your chance to go beyond your paper resume. Allow the future employer to see your personality and your communication style and to see why you're a good fit for their organization.

One final way to make a positive first impression is to be professional when introducing yourself: Offer a warm greeting, direct eye contact, and a firm handshake, and express your appreciation for the interview. Remember that in some situations, the interviewer may be as nervous as you are. This is an opportunity for you to make the interviewer more comfortable. One of the ways you can do this is by commenting on something in the interviewer's office: "I notice the picture of the sailboat. Do you sail?" This type of informal conversation has been shown to reduce the nervous energy that both interviewer and interviewee may be experiencing.[29]

RECAP: How to Make a Positive First Impression

Engage in Appropriate Waiting-Room Behavior	Greet the support staff or administrative assistant pleasantly, arrive early, leave the waiting room in good condition
Dress Appropriately	Wear clean, pressed, modest clothes, be well groomed, avoid too much jewelry
Use Technology Strategically	Monitor how you represent yourself using technology
Introduce yourself in a professional manner	Offer a warm greeting, a firm handshake, make eye contact, and express appreciation for the interviewer's time

Process the interview. As we've pointed out, an interview is like a ballroom dance. One partner usually leads while the other partner follows. During a job interview, however, you get to be both the leader and the follower. At times you follow your dance partner, which means you listen carefully to the interviewer's questions and answer them to the best of your abilities. At other times, you lead, which means you ask insightful questions of the interviewer and listen carefully to the answers. In this section, we'll provide a dance lesson on how to be a follower (how to answer questions) and how to be a leader (how to ask questions).

Be prepared to answer standard job interview questions. Numerous interview guides agree that the following are some of the most popular interview questions:[30]

- What can you tell me about yourself?

- Why are you interested in this position (or organization)?

- What are your major strengths and weaknesses?
- What are your plans for the future?
- What will your former employers (or references) say about you?
- Why did you leave your prior job?

To answer these questions, it's important to remember the five communication principles discussed in Chapters 2 through 6. First, be aware of the needs of the employer and how your skill sets meet these needs. Second, answer questions clearly, and ensure that your response directly answers the question. Use a confident voice when answering questions. A confident voice includes minimal pauses and a quick rate of speaking and can be easily heard.[31] Third, be aware of the interviewer's nonverbal messages. What is the interviewer telling you without telling you? Fourth, listen carefully to the questions; if necessary, paraphrase the questions to clarify understanding. Fifth, adapt your communication. Continuously find ways to demonstrate how you can help the organization meet its needs and goals. We'll discuss a few strategies that may help you appropriately adapt your message:[32]

Aware
Verbal
Nonverbal
Listen
Adapt

>>> COMMUNICATION AND GLOBALIZATION @ WORK

Many employers welcome the chance to see a candidate before committing to an interview. Laurine Sargent said she wished she had video clips to accompany the roughly sixty applications she received for a recent opening at her Phoenix-based real-estate firm.

"After a while [resumes] would become hypnotic," she said. "Everybody today knows to say the right things they know employers are looking for."[33]

She invited a dozen candidates for interviews and might have cut that number in half had she seen their presentation skills ahead of time.

Video resumes are a must for international or out-of-town applications. Many employers will reject a resume if the person is not a local candidate. The employer has to consider the travel costs involved in bringing a potential candidate to interview overseas or across the country. With only a paper resume, there is no guarantee you can really shine enough to get noticed. With a video resume, an employer can actually see you and your interpersonal abilities.

Others, however, remain skeptical, worried about the time it would take to view all the videos and the potential for discrimination based on race, age, and other factors that wouldn't be apparent on a traditional resume. Some employers say that they will even throw a resume in the trash if it has a picture attached, to avoid the chance of being accused of discrimination.

Tyler Redford is chief executive of ResumeBook.tv, an online resume management system that allows users to post streaming video resumes and other e-portfolio items for potential employers to access. Redford acknowledged that employers and career centers have been skeptical, and fewer than a third of his site's users have posted a video resume, even though it is a core feature of the site's services.[34]

Redford and other supporters of video resumes believe discrimination could occur at the interview stage even without video in the application process, so that alone should not deter job seekers from using them.

An electronic portfolio, also known as an e-portfolio or a digital portfolio, is a collection of electronic evidence assembled and managed by a user, usually on the web. Such electronic evidence may include text, PDF files, images, blog entries, and hyperlinks to videos showcasing the applicant's presentational style and personality. E-portfolios are both demonstrations of the user's abilities and platforms for self-expression, and, if they are online, they can be maintained dynamically over time. Some e-portfolio applications permit varying degrees of audience access, so the same portfolio might be used for multiple purposes.

In the context of a knowledge-driven society, in which being information literate is critical, the e-portfolio can provide an opportunity to demonstrate one's ability to collect, organize, interpret, and reflect on his or her learning and practice. It is also a tool for international applicants, as it allows a potential employer to get an idea of whether a person is a good fit before incurring the cost of flying the person to interview.[35]

For more information on e-portfolios, consult the following websites:

www.mahara.org
This New Zealand–based web company offers free downloadable software to assist in creating your own e-portfolio. Other features offered on the site require a small fee or membership.

www.electronicportfolios.org
Dr. Helen Barrett, of the University of Alaska, has developed a comprehensive website for students to use in their development of e-portfolios. She includes tips on what to include in your e-portfolio to make it fit your current needs, FAQs, and a list of some of the best e-portfolio software.

- *Tell a story.* Discuss your accomplishments by discussing a specific situation you were involved in, the people involved, the challenge, how you overcame the challenge, and the outcome. Use enough detail so that the interviewer can visualize your accomplishment.

- *Provide quantity.* When discussing your accomplishments, quantify them—state the number of customers served, the dollar amounts you're responsible for, or the number of new accounts you generated.

- *Emphasize results.* Provide data regarding positive results, for example, "I increased sales by 5 percent each year I was with the organization." Use numbers to quantify your results.

- *Link your results to the organization's needs.* Make sure the interviewer can connect your accomplishment to the needs of the organization, for example, "With my experiences and accomplishments, I feel confident that I can meet the needs you have expressed during this interview, specifically, the need to increase sales."

There comes a time during most job interviews when the interviewer asks if you have any questions. This is your cue to take the lead in the interview dance. The questions you ask during the job interview can be revealing, so you want to make sure you're asking questions that reflect positively on you. Here are a few things you want to *avoid* asking or saying, as they will reflect negatively on you:

- "What exactly does this company do?" This question suggests that you have not done your homework and are unfamiliar with the mission of the organization.

- "How much will I be paid?" This question is premature and usually should be reserved until a job offer has been extended. Also, it sounds presumptuous, as though you're assuming you will get the job.

- "I don't have any questions." This statement makes you appear passive and uninterested rather than actively curious and interested.

You want to ask questions that reveal that you have done your homework. For example, suppose you're interviewing for an entry-level marketing position with AT&T. The following questions reflect your curiosity and showcase your research on and background knowledge of AT&T:

- "According to *The Wall Street Journal*, Verizon, Quest, and Sprint Nextel are AT&T's chief competitors. How has this competition changed how you do business over the years?"

>>> COMMUNICATION ETHICS @ WORK

According to a 2008 poll by CareerBuilder.com, which surveyed 3,000 hiring managers from across the United States, 49 percent indicated that they had uncovered a lie on a job candidate's resume.[36] Here's what the study revealed:

- Job candidates exaggerated their job responsibilities (38 percent).
- Job candidates overstated their skill sets (18 percent).
- Job candidates listed academic degrees that they hadn't earned (10 percent).
- Job candidates inflated their job titles to sound more important (5 percent).

Harris Interactive, which conducted the survey, also asked hiring managers about the "most unusual" lies they encountered while staffing their openings. Here's a sampling of their findings:

- A candidate using someone else's photo on a resume
- A candidate claiming that he was a member of Mensa, which is a club for individuals whose IQs are well above average
- A candidate listing a degree from a nonexistent school
- A candidate pretending to be part of the Kennedy clan

Although it's tempting to stretch the truth in order to enhance your marketability, it's also misleading. If you stretch the truth too far, it's unethical. Before sending out your resume, carefully review it and make sure it presents your credentials, skills, and experiences in a truthful manner.

- "I have been reading about David Dorman's [president of AT&T] management style. Does his style reflect the style of the other managers at AT&T?"
- "What problems do you anticipate AT&T encountering in the years ahead, and what skills will employees need in order to solve these problems?"

Here are five additional questions that job-hunting experts recommend asking. Listening carefully to how these questions are answered should give you a fairly accurate picture of what's going on behind the interview:[37]

In the "dance" of an interview, sometimes the interviewer takes the lead and at other times the interviewee does.

1. "What priorities will need to be addressed immediately in this position?" Many times, the job description, which details the duties of the position, does not jibe with how the interviewer describes the duties of the job. It is important to have the duties and responsibilities clarified prior to accepting a position.

2. "How long was the previous person here?" If there is a "revolving door" with this particular position, meaning that the organization cannot keep anyone in the position, this reflects a problem with the position itself and/or the supervisory staff.

3. "Tell me about your management style. How do you bring out the best in your employees?" The answer to these questions reveals how the manager works with his or her employees. Is the manager a hands-on or hands-off manager?

4. "What types of people tend to excel here? Does the organization have a formal or an informal feel? Is the organization more traditional or is it more progressive?" Answers to these questions let you know about the work culture and if you're a fit with the culture.

5. "How long have you been here? Why do you stay?" The answer to these questions will give an indication of the health of the department or company. If there is constant turnover, then there are probably going to be a lot of inconsistencies in the work of the department and the department will feel splintered and fractured.

Listen

Close the interview. To properly close a job interview, you need to do the following: (1) express thanks and appreciation for the interviewer's time, (2) ask for the job, (3) and ask "next step" questions. Here are a few suggested task and relational messages that may help you close a job interview.

Verbal

The following relational messages reflect competent communication behaviors, because they're other-focused and illustrate your awareness of the interviewer's limited time and energies.

- "I would like to thank you for your time. I realize interviewing takes a lot of time and I appreciate the time you have given me."
- "I know you must be incredibly busy and I appreciate the time you have given me."

Although many interviewees find it awkward and difficult to ask for the job they just interviewed for, doing so is incredibly important and reinforces in the interviewer's mind your commitment to a particular position.

- "I hope I have made it clear why I feel my skills and experiences meet your needs. I would like to be given a chance to join your organization. Can you offer me the job?"
- "I would like to be given the opportunity to help you meet your needs and the needs of this organization. Could I have this job?"
- "I would like the opportunity to serve this organization in this position. Is that possible?"

In order to plan the next step of a job search, you need answers to the following questions prior to leaving the job interview:

- "Do you want me to come back for another interview, perhaps with some other members of the staff?"
- "When may I expect to hear from you?"

Following Up on a Job Interview

Following up on a job interview is very similar to following up on an information-gathering interview. You need to complete two tasks: express thanks and follow through on any additional requests made by the interviewer.

Express thanks. We noted in Chaper 4 that people have a tendency to remember and be influenced by information received at the beginning and end of a social interaction.[38] This effect is referred to as the principle of primacy and recency. There is a strong possibility that your interviewer will remember the first and last moments of his or her encounter with you. Because of this effect—and because it is common courtesy to do so—it is important to send a thank-you note to the interviewer immediately following the interview. Below are a few pointers for preparing and sending thank you notes:[39]

- *Decide whether email or regular mail makes more sense.* Depending on the timing and formality, an email message may be more appropriate. In other situations, a handwritten note may be more appropriate.
- *Use quality paper and envelopes.* Stationery stores have quality thank-you notes and cards in a variety of styles.
- *Handwritten or computer-printed is acceptable.* If your handwriting is legible, then hand-write the note. If not, then a word-processed note is acceptable.
- *Use a formal salutation.* It's preferable to write "Dear Ms. Saavedra" rather than "Dear Marisa."
- *Keep the note friendly.* Remember that the purpose of the thank-you note is to thank someone for doing something for you. Although it's best to avoid making a hard sales pitch in a thank-you note, you can provide a subtle reminder of your skills, qualifications, and accomplishments.
- *Sign the note.* Sign your first and last names and make sure that both are legible.
- *Send the note immediately.* Prepare and mail your note within the first 24 hours following an interview.
- *Avoid text messaging.* "Thx for the IView! I Wud ♥ 2 Work 4 U!!" is too casual and highly inappropriate for a thank-you note. A recent article in *The Wall Street Journal* notes that corporate recruiters and hiring managers are turning away otherwise qualified job candidates because of their lack of judgment when it comes to using technology to communicate and the informality of their communication.[40]

Figure 8.3 shows a sample thank-you note that would be appropriate following a job interview.

Follow through. In many job interviews, the interviewer asks you for additional information; or, you may have offered to provide additional information following the interview. If you said you would forward a list of professional references as soon as possible, then this is what you must do. Interviewers notice whether or not interviewees

| Figure 8.3 | Sample Thank-You Note |

March 8, 20XX

Dear Ms. Saavedra,

Thank you for giving me the opportunity to interview for the spa manager position at SPA360. After our interview, I am more convinced that I am a good fit for this position and your organization.

Although my experience managing a restaurant may at first appear to be unrelated to your position, I consider my management experience and skills to be highly transferable to your spa. I have a proven track record in managing a business that consistently provides superior service while also yielding a considerable profit at the end of each business cycle. I feel confident in my ability to manage your spa in a similar manner.

Per your request, I have enclosed a list of professional references, including their names and contact information. These individuals look forward to hearing from you soon.

Again, thank you for taking the time to meet with me. I enjoyed our visit and learning more about you and your organization.

Best wishes,

Rick Gonzalez
(956) 287-3421

follow through. In fact, one of your authors worked with a manager who purposely made a number of tedious requests during job interviews to see if job candidates followed instructions carefully. The positions the manager was trying to fill required professionals who were detailed-oriented, and this is how this particular manager assessed the job candidates' attention to detail.

Appraisal Interviews

An **appraisal interview**, also known as a *performance review*, is an interview in which a leader or employer shares information with an employee about his or her job performance. The appraisal interview serves as a feedback loop between the leader and the employee, in which two types of feedback are usually discussed—supportive and corrective. **Supportive feedback** encourages desirable behavior. **Corrective feedback** attempts to alter negative or inappropriate behavior. Leaders are wise to use both supportive and corrective feedback to achieve maximum benefit in a performance review.[41]

In most organizations, employees receive an appraisal interview from their supervisors, who detail where the employees are exceeding performance standards, where they are meeting standards, and where they are failing to meet standards. In traditional organizations, appraisal interviews usually include top-down communication with the supervisor sharing information with the employee; the structure of this type of interview is formal, and the interview occurs once a year. According to Norman Maier, an expert on appraisal interviews, this type of appraisal interview is referred to as the "tell and sell" method.[42] The supervisor's role is to tell and then to sell, or persuade the employee, that his or her observations are correct. Research reveals that the formal, top-down approach to evaluating employee performance usually leads to disgruntled employees and fails to correct inappropriate behaviors.[43]

In less traditional organizations, appraisal interviews usually include two-way communication—top-down and bottom-up—with the supervisor and the employee sharing information with each other. The structure of this type of appraisal interview is less formal; some organizations refer to these as *coaching sessions*.[44] It is not uncommon for a manager and an employee to have a number of coaching sessions throughout the year. According to

Appraisal interview an interview in which a supervisor shares information with an employee about his or her job performance; also known as a *performance review*.

Supportive feedback communication feedback whose goal is to encourage desirable behavior.

Corrective feedback communication feedback whose goal is to alter negative or inappropriate behavior.

Dayton Fandray, this type of an appraisal interview is a problem-solving conversation with the supervisor serving as a coach or counselor.[45] Many of these appraisal interviews include an employee's self-appraisal of his or her performance. Rather than the manager informing the employee of appropriate and inappropriate behavior, the employee takes the lead and informs the manager of his or her performance. This approach to appraisal interviews has been shown to produce a number of positive outcomes for both employees and organizations.[46]

Many college graduates find themselves in entry-level leadership positions in which one of their duties is to conduct appraisal interviews with their team members. To assist you in developing this important interview skill, we will discuss three communication skills: preparing the interview, conducting the interview, and closing the interview.

Preparing an Appraisal Interview

To prepare the appraisal interview, you need to identify the interview goal, analyze the individual's performance, and arrange the interview.

Identify the interview goal.   The primary goals of most appraisal interviews are for the interviewer (1) to acknowledge and reinforce employee behaviors that meet or exceed performance expectations by using supportive feedback, and (2) to identify and discuss employee behavior that fails to meet performance expectations using corrective feedback. Your secondary goals are for employees to feel supported and valued and to understand how their workplace behaviors affect others within the work unit or organization.

Analyze the individual's performance.   You begin preparing the appraisal interview by analyzing the individual's job performance. Most business and professional positions have goals or standards that employees are expected to meet. For example, one of the authors used to work for an international airline as a service manager. His annual performance review was based on how well he met the following performance standards:

- A 10 percent decrease in customer complaints
- A 20 percent reduction in employees' use of sick time
- A 5 percent increase in on-time departures
- A 15 percent reduction in employee injuries on the job

These four performance standards guided the annual appraisal interview that his manager conducted with him.

When preparing for the appraisal interview, an interviewer must be able to answer the following three questions prior to meeting with the employee:

1. Which performance expectations does the employee exceed?
2. Which performance expectations does the employee meet?
3. Which performance expectations does the employee fail to meet?

If the employee is failing to meet performance expectations, then the interviewer must also conduct what is referred to as a **gaps analysis**, which is an analysis of the identified gap between a performance standard and the employee's actual performance.[47] For example, if the airline service manager was only able to increase on-time departures by 1 percent for the year, then there would be a gap of four percentage points between the performance expectation and actual performance. To conduct a gaps analysis, an interviewer must be able to answer the following three questions:

1. Where is the employee's performance now?
2. Where does the employee's performance need to be?
3. What is causing the gap?

One of the main reasons appraisal interviews are conducted is to provide employees with corrective feedback to help them reach their performance goals. As an interviewer, you must be prepared to discuss what is causing any gap between the performance standard and an employee's actual performance and help the employee identify ways to close the gap. Ferdinand Fournies, a leading training consultant, conducted an important study in which he asked 25,000 supervisors and managers the following question: "Why don't employees do what they are supposed to do?" Here are the top thirteen reasons:[48]

Gaps analysis an analysis conducted by a supervisor of an identified gap between a performance standard and an employee's actual performance.

1. They don't know what they are supposed to do.
2. They don't know how to do it.
3. They don't know why they should do it.
4. There are obstacles beyond their control.
5. They don't think it will work.
6. They think their way is better.
7. They are not motivated.
8. They are personally incapable of doing it (personal limits).
9. There is not enough time for them to do it.
10. They are working on wrong priority items.
11. They think they *are* doing it (no feedback).
12. They have poor managers.
13. They have personal problems.

When providing corrective feedback to your employees, you can use Fournies's research to guide how you provide corrective feedback. The reasons Fournies identified may assist you in helping the employee close the performance gap.

Schedule the interview. Appraisal interviews need to be scheduled when both the interviewer and the interviewee have ample time to have a private conversation about the interviewee's job performance. Timing can be important and must be considered when arranging the appraisal interview. For example, if the interview is going to include considerable corrective feedback, is it best to conduct the interview at the beginning, the middle, or the end of the workday? If you conduct the interview at the beginning of the workday, the employee is probably rested; however, the interview may affect the employee's job performance for the rest of the day following the interview. If you conduct the interview at the end of the workday, you don't have to worry about affecting the employee's job performance, since he or she will be going home following the interview. However, the employee is likely to be tired and may not be as receptive to corrective feedback as he or she might be when feeling rested. We suggest that you be mindful of the employee and provide him or her with some scheduling options so that together you can select the time that works best.

Conducting an Appraisal Interview

Like information-gathering and job interviews, an appraisal interview includes three activities: opening, processing, and closing.

Open the interview. An appraisal interview is a more sensitive conversation than an information-gathering or a job interview, because it includes a discussion of job per-

The most effective appraisal interviews are problem-solving conversations that use both top-down and bottom-up communication.

formance. Thus, it's important to open the interview appropriately by establishing a supportive tone. Opening the appraisal interview involves three tasks: expressing thanks, stating your purpose, and describing the process.

First, thank the employee for his or her time. Although the appraisal interview is usually not optional, (meaning that employees are usually required to participate), you can show your appreciation for the employee's time. This type of courtesy indicates that you are mindful of others, which may help set the tone for the appraisal interview.

After thanking the employee, you need to state the purpose for the appraisal interview. It's also important to set the appropriate tone in this step. The following examples not only state the purpose but also set the appropriate tone:

- "The purpose of an appraisal interview is to help us develop employees. We want employees to be successful, and this interview allows us to have a conversation about what's helping you to become successful and what's getting in the way of your becoming successful."
- "The main purpose for the appraisal interview is to give us an opportunity to discuss each other's performance. I would like to share some of my impressions with you and I also want to listen to some of your impressions."

Finally, you need to inform the employee about how the interview will be structured. Again, research suggests that productive and constructive appraisal interviews tend to be less formal and structured and to feel more like a give-and-take conversation in which interviewer and interviewee spend equal amounts of time talking and listening to each other.[49] Most appraisal interviews begin with a review of supportive feedback followed by a review of corrective feedback: "I would like this to be a conversation. I will begin by sharing with you some of my observations about where I see you excelling on the job. Following these observations, I would like to hear your assessment of areas where you excel. Then I'll provide you with some feedback about areas of your job performance that need more development. Following this, I'd like to have your impressions of my feedback: Where do you agree? Where do you disagree?"

Process the interview. Processing the interview includes providing supportive and corrective feedback as well as being receptive to receiving supportive and corrective feedback. During this process you will use the principles and skills we have been discussing throughout this text, including having an awareness of your communication, using verbal and nonverbal messages, listening, and adapting appropriately.

The following strategies may help convey supportive feedback to another person in an appraisal interview:[50]

- *Make it timely.* Timeliness refers to how quickly you provide feedback to someone following the performance of appropriate behaviors. Have you ever received feedback too late? If so, you probably didn't even remember what you did to deserve the supportive feedback. It's best to provide supportive feedback immediately following the behaviors you find appropriate and desirable.
- *Make it specific.* Specificity refers to the level of detail contained in the feedback messages. Feedback messages that are more specific and detailed are preferable. For example, rather than saying, "You're doing a great job working with our customers," say, "During the past twelve months, you have grown your customer base by 50 percent and increased your sales by 62 percent over the prior year. This is exceptional performance."
- *Make it frequent.* Frequency refers to the number of times feedback is given. Unfortunately, people working in business and professional settings don't receive supportive feedback as often as is warranted.[51] To maximize the effectiveness of supportive feedback, it needs to be communicated frequently—not just once a year during the appraisal interview.
- *Be sensitive.* With all types of feedback (both supportive and corrective), it's important to be aware of the other person's feelings and to adapt the feedback accordingly. Sensitive feedback demonstrates a concern for the recipient's feelings.[52]

Although most people enjoy receiving supportive feedback, some people don't like the attention—it makes them nervous. One of your authors clearly remembers hearing in an appraisal interview that he did not accept praise well from others and that this behavior needed to be changed! When conveying feedback—whether supportive or corrective—prefacing your statements with a comment such as "I know you might be uncomfortable listening to what I have to say; however, it's important that you receive this type of feedback" is one way of showing your concern for the other person's feelings. When you receive supportive feedback, simply say, "Thank you. I appreciate receiving this recognition." If you're being recognized for a project in which others were involved, accept the supportive feedback, but also acknowledge and thank the others who helped you along the way.

One of the more challenging duties of a professional who is responsible for leading others is to provide them with corrective feedback. Research suggests that employees are more receptive to corrective feedback if they have a quality relationship with their supervisor and if they perceive their supervisor as successful, knowledgeable, and caring or understanding of others.[53] Many of these relational characteristics and the communication skills that have been shown to enhance these characteristics were discussed in Chapter 6. Put simply, a quality relationship between supervisor and employee will undoubtedly enhance how constructive the employee perceives corrective feedback to be.

Like supportive feedback, corrective feedback should be communicated in a specific, timely, and sensitive manner. Again, research suggests that rather than using a top-down, "tell and sell" approach, it's best to use a "problem-solution" approach, in which you engage the person in a conversation about his or her job performance.[54] Ferdinand Fournies refers to the appraisal interview as a coaching session in which the supervisor serves as a facilitator of a conversation. The following communication behaviors have been shown to enhance the effectiveness of the appraisal interview:[55]

1. *Describe the problematic behaviors.* Using "I" language, describe what you see the employee doing (nonverbal messages) or hear him or her saying (verbal messages) that remains a problem. For example, "I *see* you coming to meetings late and I *hear* you blocking all of the proposed ideas without offering any of your own ideas."

2. *Get agreement that a problem exists.* Ask, "Do you agree that this is a problem?"

   • If the employee agrees, ask the person to paraphrase. For example, "I'm glad you agree. In your own words, what do you hear me saying the problem is?"

   • If the employee does not agree, then adapt your communication accordingly. For example, "Let me try describing the problem from a different perspective."

3. *Mutually discuss alternative solutions.* It's best to get the person involved in generating possible solutions to the problem.

   • "What are some possible solutions or ways to remedy the problem?"

   • "What could you begin doing that would solve the problem?"

   According to Fournies, people are more likely to adopt solutions they generate than solutions that are imposed on them.

4. *Mutually agree on action to be taken to solve the problem.* To do this, the leader and the employee must carefully listen to each other and agree on which solution will be adopted to change the problematic behavior. To confirm your understanding, it's important to paraphrase. For example, "This is the solution that I hear you agreeing to in order to solve the problem . . . . Is that correct?"

5. *Be nonverbally responsive.* Many people, when receiving corrective feedback, have a tendency to become nonverbally *unresponsive.* They may take a step back, cross their arms, look away, and sigh. Usually, we interpret these verbal and nonverbal messages as defensiveness. Interestingly, defensiveness and the nonverbal behaviors that signal defensiveness are contagious. People have a tendency to "catch" each other's emotions.[56] When one person acts defensive, the other person has a natural tendency to mimic the person's nonverbal behavior (i.e., take a step back, cross arms, look away, and sigh) without being aware of it, and eventually this person becomes defensive.[57] To break this natural cycle of defensiveness, it is important to be aware that it happens. Interviewers are encouraged to remain nonverbally responsive even when their natural instinct is to become defensive.

Although communicating corrective feedback is difficult for an interviewer, equally if not more challenging is receiving corrective feedback as an interviewee. You may find the following guidelines useful when listening to corrective feedback; these are known as the four As: Acknowledge, Ask, Align, and Add.[58] First, *acknowledge* the feedback. Rather than jumping the gun and immediately explaining your behavior, making excuses for your behavior, or informing the interviewer that his or her observations are inaccurate, listen carefully. Acknowledge the corrective feedback both nonverbally and verbally, by paraphrasing what you heard. For example, "This is what I hear you saying. . . . Is that correct?"

Second, *ask* for additional information to help you better understand the problem. Your questions will also convey to the interviewer that you're interested in the corrective feedback, whether you agree with it or not. Also, the more the interviewer feels that you have fully listened to and understand the corrective feedback, the more likely the interviewer is to be receptive to your response.

Third, *align* with something the interviewer has said; in other words, find agreement. For example, "I agree with your observation that I am consistently late to meetings. I can see why this is a problem and why you might be frustrated with me." Following this agreement, offer an apology and detail how the behavior will be changed.

Fourth, *add* your point of view if you don't agree with the corrective feedback. You do this by first asking permission. For example, "Is this a good time for me to share my observations with you?" or "May I tell you my perspective?"

RECAP: Providing Supportive and Corrective Feedback

Feedback Type	Strategy	Example
Supportive Feedback	Make it timely	Praise an employee who effectively leads a meeting as soon as the meeting is over.
	Make it specific	Tell an employee that he has the department's highest percentage of policy additions this month, rather than simply referring to him as a "top seller."
	Make it frequent	Share with an employee whenever you notice effective behavior throughout the quarter, rather than waiting for her quarterly review.
	Be sensitive	Understand that all messages, even supportive feedback, may need to be adapted to the listener.
Corrective Feedback	Make it timely, specific, and sensitive	
	Describe the problematic behaviors	Say "I see you using company time to shop online," rather than, "You never do your job."
	Get agreement that a problem exists	Ask the employee to confirm that she has been doing what you describe.
	Mutually discuss alternative solutions	Ask the employee if he has some ideas for solutions to the problem.
	Mutually agree on action to be taken to solve the problem	You have not come to a conclusion until both people agree on the solution. Ask the employee if she thinks a suggested action will solve the problem.
	Be nonverbally responsive	Make eye contact, listen respectfully to the employee's views, be careful not to mimic any defensive behaviors used by the employee, which could cause you to become defensive.

Close the interview. To close an appraisal interview, you need to accomplish two tasks. First, you need to express your thanks for the interviewee's taking the time to discuss his or her job performance with you. Second, you need to inform the interviewee of how you plan to follow up the appraisal interview. Most interviews will result in an action plan or a detailed set of steps for addressing performance gaps. You want to be able to assess how well the plan works. Thus, you might tell the employee, "Before you leave, I would like to recommend that we follow up this appraisal interview. I would like to meet in two months to review your progress."

Following Up an Appraisal Interview

Unfortunately, supervisors sometimes neglect to follow up on appraisal interviews because of time constraints or other tasks that take priority.[59] However, it's essential that you, as the interviewer, follow up your appraisal interview with additional feedback if you're serious about helping another individual change his or her behavior.[60] You do this by acknowledging changed behavior and by re-addressing unchanged behavior.

Acknowledge changed behavior. Acknowledging changed behavior communicates to the interviewee that you're serious about wanting the interviewee to change. It also communicates you care about the interviewee and his or her behavior. Finally, acknowledging changed behavior serves as reinforcement for continued behavioral change.[61] You acknowledge changed behavior by communicating supportive feedback that is timely, specific, frequent, and communicated in a sensitive manner.[62]

Re-address unchanged behavior. If the interviewee has not changed the behavior discussed during an appraisal interview, then it's important to continue the dialogue. Keep in mind Fournies's research, which examined the reasons employees don't do what they're supposed to. Examining and probing some of these reasons with the interviewee may give you additional insight into why the interviewee has not changed his or her behavior.

Communication Principles and Skills for Leadership

Principle One: Be aware of your communication with yourself and others.

- In any interview, it is important to be aware of the interview goals before beginning the process.
- In a job interview, the interviewee needs to be aware of the impression he or she is creating with the other person.
- When conducting a career-search interview, be aware that it can be a precursor to an employment interview.

Principle Two: Effectively use and interpret verbal messages.

- In all interviews, note-taking is a good way to ensure the most accurate record of the other's responses.
- In an appraisal interview, you should use supportive feedback messages to support the interviewee.
- When evaluating another's performance in an appraisal interview, use descriptive "I" language to get at a problem.

Principle Three: Effectively use and interpret nonverbal messages.

- In any interview, it is good to use nonverbally responsive messages such as forward body lean and eye contact.
- A firm handshake, direct eye contact, and a confident voice are all nonverbal behaviors that make a positive impression on an interviewer.
- When receiving corrective feedback, it is important to remain nonverbally responsive and to avoid becoming defensive.

Principle Four: Listen and respond thoughtfully to others.

- In any interview, to enhance listening effectiveness and to support the interviewee, you should use verbally responsive behaviors such as paraphrasing.
- As an interviewer, asking follow-up questions or probing questions is a good way to demonstrate that you are listening.
- As an interviewee, when listening to corrective feedback, use the four As: acknowledge, ask, align, and add.

Adapt

Principle Five: Appropriately adapt messages to others.

- In an appraisal interview, in order for corrective feedback to be well received it needs to be timely, specific, and sensitive.
- All interviews are structured conversations, but you should be able to adapt each interview to the individual interviewee.
- All messages in an interview should be other-oriented rather than self-focused; keep in mind what is relevant to the other party in the interview.

Discussion Questions

1. List and define each of the three types of interviews discussed in this chapter.

2. The chapter discussed several goals of the information-gathering interview. List them, and provide an example of each.

3. Describe the career-search interview and some strategies an interviewer can use to prepare for one.

4. List the three major types of job skills discussed in the chapter. Provide some examples of each type of skill.

5. What are some ways of ensuring that you make a good impression during the job interview process?

6. Define and give an example of the two types of feedback that might be used in an appraisal interview.

7. Discuss strategies for effectively providing and receiving these two types of feedback.

Building Your Skills

1. Get together with a classmate and role-play a career-search interview. As the interviewee, take notes during the interview. Then take a few moments to take notes on your notes. Reflect on the note-taking process: Was it effective? Was your information thorough and accurate? Switch roles and do the exercise again. Present what you learned to the class.

2. Discuss impression management in the job interview process. What does the text mean by advising an interviewee to "engage in appropriate waiting room behavior"?

3. Refer to the list of career-search interview questions in Table 8.1. Which questions would you remove from the list? Based on your particular career aspirations, which questions would you add? Keep a record of these for future reference when doing career-search interviews.

4. The chapter discusses the usefulness of "weak ties" when searching for jobs. Begin to develop a network; list those whom you believe may be helpful to you in your job search, and make connections.

5. Get together with another classmate and practice providing and receiving feedback. First offer supportive messages; then provide corrective feedback. Make sure to use the strategies mentioned in the chapter for providing and receiving feedback.

6. With a classmate, invent a hypothetical organization that is currently hiring. Write out an exhaustive list of potential interview questions for a certain position. Then take turns role-playing the interview from each perspective. When you take on the role of interviewer, select questions randomly from the list, so the interviewee will need to prepare in advance, as he or she would for a real job interview.

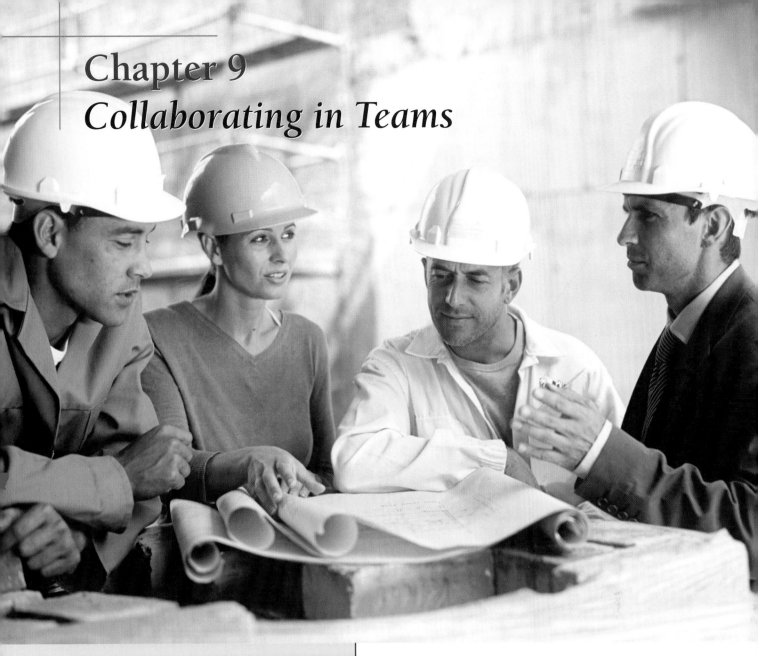

Chapter 9
Collaborating in Teams

chapter outline

After reading this chapter, you should be able to

- ■ Identify similarities and differences between a group and a team.

- ■ List and describe the eight characteristics of effective teams.

- ■ Describe and appropriately perform task and social roles in teams.

- ■ Describe team communication networks.

- ■ Develop team ground rules and a team mission statement.

- ■ Appropriately manage team status and power differences and enhance team cohesiveness.

- ■ Define and discuss the descriptive, functional, and prescriptive approaches to teamwork.

Do you or your family own any Tupperware? Chances are the answer is yes. Tupperware, invented in the 1940s, is that brand of ubiquitous plastic bowls and other kitchen storage containers that keep food fresh because of their unique way of "burping" air out of the containers. A Tupperware party—a sales meeting usually held in someone's home—is held every 2.5 seconds, resulting in annual sales of over $1.2 billion. But the pervasive influence of Tupperware in American kitchens during the past half century almost didn't happen. The inventor of Tupperware, Earl Silas Tupper, was a genius at creating new products, but he didn't know how to sell them. Then Tupper met Brownie Wise, an energetic person with a gift for sales. Through Wise's marketing ideas (home Tupperware parties), Tupperware became a household word and the Tupperware business flourished.

Without Wise, Tupperware would probably be a forgotten product. But because of Tupper and Wise's collaboration, great things happened.[1] Working together and with teams of salespeople, the two made Tupperware a household word.

In business and professional settings, most of the truly powerful transformations happen through collaboration. One person's idea connected to another person's vision has resulted in such innovations as eBay, Google, Infosys, amazon.com, and Dell computers. One person with one idea may be the seed that starts a company, but it's because two heads (or many heads) are often better than one that companies grow. Although one person may be appointed the team "leader," each person in a team can exhibit leadership skills to make a team successful. Not only *can* each team member exhibit leadership—he or she *should* do so. Leadership (influencing through communication) is a responsibility of all team members. In this chapter we discuss how to develop leadership skills when collaborating with others.

Some people enjoy working with others in groups and teams. Yet, despite the advantages of teamwork, others hate working in groups, attending meetings, or participating in *any* type of team collaboration. One researcher has even coined the term **grouphate** to label the loathing many people have for collaborating with others in groups and teams.[2] But whether you love them or would rather leave them, there is clear evidence that in contemporary organizations you *will* work in small groups and teams. Estimates suggest that lower-level to mid-level managers will spend at least one-third of their time in groups and as much as two-thirds of their day working in teams, attending meetings, or preparing for collaboration.[3] And the higher you climb in any organization, the more likely you are to spend *more* rather than less time working in small groups. Today's technology makes it easier for you to collaborate in teams even when you're not meeting face to face, regardless of whether you're collaborating with someone across the hall or across the globe. Your work will undoubtedly revolve around what your kindergarten teacher evaluated you on: "getting along with others" in group and team meetings.

Research suggests you will most likely be working in or leading a team or team-based organization at some point in your career.[4] A **team-based organization** is one that has more of a flat structure than tall, hierarchical structure (one with many layers and levels of supervisors). One research study found that at the turn of the millennium, over 70 percent of corporations were team based and the number was continuing to grow.[5] Another study found that corporations spend over $200 million annually training people to work together in teams.[6] Given increased globalization and management's increased emphasis on collaboration, it's likely the number of team-based organizations will continue to grow.

Since you'll spend considerable time collaborating with others, this chapter offers insights into how groups and teams work that can help you be successful in team-based organizations. In the next chapter we'll offer specific strategies for improving team meetings. The five communication principles for leadership can serve you well as you interact with others at work. As shown in Figure 9.1, the five principles apply to all three communication skill sets used in business and professional settings. In this chapter and the next, we will apply them to collaborating with others in groups and teams.

Principle One: Be aware of your communication with yourself and others. Chances are the people who make you want to avoid team meetings are clueless as to why they may be an obstacle to team success. Being aware of your communication is the first step to improving your communication. Especially when you are leading others, awareness of your own behavior and the behavior of other team members is the first step to understanding why you and other team members behave as you do and how to adjust your behavior for improved group performance. And, just as Earl Tupper became aware that he needed Brownie Wise to help him sell his Tupperware, you need to be aware of the power of collaboration.

Grouphate the loathing many people have for collaborating with others in groups and teams.

Team-based organization an organization that has a flat structure rather than a hierarchical structure (one with many layers and levels of supervisors).

Aware
Verbal
Nonverbal
Listen
Adapt

Figure 9.1	**Communication Principles for Leadership**

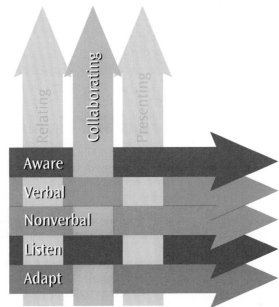

Principle Two: Effectively use and interpret verbal messages. The verbal messages you and other group members use are pivotal in shaping what roles you assume, including leadership roles, and how your work team accomplishes its work. Verbal messages are the primary communication method for accomplishing work tasks in teams. Leaders effectively use and accurately interpret verbal messages.

Principle Three: Effectively use and interpret nonverbal messages. Eye contact, tone of voice, facial expression, and the use of space and time influence what it feels like to be in a group. The overall climate of a team is often based on unspoken rather than spoken messages. When leading others, "reading between the lines" is being able to discern the unspoken, nonverbal messages of others.

Principle Four: Listen and respond thoughtfully to others. One of the most valuable skills a leader can have is the skill of listening. When everyone is talking at once, a leader has to listen to determine where conversation has gone off track: Is it one person? Is it a specific grievance? Does everyone feel the same way about the issue? How team members interact is directly shaped by group members' skill in listening and responding to what others say and do.

Principle Five: Appropriately adapt messages to others. The ability to modify messages and adjust to the behavior of others is especially important when communicating with three or more people in a team. The two chapters on groups and team communication are designed to increase your repertoire of appropriate behaviors and to help make your meetings and collaborations with others successful, especially when you are designated to lead or to influence others through your interaction in groups and teams.

Elements of Teamwork

Why do we spend so much of our work days collaborating with others? The simple fact is that two heads are indeed better than one (most of the time). We work collaboratively because research suggests that when we collaborate we usually end up with a better outcome. Here's why:[7]

- Teams have more information available to them than individuals do.

- Teams stimulate creativity.

- Teamwork increases the likelihood that we'll remember what we discuss because we're actively involved in the process.

- Team members are usually more satisfied with a decision if they are involved in the discussion.[8]

- Team members learn about themselves through feedback they receive from their fellow team members.[9]

But if all of these advantages occur when we collaborate, why do we sometimes become frustrated when working collaboratively? The answer: Because there are also disadvantages to collaborating with others:

- One individual may dominate the discussion.
- Team members may pressure others to conform.
- Team members may rely too much on just a few people.[10]
- Teamwork takes more time than working individually.[11]

Differences Between Groups and Teams

Is there a difference between a group and a team? The two terms are often used interchangeably. By exploring this question, and building on the distinction introduced in Chapter 1, you can better understand what groups and teams do and develop strategies for improving group and team performance.

What's a group? A **small group** consists of from three to fifteen people who share a common purpose, feel a sense of belonging to the group, and exert influence on each other.[12] Let's look at this definition more closely.

How many people make a group? At least three people; two people are a *dyad*, not a group. Yet, if a group becomes too large, it typically operates as a collection of subgroups rather than as a single body. When more than a dozen or so people meet together, it is difficult for all members to participate; usually, when the group gets too big for everyone to talk, it is likely that a few people will monopolize the discussion.

In order to be considered a group, people need to be united by a common goal. They must all seek the same thing. A collection of people waiting for a bus may all want to go to Dallas, but they probably haven't organized their efforts so as to meet once they get there.

Group members feel a sense of belonging. Members realize that they are part of the group. For example, the commuters waiting for the bus don't think of themselves as part of a group. Group members develop a sense of identity with their group. They know when they are in the group or not in the group.

Your presence and participation in a group influence other people in the group. Group members are interdependent; what one group member says or does affects other group members. Your comments and even your silence, facial expressions, and eye contact (or lack of it) affect what the group does. It is this quality of groups that explains why each person in a group is, to some extent, a leader. Inherent in being in a group is the idea that each person in the group influences others—sometimes by speaking, other times by listening.

Small group communication is the transactive process of creating meaning among from three to fifteen people who share a common purpose, feel a sense of belonging to the group, and exert influence on each other. The word *transactive* in our definition means that the communication that occurs has the potential to have an impact on many people simultaneously. As noted in Chapter 1, communication is a transactional process because of the possibility to express and interpret a number of messages from multiple sources at the same time when communicating in person. Because of the complexity of communicating with several people at once, there is considerable opportunity for misunderstanding. But don't assume that working in a group or team will inevitably be a frustrating experience. People can and do accomplish much when working together. Anthropologist Margaret Mead said, "Never doubt that a small group of concerned citizens can change the world. Indeed, it's the only thing that ever has." Collaborating with others does not mean you are doomed to experience frustration. There are tools and principles that can help you better navigate your way through the process of working in groups and teams and attending meetings.

What's a team? Most of us have been part of a sports team. Whether it is soccer, baseball, football, or water polo, the goal of a sports team is usually to win the game or competition. In business and professional settings, a work team has some of the same characteristics as a sports team.[13] Instead of winning the game, however, the goal may be to get the contract, decide where to build a new shopping mall, or reach a target in a capital campaign. A **team** is a coordinated group of people organized to work together to achieve a specific, common goal.[14]

Often the terms *team* and *group* are used interchangeably. Is there a difference? The answer is yes. Given the increased importance teams have in the workforce today, it's important to know precisely how groups and teams differ. Although both groups and teams are made

Small group a collection of from three to fifteen people who share a common purpose, feel a sense of belonging to the group, and exert influence on each other.

Small group communication the transactive process of creating meaning among from three to fifteen people who share a common purpose, feel a sense of belonging to the group, and exert influence on each other.

Team a coordinated group of people organized to work together to achieve a specific, common goal.

up of a small number of people who work to achieve a goal, teams are often more structured or deliberately organized to achieve the goal. For example, a team whose goal is to advertise a new MP3 player may have one person assigned to research the product, two others to develop an advertising campaign, and another team member to develop a marketing plan. Also, teams spend more time coordinating their efforts to accomplish the goal.[15] Every team is a group, but not every group is organized or coordinated enough to meet the definition of a team. Because of the prevalence of teams and the fact that the word *team* rather than *group* is used in corporate and organizational settings, we'll primarily use the term *team* to describe a collection of people who work together to achieve a specific goal.

There are several specific distinctions between groups and teams. Being aware of these differences can help you assess the nature and function of the collaboration process.

Teams develop clearly defined responsibilities for team members. On a sports team, every team member has specifically assigned duties, such as shortstop, pitcher, quarterback, or fullback. On a work team, team members' duties and roles are usually explicitly spelled out. Team members may perform more than one function or role, but each role includes well-defined duties[16]—one person researches the new building site, one person takes minutes at meetings, one person networks with people outside the team, and so on.

Team members develop explicit rules for how the work should be done.[17] For example, a team may establish a rule that if someone is going to be absent from a team meeting, he or she should tell another team member. Team members know what the rules are and know how those rules affect the team.

Teams develop clear goals. In contrast, whereas members of a group have a common goal, it may be less specific or structured.[18] Team goals are usually stated so that they can be measured: to win the game, to sell more corn flakes than the competition, to get to the North Pole before anyone else.

Teams develop a way of coordinating their efforts. Team members spend time discussing how to accomplish the goals of the team. Their work is coordinated to avoid duplication of effort. Watching a skilled sports team at work is like watching a choreographed dance. Similarly, business and professional team members develop systems for working together rather than at cross-purposes. And when such teams are permitted the freedom to manage themselves, team members report greater satisfaction than when team members are told what to do by someone outside their team.[19]

Although we have differentiated between groups and teams, don't get the idea that they are completely different entities. Both groups and teams are made up of a small number of people who are striving to achieve a goal. Think of groups and teams as existing on a continuum: in some cases the people will act more like a group; in other cases their behavior will be closer to our description of a team—more coordinated and structured, following clear rules and pursuing explicit goals. Since every team is a small group, whenever we refer to a team we are suggesting that it's a group as well.

>>> COMMUNICATION ETHICS @ WORK

Teams have a strong sense of purpose and a well-structured coordinated plan to achieve their goals. Team members are encouraged to collaborate and to unite with other team members to achieve the mission. But what if you disagree with the goal of the team or the actions of a team member? When is it appropriate to voice your concern? What if doing so means diverting the team from its stated objective?

A team of financial analysts was working on developing budget proposals for the new fiscal year. They had to cut the budget in some way. When reviewing the analysts' proposals, Alison noted that the entire training and development budget had been cut. She felt strongly that this would be a major mistake. Cutting the training and development department budget would eliminate the department. The company would either have no training, which would decrease productivity, or

would have to outsource the training, which would cost the company more money, not less. Yet if the training and development department were cut from the budget, the result would be considerable savings for the company, and the financial team would immediately achieve its goal. Alison checked with other team members; they all agreed that the training and development budget should be cut.

What should Alison do? Go along with the rest of the team, or try to argue for restoring the budget cuts? A prolonged argument with her team members could disrupt team morale and Alison could lose credibility among her team members. When you're the only person on a team who has reached a particular conclusion, do you give in to preserve team morale? Or do you stand your ground, even if doing so runs the risk of alienating you from team members?

RECAP: Comparing Groups and Teams		
	Groups	**Teams**
Roles and Responsibilities	Individual responsibilities may not always be explicitly defined.	Team member roles and responsibilities are clearly stated and explicitly discussed.
Rules	Rules are often not formal or written down; rules evolve depending on the group's needs.	Rules and operating procedures are clearly identified to help the team work efficiently and effectively.
Goals	Group goals may be discussed in general terms.	Clearly spelled out goals are the focus of the team's efforts.
Methods	Group members may or may not decide to divide the work among group members.	Team members develop clear methods of collaborating and coordinating their efforts to achieve the team goal.

Characteristics of Effective Teams

Several researchers have been interested in studying how to make teams function better.[20] One study found that team members need compatible work schedules, adequate resources to obtain the information needed to do the work, leadership skills, and help from their organization to get the job done.[21] Another study concluded that it's not how smart team members are, but how well they communicate that improves teamwork.[22] Using studies of several real-world teams (such as teams at NASA and McDonald's, and sports teams), researchers Carl Larson and Frank LaFasto identified eight characteristics of an effective team. The more of these attributes a team has, the more likely it is to be effective.[23]

A clear, elevating goal. Having a well-defined goal is the single most important attribute of an effective team.[24] This goal should be perceived by the team as *elevating* and *important*—it should excite team members and motivate them to make sacrifices for the good of the team. An elevating goal is also one that could not be accomplished by an individual. Sports teams use the elevating goal of winning the game or the championship. Teams in business and professional settings also need an exciting goal that all team members believe is important,[25] such as selling more running shoes than the competition or landing the biggest contract in company history.

A results-driven structure. Teams need an efficient method of organizing how they work together. Team structure is the way in which a team is organized to process information and achieve its goal.[26] Explicit statements of who reports to whom and who does what are key elements of team structure. It is useful, therefore, for teams to develop a clear sense of the roles and responsibilities of each team member. In order to perform well, a team needs individuals who fill task leadership roles (getting the job done) and individuals who fill maintenance leadership roles (managing the team process). A structure that is not results-driven, that tolerates ineffective meetings, busywork, and "administrivia," always detracts from team effectiveness.

Competent team members. Team members need to know not only what their assignments are but also how to perform their jobs. Team members need to be trained (to have the proper skills) and be educated (to have the information they need) so that they know what to do and when to do it. Without adequate training in both teamwork skills and job skills, the team will likely flounder.[27] One research study found that the most effective team members have experience and problem-solving skill; are open, supportive, and action-oriented; have a positive personal style; and are optimistic about team success.[28]

Unified commitment. It's vital for all team members to be "on the same page"—to have a common perception of how they are working together to achieve a goal. Josh and Amanda, for example, were on the same human resource development team. Although they shared the same goal—enhancing their company's success—they were not unified in their approach to achieving that goal. Josh's approach was to increase salaries for workers, whereas Amanda's was to try to hold down costs and limit pay increases to an absolute minimum. In successful teams, members need to be united in their commitment, dedication, and approaches to achieving the goal. When differences exist, team members should work collaboratively to clarify the overall goal and then identify differences. After the issues are identified, team members should address them using skilled approaches to managing conflict.

A collaborative climate. Effective teams foster a positive, supportive group climate and encourage development of the skills and principles needed to achieve their goals. Team members should affirm one another, support one another, and listen to one another as they perform their work.

Standards of excellence. A team is more likely to achieve its goal if it establishes high standards. Goals that cause the team to stretch a bit can serve to galvanize team members into action. Unobtainable or unrealistic goals, however, can result in team frustration. If the entire team is involved in setting goals, the team is more likely to feel a sense of ownership of the standards it has established.

External support and recognition. Teams in any organization do not operate in isolation. They need outside support to acquire the information and materials needed to do the job. Team members also need to be recognized and rewarded for their efforts by others outside the team. Positive, reinforcing feedback enhances team performance and feelings of team importance. There's evidence that receiving less support from others discourages some team members from giving their full effort; negative feedback causes more group members to not give their full effort.[29] Most coaches acknowledge the "home field advantage" that flows from the enthusiastic support and accolades of team followers. Corporate teams, too, need external support and recognition to help them function at maximum effectiveness.

Principled leadership. Teams need effective leaders. However, a team does not require an authoritarian leader to dictate who should do what. On the contrary, teams usually function more effectively when they adopt shared approaches to leadership. In most effective teams, leadership responsibilities are spread throughout the team. An effective team leader not only collaborates with team members but also has a network of support outside the team. An effective team leader keeps the team informed about how events and factors external to the team may affect the team's work.[30]

Although we've made claims about the value of teamwork and improved communication, is there any evidence that improved teamwork skills result in improved performance? The answer is a resounding yes! One internationally recognized teamwork consulting group documented dramatic increases in work productivity after providing teamwork training. Here are just a few of the reported positive outcomes of teamwork training:

- At Asea Brown Boveri, one manufacturing team doubled shipments from $1 million per month to $2 million while cutting engineering design time from 26 weeks to 14 weeks.
- At Advanced Micro Devices, one team of microchip developers improved its productivity by 20 percent and another team cut defects on microchip wafers by 30 percent.
- At Texas Instruments, a computer chip assembly team decreased its cycle time by 42 percent.
- At E-Systems' Monteck plant, team productivity increased enough to save the division over 41,000 labor hours in just over two and a half years. [31]

Teamwork works whether the organization is making microchips or potato chips. At the heart of effective teamwork is improved coordination, which occurs through improved communication.

Working in Virtual Teams

Apparently email isn't fast enough for many of us. A recent survey found that teenagers were more likely to phone someone, send an instant message, or send a text message than to send email to share a tidbit of news or just to chat. The least likely means of connecting with a friend was to visit in person.[32] And it's not just teenagers who are increasingly

Video conferencing allows virtual teams to collaborate, even when team members are in different parts of the country or the world.

relying on the Internet to communicate with friends and colleagues; when groups and teams need to collaborate in business and professional settings, especially if team members are not physically near other members, they will connect using technology rather than meeting face to face.

A **virtual team** is a team that interacts via a channel other than face-to-face communication. Email, video conferences, and a vast array of technological tools make it possible for us to be psychologically close to someone even if that person lives and works on the other side of the world. Because of the increased costs of travel, many businesses and professional organizations are doing more collaborative work using virtual teams. And even if we work in the same building with our colleagues, we may nonetheless connect electronically rather than interacting face to face.

Your personal computer, your cell phone, and other technological tools give you the ability to collaborate with other people who are not all in the same place at the same time. To give you an idea of how rapidly worldwide Internet use is increasing, note these statistics: In 2005, over 950 million people used the Internet; that number had grown to over 1.25 billion people one year later—and the numbers continue to grow exponentially.[33]

How is computer-mediated, virtual teamwork different from live, face-to-face conversation? There are four key differences:[34]

- *Anonymity*: If you are interacting by text message or email only, you may not always know precisely with whom you are communicating when you receive a message.

- *Physical appearance*: There is typically less emphasis on a person's physical appearance and nonverbal communication online.

- *Distance*: Although we certainly can and do send email messages to people who live and work in the same building, there is typically greater physical distance between people who are communicating online.

- *Time:* You have greater control over the timing and pacing of the messages you send and receive. You can decide, for example, when to retrieve email messages or when to respond to a message you receive. Your interaction with others can be **asynchronous**—which means your messages are not read exactly when you send them; often there is a time delay between when you send a message and when someone else reads it. (In contrast, *synchronous* messages, such as face-to-face conversations or phone conversations, are received the moment they are sent.)

Different types of technology make virtual communication possible. Let's take a closer look at these various technologies.

Telephone conferences. The telephone conference call—one of the first uses of technology to support group and team meetings—involves a group of people agreeing to "meet" at a certain time by phone. To hold a conference call you need a special telephone service, available from most telephone companies, so that several people in different locations can be connected at the same time.

Email and text collaboration. We don't need to tell you that email and text messaging are two of the most prevalent methods used to send and receive messages in organizations—or anywhere. If you're typical, you regularly send and receive email and/or text messages about both personal and work-related topics. The research on group use of email, however, is still in its early stages[35] and is somewhat contradictory.

- One researcher suggests that electronic correspondence minimizes status differences that may be present if people meet face to face.[36]

Virtual team a team that interacts via a channel other than face-to-face communication but rather uses email, video conferences, or other technological tools.

Asynchronous communication in which there is a time delay between when a message is sent and when it is received.

>>> COMMUNICATION AND GLOBALIZATION @ WORK

Technology has made it more difficult to escape from your work. Because of the Internet and a vast array of technological tools, you can just as easily be e-connected to your colleagues in the next room as to those on another continent. Because of the ease in using technology coupled with the increasing likelihood that you will be communicating with people from other cultures, you may need to decide when you need to meet face to face and when it may be more efficient to communicate electronically. One practical theory, called **media richness theory,** helps explain why it may sometimes be better to communicate in person rather than participating in mediated communication. According to media richness theory, a method or channel of communication is rich if it has the following characteristics:

1. There is the possibility of instant feedback.
2. Both verbal and nonverbal cues can be processed by senders and receivers.
3. It allows the use of natural, informal language rather than formal language.
4. Messages are customized to individuals rather than communicated to a mass of people.

For example, face-to-face communication is a rich medium; a memo that goes out to all employees is a lean medium.

When should you use more rich methods of communication (which may involve travel and the expense of gathering people in one place at the same time), and when is it acceptable to use more efficient, leaner communication approaches? Here are a few tips:

Use media-rich channels of communication if . . .

- Your message is likely to be misunderstood because it's highly detailed.
- Your message is important to people (such as about their compensation).
- There is a high potential for the message to lead to interpersonal conflict.
- You want to know immediately how people respond to your message.

Use media-lean channels of communication if . . .

- The information you are transmitting is routine and noncontroversial.
- You will follow up the presentation of detailed information with a face-to-face meeting later.
- You want to communicate a simple message to many people quickly.
- You already have a good interpersonal relationship with those with whom you're communicating because you have already spent time in face-to-face communication.

- Another study found that language style has a significant impact on the impression created by email. In general, someone who uses a more assertive language style is perceived as more powerful, credible, and even physically attractive than someone whose language style is weak or timid.

- Yet another research team found that groups that communicate by email while solving a problem are more likely to do a better job of analyzing the problem than groups that interact face to face.[37]

- Being able to read and re-read detailed information may help group members focus better on details and message content.

On the negative side:

- Although email and text messaging can be effective for discussing routine business, there are some messages (such as those intended to manage conflict) that are best presented in person.[38]

- There is some evidence that groups that make decisions by email are *less* likely to reach agreement.[39]

Another disadvantage of email and other forms of electronic communication, as with telephone conferencing, is the loss of emotional information communicated by facial expression, vocal inflection, gestures, and body posture.[40] And with diminished emotional information, misunderstanding may be more likely to occur.

Although emotional information may be less prevalent, we nonetheless try to express emotions when we send messages. We're sure you've noticed that some people use emoticons—keyboard symbols that are typed in certain combinations to express emotions—or just put their feelings into words: "I have a big grin on my face as I read what

Media richness theory theory that a communication medium is rich if it has (1) potential for instant feedback, (2) verbal and nonverbal cues that can be processed by senders and receivers, (3) natural language, and (4) a focus on individuals.

DILBERT: © Scott Adams / Dist. by United Feature Syndicate, Inc.

you sent me." (Some people believe that all capital letters in an email message is another way to add emotional richness. But you should be careful using all capital letters: IT'S LIKE SHOUTING AT SOMEONE.) Emotions can be expressed when using email; it just may take more time for relationships to develop and emotions to be expressed.[41]

A final disadvantage of an email message is that once a message is sent, you can't take it back. It's possible, of course, to try to retract something you've said, but as the Russian proverb puts it, "Once a word goes out of your mouth, you can never swallow it again." This is especially true of email messages that can be quickly sent to a large number of people within an organization.

Video conferences. The video conference—a relatively media-rich use of technology—takes place between two or more individuals who are linked by the Internet or by closed-circuit TV. Video conferences have the obvious advantage of permitting groups to interact over long distances when it may be very expensive to have all members travel to one destination. And video conferences have an advantage over a conference phone call because participants can see the nonverbal behavior (facial expressions, eye contact, and posture) that allows the transmission of relational messages. One research team concluded that a video meeting is more likely to be successful if group members have met one another in person prior to the meeting.[42] Being personally introduced to people can help establish trust and may also increase rapport among group members. Another study found that video conferences are better than face-to-face meetings when participants are involved in more structured discussion.[43] So, having a written agenda is especially important when holding a video conference. Group members also seem to prepare better for a video conference than for a face-to-face meeting; perhaps because of their expense and novelty, group members view video conferences as more important than an ordinary meeting.

Electronic meeting systems. Electronic meeting systems (EMS) consist of both computer hardware and software programs that help group members do their work when they are not meeting face to face.[44] Sometimes this technology is called Group Decision Support Systems (GDSS) or Group Support Systems (GSS). One popular commercial software is called Go To Meetings. Whatever the name and abbreviation, EMS, GDSS, and GSS and other systems like them are all based on similar principles. EMS permits you to send simultaneous messages, including PowerPoint slides, to an entire team.

EMS systems can also be used when people are not in the same room at the same time. They can be used synchronously (when each group member is connected at the same time) or asynchrononously (when people are not working together at the same time).

Web page collaboration. Group and team members can collaborate in the same electronic space using a common web page that functions as an electronic bulletin board. Members can go to the web page for information and may be permitted to add, edit, or delete information. Each member has access to what others have gathered and shared. If you have a Facebook or MySpace web page you are well aware of the power and uses of a web page to connect with others, share and receive information, and enhance the quality of existing relationships.

Research on the impact of technology on team problem solving is continuing. The following strategies and observations may offer some guidance to you and your team as you participate in virtual groups and teams.

- Electronically mediated communication seems to work best for more structured, linear tasks.
- The application of computer and e-technology does not inherently result in better solutions and decisions. Technology may allow greater access to

accurate information, help structure the process, and keep a group focused on facts, but problems are solved and decisions are made by people.

- The increased speed of information transfer allows less time for reflection. Thus, technology sometimes allows us to make mistakes faster.

- In computer-mediated meetings, ideas can be captured and recorded with speed and accuracy.

- Technology can enhance team efficiency, but some research suggests that team members perceive that they collaborate better when they interact face to face rather than only over the phone or through other mediated means.[45]

- Ultimately, it's not technology that makes teams better, it's the ability of team members to think critically, communicate effectively, and relate positively to others.[46]

Understanding Team Dynamics

At his first day of work at Samsung, Shuntaro was assigned to a team that was developing new computer chips. He noticed that other team members were an average of ten minutes late to the two staff meetings held that day. Although Alex was the supervisor, the other team members treated him no differently than anyone else; in fact, they sometimes ridiculed Alex behind his back. The most influential member of the team was Hailey, who although quiet and soft spoken, seemed to wield the most power because of her knowledge and experience. What Shuntaro was observing were team dynamics—the various factors that determine what it feels like to belong to a team.

Team Roles

How you communicate with others in a team is a function of your role. Your **role** is the consistent way you communicate with others on a team. Your role is based on your expectations of yourself and the expectations others have of you. There is also evidence that your personality and the personality characteristics of other team members have major influences on team role development.[47] All five of our communication principles for leadership have an impact on the development of your role in a team. How aware you are of your behavior and the behavior of others has a major impact on your verbal and nonverbal messages. Your role develops as you listen and respond and as other team members listen and respond to you, and as you adapt to the communication behavior of other team members.

Your role is worked out as you balance your own expectations of yourself and the expectations others have of you. If no leader has been assigned to a team you're part of, do you often take charge, or are you more comfortable blending in and taking directions from others? Are you the one who makes sure the team gets the work done instead of just having a good time? Maybe you're the team member who seems especially gifted in managing conflict and disagreement. Or, perhaps you have no typical pattern—your role depends on the group and who else is in the group. In business and corporate settings, your specific role may be prescribed by your job title or position. If you are the boss, you may be expected to be the procedural leader and do such things as conduct meetings, set the meeting agenda, or assign people to do certain jobs. But even if your position in the organization prescribes your role, there are still some roles that are shaped by the specific situation and job at hand. The roles people assume in teams can be classified into three types.

Task roles. **Task roles** are those behaviors that help the group achieve its goal and accomplish its work: gathering and sharing research with the group, taking minutes of meetings, and writing ideas on a chalk board are examples of task role behavior.

Social roles. **Social roles** focus on behavior that manages relationships and affects the group climate; these roles help resolve conflict and enhance the flow of communication. Soothing hurt feelings and helping the group celebrate its accomplishments are examples of social role behavior.

Individual roles. **Individual roles** are those that focus attention on the individual rather than the group. These are roles that do *not* help the group; they emphasize individual accomplishments and issues rather than those of the entire group. Dominating group

Role the consistent way someone communicates with others in a team, based on the person's own expectations and what others on the team expect of the person.

Task roles behaviors that help a group achieve its goal and accomplish its work.

Social roles behaviors that manage relationships and affect group climate; these roles help resolve conflict and enhance the flow of communication.

Individual roles behaviors that focus attention on an individual rather than the group.

discussions to talk about personal issues or concerns, telling jokes that get the group off track, and constantly complaining are examples of individual roles.

All five of the communication principles we've presented throughout the book influence whether the role you assume at a given moment in a team is primarily focused on the task, on maintaining relationships, or on individual concerns. Effective team members are aware of the role they are assuming rather than oblivious to how their communication affects the group. Role behavior is communicated by the verbal and nonverbal messages expressed. Roles change: We adjust our behavior by listening and responding to other team members and then adapting our behavior accordingly.

Over sixty years ago, group communication scholars Kenneth Benne and Paul Sheats identified a list of group roles that remains a classic way of identifying the group and individual roles that group and team members typically assume.[48] Table 9.1 presents a summary of these roles. As you look at the list of roles in Table 9.1, you may think to yourself, "Yes that's what I usually do in meetings. That's the role I usually take." And you can probably see roles that other team members usually take on. Most of us typically enact several roles when we collaborate with others. Effective team members adapt their behavior to what is happening or needed in the group.

Table 9.1	A Classification of Group Roles	
Task Roles	**Description**	**Example**
Initiator/ contributor	Offers new ideas or approaches to the group; suggests ways of getting the job done.	"How about developing an agenda to help us organize our work?"
Information seeker	Asks for additional clarification, facts, or other information that helps the group with the issues at hand.	"Can anyone tell me how many times we have had to cancel our fall conference because of bad weather?"
Opinion seeker	Asks group members to share opinions or express a personal point of view.	"So, what do you all think of the new uniform that all of the service workers have been asked to wear?"
Information giver	Provides facts, examples, statistics, or other evidence that relates to the task confronting the group.	"Within the past year, the Vice President for Information Technology has told us to use two different information management systems."
Opinion giver	Offers opinions or beliefs about what the group is discussing.	"I think the new information technology policy will decrease our productivity."
Elaborator	Provides comments or examples to extend or add to the comments of others.	"Jessica, that's a good point. The same thing happened to me when I worked for our main competitor two years ago."
Coordinator	Clarifies and notes relationships among the ideas and suggestions that have been offered by others.	"Travis, your ideas sound a lot like Sondra's suggestion. Sondra, why don't you elaborate on your idea and we'll see if Travis agrees or disagrees with you."
Orienter	Summarizes what has occurred and seeks to keep the group focused on the task at hand.	"I think we're getting a bit off track here. Let's go back to the issue on the agenda."
Evaluator/critic	Assesses the evidence and conclusions that the group is considering.	"How recent are those statistics? I think there are newer figures for us to consider."
Energizer	Spurs the group to action by making comments to motivate the group to work harder.	"Come on team. We can do it if we just keep at it! Don't stop now."
Procedural technician	Helps the group accomplish its goal by handling tasks such as distributing reports, writing ideas on a chalk board, or performing other tasks that help the group.	"I'll write your ideas on the board. After the meeting, I'll copy them and summarize them in an email to each of you."
Recorder	Makes a written record of the group's progress by writing down specific comments, facts, or the minutes of meetings.	"I'll take notes of today's meeting."

Social Roles	Description	Example
Encourager	Offers praise and support and confirms the value of other people and the ideas they contribute.	"You're doing a great job. Thanks for working overtime on this project."
Harmonizer	Manages conflict and mediates disputes between group members.	"Grover, you and Nicole seem to be agreeing more than you are disagreeing. Both of you want the same goal. Let's brainstorm some strategies that can help you both get what you want."
Compromiser	Resolves conflicts by trying to find an acceptable solution. Seeks new alternatives.	"Muriel, you want us to meet at 7:00 PM, and Samantha, you'd like us to start at 8:00. What if we started at 7:30? Would that work?"
Gatekeeper	Encourages people who talk too much to contribute less and invites those who are less talkative to participate.	"Blair, we've not heard what you think. What do you suggest we do?"
Follower	Goes along with the suggestions and ideas of other group members.	"I can support that option. You have summarized the issue about the same way I see it."
Emotion expresser	Verbalizes how the group may be feeling about a specific issue or suggestion.	"We seem to be frustrated that we are not making more progress."
Group observer	Summarizes the group's progress or lack of progress.	"We are making great progress on all of the issues except how much salary we should offer the new person we've just hired."
Tension reliever	Monitors stress within the group and offers suggestions for breaks, using humor or other appropriate strategies.	"Hey, what we need is a good laugh. Here's a joke I saw on the Internet today."

Individual Roles	Description	Example
Aggressor	Deflates or disconfirms the status of other group members or tries to take credit for the work of others.	"Lee, your idea is awful. We all know that what I suggested two meetings ago is clearly the best option."
Blocker	Is negative, stubborn, and disagreeable without an apparent reason.	"I just don't like it. I don't have to tell you why; I just don't like it."
Recognition seeker	Seeks the spotlight by dwelling on his or her personal accomplishments; seeks the praise of others.	"I offered that suggestion two meetings ago I'm the one who usually makes things happen for this team."
Self-confessor	Uses the group as a forum to disclose personal feelings and problems unrelated to the group's task.	"I'm not happy at home, so that's why I seem a bit off at this meeting. My kids are driving me crazy."
Joker	Wants to crack jokes, tell stories, and have fun instead of focusing on the task or what the group needs.	"Hey, let's just go have coffee. Then I'll tell you the gossip about Harvey in accounting. What a nutcase!"
Dominator	Tries to take control of the group, talks too much, and uses flattery or aggression to push his or her ideas on the group.	"Now here's what we're going to do: Martin, you will take notes today; Alice, you go get us some coffee; and Luke, I want you to just sit there in case I need you to run back to my office to get the Simpson file."
Special-interest pleader	Seeks to get the group to support a pet project or personal agenda.	"My boss would like it if we would support the new downtown renovation project. I'll stand a good shot at a promotion if I can get you on board."
Help seeker	Seeks to evoke a sympathetic response from others. Often expresses insecurity stemming from feelings of low self-worth.	" I'm not very good with people. I just feel like I don't relate well to others or have many friends."

What are the best or worst roles to assume? We recommend that you avoid assuming *any* individual role; by definition, these roles focus attention on an individual rather than the group. Groups need people to take on a balance of task and social roles, not draw attention to themselves.

What is the proper balance between task roles and social roles? Some experts recommend a 60:40 balance between task and social roles.[49] What is clear is that groups seem to operate most effectively when it's not all work and no play. Conversely, an out-of-balance group that focuses on just having a good time is not going to achieve its task goals. In general, more of the group's interactions should be about getting the work done than about having fun or managing the social climate—but don't forget to make sure that there are good working relationships among group members.[50]

Team Norms

When George Lucas, president of Lucasfilm, and Micheline Chau, chief operating officer of Lucasfilm, wanted to merge two separate units of the company into one unit, they decided it would be best to create new work norms by moving the teams together into one building rather than keeping them in their separate locations. They wanted the new teams to develop new collaborative norms for work productivity and procedures.[51] **Norms** are standards that determine what is appropriate and inappropriate behavior in a group. Common team norms help develop team coordination and cooperation. Norms reflect what's normal behavior in the group; they influence how group members are supposed to behave—such as the type of language that is acceptable or the casualness of the clothes they wear. Norms can evolve into more formal rules, which are more explicit prescriptions that spell out how group members should interact.[52] Lucas and Chau believed the development of new, common norms would help the new Lucas film team develop a better sense of team identity.

How can you discover what the norms of any group are? Watch the group. Listen and observe any repeated verbal or nonverbal behavior patterns. Note, for example, consistencies in the way people talk or dress. To help you spot norms in your groups, consider the following questions:

- What are group members' attitudes toward time (do meetings start and stop on time)?
- How do group members dress?
- Is it acceptable to use informal, slang terms or to use obscenity?
- What kind of humor is acceptable?
- How does the group treat the leader?

Noting when someone breaks a norm can also help you spot a norm. If a member waltzes into a meeting 20 minutes late and several folks grimace and point to their watches, that's a sure sign that a norm has been violated. The severity of the punishment corresponds to the significance of the norm.[53] Mild punishment is usually unspoken—silent glances or a frowning stare. More serious punishment can be a negative comment about the behavior in front of other group members or even expulsion from the group. You don't have to worry about whether your group will have norms or not; norms happen. You should, however, monitor the group norms to ensure that your behavior doesn't distract from the work of the group or to note whether an unproductive group norm has developed that the group should talk about.

Norms standards that determine what is appropriate and inappropriate behavior in a group.

Communication interaction pattern communication pattern that emerges based on who talks to whom.

Team Networks

Do you have your own Facebook or MySpace page? Chances are you do. If you are a member of one of these popular social networking sites, you have some idea of the power and significance of social networks. People have a need to connect to others. And just as on MySpace or Facebook, in groups and teams, **communication interaction patterns** emerge based on who talks to whom and how often. Some groups have an equal distribution of interaction among members; others develop distinct patterns of interaction between two or more people.[54] Whether we're communicating via the Internet or in person, it's normal to develop preferences for talking to certain people but not others. Group communication scholars have studied and classified the various patterns that emerge when people talk to one another in groups. Who you talk with in a group is a function of the communication networks and interaction patterns that emerge.

In most teams, people speak to certain individual people rather than to the team as a whole. We tend to speak to people who have more power and status. In addition, we talk to people we like more than to people we don't like. There will also be more communication directed toward someone on the team who holds an opinion different from the rest of the group. This person is called a **group deviate**. (Some members may call this person a pain in the neck.) Group members may spend considerable talk time trying to change a group deviate's opinion.

Cliques may create rivalries or inhibit the flow of communication among team members. Fostering inclusiveness and open communication can help prevent conflict in a group.

A group in which everyone talks to everyone else is what is known as an *all-channel network*; all channels are open and used, as illustrated in Figure 9.2. There is considerable interaction and there are no cliques or subgroups that emerge. A **clique** is a smaller group of people within a larger group who form a common bond among themselves. Perhaps you have special friends on your team whom you seek out and who seek you out when you attend meetings. During meetings you probably sit together, share private jokes and stories, and may talk about other members. Although there is nothing wrong with having special friends and colleagues at work, cliques can become detrimental to a team if they foster rivalries within the team or if they inhibit the flow of communication with others. Teams should avoid cliques that can develop divisive power plays that foster conflict. You don't want cliques ratcheting up the emotional tension as the team seeks to deliberate rationally. The first step to avoiding cliques is to be aware that one exists. Then make a conscious effort to be less exclusive and more integrated into the conversation of the entire group.

In a team with a *chain network* (Figure 9.2), people convey messages through one person at a time rather than to all group members. Many business and professional organizations have a hierarchical chain communication pattern. For example, the president of the company sends a message to the vice president, who, in turn, talks to the director; the director talks to a manager, who eventually gives the message to the other employees. As you might suspect, passing a message through many different ears and minds often results in misunderstanding by the time the message reaches the last person in the chain.

The *wheel network* pattern occurs when one person receives most of the messages from other group members; this pivotal communicator also is the prime source of information *to* other group members. Perhaps in your group of friends there is one person who seems to know everything that's going on. The wheel pattern emerges when there is a strong leader or when the group members do individual tasks and need someone to keep them informed about what others are doing.

What's the best interaction pattern? It depends. There may be times when the structured nature of the chain or wheel pattern may be called for. For example, during the huddle before a football play, when time is short, usually the quarterback does most of the talking while others listen (wheel network). But most teams function best if there is an all-channel pattern of communication, especially when the group is not too large and is trying to generate new, creative ideas.

As you participate in or lead team meetings, be aware of the general pattern of communication. Are all members participating? Do some people whisper their ideas only to a few and not share with the rest of the group? Is a group deviate monopolizing the conversation or blocking progress? By being observant of interaction patterns, you can help the team enhance cohesiveness and develop appropriate roles to get the work done.

Group deviate a team member who holds an opinion different from the rest of the group; group members may spend considerable talk time trying to change this person's opinion.

Clique a smaller group of people within a larger group who form a common bond among themselves.

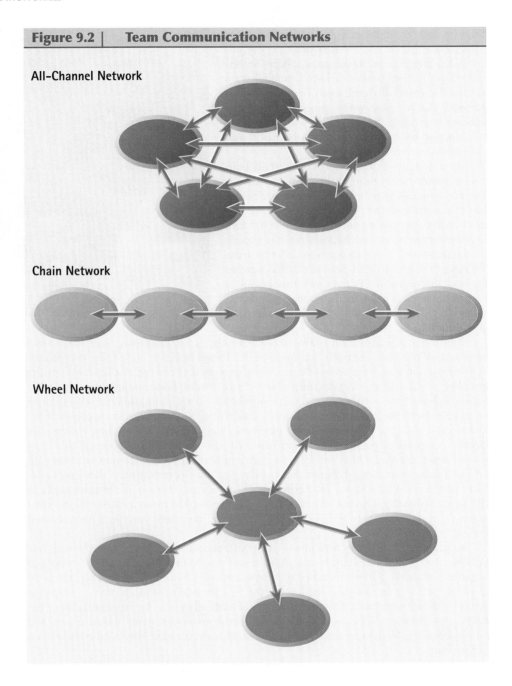

Figure 9.2 | Team Communication Networks

All–Channel Network

Chain Network

Wheel Network

Improving Team Dynamics

Aware
Verbal
Nonverbal
Listen
Adapt

Now that you can describe team roles, norms, and networks, you may wonder if there are specific ways to improve team dynamics. One way to clarify roles is to establish clear ground rules about how the team should best operate. Making sure the team has a clear mission statement contributes to good dynamics: Effective teams have a clear, elevating goal. Managing differences in status and power can also help reduce tension. And implementing strategies to enhance team cohesiveness can help teams work together more effectively. Regardless of whether you are the designated leader or not, you can have an important influence in improving team dynamics by being aware of communication strategies that can help a team operate more effectively. And you implement these strategies by using and interpreting verbal and nonverbal messages, listening, and appropriately adapting to team member behavior.

How To Develop Team Ground Rules

Team ground rules are explicit, agreed-on prescriptions for acceptable and appropriate behavior. An effective team takes the time to develop clear rules that will help to organize routine tasks and procedures. Although team norms typically develop without anyone explicitly spelling out what the norm should be, a team may decide to develop more explicit rules to help get the work accomplished. For example, although it may be a norm that meetings usually start on time, a team could decide to establish a ground rule that all meetings will *always* begin on time. There's evidence that teams are more effective if they develop explicit rules that help the team operate efficiently.[55] Rules help keep order so that meaningful work can be accomplished. Rules also state what the team or organization values. Honesty, fairness, adherence to schedules, and personal safety are typical values embedded in team ground rules.

How does a team develop ground rules? Soon after the formation of a team, the team leader may facilitate a discussion to establish the ground rules. If a team has no designated leader, any team member can say, "To help us get organized and accomplish our task, let's develop some ground rules." Teams clearly operate better if team members develop their own ground rules rather than having them imposed from "on high." Following are some questions that can help a group develop clear and appropriate ground rules:

- How should we record the results of our meetings?
- Who should set meeting agendas?
- How long should our meetings last?
- Should we have a regular meeting time and place?
- What should a member do if he or she can't attend a meeting?
- Should we make our decisions by majority vote or seek a consensus on every decision?

The questions above might result in the following team ground rules:

- Every meeting will begin on time.
- Each team member is expected to attend every meeting.
- Each team member will be prepared for every meeting.
- Only one person will speak at a time.
- We will work together to manage conflict when it arises.
- If we get off the agenda, we will return to the agenda.
- We will agree to make a written note of issues or topics that we discuss that are not on the agenda and will return to the topics later.
- We will make decisions by consensus rather than by simple majority vote.
- Each team member will follow through on individual assignments.

> **Team ground rules** explicit, agreed-on prescriptions for acceptable and appropriate behavior, which help the team organize routine tasks and procedures.
>
> **Team mission statement** a concise description of a team's goals or desired outcomes.

How To Develop a Team Mission Statement

A **team mission statement** is a concise description of a team's goals or desired outcomes. A clearly worded mission statement helps a team know not only whether it's on task or off task but also when it has completed the task.

A good team mission statement should pass the SMARTS test—it should be Specific, Measurable, Attainable, Relevant, Time-bound, and should Stretch the team.[56] A well-worded team mission statement has six elements. It is specific: It clearly describes what the team should accomplish. It is measurable: the team must be able to assess whether the mission was achieved. It is attainable—The mission statement should be realistic. It is relevant: The mission should be appropriate to what the team has been assigned to do. It is time-bound: The mission statement sets a deadline for achieving the mission. Finally, the mission statement should be a bit of a challenge, so as to stretch the team. If the mission

Verbal

is too simple, it won't inspire the team to do its best work. Here are examples of team mission statements that pass the SMARTS test:

- Our team will make 10 percent more widgets by the end of the month.
- Our team will sell more life insurance policies than any other sales team in our sales area.
- Our team will attract two new businesses to our community, which will result in an increased tax base by the end of the year.

How To Manage Team Status and Power Differences

Status refers to an individual's importance and prestige. Your status in a group influences whom you talk to, who talks to you, and even what you talk about. Although some people underestimate their perceived status and influence in a group, research suggests that you are probably quite aware of your own status level when communicating with others.[57] Your perceived importance affects both your verbal and your nonverbal messages. Typically, a person with high status

- Talks more than those of lower status.
- Directs comments to other high-status group members.
- Has more influence on the decisions the group makes.
- Is listened to by group members.
- Makes more comments to the entire group.[58]

Being aware of status differences can help you predict who talks to whom. If you can discern status differences, you'll also be better able to predict the type of messages communicated.

Status influences group communication, but just because a person has high status does not mean that his or her ideas are good ones. Don't let status differences influence your perceptions of the value of the ideas contributed. Some groups get into trouble because they automatically defer to the person with more status without reviewing the validity of the ideas presented. Similarly, don't dismiss ideas out of hand because the person who suggested them doesn't have high status or prestige. Focus on the quality of the message, not just on the messenger.

Whereas status refers to perceived importance, **power** is the ability to influence others' behavior. While status and power sometimes go hand in hand, a group member could have status and still not be able to influence how others behave. You have power if you can influence what others do—if you say or do things that get things done. A person's power stems from the resources available to him or her to influence others. Who does and doesn't have power in a group influences how people relate to one another.

A power struggle often creates ripples of conflict and contention through a group. And on the surface a conflict may seem to revolve around a simple disagreement, such as when a report is due, but underlying the disagreement may be a power struggle. The real issue may be who gets to decide when the report is due.

Power struggles also frequently focus attention on individual group members. People with less power tend to participate less in group discussion, unless they're trying to gain power. A group in which power is not balanced could have problems; the "power people" might dominate the discussion. When one or more members dominate the discussion, the group loses the contributions and insights of others. Research supports the conclusion that teams with equal power distribution usually have better quality outcomes.[59]

One classic discussion of how individuals become powerful identified five power bases: legitimate, referent, expert, reward, and coercive power. These power bases explain why certain people have power and why others don't.[60]

Legitimate power. You have **legitimate power** if someone elected or appointed you to a position of power. Your power source comes from holding a position of responsibility. The president of your university or college has the legitimate power to establish and implement school policy. Senators from your state, the chief executive officer of a company, or the manager of a department store are other examples of people who have legitimate power.

Status an individual's importance and prestige.

Power the ability to influence others' behavior.

Legitimate power power that stems from being elected or appointed to a specific position or office.

A group or team member who has been designated team leader or elected chair or president of the group is given legitimate power to influence how the group operates.

Referent power. You have **referent power** if people like you. Put simply, people we like have more power over us than people we do not like. If you are working on a committee with your best friend, your friend exerts power over you in that you may give more credence to what your friend recommends. Just the opposite occurs if you are working with someone you don't like; you will be more likely to ignore that person's advice.

Expert power. Knowledge is power. People who have **expert power** are perceived as informed or knowledgeable and have more influence than people who are perceived as uninformed.

Reward power. People who can grant favors, money, promotions, or other rewards have **reward power**. Someone who can take away a punishment or other unpleasant experience (rescinding a restrictive dress code or establishing a more flexible work schedule, for example) also has reward power. People who have greater power to reward typically are sent more positive, supportive messages than people who don't have the ability to reward others. But reward power is effective only if a person being rewarded finds the reward (or the removal of a punishment) satisfying or useful. What is rewarding to one person may not be rewarding to another person.

Coercive power. You have **coercive power** if you can punish others; coercive power is the flip side of reward power. If someone can cut your salary, lower your grade, demote you, or force you to do unpleasant jobs, that person has coercive power. The power results from the perception that the person with the power will actually use the power. If someone has the authority to punish, but if group members don't perceive that the person will use this power, then he or she doesn't really have power.

Referent power power that stems from being liked.

Expert power power derived from having knowledge and expertise.

Reward power power arising from the ability to grant favors, money, or other rewards.

Coercive power power stemming from the ability to punish others.

RECAP: Types of Power

Legitimate power	Power that arises from being elected, appointed, or ordained to lead or make decisions for a group or a team.
Referent power	Power that arises from being well liked.
Expert power	Power that arises from having information and being knowledgeable about issues or ideas.
Reward power	Power that arises from having the ability to bestow gifts, money, recognition, or other rewards that are valued by group members.
Coercive power	Power that arises from having the ability to punish others.

Even though we have categorized power into five different types, don't get the idea that group members have just one type. In reality, every group or team member typically has more than one source of power. For example, a group member who is the elected leader (legitimate power) may be able to offer rewards (reward power) or punishment (coercive power).

One of the first things to be aware of when managing power differences is the power basis. Say you're having a power struggle with your boss over when a project should be completed. Because your boss has legitimate power to fire you (coercive power) or give you a raise (reward power), it would be politically prudent to note the power resources your boss has and that you don't possess. In addition to being aware of people's power bases and the conflict resolution strategies discussed in Chapter 6, it is useful to keep in mind the other communication principles that we've discussed throughout the book. Your verbal and nonverbal messages can either create more tension or help to manage the tension that a power struggle produces. And the sensitivity established through listening and responding will help you appropriately adapt your messages to help manage power issues that arise in teams.

Aware
Verbal
Nonverbal
Listen
Adapt

Table 9.2   Suggestions for Enhancing Team Cohesiveness[61]

Cohesive Teams	Uncohesive Teams
Talk about the group in terms of "we" rather than "I."	Tend to emphasize the individual contributions of group members.
Reinforce good attendance at group meetings.	Make less effort to encourage group members to attend every meeting.
Establish and maintain group traditions.	Make less effort to develop group traditions.
Set clear short-term and long-term goals.	Avoid setting goals or establishing deadlines.
Encourage everyone in the group to participate in the group task.	Allow only the most talkative or high-status members to participate in the group task.
Celebrate when the group accomplishes either a short-term or a long-term goal.	Discourage group celebration; group meetings are all work and little or no fun.
Stress teamwork and collaboration.	Stress individual accomplishment.

How To Enhance Team Cohesiveness

Perhaps you've read about the Three Musketeers or have seen a movie about them; if so, you know that their motto was "one for all and all for one." They were a cohesive group; they liked being with each other. Group **cohesiveness** is the degree of attraction that members of a group feel toward one another and the group. In a highly cohesive group, the members feel a high degree of loyalty to one another; the goal of the team is also the goal of the individuals. Members of cohesive groups listen to one another, care about what each other think, and feel a sense of collective belonging to the team.

Teams become cohesive because of a variety of forces that attract people to the group and to each other. Similarity of goals, feelings of genuine liking, and similarity of background and culture are variables that influence group cohesion. Cohesiveness also is more likely to develop when team members' emotional needs are satisfied by participating in the group.[62] In the case of the Three Musketeers, the desire to do good deeds and assist those in need provided the clear, elevating goal that gave them satisfaction. Think of a team you belong to in which there is a high degree of *esprit de corps* and cohesiveness. You will also probably find that you both like the group members and support the overall goals and objectives that the group is trying to accomplish.

What enhances team cohesiveness? Table 9.2 summarizes some strategies that enhance team cohesiveness. Cohesiveness is more likely to occur if group members have the opportunity to talk freely with one another about the group goal and if this interaction increases affection and liking for one another. Teams that have greater control over how they conduct their work are also likely to be more cohesive.[63] Teams that aren't cohesive typically don't have a clear, shared goal, and the team members don't like one another and haven't spent much time focusing on relationship development roles. An uncohesive team is also likely to include people who perform individual roles rather than team task or relationship development roles.[64]

Can a team be too cohesive? Yes: If team members are focused only on developing a positive, cohesive relationship to the exclusion of getting their work done, group productivity can suffer. If the team becomes focused primarily on enjoying one another's company, they will produce *less* work. Strive for team cohesiveness, but balance cohesiveness with a focus on accomplishing the team's task.

Cohesiveness the degree of attraction that members of a group feel toward one another and the group.

Approaches to Teamwork

What's the best approach to analyzing teams so as to understand how they work and to make them more effective? Some team experts suggest that it's best to develop a detailed knowledge of team processes and understand how a team moves through various phases of development. So you would approach a team by getting close enough to *describe* what occurs in the team. Others suggest the best approach is to assess whether a team is using certain communication *functions*. The *functional approach* suggests that effective team members are those who meet certain task requirements in the way they communicate with other team members. Yet a third approach emphasizes using specific skills and techniques to help a team work better. This approach *prescribes* precise strategies that effective teams should employ, such as how to develop an effective meeting agenda, how to reach agreement, or steps to follow in solving a problem. A key element of being an effective team leader is understanding which approach may be best in developing the team's potential.

The Descriptive Approach: Describing Team Development

When you describe an object or experience, you look for ways to categorize or classify it. A **descriptive approach** to team development seeks to identify the typical ways teams behave when they attempt to solve a problem. It is based on the assumption that all groups experience a natural or normal process of development. Researchers have attempted to describe the way group members talk and behave to see if they can discern predictable patterns.

Some researchers have found that groups go through certain phases or sequences of talk when they meet to solve a problem.[65] Researchers don't agree on the exact nature of these phases, or even on the number of phases; some researchers have found three phases, most have found four. One of the most descriptive four-phase models was developed by group communication researcher Aubrey Fisher.[66] His four phases of group talk are (1) orientation, (2) conflict, (3) emergence, and (4) reinforcement.

Orientation. As you might suspect, when people first get together in a group, they must become oriented to what they are doing. During the **orientation phase**, group members become oriented to at least two things: who's in the group and what they will be doing. When you join a group for the first time, you have high uncertainty about how the group will be organized, who's in charge, and exactly how things will work. Research on the orientation phase suggests that your early communication is directed at orienting yourself toward others as well as to the group's task. During this first phase people often experience **primary tension**, which results from the uncertainty and discomfort they feel when the group meets for the first time.[67] Some group members who don't like uncertainty and are eager to start sorting things out may suggest an agenda: "Hello, my name is Steve. Let's each introduce ourselves." Other group members are quite content to simply sit quietly in the background and let others take the lead. As people begin to become acquainted and group members start talking about the group's purpose, typical groups experience the second phase: conflict.

Conflict. People are different. That unprofound observation has profound implications for human communication, and nowhere is it more evident than in a group discussion after the group gets down to business. The **conflict phase** typically, but not always, follows the orientation phase. During the orientation phase, group members form opinions about what the group should be doing and who should be doing it. As they become more comfortable in and oriented to the group, they start asserting these opinions.

The conflict phase is necessary for both solving problems and maintaining group relationships. The conflict phase occurs when people are honest about sharing their opinions. If there is no conflict, it usually means people aren't being honest about how they really feel. When ideas aren't challenged and tested, the group usually makes stupid decisions. Also, honest yet tactful expression of personal disagreement is more likely to foster genuine relationships rather than phony ones. You can take some comfort in knowing that conflict is an expected part of group deliberations.

Emergence. You know your group is in the **emergence phase** when decisions begin to be made and the group begins to solidify a common point of view. Though conflict is still a part of phase three, what sets the emergence phase apart from the conflict phase is the way in which group members manage the conflict. Norms, roles, ground rules, and leadership patterns that have been established in the group now help the group get work accomplished. In the emergence phase, a group settles on norms and moves toward consensus or agreement.

Descriptive approach an approach to team development that seeks to identify the typical ways teams behave in solving problems.

Orientation phase the first phase of group interaction, in which members become adjusted to one another and to the group's task.

Primary tension the tension that results from the uncertainty and discomfort people experience when they meet in a group for the first time.

Conflict phase the second phase of group interaction, in which group members experience some disagreement about social issues and group tasks.

Emergence phase the third phase of group interaction, in which conflict or disagreement is managed and decisions are made.

Reinforcement. Group members become more unified in the fourth phase, the **reinforcement phase**. During the orientation, conflict, and emergence phases, group members struggle through getting acquainted, developing cohesiveness, competing for status and prominence, and puzzling over issues and action the group could take. The group eventually emerges from those struggles and develops a new sense of direction; this results in a more positive feeling about the group. The group more clearly develops a sense of "we." In fact, one of the ways you can identify the reinforcement phase is when group members use more collective pronouns (*we, us, our*) than personal pronouns (*I, me, my*) to talk about the group.

Although we have identified four distinct phases that groups can experience, not all groups process neatly through these phases in exactly the same way. The descriptive approach to group problem solving has identified these phases and can help provide a general overview of how many groups operate, but more recent research suggests some groups don't go through these phases exactly as presented here.[68] For example, a team trying to design a new health care policy may spiral through several phases during the same meeting. Even if you have difficulty identifying these phases in your group, you will probably see some elements of these four types of talk during the history of your group meetings. Some groups may simply get stuck in orientation. Have you ever participated in a group that could never quite figure out what it was supposed to do? If so, your group may not have overcome the initial uncertainty of who does what when or determined what its goal was. Some groups remain in the conflict phase, perhaps bouncing between orientation and conflict. Eventually something will emerge from the group (phase three), even if it is not a wise decision or a quality solution. The group may decide, for example, to disband and never meet again because the members are so dysfunctional. Reinforcement (phase four) is likely to occur because people like to make sense of what happens to them. Even if the group disbands, members are likely to celebrate its demise or reinforce the decision to disband.

Many groups, especially those that emphasize efficiency and productivity, may very quickly gloss over the reinforcement phase of group interaction. Wise group leaders and participants make sure that victories are celebrated and that both group and individual efforts are recognized. The resulting cohesiveness and positive feelings that result from such celebrations will be helpful as the group prepares for its next task or phase. Again, the phases may not occur in the orderly and predictable way described by researchers, but most groups do experience some elements of these phrases.

The Functional Approach: Understanding Team Functions

The **functional approach** to team development suggests that in order for a team to be effective, certain communication functions must occur. Researchers have spent several years trying to identify what functions help teams improve communication and effectiveness.[69] Researchers have identified these essential communication functions by studying both effective and ineffective groups. Effective group members did things differently than the ineffective group members. Identifying what these behaviors are led to the labeling of key behaviors or functions that, when present, are more likely to produce better results.

An important skill of an effective group member is to be a vigilant thinker.[70] **Vigilant thinkers** pay attention to the *process* of how work is done in teams rather than focusing only on techniques used to achieve a goal. A vigilant thinker also assesses, evaluates, and tests ideas. One research team identified four essential questions that vigilant-thinking group members should consider:

1. Does something in the present situation need to be changed?
2. What goal does the group want to achieve?
3. What choices does the group have that will help achieve the goal?
4. What are the positive and negative implications of the choices?[71]

Even though these questions are usually discussed in the order listed, some groups don't follow this sequence.[72] What is clear, however, is that if one or more of these critical questions is *not* discussed, the group is less effective. These questions lead to the achievement of the critical functions that groups need to consider. The following five functions seem critical to effective group performance.

Reinforcement phase the fourth phase of group interaction, in which group members express positive feelings toward each other and toward the group.

Functional approach an approach to team development that suggests that in order for a team to be effective, certain communication functions must occur.

Vigilant thinkers people who pay attention to the process of how work is done in teams rather than focusing only on techniques used to achieve a goal.

Goal function. As we've discussed, it is important for a group or team to have a clear goal and to develop a team mission statement. Thus, taking time to talk about the team goal is an essential team function. Articulating a clear and elevating goal is one of the earliest functions that team members should enact. It is important therefore, for group members to ask and answer the question, "What's our clear, elevating goal?" The goal is developed by the group's asking itself, "Do we need to change something that is happening now?" Most group goals boil down to something that you want either more of or less of. If there is no need for a change, then there is nothing that the group wants more or less of.[73]

Analysis function. Another critical function of team communication is to analyze the data, information, or evidence that can help the group achieve the group goal.[74] To analyze something is to break it into parts and critically evaluate its causes, symptoms, and history. An effective team does at least these three things:

1. Identifies the data, information, or evidence the group currently has.
2. Identifies the additional data, information, or evidence the group needs in order to make a decision.
3. Draws accurate conclusions from the data, information, and evidence that it has.

As is true of other team communication functions, when group members don't do these things, or do them poorly, the group is more likely to make inappropriate decisions. For example, the team that coordinates the space shuttle landing has to decide whether the weather will permit the shuttle to land either in Florida or in California. If the team doesn't interpret the weather data accurately, then a poor decision may be reached. Having too little evidence—or no evidence at all—is one of the reasons groups sometimes don't analyze their present situations correctly. Even if group members do have plenty of evidence, they may not have tested the evidence to see if it is true, accurate, or relevant.

Idea-generation function. Another hallmark of an effectively functioning team is that team members generate many ideas and potential solutions after analyzing a situation. Effective teams don't just settle on one or two ideas and then move on; they list multiple approaches. We'll provide specific tips and strategies for generating ideas and enhancing team creativity in the next chapter.

The most effectively functioning teams have members who make high-quality statements. Researchers define high-quality statements as precise rather than unfocused and abstract. High-quality statements don't ramble, and they are consistent with evidence, relevant to the topic under discussion, and positively reinforce what other group members are saying.[75] When discussing how to develop a new Internet-based resume screening process, one team member began ranting about how unprepared job applicants are today. Another team member agreed and said she thought the problem is in the way students are being educated. These off-task comments epitomize low-quality statements. Teams are more productive if their comments are focused on the task at hand; mere emotional venting doesn't move the team forward.

Sometimes teams get stuck and ideas just don't flow. Rather than continuing to hammer away at the problem, the group may want to take a break from it for a while. Perhaps you've had a great idea come to you when you were taking a walk, driving, or doing the dishes or some other mindless activity. Taking a break can give your subconscious mind a chance to thrash through some of the issues and perhaps generate a breakthrough solution.[76] The principle of awareness operates here: Team members need to become aware of the group's ability to generate high-quality ideas. Leaders have a special responsibility to be mindful of the team process and help steer the team back to productive territory.

Evaluation function. Another characteristic of high-performing teams is that team members know a good idea when they see it. They are able to evaluate evidence, opinions, assumptions, and solutions and separate the good from the bad. Low-performing teams are less discriminating. A team that is eager to make a decision in order to get their job over with usually comes up with poor-quality decisions.

Effective groups, such as this team at NASA, have a clear goal, and they analyze situations, generate ideas, and evaluate those ideas to help achieve that goal. In the process, group members listen to what others have to say.

An effectively functioning team examines the pros and the cons of an idea, issue, or opinion. When the team is zeroing in on a particular course of action, an effective team member says "Let's consider the positive and negative consequences of this decision." Some teams literally make a written list of the pros and the cons on a chalk board, whiteboard, or flip chart. Teams that do this are more likely to come up with a better decision than teams that don't systematically evaluate the pros and cons of a potential solution or decision.[77]

How do you know a good solution when you see it? Early on, when identifying its clear and elevating goal, an effective team also precisely describes attributes of a high-quality solution. Criteria include such things as how much the solution should cost, when it could be implemented, and the level of success the group expects to achieve. Effective teams check to see if the solution meets the pre-determined criteria for an effective solution. In effect, the team simply asks, "Does this solution achieve the goal?" If these criteria are clearly stated (preferably written down), then they can be used to check the quality of the solution the group plans to adopt. If, after looking at the pros and the cons, you find that the pros outweigh the cons, the final test is to ensure that the solution also achieves the goal based on the criteria outlined.

Personal sensitivity function. Most of the group functions we've described so far focus on getting the work done effectively and efficiently. But team success is about more than just focusing on the task. Effectively functioning team members also are sensitive to the needs of others. They listen to what each group member has to say—even those who may hold a minority opinion. One of the benefits of working collaboratively comes from hearing a variety of ideas. If opinions of others are quickly squelched because they are not what most other team members think or believe, the team loses the power of many different points of view. Effective team members are aware of how the comments they make might be perceived by other group members. Finally, effectively functioning group members use appropriate verbal and nonverbal communication and appropriately adapt their communication to others.

Effective team members balance the concern for the task with concern for the feelings of others. As we noted when discussing cohesiveness, being too task-oriented is not beneficial to the functioning of a team.

The Prescriptive Approach: Identifying Team Strategies

Prescriptive approach an approach to team development that assumes that team members need a specific sequence of steps and techniques in order to stay on task and be productive.

The descriptive approach to teams suggests that there is a natural order or sequence to how groups and teams operate, although each group is unique and a group doesn't always follow a pattern. The functional approach to teams is based on the assumption that effective teams perform certain functions or communication behaviors that ineffective teams don't perform. A **prescriptive approach** to teams is based on the assumption that team members need to use specific steps and techniques to stay on task and remain productive while still being sensitive to other team members. Just as a prescription from your doctor is a specific medicine that is intended to treat a particular ailment, a prescriptive approach *prescribes* things to do to enhance the communication health of the team. In the next chapter we offer a wealth of suggestions, strategies, and techniques to help improve the process of collaborating with others.

Communication Principles and Skills for Leadership

Principle One: Be aware of your communication with yourself and others.
- Be knowledgeable about the differences between groups and teams.
- Be aware of the roles you and others typically assume in teams.
- Be aware of the norms and rules that develop in teams.
- Be aware of the phases of orientation, conflict, emergence, and reinforcement that many teams go through during their deliberations.

Principle Two: Effectively use and interpret verbal messages.

- Help a team establish clear ground rules.
- Clarify team goals; a clear, elevating goal is one of the key determinants of an effective team.
- Provide supportive, positive comments to help encourage team members.
- Clarify individual member roles and your own role when verbally communicating in your team.
- Talk about your team in terms of "we" rather than "I" to enhance team cohesiveness.

Principle Three: Effectively use and interpret nonverbal messages

- Accurately observe nonverbal cues to help you understand team norms.
- Provide positive, reinforcing nonverbal behaviors such as eye contact, forward lean, and appropriately positive facial cues to enhance team climate and cohesiveness.

Principle Four: Listen and respond thoughtfully to others.

- Listen attentively to others to establish a positive, supportive climate.
- Use active listening skills to clarify misunderstandings and help manage primary tension in groups.

Principle Five: Appropriately adapt messages to others.

- Adapt to the team and team members by paying attention to the roles, norms, and status differences.
- Adapt to determine if the team needs to perform certain communication functions, as identified in the functional approach to team development.
- Appropriately adapt to cultural differences within the team.

Discussion Questions

1. What are the key differences between a small group and a team?

2. What are advantages and disadvantages of working in a virtual team?

3. Describe and provide examples of task, social, and individual group roles.

4. Clarify the distinction between norms and team or group rules.

5. Differentiate between status and power.

6. What are the five bases of power discussed in this chapter?

7. Identify strategies that enhance group cohesiveness.

8. Identify three types of communication networks that occur in teams and discuss the implications of these patterns for team productivity.

9. Define, compare, and contrast the descriptive, functional, and prescriptive approaches to team communication.

Building Your Skills

1. Make a list of the groups and teams of which you are a member. Using the definitions of small groups and teams in this chapter's discussion, place your own groups and teams on a continuum, with those entities that are more like a group at one end and those that are more like a team at the other. Explain why your groups are groups and your teams are teams, based on the distinctions made in the chapter. How many of the

characteristics of effective teams and effective team members are illustrated by the teams of which you are a member?

2. Identify the many ways you have communicated using media and technology during the past week. Identify how anonymity, decreased emphasis on physical appearance, distance, and control over time have had an effect on your virtual communication.

3. Of the roles listed in Table 9.1, which do you typically assume in groups, teams, and meetings? Identify two task and two social roles that you usually do not assume. Why don't you assume these roles?

4. Identify a team that you are currently participating in or a team with which you have worked in the past. Identify norms, rules, and any explicit ground rules that were developed by the team. If the team did not have an explicit mission statement, reflect on the team goals and objectives and develop a mission statement for the team incorporating the six elements of a mission statement presented in the chapter.

5. On a scale from 1 to 10, identify the level of cohesiveness in a group or team of which you have been or currently are a member. Which of the aspects of cohesive teams described in the text are present in your team, and which are not evident?

6. At your next team meeting, try diagramming the interacting patterns of the team. Use a wheel network diagram like the one below; adjust the diagram to fit the size of your team, and put a team member's name in each oval. Draw an arrow between group members indicate their first interaction, and then make a mark on the line for each additional comment. Your ability to analyze team interaction patterns can be an important tool to help you understand a variety of team dynamics, including roles, norms, status, power, and cohesiveness.

7. Read each of the following statements once. Mark whether you agree (A) or disagree (D) with each statement. Take 4 or 5 minutes to do this. Then in a small group, try to reach consensus—everyone either agreeing or disagreeing with the statement. Try especially to find reasons for differences of opinions. If your group cannot reach consensus, you may change the wording in any statement enough to promote unanimity.[78]

_____ 1. Despite its flaws, a meeting is the <u>best</u> way to get work done in an organization.

_____ 2. There are often occasions when an individual who is a part of a working team should do what he or she thinks is right regardless of what the group has decided to do.

_____ 3. Sometimes it is necessary to change people in the direction you yourself think is right, even if they object.

_____ 4. It is sometimes necessary to ignore the feelings of others in order to reach a group decision.

_____ 5. When the leader is doing his or her best, one should not openly criticize or find fault with his or her conduct.

_____ 6. In most team conflicts, someone must win and someone must lose. That's the way conflict is.

_____ 7. Much time is wasted in talk when everybody in the team has to be considered before making a decision.

_____ 8. Almost any job that can be done by a committee can be done better by having one individual responsible for the job.

_____ 9. Body language and nonverbal messages are more important than verbal messages when communicating with others in team meetings.

_____ 10. If people spend enough time together, they will find something to disagree about and will eventually become upset with one another.

_____ 11. Most hidden agendas are probably best kept hidden to ensure a positive social climate and manage conflict.

_____ 12. If you disagree with someone in a group, it is usually better to keep quiet than to get the group off-track with your personal difference of opinion.

_____ 13. When a team can't reach a decision, members should abide by the decision of the group leader if the leader is qualified and competent.

_____ 14. Some people produce more conflict and tension than others. These people should be restricted from decision-making meetings.

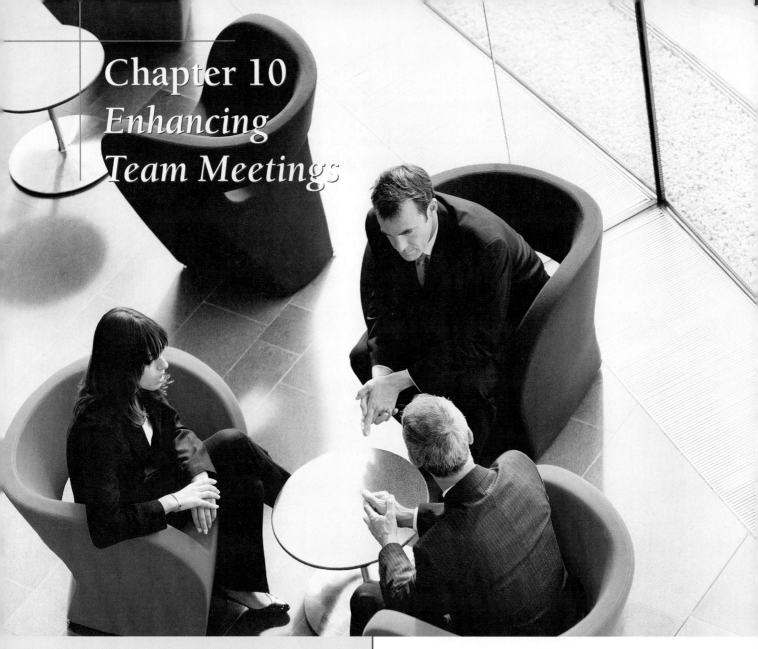

Chapter 10
Enhancing Team Meetings

chapter outline

After reading this chapter, you should be able to

- Decide whether you should or should not hold a meeting.

- Develop clear meeting goals, which may include sharing information, discussing information, and taking action.

- Describe and implement strategies for developing an effective meeting agenda.

- Identify and practice the steps of team decision making and problem solving.

- Use strategies that enhance team creativity and result in the generation of ideas and solutions to problems.

- Describe and implement strategies for facilitating team meetings.

- Identify and use skills that help a team avoid groupthink.

- Use skills that help foster team consensus.

- Identify principles and skills for leading team meetings.

Perhaps humorist Dave Barry had heard the phrase "death by meeting" when he compared business meetings with funerals. He noted that at both meetings and funerals, "you have a gathering of people who are wearing uncomfortable clothing and would rather be somewhere else. The major difference is that most funerals have a definite purpose. Also, nothing is ever really buried in a meeting."[1] Dave Barry isn't the only person who doesn't like meetings. Most people who spend a considerable amount of time in meetings would probably agree with the following sentiments:

- A committee is a collection of the unfit chosen from the unwilling by the incompetent to do the unnecessary.
- A meeting should include at least three people: but one should be sick and another should be absent.
- On judgment day the Lord will divide those entering his Kingdom by telling those on His right hand to enter the Kingdom and those on His left hand to break into small groups.

Why does meeting participation inspire such negative reactions? Often it's because meeting participants have not mastered the principles we've stressed throughout this book. Although most of you have attended meetings, let's make it clear what a meeting is.

A **meeting** is a structured conversation among a small group of people who gather to accomplish a specific task. Meetings are the ever-present format for collaborating in most contemporary organizations.[2] For a meeting to be productive, the group or team should be small enough that each participant can contribute to the conversation.[3] Meetings should have a specific goal; an agenda that identifies what will be discussed, as well as interactive conversation that is focused on achieving the meeting goal.

Meetings are more productive if participants are aware of their own behaviors. Using and interpreting verbal and nonverbal symbols, as well as listening and responding to those messages with sensitivity, are also vital for meeting effectiveness. Because of the complexity and uncertainty that can arise when several people are collaborating, being able to adapt message content and message structure is essential.

In this chapter we'll describe skills, techniques, and strategies that make meetings effective. It is important to understand how most groups and teams do their work (the descriptive approach to teams), as well as to understand the specific functions that effective groups perform (the functional approach to teams). Throughout this chapter we note that being able to adapt and respond to a group's need for organization and agendas (structure) as well as its need for creative, free-flowing ideas (interaction) is a fundamental principle of meeting management. The essential tool for giving a meeting structure is the agenda. To manage interaction, meeting participants need to be good facilitators of talk.

What specific problems occur most frequently in meetings? Here's a list of the top ten meeting "sins."[4]

1. Participants getting off the subject
2. Lack of goals or agenda
3. Running too long
4. Poor or inadequate preparation
5. Inconclusiveness
6. Disorganization
7. Ineffective leadership and lack of control
8. Irrelevance of information discussed
9. Wasting time
10. Starting late

Each of these meeting problems boils down to a lack of one or the other of the two essential things meetings need in order to be effective: structure and interaction. **Structure** is the way a group or team discussion is organized; structure is provided by the agenda and other techniques that help a group stay focused on the task at hand. A meeting that gets off topic, has no agenda, or runs too long needs more structure to keep the group focused on its goal. **Interaction** is the give-and-take conversation that occurs when people collaborate. It is vital for the exchange of ideas. However, a disorganized meeting that wastes time may have too much interaction—too much unfocused talk. One study suggests that people who communicate in groups and teams typically change topics about once a minute unless someone is helping them stay on track.[5] Too much interaction will cause the meeting to wobble.

Can a group have too much structure? Yes. If you've been to a meeting or group discussion that seemed more like a seminar than an interactive discussion, then you know what it's like to experience too much structure. If the meeting is so controlled that one or two people do most of the talking, then you're not at a meeting, you're at a speech. In a

Meeting a structured conversation among a small group of people who gather to accomplish a specific task.

Structure the way a group or team discussion is organized; provided by the agenda and by techniques that help a group stay focused on the task at hand.

Interaction the give-and-take conversation that occurs when people collaborate.

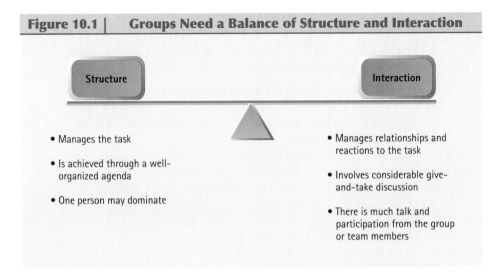

Figure 10.1 | Groups Need a Balance of Structure and Interaction

Structure

Interaction

- Manages the task

- Is achieved through a well-organized agenda

- One person may dominate

- Manages relationships and reactions to the task

- Involves considerable give-and-take discussion

- There is much talk and participation from the group or team members

Listen

meeting with too much structure, the team loses the freedom to listen and respond with sensitivity to what others are saying. In an interactive group, there are fewer long utterances; more people are contributing. In a highly structured meeting, there is more control over who talks, about what, and for how long. As suggested in Figure 10.1, the key is to find the right balance between structure and interaction.

Perhaps you're thinking you can avoid meeting problems by just avoiding meetings. Not likely: As we noted in the last chapter, you simply can't escape meetings. Research suggests that most managers spend about one-quarter of their time in meetings. Top-level leaders spend even more time; about two-thirds of their time in meetings or preparing for meetings.[6] The simple fact is, the broader your leadership responsibilities, the more time you'll spend in meetings.

Preparing for Meetings

Effective meetings don't just happen. The best way to have a good meeting is to prepare. It's like the old carpenter's adage: "Measure twice, saw once." Investing time in preparing for work before actually beginning the work will pay dividends, especially if you're in charge of leading the meeting. The first key task in preparing for meetings is deciding whether you even need to hold a meeting. If a meeting is needed, you'll need to determine what the meeting goals are and how to structure precisely what you'll talk about to achieve the meeting goals. And perhaps the most important task in preparing the meeting is to develop the meeting agenda.

Determining Whether To Have a Meeting

To meet, or not to meet? That is the first question. In your role as a leader, one of your jobs is to determine whether a meeting is needed. The cardinal rule of meetings is this: *Meet only when you have a reason to meet.* If you want to be a hero in your organization, regardless of whether you work in a small three-person office or for a large Fortune 500 corporation, don't hold a meeting if you don't need to have one.

You can accomplish quite a bit of work without meeting face to face. For example, if you just need to share information and need no commentary or interaction, sending a memo or email message may suffice. One leader we know periodically sends out what he calls a "meeting in a memo" that summarizes key announcements, reports, or reminders. You may want to ponder whether a meeting is premature: If people aren't prepared for the meeting, aren't well informed, or are embroiled in tension and conflict, holding a meeting will only make things worse. So rather than calling a meeting, you may need to share written information, delegate some tasks to one individual, talk to people individually to manage interpersonal conflict, or invite people to read existing policies and procedures before calling a meeting. But when do you really need to hold a meeting? Read on.

When collaboration is needed. Perhaps you've heard it said that many hands make light work. When a task is too big for one person and you need a team effort to gather information, evaluate information, make a decision, or solve a problem, you probably need to call a meeting to sort through the myriad of options and choices. As we've noted, groups and teams have more information available to them and can be more creative than a single individual. A meeting brings the team members together to share information and to coordinate their efforts.

When uncertainty is high. A key function of meetings is to reduce uncertainty. Actually, a primary function of *all* communication is to manage uncertainty. People who are uncertain don't know what to do or how to proceed. As we noted, sending an information-packed memo is certainly one way to help people manage uncertainty about an issue, idea, or problem. But during an interactive, collaborative meeting you can do a better job of managing uncertainty, clarifying misunderstandings, and ensuring that messages are clearly understood. When people need clear, accurate information, such as about a new company policy, and you want to ensure that the messages are clearly communicated, hold a meeting.

When people may resist a decision or a proposed solution. One research conclusion about working collaboratively is that people are more satisfied with an outcome if they participate in the process that leads to it, rather than just being told what to do.[7] A meeting is a good method for developing a solution to a problem or making a decision if you think the solution to the problem could be controversial. But don't hold a meeting simply to manipulate a group. Giving people the illusion of control without the power to shape the outcome will likely create resentment, mistrust, and dissatisfaction. Do hold a meeting when you seek honest input and participation.

When there is no individual or single source that has the answer you seek. If you want to know what the company budget is for next year, you can simply email the chief financial officer to get the information; you don't need to hold a meeting. Of, if you want to know demographic data, changes in customer buying patterns, or other work-related information that an individual expert could readily tell you, go ask the expert rather than holding a meeting. Meetings are best used to process and evaluate information. There may be times when you need a lot of information from different sources; in that situation, a team meeting can help coordinate the efforts to get the information. But if all you need is a single piece of information from a single source, call or email someone, or check a website—a meeting is not necessary.

When the task or project is complex. Simple tasks can often be delegated to one person. But if you have a multi-stage, complex project to complete, a meeting (or several meetings) may be needed to coordinate the process. Or if you need to address multiple questions, issues, or problems or make multiple decisions, using meetings to tap into the collaborative power of more than one person will probably ensure a high-quality outcome. Of course, it's the complexity of a decision or a problem, such as trying to figure out why sales are slumping and then fixing the problem, that makes managing meetings a challenge. In Chapter 9 we noted that team members typically assume different task and maintenance roles during collaboration. With a complex task or project, it is useful to establish clear roles and responsibilities, develop a clear mission statement, and establish ground rules to ensure efficient and effective collaboration.

Once you're convinced that a meeting is the best way to accomplish a task, you'll need to determine the precise outcome you want to achieve.

Determining the Meeting Goal

Every meeting should have a goal. (If you don't have a goal, don't hold a meeting!) Regardless of the task or project, most meetings are intended to achieve one or more of the following three outcomes: (1) sharing information, (2) discussing information, and (3) taking action. The first step in preparing for a meeting, especially if you're leading the meeting, is to determine its goal or goals.

Sharing information. An information-sharing meeting is like a briefing or a series of short speeches. Many weekly staff meetings are primarily gatherings during which someone shares information with others. Although these information-giving sessions are called meetings, a gathering really isn't a meeting in the true sense of the word if only one person presents information. Yes, a collection of people are present and do indeed meet, but if there's virtually no interaction and the "meeting" is so heavily structured that one person does all or most of the talking, you're really attending a presentation or briefing, not a meeting. If the person doing most of the talking is giving her spiel with PowerPoint slides, that's a good indication that the speaker views her primary purpose as imparting information rather than soliciting feedback. If the only task during such a meeting is to share information, you may not really need a meeting at all—perhaps a "meeting in a memo" or email will suffice.

There certainly are times when you want to share information in person to emphasize its importance or to get a reaction from others—such as when you need to explain a change in policy, procedures, or sales goals. If you want reactions to what you present, make sure to budget time for discussion and reactions. Sometimes you may need to give information during the early part of the meeting and then move into discussion before taking action. However, if the goal is to explain a new policy and you want or expect minimal discussion, then you're presenting a briefing, rather than holding a meeting.

Briefings have an important function in business and professional settings; sometimes, particularly in businesses with global divisions, the purpose can be simply to see other team members once a week to get an update on projects and assess team member needs. However, a briefing does differ from a collaborative meeting. There is value in the ritual of seeing other people on the team and enhancing relationships. But if people think they are going to attend a meeting and it's really a speech or a briefing, the participants may end up feeling frustrated rather than enlightened.

Discussing information. An information-discussing meeting is one in which there is considerable interaction and give and take. Whether it's nurses reviewing a medical case, real estate agents providing feedback about a new electronic multiple listing website, or student teachers discussing policies, a discussion session is typically highly interactive. The goal is to gather and assess reactions to information, policies, or procedures. It's important not to let a discussion meeting become a series of long-winded speeches. You want to encourage interaction. Also, at a discussion meeting it is easy for conversations to get off the topic. The meeting leader or meeting participants should be particularly careful to keep the goals of the discussion in mind so that the comments remain relevant. If gathering information is a key meeting goal, it's important to develop strategies to ensure that meeting participants can freely share information. There is a tendency for group members to only share information that all group members already know. It's important when the goal is to discuss information to encourage all group members to participate in the conversation and share ideas, data, opinions, and information.[8] There are structured conversation techniques that can ensure that all members feel free to participate; we'll discuss those strategies later in the chapter.

Taking action. A meeting to take action often involves making a decision, solving a problem, or implementing a decision or solution. For example, deciding who to hire for a job vacancy or figuring out how to save money on capital gains taxes involves taking action. Prior to taking action, a team must gather information, analyze the information, and discuss the information. A meeting can have a single agenda item of making a decision, but if so, team members have undoubtedly had prior conversations and have shared information and options. They would come to the meeting with the background needed to make the decision.

Many, if not most, meetings have multiple goals. Those attending a meeting may first hear information presented, then discuss the information, and finally take some action to accomplish the meeting goal. If you are the meeting leader, before beginning to draft your agenda, you need to know the meeting goal; you want to identify what you would like to have happen as a result of the meeting. A typical goal might be "At the end of this meeting we will have decided who to hire for the new advertising job," or "At the end of the meeting we will have discussed and evaluated the sales figures for the last three months." Without a specific goal, it's likely you'll accomplish little.

DILBERT: © Scott Adams / Dist. by United Feature Syndicate, Inc.

Developing the Meeting Agenda

Once you have identified goals and assessed what you need to talk about, it's time to develop an agenda—to arrange the items to be covered at the meeting in the most effective way to achieve your goals. An **agenda** is the written list of issues, questions, information, and topics to be discussed or tasks to be completed in a meeting, listed in the order in which they will be addressed. To develop an agenda, first consider all of the topics, issues, information, and questions you need to discuss to achieve your meeting goals. As you start to identify the various agenda items, don't worry about what order to place them in; first, just identify them. Once you have a first draft of your agenda items, you can arrange the topics and issues in a logical structure.

Verbal

You want to organize the agenda around your meeting goals. Use subheadings of information items, discussion items, and action items to signal to team members the goal of the discussion. If your meeting goal is to discuss the pros and cons of the new hiring policy, then your agenda would likely include such straightforward questions as "What are the benefits of the new hiring policy?" and "What are the disadvantages of the new policy?"

Before making final decisions about which items you will discuss, estimate how long you think the team will need to discuss each item. Most groups take more time than they might expect to talk about issues and ideas. Some meeting management experts suggest putting your most important item first, because usually what is introduced first takes the most time. Or, you may want to first address several small issues so that you can dispense with them before getting into the meat of the meeting. Another strategy is to place the most challenging issues for discussion in the middle of the meeting, thus giving the group a chance to get oriented at the beginning and to ease out of the discussion at the end. Another strategy is to make your first agenda item something that will immediately involve all meeting members in active discussion. By placing a high-priority item early in the meeting, you take advantage of having people talk about an issue when they are fresher. Starting the meeting with announcements and routine reports may set a climate of passivity, and boredom is the usual result—although sometimes it's necessary to start with reports before discussing an issue. One way to start your meeting is to actively involve members in finalizing the agenda: Ask them for reactions to how you have structured the discussion or if they have other agenda items to include on the agenda; this can help prevent digressions and surprise agenda additions later. Figure 10.2 presents a sample agenda that includes the location and time for the meeting as well as the meeting goals and key agenda items.

Meeting management experts John Tropman and Gershom Morningstar recommend using the "bell-curve agenda."[9] They suggest that the middle of the meeting should be reserved for the most challenging or controversial issues, as indicated in Figure 10.3. The opening and closing of the meeting includes more routine or less vital issues.

Figure 10.2	Sample Agenda

Meeting Place: The Centennial Building, Abernathy Conference Room

Meeting Time: Tuesday, September 19 at 3:30 PM

Meeting Goals: At the end of the meeting, meeting participants should be able to
1. Identify positive and negative reactions to the finance report.
2. Describe how the new employment policy will influence hiring practices.
3. Identify strategies to increase sales.

I. DISCUSSION ITEMS
   A. Are there any other agenda items we need to discuss today?
   B. What are positive and negative reactions to the finance report distributed before the meeting?
   C. How will the new employment policy influence hiring practices?

II. ACTION ITEMS
   What can be done to improve our sales figures during the next sales period?

III. INFORMATION ITEMS
   Announcements

Agenda a written list of issues, questions, information, or topics to be discussed or tasks to be completed in a meeting.

Figure 10.3 | Bell-Curve Agenda

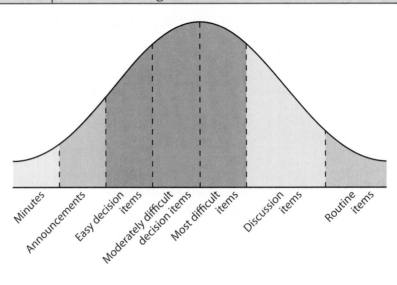

As noted earlier, in contrast to Tropman and Morningstar's recommendations, sometimes you may want to avoid placing routine announcements and reports at the beginning of a meeting.[10] In addition to creating a climate of boredom, placing routine material first on the agenda can waste time in the long run: Because they may be less sensitive to time constraints at the beginning of a meeting, participants may be tempted to spend too much time reacting to routine reports. Think about this: When you have lots of money in your bank account, you probably don't monitor every penny you spend; but when you're down to only a few dollars in your account, you're aware of everything you spend. In meetings, it's time rather than money that is the "currency." At the beginning of your meeting, you have a "full bank account" of time, so team members may be more likely to talk without monitoring how long they talk. So, rather than beginning a meeting with routine information items that are likely to spark digressions from the agenda, it may be best to make your first agenda item something of vital importance to the group that clearly relates to one or more of your meeting goals.

Always distribute an agenda to meeting participants *before* the meeting. Without an agenda or some knowledge of what will be discussed at the meeting, participants won't know how to prepare. In addition to asking for feedback about the meeting agenda before you begin the meeting, periodically ask meeting participants if the agenda is serving its

RECAP: How To Prepare for a Meeting

Determine Whether You Need a Meeting: Determine Meeting Goals

- Sharing Information: The team needs to know something it does not know now.
- Discussing Information: The team needs to express ideas and understand information.
- Taking Action: The team needs to do something or make a recommendation.

Develop the Meeting Agenda

- Identify items that need to be discussed to achieve the meeting goal(s).
- Organize the agenda items to achieve the goal(s). Consider
  - Making the first agenda item a chance for participants to offer input about the meeting agenda.
  - Placing the highest priority agenda item first on the agenda.
  - Placing an item on which the group is likely to reach consensus first on the agenda to build a positive team climate.
  - Placing routine information items last on the agenda.

Table 10.1	Meeting Agenda Pitfalls and Strategies for Managing Them
Potential Pitfall	**Suggested Strategy**
Participants tend to spend too much time on early agenda items.	Make the first agenda item something worthy of discussion rather than beginning with a trivial report or announcement.
Participants find a way to talk even if you don't want them to talk.	Invite input and discussion early in the meeting rather than having participants trying to interrupt.
Participants aren't prepared for the meeting; they have not read what they were supposed to read.	Clarify the team's ground rules about being prepared for meetings. Consider taking a few minutes to have participants read information or have them prepare by writing ideas or suggestions using the silent-brainstorming technique.
Participants won't stick to the agenda.	Remind the group what the meeting goals are, or, with input from the group, change agenda items.
A meeting is scheduled late in the day or participants are tired.	Begin with an agenda item that involves all meeting participants rather than having participants sitting silently at the beginning of the meeting.
The agenda includes a controversial item that will create conflict and disagreement.	Put one or more noncontroversial items on the agenda ahead of the conflict-producing item. Addressing easier agenda items first will establish a feeling of accomplishment and agreement before the group tackles the more controversial item.

purpose. Ask, "Are we still discussing useful information?" or "Is our agenda helping us achieve our meeting goals?"

In addition to distributing copies of the agenda before the meeting and having copies of the agenda to distribute when you meet, it's sometimes useful to display the meeting agenda using a flipchart, a PowerPoint slide, or some other visual means. Having a common image to look at can help keep a group focused on its goal.

Having adequate structure is important not only for meetings that take place in person, but also for virtual groups that meet via teleconference or the Internet. Research suggests that a virtual team will make better decisions during a meeting if it has appropriate instructions for framing the decision as well as enough time to process the information.[11] Table 10.1 summarizes potential meeting agenda problems and how to manage those problems.

How To Structure Meetings To Achieve Results

After you have decided that a meeting is needed, developed your goal(s), and prepared your agenda, you need to develop strategies to accomplish the tasks you've outlined. Whether your meeting goals include making decisions, solving problems, or developing creative approaches to issues, decisions, or problems, you'll need to develop strategies to structure the discussion to achieve those outcomes.

Structuring Decision-Making Meetings

One typical goal of team meetings is to take action by making a decision. **Decision making** is the process of making a choice from among several alternatives, such as picking the right person for a job, determining where to hold the annual conference, or selecting a new public relations firm. Although there is evidence that some people are simply better decision makers than others, teams can be taught to make high-quality decisions if they learn some basic principles of team decision making.[12] According to Randy Hirokawa, Dennis Gouran, and several other group communication scholars, group decision making usually follows a predictable pattern.[13] Groups and teams tend to make better decisions if they are aware of this pattern. Team decision making includes the following steps.[14]

Decision making the process of making a choice from among several alternatives.

1. *The team assesses the present situation.* A team analyzes a situation based on available information and realizes that it needs to make a decision. For example, the board of directors of a fast-food company is trying to decide whether to lower the price of its products to regain market share, which has recently been slipping. Thus, they look at competitors' prices to help them determine whether their existing pricing is competitive.

2. *The team identifies its goals.* After assessing the current situation, the group should identify its objectives. A team uncertain about its task will have difficulty making a quality decision. If its goal is clear, a team begins to identify alternatives or choices. The directors decide the fast-food company needs to increase its market share by 5 percent.

3. *The team identifies several alternatives.* The greater the number of alternatives a team generates, the greater the likelihood it will make a good decision. Poor decisions usually occur when a team fails to generate enough good possible choices. The fast-food company's directors look at competitors' prices and consider: Should they match those prices, find a way to offer an even greater value, or try to sell at their current prices by offering something else? The board considers developing a new ad campaign, creating a new breakfast menu, and adding gourmet coffee to the menu.

4. *The team evaluates the positive and negative consequences of alternatives.* A group must do more than identify alternatives; it should also assess the positive and negative implications of each alternative before making a decision. The board considers the costs and benefits of each strategy it has proposed. This takes time, but it's the only rational way to evaluate the ideas proposed.

5. *The team selects the best alternative (makes a decision).* The alternative selected should potentially have a maximum positive outcome with minimal negative consequences. A team is more likely to select the best alternative if it has carefully assessed the situation, considered team goals, identified several choices, and noted the positive and negative implications of each. The board ultimately decides that creating a new ad campaign, offering a new breakfast sandwich, and adding gourmet coffee to the menu are the best ways to increase the company's market share.

Teams that have reasonable confidence in their ability to make decisions as well as the skill to use these decision-making steps make better decisions. But a group that becomes overly confident or believes that it is invulnerable to problems or making mistakes is less effective. Having some confidence (but not overconfidence) in the ability to make decisions and following the steps outlined above results in the best team decisions.[15]

How teams make decisions. After the alternatives have been narrowed and weighed, what methods can groups use to make a decision? Knowing these methods can give you and your team options to consider when you need to make a decision.[16]

One person in a team may seem to be the best informed about the issue, and members can turn to this person to make the choice. This expert may or may not be a team's designated leader. Deferring to an expert from within a team may be an efficient way to make a decision, but if there is not adequate discussion, the team may not be satisfied with the outcome.

A team may decide that none of its members has the credibility, knowledge, or wisdom to make a particular decision. Members can turn to someone outside the team who has authority to make a decision. Research evidence suggests that people are often too slow to ask for expert advice. If you need information and expertise that the group doesn't have, don't hesitate to ask someone outside the group for insight, information, wisdom, and ideas.[17] However, note that although an outside expert may make a fine decision, a team that gives

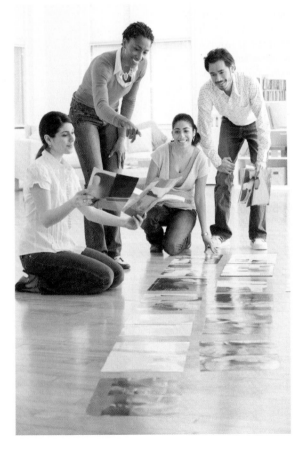

This team has already analyzed the situation, identified its goals, and generated several alternative ideas. Team members are now evaluating each alternative before selecting the best one.

>>> **COMMUNICATION ETHICS** @ WORK

Your colleague Chad, who is chairing the next meeting of the Personnel Committee, has distributed the meeting agenda before the meeting, just as he should, to help people prepare for the meeting. When he emailed the meeting agenda to all the committee members, Chad asked whether anyone had any other agenda items for the meeting. Missing from the agenda is an item about increasing employee benefits, which you are in favor of; you know that Chad opposes this move. You're certain that if you ask to have the item placed on the agenda, Chad will not do so. Is it ethical for you to wait until the meeting begins to have your agenda item added to the discussion, or should you tell Chad before the meeting begins that you'd like to have your item about employee benefits added to the meeting agenda? What is the most ethical way to proceed?

up its decision-making power to one person loses the advantages of the greater input and variety of approaches that come from being a team in the first place.

Team members can rank or rate possible alternatives. After the team averages the rankings or ratings, it selects the alternative with the highest average. This method of making decisions can be a useful way to start discussions and to see where the team stands on an issue. However, it is not the best way to make a final decision, because it does not take full advantage of the give and take of group discussion.

The method of team decision making most often used is majority rule. Majority rule can be swift and efficient, but it can also leave an unsatisfied minority. Unless it allots time to discuss an issue, a group that makes a decision on the basis of majority rule may sacrifice decision quality and group cohesiveness for efficiency.

Sometimes a minority of team members makes a decision. The minority may yell the loudest or threaten to create problems for the group unless it gets its way. Team members may ask, "Does anyone have any objections?" and if no one answers immediately, consider the decision made. Minority members whose decision is adopted may temporarily rejoice, but over time the group will have difficulty implementing a decision that is not widely accepted. On the other hand, research suggests that when a majority of members of a group supports an idea and then the majority evaporates because several group members change their minds, the group is in a vulnerable position; a view that was previously held by a minority can swiftly become the majority view. So, in cases when you side with the minority, keep in mind that things change. Don't side with the majority simply because it's the majority opinion. Groups work best when there is honest dialogue in the search for the best solution.[18]

Consensus occurs when all group members can support a course of action. Reaching consensus is time-consuming and difficult, but team members are usually more satisfied with the decision than if a decision is imposed from someone in authority outside the group. If group members must also implement the solution, taking the time to develop consensus is worth the extra effort.

To reach a decision by consensus, group members must listen and respond to individual viewpoints and manage conflicts that arise. Consensus is facilitated when group members are able to remain focused on the goal, emphasize areas of agreement, and combine or eliminate alternatives identified by the group.

Sometimes teams become so frustrated that they make no decisions. They resort to coin tosses or other random approaches. These methods are not recommended for groups that take their decision making seriously. Teams that resort to random methods usually are desperate.

Structuring Problem-Solving Meetings

Problem solving is the process of overcoming obstacles to achieve a specific goal. In contrast to decision making, which involves making a choice from among alternatives, problem solving usually requires a team to make several decisions or choices as it identifies a problem and decides how to solve it.

A problem consists of three elements; (1) an undesirable existing situation, (2) a goal the team wants to accomplish, and (3) one or more obstacles that prevent a team from achieving its goal.[19]

Consensus group agreement that occurs when all group members support and are committed to a collective decision.

Problem solving a process of overcoming obstacles to achieve a goal.

RECAP: Methods of Team Decision Making

Method	Advantages	Disadvantages
Decision by expert: The team defers to a person who has the most expertise or experience.	• Decision is made quickly. • Team benefits from the expertise of a knowledgeable source of information.	• Team members may not be satisfied with the decision. • The expert could be wrong.
Average individual rankings or ratings: Team members rate or rank possible outcomes and select the decision with the highest ranking or best rating.	• Uses a democratic process that taps all team members' thinking. • Useful when the team needs to assess where it stands on an issue.	• The average ranking or rating may be a decision that no team member supports. • Team loses the opportunity for give-and-take discussion.
Majority rule: Decision is made by the majority of team members.	• Is often perceived as a fair way of making decisions. • Can be an efficient way of making a decision.	• Those who do not support the majority opinion may feel left out of the process. • Team may lose cohesiveness.
Decision by minority: Team decides to support a position voiced by a vocal minority of team members.	• Decision is made by those who feel most passionate about the outcome. • Helps the group acknowledge opposing points of view.	• The majority of team members may feel disenfranchised from the decision. • Team decision may be difficult to implement because the majority of team members do not support the outcome.
Decision by consensus: Through discussion, team members reach a decision that all members can support.	• Team members are more likely to be satisfied with the outcome. • Team members are more likely to participate in implementing a decision that all members support.	• Takes time. • May require conflict-management skills.
Random choice: Team members flip a coin or use some other technique so the group can move forward.	• Easy • Fast	• More likely to result in ineffective outcome because team members have not discussed the issues thoroughly. • Suggests that the team does not care about making a high-quality decision.

Like decision making, the problem-solving process begins with assessing the present situation. What's wrong with what we currently are experiencing? *Almost every problem can be phrased in terms of something you want more of or less of.*[20] Note whether your list of problems boils down to something you want more of or less of—more time, money, sales, information; or fewer expenses, errors, customer complaints, or less absenteeism.

What are the most common barriers that keep teams from solving problems? Communication researchers Benjamin Broome and Luann Fulbright spent over six years asking business and professional people who participated in group and team discussions what barriers kept their teams from operating at full capacity. The researchers found the most often cited barriers were lack of a clear goal and lack of opportunity for meaningful interaction. Not having a clear goal or agenda (lack of clear structure) was the most common barrier to effective problem solving. Other problems included poor communication, lack of cultural sensitivity to others, time pressures, and team members' not being supportive of each other.[21]

The prescriptive approach to teamwork focuses on giving a team specific structures, agendas, or techniques to help it do its work. One researcher suggests that problems can be classified on a continuum of structured or unstructured.[22] An unstructured problem is one that leads to high uncertainty about how to solve the problem; there is little information and the team is confused. The team needs information to help orient its members. The more uncertainty team members feel (the more unstructured the nature of the problem), the greater the need for a structured approach to help the team solve its problem. For example, how best to merge two well-functioning departments in an advertising firm that has never merged departments is an unstructured problem; there is no single right answer—there are many possible strategies that could accomplish the outcome—so uncertainty is high. A more structured problem might be determining whether it is worthwhile to install new energy-saving light bulbs in a manufacturing plant. This problem is more straightforward; doing a simple cost-benefit analysis is a more structured process than trying to predict how well two departments can merge.

One researcher has identified over seventy methods or sequences of prescriptive steps and techniques that can be used to solve problems.[23] Which one works best? Several researchers have sought to answer that question. Their conclusion? *No single prescriptive method works best. But having some structured sequence of steps or questions works better than having no structure.* Any of the following problem-solving strategies can help you prepare a problem-solving agenda.

The standard problem-solving process. The standard problem-solving process was developed to help individual people structure problem solving, but it has been adapted for use by groups and teams. These steps were developed by educator and philosopher John Dewey in his 1910 book *How We Think*.[24] In essence, his steps follow the scientific method of defining and analyzing a problem, identifying solutions, picking a solution, and putting the solution into practice—a method scientists still use. Dewey's approach, which he called *reflective thinking*, is not a one-size-fits-all prescription. However, it is one useful way of structuring the problem-solving process to manage uncertainty and to ensure that the key functions identified in Chapter 9 (identify the goal, analyze the issues, generate ideas, evaluate ideas, and be sensitive to interpersonal dynamics) are included in your team discussion.

Step 1: Identify and define the problem. As we pointed out in Chapter 9, teams work best when they have identified a clear, elevating goal that focuses their problem-solving effort. And, as we've also noted, the goal is often to have more of something (money, time, work quality) or less of something (errors, conflict, wasted time). To reach a clear specification of the problem, consider asking the following questions:

- What is the specific problem that concerns us?
- What do we want more of, or less of?
- What terms, concepts, or ideas do we need to define in order to understand the problem?
- Who is harmed by the problem?
- When do the harmful effects of the problem occur?

Most team experts agree that an effective way to give your problem-solving task appropriate structure is to phrase your problem in the form of a policy question. A policy question is phrased so that the answer is some action (policy) intended to eliminate, reduce, or manage the problem. Policy questions begin with the words "What should be done about . . ." or "What could be done to improve . . . ." Here are some examples of policy questions:

- What should be done to lower the cost of tuition at our university?
- What could be done to decrease property taxes in our state?
- What should be done to make health care more affordable for all U.S. citizens?

One specific technique for structuring a discussion to identify a problem is the Journalists' Six Questions technique.[25] Most news reporters are taught to include the answers to six questions when writing a news report: Who? What? When? Where? Why? and How? Posing these six questions about the problem your team has identified can help further define and limit the problem as well as help you move to the next step in the process—analyzing the problem. You could make a chart, like the one in Figure 10.4, that includes these sample questions and invite group members to answer each question individually, then pool their responses.

Step 2: Analyze the problem. For some reason, many teams want to "cut to the chase" quickly and start spinning out solutions before taking the time to thoroughly analyze

| **Figure 10.4** | **Journalists' Six Questions** |

Who?

What?

When?

Where?

Why?

How?

a problem under consideration. But research clearly suggests that analyzing the problem well is an important prerequisite to finding an effective solution. To analyze something is to break it down into smaller pieces; to analyze a problem is to consider its causes, effects, symptoms, history, and other information that will inform the team about how to best solve the problem. Here are some essential questions that can help your team analyze problems:

Verbal

- How long has the problem existed?
- How widespread is the problem?
- What are the causes of the problem?
- What are the effects of the problem?
- What are the symptoms of the problem?
- What methods already exist for managing the problem?
- What are the limitations of existing methods?
- What obstacles keep the team from achieving the goal?

In addition to considering these questions, when analyzing a problem team members should develop criteria—standards and goals—for an acceptable solution. Identifying clear criteria can help you spot a good solution when you see one. Here are some sample criteria for solutions:

- The solution should be inexpensive or within our budget.
- The solution should be implemented by a certain date.
- The solution should be agreed on by all team members
- The solution should be agreed on by all persons affected by our recommendations.

One tool that can help structure the analysis of a problem and also help your team identify criteria is **force field analysis**.[26] This technique works best when your team has identified a clear goal. After identifying a goal, the team lists all of the forces currently at work that would help attain the goal. Then the team does just the opposite; it identifies forces that are keeping the team from achieving the goal. When complete, the analysis can help the team see what needs to be increased (the forces that currently favor attaining the goal) and what needs to be decreased (the forces working against the goal). Figure 10.5 illustrates force field analysis by a team that wanted to increase the number of employees who volunteered for community projects; the goal is written on the top. On the left side of the diagram is a list of factors that the team identified that increase the chances of achieving the goal. On the right side is a list of the restraining forces, or forces that keep the team from achieving the goal. The task of the team is to foster or increase the number of driving forces and lessen the impact of or decrease the number of restraining forces.

Step 3: Generate possible solutions. You've now identified a specific problem, analyzed it (causes, history, and so on), and are ready to identify possible ways to solve the

Force field analysis a tool that structures the analysis of a problem by identifying the driving forces that increase the probability that a goal will be achieved and the restraining forces that decrease that probability.

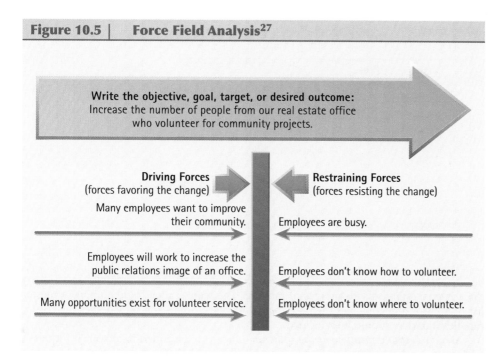

Figure 10.5 | Force Field Analysis[27]

problem. The classic technique for identifying possible solutions is called *brainstorming*. It was developed by an advertising executive more than half a century ago to encourage a team to be creative. You've probably already used this technique. With brainstorming, team members are encouraged to suggest many options or ideas without evaluating them first. We'll discuss this technique in more detail later in the chapter.

Step 4: Select the best solution. Once they have completed step 3 and generated different options to solve the problem, the team takes the list of ideas generated and determines which ones best meet the criteria identified in the initial analysis of the problem (step 2). They also determine which solutions best achieve the team's clear, elevating goal.

It is usually easier for teams to expand alternatives (brainstorm) than it is to narrow alternatives. Teams can use one of the following three methods to whittle down a long list of alternatives to a manageable number for more serious debate:

- *Ranking:* Tell team members to rank their top five choices from 1 to 5.
- *Rating:* Ask team members to rate each solution on a scale from 1 to 5. The solutions rated best get the most serious discussion.
- *Voting:* Team members simply vote for the alternatives they like.

What seems to work best is for team members to first discuss the criteria and remind themselves of their analysis of the problem before taking a vote or even before rating or ranking. The following questions can help focus the discussion on analysis before selecting a solution:

- Which of the solutions deals best with the obstacles identified?
- Does the suggestion solve the problem in both the short term and the long term?
- Does the solution meet our criteria?
- Do we have the resources to implement the solution?

Once you've narrowed your list of solutions to a handful or a couple of options, it's time to systematically evaluate the pros and the cons of each potential solution. An easy way to structure this discussion is to use a T-chart like the one shown in Figure 10.6. Simply write down the possible solution at the top of the chart (displayed on a flipchart, chalkboard, or overhead projector) and then list both the pros and the cons. This technique will help you look at the positive and negative consequences of an action. For example, suppose one option for a company that needs to cut costs is to move the corporate

Figure 10.6	T-Chart

Pros	Cons

headquarters to a new location. Team members studying this issue could list on a T-chart the advantages and disadvantages of moving. The team leader could compile a master list of all pros and cons and then use the list to spark discussion on whether the corporate headquarters should be relocated.

Step 5: Test and implement the solution. Once you have identified your solution(s), your team needs to consider the question "Will it work?" You may want to do a pilot test or ask a small group of people what they think of your idea before you "go public" with it. Bouncing your proposed solution off an expert and checking to see if the solution was successful for others who may have adopted it can help you test the solution's likely effectiveness.

If the team not only has to identify a solution but also put it into action, it will need structure to make sure that the job gets done and that everybody has a role and assumes specific responsibilities. Perhaps you know the people in the following story:

> This story is about four people: Everybody, Somebody, Anybody, and Nobody. There was an important job to be done and Everybody was asked to do it. Everybody was sure Somebody would do it. Anybody could have done it but Nobody did it. Somebody got angry about that because it was Everybody's job. Everybody thought Anybody could do it but Nobody realized that Everybody wouldn't do it. It ended up that Everybody blamed Somebody when actually Nobody asked Anybody.

Making sure you have clearly identified who does what can keep everybody from blaming somebody and ensure that the solution is implemented.

RECAP: Reflective Thinking Problem-Solving Steps and Techniques

Steps	Techniques
1. Identify and define the problem.	• Phrase the problem as a policy question. • Use the Journalists' Six Questions (Who? What? When? Where? Why? How?) to help define the issues.
2. Analyze the problem.	• Develop clear criteria that clarify the issues and can help in evaluating solutions. • Use force field analysis to identify driving and restraining forces.
3. Generate possible solutions.	• Use brainstorming.
4. Select the best solution.	• Narrow alternatives using ranking, rating, or voting. • Evaluate the pros and cons of each solution.
5. Test and implement the solution.	• Develop a clear action plan. • Make a written list of who should do what.

Structuring Creative Meetings

Ingvar Kamprad, the founder of IKEA furniture stores, had a creative idea: He would sell quality furniture disassembled in flat containers at a price lower than any of his competitors. IKEA started in a shed used for storing milk churns and is now an international corporation worth over $17 billion. IKEA (an acronym—the first two letters stand for Ingvar Kamprad; the E is for Elmtaryd, the Swedish farm where Kamprad was born, and A is for Agunnaryd, the name of the village in which the farm was located) is successful because Ingvar Kamprad, working with a team of colleagues, was able to implement his creative idea.[28]

Creativity may seem like a mystical process, but it can be developed. Group and team members often want to know "What techniques will enhance our creativity?" Beyond understanding general principles of creativity and promoting conditions to enhance creativity, what are specific methods, approaches, or techniques that can boost creativity? As we noted earlier, sometimes groups and teams need the structure of a technique in order to stimulate a creative breakthrough.[29] Such techniques include brainstorming, the nominal-group technique, the Delphi technique, and electronic brainstorming. There is evidence that sometimes creative groups make intuitive decisions—decisions that just feel "right" based on hunches and team members' gut feelings. And sometimes creative teams simply stumble on a discovery while looking for something else. For example, Spence Silver was a researcher at 3M trying to develop a new glue for adhesive tape when he discovered a "low-tack" adhesive. His colleague Art Fry was irritated when the little bookmarks he used to keep his place in a hymnbook kept falling out of his book. Fry had a creative idea: He thought that if he used Silver's "low-tack" adhesive on little pads of paper, he would have sticky bookmarks that wouldn't fall out. Eureka! Post-it Notes were born.[30]

Gut feelings and chance discoveries aside, in the long run, teams are more creative if they take the time to thoughtfully consider a number of alternatives when trying to solve a problem, make a decision, or invent a new process or product.[31] In this section we'll identify strategies and techniques to help develop creativity in groups.

Brainstorming. Imagine that your employer assigns you to a task force whose goal is to increase the productivity of your small manufacturing company. Phrased as a policy question, the problem is "What can be done to increase efficiency and productivity for our company?" Your group is supposed to come up with ideas to help solve the problem. Assume that your boss has clearly identified the problem and has provided your group with several documents analyzing the problem in some detail. Your group may decide that reflective thinking, which focuses on identifying and analyzing problems, is not the best process to follow—you need innovative ideas and creative, original solutions. Perhaps your group could benefit from brainstorming.[32]

Brainstorming has been used by businesses, committees, and government agencies to improve the quality of group decision making. Although it can be used in several phases of many group discussions, it may be most useful if a group needs original ideas or has trouble coming up with any ideas at all. Research suggests that a trained facilitator can improve the execution of group brainstorming.[33] Because it's an interactive strategy, brainstorming can help energize a group by actively involving team members in the discussion process. Yet it takes skill to lead and participate in an effective brainstorming session.

Traditional brainstorming. Traditional brainstorming is a process that follows certain specific guidelines.

1. *Identify the problem that needs solving.* Be sure that all group members can identify and clearly define the problem.

2. *Set a clear time limit.*

3. *Ask group members to temporarily put aside all judgments and evaluations.* The key to brainstorming is ruling out all criticism and evaluation. Alex Osborn, the advertising executive who originally conceived of brainstorming, had these suggestions:[34]

   - Acquire a "try anything" attitude.

   - Avoid criticism, which can stifle creativity.

   - Remember that all ideas are thought-starters.

   - Today's criticism may kill future ideas.

4. *Have group or team members think of as many possible solutions to the problem as they can and share the ideas with the group.* Consider the following suggestions:

   • The wilder the ideas, the better.
   • It is easier to tame ideas down than to think ideas up.
   • Think out loud and mention unusual ideas.
   • Someone's wild idea may trigger a good solution from another person in the group.

5. *Make sure that the group understands that "piggybacking" off someone else's idea is useful.* Combine ideas; add to previous ideas. Adopt the philosophy that once an idea is presented to the group, no one owns it. It belongs to the group and anyone can modify it.

6. *Have someone record all the ideas mentioned.* Ideas could be recorded on a flipchart, chalkboard, or an overhead projector so that each group member can see them. You could also tape-record your discussions.

7. *Evaluate ideas when the time allotted for brainstorming has elapsed.* Consider these suggestions:

   • Approach each idea positively and give it a fair trial.
   • Try to make ideas workable.
   • Encourage feedback about the success of a session.
   • Remember that if only a few of the ideas generated by a group are useful, the session has been successful.

The nominal-group technique. The **nominal-group technique** is a procedure that uses some of the principles and methods of brainstorming but has members write their ideas individually before sharing them with the group.[35] The nominal-group technique gets its name from the notion that because members work on problems individually rather than during sustained group interaction, the group is a *nominal* group (it is a group in name only). This technique uses "silent brainstorming" to overcome some of the disadvantages researchers have discovered with exclusively oral brainstorming.

Why does silent brainstorming often produce better results than oral brainstorming? During traditional brainstorming, group and team members blurt out their ideas. But if someone laughs at an idea, nods in appreciation, says, "That's cool," or comments "That won't work," the idea has been evaluated. *The key to making brainstorming work is to separate the generation of ideas from the evaluation of ideas.* In oral brainstorming it's hard not to evaluate ideas—but evaluation can stifle the sharing of ideas. Criticism and evaluation diminish creativity.[36] Even if group members do not verbalize their evaluation, their nonverbal expressions often convey positive or negative reaction to ideas. Another problem is that some people are apprehensive or nervous about speaking up in a group, and using traditional oral brainstorming makes it less likely that the communication-apprehensive members will participate. In addition, researchers have found that sometimes with traditional brainstorming, the creative talents of some members seem to be restricted just by the very presence of others.[37] Silent brainstorming overcomes these problems by encouraging even apprehensive team members to participate by first writing their ideas. Once they have a written "script," they are more comfortable sharing their ideas. Researchers have also found that people work more diligently if they have an individual assignment than if they have a group assignment.[38] Team members using the nominal-group technique are also more likely to remember the ideas suggested.[39]

Research suggests that group and team members may generate more ideas if members first work alone and then regroup. However, although the nominal-group technique can result in more ideas being generated, they may not always be better ideas. It still takes creative, intelligent team members to develop high-quality ideas. No simple technique automatically makes ideas better.[40]

After writing their own ideas individually, group members can come together to modify, elaborate on, and evaluate ideas. The generation of ideas (writing them down) has been separated from the evaluation of ideas. Silent brainstorming can be done even before a group meets for the first time; you could describe a problem and ask group members to brainstorm individually before assembling. Email makes this approach easier. Communication researchers Henri Barki and Alain Pinsonneault found that electronic

Nominal-group technique a brainstorming method in which members work individually on ideas, rank suggested solutions, and then report their findings in a group discussion.

brainstorming worked just as well as face-to-face brainstorming in generating ideas.[41] The following steps summarize how to use the nominal-group technique.

1. All group members should be able to define and analyze the problem under consideration.

2. Working individually, group members write down possible solutions to the problem.

3. Group members report the solutions they have identified to the entire group, one at a time. Each idea should be noted on a flipchart, chalkboard, or whiteboard for all group members to see.

4. Group members discuss the ideas gathered, not to advocate for one idea over another but rather to make sure that all the ideas are clear.

5. After discussing all proposed solutions, each group member ranks the solutions. If the list of solutions is long, group members can rank the five solutions they like best. The results are tabulated.

6. The entire group discusses the results of the rankings. If the first round of ranking is inconclusive or if the group is not comfortable with the results, the options can be ranked again after additional discussion. Research suggests that using this organized method of gathering and evaluating information results in better solutions than attacking a problem in a disorganized fashion.[42] One researcher has found that the nominal-group technique works better than other prescriptive approaches such as reflective thinking.[43]

Both traditional brainstorming and the nominal-group technique can be used at any phase of the problem-solving process. For example, you could combine the nominal-group technique with force field analysis by asking group members to silently brainstorm about the forces driving and restraining attainment of a group goal. Or, you could ask members to brainstorm possible causes or symptoms of the problem during problem analysis. Or, you could use brainstorming or the nominal-group technique to generate possible strategies for implementing a solution the group has settled on.

The Delphi technique.   Whereas the nominal-group technique invites participants to contribute ideas by first writing them down and then sharing them with the group, the Delphi technique takes this idea one step further. This method, named after the ancient oracle at Delphi, has been called "absentee brainstorming," because individuals share ideas in writing or via email and do not meet face to face. One person coordinates the information and shares it with the rest of the group. This approach is especially useful when conflict within a group inhibits effective group interaction, or when time and distance constraints make it difficult for group members to meet. Here is a step-by-step description of the Delphi technique.[44]

1. The group leader selects a problem, issue, policy, or decision that needs to be reviewed. For example, the leader may pose this question: "Should we support the development of a new convention center to be located near the environmentally sensitive river that runs through our community?"

2. The leader corresponds with group members in writing, informing them of the task and inviting their suggestions and input; often a specific questionnaire is developed. Group members are asked to individually brainstorm suggestions or reactions to the issue confronting the group.

3. The respondents complete the questionnaire or generate a list of their brainstormed responses and send it to the leader.

4. The leader then summarizes all the responses from the group and shares the summary with all group members, asking for additional ideas, suggestions, and reactions. Team members are asked to rate or rank the ideas and return their comments to the leader.

The leader continues the process of summarizing the group feedback and asking for more input until general consensus emerges. Several rounds of soliciting ideas and evaluating them may be needed to achieve consensus.

This method often produces many good ideas. All participants are treated equally, because no one is aware of who submitted which idea. It is, however, a time-consuming process. And because there is no face-to-face interaction, some ideas that are worthy of elaboration and exploration may get lost in the shuffle. Using the Delphi technique in combination with face-to-face meetings can help eliminate some disadvantages of the procedure.

One of the benefits of electronic brainstorming is that team members—those in the office and those working elsewhere—can look at lists of ideas together and then build on those ideas.

Much research seems to suggest that oral brainstorming typically results in the generation of *fewer* ideas than such silent brainstorming techniques as the nominal-group technique or the Delphi technique, for several reasons:[45]

- Group members may not share their ideas orally because they fear that their suggestions will be criticized by others.
- Group members may compare their ideas with those they hear from others and think their own ideas are inferior and thus not share them.
- Group members may just loaf when they hear others suggesting ideas.
- Some group members may not be able to create ideas while listening to others—they can't do two things at once.

Electronic brainstorming. Electronic brainstorming is a technique whereby team members generate ideas and enter them in their computers; the individual lists are then displayed to the entire group. This high-tech method resembles the nominal-group technique in that group members write ideas before sharing them with the group. It also is similar to the Delphi technique, but it improves on that information-structuring method because team members can see ideas in written form; with other ideas in view group members can piggyback off the ideas of others. Electronic brainstorming can be performed by group members who are all in the same room or by members at their own home or office computers.

Research suggests that groups using electronic brainstorming generate more ideas than traditional face-to-face brainstorming groups.[46] One research team found that when some members of a group meet face to face and are supported with ideas from group members who are not physically present but who are using electronic means to share information, more ideas are generated and these are of higher quality than if all members meet face to face.[47] Some electronic meeting software programs permit team members to submit ideas and suggestions without other team members knowing who made them. Members feel less fear or anxiety about being criticized for unconventional ideas, because no one knows who suggested them.[48] Thus, when group members move to the phase of evaluating ideas, they are not sure whether they are evaluating an idea coming from a boss, a group leader, or a new intern. All ideas are considered on their own merit. Another reason more ideas may be generated is because of the "piggyback effect." Group members may be stimulated to build on the ideas of other group members.

One obvious disadvantage of electronic brainstorming is the need for all group members to have access to a computer network and appropriate software. But recent evidence strongly supports the value of this variation of the brainstorming method, in which computers add structure to the process.

How To Manage Meeting Interaction

Without interaction—the give and take of dialogue and the contributions that participants make during meetings—meetings become monologues. But with too much interaction, meetings can become disorganized, with rambling, redundant, or digressive discussions that waste time and are inconclusive. Meeting leaders and participants can help ensure a balance of structure and interaction by using facilitation skills such as gatekeeping, reminding the group of meeting goals, helping the group to be sensitive to the passage of time during discussion, and using strategies that structure group interaction.

Facilitating Meeting Interaction

The essential task of a meeting facilitator is to manage the interaction in order to achieve the goals of the group. A meeting facilitator may be someone other than the leader, boss,

---

RECAP: Comparing Creative Techniques

	Advantages	Disadvantages
Brainstorming	• Easy to use • No special materials needed • Group members can piggyback off each other's ideas	• High potential for group members to evaluate ideas as they are being generated • Takes more time than more highly structured methods such as the nominal-group technique or the Delphi technique • Quiet group members less likely to participate
Nominal-group technique	• Group members can build on ideas of others • Provides a written record of ideas suggested • Controls more talkative, dominating group members by limiting participation	• A good leader is required to organize the process • Less time is allotted for free flow of ideas • Difficult to implement with a large group
Delphi technique	• Group does not have to meet in person • Provides a written record of ideas suggested • Helps group members prepare for upcoming meeting	• No synergy created by hearing the ideas of others • Minimizes opportunities for elaborating on ideas • Group members may be suspicious that someone has manipulated the results
Electronic brainstorming	• Very efficient • Anonymity increases number of ideas generated	• Need computers and software and training to use them • It takes time to describe procedures of electronic brainstorming to team members

or the supervisor of the team. A facilitator's job is to help manage the flow of conversation and keep the group on track. Research suggests that one of the key duties of a meeting facilitator is to ask questions that help the group uncover information, ideas, and strategies for making decisions and solving problems. Specifically, facilitators who can accomplish the following enhance team processes:[49]

- Ask questions that help the group identify information it needs at the beginning of team deliberations.
- Get as many people in the team as possible to participate in the conversation.
- Make sure team members understand the comments and suggestions offered by other team members.
- Solicit high-quality, on-task, relevant contributions from team members.

Communication researchers Fred Niederman and Roger Volkema, in studying the effects of meeting facilitators on group productivity, found that the most experienced facilitators helped orient the group toward the goal, helped members adapt to what was happening in the group, and involved the group in developing the agenda for the meeting.[50]

Be a gatekeeper. Meetings should not consist of a monologue from the meeting leader or be dominated by just a few participants. A gatekeeper encourages less-talkative members to participate and tries to limit lengthy contributions by other group members. A meeting facilitator needs to be a skilled listener who is sensitive to both individual members' needs and the overarching team goals and knows when to step in. Gatekeepers make comments such as "Alice, we haven't heard your ideas yet. Won't you share your thoughts with us?" Or, "Mike, thanks for sharing, but I'd like to hear what others have to say." Polite, tactful invitations to talk or limit talk usually work. If worse comes to worst, a facilitator may need to speak to an unruly ororverbalizer privately to let him or her know that a more balanced discussion is preferable.

Focus on the goal.   Team members need to understand the group's goals. Once they do, the group's agenda for each meeting should provide a road map for moving toward those goals. A leader often has to keep the group on course, and one of the most effective tools for doing so is summarizing. Periodically, use metadiscussional skills (discussion about discussion, which we will consider shortly) and review your understanding of the group's progress with brief comments such as "Okay. Dennis agrees with John that we need to determine how much our project will cost. Are we ready for the next issue?" Such summaries help a group take stock of what it has done and what it has yet to accomplish.

Monitor time.   Another job of a meeting leader is to keep track of how much time has been spent on the planned agenda items and how much time remains. Think of

>>> COMMUNICATION SKILLS @ WORK

For meetings to be effective, at a minimum, participants must be able to tackle the agenda without angering one another. If the leader can't recognize and control disruptive personality types, inefficiency and friction result. Reuben, head of the program committee for a large nonprofit organization, enjoyed his responsibilities, except for one tough obstacle: Trisha. She had lost out to Reuben for head of the committee but took charge anyway by putting down everyone's ideas and arguing openly with Reuben about his "unassertive leadership." Group members started complaining about her. To preserve the health of his committee, Reuben needed to learn about "meeting manglers" and how to manage them.[51]

Type 1: The Bull
Identifying characteristic: Runs down people's ideas. To keep the bull penned in:

- Give the bull some authority (like being head of a project), which may lessen the need to take over by force.
- Don't lock horns by replying with hostility; instead, act and sound calm.
- Find some value in the bull's ideas and rephrase them to the group in a less threatening way.

The Bull: "Sue's idea to bring in Karl Rove as a speaker is absurd. He's too political for this town, and he probably charges a fortune."
Leader: "So you think Rove is too expensive and political. Sue, what's your reaction to those concerns?"

Type 2: The Astronaut
Identifying characteristic: Speaks tangentially, is never on track, seems to be "up in the air." To ground the astronaut:

- Avoid responding to the astronaut's tangents. Express appreciation and get right back on the topic.

- If the astronaut gets others involved in discussion, say, "Though this is interesting, can we get back to the major problem we need to solve?"
- Astronauts do well when asked specific questions, such as "Nell, do you think we need another receptionist in the front lobby?" instead of open questions, such as "What do you think we need for the front lobby?"

Type 3: The Joker
Identifying characteristic: Sees every meeting as an opportunity to get attention, make people laugh, and just have a good time. If you want the joker to get serious:

- Ask in advance if the person can help you out with presenting data, overheads, and so forth.
- Ask advice on how to make meetings more productive. He or she might behave like a joker because he or she feels time isn't being used well.
- Avoid giving false cues that you're being entertained and explicitly convey your desire for seriousness: "Let's get serious" or "OK, enough fooling around."

Type 4: The Blob
Identifying characteristic: Just sits there, silent, and watching, watching, watching. To jog the blob:

- Try gently drawing the blob out: "What are your thoughts about that, Nancy?" (If the person is super-shy, ask privately in advance if that's OK.)
- Give the blob a small but significant task to perform in the group that forces more interaction (such as being in charge of a sign-up list, collecting reports, or the like).
- Talk to to the blob between meetings to get his or her thoughts on how he or she thinks the group is going and how meetings could be more useful.

your agenda as a map, helping you plan where you want to go. Think of the clock as your gas gauge, telling you the amount of fuel you have to get where you want to go. In a meeting, just as on any car trip, you need to know where you are going and how much fuel you need to get you to your destination. If you are running out of fuel (time), you will either need to fill up the tank (budget more time) or recognize that you will not get where you want to go. Begin each meeting by asking how long members can meet. If you face two or three crucial agenda items, and one-third of your group has to leave in an hour, you will want to make certain to schedule important items early in the meeting.

Structure interaction.   To ensure that all members participate in the discussion, you may need to use some of the decision-making and problem-solving tools and techniques mentioned earlier in the chapter, such as force field analysis or the Journalists' Six Questions, or the various techniques for generating creative options. For example, if your meeting goal is to identify new ideas for reducing customer complaints, consider using brainstorming or the nominal-group technique as a way to generate ideas. A key task of the meeting facilitator is to orchestrate meaningful interaction during the meeting so that all participants have the opportunity to give input. Structured methods of inviting involvement are effective in garnering contributions from all group members.

RECAP: Strategies for Effective Meetings

How To Give a Meeting Structure

Prepare an effective agenda by

- Determining your meeting goals
- Identifying what needs to be discussed to achieve the goals
- Organizing the agenda to achieve the goals

How To Ensure Managed Interaction

Keep discussion on track by

- Using effective gatekeeping skills
- Using metadiscussion to help the group focus on the goals
- Reminding the group of elapsed time and time remaining for deliberation
- Using strategies to manage interaction (for example, nominal-group technique or silent brainstorming)

Structure   Interaction

Avoiding Groupthink: Encouraging Interaction

Be cautious if all team members agree too quickly. Your team may be experiencing groupthink instead of consensus. **Groupthink** is a faulty sense of agreement that occurs when team members seemingly agree but they primarily just want to avoid conflict. On the surface it seems as if team members have reached consensus—but it's an illusion of agreement, or an ineffective consensus.

Too little disagreement often reduces the quality of team decisions. If a team does not seriously examine the pros and cons of an idea, it's likely that the quality of its decision will suffer.[52] Effective groups do experience conflict, and then they seek productive ways to manage the conflict. When conflict occurs in a group, the entire group may experience a feeling of dissonance or discomfort. Some group members may want to manage the dissonance by quickly agreeing. But members of well-functioning group realize conflict is part of the process of collaborating in groups and teams.[53]

Groupthink a faulty sense of agreement that occurs when team members seemingly agree but they primarily want to avoid conflict.

The tragedy of the Challenger explosion might have been avoided had group members been willing to challenge the decision to launch in cold weather.

There are some causes of groupthink. Sometimes it occurs because team members are not particularly interested in the topic. Or the team may just be tired and want to get on with other work. If a team has a highly revered leader, someone that all team members respect, the team is more likely to agree with the leader rather than testing and challenging the leader's ideas. Groupthink also occurs when team members feel they can do no wrong; they feel invincible. Rather than taking time to test and evaluate ideas, the team may quickly decide and assume that the decision is a good one. Groupthink is also likely to occur when (1) the team feels apathetic about its task, (2) team members don't expect to be successful, (3) one team member has very high credibility, so team members tend to believe what he or she says, (4) one team member is very persuasive, or (5) team members don't usually challenge ideas; it's expected that team members will agree with one another.[54] Be on the lookout for these symptoms in your groups and teams.

Failure to test ideas and the resulting groupthink can have serious consequences: Wrong, dangerous, or stupid decisions can be the result. On January 28, 1986, school children all over the United States were watching the televised launch of the first teacher into space on the space shuttle *Challenger*. Their excitement soon turned to horror when, only moments after liftoff, the space shuttle exploded, killing all astronauts on board. A technical flaw in the design of the shuttle was traced to a problem with O-rings, which provide a seal between components of the shuttle. But the root cause of the accident was groupthink. A review of meeting minutes and memos revealed that at least some people at NASA knew that the O-rings would not work in cold weather. It was below freezing the morning of *Challenger*'s launch. It is now evident that groupthink occurred: Despite the weather, no one spoke up to challenge the decision to launch. Tragedy was the result.[55]

To overcome groupthink, consider the following strategies:[56]

1. *Encourage team members to be independent, critical thinkers.* Reward people for being honest and stating their true feelings. Establish a climate of acceptance of others' ideas.

2. *Don't agree with someone just because he or she has high status; examine the ideas of others carefully, regardless of their position.* Consider the merit of the idea, not the rank or title of the person making the suggestion. Of course, you have to be tactful when disagreeing with individuals who may have more power and status than you do.

3. *Consider asking someone from outside the group to evaluate the group's decisions and decision-making process.* Or, take a few moments to evaluate the group's decision-making skill at the end of the meeting.

4. *Assign someone to be a devil's advocate—to purposely look for disadvantages of a proposed idea.* This strategy is especially useful if no one disagrees with an idea. There is evidence that teams that have team members who are skilled in arguing for and against ideas and evidence make better-quality decisions.[57]

5. *Ask team members to break into smaller teams or pairs to consider both the pros and the cons of a proposed solution.* Sometimes team members may feel more comfortable expressing their disagreement in a smaller group than in a larger group or team.

Reaching Consensus: Managing Conflict

Consensus occurs when all group members support and are committed to a decision. To manage conflict and disagreement in order to reach consensus takes time and skill, but to reap the benefits of group and team deliberations, it's useful, if time permits, to strive for team consensus on key issues and decisions.

Table 10.2 compares the behavior of effective and ineffective members in a group that is attempting to achieve consensus. Three strategies can help teams reach consensus. First, because teams often bounce from topic to topic, it's important to keep the team oriented toward the goal. When you see the team starting to stray from its task, whether you are the official team facilitator or not, remind the team what the goals are. It also helps to write ideas and facts on a flipchart or chalkboard to keep the team focused.

A key strategy to keep a team focused on its goal is to use metadiscussion. **Metadiscussion** literally means "discussion about discussion"—it is comments about the discussion *process* rather than the topic under consideration. A metadiscussional comment helps the group stop and reflect on what it's doing or become aware of how it's operating. The fundamental communication principle of being aware that we've emphasized throughout the book is especially important when several people are talking (sometimes at the same time) and people are thinking about what they are saying rather than really listening to what others are saying.[58] A metadiscussional statement might be "I'm not following this conversation. What is our goal?" or "Can someone summarize what we've accomplished so far?" Periodically using metadiscussional statements can help keep the team on track and focused. For example, saying, "Peggy, I'm not sure I understand how your observation relates to our meeting goal" can help gently guide a team member back to the topic at hand.

Obviously, we're not suggesting that you attack others personally. Don't just blurt out "You're off task" or "Oh, let's not talk about that anymore." Metadiscussional phrases need to be tactful and respectful. Use "I" messages rather than "you" messages to bring the team back on track. Rather than saying, "You're not following the agenda" or "Your point doesn't make any sense," you can express these same ideas, but with less of a negative edge, by saying, "I'm not sure where we are on the agenda" or "I'm not sure I understand how your point relates to the issue we are discussing." Being able to use metadiscussion is an exceptionally powerful skill, and you can offer metadiscussional statements even if you are not the appointed leader.

Metadiscussion discussion about discussion; comments that describe the discussion process rather than the topic under consideration.

Table 10.2   Suggestions for Reaching Group and Team Consensus

Effective Group Members	Ineffective Group Members
Keep the group oriented toward its goal: • Remind the group what the goal is. • Write facts and key ideas on a flipchart or chalkboard. • Talk about the discussion process; ask questions that keep the group focused on the agenda.	• Go off on tangents and do not stay focused on the agenda. • Fail to summarize or rely on oral summaries to keep group members focused on the goal. • Do little to help clarify group discussion.
Listen to the ideas of others: • Clarify misunderstandings. • Emphasize areas of agreement. • Maintain eye contact when listening to someone and remain focused on the speaker without interrupting.	• Do not clarify misunderstandings or check to see whether others understand their messages. • Ignore areas of agreement. • Avoid eye contact with a speaker, do not focus attention on the speaker, interrupt the speaker.
Promote honest dialogue and discussion: • Seek out differences of opinion. • Do not change their minds simply to avoid conflict. • Try to involve everyone in the discussion.	• Do not seek other opinions from group members. • Quickly agree with other group members to avoid conflict. • Permit one person or just a few people to talk too much and dominate the conversation.

Source: Adapted from Steven A. Beebe and John T. Masterson, *Communicating in Small Groups: Principles and Practices 9e* (Boston: Allyn and Bacon, 2009).

A second general strategy for promoting consensus is to listen carefully to the ideas of others. Work to clarify misunderstandings. When you do agree with something that is said, say so. Maintain eye contact with the speaker and give him or her your full attention. The active listening technique, whereby you sometimes paraphrase key ideas to ensure that you understand what someone is saying, is another useful tool to help a team get unstuck when consensus seems elusive. When listening to others, try to find areas of agreement rather than just trying to convince someone that his or her idea is wrong and yours is right. Consensus is more likely to blossom when the team can find some areas of agreement rather than just hammering away at the most contentious issues. Team members who help promote a positive climate, express agreement, are open to new ideas, and look for ways to support other team members enhance the likelihood that consensus will occur.[59]

A third general strategy is to promote honest dialogue and discussion. True consensus is more likely to occur if many ideas are shared and team members don't just give in or change their minds to avoid conflict. Those tactics are likely to result in groupthink. Some teams may be tempted to take a quick vote to settle issues. Although voting can be a useful way of seeing where team members stand on an issue, be wary of taking a vote too quickly before the team has had an opportunity to discuss it. Consensus is most likely to be genuine if the team has explored several alternatives, despite the time it takes to have these discussions.

Tips for Leading Team Meetings

In many respects, this entire chapter is about leading team meetings. Determining whether you need a meeting, developing meeting goals, and establishing an agenda are key tasks of a meeting leader. Also, a meeting leader needs to be especially sensitive to balancing meeting structure with interaction. Here we provide an overview of the key procedural expectations of meeting leaders.

To be effective, a meeting leader should facilitate rather than dictate how the group will conduct the meeting. One study found that groups in which team leaders simply listened and waited for team members to contribute ideas before stating their own ideas generated more and better ideas than groups in which the leader spoke first.[60] Different groups accept (or tolerate) different levels of directions from their designated leaders. One simple rule of thumb is this: A group will generally allow a leader who emerges naturally from the group or who leads a one-time-only, ad hoc group to be more directive.

Beyond giving direction, certain tasks are generally expected of leaders. In general, meeting leaders are expected to do the following:[61]

- Call the group together, which may involve finding out when participants can meet.
- Call the meeting to order.
- Review the agenda. Ask if there are additional agenda items to discuss.
- If it is a formal meeting, determine if there is a quorum—the minimum number of people who must be present to conduct business.
- Keep the meeting moving; go on to the next agenda item when a point has been thoroughly covered. Use effective facilitation and gatekeeping skills.
- Summarize meeting progress, preferably using a flipchart, chalkboard, or dry-erase board; the written notes of a meeting become the "group mind" and help keep the group on track.
- If the meeting is a formal one, decide when to take a vote. Make sure the issues are clear before a vote is taken.
- Prepare a committee report (or delegate someone to prepare a report) after one or many meetings. Groups need a record of their progress. Many groups designate someone to be secretary and prepare the minutes or a summary of what occurred at the meeting.

Parliamentary procedure a comprehensive set of rules that prescribe how to take action on specific issues that come before a group. For a complete guide to parliamentary procedure, see *Robert's Rules of Order.*

One of the time-tested strategies for leading a large group is **parliamentary procedure**—a comprehensive set of rules that prescribe how to take action on specific issues that come before a group. Parliamentary procedure provides the needed structure to help large groups (twenty or more people) stay focused on the business at hand, although it is less useful for small groups (in which it leads to win-lose patterns of decision making rather than consensus). Research suggests that parliamentary procedure can be an effective method of adding structure and rules to coordinate quality discussion in a large group but may be overkill in small team meetings.[62]

>>> COMMUNICATION AND GLOBALIZATION @ WORK

Larry was working from his home computer in Grain Valley, Missouri; Peter was at his office computer in Oxford, England. Tomoko was using her iPhone while traveling on the train near Tokyo, while Samuel sat in a park in Johannesburg, South Africa and logged on to his BlackBerry. The four were part of a team working to design new software for tracking food inventories in grocery stores. Like the members of this global design team, it's increasingly likely that you'll participate in virtual meetings in which you interact with people in other locations and the interaction is mediated by the Internet or a video conference. Some of your colleagues may have cultural values that differ from yours or those of other members of your team. Whether you're the meeting leader or not, it's important to be aware of how cultural factors coupled with the use of mediated message may shape your meetings. Drawing on the cultural factors identified by intercultural researcher Geert Hofstede, which we introduced in Chapter 5, we list below some implications for meetings of the intersection of culture and use of technology.

Individualism-Collectivism

People who are from cultures that value collectivism may be most comfortable in face-to-face meetings rather than in mediated meeting settings. Periodically, ask participants in virtual meetings if it's necessary to meet face to face now and then. Or, if that is not practical, ask participants if they would prefer to hold a video conference instead of just collaborating via email or text messages.

Uncertainty Avoidance

People from cultures with a lower tolerance for uncertainty and who need to know what will happen in the future will need more background details and information. Using email and the Internet, a group can share a significant amount of information before meetings to help manage uncertainty. Rather than assuming who needs what level of detail, take the time to ask team members if they each have

enough information about both the task and the process of team collaboration.

Power Difference

People from cultures in which power and status differences are pronounced and power is in the hands of fewer people may expect more formal use of titles even when communicating via email or in other technologically mediated contexts. It's usually better to start with more formal titles and then, if team members are comfortable doing so, use more informal names. Listen and be aware of how others in your virtual team respond to power differences.

Masculinity-Femininity

People from cultures with a more "feminine" orientation (who are concerned with nurturing, cooperation, and sharing) as contrasted to a "masculine" orientation (concerned with task messages and accomplishment) may have a greater preference for face-to-face meetings than virtual meetings.

High Context Versus Low-Context Cultures

People who are from high-context cultures (people who pay specific attention to nonverbal cues and the surrounding context) will likely be more comfortable in face-to-face meetings in which they can observe the nonverbal cues of other meeting participants. Meeting members from low-context cultures (people who place considerable emphasis on words rather than nonverbal cues) may prefer to focus on task accomplishment and may work well in mediated contexts.

Short-Term Versus Long-Term Time Orientation

People from cultures with a long-term orientation to time tend to value a broad perspective on issues and saving money for the future. Multiple meetings may be needed over a longer period of time to solve problems. People from cultures with a short-term orientation to time value the past and present, respect for tradition, "saving face," and spending rather than saving money. They may value less prolonged meetings and quick action.

Communication Principles and Skills for Leadership

Principle One: Be aware of your communication with yourself and others.

- Be aware of the need for structure to keep meetings on track and moving forward when people get off task and off topic.
- Be aware of team members' need for interaction when one or more members are talking too much or are talking too little.

Principle Two: Effectively use and interpret verbal messages.

- Use appropriate verbal messages to define and analyze problems, generate solutions, select the best solution, and test and implement the solution.

- Assess solutions by systematically evaluating their pros and cons.
- Develop an agenda to give a meeting appropriate structure.
- Use metadiscussional skills to keep a meeting focused on the agenda.

Principle Three: Effectively use and interpret nonverbal messages.

- Use appropriate nonverbal behavior to establish and maintain a positive team climate.
- During brainstorming sessions, avoid evaluating others using nonverbal behaviors such as frowning or shaking your head.
- Monitor the eye contact of team members to assess leadership, power, status, and norms.

Principle Four: Listen and respond thoughtfully to others.

- Listen to other team members to demonstrate your respect for their ideas and opinions.
- Listen and respond to provide appropriate team leadership.
- Listen and respond to assess whether the team needs more structure or more interaction to help it achieve its goals.

Principle Five: Appropriately adapt messages to others.

- Adapt your messages to help the group identify, define, and analyze a problem, create solutions, select the best solution, and take appropriate action.
- Adapt your messages to give team meetings an appropriate balance of structure and interaction.
- Adapt your messages to help keep the team focused on the agenda during meetings.

Discussion Questions

1. What are the three primary meeting goals?

2. What are some strategies for deciding which items should typically be placed first on an agenda, and what agenda items should be placed toward the end of the meeting?

3. What is the difference between problem solving and decision making?

4. What are the steps of team decision making?

5. What are the steps in the standard problem-solving process?

6. What are the rules of traditional brainstorming?

7. What are techniques or strategies that can help improve team brainstorming?

8. What are strategies for reducing groupthink?

9. What are strategies for increasing consensus during team discussions?

Building Your Skills

1. Think of group or team meetings you have attended. Have these had a good balance of structure and interaction? If a meeting was out of balance (either too much structure or too much interaction), what specific strategies could have been used to make the discussion more balanced?

2. Develop a meeting agenda for an upcoming meeting. Develop a meeting goal or goals and settle on the sequence of agenda items. After you have written your agenda, write a brief explanation of why you structured your agenda as you did.

3. Identify a specific problem that you currently have and, referring back to the force field analysis diagram in Figure 10.5, identify driving forces and restraining forces to analyze the problem. Which driving forces are you able to increase and which restraining forces can you decrease?

4. Attend a public meeting, such as a meeting of your local school board, city council, or campus council. Keeping in mind the principles and skills discussed in this chapter and the five principles of leadership discussed in this book, evaluate the meeting. Were group members self-aware and aware of comments and actions of others? How effectively did group members use verbal messages to make their points and organize their ideas? Did nonverbal messages provide supportive and positive reinforcement of others' comments? How effectively did group members listen and respond to messages? What evidence did you find that group members appropriately adapted their messages to others during the course of their conversations?

5. Working in a group with three to five other classmates, hold a meeting to consider the following Hurricane Preparedness Case. During the course of the meeting, make a point to do the following:

   • Take turns facilitating the group discussion using the facilitation skills presented in the chapter.

   • Practice the nominal-group technique.

   • Evaluate your group's top two or three highest-priority tasks using pro and con analysis.

   • Assess your group's ability to avoid groupthink.

   • At the conclusion of your meeting, evaluate the group's skill in reaching consensus.

Hurricane Preparedness Case

Although you have idly watched local meteorologists track Hurricane Bruce's destructive course through the Caribbean for several days, you have not given any serious thought to the possibility that the category 3 storm might directly affect your coastal city. However, at about 7 o'clock this morning, the storm suddenly veered northward, putting it on course for a direct hit. Now the National Hurricane Center in Miami has posted a Hurricane Warning for your community. Forecasters are predicting landfall in approximately 9 to 12 hours. Having taken no advance precautions, you are stunned by the amount of work you now have to do to secure your three-bedroom suburban home, which is about a half-mile from the beach. You have enough food in the house for two days. You also have one candle and a transistor radio with one weak battery. You have no other hurricane supplies, nor have you taken any hurricane precautions. Your task is to identify specific strategies for (1) ensuring your survival and (2) ensuring the safety of the property. List tasks that you should accomplish to achieve both of these goals. Your list should be arranged in priority order—what should you do first? What should you do second? and so on.

6. Consider the typical meetings you attend. In the following list of characteristics of effective meetings, check those statements that apply to meetings you normally conduct or attend.

_____ 1. An agenda is prepared prior to the meeting.

_____ 2. Meeting participants have an opportunity to contribute to the agenda.

_____ 3. Advance notice of meeting time and place is provided to those invited.

_____ 4. Meeting facilities are comfortable and allow adequate space for the number of participants.

_____ 5. The meeting begins on time.

_____ 6. The meeting has a scheduled ending time.

_____ 7. The use of time is monitored throughout the meeting.

_____ 8. Everyone has an opportunity to present his or her point of view.

_____ 9. Participants listen attentively to each other.

_____ 10. There are periodic summaries as the meeting progresses.

_____ 11. No one tends to dominate the discussion.

_____ 12. Everyone has a voice in decisions made at the meeting.

_____ 13. The meeting typically ends with a summary of accomplishments.

_____ 14. The meeting is periodically evaluated by participants.

_____ 15. People can be depended on to carry out any action agreed to during the meeting.

_____ 16. A memorandum of discussion or minutes of the meeting are provided to each participant following the meeting.

_____ 17. The meeting leader follows up with participants on actions agreed to during the meeting.

_____ 18. The appropriate and necessary people can be counted on to attend each meeting.

_____ 19. The decision process used is appropriate for the size of the group.

_____ 20. When used, audiovisual equipment is in good working condition and does not detract from the meeting.

How you scored: Multiply the number of statements you checked by 5 to get your total meeting score. A score of 80 or more indicates that the meetings you attend are generally of high quality. A score below 60 suggests that the quality of the meetings you attend could be improved.

7. Communication researchers Katherine Hawkins and Bryant Fillion surveyed personnel managers to find out what the managers considered the most important skills necessary for success in groups and teams.[63] The results are reflected in the following scale. Rate each member of a group you are in on the following skills, using a scale from 1 to 5 (1 = not at all effective; 2 = generally not effective; 3 = uncertain; 4 = effective; 5 = very effective).

Skill	Group Member	Group Member	Group Member	Group Member	Group Member
1. Listens effectively	____	____	____	____	____
2. Understands roles and responsibilities	____	____	____	____	____
3. Actively contributes to the group	____	____	____	____	____
4. Asks clear questions	____	____	____	____	____
5. Establishes and maintains rapport with others	____	____	____	____	____
6. Is sensitive to people with different cultural backgrounds	____	____	____	____	____
7. Uses clear, concise, accurate, and professional language	____	____	____	____	____
8. Communicates well with people who have different professional backgrounds	____	____	____	____	____
9. Gives clear and accurate instructions	____	____	____	____	____
10. Presents a positive professional image nonverbally (through appropriate grooming and attire)	____	____	____	____	____
11. Helps resolve conflicts	____	____	____	____	____
12. Accurately summarizes information to the group	____	____	____	____	____
13. Gives brief, clear, and well-organized, informative presentations to the group when appropriate	____	____	____	____	____
TOTAL	____	____	____	____	____

Scoring: Total the score for each group member. A perfect score is 65; the lowest possible score is 13. Your instructor may invite you to share your ratings of other group members anonymously. Also, note how you evaluate your skill in comparison to your ratings of other group members.

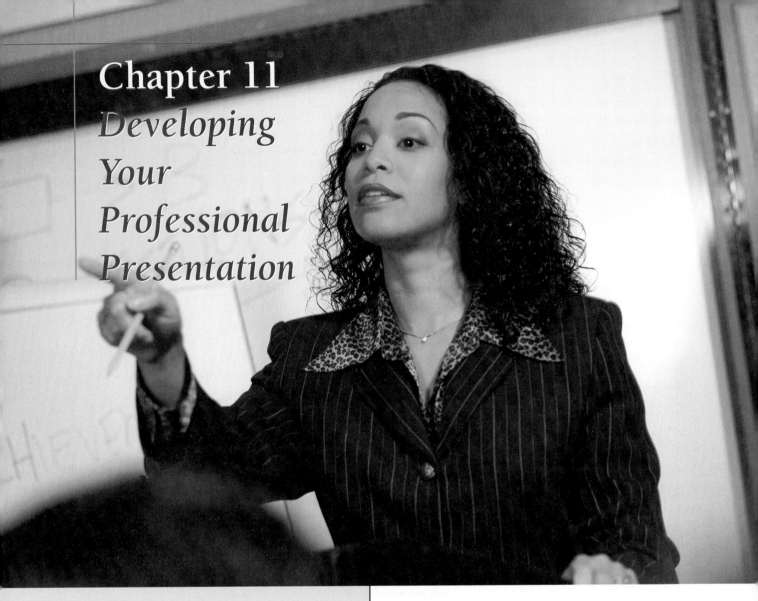

Chapter 11
Developing Your Professional Presentation

After reading this chapter, you should be able to

- ■ Identify the reasons people sometimes get nervous when delivering presentations.

- ■ Implement several strategies to help manage communication apprehension.

- ■ Explain why being audience-centered is essential to being an effective speaker.

- ■ Identify several strategies for analyzing an audience before, during, and after a presentation.

- ■ Identify and implement several strategies for adapting to an audience to enhance the communication process.

- ■ Use communication strategies to enhance your initial, derived, and terminal credibility.

- ■ Select and narrow a presentation topic.

- ■ Determine the specific purpose and central idea for a presentation.

- ■ Generate main ideas for a presentation.

Pierre Omidyar and Jeff Skoll had a major presentation to make. They were giving a talk to executives from Benchmark Capital to persuade them to invest millions of dollars in their new idea. It was originally called AuctionWeb. After presenting all of the facts and figures regarding their investment deal, Omidyar and Skoll were delighted to learn that Benchmark Capital would invest in their little company—which is not so little today. You know it as eBay.[1]

Although there may not be as much at stake with your presentations as in the investment pitch made by Omidyar and Skoll, regardless of your professional or business role, you will be expected to make presentations to others. Some of your talks will be presented to only one person, but many will be presented to larger audiences. During some presentations you'll likely be seated around a conference table, perhaps promoting a new product that you hope your customers will buy. If you aspire to a major leadership role in an organization, it's possible that you may find yourself speaking to a large audience who are anxiously waiting for you to tell them whether they still are employed. Or, you may present your message via phone, web cam, or video phone. As management consultant Tony Jeary has noted, "Life is a series of presentations."[2]

To lead is to speak. Of course you can lead, or influence others, while listening—but effective leaders are also effective speakers. Delivering public presentations is an essential part of being a leader in contemporary business and professional settings. Although it's true that you could simply hand your listeners a written report that provides the information you want to share, the written word alone does not have the same impact as a live presentation. This chapter is about the inevitable public presentations that will punctuate your professional life.

> *Everything that can be said can be said clearly."*
>
> — LUDWIG WITTGENSTEIN

As with the other communication skill sets that we've discussed in this book (skills for relating discussed in Chapters 6 through 8, and skills for collaborating, discussed in Chapters 9 and 10), when presenting a message to an audience you will draw on all five fundamental communication principles. Applying these principles is the primary means of leading or influencing others. In this final unit of the book we focus on presenting skills and note how these skills draw on our five principles for communication and leadership, as suggested in Figure 11.1.

Principle One: When speaking to an audience, be aware of your own communication as well as the communication behavior of others. To present information publicly and not be fully aware of what you are saying is a formula for disaster. Mindlessly blathering about your topic in front of an audience can be embarrassing, or worse—it could lead to the loss of your job if you say the wrong thing. It's also vital to be aware of how your audience is reacting to you and your message as you present your ideas. Speaking without considering the impact of your message on others is like talking to an audience from inside a darkened, soundproof booth—you'll have no notion of whether your message is being heard or not. Effective leaders are mindful of their own communication behaviors as well as the behaviors of those whom they lead.

| Figure 11.1 | Communication Principles and Skills |

Principle Two: When speaking to an audience, effectively use and interpret verbal messages. Leaders lead by their skill in expressing their ideas to others. A speech is called a speech because spoken words express the ideas of the presenter. In the chapters ahead we'll discuss how to conduct research, organize your ideas, and craft your speech for maximum message impact.

Principle Three: When speaking to an audience, effectively use and interpret nonverbal messages. Leaders lead not only through words but also through their actions. If there is a contradiction between what you say and what you do, people will believe what you do rather than what you verbalize. Your delivery plays a key role in expressing emotions, establishing rapport, and developing a relationship with your audience. Effective speakers skillfully make eye contact with their listeners and use appropriate movement, posture, and gestures to emphasize and illustrate their ideas.

Principle Four: When speaking to an audience, listen and respond thoughtfully to others. Although being a good listener seems intuitively important in interpersonal and team communication situations, you may wonder "How does this principle of communication relate to presentational speaking?" It has several applications. You'll listen to others who will give you tips and insights about the audience you'll face. You'll listen to people who speak immediately before you do so that you can ensure that your message makes sense in the context in which you present it. You'll listen and observe what audience members might say or do during your speech and for their reactions following your presentation. Leaders who are effective listeners are also better speakers.

Principle Five: When speaking to an audience, appropriately adapt your message to the audience. This principle is a key concept in any communication situation, but it's especially important when speaking to an audience. One definition of public speaking describes it as "adjusting ideas to people and people to ideas."[3] The degree to which a speaker ethically adapts his or her message to an audience can determine whether listeners remain listeners, or whether they drift away into boredom or become hostile to what you are saying. Skilled leaders appropriately and ethically adapt what they say and how they say it to their audience.

The five fundamental communication principles provide a strong foundation to support the practice of speaking to an audience. Yet a huge hurdle many speakers face—one that you may have experienced and may worry about—is the fear and anxiety they experience when speaking to a group of people. So first, we'll address the causes of communication apprehension and offer several strategies to help you manage your apprehension and communicate your verbal and nonverbal messages as effectively as possible.

Managing Communication Apprehension

Some people believe that if they don't talk about "it," then "it" will go away. The "it" we're talking about is the anxiety and apprehension many people feel when they give a presentation. If you get nervous when you speak in public, you are not alone, many—if not most—people are nervous about giving presentations. Someone once noted "The mind is a wonderful thing. It starts working the minute you're born and never stops . . . until you get up to speak in public." In a frequently cited survey seeking to identify people's fears, public speaking ranked as the top anxiety-producing experience most people face.[4] Forty-one percent of all people responding said public speaking was their greatest fear; fear of death ranked only sixth! Other research suggests that more than 80 percent of people feel nervous when they give a presentation.[5] And about 20 percent of all college age students are highly apprehensive about speaking with others.[6] Because there may be much at stake when you speak in business and professional contexts (such as getting the sale, getting the contract signed, or negotiating a major deal), the anxiety of giving a public presentation may seem overwhelming. Although you may find some comfort in knowing that you are not alone in experiencing public speaking anxiety, you may still welcome some tips and strategies to help you manage your nervousness. One of the biggest comforts can simply be having more information about *why* you experience nervousness and anxiety.[7]

Understanding Your Nervousness

Why do you feel apprehensive when delivering a presentation? Believe it or not, your anxiety stems from your brain trying to help your body adapt to a stressful situation. Sometimes, however, your body adapts more than you need it to.

Your view of the speaking assignment, your perception of your speaking skill, and your self-esteem interact to create anxiety.[8] You want to do a good job, but you're not sure that you can or will. Presented with this conflict, your body responds by increasing your oxygen supply through deeper and more rapid increased breathing, pumping more adrenaline to give you energy, and causing more blood to rush through your veins (to distribute the oxygen and adrenaline). Your brain switches to its fight-or-flight mode: You can either fight—respond to the challenge—or flee to avoid it.

You are experiencing physiological changes because of your psychological state. The increased level of adrenaline in your body explains why you may have a quicker heartbeat, wobbly knees, trembling hands, a higher, quivering voice, and increased perspiration. As a result of your physical discomfort, you may make less eye contact with your listeners, use more vocalized pauses ("Um," "Ah," "You know"), and speak more rapidly than normal. And although you view these physical responses as problems, your body is simply trying to help you with the task at hand—to speak effectively.

You are most likely to feel nervous about giving a presentation just moments before you deliver it. Anxiety is also likely to surge when you learn you have a presentation to deliver, such as when your boss assigns you to talk about a project your team is working on.[9] As you begin preparing your presentation, your anxiety decreases somewhat; that's because you are taking positive action to respond to the speaking opportunity.

To help you mentally prepare for a presentation, consider the following: **You are going to feel more nervous than you look.** Realize that your audience cannot see what you feel. In fact, worrying about your speech and continuing to focus on your fear may actually increase your fear.

Virtually every speaker gets nervous, including many well-known, polished presenters. Katie Couric, Conan O'Brien, Jay Leno, and Oprah Winfrey have all admitted to getting nervous before a speech.[10] Both President John F. Kennedy and British Prime Minister Winston Churchill were hailed as outstanding orators. Both got very nervous before speaking.

Use your anxiety to help you. Extra adrenaline, increased blood flow, increased endorphins to block pain, increased heart rate, and other physical changes triggered by anxiety actually enhance your energy level and help you function better than you might otherwise. Speakers who label their feelings of physiological arousal as "nervousness" are more likely to feel anxious and fearful; but speakers who don't label the increased arousal in a negative way experience it as enthusiasm or excitement. Don't let your initial fear convince you that you cannot speak effectively.

Aware

Tips for Building Your Confidence

Other than understanding what is causing your fear, are there specific things you can do to enhance your confidence? We're happy to report that the answer is "yes"! Here are some tips and strategies to decrease anxiety and increase your poise.

Don't procrastinate.   One research study reached this common-sense conclusion: Speakers who are more apprehensive about speaking put off working on their speeches.[11] There is a link between how far in advance you start preparing and the amount of anxiety you'll experience. The lack of thorough preparation often results in a poorer performance, thereby reinforcing the perception that making a presentation is difficult. Take charge by preparing for your talk early; give yourself every chance to be successful.

Know your audience.   Learn as much as you can about your listeners. The more you can anticipate their reactions to your presentation, the more comfortable you will be in delivering your message. Consider their needs, goals, and hopes as you prepare your message. As you are rehearsing your speech, periodically imagine what your audience members may be doing or how they may respond to your presentation. In other words, be audience-centered, not speaker-centered. Don't keep telling yourself how nervous you are going to be; that's being speaker-centered.[12] An audience-centered speaker focuses on connecting to listeners.

Adapt

Re-create the speech environment when you rehearse.   When you practice your presentation, imagine that you are actually delivering the speech to the audience you will be addressing. Picture what the room looks like. Practice rising from your seat, walking to the front of the room, and beginning your speech. Stand up, and practice out loud; don't

Nonverbal

just think about what you are going to say. The more your brain and body experience actually presenting your speech, the less they will try to deal with the challenge by increasing adrenaline, heart rate, and breathing. A realistic rehearsal will increase your confidence when your moment to speak arrives.

Visualize success. Imagine not just giving your speech, but giving it effectively and comfortably. Studies have found that positive visualization can help you feel more confident and reduce anxiety.[13]

Breathe. You can't not breathe—or else you'd be dead. Yet, nervous speakers often tend to take short, shallow breaths. To help break this anxiety-induced breathing pattern, consider taking a few slow deep breaths before you speak. No one will be able to detect that you are taking deep breaths if you just slowly inhale and exhale before beginning your talk. While breathing deeply, relax your entire body. Deep breathing coupled with visualizing your success can help you relax.

Channel your nervousness. Typical symptoms of anxiety are shaking hands and wobbly knees. Your muscles may move whether you've asked them to move or not. One way to release tension is to take a leisurely walk before you arrive wherever you will be speaking. Another technique is to grasp the edge of your chair (without calling attention to what you are doing) and gently squeeze the chair to release tension. Just squeeze and relax, squeeze and relax. You can also purposely tense and then release the muscles in your legs and arms while you're seated. You may also want to keep both feet on the floor and ever so gently wiggle your toes. These tactics will ensure that every body part will be wide awake and ready to go when it's your turn to speak.

Give yourself a pep talk. Mentally tell yourself positive, encouraging messages rather than negative, fear-laced messages. There is research evidence to support this advice: Worry begets more worry and anxiety. There's also research to suggest that if you can *cognitively restructure* the defeating messages you tell yourself, you can decrease your anxiety.[14] Cognitive restructuring is the technical term for telling yourself positive messages instead of negative messages. So break the chain of negative thoughts by mentally telling yourself "I've practiced this speech. I've got good notes. I'm prepared." Or, "I can do this! My listeners want me to succeed." If you find yourself drifting back into self-defeating negative self-talk, stop those thoughts and replace them with more positive, encouraging messages.

Look for friendly faces when you speak. If you think your audience is not going to like you or agree with your message, you are more likely to feel nervous.[15] So, look for friendly, positive support when you speak. Find the people who will nod affirmatively in agreement with your message. Look for smiles, reciprocal eye contact, and other positive reinforcement. Although you may find some audiences that won't respond positively to you or your message, the overwhelming majority of listeners will be positive. Finding reinforcing feedback can help you feel more confident.

Seek speaking opportunities. The way you get better at anything is through practice. There is evidence that as you gain public speaking experience your anxiety will decrease.[16] So, rather than fleeing from speaking opportunities, look for ways to increase rather than decrease your public speaking experience. At the end of each speech, resist the temptation to focus on your initial fear; instead, celebrate your accomplishment. Mentally replay your success in connecting to an audience.

© 2003 King Features Syndicate

RECAP: Tips for Speaking with Confidence

Before You Speak

- Don't procrastinate—start early.
- Know your audience.
- Rehearse by re-creating the environment in which you will speak.
- Visualize your success.
- Use breathing techniques to help you relax.
- Channel nervous energy.
- Give yourself a mental pep talk.

During Your Speech

- Focus on connecting to your audience rather than on your fear.
- Look for and respond to positive listener support.

After Your Speech

- Seek other speaking opportunities to boost your experience level and confidence.
- Focus on your success and accomplishments.

An Overview of Professional Speaking

Before taking a trip, many travelers purchase a travel guide that gives them an overview of the places they will visit. To provide you with a preview of the tour we will take of the professional speaking process, here we introduce the steps and processes in designing and delivering a professional presentation. An overview of the process should help you see the various steps and help you think and prepare systematically and present a professional presentation.

As shown in Figure 11.2, at the heart of the professional speaking process is considering your audience. You'll notice that double-headed arrows connect the center of the model with every other element in the public-speaking process. Focusing on the audience is where you start and end the speaking process and how you stay centered throughout speech preparation and presentation. Effective leaders ethically adapt or customize their message to their audiences. View the model as you would a clock. You'll find "Select and Narrow Topic" at 12 o'clock. The process proceeds clockwise in the direction of the arrows to "Deliver Speech." Each element is one of the key tasks of a presenter:

1. *Select and narrow your topic*. In business and professional settings, your topic may already be determined because of your job or leadership position. For example, if you're selling a product or presenting an update on a project, you already have your topic. Your task may be to narrow your topic to fit the expected time limits of your talk.

2. *Identify your purpose*. Most presentations have one of three primary purposes: to inform, to persuade, or to entertain. It's likely you will primarily inform (when you give reports or briefings, for example), but you will also undoubtedly seek to persuade others (such as during a sales presentation or when advocating for a specific policy).

3. *Develop your central idea*. Effective speakers are able to boil their message down to a single sentence.

4. *Generate your main ideas*. Effective presentations are not a rambling jumble of ideas but are thoughtfully organized on the basis of one or more key ideas.

Figure 11.2	An Audience-Centered Model of the Presentational Speaking Process

5. *Gather your supporting material.* Most of what you say during a presentation consists of stories, facts, statistics, and definitions to support your main ideas.

6. *Organize your presentation.* A speech, said famed Roman orator Cicero, is like a living creature: It has a head, a body, and a foot. Your presentation should have an introduction, the main body of your message, and a conclusion that summarizes your key ideas.

7. *Rehearse your presentation.* A well-delivered presentation takes practice.

8. *Deliver your presentation.* Your use of eye contact, posture, gestures, and vocal cues will reflect your credibility as a speaker.

Developing and delivering a professional presentation may seem daunting. But if you take it one step at a time and keep your focus on your audience—the element in the process that will determine your success—you'll be rewarded with an effective presentation. As the wheel model in Figure 11.2 suggests, considering the needs, wants, expectations, and backgrounds of your audience is at the heart of designing and delivering an effective presentation.

Consider Your Audience

When attempting to sell a product, a good businessperson knows that one of the keys to success is marketing—which is considering who will buy the product and having a detailed sense of the needs, interests, and goals of the people in that market. When giving a professional presentation, you'll need to practice good marketing skills by considering the specific market for your ideas—your audience. The audience "writes" the

These audience members, who are clearly engaged in a presentation, appear to be listening to a speaker who considered their needs, interests, and goals when developing his or her presentation.

speech[17]—not literally, but certainly metaphorically. By suggesting that the audience "writes the speech," we mean that the audience plays a central role in determining what you should say. If the audience is not foremost in your thoughts as you design and deliver your presentation, you are less likely to accomplish your purpose. Constantly think about connecting your message to your listeners; you'll be more likely to achieve your speaking goal.

Why should the central focus of professional speaking be the audience? Because ultimately your listeners will determine whether you get the sale, land the contract, convince a philanthropist to give your organization money, or achieve whatever your speaking goal is.

Being audience-centered involves making decisions about what you say and how you say it before you speak. It also means being aware of your audience's responses during the presentation so that you can make appropriate adjustments to your message or your style of delivery. Finally, effective speakers acknowledge that cultural, ethnic, and other traditions affect the way people process messages. In addition, each organization, whether a for-profit business or a nonprofit organization, has its own organizational culture. Audience-centered professional speakers are inherently sensitive to the variety of ethnic and cultural backgrounds of contemporary audiences.

Analyzing Your Audience Before You Speak

As we've noted, before thinking about how to narrow your topic or proceeding with any other task in preparing for your presentation, you *consider your audience*. One way to do this is to gather information about them: **demographic information** such as age, gender, and cultural background, and **psychological information** such as likes, dislikes, and possible biases against you, your topic, or your speaking goal. You'll also want information about the speaking situation (including where you will speak and the overall environment in which you'll talk).

After you have gathered the information, you'll need to think about how the information you've gathered can help you. Reflecting on this information is a key task—something less experienced speakers fail to do. The information you gather about your audience won't help you if you don't take it into account at each step of developing your presentation.

Gather demographic information. As every good salesperson knows, before trying to sell someone something, it's important to qualify the customer. To **qualify** customers is to learn as much as you can about them—their backgrounds, likes, dislikes, interests, needs, and goals. If you have the right information, you can determine if customers are interested in what you are selling. Whether you are qualifying a customer to make a sale, or

Demographic information statistics about audience characteristics such as age, gender, and cultural background.

Psychological information listener attributes such as attitudes, beliefs, and values.

Qualify to learn as much as possible about a customer or an audience, such as backgrounds, likes, dislikes, interests, needs, and goals.

presenting a short report to a corporate board, the more background information you have about your listeners, the better able you will be to adapt to them and ethically achieve your speaking goal. Among the key types of information to learn are demographic details, or statistics about such audience characteristics as age, gender, and ethnicity. Consider the following questions about your listeners:

- How old are your listeners?
- What is the ratio of men and women in the audience?
- Are there differences in cultural background related to a national or religious heritage?
- What is the typical education level of your audience?
- Are listeners members of religious, political, social, or service groups?
- What are the range of income and the occupations of your audience?

Once you've gathered demographic information about your listeners, you'll need to ponder how to use the information to help you adapt your message to them. One of the biggest challenges speakers face is how to adapt to an audience that is highly diverse. You may have to focus on a target audience within the larger audience. A **target audience** is a specific segment of your audience that you most want to influence. The challenge when focusing on a target audience is not to lose or alienate the rest of your listeners—to keep the entire audience in mind while simultaneously making a specific attempt to appeal to the target segment.

Another strategy when speaking to a diverse audience is to use a variety of different approaches. Consider using many different types of supporting materials such as illustrations, examples, statistics, opinions; we'll discuss these in more detail in the next chapter. Tell stories. Most people like to hear a good, well-told, relevant story. With an exceptionally diverse group, consider relying on visual materials that transcend language and cultural differences. Pictures and images can communicate universal messages—especially emotional ones. Finally, with a highly diverse audience, seek common ground: Identify values that many people in the audience may hold.

Consider the psychological profile of your audience. Since you are probably not a trained psychologist, you may wonder how to develop a psychological profile of your listeners. It's not as tricky as it may seem. You need not conduct a detailed personality inventory of your audience to gain a general sense of whether they are interested, uninterested, favorable, or unfavorable toward you and your topic. But you can ask someone who knows your audience well about their attitudes, beliefs, and values. Or you could speculate about their position on the issues you will discuss based on their demographic characteristics as well as the nature of their jobs and their roles in the organization. What are their attitudes (likes and dislikes)? What are their beliefs (what they hold to be true or false)? What are their values (concepts of good and bad, right and wrong)? Overall, does your audience have a positive attitude toward what you are going to say? Are they hostile or opposed to you and your ideas? Or are they, like many audiences, simply neutral or apathetic toward you and your message? For example, if it's your job to announce that there will be a 10 percent cut in employment in your department, your listeners will be both attentive and fearful that their jobs are on the line. Or, if it's your turn to present a mandatory routine reminder of safety tips for your work team, your listeners are likely to be somewhat apathetic, since they've heard this message before. Knowing your audience's attitudes toward you or your topic is important—it determines how you organize your message, the types of examples and illustrations you use, and many other facets of your talk that we will discuss in this chapter and the chapters ahead.

Consider the situation. Situational audience analysis includes a consideration of the time and place of your presentation, the size of your audience, and the reason you are speaking. Although these elements are not technically characteristics of your audience, they can have an important effect on how your listeners react to what you say.

Key factors in the situation are the time at which you are expected to speak and the length of your presentation. If you're speaking to people who are not quite awake or are tired, you may have to throttle up your energy level when talking. Another key piece of information to know before any presentation is when your listeners expect you to conclude. A general rule of thumb is to *never exceed your time limit*—in fact, if possible, conclude just slightly before your listeners expect you to end. Most listeners

Target audience a specific segment of your audience that you most want to influence.

Figure 11.3 | A Standard Classroom Arrangement

don't complain if a talk is too short; but they will not appreciate you if you take too much of their time.

The size of your audience directly affects your speaking style. Usually, the larger the audience, the more likely they are to expect a more formal style. With an audience of ten or fewer, you can be more conversational; but in a professional or business setting, formality may be expected. If, as during many professional presentations, you and your listeners are so few that you are all sitting around a table, you'll probably be expected to stay seated for your presentation.

The location of your presentation will also influence your overall style and speaking approach. If you're delivering your message in a boardroom, with audience members seated around a huge table, you'll probably have a more formal style than if you are speaking to a group in a small conference room or seated at a table in someone's office. The arrangement of chairs, placement of audiovisual materials, and the control of the lighting are ultimately up to you. Note the different types of seating arrangements you are likely to experience in the following illustrations.[18] If you want to limit interaction among your audience members, then a standard classroom arrangement (shown in Figure 11.3) works best. Angling the chairs, (as shown in Figure 11.4), which slightly increases eye contact among participants, may be useful if you plan to have a

Figure 11.4 | An Alternative Classroom Arrangement

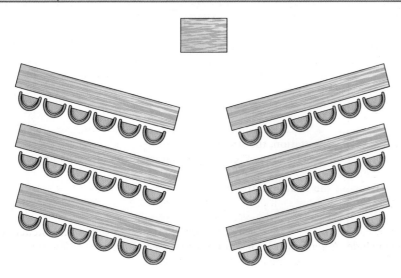

Figure 11.5	A Standard Conference Table Arrangement

question-and-answer session following a presentation. If you're holding a meeting at which you will do most of the talking, the standard conference table arrangement in Figure 11.5, with you at the head of the table, will be what meeting participants will expect. But if you want the meeting to be more interactive, having people sit on all sides of the table, as in Figure 11.6, will signal that you expect participants to interact with one another. And if you have a panel discussion of experts or a symposium presentation in which several people will give short presentations, the T-shaped conference table setup (Figure 11.7) may be best. Consider how the arrangement of the room where you are speaking can help you achieve your purpose, and if it's possible, make the necessary changes.

Figure 11.6	A Square Conference Table Arrangement

Figure 11.7	A T-Shaped Arrangement of Conference Tables

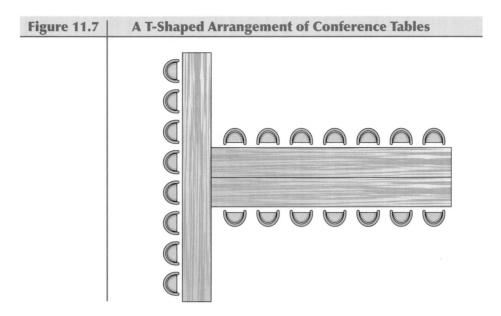

Analyzing Your Audience as You Speak

Being audience-centered involves more than thinking and planning your message before you speak; it also is a process that occurs as you are speaking. An effective speaker looks for cues from the audience during the speech to help him or her adjust speaking content or delivery. Delivering a presentation is a lot like playing in a jazz ensemble and responding to what the other musicians are playing. If you know what to look for, you can find cues from your listeners that will help you know how to connect with them. Here's where Principle Four is applicable to presentational speaking: A good speaker is listening with both ears and eyes to monitor the audience so that he or she can customize the message for maximum effectiveness.

For speeches in business and professional settings, it's often a good idea to *overprepare* your message. By this we mean you may need to have stories, examples, statistics, or facts that you could add to your message once you actually see your audience and observe how they are responding. You may not use all the information you've prepared. You may, for example, have a handout that spells out detailed costs of the project you're proposing; you'll distribute the handout only if you find that your listeners have questions about your project's expenses. Yes, it takes additional time to overprepare. But an investment in extensive preparation can be worth it. As we've noted, effective leaders adapt and respond to others.

Analyzing Your Audience's Nonverbal Cues as You Speak

During most presentations, your listeners will not be talking back to you. Unless your presentation is part of an interactive meeting in which there is lots of discussion, you'll talk and others will listen. It's your audience's nonverbal cues that will tip you off to how successful you are and whether you need to modify your message or delivery. Nonverbal cues are the primary way people communicate likes and dislikes, feelings, and emotions, and if you know what to look for you'll be able to accurately interpret your listeners' unspoken cues.

Eye contact. The best indicator that your listeners are with you is their eye contact. The more eye contact your listeners make, the more likely it is they are connecting to your message. If they are flipping through notes, looking out the window, looking at someone else, or sitting with eyes closed, it's a good bet that you're not connecting with them.

Facial expression. Another key indicator of interest is audience members' facial expressions. Someone who is looking at you with a slight head tilt and a frozen, "in-a-stupor" expression is probably not mentally in the same room with you. An interested listener not only looks at you, but also responds to your messages with facial expressions. Smiling at appropriate times, laughing at your humor, nodding their heads in agreement, or even shaking their heads in disagreement means audience members are listening. A bored listener has an expression that doesn't change, no matter what you are saying.

Movement. A bored audience expresses its boredom with movement, especially finger tapping, toe jiggling, foot wagging, and other squirms and jitters. An attentive audience doesn't move much while you are speaking, but if you ask for a show of hands in response to a question, an attentive audience will respond. When you "have" an audience, they look at you and focus on your message. When you don't "have" them, their inattentiveness manifests itself with nervous, restless movement.

An inattentive, unengaged audience just sits there. An inert, motionless, nonresponsive audience is a bad sign. If you see bad signs, you'll need to modify your message content or your delivery. Effective speakers use and interpret others' nonverbal messages.

Verbal responsiveness. During smaller, informal presentations your listeners may respond verbally to questions you ask or ideas you express. Even in a large group, audience members may respond verbally; they may mouth "yes" or "no" to a question you ask or respond aloud to something you've said. If your listeners express disagreement with an idea, you now have information you can use to adapt to them. The effective speaker not only watches the audience, but also listens for any audible information that may indicate that the audience is in agreement or opposition.

Responding to Your Audience's Nonverbal Cues

More important than just observing your listeners is responding to them. If audience members are responsive to you and in agreement with your ideas, you have the luxury of continuing to present the message you planned. But if you see indications of disagreement or inattentiveness, you'll be wise to adapt and adjust either your message, your delivery, or both. It takes experience to "read" an audience and then respond appropriately. Here are several strategies and tips to consider when responding to audience reactions during your talk.[19]

If Your Listeners Appear Bored

- Tell an appropriate story.
- Use a personal example.
- Remind your listeners why your message is of interest to them.
- Eliminate abstract facts, statistics, and details.
- Consider using appropriate humor.
- Make a direct reference to the audience; consider using members' names or mentioning something about them.
- Get audience members to participate by asking them for an example.
- Ask a rhetorical question.
- Speak a bit faster and with more intensity and energy than you have shown so far.
- Pause for dramatic effect.

If Your Listeners Don't Seem to Understand You

- Ask someone in the audience to summarize a key point you are making.
- Repeat your main points.
- Restate your information using a different example, if you have one. Effective speakers have backup examples and illustrations that they can use if they need to add depth to or clarify their ideas.
- Use a presentation aid such as a whiteboard, chalkboard, or flipchart to focus listener attention.

- Clarify the overall organization of your message by noting what point you are on now and what point you will make next.

If Your Listeners Appear to Disagree with You

- Identify those parts of your message on which you and your listeners do agree.
- Provide additional data and evidence to support your key point.
- Rely less on anecdotes and emotional support and more on facts to document your case.
- Write key facts on a whiteboard, chalkboard, or flipchart.
- If you don't have answers to their questions, tell your listeners you will get back to them with more information.

Analyzing Your Audience After You Speak

You may think that after you give your talk there is nothing left to be done. But post-presentation analysis can help you prepare your next presentation. Following are ways of assessing how effectively your listeners received your presentation.

>>> COMMUNICATION SKILLS @ WORK

A sales presentation on iMacs to a group of "techies" in charge of purchasing computer technology should be different from one presented to a group of inexperienced new teachers with little technical background who want to equip the student computer lab. The more skillfully you can customize your message to your audience, the more successful you will be in achieving your communication goal. You've undoubtedly heard a "canned" presentation which you knew the speaker had memorized. Even if the key ideas and overall structure of a sales talk or informative briefing are the same from audience to audience, the skilled speaker finds ways to make a message connect to a specific audience. If you can give exactly the same speech to several audiences, then your presentation isn't specific enough. A good speaker customizes his or her message for a specific audience.

Following are some suggestions of strategies and techniques for customizing your message to a particular group.

Use Audience Members' Names
If appropriate, consider using the names of members of your audience in your talk. You certainly don't want to single someone out and make the person feel awkward. But you may be able to use a person's name in an example, illustration, story, or anecdote. Remember, however, that it's always wise to get someone's permission to use his or her name in an example rather than surprising the person.

Refer to the Organization, Company, City, or Community
Use the company name or refer to the city early in your presentation, and offer a sincere compliment. Most listeners can smell phony flattery, so don't say things just to patronize a group. Find an honest way to say a positive word about the city or company.

When speaking to the Lafayette, Indiana, Rotary, then president of Purdue University Dr. Martin Jischke began his speech with these words:

> I am a Rotarian. I believe in the work that Rotary is doing. Rotary efforts have important focuses on youth, education, and international exchanges. That is why I have chosen this opportunity to talk with you today about the future of our nation and the dreams for our future.

Establishing common ground with his listeners by explicitly noting the links between his own interests and his membership in Rotary International helped Dr. Jischke customize his message.

Refer to a Recent Event
Make a point to read the company newsletter and explore the website of the organization where you will be speaking to find out if there is an event to which you can refer.

Refer to an Event That Happened on the Date of Your Presentation
On the Internet (for example, at Historychannel.com), you can quickly find out what significant event happened in history on the day of your presentation. For example, on the day this paragraph was written, April 15, the Titanic sunk. So you might make a reference to how even great ideas are vulnerable. Or, because April 15 is the deadline for filing U.S. income tax returns, you could note that there comes a time when payment must be made. Other sources of historical events are columns in the local paper or books such as the *Speaker's Lifetime Library*, which provides a description of events for each day of the year.

Nonverbal responses. Did your audience applaud? Gauging the level and intensity of applause you received is a simple way to determine if your audience liked what you had to say. Smiles, head nods, and eye contact are also cues to observe when you conclude. Although the nonverbal response can give you a general sense of how well your message was appreciated, you may not be able to determine which parts of your talk were the best or if there were things you said that were less well received.

Verbal responses. You may need to listen to audience members' comments and ask them for feedback to gather more specific information about your message. If a listener says, "Nice job," or "Good talk," follow up by asking what part of the speech was the most helpful or what part she agreed with the most. Asking, "Is there anything you disagreed with?" may also help you glean useful feedback.

Survey responses. If you presented a more formal presentation to a large audience, you may want to survey your audience after you speak. A short written survey that can be distributed right after your talk, a telephone survey, or an Internet survey can help you gather precise information about your message.

Behavioral responses. The ultimate test of whether your message was effective is whether your listeners do what you wanted them to do following your presentation. If you were selling a product or service, did they purchase it? Did they sign the petition or vote as you wanted them to vote? If you presented training, can they now perform the skill you taught them? Or, if you were delivering an informative briefing or report, can they remember and use the information you shared? Your listeners' subsequent actions are the best indicators of your success.

Establish Your Credibility

Credibility a listener's perception of a speaker as competent, trustworthy, and dynamic.

Competence the perception that a person is skilled, knowledgeable, and informed about the subject he or she is discussing.

Trustworthiness the aspect of credibility that reflects whether a speaker is perceived as believable and honest.

Dynamism an aspect of a speaker's credibility that reflects whether the speaker is perceived as energetic.

Charisma a form of dynamism; a charismatic speaker possesses charm, talent, magnetism, and other qualities that make the person attractive.

Initial credibility the impression of a speaker's credibility that listeners have before a speech begins.

Derived credibility the perception of a speaker's credibility that the audience forms as he or she presents a speech.

Terminal credibility the perception of a speaker's credibility listeners have at the conclusion of a speech.

If you were going to buy a new computer, to whom would you turn for advice? Perhaps you would consult your brother, who's a computer nerd, or your roommate, a computer science major. Or, you might seek advice from *Consumer Reports*, the monthly publication of studies of various consumer products. In other words, you would turn to a source you consider knowledgeable, competent, and trustworthy—a source you think is credible.

Credibility is a listener's perception of a speaker as competent, trustworthy, and dynamic. It is not something a speaker inherently possesses or lacks; rather, it is based on listeners' mindset regarding the speaker. Your listeners, not you, determine whether you have credibility. Regardless of your professional goal as a communicator, it is important that you be perceived as credible. The more credibility you have, the more likely it is that your listeners will believe you, trust you, and like you.

How do you establish your credibility? It's a centuries-old question. The ancient Greek philosopher Aristotle thought that a public speaker should be ethical, possess good character, display common sense, and be concerned for the well-being of his audience. Quintilian, a Roman teacher of public speaking, advised that a speaker should be "a good person speaking well." These ancient speculations about the elements that enhance a speaker's credibility have been generally supported by modern research.

Elements of Your Credibility

Walter Haskell is a genius at marketing automobiles—he knows how to sell cars. So when he spoke at the annual sales meeting about his marketing techniques, he had a packed hotel ballroom filled to overflowing with salespeople hanging on every word he uttered. He had credibility. But later that evening when he spoke to the Parent-Teacher Association meeting at his daughter's school in support of a new school, his audience listened politely but didn't seem all that interested in his analysis. What Walter experienced is the multifaceted and contextual nature of credibility: He was perceived as a credible speaker when he talked about selling cars but not when he talked about junior high school renovations.

Credibility is not a single factor but consists of multiple elements. It is your listeners who determine if you are credible. Your goal is to be perceived as displaying each element of credibility when you speak. Ideally, you should be perceived as competent, trustworthy, and dynamic.

Competence is the perception that a person is skilled, knowledgeable, and informed about the subject he or she is discussing. Olympic swimmer Michael Phelps and professional golfer Tiger Woods are both perceived as highly competent in their respective fields. You will be more persuasive if you can convince your listeners that you are an expert on or at least know something about *your* topic. How do you do this? You can talk about relevant personal experience with the topic. If you have lived in a high-rise condominium, you'll have more credibility as a high-rise condo salesperson than someone who has only lived in a ranch-style house. You can also cite evidence to support your ideas. Even if you have not lived in a high-rise condo yourself, you can be prepared with information about the advantages of apartment living, such as convenience and efficiency.

A second element in credibility is **trustworthiness**. While delivering a speech, you need to convey honesty and sincerity to your audience. You can't do this simply by saying, "Trust me." You have to earn trust. You can do so by demonstrating that you are interested in and experienced with your topic. Again, speaking from personal experience makes you seem more trustworthy. Conversely, having something to gain by persuading your audience may make you suspect in their eyes. That's why salespeople and politicians often lack credibility. If you do what they say, they will clearly benefit from their sales commissions or political influence.

A third factor in credibility is a speaker's **dynamism**, or energy. Dynamism is often projected through delivery. A speaker who applies the communication principle of effectively using and understanding nonverbal messages maintains eye contact, has enthusiastic vocal inflection, and moves and gestures purposefully and is likely to be seen as dynamic. **Charisma** is a form of dynamism; a speaker with charisma possesses charm, talent, magnetism, and other qualities that make the person attractive and energetic. Former General Electric CEO Jack Welch and well-known talk show host Oprah Winfrey are considered charismatic speakers by many people.

Michael Phelps's competence in competitive swimming was established when he won eight Olympic gold medals in 2008. He uses his credibility to boost interest in and gain media attention for the sport.

Phases in the Establishment of Credibility

A speaker has opportunities throughout a speech to enhance his or her credibility. **Initial credibility** is the impression of your credibility your listeners have even before you begin speaking. They grant you initial credibility based on such factors as your appearance and your credentials. Dressing appropriately and having someone introduce you with a brief summary of your qualifications and accomplishments are two strategies for enhancing your initial credibility.

Derived credibility is the perception your audience forms as you present your speech. If you appropriately adapt your message to your audience, you will enhance your derived credibility. Specific strategies include establishing common ground with your audience, supporting your arguments with evidence, and presenting a well-organized speech. Using effective eye contact, posture, and vocal delivery also enhances your derived credibility.

The last phase of credibility, called **terminal credibility**, is the perception of your credibility your listeners have when you finish your speech. A thoughtfully prepared and well-delivered conclusion can enhance your terminal credibility, as can maintaining eye contact throughout the speech and even after your closing sentence. Also, apply the communication principle of listening and responding thoughtfully to others. Be prepared to answer questions after your speech, regardless of whether there is a planned question-and-answer period.

A key principle to remember about credibility is this: *Credibility is in the eye of the beholder*. You have as much credibility as other people give you. Yet once you have established high credibility, it's possible to lose it—just ask talk show host and designer Martha Stewart, former President Clinton, or Vice President Biden. At one point in each of their careers they were held in exceptionally high esteem; they had high credibility and influence. Then each of them experienced a loss of credibility. Martha Stewart went to prison for perjury. President Clinton, who started his presidency with very high credibility, lost a lot of that credibility because of the Monica Lewinsky scandal during his second term as president. And when Vice President Joe Biden, as a Senator from Delaware running for president in the late 1980s, admitted that he plagiarized a speech by British politician Neil Kinnock, he lost considerable credibility and dropped out of the 1988 presidential race. Yet, each of these leaders has worked hard to rebuild credibility. Martha Stewart now has a successful television show, President Clinton now draws large crowds at his speaking engagements. And Vice President Biden? Well, his title indicates he's recovered the credibility he lost years earlier. Credibility can change. It is other people who give, perhaps take away, and then may restore your credibility as a leader, based on your efforts to build a reputation as a competent, trustworthy, and dynamic person.

RECAP: Enhancing Your Credibility

Before You Speak: Enhancing Your Initial Credibility

- Dress appropriately.
- Have a brief summary of your qualifications and accomplishments ready for the person who will introduce you.

As You Speak: Enhancing Your Derived Credibility

- Establish common ground with your audience.
- Support your arguments with evidence.
- Present a well-organized speech.
- Use effective delivery skills (eye contact, good posture, appropriate vocal inflection).

After You Speak: Enhancing Your Terminal Credibility

- Prepare your conclusion, and deliver it well.
- Maintain eye contact throughout your speech and even after your closing sentence.
- Be prepared to answer questions after your speech.

Craft Your Message

With a clear understanding of your audience and having given thoughtful consideration to establishing your credibility, you're ready to move on to the key task of developing your message. The essential steps including selecting and narrowing your topic, determining the purpose of your presentation, developing your central idea, and generating the major points for your talk.

Select and Narrow Your Topic

The best presentation topics are those that are of interest to both you and your audience. Your topic should also have a link to your job, background, or expertise so you can establish your credibility. When speaking professionally, you typically don't have to rack your brain trying to think of a presentation topic. Unlike a high school or college public speaking class, in which your instructor asks you to give an informative or persuasive speech on a topic of your choice, your professional presentation topic is typically established for you, in that you are speaking for a specific reason: to sell a product or a service, to enhance the image or reputation of your organization, to solicit donations, or to report on a project. What is less obvious, however, is how you narrow your topic and adapt your specific purpose to achieve the outcome you wish to achieve.

Adapt

Although the topic of your presentation may be evident, you will need to narrow and customize it to fit your time limits and to adapt to your listeners. For example, if you've been working for three weeks with a team of people studying ways to trim the budget and you only have five minutes to give your report, you'll have to be selective. To narrow your topic, you'll need to consider three things: your audience, the occasion, and yourself.

Given what we've already said about the centrality of the audience, it shouldn't be surprising that your topic should be one your listeners are interested in. The occasion will also dictate the type of presentation you make. Whether you are giving a sales talk, briefing stockholders, presenting a short report, or addressing the media, the specific purpose helps you decide how to approach your topic. The third element is you: your own interests and skills, your role in the organization you represent, and whether you are presenting information or persuading others all help you tailor your topic.

Determine Your Purpose

Your presentation topic and your presentation purpose are two different things. Your *topic* is what you are talking about; your *purpose* is the goal you seek to accomplish. In business and professional contexts, that goal will likely be to inform (as when sharing information at a briefing, seminar, or lecture) or to persuade (as when trying to convince your listeners to do something or believe something). (Some presentations have a third goal: to entertain. This might be your goal if you were delivering a speech that your audience expected to be funny, such as an after-dinner speech. And you could certainly use entertaining humor when informing or persuading.) So with your topic settled, you'll need to decide what your overarching purpose is—to inform, persuade, or to entertain others.

Many presentations may have more than one purpose. You may first need to inform listeners about a product or service before you persuade them to purchase it. Although you may have multiple purposes, it's a good idea to think about and be aware of the ultimate purpose or purposes of your presentation.

After making sure you understand your general purpose, you will need to develop your specific purpose. A **specific purpose** is a concise statement that indicates precisely what you want your listeners to be able to do, remember, or feel when you finish your speech; your specific purpose statement indicates the *audience response* you seek. Once again, we emphasize the importance of focusing on the audience as you develop your specific purpose. If you don't know what your precise purpose is, chances are your audience won't know either.

A specific purpose is also called a *behavioral objective* because you identify the specific behavior you seek from your listeners. Here are some examples of specific purpose statements:

- At the end of my presentation, the audience should be able to identify the three reasons our stock price increased during the last quarter.
- At the end of my presentation, the audience should be able to restate the two new security measures our company has instituted to enhance employee safety.
- At the end of my presentation, the audience should increase their order for one or more of the products our company makes.

Note that each of the above examples all begin with the same words: "At the end of my presentation, the audience should be able to . . . ." The next word should be a verb that describes an observable, measurable action that the audience should be able to complete when you finish your presentation. If your general purpose is to inform, then you will use verbs such as *list*, *explain*, *describe*, or *write*. If your general purpose is to persuade, then you'll use such verbs as *purchase*, *order*, *act*, or *write*. Don't use words such as *know*, *understand*, or *appreciate*, because you cannot measure what an audience knows, understands, or appreciates unless your listeners perform a specific behavior such as explaining, describing, or listing.

A specific purpose sentence states what you want the *audience* to be able to do, not what you, the speaker, will do. A sentence such as "I want to describe the history of our company" is not a specific-purpose statement because it is not audience-centered; it's a speaker-centered statement. It's not effective because it is not focused on the primary reason for speaking—the audience. If you phrase your specific-purpose sentence as "At the end of my presentation, the audience should be able to describe the four transforming events in our company's history," then the focus of the presentation shifts to the listeners rather than the speaker.

Specific purpose a concise statement of precisely what you want your listeners to be able to do, remember, or feel when you finish your speech. Your specific purpose statement indicates the *audience response* you seek.

Use your specific purpose sentence to guide you in accomplishing your speaking goal. Some speakers write their specific purpose sentence on a note card or a Post-it note so that they can refer to it as they prepare their message. The shorter the speech, the more important it is to have a clear sense of direction, because a short talk needs to be tightly focused; you don't have extra time to be off topic. If you have a clear specific purpose, you can make sure that as you are gathering information, examples, and ideas for your talk, your research is helping you achieve your specific purpose. If what you are gathering is not related to your specific purpose, don't include it in your talk.

Develop Your Central Idea

Verbal

Imagine you hop on an elevator at the first floor of your office building and are traveling to the twentieth floor. Traveling with you is a client to whom you'd like to sell your company's services. What would you say during the short ride to communicate your key ideas? Whether you have one minute or one hour to pitch your ideas to listeners, you need to distill your message into a short, specific statement. The essence of your message is your **central idea** (sometimes called a *thesis sentence*): a one-sentence summary of your presentation. The difference between a central idea and a purpose statement is that the central idea focuses on the content of your presentation, whereas the purpose statement focuses on audience behavior.

The central idea should be a complete sentence—not a phrase, a sentence fragment, or a question. The language in the central idea sentence should be clear and direct. The central idea sentence should also contain just one major idea. Here's a good example of a central idea sentence: "The Acme Computer Store is the best computer store because of our low prices, high quality, and excellent customer service." This sentence summarizes the key content of the presentation. It has one idea that is supported by several reasons. Here's another example: "New federal laws require every company to increase security at manufacturing plants." It's an effective statement because it's short, clear, and contains only one idea.

Central idea a one-sentence summary of your presentation; sometimes called a thesis sentence.

A less effective central idea might be "Federal laws and business." The statement is not a complete sentence and it doesn't provide a sense of the key content of the message; it's a description of a topic, not a central idea sentence. A statement such as "In my opinion, our West Coast factory is overstaffed and we spend too much money on staff development" is also not well phrased because it contains two different ideas (overstaffing of the factory and expensive staff development). The phrase "in my opinion" is not needed; you don't need to include qualifiers such as "I think," or "from my point of view" in a central idea sentence. Just state your key conclusion or essential idea in a clear, direct, well-worded sentence.

RECAP: Identify Your Purpose and Central Idea

Your General Purpose

- To inform: To define, describe, or explain a thing, person, place, idea, or process
- To persuade: To change or reinforce a listener's attitude (likes or dislikes), beliefs (sense of what is true or false), values (view of what is good or bad), or behavior
- To entertain: To amuse an audience

Your Specific Purpose

- A description of the specific behavior you want your audience members to be able to do by the end of your presentation: "At the end of my presentation, the audience should be able to . . ."
- Includes a verb such as *list, describe, identify, purchase,* or *build*

Your Central Idea

A one-sentence summary of your presentation that

- Is a declarative sentence
- Is short, clear, and direct
- Contains only one idea
- Focuses on the audience's interests and needs

Finally, your central idea sentence should be audience-centered. The content of your speech, as summarized in your central idea sentence, should be tailored to your listeners. If the key idea of the message doesn't relate to your audience, your presentation will not connect with them effectively. For example, speaking to plant workers about four ways to increase security at manufacturing plants is appropriately audience-centered. But the same central idea is not appropriate for a talk to the plant's customers gathered for a new product demonstration. Your audience should be the prime factor that determines how you develop your central idea sentence.

Generate Your Main Ideas

With your central idea sentence in hand, you are now ready to add depth and dimension to your presentation by identifying the key ideas you will talk about. Although we've suggested that your central idea sentence should contain a single idea, it will probably be an idea that you can subdivide and organize into smaller ideas that you will present to your audience one at a time. Most listeners like a clearly organized presentation rather than a hodgepodge of information. At times it's a challenge for speakers to figure out what the major points of their talk will be. But if a speaker hasn't taken the time to think about how to divide the information into manageable pieces, it will be more difficult for listeners to follow the speaker's train of thought. In fact, "train of thought" is an apt metaphor: Think about your speech as a train with separate cars being pulled by the engine; the major ideas are the cars. Each car is separate, but all are connected to make up the entire train. Your speech will have separate pieces as well; each piece is a main idea.

An effective strategy is to ask yourself three questions about your central idea sentence to help you divide your speech into manageable pieces.

- Does the central idea have *logical divisions*? (These may be indicated by such phrases as "three types of software" or "four different ways to perform the same computer function using this technology.")

- Can you think of several *reasons* the central idea is true? (You could say, "There are three reasons you should buy this computer.")

- Can you support your central idea with a series of *steps* or a chronological progression? (For example, "There are four steps to installing this computer program, which should be performed in sequence.")

Virtually any central idea sentence can be subdivided by finding out the answer to one of these questions.

Does the Central Idea Have Logical Divisions?

If your central idea is "There are three parts to the new corporate insurance claim forms," your presentation can be organized into three parts; each of the three parts of the insurance form will be a major idea of your talk. Another example might be "There are four types of strategies to help manage interpersonal conflict at work." The phrase "four types" is a clue that this talk can be divided into four main ideas—one for each strategy for managing interpersonal conflict. At this point in developing your presentation, you don't need to worry about the order of the points, just note that there are separate main ideas to discuss.

Are There Several Reasons Why the Central Idea Is True?

If you are trying to persuade someone to do something, you may identify several reasons why they should do what you are suggesting. Here's an example of a central idea sentence that can be divided into reasons that the central idea sentence is true: "The San Marcos Advertising Agency is the best advertising agency for any company to use to advertise their product or service." A speaker could cite the reasons this central idea is true:

1. The San Marcos Advertising Agency gets results.
2. The San Marcos Advertising Agency is affordable.
3. The San Marcos Advertising Agency is creative.

Note that each of the reasons is written as a brief complete sentence. Once you have chiseled your talk into these smaller pieces, you are well on your way to begin organizing the overall structure of your message.

Can You Support the Central Idea with a Series of Steps?

If you are giving a talk on how to perform a task, you'll probably be able to organize your presentation into a series of steps by noting what should be done first, second, third, and so on to perform the task. An example of a central idea sentence that can be supported by describing the steps in the process might be "Requesting an office transfer is easy." The speech would describe, in order, the things that an employee needs to do. First, the employee must ask his or her supervisor to fill out a form. Second, the employee must submit that form and a transfer request to the corporate office. And finally, the employee must schedule an interview with the personnel office to discuss the transfer. Training presentations and orientation programs typically use a chronological pattern organized by the sequence of steps involved in accomplishing a task.

>>> COMMUNICATION AND GLOBALIZATION @ WORK

One of the principles we've stressed throughout this book is the importance of adapting your messages to others. Many, if not most, of the professional presentations you give will include audience members who represent a mix of cultures and backgrounds rather than a single cultural tradition. Although you may not have immediate plans to travel to Paris, Moscow, Tokyo, or Sydney, it will not be unusual for you to face audience members who come from one of these cities when you speak at work. Eventually you may be assigned to work in another country. Or perhaps you work for an internationally based company that has cultural traditions and norms that are different from yours. Or you may have a job that requires you to make telephone calls to people around the world. Your "speech" may be delivered via a phone, text message, fax, or other electronic means. The principles we've presented in this chapter for planning a speech apply to both in-person presentations and mediated messages.

People from the predominant culture in the United States usually prefer a structured speech that follows an outlined pattern; they also prefer an introduction that previews the ideas you'll present and a conclusion that summarizes the essential points you've made. But if you were addressing a Russian or Eastern European audience, they would expect a less tightly structured presentation. You might tell several stories rather than enumerating specific points. When you're in doubt about listener preferences, we recommend being structured and organized. But realize that not all audience members may expect information to be presented as *you* prefer. For example, Japanese speakers addressing a predominantly Japanese audience expect to begin a speech by making respectful references to their audience such as explicitly telling them what an honor it is to speak to them.

You may be still wondering, "So, what should I do when I present a speech to people who have a cultural background different from my own?" Here are some ideas that may help you.[20] First, consider using a variety of different types of supporting materials. A mix of stories, examples, statistics, and other supporting illustrations can appeal to audiences with a wide range of backgrounds. Also, consider the power of images; use visual aids to help illustrate your talk. Pictures and images can communicate universal messages—especially emotional ones.

Telling a good story to illustrate your ideas is another effective strategy to appeal to a wide range of audience preferences. Most audiences value a good story with a point or moral that is relevant to the point you want to make. Humorist, novelist, and renowned storyteller Garrison Keillor masterfully tells stories about his fictional hometown of Lake Wobegon. Keillor is internationally respected because of the universal themes of friendship and humanity that he uses in his stories. Whether you're the CEO of a company or a new staff member, you can use Keillor's technique of telling stories to express universal themes of brotherhood, family, and other basic human values. For example, when a CEO of a large steel company made speeches at her company's European manufacturing plants, she was able to connect with her audience by opening her talk with a story about her children.

Our bottom-line advice is this: Be aware of who will be in your audience and adapt your message to them. If you're unsure of what speaking style your listeners might prefer, ask for tips and strategies from audience members or people you trust before you design and deliver your presentation.

SAMPLE SPEECH *by* DOUGLAS STARR

Presented to the International Association of Business Communicators, August 5, 2005[21]

Writing for the Web

The best news is that you don't need to learn a different writing style to write for the World Wide Web.

Starr began his speech by simultaneously catching attention and summarizing his key idea.

Writing news stories and news releases for the World Wide Web, writing online, is no different from writing for print, particularly writing for newspapers. It is amazing how many newspaper techniques are recommended for web writing.

And the best part is that you already know all of those techniques. You learn them in journalism school, and you've been doing it all your professional lives—at least, you should have.

The speaker makes a personal, direct connection with his listener.

I am speaking about only the writing, not the audio, the video, the blinking buttons, and other gimmicks of websites. Moreover, researchers agree that web readers, like newspaper readers, are attracted by the headline and the text rather than by graphics or pictures.

The technique of writing for newspapers—as taught in schools of journalism throughout the country—is simple: Write tight, be clear and concise, write short sentences and short paragraphs, use words correctly, obey the rules of grammar and spelling, and get to the point quickly with the inverted pyramid lead: the Who, What, Where, When, How, and Why of the story.

The addition of the web to the time-honored tools of writing has no effect on those techniques of writing. They remain the same. The web does not require a different style of writing; it only provides a more broadly based medium for much wider dissemination of information.

In past centuries, some of the finest writing was done with a goose quill pen and a pot of ink. Over time, as technology advanced, the goose quill pen and pot of ink gave way to pens and pencils, to movable type and linotype machines, to typewriters, to computers, to desktop printing, and, finally, to the Internet and the World Wide Web. Along the way, a curious thing happened. With each change in technology, writers and scholars equated the tools with the techniques of writing, holding that if the tool changed, so must the writing change.

Nothing could be further from the truth. The tool of writing has little to do with the technique of writing. Writing is writing. It is a means of communicating information to a large number of readers. The challenge to the writer using the Internet remains the same as the challenge to the writer using the goose quill pen—to communicate, to hold onto and to inform the reader.

This conclusion is borne out by continuing research by writing research centers—the Pew Research Center, the Poynter Institute for Media Studies, Sun Microsystems—and by individual scholars, teachers, and professionals who publish in *Communication World, Public Relations Tactics, Poynter Report, Writer's Digest*, and *Quill Magazine*, and on various websites.

Here the speaker is effectively enhancing his credibility by citing research by other sources that his audience would find credible.

A survey of that research and those publications shows almost unanimous agreement on the techniques for writing on the web. They grew out of the demands of reporting from the field and have been taught in journalism schools almost from the beginning.

Today, in general, researchers and professionals agree that web readers, like newspaper readers, want to know quickly what the story is about, and most of them do not want the details of a full story. Therefore, the recommendation is that web stories follow the traditional inverted pyramid style of writing news—summary lead to get to the point quickly, short sentences, short paragraphs, and no more than one screen of copy. That's 250 words, or one sheet of paper, double-spaced.

Most public relations news releases are too long. Studies show that newspapers seldom use more than half of any news release, and most use only the first one or two paragraphs, preferring not to give away too much space to an outside writer.

One of the pioneer researchers in web writing, Jakob Nielsen, recommends that because readers read 25 percent slower on the web than in newspapers, writing for the web ought to be half as long as newspaper stories.

Starr makes his point by comparing the words in a typical news story with the number of words in the Bible creation story.

A researcher for the Poynter Institute for Media Studies in St. Petersburg, Florida, Roy Peter Clark, believes that any story can be told in 800 words. The Bible story of creation is told in 754 words.

Because large blocks of type tend to lose readers, the recommendation is that no paragraph be longer than five lines on screen and that paragraphs be separated with a blank line. All of that is nothing more than the electronic equivalent of newspaper white space.

There is no question about the writing; it must be accurate, clear, concise, vivid, and with strong verbs. Researchers recommend using a conversational style that avoids overuse of punctuation marks, all of which provides for a smooth flow of language and ease of understanding.

The speaker does a good job of providing specific recommendations that his audience would find practical and useful.

If you do need a lengthy story, the recommendation is that you rely upon the old newspaper technique of using subheads to break up the copy, to provide more white space, and to alert readers as to what is coming next. In addition, you should write in "chunks," that is, completing one topic before moving on to another. Chunk writing normally is restricted to under 100 words, further attesting to the value of tight writing.

But be careful. Web readers generally are newspaper readers, and they read the web the way they read newspapers. Most newspaper readers don't scroll; they read no more than the first four or five paragraphs and move on to another story.

On the web, those who do scroll read an average of six websites, though some read up to three times that many. These readers are seeking additional information because they are interested in that specific topic. Those additional websites are called "hypertext," meaning "beyond text" or "additional text," and they are nothing more than the electronic name for the newspaper "sidebars."

Starr continues to keep his audience's attention by providing a list of cogent ideas that will help them with their work as well as summarizing his key advice.

Here are specific suggestions for making website news releases readily understandable and interesting.

- Write in the conversational active voice: subject, verb, object. Tell, rather than write, your story.
- Avoid synonyms; repeating key words reinforces understandability.
- Obey the rules of grammer, punctuation, syntax, precise word use and spelling, subject-verb agreement, noun-pronoun agreement.
- Write objectively; no opinion words.
- Use strong verbs.
- No paragraph longer than five lines on screen.
- No line longer than five inches on screen.
- Paragraphs separated with a blank line.
- Write tight. No story longer than one screen, 250 words.
- For lengthy stories, use subheads and hypertext sidebars.
- Get to the point quickly with the summary lead—the Who, What, Where, When, How, and Why of the story—and the inverted pyramid.

Communication Principles and Skills for Leadership

Principle One: Be aware of your communication with yourself and others.

- Give yourself a pep talk before getting up to speak.
- Consider your own interests and experiences when searching for a topic.

Principle Two: Effectively use and interpret verbal messages.

- Focus on your message to help manage your anxiety.
- Expressing your specific purpose in terms of your audience will help you keep your focus on them.
- A central idea should reflect a single topic, be a complete declarative sentence, and use specific language.

Principle Three: Effectively use and interpret nonverbal messages.

- Determine whether your audience is interested in you by observing whether they make eye contact with you and whether they are focused on you or are fidgeting and restless.

Principle Four: Listen and respond thoughtfully to others.

- Seek out information about your audience and how they are likely to respond to your message to increase your comfort with speaking in public.
- Listen for topic ideas in the course of casual conversation with friends.

Principle Five: Appropriately adapt messages to others.

- Revise your ideas or strategies at any point in the presentation preparation process, as you learn more about your audience.
- Be audience-centered to reduce speaker anxiety.
- Be sensitive to and adapt to the diversity of your audience.
- Keep in mind your audience's knowledge, interests, and expectations as you select a topic for your presentation.

Discussion Questions

1. How are the five principles for communication and leadership applicable to designing and presenting a speech?

2. What are some reasons people sometimes experience communication apprehension before giving a presentation?

3. What are some specific tips and strategies for building your confidence when giving a speech?

4. Why are analyzing and adapting to your audience central tasks in designing and delivering an effective presentation?

5. What are specific nonverbal cues that you should look for in order to assess your audience's interest as you are delivering your presentation?

6. What are key strategies to keep in mind when selecting the topic for a presentation?

7. What are the differences between a general purpose and a specific purpose?

8. What is the function of your central idea for a presentation?

9. What are three strategies you could use to generate main ideas for a presentation?

Building Your Skills

1. The following list identifies behaviors that are likely to make communication apprehension *worse*. Indicate which of these counterproductive behaviors you do when preparing a speech, and rank the top five by placing a 1 on the line beside the thing you do most often, a 2 beside the thing you do next most often, and so on until you have ranked your top five ineffective behaviors.

_____ 1. I usually procrastinate and often wait until the last minute to prepare my speech.

_____ 2. I typically don't learn much information about my audience or think about my audience.

_____ 3. I often select a topic that I don't know much about.

_____ 4. I often have a poor or disorganized outline for my speech.

_____ 5. I often don't have a clear notion of how I will begin my speech.

_____ 6. I often haven't carefully thought out how I will end my speech.

_____ 7. I don't rehearse aloud while standing up; I just think about my speech rather than practice it.

_____ 8. I usually don't use deep-breathing techniques to help me relax.

_____ 9. I usually don't channel my nervous energy.

_____ 10. I rarely visualize myself confidently giving my speech before I present it.

_____ 11. I usually don't give myself a pep talk to boost my confidence.

_____ 12. When I get nervous, I often focus on my nervousness rather than thinking about connecting my message with my audience.

_____ 13. I usually don't try to find friendly faces in the audience while I'm speaking; I just focus on my notes and try to get through the speech.

_____ 14. I avoid every speaking opportunity that comes my way because I'm so nervous.

_____ 15. When I'm finished with a speech, I focus on what I did wrong rather than congratulating myself on what I did well.

Now that you've identified the top five things you do to make your nervousness worse, develop a specific plan to change your behavior, based on information presented in this chapter.

2. Use the following worksheet to analyze an audience for a speech you expect to give and adapt a message to them.

Audience Characteristic	What strategies will you use to adapt your message to your audience?
Demographic Characteristics Age range: Average age: Percentages of women and men: Predominant ethnicity: Educational backgrounds:	

Group memberships:	
Socioeconomic status:	
Psychological Characteristics	
Attitudes toward my topic:	
Beliefs about my topic:	
Common audience values:	
Situational Analysis	
Time speech will be delivered:	
Size of audience:	
Location of speech:	
Occasion or reason for speech:	

3. Generate at least three main ideas from each of the following central ideas. Apply the questions suggested in this chapter: Does the central idea have *logical divisions*? Can you think of several *reasons* the central idea is true? Can you support the central idea with a series of *steps* (a *chronological sequence*)?

   • Our company's new digital camera is the best on the market.
   • There are several things you need to do as a new employee to complete your benefits package.
   • There are several elements to designing and delivering an effective sales presentation.
   • Business ties between the United States and Iran have been strained over the last decade.
   • Sleep deprivation can lead to dangerous conditions on the job.
   • Three specific strategies can help you deal with unsolicited visits by sales managers.
   • There are three reasons why our product underperformed and did not meet sales targets.

4. Develop a general and a specific purpose sentence for the following speech topics.

   • The history of consumer credit cards in the United States.
   • Increasing real estate sales in our community
   • Investing in U.S. savings bonds
   • Corporate mergers
   • Slowing sales of houses in the United States
   • The impact of globalization on the economy

5. Based on this chapter's discussion of initial, derived, and terminal credibility, identify two strategies you could implement to enhance your credibility when you deliver your next speech (whether it's a speech you present in your business and professional communication class or a speech you present to another group).

6. Imagine that as you are presenting a sales talk, you notice that your listeners seem to be losing interest in your presentation. Based on the discussion in this chapter, identify several possible strategies that could increase interest in your presentation.

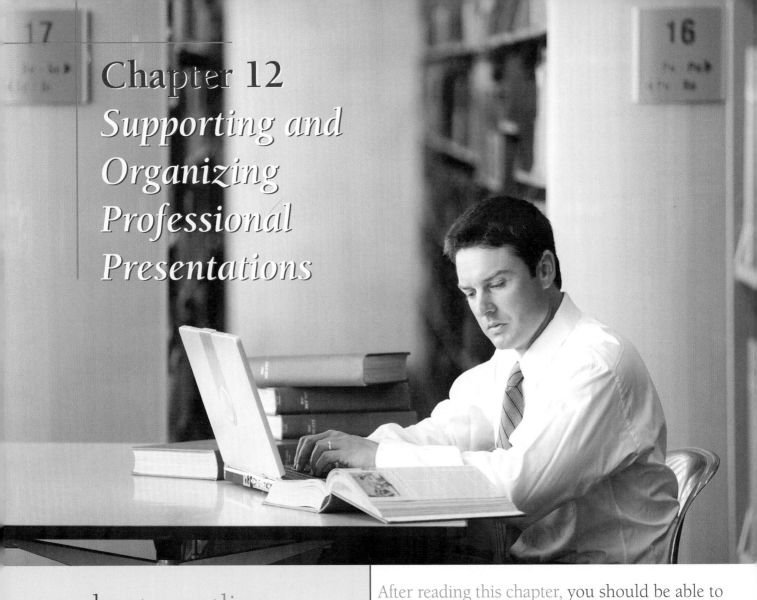

Chapter 12
Supporting and Organizing Professional Presentations

chapter outline

After reading this chapter, you should be able to

- Identify research strategies that will help you choose supporting material for your professional presentations.

- List and describe five criteria for evaluating information you find on the Internet.

- List and explain how to use illustrations, descriptions, explanations, definitions, analogies, statistics, and opinions as supporting material in a presentation.

- List and explain five strategies for organizing main ideas in a presentation.

- List and describe five specific strategies for organizing supporting material in a presentation.

- Identify how to organize a presentation for the ears of listeners.

- List and describe five functions of a presentation introduction.

- Identify strategies for concluding a presentation.

- Define and prepare a preparation outline and a delivery outline.

When Jack Welch was the CEO of General Electric, he was awakened early one morning with the news that there was an emergency at the General Electric jet engine plant in Ohio. He flew to Ohio on his corporate jet, and two hours after hearing about the problem, he was speaking to his beleaguered plant workers in Ohio. How did he begin his message to address the problem that had developed? Did he present statistics about sales figures? PowerPoint slides showing his solution? No: He began with a story about his grandmother. His grandmother had always told him to be prepared for the unexpected. Jack Welch knew the power of a well-told story to provide encouragement and motivation.[1]

Being able to tell a great story or use a clear example can be your best insurance that you will never give a lackluster presentation. It's usually not a speaker's main ideas that make a listener want to doze off—it's more than likely dry and dusty supporting material that makes a presentation boring. Most of what you say when delivering a presentation is stories, examples, illustrations, definitions, statistics, and other forms of supporting material. To gain and maintain interest, however, a speaker does more than just start telling stories and dumping information into the ears of listeners. A skilled speaker carefully thinks about the sequence of information, the overall organizational strategy for presenting the information to the audience. In this chapter we focus on what many people consider to be vital to presentational speaking: how to support and organize your message. We will emphasize how to develop well-crafted verbal messages and adapt them to listeners. Specifically, we'll discuss sources and types of supporting material, describe how to organize your message, and give special attention to how you introduce and conclude your presentation. You will learn how to prepare a well-developed outline of your ideas and how to find interesting things to say to your audience. Whether you're developing a sales presentation, delivering a short briefing to colleagues, or presenting the fourth-quarter financial report to the corporate board of directors, the supporting material you use and your organizational strategy can make the difference between a boring and rambling talk or an interesting, memorable message. One of the key elements that sets a leader apart from others is that a leader is prepared. It is through your selection of supporting material that you let others know you are well prepared and have research to support your ideas.

> *Say not always what you know, but always know what you say."*
>
> — ROMAN EMPEROR CLAUDIUS I

Supporting Your Presentation

Supporting material includes illustrations, explanations, descriptions, definitions, analogies, statistics, and opinions—material that will clarify, amplify, and provide evidence to support your main ideas and your thesis. You could simply rattle off your main points and subpoints without supporting material, but it's likely your message would be unclear and unconvincing. It's your supporting material that helps clarify your ideas and makes your message memorable, interesting, and credible.

What's the secret to keeping your listeners interested in you and your message? Pace the flow of new ideas and information. Communication expert Frank E. X. Dance recommends a 30:70 ratio: 30 percent of your speaking time should be spent presenting new ideas and information, and 70 percent of your time should be spent supporting the ideas with vivid examples and interesting stories.[2] We'll first discuss sources of supporting material and then offer tips and strategies for using the material you find in your professional presentation. What makes supporting material interesting? The best supporting material is personal and concrete and appeals to listeners' senses. Tell stories based on your own experiences and provide vivid descriptions of things that are tangible so that your audience can visualize what you are talking about. Besides sight, supporting material can appeal to the senses of touch, hearing, smell, and taste. The more senses you trigger with words, the more interesting your presentation will be. A description of an executive who was fired from his job could have a powerful impact on the audience: "You could see the sadness in his tired eyes as the board dismissed the worn-out, overwhelmed executive. His audible sigh, his bewildered blinking eyes, and the worry lines etched into his face told the story of dejection and disappointment at having given so much of himself for over two decades." Carefully chosen descriptive terms help listeners mentally "see" and "hear" and add to the power of the description.

Sources of Supporting Material

How do you go about finding just the right supporting material for a presentation? By developing good research skills. President Woodrow Wilson once revealed "I use not only

Supporting material illustrations, explanations, descriptions, definitions, analogies, statistics, and opinions that clarify, amplify, and provide evidence to support the main ideas and the thesis of a presentation.

all the brains I have, but all that I can borrow." It is not only important to have good ideas, it is also important to build on your existing knowledge by searching for good ideas. Three potential sources of supporting material are the Internet, the library, and people you know.

The Internet. Typically, the Internet is the first place you turn when faced with a research task. Rather than heading off to the library, in the comfort of your own office, you tap out a few key terms and quickly are deluged with information. You have probably accessed material on the web through a directory or search engine such as Google, Yahoo!, Ask.com, or another popular site.

You can use directories and search engines in two ways: by clicking on categories that are in turn broken down into ever-more-specific subcategories, or by entering key words or phrases into a designated space, clicking on "Search" or "Find," and then sorting through the resulting list of websites and web pages that deal with the topic you entered.

The websites and web pages you discover may include personal pages, books, periodicals, newspapers and wire services, reference material, and government documents. In addition, you may discover indexes and catalogs for accessing these various kinds of resources. You can even find sites designed to help you prepare and deliver your speeches. Although the sheer volume of material may be overwhelming for even the most experienced researcher, two strategies can help.

First, explore the advanced, or **Boolean search**, capabilities of your directory or search engine. Most will offer directions on how to limit your search to sites that are most relevant to what you are looking for. Boolean searches let you enclose phrases in quotation marks or parentheses so that a search yields only those sites on which all the words of the phrase appear together, rather than sites that contain any one of the words. You can also insert the word *or* between two parenthetical phrases, directing your search to include documents in which either phrase appears. Or you can insert the word *and* between parenthetical phrases to indicate that you wish to see results that contain both phrases. These relatively simple strategies can help you narrow a list of hits from, in some cases, millions to a more workable number.

Verbal
Nonverbal

A second strategy for sorting through information you discover on the World Wide Web has to do with the principle of appropriately interpreting verbal and nonverbal messages. Specifically, you need to evaluate the sites you discover according to a consistent standard. The following five criteria can serve as such a standard:[3]

1. *Accountability.* Find out what organization or individual is responsible for the website. What do you know about that sponsor? If it is an organization, is it a commercial enterprise? A nonprofit? An educational entity? Is the page an official statement of that organization? If the sponsor is an individual, what are the person's qualifications for writing on this topic? If you cannot discover an author, be wary of the site.

2. *Accuracy.* Sources of facts should be documented on a website just as they are in print publications. An additional advantage of the web is that some sites provide hyperlinks to original sources. Clicking on a hyperlink will take you directly to the linked site. Websites should also be relatively free of errors in usage and mechanics.

3. *Objectivity.* As noted above, you need to know who or what organization has posted the site. For example, a website sponsored by a pharmaceutical company may have a bias in favor of such companies. Consider the philosophies and possible biases of the organization or individual responsible for any site you plan to use as a source. The more objective the author, the more credible the facts and information.

4. *Recency.* Many sites state when they were posted and/or last updated. In most cases, when you are concerned with factual data, the more recent, the better.

5. *Usability.* If you have spent much time on the Internet, you have probably at one time or another called up a site that contained such complex graphics that it took a long time to load or even caused your computer to crash. Frames, graphics, and multimedia resources can enhance a site, or they can simply complicate it. Consider the practical efficiency of the sites you explore.

The library. Despite the explosion of World Wide Web resources in recent years, the library remains a rich source of supporting material. Most libraries, from the largest research university library to the smallest village public library, house the following kinds of resources:

Boolean search an advanced web-searching technique that allows a user to narrow a key word search by specifying certain parameters.

Books
Periodicals
Full-text databases
Newspapers
Reference resources
Government documents
Special services

Books. The word *library* is almost synonymous with the word *book*. In spite of predictions that electronic resources will someday make books obsolete, for now, books remain central to the holdings of most libraries. Here's a brief review of library basics.

A library's books are housed in the stacks, often several floors of seemingly endless shelves of books. Libraries' stacks may be either open or closed. In an open-stack library, patrons may browse freely through the stacks. Since books on a particular subject are shelved next to one another, open stacks give researchers the opportunity to make lucky discoveries. For example, if you are looking for a specific book on the history of digital audio, you may find on the same shelf two or three other books that contain relevant information. In a closed-stack library, on the other hand, users must copy onto retrieval cards information on the books they want. They present these cards at the circulation desk, and library staff find the desired books and return them to the circulation desk, where the users can check them out.

A library's central catalog of all its books is called the card catalog. Today, card catalogs at most libraries contain not literal cards but electronic ones. Banks of computers in a central location in the library allow users to look up the books they need.

You may be able to print the electronic records for the books you want. If you have to copy information from the computer screen, be sure to include the author's name, title of the book, publisher and date of publication, and the library's call number. Use a consistent format so that later you can easily interpret the information. Figure 12.1 illustrates a sample entry from a computerized card catalog and a corresponding bibliography card for the same book.

Books will be important sources as you prepare your speeches. They can provide in-depth coverage of topics, which is not possible in shorter publications or on websites. However, because most books are written two or three years before they are published, they are inherently outdated. If your speech addresses a current topic, or if you want to use current examples, you will probably not find the information you need in books. You will turn instead to periodicals and newspapers, available both online and in hard copy.

Periodicals. The term *periodicals* refers both to magazines, such as *Time*, *People*, and *Sports Illustrated*, and to professional journals, such as *BusinessWeek* and the *Quarterly Journal of Economics*. Both types of periodicals can be useful for professional speeches.

Periodical indexes are the equivalent of card catalogs; a number of such indexes cover many topics and most of the thousands of periodicals published. Most periodical indexes are available online, and many can be accessed either from the library or from other locations. Periodical index entries are arranged alphabetically according to both subject and author. Most people use them by searching for subjects or key words, much as they would conduct a web search. Some periodical indexes are full-text databases, meaning that you can access not only bibliographical information but the texts of the articles themselves.

Full-Text Databases: Among the most frequently used periodical indexes and full-text databases are the following:

- *The Reader's Guide to Periodical Literature* is the oldest periodical index and the one that many researchers first learn to use. It indexes popular magazines and a few trade and professional journals.

- *InfoTrac*, an electronic index, includes full-text articles from more than 1,000 business, science, government, and general-interest periodicals.

- The *Public Affairs Information Service (P.A.I.S.) Bulletin*, available in both hard copy and electronic formats, indexes both periodicals and books in such fields as sociology, political science, and economics.

Although electronic resources are quickly becoming the medium of choice for speakers seeking supporting material for a presentation, books can provide in-depth coverage of a topic, which is not readily available online.

Figure 12.1	Entry from an Electronic Card Catalog and Corresponding Bibliography Card

Author: Angell, Pamela
Title: Business Communication Design: Creativity, Strategy, and Solutions
Publisher: Boston: McGraw-Hill/Irwin, 2007.
Subjects: Business communication

Library holdings:
General Collection, Floor 5

1. Call number:
HF5718 .A746 2007

HF5718
.A746
2007

Angell, Pamela. Business Communication Design: Creativity, Strategy, and Solutions. McGraw-Hill/Irwin, 2007.

- *Lexis/Nexis* is an extensive full-text subscription database of periodicals, newspapers, and government documents. It is an excellent source of very current information.
- *CARL UnCover* is a multidisciplinary full-text database of articles from more than 15,000 journals. The index function of *CARL UnCover* is free. Full texts can be ordered and faxed to a local fax machine for about $10 each.

Newspapers. You can find information that is only hours old by reading the latest edition of a daily newspaper. Newspapers also offer the most detailed coverage available of current events.

In most libraries you'll find newspapers in three formats. The first is the traditional newsprint format. However, libraries usually keep only the most recent newspapers (probably less than a week old) in their racks because they take up so much storage space. Back issues are kept on microfilm, which is the second format. Most newspapers, from major national newspapers to local and college newspapers, have also become available online.

As with books and periodicals, you need an index to help you find newspaper articles relevant to the topic you are researching. Newspaper indexes are published for a number of medium-size and large newspapers. Your library may subscribe to several of these. In addition, several electronic indexes, including the *National Newspaper Index* and *NewsBank*, index multiple newspapers. If you need information about a specific event and you know the day on which it occurred, you can locate a newspaper from that day or the following day and probably find a relevant news story about the event.

Reference Resources. A library's reference resources include encyclopedias, dictionaries, directories, atlases, almanacs, yearbooks, books of quotations, and biographical dictionaries. As a speaker, you may at one time or another use most of these types of materials. Like periodicals, newspapers, and microfilm, reference resources are usually available only for in-house research and cannot be checked out.

Government Documents. The federal government publishes information on almost every conceivable subject, as well as keeping records of most official federal proceedings.

Once a dauntingly complex collection of pamphlets, special reports, and texts of speeches and debates, government documents today are much more readily accessible through the web.

The most important index of government documents is the *Monthly Catalog of U.S. Government Publications*. The *Monthly Catalog* is now available online, as is the *American Statistics Index*, which indexes government statistical publications.

Special Services. Interlibrary loan and reciprocal borrowing privileges are among the special services that can help you find resources not otherwise available through your own library or online. If you are reading an article and discover a reference to a book you would like to see, but your library does not own the book, you may be able to use interlibrary loan to locate the book at another library and have it sent to your library within a few days. Or, if your library has reciprocal borrowing privileges with another nearby library, you may be able to go yourself to that library and locate the book.

You and people you know. For some presentations you can find rich sources of material by talking to friends, colleagues, and other people you know. If you are going to present a training program about how to boost sales of your company's products, you could talk to the top salespeople to identify stories and strategies that would help you develop useful sales tips. Or, if you were going to give a presentation about how to improve the quality of service your organization provides, you could talk to some of the front-line receptionists to identify common complaints or concerns of customers. You can also draw on your own experiences when looking for great stories or examples for a talk. Listeners usually like to hear personal stories and anecdotes from a speaker (assuming the stories are relevant to the topic). As we noted at the beginning of this chapter, the story Jack Welch told about his grandmother and the importance of being prepared for the unexpected was a well-chosen way to make a key point. Good speakers reflect on their personal experiences, including experiences with family and friends, other jobs they've held, and everyday experiences as sources of interesting supporting material.

The point is that you don't necessarily need to search the Internet or run to the library for every piece of supporting material for every topic on which you speak. It is true that most well-researched presentations include some objective material gathered from the Internet or from library resources. But don't overlook your own expertise and experience or those of the people you know. As an audience-centered speaker, realize, too, that offering personal knowledge or experience has the added advantage of heightening your credibility in the minds of your listeners. They will respect your authority if they realize that you have firsthand knowledge of the topic on which you are speaking.

Types of Supporting Material

If you have discovered material on the Internet, examined a variety of library resources, and explored your own knowledge and the insights of people you know, you will probably have a wealth of potential supporting material. Now you need to decide what to use in your speech. Keeping in mind your audience's knowledge, interests, and expectations will help you to determine where an illustration might stir their emotions, where an explanation might help them to understand a point, and where statistics might convince them of the significance of a problem.

Illustrations. An **illustration** is a story or anecdote about an idea, issue, or problem a speaker is discussing. It can be as short as a sentence or two, or as long as several well-developed paragraphs. Sometimes speakers will offer a series of brief illustrations. Other speakers may present longer and more detailed illustrations. Here's an example of a short illustration used by business executive Tami Longaberger when speaking about her friend and former editor of *The Washington Post* Kay Graham and about the importance of leadership:

> A great leader reflects integrity in the hardest times, as well as when times are good. Let me go back to Kay Graham at *The Washington Post*. Not a day went by when Kay Graham wasn't challenged by some major government or business official to change a story or do something that was outside the ethics or integrity of the paper. She never compromised. Her editors and reporters took great heart from this and redoubled their efforts. That's one of the reasons *The Washington Post* continues to stand for a level of quality and integrity that is now known around the world.[4]

Illustration a story or anecdote about an idea, issue, or problem a speaker is discussing.

Here's a more detailed example of a well-told personal illustration:

> When Martin Luther King, Rosa Parks and the citizens of Montgomery succeeded in their fight to define some of those rights by integrating the buses of that southern city, I was a fifth grader in the segregated community of Muskogee, Oklahoma. Like many African American children of my generation, I remember water fountains from which we could not drink, doors through which we could not pass, movie theaters we could not attend, restrooms we could not use, and lunch counters at which we could not eat.
>
> I also recall very vividly the expressions of protest over these conditions in which many of us throughout the South participated—the sit-ins, the boycotts, the marches, and the demonstrations. It is impossible to forget the reactions to that quest for equality, particularly the acts of intimidation: the days in jail, the use of torture, the fire hoses, the attacking dogs, the burning crosses, the white hoods, the lynchings, and the firebombs.[5]

Sometimes, instead of a real example, a speaker will use a **hypothetical illustration, a description of something that has not actually occurred but that could happen.** If you decide to use a hypothetical illustration, it is important to make clear to your audience that the scene you describe never really occurred. Using such phrases as "Imagine what you would do . . ." or "What would you do if the following experience happened to you?" are typical ways of signaling that your illustration is hypothetical. A speaker effectively gained and maintained his listeners' attention with this hypothetical illustration:

> Imagine that you've just received a call from your boss informing you that she has to reduce the number of employees in your organization by the end of the day. She's asked you to report to her office in one hour to document your worth to the company. What evidence would you offer? Do you know how to prove your worth to your organization on a moment's notice?

Business leader Soloman Trujillo's audience would certainly know that the following is a hypothetical example about Paul Revere:

> Imagine if Paul Revere, at the beginning of the American War of Independence, had at his disposal the technology we have today. His horse would certainly not be as footsore. Revere could record himself on his 3G phone, addressing the approaching British troops and then send a broadcast email of that recording to all of his contacts. They might receive those messages on their own mobile handsets or their BlackBerrys—at work or at home. If the recipients were sleeping, the receiving device would be smart enough to alert its owner to the importance of the message by using a sensor network, which turned on the lights in the house and stirred up its inhabitants to respond to the call to arms.[6]

Whether you choose to use brief or extended illustrations, actual or hypothetical ones, remember this principle: *Everybody likes to hear a story.* A well-told and relevant story almost always ensures audience interest. In addition, the following suggestions should help you use illustrations effectively in your speeches.

Verbal

- Be sure that your illustrations are directly relevant to the idea or point they are supposed to support.
- Choose illustrations that are typical, not exceptions.
- Make your illustrations vivid and specific.
- Use illustrations with which your listeners can identify.
- Remember that the most effective illustrations are often personal ones.

Should you tell jokes to illustrate your talks? One well-known professional speech writer suggests using anecdotes rather than jokes to make your point. The speechwriter notes the difference this way:

> What's the difference between a joke and an anecdote? It is the difference between fiction and fact. An anecdote is supposed to be true—even if many are apocryphal (an anecdote doesn't have to be authentic to be told). The subject of an anecdote is famous or at least real, and what that subject did has to

Hypothetical illustration
a description of something that has not actually occurred but that could happen.

be believable. As professional speech writer James Humes suggests, a story about "Jesus on the golf course" . . . fails to meet the test.[7]

Nonetheless, a joke can be a good attention-getter and can relax your audience and win their good will. Here's an example of the nice use of humor in a speech by Marion Blakey, then Administrator of the Federal Aviation Administration, in a presentation she gave to the Commercial Aviation Forecast Conference in Washington, DC:

> I heard a story that gave me a chuckle. When the snow was at its heaviest, one of the locals from this area was headed to Morgantown. He stopped at a shopping mall around here to pick up a package. Now, it's dark, but he's ready to go. The snow's coming down pretty hard . . . visibility is just about zero. Lucky for this guy, he sees a snowplow, and he does what most of us, I guess, would do. He falls in line right behind it. Why fight the snow when a machine can do it for you? So he follows the snowplow for about 45 minutes, through each and every turn. He just follows the red taillights right in from of him. It's a tough ride, but at least he has a clear path to follow. Then the snowplow stops, and the driver gets out. The snowplow driver walks back to the guy and says. "Where are you going? You've been following me for almost an hour." The local says, "Morgantown." The snowplow driver says, "Well, you'll never get there following me. I'm plowing out this parking lot."[8]

Descriptions and explanations. Probably the most commonly used forms of supporting material are **descriptions** and **explanations**. To describe or explain is to provide detailed images that allow an audience to see, hear, smell, touch, or taste whatever you are describing. Descriptions can make people, places, and events come alive for an audience, as does this description of being a drug addict, from a speech presented by Nora Volkow, director of the National Institute on Drug Abuse, to a group of business people:

Verbal

> I want to share with you what it is to be an addicted person from the perspective of the individual suffering from it. This happens to be an individual who sent me an email and I chose this particular email because it does highlight some of the characteristics of addiction: "I am a Dutch thirty-year-old male, very addicted to marijuana, alcohol, and crack cocaine. I have no social life and no job and feel more and more isolated. I have less and less hope to break free of this hell. My life is a mess and I did several attempts to break with my addictions in the past. Now, as I am so tired of trying, I find it very difficult to keep on fighting, even more so because of the depressed mood and feelings of dissatisfaction while being clean. I do not feel whole without the damn drugs anyway."[9]

Although descriptions and explanations are found in most speeches, they lack the inherent interest of illustrations. To keep audiences from yawning through your descriptions and explanations,

- Avoid too many descriptions and explanations.
- Keep your descriptions and explanations brief.
- Describe and explain in specific and concrete language.

Definitions. Speakers should offer definitions of all technical or little-known terms in their presentations. A **definition** is a brief explanation that identifies and clarifies what something is through classification or description. If you determine that you should define a word or phrase for your audience, consider whether you can best define it by **classification**, which is the approach used in a standard dictionary definition of first placing a term in the general class, group, or family to which it belongs and then differentiating it from other members of its class. Or you might use an **operational definition**, which explains how the item being defined works or what it does.

To define something by classification, you could turn to the *Oxford English Dictionary*, *Webster's*, or another dictionary, or you might consult a specialized dictionary, such as *Black's Law Dictionary*. However, you need not limit yourself to dictionary

Description a word picture; a detailed image that allows an audience to mentally see, hear, smell, touch, or taste whatever a speaker is describing.

Explanation a statement of how something is done or why it exists in its present form or existed in its past form.

Definition a brief explanation that identifies and clarifies what something is by classifying it or describing how it works.

Classification defining something by placing it in a group or category based on its qualities or characteristics.

Operational definition an explanation of how an item being defined works or what it does.

Humor is the spice of speeches: Too little humor and a speech may seem bland, too much and it can be too hot to handle. The trick is to get just the right kinds of humor in the right amounts. Such details may seem small, but they are a vital part of crafting an interesting and memorable speech.

Use Humor Wisely
Should you use humor in your presentation? The answer is yes and no.

Humor can be fun. It can be entertaining. People respond favorably to other people who make them laugh. That accounts for the popularity of comedy clubs and the universal love of good comedians. Humor can make us feel good. But, it can also be offensive. Racist, sexist humor or a joke that demeans a person's sexual preference is never in good taste.

Humor is tricky—even for the best comedians. Consider that professional comedians such as David Letterman and Jay Leno have paid writers who crank out bits for them. They select the best of these and weave them together in an opening monologue. They rehearse the jokes and then deliver them, drawing on years of experience in making audiences laugh. Even with all these resources and the talent and preparation devoted to them, observe how many of the jokes of professional comics don't elicit a laugh from the audience.

As a speaker, you can't roll out a whole string of jokes and hope that one or two tickle people's fancy. You have room for one or two, if that. And you don't have years of experience at making audiences laugh. So your risks are much higher.

Humor can also backfire. What might be funny to you, the storyteller, could potentially be offensive to the listener. There are several ways to take advantage of the power of humor while minimizing the risks:

Use Humor to Make a Point
Some speakers start their presentation with their favorite joke, even if it bears no relationship to the topic. This approach is based on the assumption that the audience needs to be primed or warmed up before you can turn to the serious (and perhaps boring) topic at hand. But unless you are a professional comedian, the audience is probably expecting to hear about your topic. The joke then becomes an unnecessary, perhaps risky, and even annoying diversion.

If, on the other hand, you can use humor to drive home a point, then it serves a purpose. It can be a way to warm up the audience while moving your speech forward. This is the best kind of humor.

For example, you might start off a discussion of using cross-functional teams to solve company problems this way:

> I read recently about a veterinarian and a taxidermist who decided to share a shop in a small town in Ohio. The sign in the front window read: "Either way, you get your dog back."
>
> There is an important lesson there. We need to work together to solve our problems. People from

definitions. Business executive William Harrison clearly defines globalization by classifying what it is:

> Let's begin with a simple and easy-to-understand definition. As I am going to use the word, *globalization* relates to "the death of distance." It relates to intensified global connectedness and the whole raft of changes—economic, social, political, and cultural—that spring from that. As Tom Friedman declared in *The World Is Flat*, globalization has "accidentally made Beijing, Bangalore, and Bethesda next-door neighbors." Inside this accidental, virtual neighborhood, we find that we—as Americans—no longer have a lock on many of the best jobs inside the United States. Candidates from other countries are now just a "mouse-click" away.[10]

Here's an example of an operational definition—defining something based on how it works or its general operation:

> Here's what I mean by high-performing local economy: New housing starts increase 10 percent over the previous year, the Chamber of Commerce fields several calls a day from businesses that want to relocate to our community, and sales tax revenue is up by double digits for the past three years. Now that's what I call a high-performing economic base.

Verbal

To use definitions effectively, consider the following tips:

- Use definitions only when necessary, because they can be uninteresting and abstract.

marketing need to work with operations people. Designers need to work with engineers. Then, when we find a problem that one part of the organization can't solve, someone else may suggest a solution. It doesn't matter who comes up with the solution. The important thing is to "get the dog back."

Use Humorous Stories

A real story is less risky than a joke, just as nonfiction is less risky to write than fiction. Even if people are not impressed by a real story, at least it is real. But a fictitious story that falls flat is twice cursed—first because it failed, and second because someone took the trouble to make up this failure. Audiences are more forgiving about real life than they are about fantasy.

The best stories are personal, humorous ones. Sometimes even a story about an unrelated event can be tied in. An economist explaining an obscure concept to a lay audience starts out this way:

> I was told to present this material so even a four-year-old could understand it. Well, I tried it out on my four-year-old daughter. I have to admit, it's not quite there yet. Her response was, "That's nice, Daddy. Now can I have a lollipop?" I hope you'll be able to follow the presentation—but if I lose you anywhere, please ask. And if you need some incentive to stay with me, I still have a few lollipops left in my pocket.

Personal experiences or anecdotes are suitable grabbers. And if you don't have any great stories in mind, keep your eyes open on your way to the speech or after you get there. Successful comics used to start their routines by recounting "A funny thing happened to me on the way to the show tonight." If something funny *did* happen to you, try to work it in. It may be corny, but it is also effective. Most important: It's real. It's personal. It's you.

Anecdotes make you interesting because people like stories. Anecdotes also carry conviction because you're talking about events you experienced firsthand.

Make Yourself the Butt of the Joke

Obviously, if you are standing on the podium telling ethnic jokes, you're asking for trouble. But even jokes that appear to you to be innocuous can offend listeners. It is very hard to overestimate the sensitivity of audiences. Therefore, it's best to make yourself the butt of the joke. Making fun of yourself is least likely to offend anyone else. Personal stories, focusing on your own life or shortcomings, can often accomplish this.

Use Quotes

Quotes, proverbs, or sayings are also good grabbers, as well as good vehicles for using humor, because someone else actually does the talking.

> Humorist Erma Bombeck suggests never using a doctor whose plants have died in the waiting room.

Should anyone take exception to the quote, you are not the offending party, the person quoted is. And if that someone is Mark Twain or Ben Franklin, chances are he—and you—will be forgiven.[11]

- Be certain that your definitions are clear to your listeners.
- Be sure that your definition accurately reflects your use of the word or phrase throughout the presentation.

Analogies. **Analogies** are comparisons that demonstrate how unfamiliar ideas, things, and situations are similar to something the audience already understands. Speakers can use two types of analogies in their speeches. The first is a **literal analogy,** or a comparison of two similar things—for example, comparing the available memory in a flash drive to a CD's storage capacity.

One business leader who wanted to illustrate the value of the European Union to a group of chief financial officers used the following literal analogy:

> What if each state in the United States had its own currency, had different requirements and rules for weights and measurements, and had no unified constitution that provided basic rights for its citizens? That would not encourage economic prosperity, would it? So perhaps you can understand why the countries in the European Union want to band together to develop common political and economic principles: It's good for business. It's important to collaborate to succeed economically.

A literal analogy can help clarify an idea or persuade listeners to support the speaker's point.

A **figurative analogy** is one that compares two unlike things or events that nevertheless share some feature. Figurative analogies, although less useful to prove a point, can be espe-

Analogy a comparison between an unfamiliar idea, thing, or situation and something the audience already understands.

Literal analogy a comparison between two similar things.

Figurative analogy a comparison between two essentially unlike things or events that nevertheless share some feature.

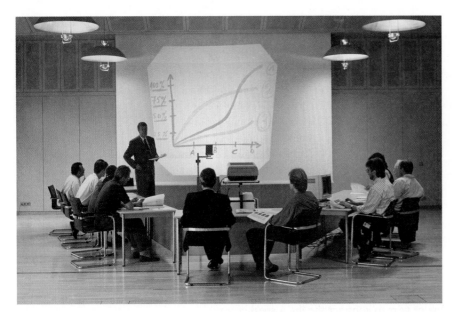

Visual aids, such as the line graph this man is using for his presentation, can be very effective when presenting statistics to an audience.

cially useful when clarifying an idea. Comparing the memory capacity of a computer to a person's mental capacity to remember something would be a figurative analogy. Eric opened his speech on the National Flood Insurance Program with this figurative analogy comparing gambling on horse races to gambling with nature:

> If someone were to lose thousands of dollars gambling on horse races, would you want your tax dollars to bail them out? . . . Currently in the United States there are millions of people gambling, not on horse races, but on Mother Nature, by living on flood plains or coasts. When these people lose, they lose big: beach houses, farm houses, and apartment houses go out to sea, down the river, or simply soak up catastrophic damages.[12]

Two suggestions can help you use analogies more effectively in your speeches:

- Be certain that the two things you compare in a literal analogy are very similar so that listeners can immediately see the connection.
- Make the similarity between the two objects in a figurative analogy apparent to the audience by providing specific detail and explanation.

Statistics. **Statistics** are simply numerical data that summarize several examples. Numbers can represent hundreds or thousands of illustrations and can thus help a speaker express the significance or magnitude of a situation. Statistics can also help a speaker express the relationship of a part to the whole. Note communication expert Richard Weaver's clever use of statistics from his speech titled "Sticky Ideas":

> Trying to get listeners to understand what the word *billion* means is a good example of making statistics meaningful. Politicians use the word *billion* in a casual manner, and there is no doubt it is a difficult number to comprehend. Did you realize that a billion seconds ago it was 1959? A billion minutes ago, Jesus was alive; a billion hours ago, our ancestors were living in the Stone Age; a billion days ago, no one walked on the earth on two feet; a billion dollars ago was only 8 hours and 20 minutes, at the rate our government is spending it—and that does not include spending for the war.[13]

Skilled speakers learn how to use statistics to their advantage. For example, they try to make huge numbers more readily understandable and more dramatic to their audiences. Note this example from a business executive who effectively makes a point about the serious problem of world poverty:

> We are surrounded by a flood of global troubles, crises and problems: Every 30 seconds, an African child dies of malaria. Every 3.6 seconds, a person dies of starvation.[14]

Another speaker presented statistics about the geographical distribution of the world's population in these terms, in order to illustrate how small our global business village is:

> If we could shrink the Earth's population to a village of precisely 100 people with all existing human ratios remaining the same, it would look like this: There would be 57 Asians, 21 Europeans, 14 from the Western Hemisphere (North and South), and 8 Africans.[15]

Statistics numerical data that summarize several examples.

In addition to simplifying and dramatizing your information, statistics can be effective if you utilize the following two suggestions:

- Round off large numbers.
- Use visual aids such as bar, line, or pie graphs to present your statistics.

Cite the sources of your statistics. To integrate an **oral citation** into your speech, simply tell your listeners the source of your information. For example, when providing evidence about the growth of popular online social networking sites, you might say, "According to a report entitled 'Social Networking Site Hi5 Nearly Doubles Monthly Visitors,' published online in August 2008 by *Information Week*, 'Hi5.com's monthly visitors rose from 31 million to more than 56 million in the first half of 2008, which marks an almost 80 percent increase and ranks the site ahead of its competitors for its speed of growth worldwide.'"[16] Note that this citation includes three things: the title of the report, the date when it appeared, and the organization responsible for the website. The web address itself need not be given in the oral citation, although the speaker should have that information available if someone wants to confirm the information.

Opinions. The opinions of others can add authority, drama, and style to a speech. A speaker can use three types of opinions: expert testimony, lay testimony, and literary quotations. **Expert testimony,** the opinion of a recognized authority on a topic, is perhaps the most frequent type of opinion employed by speakers. If you yourself lack authority on your topic, cite someone who can offer such expertise. For example, to convince company employees that the winter months are the most common time of year to contract the flu, a speaker noted "Influenza virus is more likely to be transmitted during winter on the way to the subway than in a warm room, according to Dr. Peter Palese, a flu researcher who is professor and chairman of the microbiology department at Mount Sinai Medical College in New York City."[17]

Lay testimony is an opinion or a description offered by a nonexpert who has firsthand experience. Like illustrations, lay testimony can stir an audience's emotions. And, although neither as authoritative nor as unbiased as expert testimony, lay testimony is often more memorable.

Finally, speakers may wish to include **literary quotations**—opinions or descriptions by writers—in their speeches.

> Certainly it's true that some newspapers are more oriented in one direction than the other.
>
> Humor columnist Dave Barry perhaps best articulated this diversity within the American newspaper industry. "The more boring a newspaper is," Barry explained, "the more it is respected." The most respected newspaper in the United States, Barry pointed out, is *The New York Times*, which has thousands of reporters constantly producing enormous front-page stories on bauxite. On the other hand, Barry said, "the least respected newspaper in America, *The New York Post*, would write about bauxite only if celebrities were arrested snorting it at an exclusive New York nightclub."[18]

Whether you use expert testimony, lay testimony, or literary quotations, consider the following suggestions for using opinions effectively in your speeches:

- Be certain that any authority you cite is actually an expert on the subject you are discussing.
- Identify your sources with an oral citation.
- Cite unbiased authorities.
- Cite opinions that are representative of prevailing opinion. If you cite a dissenting viewpoint, identify it as such.
- Quote or paraphrase your sources accurately and within the context in which the remarks were originally made.
- Use literary quotations sparingly.

As you select your illustrations, descriptions, explanations, definitions, analogies, statistics, and opinions, be guided not only by the suggestions we've provided for each type of supporting material, but also by the five fundamental communication principles. The best supporting material reflects self-awareness, taking advantage of your own knowledge and experience. Effective verbal supporting material is appropriately worded, concrete, and vivid enough that your audience can visualize what you are talking about.

Verbal

Oral citation an oral statement of the source of information used in a speech.

Expert testimony an opinion offered by someone who is an authority on the subject under discussion.

Lay testimony an opinion or a description offered by a nonexpert who has firsthand experience.

Literary quotation an opinion or description by a writer, expressed in a memorable and often poetic way.

RECAP: Supporting Your Speech

Type of Supporting Material	Guidelines for Use
Illustrations	• Make them directly relevant to the idea you are discussing or point you are making. • Choose illustrations that are typical, not exceptions. • Make them vivid and specific. • Use illustrations with which your listeners can identify. • Remember that the most effective illustrations are often personal ones.
Descriptions and Explanations	• Avoid too many descriptions and explanations. • Keep descriptions and explanations brief. • Describe and explain in specific and concrete language.
Definitions	• Use definitions only when necessary. • Be certain that definitions are clear to listeners. • Be sure that a definition is accurate.
Analogies	• When using a literal analogy, be certain that the two things you compare are very similar. • When using a figurative analogy, make the similarity between the two objects apparent to the audience.
Statistics	• Round off large numbers. • Use visual aids to show comparisons and trends. • Cite your sources.
Opinions	• Be certain that any authority you cite is actually an expert. • Identify your sources. • Cite unbiased authorities. • Cite representative opinions, or identify dissenting viewpoints as such. • Quote or paraphrase accurately and in context. • Use literary quotations sparingly.

Effective visual supporting material enhances, rather than detracts from, your verbal message. Sensitivity to your audience will help you choose the supporting material that is most appropriately adapted to them.

Organizing Your Presentation

Developing a presentation is like building a house. Just as a construction contractor develops the frame for a house early in the building process, a speaker develops the frames for a presentation by completing the first four stages of the speech-preparation process—selecting and narrowing a topic, identifying a general and a specific purpose, determining a central idea, and generating main ideas. Framing completed, the contractor assembles all the materials needed for the house: windows, doors, cabinets, hardware, and flooring; the speaker finds and adds supporting materials to the speech "frame." Once the house is framed out and the building materials are ready, the contractor must organize the work of the electricians, plumbers, carpenters, and carpet layers. Similarly, the speaker must organize ideas and supporting material.

Grounded in the five fundamental communication principles with which you are now familiar, the suggestions and strategies we discuss in the following sections will result in an essentially complete "house"—a presentation that is ready for rehearsal and delivery.

Organizing Your Main Ideas

An organized message is easier for your listeners to remember *and* easier for you to remember. Note the following two columns of words. Don't you find the words in column B easier to remember than the ones in column A?[19]

Column A	Column B
be	to
question	be
to	or
that	not
not	to
the	be
be	that
is	is
to	the
or	question

Giving careful thought to how you structure your message, whether you use a pattern that is already familiar to your audience or one that you create to help your listeners make better sense of your message, is the mark of an effective communicator.

We'll first discuss strategies for organizing the main ideas of a speech and then focus on organizing supporting material and developing signposts and transitions. Next, we will identify how to effectively introduce and conclude your presentation and, finally, how to outline your ideas and supporting material.

Organize ideas chronologically. If you determine that you can best develop your central idea through a series of steps, you will probably organize those steps—your main ideas—chronologically. **Chronological organization** is organization by sequential order, according to when each step or event occurred or should occur. If you are explaining a process, you will want to organize your explanation of the steps of that process from first to last. If you are providing an historical overview of an event, movement, or policy, you might begin with the end result and trace its history backward in time.

Examples of presentation topics that might lend themselves to chronological organization include a training presentation on how to perform a skill or task or a description of the development of an idea or process. Here's an outline of a speech that follows a chronological organizational pattern.

Central Idea: There are three steps to developing a business meeting agenda.

I. Determine whether the goal of the meeting is to give information, to get information, or to take some action.

II. Identify the agenda items that need to be discussed to achieve the meeting goal or goals.

III. Organize the agenda items.

Organize ideas topically. If your main ideas are natural divisions of your central idea, you will likely want to use **topical organization**. Topical organization may be simply an arbitrary arrangement of main ideas that are fairly equal in importance. For example, if you are giving a briefing in which you describe the athletic apparel your company makes,

Chronological organization organization by sequential order, according to when each step or event occurred or should occur.

Topical organization organization by natural divisions of a central idea presented according to primacy, recency, or complexity, or arbitrary arrangement of ideas that are equal in importance.

Like a contractor who builds the framework for a house, a speaker constructs the framework of his or her presentation by completing the first four stages of the speech-preparation process.

you could use a topical organization plan to group the three primary types of products your organization manufactures—running shoes, clothes, and hats. The order in which you discuss the products may not really matter.

Here's an example of a topical organization plan for a talk designed to recruit salespeople to join the organization:

Central Idea: People who join our company have several education options for their children.

  I. Parents can send their children to the local, nationally recognized public school.
  II. Parents can send their children to one of two private schools.
  III. Parents can apply for low-interest loans from our company to cover college tuition.

In this example, the order of the ideas may not be important. At other times, topical organization is less arbitrary; you may decide to arrange your major points in a specific order.

The principle of **recency** suggests that audiences remember best what they hear last. So if you want your audience to remember a specific point, put it last.

Another principle that can help guide your topical organization is the principle of **primacy**. Primacy suggests that you discuss first your most convincing and/or least controversial idea. To adapt to an audience who may be skeptical of some of your ideas, discuss first those points on which you all agree.

One other type of topical organization is organization according to **complexity**, moving from simple ideas and processes to more complex ones. Many skills you have learned in life have been taught in order of complexity. In first grade, you learned to read easy words first, then moved on to more difficult ones. In third grade, you learned single-digit multiplication tables before moving on to more complex double- and triple-digit multiplication problems. In junior high school, you learned to use the library's card catalog before you undertook a multi-stage research project. And in high school, you learned to drive by practicing simple maneuvers in the parking lot before cruising on the highway.

Organize ideas spatially. "Go down the hill two blocks and turn left by the florist. Then go three blocks to the next stoplight and turn right. The place you're looking for is about a block farther, on your right." When you offer someone directions, you organize your ideas spatially. **Spatial organization** is arrangement according to location, position, or direction. Speeches that rely on description are good candidates for spatial organization; for example, a speech about the layout of a manufacturing plant or a new shopping center would lend itself to spatial organization.

Here's an example of spatial organization:

Central Idea: Our corporate headquarters includes buildings that have three major functions.

  I. At the western edge of the campus is the employee recreation and sports complex.
  II. In the central part of the campus are the buildings that house the financial operations.
  III. At the eastern edge of the campus are the top executive offices.

Organize ideas to show cause and effect. **Cause and effect organization** actually refers to two related patterns: identifying a situation and then discussing the resulting effects (cause–effect), and presenting a situation and then exploring its causes (effect–cause).

A speaker who discusses the consequences of tax increases and their impact on the local economy will probably use a cause–effect pattern, establishing first that the tax rate is a major burden on local business and then providing evidence that the high taxes are causing business owners to close their doors. A speaker who does the opposite, documenting the loss of businesses in a downtown area and then providing statistics on recent tax increases instituted by the local county commissioners, is using an effect-cause organizational pattern. A cause–effect pattern emphasizes effects; an effect–cause pattern emphasizes causes.

Here's how one speaker organized a presentation using a cause–effect organizational pattern:

Recency arrangement of ideas from least to most important, based on the principle that audiences remember best what they hear last.

Primacy arrangement of ideas from most important or convincing to least important.

Complexity arrangement of speech ideas from simple to complex.

Spatial organization organization based on location, position, or direction.

Cause and effect organization identifying a situation and then discussing its effects (cause–effect) or presenting a situation and then exploring its causes (effect–cause).

> **>>> COMMUNICATION ETHICS @ WORK**
>
> The principle of recency suggests that you should discuss last what you want your audience to remember best. However, if a speaker has a statistic that offers overwhelming evidence of the severity of a given problem, is it ethical for the speaker to save that statistic for last? Or is the speaker ethically obligated to reveal immediately to the audience how severe the problem really is?

Central Idea: Higher taxes will force many businesses in our community to close.

    I. (Cause) Our school board and city council have raised our tax rate for the past five years.

    II. (Effect) The hardware store has closed because it can no longer afford the business tax levied by the school board and city council.

    III. (Effect) One of our two grocery stores has closed because it can no longer afford the business tax.

Organize ideas by problem and solution. If, instead of exploring causes or consequences of a problem or issue, you want either to explore how best to solve the problem or to advocate a particular solution, you will probably choose **problem-and-solution organization.** When addressing the dip in your company's stock price, you could first identify the problems associated with the downturn in the stock and then suggest strategies that could boost the stock price. Or, when delivering a motivational speech to new employees, you could first describe the implications of poor customer service—loss of company revenue and the potential loss of employment for workers. You could then offer specific solutions so that the problem of poor customer service doesn't occur.

Here's an outline of a speech organized using a problem-and-solution organizational framework:

Central Idea: Because of higher mortgage rates, the U.S. economy has experienced a significant downturn.

    I. (Problem) When the mortgage rates in adjustable rate mortgages increase, many people can no longer afford to pay the mortgage and end up losing their homes.

    II. (Solution) The federal government should implement a new guaranteed home mortgage plan to help homeowners avoid foreclosures.

RECAP: Organizing Your Main Ideas

Pattern	Description
Chronological	Organization by time or sequence
Topical	Organization of natural divisions of an idea according to recency, primacy, or complexity or in an arbitrary arrangement
Spatial	Organization according to location, position, or direction
Cause and effect	Organization by discussing a situation and its causes or a situation and its effects
Problem and solution	Organization by discussing a problem and then various solutions

Organizing Your Supporting Material

Once you have organized your main ideas, you are ready to organize the supporting material for each idea. Suppose you find that you have two brief illustrations, a statistic, and an opinion in support of your first main idea. How should you organize these materials to communicate your verbal message most effectively?

Problem-and-solution organization organization that describes a problem and then offers one or more solutions to it.

>>> COMMUNICATION AND GLOBALIZATION @ WORK

What's the shortest distance between two points? Why, a straight line, of course. In organizing a message, it may seem that the most logical strategy is to develop a structure that moves from one idea to the next in a logical, "straight" way. But not every culture organizes ideas using that logic. In fact, each culture teaches its members unique patterns of thought and organization that are considered appropriate for various occasions and audiences. In general, U.S. speakers tend to be more linear and direct than do Semitic, Asian, Romance, or Russian speakers.[20] U.S. listeners prefer direct cause and effect examples. For example, a U.S. speaker might say, "There are two reasons you should move your company to our city. First, we have a university located in our town so you'll have a steady supply of educated employees. And second, the nearby international airport means you can easily travel from our city to anywhere in the world." In contrast, Semitic speakers support their main points by pursuing tangents that might seem "off topic" to many U.S. listeners. When speaking to someone from a Semitic culture, instead of ticking off points one and two, you could offer several anecdotes about others who have enjoyed having corporate headquarters in your city. Or, a short story about how college-educated workers help companies flourish may

implicitly make the point that your city is advantageous because of its ample supply of well-educated workers. Asians may only allude to a main point through a circuitous route of illustrations and parables. Instead of using well-documented points when speaking to Asian listeners, you could tell a story about how those who are in the best location flourish and those in the wrong place are subject to disaster. And speakers from Romance and Russian cultures tend to begin with a basic principle and then move to facts and illustrations that are only gradually related to a main point and that to a North American listener may seem less relevant. Yet listeners from Romance and Russian cultures may find the illustrations more compelling than too quickly getting to the "bottom line" with explicit facts and statistics. A more gentle, circuitous route to get to the point may be best. The figure illustrates these culturally diverse patterns of organization.[21]

Of course, these are very broad generalizations. As an effective speaker who seeks to adapt to your audience, you should investigate the organizational strategies best suited to your particular audience. In addition, when you are listening to a speech, recognizing the existence of cultural differences can help you appreciate and understand the organization of a speaker from a culture other than your own.

The same organizational patterns you considered as you organized your main ideas can also help you organize your supporting material. For example, you might arrange a group of brief illustrations chronologically. At other times, you might find it more useful to organize supporting material according to the principle of recency, primacy, or complexity. You would employ the principle of recency if you saved your most convincing statistic for last. You would use primacy if you decided to present first the opinion with which you were certain your audience would agree. And you might arrange two explanations according to the principle of complexity, presenting the simplest one first and working up to the more complex one.

Organizing Your Presentation for the Ear

You now have a fairly complete, logically organized plan for your speech. But if you tried to deliver the speech at this point, your audience would probably become confused. What are your main ideas? How is one main idea related to the next? What supporting material develops which main idea? To adapt your logically organized message to your audience, you need to provide organizational cues for their ears. You do this by adding **signposts**— previews, verbal or nonverbal transitions, and summaries that allow you to move smoothly from one idea to the next throughout the speech.

Previews. A **preview** is a statement of what is to come in a speech—it "tells them what you're going to tell them." Previews help your audience members anticipate and remember the main ideas of your speech. They also help you move smoothly from the introduction to the body of your speech and from one main idea to the next.

The **initial preview** is a statement of the main ideas of a speech, usually presented in conjunction with, and sometimes as part of, the central idea of the speech. In addition to offering an initial preview, a speaker may also offer **internal previews** at various points throughout a speech. These previews introduce and outline ideas that will be developed as the speech progresses.

Verbal and nonverbal transitions. Effectively using and understanding verbal messages includes using **verbal transitions**, words or phrases that show relationships between ideas in your speech. They include simple enumeration (*first, second, third*); repeated words or synonyms or pronouns that refer to earlier words or ideas (the word *they* at the beginning of this sentence refers to the phrase "verbal transitions" in the previous sentence); and words and phrases that show relationships between ideas (*in addition to, not only . . . but also, in other words, in summary, therefore, however*). As you begin to rehearse your speech, you might need to experiment with various verbal transitions to achieve coherence that seems natural and logical to you. If none of the verbal alternatives seems quite right, consider a nonverbal transition.

Nonverbal transitions are behaviors that are used alone or in combination with verbal transitions help to show relationships among ideas in a speech. An effective nonverbal transition might take the form of a facial expression, a pause, a change in vocal pitch or speaking rate, or movement. Most good speakers use a combination of verbal and nonverbal transitions to help them move from one idea to the next throughout their speeches.

Summaries. Like previews, summaries provide an additional opportunity for an audience to grasp a speaker's most important ideas. Most speakers use two types of summaries: internal summaries and a final summary.

Internal summaries, like internal previews, occur within and throughout a speech. You might want to use an internal summary after you have discussed two or three main ideas, to ensure that the audience keeps them firmly in mind as you move into another main idea. You can combine an internal summary with an internal preview.

You may also want to provide your audience with a restatement of your main ideas, in the form of a **final summary** in your conclusion. Just as your initial preview gave your audience their first exposure to your main ideas, your final summary will give them their last exposure to those ideas.

Adding previews, transitions, and summaries to your well-organized speech applies the fundamental principles of using both verbal and nonverbal messages effectively and of adapting your message to others, increasing the likelihood that your audience will grasp your main ideas and the logic of your organizational strategy.

Introducing and Concluding Your Presentation

At this point, you have well-developed ideas and content for your presentation, and you have strategies for organizing that material. But you have not yet given much thought to how you are going to begin the speech. That's OK. Even though you will deliver your introduction first, you usually plan an introduction last. You first need to know what you're introducing—especially your central idea and main ideas. While they make up a relatively small percentage of the total speech, your introduction and conclusion provide your audience with important first and final impressions of you and your speech. They are important considerations in adapting your message to others.

Signpost a verbal or nonverbal signal that a speaker is moving from one idea to another.

Preview a statement of what is to come in a speech.

Initial preview the first statement of the main ideas of a presentation, usually presented in conjunction with or as part of the central idea.

Internal previews previews that introduce and outline ideas that will be developed as a speech progresses.

Verbal transitions words or phrases that show relationships between ideas in a speech.

Nonverbal transitions nonverbal behaviors (facial expressions, pauses, changes in vocal pitch or speaking rate, or movement) that are used either alone or in combination with verbal transitions to show relationships among ideas in a speech.

Internal summaries summaries that occur within and throughout a speech to help listeners keep ideas in mind as the speech progresses.

Final summary the final part of a speech, which restates a speaker's most important ideas.

Introductions

Your **introduction** should convince your audience to listen to you. More specifically, it must perform five functions: get the audience's attention, introduce the topic, give the audience a reason to listen, establish your credibility, and preview your main ideas.

Get the audience's attention. If an introduction does not capture the audience's attention, the rest of the speech may be wasted on them. You have to wake up your listeners and make them want to hear more.

There are several potentially effective ways to gain an audience's attention. One commonly used and quite effective one is to open with an illustration. Other strategies include asking a rhetorical question, stating a startling fact or statistic, quoting an expert or a literary text, telling a humorous story, or referring to an historical or recent event. Note the following clever introduction that refers to the date of the speech.

> It is perhaps fitting that we are meeting on this particular day, because this is the 15th of March, the dreaded "Ides of March". . . and I am going to address a subject of growing concern and distress to many people—the subject of globalization. In the play *Julius Caesar,* the Ides of March are a "strange-disposèd time." Thunder and lightning fill the air, and people are amazed to see the owl, or "the bird of night," sitting in the marketplace at noon, "hooting and shrieking."[22]

Still other speakers might get their audience's attention by referring to a personal experience, referring to the occasion, or referring to something said by a preceding speaker. While these strategies will not work for every speech, at least one of them should be an option for any speech you deliver. And with a little practice, you may find yourself being able to choose from several good possibilities for a single speech.

Introduce the topic. Within the first few seconds of listening to you, your audience should have a pretty good idea of what your topic is. The best way to achieve this objective is to include a statement of your central idea in your introduction.

Give the audience a reason to listen. Not only do you have to get your audience's attention and introduce your topic, you have to motivate your listeners to continue to listen. Show the audience how your topic affects them directly. By the end of your introduction, your audience should be thinking, "This concerns *me!*"

Establish your credibility. A credible speaker is one whom the audience judges to be competent, trustworthy, and dynamic. Be aware of your skills and talents and the experiences you have had that are related to your topic. You can increase your credibility by telling your audience about your expertise.

Preview your main ideas. As we discussed above, you should provide an initial preview of your main ideas at or near the end of your introduction, to allow your listeners to anticipate the main ideas of your speech.

Conclusions

Whereas your introduction creates a critically important first impression, your conclusion leaves an equally important final impression. Long after you finish speaking, your audience may mentally hear the echo of effective final words. An effective **conclusion** serves four functions: it summarizes your speech, reemphasizes the main idea in a memorable way, motivates the audience to respond, and provides closure.

Summarize the speech. The conclusion offers a speaker a last chance to repeat his or her main ideas. Most speakers summarize their main ideas between the body of the speech and its conclusion or in the first part of the conclusion.

Reemphasize the central idea in a memorable way. The conclusions of many famous speeches contain many of the lines we remember best:

> . . . government of the people, by the people, for the people, shall not perish from the earth. (Abraham Lincoln)[23]

> Old soldiers never die; they just fade away. (General Douglas MacArthur)[24]

> Free at last! Free at last! Thank God almighty, we are free at last! (Martin Luther King Jr.)[25]

Introduction the opening sentences of a speech, intended to get the audience's attention, introduce the topic, give the audience a reason to listen, establish the speaker's credibility, and preview the main ideas.

Conclusion the closing sentences of a speech, intended to summarize the speech, to reemphasize the main idea in a memorable way, to motivate the audience to respond, and to provide closure.

Although business and professional presentations don't usually have such memorable or emotion-packed conclusions, consider how even the most routine briefing or report can be enhanced by a strong call to action or reiteration of the expense budget statistics or other points. Word your final thoughts so that your audience cannot help but remember them.

Motivate the audience to respond. Think back to your specific purpose. What do you want your audience to be able to do by the end of your speech? If your speech is informative, you may want your audience to think about your topic or to seek more information about it. If your speech is persuasive, you may want your audience to take some sort of action—to write a letter, make a phone call, or volunteer for a cause. Your conclusion is where you can motivate your audience to respond.

Provide closure. You may have experienced listening to a speech and not being certain when it was over. That speaker did not achieve the last purpose of an effective conclusion: providing **closure,** or cueing the audience that the speech is ending by making it "sound finished." One good way to provide closure is to refer to your introduction by finishing a story, answering a rhetorical question, or reminding your audience of the startling statistic you presented in your introduction.

You can also achieve closure by using verbal and nonverbal signposts. For example, you might use such transitions as "finally" and "in conclusion" as you move into your conclusion. You might pause before you begin the conclusion, slow your speaking rate as you deliver your final sentence, or signal by falling vocal inflection that you are making your final statement. Experiment with these strategies until you are certain that your speech "sounds finished."

RECAP: The Purposes of Introductions and Conclusions

Your speech introduction should	• Get your audience's attention
	• Introduce your topic
	• Give your audience a reason to listen
	• Establish your credibility
	• Preview your main ideas
Your speech conclusion should	• Summarize your speech
	• Reemphasize your central idea in a memorable way
	• Motivate your audience to respond
	• Provide closure

Outlining Your Presentation

With your introduction and conclusion planned, you are almost ready to begin rehearsing your speech. By this point, you should have your preparation outline nearly complete. A **preparation outline** is a fairly detailed outline of your central idea, main ideas, and supporting material; it may also include the specific purpose, introduction, and conclusion of your speech. A second outline, which you will prepare shortly, is a **delivery outline,** a condensed, abbreviated outline that provides the notes you will use when you present your speech.

Preparation Outline

Although few speeches are written out word for word (manuscript form), most speakers develop a fairly detailed preparation outline that helps them to ensure that their main ideas are clearly related to their central idea, and that their main ideas are logically and adequately supported. A speaker who creates a preparation outline is applying the first fundamental principle of communication: becoming aware of his or her communication. In addition to helping the speaker judge the unity and coherence of the speech, the preparation outline serves as an early rehearsal outline.

Closure a sense of being complete or "sounding finished" provided in the conclusion of a speech by finishing a story, answering a rhetorical question, or reminding the audience of a statistic presented in the introduction.

Preparation outline a detailed outline of the central idea, main ideas, and supporting material for a speech; may also include the specific purpose, introduction, and conclusion.

Delivery outline a condensed, abbreviated outline that provides the notes a speaker uses when presenting a speech.

A preparation outline of your speech helps you rehearse the speech; a delivery outline provides notes that you can use as reminders as you deliver your speech.

When outlining a speech, it is helpful to use **standard outline format.** Standard outline format lets you see at a glance the exact relationships among various main ideas, subpoints, and supporting material in your speech. Even if you haven't had much experience with formal outlines, the following guidelines can help you produce a correct outline.

Use standard numbering. Outlines are numbered by using Roman and Arabic numerals and uppercase and lowercase letters, followed by periods, as follows:

> I. First main idea
>> A. First subdivision of I
>> B. Second subdivision of I
>>> 1. First subdivision of B
>>> 2. Second subdivision of B
>>>> a. First subdivision of 2
>>>> b. Second subdivision of 2
>
> II. Second main idea

You will probably not need to subdivide beyond the level of lowercase letters in most speech outlines.

Use at least two subdivisions, if any, for each point. You cannot divide anything into fewer than two parts. On an outline, every I should have a II, every A should have a B, and so on. If you have only one subdivision, fold that information into the level above it.

Line up your outline correctly. Main ideas, indicated by Roman numerals, are written closest to the left margin. The *periods* following these Roman numerals line up, so that the first letters of the first words also line up:

> I. First main idea
> II. Second main idea
> III. Third main idea

Letters or numbers of subdivisions begin directly underneath the first letter of the first *word* of the point above:

> I. First main idea
>> A. First subdivision of I
>> B. Second subdivision of I

Standard outline format
numbered and lettered headings and subheadings arranged hierarchically to indicate relationships among main ideas, subpoints, and supporting material in a speech.

If a main idea or subdivision takes up more than one line, the second line begins under the first letter of the first word of the preceding line:

I. First main idea

    A. A rather lengthy subdivision that runs more than one line

    B. Second subdivision

Within each level, make the headings grammatically parallel. Regardless of whether you write your preparation outline in complete sentences or in phrases, be consistent within each level. In other words, if I is a complete sentence, II should also be a complete sentence. If A is an infinitive phrase (one that begins with *to* plus a verb, such as "To guarantee greater security"), B should also be an infinitive phrase.

Delivery Outline

As you rehearse your speech, you will find yourself needing to look at your preparation outline less and less. You have both the structure and the content of your speech well in mind. At this point, you are ready to develop a shorter outline—your delivery outline.

Your delivery outline should provide all the notes you will need to present your speech as you have planned, without being so detailed that you will be tempted to read it rather than speak to your audience. Here are a few suggestions for preparing a delivery outline:

Use single words or short phrases whenever possible.

Include your introduction and conclusion in abbreviated form. You may feel more comfortable delivering the speech if you have your first and last sentences written out in front of you.

Include supporting material and signposts. Write out any statistics and direct quotations and their sources. Write out your key signposts—your initial preview, for example—to ensure that you will not have to grope awkwardly as you move from one idea to another.

Do not include your purpose statement. Since you will not actually deliver your purpose statement ("At the end of my speech, the audience should be able to . . ."), do not put it on your delivery outline.

Use standard outline form. Standard outline form will help you find your exact place when you glance down at your speaking notes. You will know, for example, that your second main idea is indicated by II.

Although you may write the first version of your delivery outline on paper, eventually you may want to transfer it to note cards. They don't rustle the way paper does, and they are small enough to hold in one hand if there is no lectern. Three or four note cards will probably give you enough space for your delivery outline. Type or print neatly on one side only, making sure that the letters and words are large enough to read easily. Organize your note cards to reflect blocks of material, using one note card for your introduction, one or two for the body of your speech, and one for your conclusion. Number your note cards to prevent getting them out of order while you are speaking.

A final addition to your note cards as you rehearse your speech will be **delivery cues**, such as "Louder," "Pause," or "Walk two steps left." These will remind you to communicate the nonverbal messages you have planned. Write your delivery cues in a different color ink so that you don't confuse them with your verbal content.

Delivery cues notes a speaker uses to remind himself or herself of nonverbal behaviors to use while making a presentation.

RECAP: Two Types of Speech Outlines

Preparation outline	Allows a speaker to examine a speech for completeness, unity, coherence, and overall effectiveness; it may serve as a first rehearsal outline.
Delivery outline	Serves as speaking notes and includes delivery cues.

SAMPLE INFORMATIVE SPEECH *by* **JIM McNERNEY**

Chairman and CEO of Boeing Company

Delivered to the Invitational Symposium of the National Center for Healthcare Leadership[26]

Secrets of High-Performing Executive Teams

McNerney begins his message with a short story about the Apollo 13 astronauts to capture his listeners' attention and introduce his topic of teamwork.

Thank you, Gail. I really appreciate the comments about my father. Good afternoon, ladies and gentlemen. I'd like to start with a bang—specifically, the onboard explosion that rocks the *Apollo 13* spacecraft as it is hurtling toward the moon on April 14, 1970. Imagine you are at Mission Control when Jim Lovell radios in to say, "Houston, we have a problem."

The explosion results in a sudden loss of oxygen, power, and water. To conserve remaining supplies, Lovell and his fellow astronauts shut down the main ship and move into the lunar module. It is chilly and cramped. And they are 200,000 miles from home.

Now, a new danger arises: poison gas, a byproduct—ironically—of the act of breathing. On a screen at your console at Mission Control, you can see the rapidly rising level of carbon dioxide inside their tiny cabin. You know they are in imminent danger of choking to death.

Those of you who saw the movie *Apollo 13* will remember the next scene. With just two hours to find a solution, experts from different disciplines at Mission Control frantically pile together materials identical to those on board the spacecraft, and set about building a crude but workable air filtration system. Then they guide the astronauts through the same sequence of steps they have just discovered. Miraculously, it all works, and the astronauts are saved from asphyxiation. They splash down in the Pacific three days later—cold, tired, dehydrated . . . but safe.

Here the speaker connects his message with the theme of the conference this audience is attending. This helps him customize his message for this particular audience.

Now clearly, the *Apollo 13* saga mirrors some of the drama that goes on—every day—in operating rooms around the country. You live in a high risk, . . . high stakes . . . world of your own. But what does the story really tell us about "Achieving Organizational Excellence," the theme of this conference?

Well, to be sure, it demonstrates the value of putting a great deal of emphasis on teamwork. As a recent headline in the *Wall Street Journal* said, "Teamwork Raises Everyone's Game." That was from a story in the *Journal* on November 7 regarding recent research by Harvard professors on levels of performance in fields supposedly dominated by individual "stars"—such as stock market analysis . . . and heart surgery. What the researchers found was that teamwork is crucial to outcomes—whether it is the analyst's interactions with other analysts within the same firm . . . or the surgeon's interactions with anesthesiologists, nurses, and technicians. The best results are achieved by those who work in well-defined teams.

Is anyone surprised by that finding?

Now, there are two closely related lessons I would take away from the *Apollo 13* saga.

First: You can manage and teach leadership. You can measure and demand leadership. That's something that NASA did exceptionally well in fulfilling President Kennedy's promise to send a man to the moon within a decade. Growing great leaders is the first step on the road to organizational excellence.

And second: Contrary to popular belief, innovation is a team sport, not a solo sport. It takes people working together across different groups and organizational lines to make it happen. It requires genuine sharing, combined with an openness to change.

Be they hospitals, corporations, or whole armies, it is always difficult for big organizations to embrace change. Mass—as we know from physics—is the measure of inertia. And it is not as though large aggregations of people are united in the desire to remain stationary. Rather, the writer Warren Bennis put it, "We all see and understand the need for change, and instinctively avoid it at all costs."

So how do you overcome inertia in your own organization? How do you get ignition in stimulating innovation and the formation of high performing teams? How—in a word—do you act as a leader . . . someone who produces useful change within a larger group?

McNerney uses several rhetorical questions as a transition technique to move to his next major point.

I can list some leadership attributes—things like Chart the Course, Raise the Bar, Be Inclusive. But I must admit: I always feel a little funny in doing so. Every one of these attributes sounds so fundamental. But that's really the point. They ARE fundamental. There's no magic.

Marie Sinioris asked me to talk about "legendary leadership." So let me tell you a few things I have learned from two leaders—two legendary leaders—who had a huge impact on my own life and career.

A *mentor*—and that is a name that has come to us from Homer—is a father substitute. But my first mentor really was my own father. Walter McNerney excelled in a number of roles, and one of them—as many of you who were his students know—was as a teacher. And leadership was often a theme. On the first day of class in hospital-management courses, he would tell his students, "You have got to decide early on whether you want to lead or follow, and that simple decision will go a long way to deciding what the rest of your career will be like."

Using a personal story or anecdotes adds interest to the speech and helps to illustrate McNerney's ideas about mentorship.

It's a whole lot harder to be a leader than a follower, my father would say, because the leader aims to do what others regard as the impossible.

But then he would go on to say, "Don't overestimate the opposition. If you have the will and the courage to lead, you will gain a lot of support along the way."

My father cared very deeply about the poor, the disadvantaged, and the elderly, and he devoted a large portion of his life to the crafting and selling of Medicare legislation. He did the seemingly impossible in bringing that legislation to fruition. Later on, he succeeded in bringing Blue Cross and Blue Shield together when most experts were agreed that a merger between those two organizations could never happen. Once again, his idea was to force through a more rational and equitable delivery of health care . . . in the face of substantial resistance on the part of almost everyone who felt reasonably comfortable within the status quo.

Let me turn now to my longtime boss and friend, Jack Welch. Though no one would accuse Jack of being a diplomat, I will cite a few striking similarities between the two men . . . other than their love of conviviality and late nights. (That's another speech with a smaller group!)

Using another personal example, McNerney continues to keep his listeners' attention.

- One was in having the foresight to see the need for change . . . when almost no one else did.
- Another was in having that will, and courage, and self-confidence to lead.
- And finally, they both had the ability to communicate the call to action in simple, inspirational terms.

As a newly minted CEO in 1981, Jack was way ahead of his time in recognizing the colossal challenges facing U.S. companies of every description—even the greatly admired and highly diversified General Electric company. American industry had become an overconfident group in major denial, even as global forces were eroding its competitiveness.

Given these new realities of global competition and rapid technological change, he believed it was absurd to think that you could lay out detailed business plans looking

continued

four or five years ahead, or that you could devise clever ways to control the thinking and behavior of your customers.

So he didn't just decimate GE's celebrated corporate strategies department; he abolished it—telling GE's vaunted planners (all 75 of them) to start looking for another line of work. In his first big presentation to Wall Street analysts, he quoted the elder Von Moltke, of the Prussian General Staff, to the effect that strategy was not a "lengthy action plan," but rather "the evolution of a central idea through continually changing circumstances."

With this came the idea that GE would be "number one" or "number two" in every one of its globally defined businesses (a first for GE back then)—a strategy of "Fix, Sell, or Close." Talk about simple, clear communications!

And in his first few years as CEO, he closed or sold a lot of businesses—earning the nickname of "Neutron Jack" . . . the guy who got rid of people but left the buildings standing.

After using a personal example, the speaker makes sure that his listeners understand the main point of the message by explicitly identifying the key message embedded in his example.

Now, the point I want to make here is that Jack didn't just chart the course, he stayed the course . . . when that made him an unpopular and even a hated figure. He wouldn't settle for anything less than the radical and thoroughgoing change that was needed to make GE truly competitive.

To borrow from Shakespeare, it is all too easy to be "unkindly kind." In a competitive marketplace, you don't do anybody a favor by trying to prop up nonperforming businesses or people. All that does is prolong the agony of those who aren't performing while putting everyone else at risk.

That said, it must be recognized that the development of people is the single most important job a leader has. More than anything else, that's the one thing that really defines the best companies and the best organizations. One of the (true) stories that have passed into GE lore is the hourly worker who told Welch, "For 25 years, you paid for my hands when you could have had my brains—for free."

The fact is, in a super-competitive world, no one has the luxury . . . if that is what it is . . . of allowing any of their people to leave their brains at the door. That's just not good enough anymore.

So let me return to one of those leadership attributes that seem so fundamental—so obvious. I mentioned being inclusive. We can all talk about how it is better to include and inspire people than it is to lead through fear and intimidation. But what are you really doing about it? If that is one of the things you value, then it must be one of the things you measure, reward, and factor into the whole pay and promotion process.

Here McNerney uses the transition phrase "you must be prepared to go to the next step" to move from his previous point about leadership attributes to how to identify ineffective leaders.

If you say you want an empowered and inclusive workforce, you must be prepared to go to the next step—and this is the hard part: Not only should you reward the inspirational leaders, but you should be equally aggressive in weeding out the tyrants and abusive leaders . . . because even if they are achieving good results in the short run, they are a cancer in the organization.

And speaking of "cancer" and "weeding out" certain kinds of behavior, I believe it makes sense to think of an organization as a living entity—one that is biological rather mechanistic in nature. I fundamentally believe that a company grows when its people grow and that there are different things that you can do that will either encourage or discourage the growth that is needed for continued survival.

In addition to leadership, one other factor is critical to growth. That is innovation. To innovate literally means "to renew" or "to make new again." And that really says it all. With deferential apologies to Bill McGuire, it is unusual to get sustainable growth through mergers and acquisitions. That usually comes from organic growth, and innovation is the magic elixir that is needed for continued renewal through organic growth—for organizations of any age, from 1 to 150 or more.

So how do you cultivate innovation? Let me repeat part of the Hippocratic Oath. For starters, you should do no harm. Unfortunately, there are a number of popular but damaging misconceptions about innovation. From personal experience, I have seen how these romantic but misguided notions can lead to dysfunctional behavior—serving only to discourage creativity and growth.

Using another rhetorical question as a transition technique, McNerney segues into his next point.

So here are five great innovation myths. (Do you see these in your organization?)

- Myth #1: It's the solitary genius who is responsible for most innovation.
- Myth #2: It's all about technology. The techies are the only innovators.
- Myth #3: If it isn't "new to the world," it's not innovation.
- Myth #4: Innovation can't be "managed." It's a matter of serendipity. An accident. Or luck.
- And Myth #5: As a follow-on to Number 4, creativity and discipline are mortal enemies.

Leaders who take over at companies with a long pedigree of success often find mid-life crises in the form of these myths . . . largely because they are rooted in a desire for life to remain less cluttered and simpler than it's become. Companies that have faced this transition in recent years include IBM, GE, 3M, and Microsoft, to name a few.

In the case of 3M, we still had a great reputation for innovation. But some had begun to mistake legend for the truth. During the 1990s, discounting acquisitions, the company stopped growing. It turned inward, waiting for the myth to repeat, while losing the edge on the real reasons why innovations happen.

The speech is effective because of the liberal use of specific examples and illustrations about people the speaker has known, as well as specific company examples.

The team and I set out to change the mindset of the company in two basic ways:

- First was to switch the emphasis from the individual to the team, and to make the team an all-inclusive concept.
- Second was to move away from the thought of innovation-for-innovation's-sake and to replace that with a disciplined focus on customer-inspired innovation.

Now if I may go back to another one of those fundamental leadership attributes, in taking a more disciplined, customer-based approach, we really did "Raise the Bar"—aiming to double the number of new product introductions and to triple the sales from new products in the marketplace (all external measurements). To achieve stretch objectives like those, everyone—across all functions and disciplines—has to work together.

So innovation really is a team sport, not a solo sport. It can and should occur in all areas of the business. And it is—or ought to be—a fun part of everyone's job.

Most innovation involves incremental improvements. Incremental does not mean insignificant. Neverending incremental improvements important to your customers' ongoing competitiveness are vital both to sustaining current business and to opening up whole new opportunities.

I opened this discussion with the *Apollo 13* story because it illustrates what an organization on top of its form can do, in bouncing back from a near-catastrophe. The astronauts and the ground crews came up with one innovation after another—and none of those innovations, I might add, was especially high-tech. What they really involved was the brilliant use of scarce resources, a magnificent display of teamwork across a large organization, and the kind of gutsy decision-making that is the true mark of an organization with a high leadership component.

McNerney uses the effective technique of closing his message by making a reference to his opening example of Apollo 13.

It is not easy to achieve that kind of organizational excellence.

But as my father would have told you: Whoever said that it was supposed to be easy?

Communication Principles and Skills for Leadership

Principle One: Be aware of your communication with yourself and others.

- Remember that the most effective illustrations are often personal ones.
- Be aware of the skills, talents, and experiences you have that can enhance your credibility with your listeners, and use the introduction of your presentation to help establish your own credibility.
- Use a preparation outline to demonstrate to yourself that your main ideas are clearly related to your central idea and are logically and adequately supported.

Principle Two: Effectively use and interpret verbal messages.

- Be sure that your illustrations are vivid and directly relevant to the idea or the point they are supposed to support.
- Organize your presentation logically by using verbal transitions to show relationships between ideas.
- Introduce your topic and preview your main ideas in your introduction.
- Use stories, examples, illustrations, statistics, a quotation, or other techniques to capture your listeners' attention when you begin your talk.
- In your conclusion, summarize your presentation and reemphasize your main idea in a memorable way.

Principle Three: Effectively use and interpret nonverbal messages

- Use nonverbal transitions—pauses, facial expressions, altered vocal pitch or speaking rate, and movement—to indicate when you are moving from one idea to the next.
- Use nonverbal cues, such as pausing, slowing your rate of speech, and letting your vocal inflection fall, to signal that you are approaching the end of your presentation.
- Add delivery cues and reminders to your final delivery outline.

Principle Four: Listen and respond thoughtfully to others.

- Seek out information about your audience and how they are likely to respond to your message to increase your comfort with speaking in public.
- As you listen to presentations, consider differences in the organization schemes used by speakers from cultures other than your own.

Principle Five: Appropriately adapt message to others.

- Keep in mind your audience's knowledge, interests, and expectations as you select supporting material for your presentation.
- Use illustrations with which your audience can identify. Consider making your audience members part of the scenario in a hypothetical illustration.
- Make the similarity between the two things compared in a figurative analogy apparent to your audience.
- Investigate and consider using organizational strategies familiar to members of your audience's culture.
- Discuss last the idea that you most want your audience to remember.
- If you know your audience will be skeptical of some of your ideas, first present ideas on which you can agree.
- Provide signposts as organization cues for your audience.
- Use your introduction and conclusion to help adapt your presentation to your audience.

Discussion Questions

1. What are the primary sources of supporting material for your presentation?

2. List and explain the five criteria for evaluating Internet resources.

3. What types of supporting material could you use to support your ideas?

4. What are five strategies for organizing the main ideas in a presentation?

5. List and explain five strategies for organizing supporting material in a presentation.

6. What are the functions of the introduction to a presentation?

7. What are the functions of the conclusion of a presentation?

8. Identify three verbal signpost techniques.

9. What is typically included on most preparation and delivery outlines?

Building Your Skills

1. Select a story from the newspaper or a weekly newsmagazine such as *Time* or *Newsweek*. Based on this chapter's discussion of supporting material, identify the different types of supporting material you find in the article. Determine whether the supporting material you identify could be used in an oral presentation.

2. Draft an introduction for a presentation on one of the following:

   • Promoting your city, town, or community as the location for a new shopping mall

   • Selling a product to a company that you hope will market it for you

   • Giving a report describing the accomplishments of your college or university to the city council

   In addition to introducing the topic and previewing your main ideas, select a specific strategy to capture your audience's attention and establish your credibility.

3. Select several statistics that you find in a newspaper. Identify strategies for adapting the statistics for a presentation, such as rounding off the statistics and developing a way to relate the numerical data to something an audience can visualize.

4. Outline a lecture by one of your instructors using the standard outline format described in this chapter. Then convert the outline to a delivery outline. Analyze the organizational strategy used in the lecture: Is it chronological, topic, spatial, cause and effect, problem and solution, or a combination of those strategies?

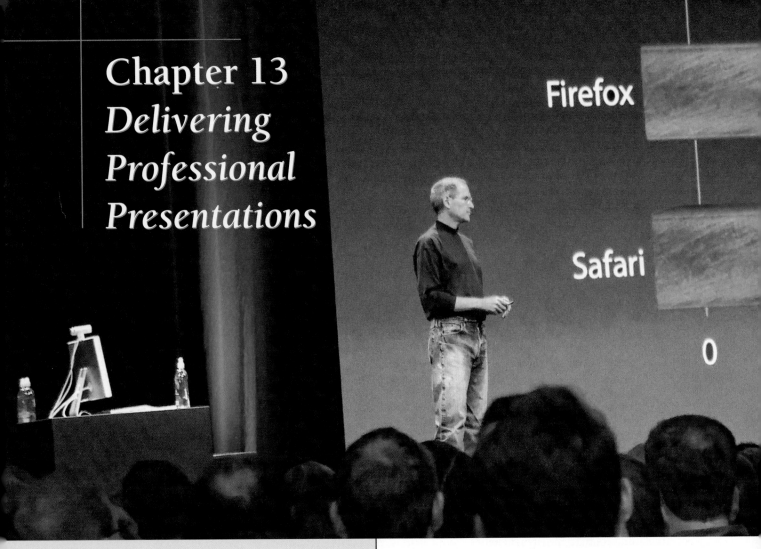

Chapter 13
Delivering Professional Presentations

chapter outline

After reading this chapter, you should be able to

- List and describe four methods of delivery and provide tips for effectively using each one.

- Identify and describe characteristics of effective eye contact, posture, movement, gestures, facial expression, vocal delivery, and personal appearance.

- Identify strategies for adapting your speaking style when your presentation is televised.

- List and describe strategies for responding to questions following your presentation.

- Identify the types of presentation aids a speaker might use, and provide suggestions for using each type effectively.

- Offer general guidelines for preparing effective presentation aids for a professional presentation.

- Identify tips and strategies for designing effective presentation aids using presentation software such as PowerPoint.

"The medium is the message" communication theorist Marshall McLuhan said. In essence, McLuhan was saying that *you* are the message. When delivering a presentation, you are the "medium," or the means of communicating a message to listeners. Long after your listeners forget the facts, details, and even the main points of your business presentation, sales pitch, or conference briefing, they will most likely remember *you*—your demeanor, credibility, sincerity, and an overall impression of whether you were boring or interesting. Your use of eye contact, voice, and gestures, your facial expressions, and your overall appearance may leave a longer-lasting impression than your words. In professional speaking situations, whether you're selling something, motivating people, or making a brief report, your delivery will influence what people remember and ultimately how they will respond to you and your message. Leaders lead by example; it is your delivery that provides the example—your energy, charisma, and the overall perception of leadership competence that you convey.

> *You can speak well if your tongue can deliver the message of your heart."*
>
> — JOHN FORD

In this chapter we focus on the delivery skills that can help you create a favorable impression of you and your message, regardless of whether you're giving a formal speech to hundreds of people, sharing a few impromptu ideas in an informal meeting, or convincing your boss to give you a raise. Specifically, we'll focus on methods of delivery and the use of delivery cues such as eye contact, gestures, posture, movement, facial expression, vocal delivery, and your overall appearance. In addition, we'll discuss the visual support typically used by business and professional speakers, such as PowerPoint and other types of visual and technological tools to enhance their presentations. This chapter is about you as the communication medium and how to make your message memorable, credible, and well received by your listeners. Specifically, we're focusing on how to effectively use and interpret nonverbal messages.

Nonverbal

As we begin this chapter, consider this age-old question: What's more important, the content or the delivery of your message? Speakers, educators, and scholars have debated that question since ancient times. Many people have concluded that when all is said and done, what is done (a speaker's delivery) is more important than what is said. There is considerable research to support the observation that delivery is the foremost factor in determining the overall impact of your message. One classic research study found that listeners believe that the most important factors that make a speaker effective are direct eye contact, alertness, enthusiasm, a pleasant voice, and animated gestures.[1] Another researcher concluded that delivery was almost twice as important as content when students gave persuasive presentations.[2] Still other communication researchers have concluded that speaker delivery provides essential information about a speaker's feeling and emotions, which are the primary factors that determine how listeners respond emotionally to a message.[3] Although there is clear support to tip the scales toward delivery over content, especially when a speaker is expressing emotion, most contemporary communication teachers suggest that *both* content and delivery are important. They are both vital because, as one executive communication coach has suggested, "In the real world—the world where you and I do business—content and delivery are always related. And woe be to the communicator who forgets this."[4]

So how do you achieve a delivery style that makes your message memorable and interesting? That's what you're about to find out.

Methods of Delivery

Pick up any public speaking book and open it to the chapter about speech delivery and you'll find a section about the methods of speech delivery just like the one you are about to read. Why? Because regardless of whether you are selling insurance, summarizing quarterly profits, or just making a few brief remarks, you have a decision to make about your delivery. You first need to determine, from among the four common methods, the delivery method you'll use to communicate your ideas to others. The four methods of presentation delivery are as old as the hills but also as contemporary as today's news headlines. Whether you choose to read your speech, memorize it, make it up on the spot, or speak conversationally from an outline, the method of delivery you choose will have an impact on the overall effect of your message on your listeners. And in keeping with our emphasis on adapting to your audience, focusing on your listeners' expectations and the specific speaking situation will help you determine which delivery method to select.

Adapt

Reading: Manuscript Speaking

You could write your speech word for word and then read your speech. This method is called **manuscript speaking**. One advantage of manuscript speaking is that you don't have to worry if you forget what you're going to say. You simply write exactly what you're going to say and then read it. Manuscript speaking also has the advantage of letting you carefully craft each word so that you can prepare a speech that has power and pizzazz while also focusing on precise word choices. If you are a company spokesperson and your company is unveiling a new product, the corporate communication department may have prepared a few remarks for you to read. Or, if the organization you work for has had a problem or been involved in scandal and you're facing the media to describe the problem, you would probably want to have a carefully prepared statement to ensure that you get the facts right and that you are telling the story accurately. Having a manuscript that you can read to reporters or other members of the media that can then be distributed is a good way to get out a message that is clear, accurate, and precise. When possible, during times of crisis, statements to the press by government, business, or education leaders should be carefully crafted rather than tossed off casually. An inaccurate or misspoken message could have serious consequences. Yet, despite these advantages, manuscript speaking is *not* a preferred method, because listening to someone reading a speech is not inherently interesting.

Most public speaking teachers describe manuscript speaking as one of the *least* effective methods of maintaining audience interest. With the exception of children, who like to hear mom or dad read a bedtime story, most listeners don't want to hear a speech read to them. It takes considerable skill to make a manuscript speech sound interesting and lively. Another disadvantage: When reading a speech, you'll have minimal eye contact with your audience. Also, when you read a message your voice tends to fall into a sing-song pattern that sounds like you're reading rather than talking naturally with your listeners. So, consider a manuscript speaking style only when you need to make sure your message is clearly worded, or when you need to be very careful about what you are presenting.

When you do use a manuscript speaking style, consider these tips from media consultant Roger Ailes, who has advised leaders including U.S. presidents and corporate CEOs:[5]

- Type your speech in short, easy-to-scan phrases on the upper two-thirds of the paper so that you don't have to look too far down into your notes.
- Rehearse your speech so that you can have maximum eye contact when reading your message.
- Use an index finger to follow along on each line of your message so that when you do break for eye contact you'll be able to quickly find your place and seamlessly keep on reading without missing a beat.
- Don't read too quickly; try to speak as you typically do when not using a manuscript.
- Vary your vocal inflection to mirror the way you normally talk.
- Use appropriate gestures and movement to add interest and emphasis to your message.

The goal when delivering a manuscript speech is to sound like you are not reading a speech.

Recalling: Memorized Speaking

If you've ever been in a play and had to memorize lines, you already know both the advantages and the disadvantages of delivering a speech from memory. **Memorized speaking** has the advantage of allowing you to have constant eye contact with your audience while also saying precisely what you want to say. As with manuscript speaking, you can carefully develop your message and work on both word choice and the overall message.

A prime disadvantage of memorized speaking is that you might forget what you've rehearsed. Another disadvantage: Most memorized speeches sound like they are memorized—stiff, stilted, and over-rehearsed. Also, you won't be able to adapt to your listeners if you've memorized every word.

Given those disadvantages, are there instances when it is appropriate to memorize your message? If you have a very short message to present, such as when accepting an award, introducing a speaker, or making an announcement, a memorized talk may be best.

Manuscript speaking reading a speech from a written text.

Memorized speaking delivering a speech word for word from memory without using notes.

But even in those situations you may want to have notes available so that you can use them if you need them. And if you do memorize your message, avoid rehearsing it using exactly the same vocal inflection each time you practice. Vary your voice to sound as natural and as conversational as possible. Memorize this: *Unless a speech is short, don't try to memorize it.*

Improvising: Impromptu Speaking

You've given more impromptu speeches in your life than any other type of speech. **Impromptu speaking** is delivering a speech without any advance preparation. You simply respond to a question, comment, or invitation to speak. Impromptu speaking is also called "thinking on your feet" or "speaking off the cuff." Whether in a meeting when someone turns to you for a short briefing on a topic or when you respond to something said during a conference call, you'll undoubtedly give many impromptu speeches. Leaders are expected to think on their feet and to speak fluently.

The key advantage of impromptu speaking is that you can speak conversationally (since you didn't prepare your message ahead of time) while maintaining direct eye contact with your listeners. You can also adapt your comments to your listeners, based on the remarks of a previous speaker or something that has just occurred. A skilled impromptu speaker can customize a message to hold an audience's interest and attention. But the problem is that a speaker needs to be especially skilled and talented to be a good impromptu speaker. Another potential disadvantage is that an impromptu speech may lack a coherent organizational structure. You're also not able to carefully gather facts and other information for an impromptu speech; you can include only the supporting material that comes to mind when you're speaking.

Mark Twain said, "A good impromptu speech takes about three weeks to prepare." What Twain knew is that the best impromptu speakers are always thinking about what they might say if they were called on to say a few remarks. In business and professional settings, when you find yourself in a situation with an audience present and others are speaking (such as when your team is reporting its findings to stockholders), you would be wise to think about a few remarks you could present, even if you were not invited in advance to talk.

The following tips can help you present impromptu speeches that sound professional and polished.

Identify the number of points you wish to make. Before you open your mouth to respond to another speaker or to ask to speak, think about how many major ideas you will mention. Maybe you'll just have one major idea; you'll probably not have more than three or four. Just as in any speech, as you develop a brief introduction to your comments, you could say, "I have two responses" or "There are three points I want to make." You'll impress listeners with your clarity of thought and give your message an immediate structure.

Organize before you speak. In addition to enumerating your major points, think about the order of your major ideas. For example, consider using the primacy-recency principle: Whatever you present first or last is most likely to be remembered. If you think your audience may be opposed to your message, start with your strongest idea. Or, you may want to build to a strong conclusion, saving your strongest point for last. Or, use a simple problem-solution, topical, or chronological pattern. With just a few seconds of reflection, you can develop a mental outline of your key points and place them in an order for maximum impact.

Be brief. Since it's an impromptu speech, most listeners won't expect (or want) your message to be lengthy. A typical impromptu speech lasts from one to three minutes, although depending on the issue, or your leadership role, and the specific audience you are addressing, an impromptu speech could be longer than three minutes.

Speak honestly and draw on personal experience. More than likely, you will support your key ideas with personal experience or stories, since you've not had time to conduct research. But be careful to self-censor your remarks to make sure you're not making a heat-of-the-moment response. Don't let your emotions lead you to say something you'll later regret. In speaking impromptu to local supporters on the evening of the Iowa Caucus vote during the 2004 presidential campaign, Howard Dean, in the emotion of the moment, let forth a screaming "Yeeeeeeeehaaaaa!" Many think his emotional outburst cost him support in later primaries. (His scream, played and replayed on TV out of context, made him look overly and oddly exuberant.) When you do provide impromptu personal examples and

Impromptu speaking
delivering a speech without advance preparation.

illustrations, we recommend using short—and we emphasize *short*—anecdotes or stories to make your point; long, rambling offerings will likely not be well received.

Always keep your audience in mind. As we've stressed throughout our discussion of professional speaking, be audience-centered. Always think about your audience's needs, interests, and background as you begin an impromptu message. A quick way to be audience-centered and adapt your message to your listeners is, for just a few moments, to *be* your audience: Imagine that you are different members of your audience, with their different roles and experiences. If you were them, what would you expect or want a speaker to say? Being audience-centered is always good advice when speaking on short notice.

Conversing: Extemporaneous Speaking

The delivery style advocated by most communication experts is extemporaneous delivery. **Extemporaneous speaking** is speaking from a written or memorized outline without having memorized the exact wording of what you are going to say. You have rehearsed your message so that you know the key ideas and how to organize them, but not to the degree that your speech sounds memorized. An extemporaneous delivery style gives your audience the impression that the speech is being created as you're presenting it. But you've worked hard to gather research, refine your ideas, organize your message, and even practice saying what you'll say. Extemporaneous speaking sounds conversational, fluid, and thoughtful. Yet, because you haven't memorized the exact wording of your talk, you really are creating your message in front of the audience.

How do you make an extemporaneous speech sound conversational yet evidence ample research and reflection? You should follow the steps of the audience-centered speaking process discussed in Chapters 11 and 12. You develop your message with a fine-tuned objective in mind. After developing your major ideas, organizing them, and supporting them with interesting and applicable supporting material, you prepare your outline, usually a full-content outline. With the content of your message in hand, you move to the rehearsal phase of preparation. As you rehearse your message, try to rely less on your notes, but don't memorize your message word for word. In fact, if you find yourself starting to say exactly the same things during rehearsal, stop rehearsing. You don't want to sound like a computer-generated voice—you want to sound live and immediate. As you master the overall structure of your message, you'll rely less on your notes and focus more on adapting your ideas to your audience. The final draft of your speaking notes may be an abbreviated outline or a few key words, facts, quotations, statistics, or other bits of information you don't want to commit to memory.

Effective Delivery Strategies

"Should I look over their heads so I don't get nervous?"

"Should I stand or sit when delivering my presentation?"

"What do I do with my hands while speaking?"

"Should I vary the pitch, rate, and intensity of my voice?"

The answers to these common questions about delivering a speech (No; It depends; It depends; and Yes) have important implications for you the next time you deliver a speech. However, you may need more than one-word responses to gain worthwhile insights about how to best deliver a presentation. In this section we'll offer tips about eye contact, gestures, posture, facial expression, vocal cues, and your personal appearance to help you deliver a speech with power and credibility.

Look Up: Maximize Eye Contact

Extemporaneous speaking
speaking from a written or memorized speech outline without having memorized the exact wording of the speech.

The most important tip to remember, if you do nothing else during a presentation, is to look at your listeners. As James Humes, famed speech writer for business leaders and several presidents, says, "There is only one rule you have to follow: *Never, never,*

RECAP: Methods of Delivery

Delivery Method	Description	Tips	Advantages	Disadvantages
Manuscript speaking	Reading your speech	Write like you speak. Use shorter sentences. Use personal pronouns (*I*), contractions (*don't* instead of *do not*), and be more redundant than when you write.	You can carefully craft your message, which is especially important when speaking to the media or when many people will monitor what you say. You can polish your language style.	Your speech may sound like it's being read. It takes considerable skill and effort to deliver a well-polished manuscript speech.
Memorized speaking	Giving a speech from memory with no notes	Use only for short messages. Budget time to rehearse your memorized message.	You can have eye contact with your listeners. Since you won't have notes, you can use gestures and move freely.	You run the risk of forgetting your speech. You may sound stilted and unnatural.
Impromptu speaking	Delivering a speech without advance preparation	Enumerate your main points. Be audience-centered. Organize. Be brief. Be honest, but monitor what you are saying.	You can easily and quickly adapt to your immediate audience. You'll deliver a spontaneous presentation without notes and with good eye contact.	Impromptu speeches may not be well organized. Because you've not prepared in advance, it's more difficult to offer appropriate evidence and other supporting material.
Extemporaneous speaking	Knowing the major ideas, which you have outlined, but not memorizing the exact words of a speech	Follow the steps for preparing a speech, including developing a full-content outline. Rehearse the speech until you know the overall structure of the message, but stop rehearsing when you start saying exactly the same words each time you rehearse.	It is well organized and well researched. Your speech sounds spontaneous and natural and yet is appropriately polished.	It takes considerable time to prepare an extemporaneous speech. It takes skill to deliver an extemporaneous speech so that it sounds natural.

never let words come out of your mouth when your eyes are looking down."[6] Known for being an excellent speaker, President Ronald Reagan used a specific technique to ensure maximum eye contact when delivering his presentations. He would look at his notes, make a mental "snapshot" of what he would say next, and then look up to deliver his lines.[7] For most Americans, having direct eye contact with audience members has been shown to increase speaker credibility and listener comprehension.[8] A study by one of your authors found that speakers with less than 50 percent eye contact are considered unfriendly, uninformed, inexperienced, and even dishonest by their listeners.[9] Don't look over listeners' heads (listeners know if you're not looking directly at them). Look at them and they will like you more and will be more likely to remember what you tell them.

Is there such a thing as too much eye contact? Probably not for most North American listeners. But you don't want to stare at just one person; that will likely make him or her uncomfortable. And be aware that not all people from all cultures prefer as much eye contact as North Americans do. Asians, for example, typically prefer less.

When it's your time to speak, walk to the lectern or the area where you've been asked to stand while speaking, pause briefly, and look at your audience before you say anything. Eye contact nonverbally sends the message "I am interested in you; tune me in; I have something I want to share with you." You should have your opening sentence firmly in mind so you can deliver it without looking at your notes or away from your listeners.[10]

Keep these eye contact tips in mind as you speak:

- Establish eye contact with the entire audience, not just with those in the front row or only one or two people.

- Make eye contact with individuals, establishing person-to-person contact with them—not so long that it will make a listener feel uncomfortable, but long enough to establish the feeling that you are talking directly to that individual.

- *Don't* look over your listeners' heads.

Move Meaningfully: Use Appropriate Gestures, Movement, and Posture

Nonverbal

When you write, you use punctuation, CAPITALIZATION, *italics*, and **boldface** to help your reader interpret your message and add emphasis to words. When you speak, gestures, movement, and your overall posture often serve those functions. You move to emphasize ideas, enumerate items, and describe objects.

Gestures. Some people (maybe you're one of them) gesture easily and appropriately during the course of everyday conversations, yet aren't sure what to do with their hands when they find themselves in front of an audience. If you don't know what to do with your hands, think about the message you want to express. As in ordinary conversation, your hands should simply help emphasize or reinforce your verbal message. As we discussed in Chapter 3, the specific functions of gestures include repeating, contradicting, substituting, complementing, emphasizing, and regulating your message.

- *Repeating:* You can say, " I have three major points to talk about this afternoon," while holding up three fingers.

- *Contradicting:* Because your listeners will believe what you communicate nonverbally, monitor your gestures to make sure that you are not contradicting what you say. It is difficult to convey an image of control and confidence while using flailing gestures and awkward poses.

- *Substituting:* Without uttering a word, you can hold up the palm of your hand to calm a noisy crowd. You can probably think of other gestures that substitute for a specific phrase or word and that powerfully communicate a message to listeners.

- *Complementing.* Complementing means using a gesture that adds to the meaning of your message. A CEO, for example, who declines to comment on a reporter's question while holding up her hands to augment her verbal refusal is relying on the gesture to add meaning to her verbal message.

- *Emphasizing.* A shaking fist, a fist pounded into the palm of your hand, or a slicing gesture with one or both hands can emphasize a point you're making.

- *Regulating.* If you want the audience to respond to a question, you can extend both palms to invite a response. Or, during a question-and-answer session, your gestures can signal when you want to talk and when you want to invite others to do so.

When you give a speech, your gestures should simply help emphasize or reinforce your verbal message, just as they do in ordinary conversation. A presentation to a small group requires much less dramatic gestures than one given to a large audience.

Here are some tips for using gestures when you speak in public:

- Focus on the message you want to communicate. Your gestures should naturally coincide with what you are saying.

- Be definite. If you want to gesture, go ahead and gesture. Avoid minor hand movements that may appear accidental to your audience.

- Vary your gestures. Don't use the same hand to gesture or one all-purpose gesture all of the time.

- Don't overdo your gestures. Listeners should focus on your message, not your gestures.

- Adapt your gestures to fit the situation. When speaking to a large audience in a formal setting, use bolder and larger gestures. For a smaller group, your gestures would likely be less dramatic.

- Adapt your gestures to the cultural expectations of your audience. Listeners from Asia, for example, typically prefer a quieter, less flamboyant use of gestures. British listeners seem to prefer a speaker to stay behind a lectern and use few gestures. Europeans often say they can spot an American speaker because Americans typically are more animated in the use of gestures, movement, and facial expression.

We've provided several do's and don'ts for using gestures, but the most important point about gestures is this: Use gestures that work best for you. Your gestures should fit your personality. It may be better to use no gestures—to just put your hands comfortably at your side—than to use distracting, awkward gestures or to try to mimic someone else's gestures.

Movement. Oprah Winfrey does it and so do many newscasters: They move around when they talk. When speaking in a business or professional situation, should you move when you speak? The best advice we can give you is to be aware of and adapt to the expectations of your listeners. If you're seated at a conference table and all of the other speakers have delivered their presentations while seated, then probably you should remain seated too, unless you purposely want to change the mood or momentum of the meeting. Consider these tips as you evaluate whether to add movement to your message.

Aware

Nonverbal

Adapt

- *Move—but don't distract listeners from your message.* You don't want your listeners to be thinking about your graceful movements; you want them to listen to your message. Movement should make sense—it should be neither artistic expression nor aimless meandering.

- *Move to reduce physical barriers.* Barriers such as a lectern, rows of chairs, or a projector may act as obstacles between you and your audience. If such physical barriers make you feel too far removed from your audience, move closer and reduce the physical separation.

- *Move to signal a new idea or tone.* Your movement can signal the beginning of a new idea or major point in your speech. As you move into a transition statement or change from a serious subject to a more lighthearted one, movement can be a good way to signal that your approach to the speaking situation is also changing.

Posture. Your posture is a strong nonverbal cue that communicates your credibility, power, and the overall intensity of your message. Research has found that a slumped-over, casual posture violates what listeners expect to see and can lower your credibility.[11] Whereas your face and voice play the major role in communicating a specific emotion, your posture communicates the intensity of that emotion. If you are happy, your smile and your laughter reflect your happiness; your upright posture and quick movements communicate the intensity of your joy. So make sure that your posture is consistent with your verbal message. Slouching lazily across a lectern does not communicate enthusiasm for or interest in your audience or topic. If you announce how happy you are to speak to an audience, yet your frozen posture expresses your discomfort, your listeners will believe your nonverbal message rather than your claim that you're pleased to be there.

Adapt your posture to your topic, your audience, and the formality or informality of the speaking occasion. For example, it may be perfectly appropriate, as well as comfortable and natural, to sit on the edge of a desk during a very informal presentation, such as a brief update on a project to a small team of colleagues. For a class presentation, however, most teachers frown on casually sitting on a desk and dangling your feet. In professional speaking sessions, always consider the expectations and culture of the audience members to guide you in the posture you adopt. An effective and audience-centered leader would tend to adopt a more formal posture to convey a professional approach.

Regardless of the specific situation, consider these suggestions to enhance your posture when speaking to others:

- *Plant your feet.* When standing, place your feet on the floor with one foot slightly in front of the other one; this will keep you from being tempted to sway from side to side. With one foot in front of the other one, you may move slightly forward and back, but this is less noticeable or distracting than swaying.

- *Stand tall.* To enhance your posture, pull your shoulders back a bit (as one posture expert suggests, "put your shoulders in your back pocket") and then imagine a string holding up the top of your head. Shoulders back, head up.

Like your gestures your posture should not call attention to itself. It should reflect your interest in and attention to your audience and your message.

Express Emotions: Use Appropriate Facial Expressions

Telling you to have a facial expression is like telling you to breathe; you can't help but have some kind of expression on your face. But the specific facial expression you display can be positive or negative, energetic or lethargic, expressive or neutral. Your audience sees your face before they hear what you are going to say. Thus, through your facial cues, you have an opportunity to set the emotional tone of your message before you utter a word.[12]

Throughout your presentation, your facial expression, like your body language and eye contact, should be appropriate to your message. Your face is the primary source of whatever specific emotion you communicate to your audience. The Roman orator Cicero said that you could help your listeners experience the emotion you wish them to experience by displaying the emotion yourself. If you want listeners to be joyful, you must express joy. To have them feel sorrow, communicate your sadness with your face. Not in a fake way—audience members can spot a phony—but with a facial expression that genuinely expresses how you feel. Present somber news with a serious expression. Tell a funny story with a smile.

Although humans are capable of producing thousands of different facial expressions, researchers have classified six primary emotions that are expressed on the face: happiness, anger, surprise, sadness, disgust, and fear.[13] But when we speak to others, our faces communicate a blend of expressions, rather than a single emotion. According to cross-cultural studies by social psychologist Paul Ekman, facial expressions conveying emotions are virtually universal; in most situations even a culturally diverse audience will be able to interpret your emotional expressions.[14]

Consider these suggestions to enhance your use of facial expressions when speaking to others:

- *Be aware of your facial expressions.* When you rehearse your speech, stand in front of a mirror or, better yet, videotape yourself. Note whether you are allowing your face to help communicate the emotional tone of your thoughts.

- *Ensure that your facial expression supports your verbal message.* As we've suggested throughout our discussion of delivery, your nonverbal message should be consistent with your verbal message.

- *Ask someone to watch you rehearse, paying special attention to your facial expressions.*

Look Good: Monitor Personal Appearance

What you wear tells people how you wish to be treated. For example, wearing jeans and a T-shirt to class says, "I just want to blend in with other students." Wearing a business

---

Audience members attending a speech by Steve Jobs, CEO of Apple, would likely be surprised if he appeared in a suit and tie. Remember to adapt your personal appearance to the norms of the situation so that you meet your audience's expectations.

suit to an upscale office says, "I want to be perceived as credible and competent like my colleagues." Your personal appearance affects how other people respond to you and your message. A key principle to keep in mind when monitoring personal appearance is to adapt to the norms of your situation. At the California corporate offices of Google, for example, casual clothing is the norm. Someone who wore a coat and tie or a dressy suit would not be perceived as part of the team. Whenever possible, monitor the audience's dress code before deciding what to wear or what not to wear.

Go to any bookstore or browse through magazines such as *GQ*, *Vogue*, *Vogue for Men*, or *Cosmo* and you'll find many fashion mavens prescribing how to "dress for success." Some advocate specific colors and styles of suits, ties, dresses, and skirts. Although these books and magazines offer some useful contemporary fashion guidelines, the ultimate judge of your style choices is not a fashion editor from New York or Paris, but the people in your audience. Steve Jobs, CEO of Apple, typically wears jeans and a black turtleneck sweater. Bill Gates often leaves his tie at home in favor of an open-collared shirt. Our point is that you should be wary of "one-size-fits-all" prescriptions for how to dress. Fashion styles change. What doesn't change is this: If you violate your listeners' expectations or the style or culture of the organization where you are making a presentation, you will be less successful in achieving your purpose.

Consider these general guidelines to help you adapt your personal appearance for maximum credibility.

- *Take cues from your audience.* If you're presenting to the sales force and they will be dressed casually, you should be, too. If you know that they will be dressed in more formal business attire, dress similarly.

- *If you're in doubt about the dress code, ask someone who is familiar with the audience and the occasion to help you decide whether to dress up or dress down.*

- *Dress better than your audience members.* Your grooming and attention to appearance suggest that you care about your listeners and have given special thought to how you will be perceived by them.

- *Never wear clothing that would be potentially distracting—for example, a shirt or blouse that displays printing that advertises something unrelated to your topic.* You want your listeners to listen to you, not read you.

- *When in doubt, select clothing that is conservative.* You want your listener to focus on your message, not on your wardrobe.

Speak Clearly: Use Appropriate Vocal Delivery

Have you ever heard a radio announcer's voice and conjured up a mental image of what the person looks like, based only on the sound of his or her voice, only to see a photo and discover that your mental picture is completely inaccurate? Your voice is a powerful projector of personality, energy, and overall credibility. As a leader, you can influence others not only with the power of your ideas, but with the power of your vocal delivery. We don't mean you need to shout or try to sound like someone you're not—but thoughtfully monitoring your voice can help you enhance your leadership image.

Vocal delivery includes volume, pitch, rate, articulation, pronunciation, and dialect. A business or professional speaker has at least two important vocal obligations to an audience: Speak to be understood, and speak to maintain interest.

Speaking to be understood. To be understood, consider four aspects of your vocal delivery: volume, articulation, pronunciation, and dialect.

Your speaking *volume*—how loud or soft your voice is—is the most fundamental aspect of your voice. The volume of your speech is determined by the amount of air you project through your larynx, or voice box. More air results in a louder sound. Your diaphragm, a muscle in your upper abdomen, helps control sound volume by increasing air flow from your lungs through your voice box. Breathing from your diaphragm—that is, consciously expanding and contracting your abdomen as you breathe in and out—can increase the volume of sound as well as enhance the quality of your voice.

With many speakers the problem is not the volume of the voice, but a lack of intensity. You can enhance the intensity of your voice by increasing vocal energy using a combination of increased volume, varied pitch, and clear articulation of speech sounds.

Articulation is the enunciation of speech sounds. You should articulate distinctly to ensure that your audience can clearly determine what words you are using.

Many errors in articulation result from bad habits, from emulating the sounds of others who use poor articulation, or from simple laziness. It takes more energy to articulate speech sounds clearly. Sometimes we are in a hurry to express our ideas, but more often we simply get into the habit of mumbling, slurring, or abbreviating—saying "dint" instead of "didn't" or "lemme" instead of "let me." Such vocal flaws may not keep your audience from understanding you, but poor enunciation does reflect on your credibility as a speaker.

How do you improve your articulation? First, identify words or phrases that you have a tendency to slur or cut short. Once you have identified these, practice saying the words correctly. Work to hear the difference between improper and proper articulation. Listen to the way newscasters or other media announcers articulate speech sounds. Consult a dictionary, which, in addition to defining words, provides guidelines for articulating the sound of words.

Whereas articulation refers to the clarity of speech sounds, *pronunciation* is the degree to which words conform to standard English. Mispronouncing words can detract from your credibility. You may not be aware that you're mispronouncing a word unless someone tells you.

Some speakers reverse speech sounds, saying "aks" instead of "ask." Some allow an *r* sound to intrude into some words, saying "warsh" instead of "wash," or "Warshington" instead of "Washington." Another common pronunciation error is to leave out sounds in the middle of words, as in "ackchally" instead of "actually" or "Febuary" instead of "February." Some speakers accent syllables in nonstandard ways; they say "po´lice" instead of "police" or "um´brella" rather than "umbrella."

If English is not your native language, you may have to spend extra time working on your pronunciation and articulation. Try these strategies:

- Make an effort to prolong vowel sounds. Speeeeeak tooooo proooo-loooooong eeeeach voooowel sooooound yoooou maaaaake. Such exaggerations of speech sounds will help you become more aware of how to avoid clipping vowel sounds.[15]

- To reduce choppy-sounding pronunciation, blend the end of one word into the beginning of the next. Make your speech flow from one word to the next, instead of separating it into individual chunks of sound.

A **dialect** is a consistent style of pronouncing words that is common to an ethnic group or a geographic region such as the South, New England, or the upper Midwest. In the southern part of the United States, people prolong some vowel sounds when they speak. And in the northern Midwest and Canada, the word *about* sometimes sounds a bit like "a boat."

Although a speaker's dialect may classify the person as being from a certain part of the country, it won't necessarily affect an audience's comprehension of information unless the dialect is so pronounced that the listeners can't understand the speaker's words. Research does suggest, however, that listeners tend to prefer a dialect similar to their own.[16] If your word pronunciation is significantly distracting to your listeners, you might considering modifying your dialect (although radically altering a dialect is difficult and time consuming). However, you don't want to try to develop a fake dialect—unless you have the acting skill of Meryl Streep or Tom Hanks, people will be able to detect that your dialect is phony.

Articulation the enunciation of speech sounds.

Dialect a consistent style of pronunciation and articulation that is common to an ethnic group or a geographic region.

Speaking to maintain interest. Listeners dislike a monotone delivery. Effective speakers have vocal variety—they vary their vocal pitch and speaking rate and use pauses for emphasis. Vocal variety is a key way we express our emotions and our interest. Appropriate vocal variation adds zest to your speech and helps your listeners maintain their focus on your message.[17]

Vocal **pitch** is how high or low your voice sounds. When you sing, your pitch changes to produce a melody. When you speak, your pitch also has a natural variation. Not varying your vocal pitch is one of the worst things you can do while speaking; a monotone voice is boring.

Everyone has a habitual pitch. This is the range of the voice during normal conversation. Regardless of your habitual pitch, it's important to have a varied inflection when you speak. Vocal **inflection** is the variation in pitch as you pronounce words or sounds. Your inflection helps determine the meaning of your utterances. A disappointed "Ah" sounds different from a surprised "Ah!" or a quizzical "Ah?"

For English-speaking people, vocal inflection adds interest and helps communicate emotions and subtle nuances of meaning. In some languages, vocal inflection plays a significant role in determining the meanings of words. Thai, Vietnamese, and Mandarin Chinese languages use such inflections as monotone, low, falling, high, and rising inflections to vary the meaning of messages.[18] If you are a native speaker of a language in which pitch influences meaning, be aware that listeners do not expect these kinds of variations in many Western languages, although all languages rely on some variation in inflection to communicate emotions and nuances of meaning.

In addition to pitch, another way you express your interest and energy is by your speaking *rate*. Most speakers average between 120 and 180 words per minute. At the upper end of that range you'd be speaking at a fairly fast clip. The ideal speaking rate depends on the topic, the occasion, your own natural style of speaking, and the preferences of your audience.

Sometimes when speakers are nervous they speak rapidly. This is because their anxiety leads to an increase in adrenaline and thus extra energy; speaking rapidly is a manifestation of their anxiousness.

Effective speakers vary their speaking rate. You need not deliver your entire speech at the same pace. When you are excited or wish to communicate excitement and interest, speak faster. Slow your pace to emphasize an idea. As with any aspect of delivery, you don't want listeners to focus on your speaking rate—you want them to focus on your message. The pace of your delivery should make sense in terms of the ideas you are sharing with your listeners.

Your use of well-timed *pauses* can greatly enhance the overall impact of your message. Whether you are trying to tell a joke, a serious tale, or a dramatic story, your use of a pause can determine the effectiveness of your anecdote.

Although pauses can add impact and dramatic effect, many beginning speakers are uncomfortable with silent pauses and fill them with "Umm," "Er," "You know," and "Ah." Try to avoid making these unnecessary vocalizations.

Silence can be an effective tool in adding emphasis to a particular word or sentence. A well-timed pause coupled with eye contact can powerfully accent your idea. Silence is a way of saying to your listeners, "Think about this for a moment."

Speak Up: Tips for Using a Microphone

In many business and professional settings, especially with a large audience, you will be expected to use a microphone so that all your listeners can hear you clearly. There have been some classic blunders when speakers didn't know the microphone was on, including the story of President Ronald Reagan, who, while doing a microphone check, instead of saying the proverbial "Testing, one, two, three," said, "My fellow Americans, I am pleased to tell you today, I've signed legislation that will outlaw Russia forever. We begin bombing in five minutes." The microphone was live! Not funny—for either the Russians or President Reagan's spokesperson, who had some explaining to do.[19]

You would do well to be mindful of the power of a microphone to amplify your message. If, during a panel discussion, you make an amplified unflattering comment about a fellow panelist (or anybody else), you will not have the clout of a U.S. president to help you. A good guideline: Any time you're near a microphone, assume that it's on.

Pitch how high or low a speaker's voice is.

Inflection variation in vocal pitch.

You will likely encounter one of two kinds of microphones. A lavaliere microphone is the clip-on type often used by newspeople and interviewees. Worn on a collar or lapel, it requires no particular care other than not thumping it or accidentally knocking it off. In contrast, a stationary microphone is attached to a lectern, sits on a desk, or stands on the floor. Generally, the stationary mikes used today are multidirectional. You don't have to remain absolutely anchored to the floor in front of a stationary microphone while delivering your speech—it can pick up your voice even if you're a couple of feet away. Regardless of the type of microphone you use, here are a few tips for using it well.

- Microphones amplify sloppy habits of pronunciation and articulation. You'll need to speak clearly and crisply when using a mike. Be especially careful when articulating *b* and *p* sounds; they can be overamplified and produce slight popping sounds. Microphones can also intensify the sibilance of the *s* sound at the beginning or ending of words. You may have to articulate these sounds with slightly less intensity to avoid overamplifying them.

- If you must test a microphone, ask the audience whether they can hear you. Blowing on an active mike produces an irritating noise. Just say "microphone test" or "one, two, three" in your normal speaking voice.

- Don't tap or pound the microphone or shuffle anything nearby. If you are using note cards, quietly slide them aside as you progress through your speech. Full sheets of paper are more difficult to handle quietly; if you must use them, try to shuffle them as quietly as you can.

- When you are delivering your presentation, talk directly into the microphone at your normal volume. Some speakers lower their volume and become inaudible when they have a microphone in front of them.

- If you can, practice before you speak with the type of microphone you will use. If you have the opportunity, conduct the microphone test before your audience arrives. Practicing in the room where you will be speaking will help you adapt to echoes or other distortions so that these sounds don't surprise you during your presentation.

Adapting Your Presentation for Television

Whether your message will be broadcast on national TV, transmitted throughout your company on the Internet, or presented during a videoconference, it is increasingly likely that you will deliver a presentation that will be conveyed via video transmission. Should you use a different style of speaking when your message will be on TV? For the most part, you'll follow the same guidelines for delivery we've already discussed. Good eye contact, varied vocal inflection, and appropriate posture and gestures are expected, but consider these strategies if there is a video camera present.

Consider toning down your gestures. You don't need to use large sweeping gestures when speaking via TV. Dramatic gestures that are appropriate when addressing a large audience will likely appear too demonstrative on TV. Most newscasters use subtle head nods and facial expressions rather than gestures to emphasize their points. Use fewer gestures, and don't fidget with pens, your hair, or your clothing. Also, keep your hands away from your face. When you watch someone on TV, it's more like having an interpersonal conversation than hearing a formal oration. If your primary audience is the live audience in the room when you present your message, then that should be the key audience to whom you adapt your speaking style. But if the target audience is watching on monitors elsewhere, tone down the gestures a bit.

Dress for TV success. White clothing can sometimes create a glare on TV depending on the quality of the camera. Men who do not plan to wear a jacket may want to wear a light blue rather than a white dress shirt, and women should also consider nonwhite clothing. Avoid large patterns, jangling or shiny jewelry, and overly frilly or complicated necklines, especially if you're being televised in high-definition TV. Solid colors typically look best.

The camera can add five to ten pounds to your appearance. You don't need to go on a crash diet, but do wear clothes that make you look and feel your best.

Monitor your facial expressions.   Because TV amplifies your facial expressions, your listeners are seeing your expression up close rather than from a distance. Therefore, if you have a tendency to use exaggerated or dramatic facial expressions, realize that they will be seen from the camera's perspective rather than from the audience's perspective. Smile appropriately, but make sure you're not smiling at inappropriate times. If you are asked a serious question about company layoffs but you have a big grin on your face when the camera cuts to you, it will appear that you are insensitive to the question.

Keep it short.   If you are speaking for the media, realize you will only be given a few seconds (or sound bites) of airtime. Short answers, short phrases, quotable lines are what editors are looking for.

Choose your words with care and style.   The sound bites that often are broadcast are those phrases that are particularly memorable or attention catching. Repeating key words, speaking in parallel structures, and using alliteration and other stylistic devices enhance the likelihood that your message will be quoted or broadcast.

Become familiar with the technology before you speak.   If you are being taped or broadcast from a studio, be sure to arrive in plenty of time so that you won't have to rush around making last-minute adjustments to your microphone.

RECAP: Characteristics of Effective Nonverbal Delivery

- Gestures should be relaxed, definite, varied, and appropriate to your audience and the speaking situation.
- Movement should be purposeful.
- Posture should feel natural and be appropriate to your topic, your audience, and the occasion.
- Eye contact should be established before you say anything and sustained as much as possible throughout your presentation.
- Facial expression should be alert, friendly, and appropriate to your message.
- Volume should be loud enough that you can be easily heard and should be purposefully varied.
- Vocal pitch should be varied so that the inflection in your voice helps to sustain your audience's interest.
- Speaking rate should be neither too fast nor too slow and can be varied to add interest and emphasize key ideas.
- Speech articulation should be clear and distinct.

Responding to Questions

Often the sale is made or lost, or your client decides whether you get the contract, during the Q & A (question and answer) portion of your presentation. During a Q & A period following a prepared presentation, your delivery methods change to impromptu speaking. In addition to the strategies for impromptu speaking that we offered earlier, here are additional tips to make a Q & A period effective. [20]

Prepare. How can you prepare for a question that hasn't been asked yet? Anticipate the kinds of questions listeners may have and prepare responses to those. How do you anticipate questions? You analyze your audience. Think of possible questions those particular listeners might ask you, and then rehearse your answers.

Repeat or rephrase the question.   There are several reasons why it's a good idea to repeat questions. First, your restatement makes sure that everyone can hear the question. Second, paraphrasing ensures that *you* understand the question before you respond. Third, by paraphrasing, you can succinctly summarize long, rambling questions. And finally, by repeating the question, you give yourself more time to think about your answer.

Ask yourself the first question. One way to prime the audience to ask questions is to ask yourself a challenging question first. For example, you might say, "As we move into the question and answer portion of the presentation, several of you may be wondering . . . ." State the question and answer it. Doing this also gives you a comfortable way to make a transition between the presentation and the Q & A period. Asking yourself a tough question tells the audience that you're open for serious questions and that they'll have your attention.

Stay on message. Sometimes listeners may ask questions unrelated to your talk. If so, you'll want to find a way to gently guide your questioner back to the message you have presented. Your answers, rather than the questions, are what are important. We're not suggesting that you dodge questions, but you can ensure that your key ideas remain the focus of the Q & A session. Some seasoned speakers suggest that you save a bit of your presentation to deliver during the Q & A session. It's called giving a "double-barreled" talk.[21] You first deliver your presentation, and then, during the Q & A period, you give your second, much briefer talk.

Listen carefully and nonjudgmentally. Your listeners expect you to be polite and attentive. When you listen to questions, keep your eyes focused on the person asking the question and lean forward slightly to communicate your attentiveness. If you think a question is stupid, don't say so. Just listen and respond courteously. Audience members will judge for themselves whether a question was appropriate or not. Don't wince, grimace, or scowl at the questioner. You'll gain more credibility by keeping your cool than by losing your composure.

Neutralize hostile questions. We're not suggesting that you should celebrate when you get a hostile or mean-spirited question, but such a question gives you opportunity to score points with your listeners. Why? Because you'll have your listeners' attention; use that attention to your advantage. Here are some tips to help you do that.

- *Restate the question.* If the question was a lengthy diatribe attacking you, focus on the essence of the issue. If the question is "Your ideas are just stupid! I'm angry that you have no idea how to proceed. The program has been a complete failure. Why are you still trying to make it work?" a paraphrase could be, "You're asking me why I'm still trying to make a program successful. From your perspective, the program has failed."

- *Acknowledge emotions.* For example, you could say, "I can certainly understand why you're angry. I share your anger and frustration. It's because of my frustration that I want to give my proposal more time to work."

- *Don't make the issue personal.* Even if the question has made you the villain, don't counterattack the questioner. Keep the conversation focused on issues, not personalities.

- *Get to the heart of the issue.* Respond directly to a hostile question. Consider restating the evidence you presented. Or provide a new example to support your position. A hostile listener is more likely to be persuaded with evidence and facts than by opinions or increased vocal volume.

- *When you don't know the answer, admit it.* It's better to admit you don't know an answer to a question than to try to fake it. Promise to find out more information and get back to the person later. And if you make such a promise, follow through on it.

- *Be brief.* Make your responses short and to the point.

Use organizational signposts. Listeners will be impressed if you can enumerate the number of points you'll make in response to a question. For example, you might say, "I have two responses to your question." When you get to your second point, say, "My second point is . . . ." Signposts will both help you stay organized and impress your listeners with your clarity.

Signal when the Q & A period is concluding. You might say to the audience, "I have time for two more questions." Let them know that the Q & A session will soon conclude. Even if you have someone helping you moderate the discussion, you should remain in control of concluding the presentation.

Presentation Aids

Because of the power of visual image, Jared Fogel has helped to make Fred Deluca, cofounder of Subway sandwiches, rich. Photos of Jared when he weighed 425 pounds, before he shed 245 pounds eating Subway sandwiches, are startling when compared to the new, slimmer 180-pound Jared who appears in Subway's TV ads. Subway's pitch that their sandwiches are a healthy alternative to other fast food choices has been successful— Subway is second in sales to McDonald's—because people can *see* for themselves that if you eat lower-fat sandwiches you can lose weight. So thanks in part to a trimmer Jared, Fred Deluca now makes an estimated one million dollars a week.[22]

Seeing is indeed believing when it comes to communicating to others. Because visual information can be so powerful, we now turn our attention to the visual (and sometimes auditory) support that audience members see (and hear) when you supplement your speech with presentation aids.

In many professional settings, you'll be expected to use some kind of presentation aid when you speak. A **presentation aid** is any object or image that reinforces your point visually so that your listeners can better understand it. Today's audiences often expect to see PowerPoint slides, those ubiquitous computer-generated lists of bulleted words, phrases, images, and even video; if you don't use professional-looking presentation aids, you'll lose credibility. In this section, we offer tips, pointers, and strategies to make sure you gain rather than lose credibility when using presentation aids.

Why Use Presentation Aids?

The short answer to the question "Why use presentation aids?" is "For many professional presentations, you're expected to." But there are several research-based reasons why presentation aids enhance professional presentations.[23]

Enhanced understanding. People are more likely to comprehend what they can both see and hear. Because your audience has become accustomed to visual reinforcement by watching TV and images on the Internet, it is wise to consider how you can increase their understanding of your message by using presentation aids.[24]

Enhanced memory. It's well known that you remember most what you understand best. Your listeners will not only have an improved understanding of your presentation, they will also better remember what you say as a result of visual reinforcement.

Enhanced organization. Listing major ideas on a chart, a poster, or a PowerPoint slide can add clarity to your talk and help your audience understand your overall organizational strategy. Using verbal signposts ("I have three points. My first point is . . .") and clear transition statements is helpful, but visually displaying your major points ensures that your listeners understand your presentation's architecture.

Enhanced attention. Appropriate and well-chosen presentation aids not only can grab the attention of your listeners but also can maintain interest when words alone might not. Rather than just describe the new manufacturing plant, show a picture of it.

Enhanced sequencing. If you're giving a "how to" or training presentation, visually listing the steps or procedures in a process can help your audience understand a step-by-step process. Showing rather than just describing how to do something is more likely to teach your audience how to perform a task or function.

Types of Presentation Aids

Almost anything tangible can be used as a presentation aid, including objects, models, photos, graphs, charts, videos, and audio recordings. Perhaps the most pervasive presentation aid in business and professional settings is PowerPoint slides. Because of the importance and ubiquity of PowerPoint, we'll give special emphasis to the dos and don'ts of PowerPoint in a later section. For now, let's consider the various types of presentation aids a speaker might use.

Objects. Objects add interest because they are tangible. They can be touched, smelled, heard, or even tasted, as well as seen. Make sure any object you use is large enough to be

Presentation aid any tangible item or image used to help communicate ideas to an audience.

seen clearly by your listeners. One powerful prop you can use is a copy of the daily newspaper if you are referring to a late-breaking news event—it adds immediacy, and you can connect the events of the day with your topic.

Models. If it is not possible to bring the object you would like to show your audience, consider showing them a model. Again, make sure the model is big enough for your listeners to see.

Drawings. Today, unless they are artists, most speakers use computer-generated drawings. Yet there may be some situations in which a small freehand drawing on a flipchart or whiteboard may be more appropriate, such as when you want to show a very simple diagram.

Photographs. A photo can show objects, places, and people that can't be illustrated with drawings or that an audience cannot view directly. To be sure that a printed photo will be effective as a presentation aid for a large audience, enlarge it or project it. A digital photo can be easily added to a PowerPoint presentation.

Graphs. A graph is a pictorial representation of statistical data in an easy-to-understand format. Most listeners find that graphs help make data more concrete. Graphs are particularly effective in showing overall trends and relationships among data. The four most common types of graphs are line graphs, bar graphs, pie graphs, and picture graphs. Presentation software programs such as PowerPoint let you quickly and easily create charts and graphs.

Line graphs show relationships between two or more variables and they organize statistical data to show overall trends. A line graph can cover a greater span of time or numbers than a bar graph without looking cluttered or confusing. A simple line graph, as in Figures 13.1 and 13.2, communicates better than a cluttered one.

A **bar graph** consists of flat areas—bars—of various lengths to represent data or information, as shown in Figure 13.3.

A **pie graph** shows the general distribution of data. Pie graphs are especially useful in helping your listeners quickly see how data are distributed in a given category, as in Figure 13.4.

Picture graphs look less formal and less intimidating than other kinds of graphs. One of the advantages of picture graphs is that they need few words or labels, which makes them easier for your audience to read.

Figure 13.1 | Line Graph

Sales Growth of Designer Jeans

(Line graph showing Online sales and In-store sales, Millions on y-axis from 1 to 7, years 2005–2009 on x-axis)

Line graph a graph that shows trends over time and relationships among variables.

Bar graph a graph that uses bars of different lengths to represent statistical data.

Pie graph a circular graph that shows the distribution of data as a proportion of a total.

Figure 13.2	**Line Area Graph**[25]

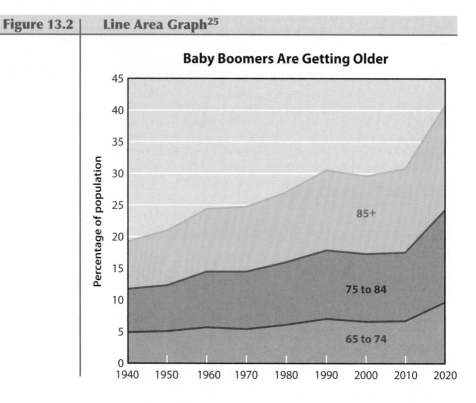

Charts. Charts summarize and present a great deal of information in a small amount of space. They are easy to use, reuse, and enlarge. They can also be displayed in a variety of ways. You can use a flipchart, a poster, or an overhead projector, which can project a giant image of your chart on a screen. Simple, professional-looking, large charts using a large font, such as 24-point type, are best. Figure 13.5 shows an example of a chart.

Flipcharts. A flipchart consists of a large pad of paper resting on an easel. You can either prepare your visual aids on the paper before your presentation or draw on the paper while speaking. Flipcharts are easy to use; during your presentation, you need only flip the page to reveal or create your next visual. Flipcharts are best used when you have brief information to display or when you want to summarize comments from audience members during a presentation.

Figure 13.3	**Bar Graph**[26]

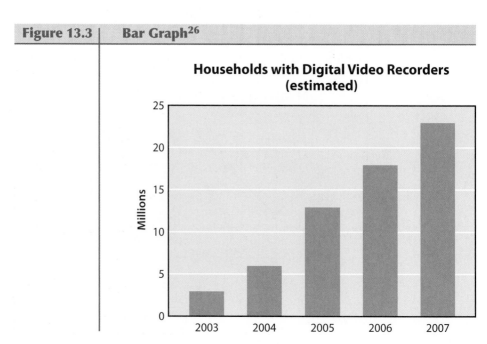

Figure 13.4 | Pie Graph[27]

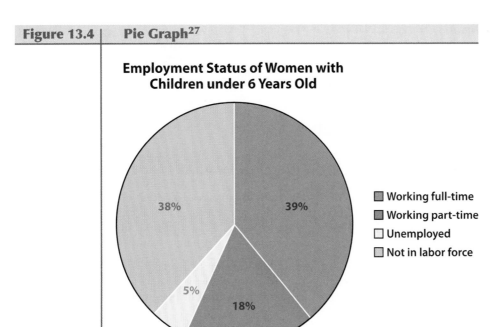

Employment Status of Women with Children under 6 Years Old

39%

38%

18%

5%

- ◼ Working full-time
- ◼ Working part-time
- ☐ Unemployed
- ◼ Not in labor force

Overhead transparencies.   Overhead projectors project images drawn on clear sheets of plastic, called *transparencies*, onto a screen so that a large group can see the images. They enable you to maintain eye contact with your audience yet still see your visuals. The overhead doesn't require that you turn off the lights in the room. Overhead projectors also permit you to prepare your transparencies ahead of time and to mark on them during your presentation. If you do write on your transparencies during your presentation, limit yourself to writing a few short words or underlining key phrases.

Like other types of presentation aids, overhead transparencies are being replaced by PowerPoint slides. But many speakers make a backup set of overhead transparencies to use in case there is a problem with the PowerPoint slides.

Video.   DVDs (digital video disks) let you project short clips of movies or other video images for your audience. DVDs have replaced videotapes as the means of showing an audience a movie because of the ease of finding, freezing, and cueing up a video image. With a video camera, you can, if you need to, make your own video images of things you'd like your audience to see and hear. The key to using any video image is to make sure that the video selection doesn't take over your presentation. In most instances, short clips will be best.

Figure 13.5 | Chart[28]

Marital Status in the United States

Status	Number (rounded)	Percent
Population 15 years old and over	221,000,000	100.0
Never married	60,000,000	27
Married (not separated)	120,000,000	54
Married but separated	5,000,000	2
Widowed	15,000,000	7
Divorced	22,000,000	10

Audio. You may decide to support your message with sound as well as visual images. A CD player or a tape player may be just what you need to play a short excerpt of music or an interview you've recorded. As with video, don't let the audio sound track become the primary focus of the message. Used sparingly, audio aids can help set a mood or illustrate a point.

Using Presentation Aids

It's one thing to select a presentation aid and prepare it; it's quite another task to actually use your presentation aid in your talk. Just as there is an art to developing presentation aids, there is an art to using them. As you review the following list of suggestions, you may think that some of them are fairly obvious (like making sure that the presentation aid is big enough to be seen). However, even some of the most seasoned presenters violate these tips and techniques. Use these suggestions as a final checklist to ensure that you don't end up as a textbook example of what not to do when using presentation aids.

Rehearse with your presentation aid. The opening sentences of your sales presentation to the marketing team extolling the virtues of the new product should *not* be the first time you use your PowerPoint slides. Practice with your presentation aids until you feel at ease with them.

Make eye contact with your audience, not with your presentation aid. Don't be tempted to talk to your presentation aid rather than to your audience. Your focus should remain on your audience. Of course, you will need to glance at your visual aid to make sure that it's the correct one and it isn't upside down. But do not keep looking at your PowerPoint slide, chart, or poster; keep making eye contact with your audience.

Talk about your presentation aid, don't just show it. "Well, here are our production statistics for the second quarter," says Meredith. "Now let's move to the third quarter. And here are the fourth-quarter statistics." Don't do what Meredith just did—she simply projected information and data without explaining. Remember that a presentation is a talk, not just a slide show. Visual support performs the same function as verbal support. It helps you communicate an idea. Make sure that your audience knows what that idea is.

Be sure to rehearse with your presentation aid and to time its display to control your audience's attention. A skilled presenter knows when to show a presentation aid and when to put it away.

Do not pass objects among members of your audience. It's usually not a good idea to pass a small object or handout around from listener to listener while you are speaking. Why? Because the listeners will stop being listeners and will focus on the object that is coming their way; you lose control over your listeners. It may be best to let people observe your object after your talk. Or, if the audience is only two or three rows deep, you can hold up the object and move in close to audience members to show it while you maintain focus and control.

Use handouts effectively. Audiences in many business and professional settings often expect to be looking at written material you've distributed while they are listening to your presentation. The problem is, however, that your listeners may focus on the written message instead of on your oral message. Consider these tips for using handouts:

• Only distribute handouts during the presentation if your listeners must refer to the material while you're talking about it. If your listeners don't need to have the handout material while you speak, tell them you will distribute a summary of the key ideas at the end of your talk.

- If you see that your listeners are giving the written material more attention than they are giving you, tell them where in the handout you want them to focus. For example, you could say, "I see that many of you are interested in the third page of the report. I'll discuss those points in just a few moments. Let's look at the information on page one."

- After distributing your handouts, ask audience members to keep the material face down until you're ready to talk about it; this will help listeners focus on you rather than on your handout.

- Number the pages of your handout material so you can easily and quickly direct audience members to specific pages. You may even add numbers to paragraphs to help point your listeners to specific passages.

- By projecting the handout on an overhead projector or a PowerPoint slide, you can nonverbally let your audience members know which page of the material they should be looking at.

Time the use of visuals to control your listeners' attention. A skilled presenter knows when to show a supporting visual and when to put it away. It's typically not a wise idea to begin your speech with splashy, eye-popping graphs or charts while you are presenting your opening remarks. Your visuals would just compete with your verbal message. Time the display of your visuals to coincide with your discussion of the information contained in them.

- Remove your visual aids when you move to your next point.

- Have your PowerPoint or overhead projector image already cued up and ready to display.

- If necessary, ask a colleague beforehand to help you change slides or transparencies; if you do ask someone to assist you, it's best to have a short rehearsal so that the presentation is professional and polished.

No matter what medium you plan to use, you should give your audience enough time to absorb what you place in front of their eyes and to listen carefully to your verbal message before asking them to shift their attention to another image.

Designing Presentation Aids

Whether you are using PowerPoint slides, a whiteboard, or a flipchart, there are some basic principles to keep in mind when designing visual images for a speech. Although we'll offer several specific suggestions for developing PowerPoint slides later in the chapter, the following suggestions are basic principles of "visual rhetoric" that can help you develop appealing as well as effective visual messages.[29]

Make them easy to see. The most violated principle of visual aids is also the most basic: Make visual images and words large enough to be seen easily by everyone in your audience. If you don't do anything else, do this: Make messages big.

Make them simple. Simple and brief are usually better than cluttered and lengthy. Limit text to essential words or phrases. If you have a considerable amount of information, use two or three simple charts or slides rather than putting all of your information on one visual. Keep the emphasis on your speech rather than on your visual message. Simple drawings and easy-to-grasp images or pictures have more power than images that take the viewer a long time to decipher.

"For God's sake, Edwards. Put the laser pointer away."

Cluster related elements. By grouping related points, you can help your audience understand key concepts and grasp relationships as you convey your information. Grouping points also frees up space, which in turn highlights text blocks and provides a resting place for the eye.

The alignment you choose for your text and images also affects the open space on the visual aid and directs the reader's eye. Alignment can be flush left, flush right, or centered. Centered alignment is often effective for titles, but centered body text can be difficult to read. A flush left or right alignment makes the text look crisp and allows the eye to move easily from point to point.

Develop a consistent visual theme.   Choose one basic design and color scheme and use it throughout your presentation. Repeating words, symbols, styles, or fonts throughout the presentation conveys a sense of unity. Yes, repetition can be boring, so you may want to vary your visuals a little, but keep in mind that a consistent graphic theme will help your audience process and remember complex information.

Communicate numerical data visually.   Numbers and statistical summaries are abstract. Listeners like concrete, visual information. A well-developed graph can often convey the information that you wish to present without requiring your audience to absorb and interpret complex numerical data. If your listeners need or want more detailed data, consider sharing it with them in a handout that you distribute after your talk. If you absolutely must present complex data during your talk, walk the audience through the information rather than just pointing to a number-laden sheet of paper or briefly displaying a complex graph.

Choose a font with care.   A font is a typeface of a particular style and design. Font size is measured in points; a point is 1/72 of an inch. The larger the point size, the larger the letters.

A single font (typeface) includes a collection of uppercase and lowercase letters, as well as numbers, symbols, and punctuation that have a consistent structure and form. Each font has a name, and many have variations in size, weight, and spacing. Fonts are divided into four types: serif, sans serif, script, and decorative, as shown in Figure 13.6.

1. **Serif fonts** (like those in the text you are reading) have lines (serifs) at the tops and bottoms of the letters. Serif fonts are easier to read for longer passages, because the serifs guide the eye from one letter to the next.

2. **Sans serif fonts** do not have extra lines, and all the lines in the letters are of uniform thickness.

3. **Script fonts** imitate handwriting, but are precise and uniform. They can be fancy and complicated as well as hard to read, so be cautious about using them.

4. **Decorative fonts** are designed to convey a feeling or tone. The letters in a decorative font may even be stylized drawings (for example, flowers) in the shape of letters. Use these fonts sparingly for emphasis.

Regardless of the style of font you use, your visuals must be big enough to be seen by people in the back row of your audience. Consider using 44-point type for titles, 32-point type for subtitles or for text if there is no subtitle, and 28-point type for the text if there is also a subtitle.

Avoid using all uppercase letters for emphasis, except in short titles. Longer stretches of text in ALL CAPS are hard to read, because our eyes are accustomed to seeing contrasting letter shapes. When we read, we recognize not only the individual letters, but also the shapes of the words.

Use color to create a mood and maintain attention.   Graphic designers have long known that warm colors (oranges and reds) communicate excitement and interest. (Note that fast-food restaurants often use red, yellow, or orange in their color schemes to create excitement and stimulate hunger.) Warm colors tend to come forward, whereas cool colors, such as green and blue, have a more calming effect and recede into the background. Consider using warm colors for positive messages (for example, "Profits are up") and cool colors for more negative messages ("We're losing money").

Design for contrast.   If you're designing PowerPoint slides or overheads, consider using dark type on a light background. Black, dark blue, or dark red type will stand out crisply from a white, light gray, or light yellow background. Two different colors of text on one background color are usually sufficient. To unify your presentation, consider using the same color for all of your backgrounds, and then varying the complementary colors you use for the text. The use of purple, for example, against a blue background is not effective; both colors are dark, so the purple letters don't stand out. Yellow against a blue background is more effective because the colors are contrasting yet harmonious. Be cautious about using green and red together; the combination is difficult to read and people who are color-blind will not be able to distinguish between these two colors.

Serif font a font that has lines (serifs) at the tops and bottoms of the letters.

Sans serif font a font without lines (serifs) at the tops and bottoms of letters and with letters of uniform thickness.

Script font a font that imitates handwriting, but is precise and uniform.

Decorative font a font designed to convey a feeling or tone.

Figure 13.6 | Typefaces Grouped by Font Type

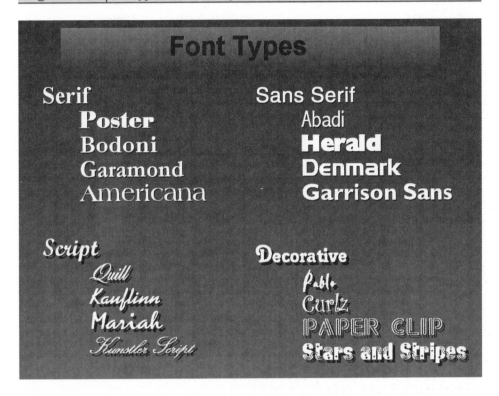

Use black and white effectively. If your budget or equipment limits you to using only black and white, you can still use contrast to create attractive graphics. By choosing contrasting typefaces, spacing text widely or more compactly, using larger or smaller text, and using both bold and lightface text, you can create differences in textual emphasis.

Use a storyboard to plan your message. A *storyboard* is a technique for planning how words and pictures will be used in a presentation. Each page of a storyboard is a sheet of paper or a flipchart page that discusses a single point in the presentation. The point is described in sentences, phrases, or key words and then illustrated with rough sketches to help you visualize how the words and images will work together in your presentation. Experienced speakers sometimes use storyboards as a substitute for a detailed formal outline when they are preparing a presentation.

To use this method of planning a message, first, as when planning any message, think about your audience. Then, with your audience in mind, make a list of the main points you'd like to cover, knowing that each one will become a page on your storyboard.

Once you have decided on your main points, you can begin creating your storyboards. Divide a piece of paper down the middle and label it "Storyboard." In the left column, write the main idea followed by notes about supporting points. In the right column, sketch the visuals you plan to include. Don't worry if you are not a skilled artist. These sketches are simply placeholders for the finished visual aid that you will prepare later on a computer.

When you draft your sketches, be conservative about the number of visuals you plan to use. Select key supporting points to be illustrated with a few memorable words or images.

When you finish your storyboards, convert them into a more formal presentation outline. Prepare your PowerPoint slides or whatever other form of visual you plan to use. Then practice with your outline and visuals to ensure that your visuals are large enough, that they communicate your key points, and that you talk about them as you show them.

Using Presentation Software

When most people think about business presentations, the first image that may come to mind is a talk illustrated with accompanying computer-generated graphics created with PowerPoint or similar software. Although PowerPoint presentations can be overused and

Figure 13.7 | Clip Art Can Be Used To Illustrate Visuals

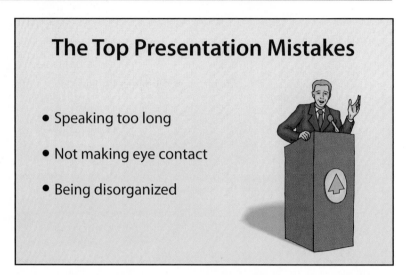

can distract from your message if used improperly, PowerPoint provides professional looking possibilities for illustrating your presentation.[30]

Using a program such as PowerPoint, you can design and create complete presentation aids on your personal computer. It's easy to store a PowerPoint presentation on a flash drive, a very compact computer memory device, or on your computer's hard drive. You could also attach your PowerPoint presentation to an email message. You can, for example, develop a key word or phrase outline to emphasize your main points as you speak. You can create graphs, charts, or drawings to display statistical information or illustrate your points. Using a scanner, you can convert photos or use digital photographs and incorporate them into your presentation. In addition, you can easily incorporate video or audio clips.

Presentation software has several advantages. It's relatively easy to use, and it adds a professional look to a presentation. But it also has the potential to create problems if used improperly. PowerPoint images can distract from your verbal messages; listeners may be tempted to focus on the visual message and not hear your verbal message. Many presenters overuse PowerPoint to the extent that listeners may feel they're watching a competing TV program being projected behind the speaker while they are trying to hear the message. If overused, PowerPoint can turn a live speaking event into a canned media presentation that may lack immediacy. Used effectively and appropriately, however, PowerPoint slides can add to rather than detract from your presentation.

Keep sights and sounds simple. In most aspects of communication, simple is better. The purpose of a presentation aid is to support rather than to compete with your message. Resist the temptation to add sound effects. Cute sounds often lose their novelty after the first slide or two and can become irritating. *You* should be the soundtrack, not your computer.

Repeat visual elements to create unity. Use a common visual element, such as a bullet or a symbol, at the beginning of each word or phrase on a list. Use common color schemes and spacing to give your visuals coherence. Also, avoid mixing fonts in the same presentation. You get a professional, polished look if you use a similar visual style for each of your images.

Use clip art and other images. Clip art consists of images that are in print form or stored in a computer file. You can easily incorporate these images into your visuals, as shown in Figure 13.7, even if you did not excel in art class. Repeating the visual images can provide a consistent look and feel to your presentation.

Allow plenty of time to prepare your presentation aids. Consider developing your PowerPoint slides as you are developing your message. Using the storyboarding method we discussed earlier can help you integrate your visual message with your verbal message. Waiting until the last minute to develop your visuals can result in a sloppy, amateurish presentation that will detract from your credibility.

Use words sparingly. Research suggests that the best use of PowerPoint is to present pictures, images, and other non-text information.[31] Don't clutter a slide with lots of text; let your speech communicate your message and use PowerPoint to support your points. Using too many words on your slides tempts listeners to become readers instead of listeners. A presentation is powerful because it's live and happening now. Used poorly, PowerPoint slides can make listeners assume the catatonic pose of watching TV rather than participating in a live presentation. Using words sparingly on your PowerPoint slides keeps the cognitive and linguistic focus on you rather than on prepared words and text.

Preparing a Presentation with PowerPoint

PowerPoint is ubiquitous—it's everywhere. Although you can easily learn to use this software program with the built-in tutorial that comes with the software, here are a few tips.[32]

Create consistency. PowerPoint is designed to give your presentations a consistent appearance. In addition to choosing from the menu of design templates, you can use the program's Slide Master, Title Master, and Color Schemes features to control the look of your slides.

The Slide Master controls the format and placement of the titles and text you type on slides; the Title Master controls the format and placement of the title slide and any other slide you designate as a title slide. Masters also hold background items such as graphics that you want to appear on every slide.

Color Schemes are sets of eight balanced colors designed to be used as the main colors of a slide presentation—for text, background, fill, accents, and so on. Each different element on a slide is automatically given a color in the scheme. You can pick a color scheme for an individual slide or for an entire presentation. If you create unique slides—for example, slides with backgrounds that differ from the master or fill colors that aren't part of the master color scheme—these slides retain their uniqueness even when you change the master. If you change your mind later, you can always restore slides you altered to the master format.

Add text. The easiest way to add text to a slide is to type directly into any placeholder on the slide. When you want to add text outside a placeholder or shape, you can use the Text Box tool on the Drawing toolbar. But as we've noted, use text sparingly. Too many words may cause your listeners to tune you out and turn them into readers rather than listeners.

Insert pictures. PowerPoint comes with its own set of pictures in the Clip Gallery, a wide variety of clip art that makes it easy for you to dress up your presentations with professionally designed images.

Select a picture by clicking Insert Clip Art and then clicking on Clip Art or Pictures. The Clip Gallery includes a handy Find feature to help you locate just the right images for your presentation. You can also insert pictures and scanned photographs from other programs and locations.

Insert charts and graphs. PowerPoint includes subprograms you can use to add charts, scanned pictures, and equations to your presentations. Organization Chart, Graph, Photo Editor, and Equation Editor all create embedded objects that you can insert into a presentation. When you embed data in a PowerPoint document, you can edit it in your document without having to return to the source files. When you create or modify a chart, a scanned picture, or an equation in your presentation, PowerPoint subprogram toolbars replace the PowerPoint menus and toolbars.

Print a presentation. You can print your entire presentation—the slides, outline, speaker's notes, and audience handouts—in either color or black and white. To print your presentation, open the file and choose whether you want to print slides, handouts, note pages, or an outline. Then identify the slides to be printed and the number of copies you want. When you print handouts, you can print one, two, three, or six slides on a page; or you can use the Microsoft Word Send To command (under the File menu) and then use Word to print other layout variations.

You can create notes pages while you're creating your presentation and then use these pages as speaker notes when you give a slide show. You can also print handouts of your slides for the audience.

Use special effects sparingly. Transitions and animations, when used in moderation, can add interest to your presentation, help highlight important points, and control the flow of information. PowerPoint comes with music, sounds, and videos you can play during your slide shows. You can also animate text, graphics, sounds, movies, and other objects. You can insert a sound or video clip where you want it to play during a slide. But use these special effects the way you would add hot chili powder to chili—sparingly. Too much "spice" distracts from the main meat of your message.

RECAP: Tips for Preparing and Using Presentation Aids

Preparing Presentation Aids

- Keep drawings simple and large.
- Be sure photographs are large enough to be seen easily.
- Limit the amount of information you put on a single chart or PowerPoint slide.
- Keep graphs simple and uncluttered.
- Use only brief excerpts and clips from DVDs or video or audio tapes.
- Be sure that any models you use are large enough to be seen easily.

Using Presentation Aids

- Rehearse with your presentation aids.
- Rehearse with people who will assist you with presentation aids.
- Have any needed equipment set up and ready to go before you speak.
- Maintain eye contact with your audience, not with your presentation aids.
- Explain your presentation aids.
- Time the display of your presentation aids to coincide with your discussion of them.
- Do not pass objects, pictures, or other small items among your audience.
- Use handouts effectively.

Communication Principles and Skills for Leadership

Principle One: Be aware of your communication with yourself and others.

- If your subject is sensitive or your information is classified, be cautious and noncommittal in any impromptu remarks you might be asked to make.
- Be aware of your speaking rate, and adjust it if necessary.
- Be certain that your presentation aids, including those that utilize technology, contribute to your specific purpose.
- Pay attention to your nonverbal delivery when you rehearse your presentation.

Principle Two: Effectively use and interpret verbal messages.

- Give a manuscript or memorized speech when exact wording is critical.
- Phrase your ideas so that they will be clear, accurate, and memorable.
- Do not try to memorize an extemporaneous presentation word for word; vary the ways in which you express ideas and information.

Principle Three: Effectively use and interpret nonverbal messages.

- When you deliver a manuscript speech, try to memorize an entire sentence at a time so that you can maintain eye contact throughout the sentence.

- Use gestures and movement to add interest and emphasis to both manuscript and memorized speeches.

- Move during your presentation to signal the beginning of a new idea or major point, or to signal a transition from a serious idea to a humorous one or vice versa.

- To heighten your credibility and to increase listener comprehension, use eye contact to let your audience know that you are interested in them and ready to talk to them.

- Speak loudly enough to be heard easily by all members of your audience.

- Vary the volume and rate of your voice to emphasize ideas and sustain the audience's interest.

Principle Four: Listen and respond thoughtfully to others.

- Use eye contact to help you determine how your audience members are responding to you.

- Listen to what audience members tell you before and after your presentation to give you insights about how best to deliver your message.

- If possible, rehearse your presentation for someone and seek feedback about both your content and your delivery.

Principle Five: Appropriately adapt messages to others.

- Although audiences today generally expect speakers to use everyday language and a conversational delivery style, you will need to adapt your delivery to audiences of different sizes and from different cultures.

- Consider your audience and the speaking context when you select a method of delivery.

- Consider your audience's interests, expectations, and knowledge to ensure that an impromptu presentation is audience centered.

- Adapt your gestures to your audience. Use bolder, more sweeping, and more dramatic gestures with large audiences. Tone down gestures if you are speaking to a culturally diverse audience who might prefer a more subdued style.

- Adapt to your audience's expectations for your appearance.

- Let your audience's interests, experiences, and knowledge guide your preparation and selection of presentation aids.

Discussion Questions

1. In what way does delivery contribute to the success of a speech?

2. What style of delivery do most North American audiences expect?

3. Under what circumstances might a speaker want to deliver a manuscript or memorized speech?

4. How does an extemporaneous speech differ from an impromptu speech?

5. List and define some key forms of body language, and provide suggestions for effectively using each one.

6. What can facial expression communicate during a speech?

7. List and define four elements of vocal delivery, and provide suggestions for using each one effectively.

8. How should you dress when you are going to deliver a speech?

9. List types of presentation aids a speaker might use, and provide suggestions for effectively using each type.

10. State six general guidelines for using visual aids effectively in a speech.

Building Your Skills

1. Either in person or on television, watch a political campaign speech or a speech by a business or professional leader. Pay particular attention to the leader's delivery. Critique his or her use of gestures, movement, posture, eye contact, facial expression, vocal delivery, and appearance. What advice would you give this speaker based on the principles of effective delivery presented in this chapter?

2. Imagine you are a speech consultant to the chief executive officer of a large paper company. Your boss is about to begin working on her annual "State of the Company" address, which she gives to an audience of about 500 employees, stockholders, and community members. This year, she wants to enliven her presentation of sales statistics, stock prices, and the state of the physical plant with some presentation aids. Make a list of suggestions of the types of visual aids she might employ, and offer suggestions for using each one effectively.

3. Make a video of yourself as you rehearse a speech you plan to give. Use the following list to evaluate your delivery.

DELIVERY STYLE

_____ Did I use an extemporaneous delivery style?

_____ Did I use appropriate notes, but not read or memorize my speech?

EYE CONTACT

_____ Did I establish eye contact with my audience before I began my speech?

_____ Did I maintain eye contact during my speech?

PHYSICAL DELIVERY

_____ Did I use gestures in a natural way?

_____ Did I have appropriate posture?

FACIAL EXPRESSION

_____ Did I have an appropriate facial expression?

_____ Did I vary my facial expression?

VOCAL DELIVERY

_____ Did I speak loud enough to be heard clearly?

_____ Did I speak with vocal variety?

---

4. Imagine that your business colleague will be delivering a ten-minute report from the national office to twenty branch offices via web cam. The audience for this message will be seated in conference rooms around the country, and your colleague's image will be projected on large screens. Based on the principles and strategies discussed in this chapter, what suggestions would you give your colleague who will be making the web cam presentation?

5. Imagine that you are the regional manager for a small fast-food company. Profits are down and sales are sluggish. You are about to deliver a message in which you'll announce a 10 percent cut in employees. Given the unpleasant news you will discuss, you anticipate that you'll receive several hostile questions and face a skeptical and negative audience. Based on this chapter's discussion of responding to questions following a presentation, what can you do to prepare for the questions you are likely to face following your speech?

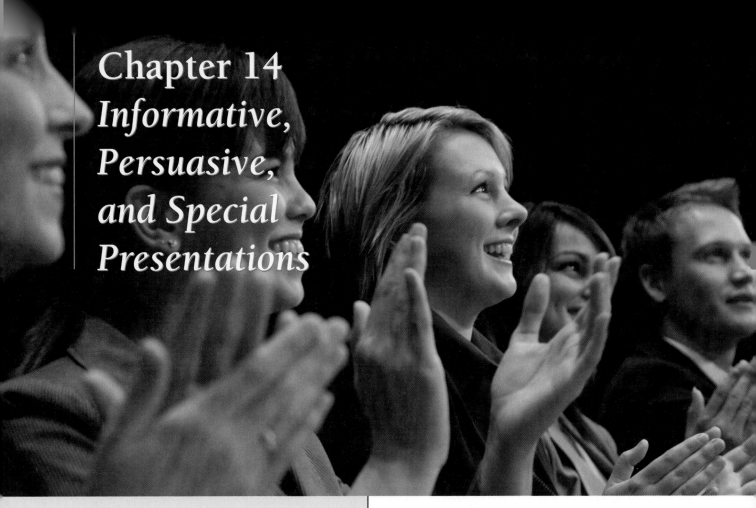

Chapter 14
Informative, Persuasive, and Special Presentations

chapter outline

After reading this chapter, you should be able to

◼ Describe and use effective strategies to present a briefing, a report, and a public relations presentation.

◼ List and illustrate the nine steps in designing and delivering a training presentation.

◼ Identify and describe four strategies to motivate and persuade listeners.

◼ Define and provide an example of inductive reasoning, deductive reasoning, reasoning by analogy, and reasoning by cause and effect.

◼ List and explain eight logical reasoning fallacies.

◼ Explain three ways to ethically and appropriately use emotional appeals in a persuasive presentation.

◼ Describe and illustrate four ways to organize a persuasive message.

◼ Design and deliver an effective sales presentation.

◼ Identify and describe strategies for developing and presenting a team presentation.

◼ Describe and give examples of special occasion speaking situations, including introducing others, presenting and receiving an award, and giving a toast.

When we talk we usually expect something to happen. We may want people to remember what we say; more typically, we want people to respond to our message. In a business or professional context, sometimes our goal may simply be to develop a positive relationship with a colleague, a customer, or a client. Or the goal may be to share information. The goal may also include persuading the listener to do something in response to our message, such as buy our product or donate time and money to a good cause. We've defined leadership as influencing others through communication. How we communicate with others has a direct impact on how we influence others.

In the three previous chapters we've discussed the steps in preparing and delivering a presentation. In this chapter we will discuss how to apply the skills and principles of communicating with your audience to achieve two specific goals: to inform and to persuade.

As we discussed in Chapter 11, the primary goals of speaking to others are to inform, to persuade, and to entertain. To **inform** is to share information with others to enhance their knowledge or understanding of the information, concepts, or ideas presented. When you inform someone, you assume the role of a teacher by defining, illustrating, clarifying, or elaborating on a topic. In a professional context, briefs, reports, lectures, and training presentations are typical formats for informing others. Speaking to inform others can be a challenging task. The information you communicate to someone else is rarely, if ever, understood exactly as you intend it: Simply presenting information does not mean that communication has occurred. Communication happens when listeners make sense of the information they receive.

To **persuade** someone is to change or reinforce the person's attitudes (likes and dislikes), beliefs (what is perceived to be true or false), values (what is considered good or bad), or behavior. A sales presentation is a type of persuasive presentation you'll commonly encounter in a professional setting. When you interview for a job, you're doing more than simply presenting information about yourself; you're presenting a sales pitch on why the organization should hire you. Informative and persuasive speaking are related processes. A key difference is that in a persuasive presentation, you want the listener to do more than merely remember what you say; you want to change or reinforce what the listener likes, believes, values, or does. Persuasive speakers *intentionally* try to change or reinforce listeners' feelings, ideas, or behavior.

In professional settings there are also times when people working collaboratively in a team present information or seek to persuade. Although the overall steps for planning and delivering a group presentation are the same as for an individual presentation, it usually takes more effort to coordinate a team presentation. This chapter will offer suggestions for working collaboratively to inform or persuade.

In addition to informing and persuading, whether individually or as a team, there are special occasions on which you will be called on to say a few remarks. These special occasions can be informative, such as when you introduce someone before he or she speaks, but more often they will be ceremonial, such as when you are presenting or receiving an award, giving a toast, or giving a short speech of thanks or congratulations. Throughout the discussion of informative, persuasive, and special occasion speaking, keep in mind the five communication principles for leadership.

Informing Others

Think of the best teacher you ever had. He or she was probably a great lecturer with a special talent for making information clear, interesting, and memorable. As a leader, you no doubt will be called on in your professional life to present information to others. Leaders explain and help keep others informed. Skilled leaders are also expected to be skilled educators. What do effective leader/educators do to communicate information to others? They simplify so listeners understand the message, pace the information to avoid information overload, directly address the needs and problems of their listeners, and reinforce their messages nonverbally or visually.

Use simple ideas. Mark Twain told a story about a Missouri farmer who ran for the state legislature five times but lost each election. He didn't lose because he didn't practice his campaign speeches; he gave his speeches to his cows each morning. The problem was,

> *Make sure you have finished speaking before your audience has finished listening."*
>
> — DOROTHY SARNOFF

Inform to share information with others to enhance their knowledge or understanding of the information, concepts, or ideas presented.

Persuade to change or reinforce a person's attitudes, beliefs, values, or behavior.

according to Twain, that he used "high-falutin'" words when he should have used shorter terms. He described his audience as "my enlightened constituents" and suggested he was trying to "obtain a mandate" for his "legislative mission." During one of his morning oration rehearsals, one of his cows knocked out his front teeth. He could then only use one-syllable words. The result: He won every election in his career from that day on.[1]

When you inform others, your job is to get your ideas across to your audience, *not* to see how much information you can cram in. The simpler your ideas and phrases, the greater the chance that your audience will remember them. We don't mean you should talk down to your audience. Listeners can sense a speaker's superior know-it-all attitude, and they won't like it. Simplify your message, but don't be condescending.

Pace information flow. Organize your talk so that you present an even stream of information, rather than bunch up a number of significant details around one point. If you present too much new information too quickly, you may overwhelm your audience, and your listeners' ability to understand may falter.

Use adult learning strategies. If your audience consists of adult listeners, you will need to ensure that you deliver your message in the way that adults learn best. **Adult learners** prefer the following:[2]

- To be given information they can use immediately
- To be actively involved in the learning process
- To connect their life experiences with the new information they learn
- To know how the new information is relevant to their busy lives
- To know how the information will solve a problem
- To receive information that is relevant to their needs

Most people who work in business have in-baskets on their desks to hold work that must be done. Similarly, each of us has a kind of "mental in-basket," an agenda of what we want or need from a presentation. Remember the characteristics of adult learners and the importance of adapting your message to others. You will hold your audience's interest, and also have more success in informing them, if you tailor your information to address what is in your audience's literal or metaphorical "in-basket."

Reinforce ideas nonverbally. You can also signal the importance of a point with nonverbal emphasis. Gestures serve the purpose of accenting or emphasizing key phrases, as italics do in written communication. A well-placed pause can emphasize or reinforce a point. Pausing just before or just after making an important point will focus attention on your thought. Raising or lowering your voice can also reinforce a key idea. Movement can help emphasize major ideas. Moving from behind the lectern to tell a personal anecdote can signal that something special and more intimate is about to be said. Finally, in business and professional settings you will likely present briefings, reports, public relations presentations, and training sessions. Photos, images, charts, and other visual information may be just what your listeners need to better understand your key ideas. We next focus on applying these principles to preparing informative briefings, reports, public relations speeches, and training sessions.

Presenting Briefings

A **briefing** (or a *brief*), as you might guess from the name, is a short talk that provides information to an audience. A briefing can focus on what has happened in the past, what is currently happening on a given project or topic, or what may happen in the future. The military, public safety organizations (police departments, security departments), medical organizations, and other organizations that need clear, short summaries of information almost exclusively rely on briefings to ensure the exchange of information.

Because briefings are short (from five to fifteen minutes), they typically don't have an extended or formal introduction. You should still be mindful of catching your listeners' attention, but not with a lengthy story or illustration. Just get to your points after a very short overview. Listeners expect a brief to be quick. Whereas in a more formal fifteen-minute presentation the introductory remarks and overview could take one-and-a-half minutes, for a briefing the introductory remarks may take thirty seconds or less. Beginning with a short question or stating the purpose of your briefing is typically expected.

Adult learners people who prefer to be given information they can use immediately, to be actively involved in the learning process, to connect their life experiences with the new information they learn, to know how the new information is relevant to their busy lives, to know how the information will solve a problem, and to receive information that is relevant to their needs.

Briefing a short talk that provides information to an audience.

Because several briefs are often presented one after another, the first brief may provide a longer introduction to introduce the briefings that will follow. For example, if you're giving a briefing about the income and loss statement for the past quarter and you're part of a four-person team, each of whom is sharing information, provide a short overview of your message, present your key ideas, summarize them, link to what the next person will say, and sit down.

The organizational pattern for briefings is usually topical or chronological. It's still appropriate to use transition phases and signposts ("I have three points to make. First, . . .") but the transitional phrases are shorter and less pronounced than in a more extended informative presentation.

Some briefings can be quite formal, and listeners may expect a no-nonsense delivery style with little use of humor and lots of information. In some organizational cultures, however, a briefing is expected to be informal and casual. It's important to be aware of your audience as you make decisions on how to customize your briefing content.

Presenting Reports

Report a summary of what has been accomplished in the past or an update on a project.

A **report** is a summary of what has been accomplished in the past or an update on a project. In contrast to a briefing, a report is often a longer, more detailed summary of a past, present, or future event. For example, a briefing might include a short update on a new development at a manufacturing plant; a more lengthy report may summarize the history of the plant, what it produces, why the plant is being upgraded, and what is expected to happen to plant operations in the future. A briefing could provide a summary of reactions to the new employee training program; a report on the same topic could include information about the rationale for the new training, a summary of the training content, and a review of methods of assessing the training. Briefs are brief; reports are longer. Some organizations, however, use the terms *report* and *briefing* interchangeably. You may be asked to report on how to increase sales in the next quarter or to present the findings of a market survey your division has conducted in the past several months. Whatever the specific objective of the report, the general purpose is to communicate information or policy; some reports include a persuasive appeal to try some new course of action. Consider the following when preparing a report:

- *Adapt to your audience.* When you are presenting your report, keep in mind that your audience is there to hear you address a particular need or problem. Begin by briefly acknowledging that situation.

- *Present conclusions, then explain how you reached those conclusions.* If you are reporting on a particular project or study, first discuss what your research group decided to do to explore the problem. Then explain how you gathered the information.

When presenting a report, first acknowledge the particular need or problem the report addresses, then deliver your conclusion and discuss how you reached it. Finally, give your audience the bottom line and provide a solution or identify what will happen next.

- *End a report with solutions or identify what happens next.* Your listeners often want to know what the bottom line is. The most important part of some reports is this outline of new courses of action or changes in present policy. When your report proposes changes, tell your audience what's in it for them—what benefits will accrue to them directly as a result of the new proposal. One business consultant suggests this report technique:

> Tune your audience into radio station WIIFM— What's In It For Me. Tell your listeners where the benefits are for them, and they'll listen to everything you have to say.[3]

In addition to listening to a report, audience members usually expect to receive a hard copy or email version of the report, or at least a summary of the report's key conclusions.

Presenting Public Relations Presentations

A **public relations presentation** is one in which the speaker is specifically providing information to promote a positive public image for the person or organization the speaker is representing. People who work for professional associations, blood banks, utility companies, government agencies, universities, religious organizations, or charitable institutions, as well as those employed by commercial enterprises, are often called on to speak to an audience about what their organization does or about a special project the organization has taken on. Public relations (PR) speeches are designed to inform the public and improve relations with them—either to present general impressions of the organization, or, because a particular program or situation has raised some questions or concerns, to emphasize the positive features of the organization. So although the purpose of many public relations presentations is to present information, there is often a persuasive edge to public relations messages. The speaker may be trying to enhance or maintain a positive, polished public image.

Like the presenter of a report, the public relations speaker first discusses the need or problem that has prompted the speech. Then he or she goes on to explain how the company or organization is working to meet the need or solve the problem, or why it believes there is no problem.

It is important in public relations speaking to anticipate criticism and objections, especially if the purpose of the PR speech is to change opinions or address a controversial issue. The speaker may acknowledge listeners' points of view and then counter potential problems or objections, especially if he or she has witnessed past presenters encountering some opposition to the policy or program. The speaker should emphasize the positive aspects of the policy or program and take care not to become defensive. He or she wants to leave the impression that the company or organization has carefully worked through potential pitfalls and drawbacks. It should be noted that not all public relations speeches make policy recommendations. Many simply summarize information for those who need to know.

Presenting Training Sessions

Many organizations have extensive training departments whose function is to orient new employees to the organization and teach specific job skills, including communication skills. Business and professional organizations invest billions of dollars each year in training employees.[4] **Training** is a special type of informative speaking through which the trainer seeks to develop specific skills in listeners to help them perform a specific job or task more effectively.[5] The goal of a training session is for listeners to be able not just to recall information but to perform specific tasks. Since the goal of training is to implement behavior change, training presentations also seek to motivate listeners to perform the skill or task being taught.

Training is similar to any presentation, in that it's essential to focus on the needs, interests, and backgrounds of listeners. More specifically, what do trainers do, and how does training differ from other types of presentations? Figure 14.1 presents a needs-centered model of training that closely resembles the audience-centered model of communication that we introduced in Chapter 11. The model in Figure 14.1 is called a *needs-centered model* because the primary purpose of any training program is to respond to the learning needs of the trainee. Training that does not address a trainee's needs or specific job functions is not effective training.

What are the differences between training and traditional classroom education? In a nutshell, training focuses more on behavioral learning, whereas education emphasizes the cognitive domain. Differences between training and education include the following:[6]

- Training emphasizes doing; education emphasizes knowing.
- Training emphasizes achieving a certain level of skill; training does not evaluate mastery of a skill by comparing one trainee with another, as is done in a classroom.
- Training is more of a closed system that is applicable to a specific situation or task; there are right or wrong ways of performing a skill to accomplish a task. Education operates more as an open system, in that what is taught has multiple applications in a variety of contexts.

Public relations presentation a presentation in which the speaker is specifically providing information to promote a positive public image for the person or organization the speaker is representing.

Training a type of informative speaking in which a trainer seeks to develop specific skills in listeners to help them perform a specific job or task more effectively.

Figure 14.1 | A Needs-Centered Training Model

- Training emphasizes analyzing how to perform skills following a prescribed, step-by-step approach; education is typically less concerned with performing a linear sequence of behaviors.

Drawing on adult learning theory, a trainer should view himself or herself less as a lecturer and more as a facilitator. Adult learners bring their own experiences to the training session; they also want to focus on real problems that are in their literal or metaphorical "in-baskets" or on their "to-do" lists. A trainer follows the steps in Figure 14.1 in order to draw on those experiences and equip trainees to address problems.

Analyze organizational and trainee needs. At the center of the model in Figure 14.1—and the first and ongoing step in any training—is the process of identifying the needs of the organization and those of the specific trainees who will attend the training session. How do you know what trainees need? One way to assess their needs is to ask them what those needs are, using surveys, questionnaires, or interviews. The process of identifying trainee needs is quite similar to analyzing your audience when delivering a presentation. Analyzing trainee needs is so central to the process of training that it is in the center of the model. *Every other aspect of designing and delivering a training presentation depends on the needs of the trainees.* In addition to analyzing the needs of individuals, it's also important to consider the needs of the organization.

Analyze the training task. Viewing the model in Figure 14.1 as a clock, begin at the top and work your way around clockwise to explore the steps of designing and delivering a training presentation. After you've figured out what trainees need (for example, skill in listening or conflict management), an early critical step in designing a training program is to thoroughly analyze the specific task you want the trainees to perform. You conduct a task analysis. A **task analysis** is a detailed, step-by-step description of precisely what a trainee should do and know in order to perform a particular skill. As the trainer, if you are going to teach someone how to prepare and deliver a sales presentation, you first need to know what the steps in that process are before you teach them to others. You perform a task analysis to create a comprehensive outline of what you would be teaching others if you had unlimited time. You may only have three or four hours to teach a skill, so you may have to

Task analysis a detailed, step-by-step description of precisely what a trainee should do and know in order to perform a particular skill.

focus only on the most critical steps. A task analysis lets you discover what the essential elements of a task are. (Our needs-centered training model is itself a simplified task analysis of how to train someone. Each piece of the model represents an essential step in the process.)

Develop training objectives. After you have figured out the steps in teaching a particular skill, it's important to develop objectives or learning outcomes that you want your trainees to achieve. It's important to specify the precise behavior you want trainees to perform at the end of the training. What do training objectives look like? We begin each chapter in this book with a list of learning objectives. Reviewing those objectives will give you an idea of the format and style for training objectives. Training objectives are also similar to the specific purpose statement for a presentation, discussed in Chapter 11. Training objectives specify what you want trainees to be able to do following the training presentation.

When training adult learners, a trainer's job is to facilitate rather than to lecture. Demonstrating a skill and then having trainees practice performing it is much more effective than merely describing the skill.

Organize training content. Once you have your precise training objectives in hand, you can begin drafting the information that trainees need to know and describing in more detail the behaviors that they will be expected to perform. The most typical organizational patterns for training content include (1) chronological (a step-by-step sequence of what someone does first, second, and so on) (2) by complexity (from simplest or easiest to learn to more complex or more detailed information), and (3) topical (identifying the natural divisions in a topic).

Determine training methods. To train someone, you don't just talk to them. Adult learners are not interested in hearing a three- or four-hour lecture; that's not good training. So you'll need to develop effective methods of presenting information to your trainees. You may decide that, rather than presenting a lecture, it would be better to have trainees participate in role-playing situations, discuss a case study, or brainstorm solutions to a problem that you pose. A typical training session may involve a mix of methods, including the following:

- *Tell.* At times it may be important to lecture—but lecture should not be the prime focus of a training presentation. Trainees need to see how to perform a skill and practice their new behavior.

- *Show.* Provide models, videos, or demonstrations of how to perform a skill.

- *Invite.* Ask trainees to practice performing the new skill you are teaching.

- *Encourage.* Provide positive reinforcement when trainees perform the skill the proper way.

- *Correct.* Provide feedback that lets a trainee know when he or she is not performing a skill properly.

Select training resources. Perhaps you've discovered an excellent video that masterfully illustrates the skill you want to teach in the training session. Or, maybe you've decided to use a small-group method and you want trainees to respond to discussion questions. Whether it's a video, a list of discussion questions, PowerPoint presentation slides, or some other type of resource, you'll need to decide what materials you'll need to prepare for the training presentation.

Complete training plans. After you've developed your objectives and settled on the content of the training, the methods you will use to present your message, and the resources you need, it is important to develop a comprehensive written plan that describes how you will present your session: a training plan (sometimes called a *lesson plan* in educational settings). There are many different formats. Some training plans are simply detailed outlines of the training content and methods. Other plans offer a complete narrative transcript of the training lesson. Most training plans include a description of the objectives, methods, training content, and training resources needed, along with an estimate of how much time each part of the training will take.

Nonverbal

Deliver training. After developing a well-crafted plan, you are now ready to bring the training presentation to life. You deliver your training not only by presenting lectures, videos, and activities, but also by asking good questions to facilitate class discussion. An effective training presentation should be much more interactive than a speech, although the elements of effective speech delivery (such as eye contact, good posture, effective gestures, and varied vocal inflection) are essential when training others.

Assess the training process. When the training session is over, a trainer's job is not complete. Effective trainers evaluate how their training was received (Did trainees like it?) and even more importantly, whether trainees learned what they needed to. The ultimate test of a training session is whether trainees can use the new skills on the job. Did the training make a difference?

Each piece of the needs-centered model of training in Figure 14.1 reflects an essential element in what a trainer does. Trainers first and foremost focus on the needs of learners and then carefully develop a training program that meets those needs. Training others well involves more than just talking to them. Effective training develops a specific skill by having trainees practice and receive feedback to master the skills being taught.

Persuading Others

Go to any bookstore and peruse the shelves of books on management and leadership and you'll find books about how to influence others. The best-selling business management book of all time is Dale Carnegie's classic *How to Win Friends and Influence People*. At the heart of influencing others is being able to persuade them. We've noted that to lead is to influence, so being able to persuade others is a vital leadership skill. As we're noted, persuasion is the process of changing or reinforcing attitudes, beliefs, values, or behavior. Think of any great leader, in business or politics, past or present, and undoubtedly you'll be thinking of someone who possessed effective persuasion skills. Not all leaders use the same persuasive methods. Martin Luther King Jr. and Mahatma Gandhi led through promoting nonviolent means of achieving their goals. In leading the United States out of the Depression and through World War II, Franklin Roosevelt used his skill as a communicator as well as his behind-the-scenes power and influence to achieve his goals. Lee Iacocca, former CEO of Chrysler Corporation, Jack Welch, former CEO of General Electric, and the late Sam Walton, founder of Wal-Mart, are examples of business leaders who could inspire and motivate others.

To develop strong leadership and persuasive skills, you need first to understand principles of persuasion and then learn specific strategies for persuading others.

Principles of Persuasion

How does persuasion work? What makes you reach for your phone so you can call and order a gadget you've just seen advertised on TV? What motivates people to do things that they wouldn't do unless they are persuaded to do so? Let's look at four possible explanations.

People respond to resolve dissonance. When you are confronted with information that is inconsistent with your current thinking or feelings, you experience a kind of psychological discomfort called **cognitive dissonance**. You can be persuaded by being convinced that you have a problem and then pointed in a direction that will solve your problem. For example, if you have ever driven an automobile after consuming a drink or two, then seen a public service announcement from Mothers Against Drunk Driving documenting how even two drinks can contribute to serious traffic accidents, you've likely experienced cognitive dissonance. The incompatibility of your behavior and your knowledge is likely to make you feel uncomfortable. And your discomfort may prompt you to change your thoughts, likes or dislikes, feelings, or behavior so that you can restore your comfort level or sense of balance—in this case, by not driving after drinking.

Cognitive dissonance
psychological discomfort experienced when a person is presented with information that is inconsistent with his or her current thinking or feelings.

Skilled persuasive speakers know that creating dissonance and then offering their listeners a way to restore balance is an effective persuasive strategy.

People respond to meet needs. Besides creating cognitive dissonance, effective persuaders attempt to identify your needs and then convince you that they can meet your needs. For example, executives of a manufacturing company who observe people moving out of your town in search of jobs elsewhere might be able to persuade the town council to provide tax incentives to build a new plant in the area, reasoning that the town's need for jobs will make council members receptive to the request. The manufacturing company's executives can see the town's need for jobs and can craft a message explaining how the company will meet the need. As a speaker, the better you understand what your listeners need, the better you can adapt to them and the greater the chances that you can persuade them to change an attitude, belief, or value or get them to take some action.

Abraham Maslow developed the classic theory that outlines basic human needs.[7] If you've taken a psychology course, you have undoubtedly encountered this theory, which has important applications to persuasion. Maslow suggests that all human behavior is motivated by a **hierarchy of needs**. Basic physiological needs (such as the need for food, water, and air) have to be satisfied before we attend to any other concern. Once our physiological needs are met, we think next about safety needs. We need to feel safe and to be able to protect those we love. Comfortable and secure, we attend next to social needs, including the need to be loved and to belong to a group. The next level of need is for self-esteem, or thinking well of ourselves. And finally, if these first four levels of need have been satisfied, we may attend to the need for self-actualization, or achieving our highest potential. Although research does not completely support the notion that humans have a fixed hierarchy of needs, as Maslow originally thought, the theory does serve as a useful way of classifying basic human needs. Figure 14.2 illustrates Maslow's five levels of needs, with the most basic at the bottom.

As a persuasive public speaker, understanding and applying the hierarchy of needs helps you to adapt to your audience. One practical application is to do everything in your power to ensure that your audience's physiological needs are met. For example, if your listeners are sweating and fanning themselves, they are unlikely to be very interested in listening to your sales presentation. If you can turn on air conditioning or fans, you will have a greater chance of successfully making a sale.

Another way in which you can apply the need hierarchy is to appeal to an audience's higher-order needs. The U. S. Army once used the recruiting slogan "Be all that you can be" to tap into the need for self-actualization, or achievement of one's highest potential.

People respond to fear messages. One of the oldest ways to convince people to change their minds or their behavior is by scaring them into compliance. Fear works. The appeal

Figure 14.2 | **Maslow's Hierarchy of Needs**

Self-actualization needs

Self-esteem needs

Social needs

Safety needs

Physiological needs

Hierarchy of needs Abraham Maslow's classic theory that humans have five levels of needs and that lower-level needs must be met before people can be concerned about higher-level needs.

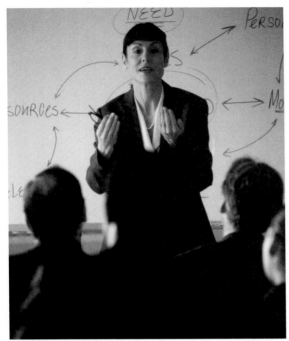

Strong gestures can be helpful in conveying your message, but you must also understand the principles of persuasion and learn specific strategies for persuading others.

Ethos the credibility or ethical character of a speaker.

Logos the use of logical arguments.

Pathos the use of emotional appeals to move an audience.

Proof evidence and the conclusions you draw from it.

Evidence the illustrations, definitions, statistics, and opinions presented as supporting material in persuasive speaking.

Reasoning the process of drawing conclusions from evidence.

Inductive reasoning reasoning that arrives at a general conclusion from specific instances or examples.

to fear often takes the form of an "if-then" statement: *If* you don't do X, *then* awful things will happen to you. "If you don't buy this insurance policy, then your loved ones may not be able to pay the mortgage and they may be homeless." "If you don't wear a seatbelt, then you are more likely to die in an automobile accident." "If you don't support the development of a new hospital in our community, lives could be lost if we have to travel to the next county for medical attention." These are examples of fear appeals. A variety of research studies support the following principles regarding the use of fear as a motivator.[8]

- A strong threat to a family member or someone whom members of the audience care about will often be more successful than a fear appeal directed at the audience members themselves.

- The more respected the speaker, the greater the likelihood that the appeal to fear will work.

- Fear appeals are more successful if you convince your audience that the threat is real and will affect them unless they take action.

People respond to positive messages. A TV commercial for a "big box" department store pledges "For every dollar you spend in our store, we will return 5 percent to the public schools in your community; your students will have new computers to help them learn." A candidate for chair of the board of directors asserts "If you support me for board chair, I can assure you our stock price and sales will increase." We've all encountered these kinds of positive appeals. Politicians, salespeople, and most successful business and professional persuaders know that one way to change or reinforce your attitudes, beliefs, values, or behavior is to use a positive motivational appeal. Positive motivational appeals are verbal messages promising that good things will happen if the speaker's advice is followed. The key to using positive motivational appeals is to know what your listeners value. Most people value a comfortable, prosperous life; stimulating, exciting activity; a sense of accomplishment; world peace; and overall happiness and contentment. In a persuasive speech, you can motivate your listeners to respond to your message by describing what positive things will happen to them if they follow your advice.

Strategies for Persuading Others

Greek philosopher and scholar Aristotle said that rhetoric is the process of discovering the available means of persuasion.[9] What are those available means? Aristotle singled out three primary strategies: (1) emphasize the credibility or ethical character of a speaker, which he called **ethos**; (2) use logical arguments, or **logos**; and (3) use emotional appeals, or **pathos**, to move an audience. The following strategies for developing your credibility as a speaker, using logic, evidence, and emotion to persuade and motivate listeners, are based on Aristotle's three strategies and bolstered by contemporary research. We'll also revisit some of our strategies of message organization and discuss how to adapt ideas to people and people to ideas.

Using evidence and reasoning to persuade. Besides knowing how to motivate listeners, an effective persuader knows how to structure a persuasive message for maximum effect. In addition to being considered a credible speaker, you will gain influence with your audience if you can effectively use logically structured arguments supported with evidence. As we noted earlier, Aristotle called this *logos*, which is usually translated as "word" but also means "topic of discourse." Using words effectively to communicate your arguments to your listeners is vital to persuading thoughtful and informed listeners. The goal is to provide logical proof for your arguments. **Proof** consists of both evidence and the conclusions you draw from it; **evidence** is the illustrations, definitions, statistics, and opinions that are your supporting material. **Reasoning** is the process of drawing conclusions from your evidence. There are three major ways to draw logical conclusions: inductively, deductively, and causally.

Reasoning that arrives at a general conclusion from specific instances or examples is known as **inductive reasoning**. You reason inductively when you claim that a conclusion is probably true because of specific evidence. For example, if you were giving a sales pitch to convince your customer that Hondas are reliable cars, you might use inductive reasoning to make your point. You have a 1998 Honda Civic that has 140,000 miles on it and has required little repair other than routine maintenance. Your brother has a Honda Accord and has driven it twice as long as any other car he has ever owned. Your friend just returned from a 3,000-mile road trip in her Honda Odyssey minivan, which performed beautifully. Based on these specific examples, you ask your listener to agree with your general conclusion: Hondas are reliable cars.

Reasoning by analogy is a special type of inductive reasoning. As you recall from Chapter 11, an analogy demonstrates how an unfamiliar idea, thing, or situation is similar to something the audience already understands. Analogy is not only a type of supporting material; it can also be used to reason inductively. For example, you might reason "Even though we're a small business, we should start a retirement plan for our company. If we don't we could lose our top employees. Our top competitor started a new 401(K) retirement plan for her employees and she's had much less employee turnover." The key to reasoning by analogy is to make sure that the two things you are comparing (your company and your competitor's company) are similar so that your argument is a sound one.

Reasoning from a general statement or principle to reach a specific conclusion is called **deductive reasoning**. Deductive reasoning can be structured as a **syllogism**, a three-part argument that has a major premise, a minor premise, and a conclusion. In attempting to convince the marketing department at a car dealership to advertise on television, you might offer this syllogism:

Verbal

MAJOR PREMISE: All of the top-selling automobile dealers in our county advertise on television.

MINOR PREMISE: Your automobile dealership is in this county.

CONCLUSION: Your automobile dealership should advertise on television.

Contemporary logicians note that when you reason deductively, your conclusion is certain rather than probable. The certainty of the conclusion rests primarily on the validity of the major premise and secondarily on the truth of the minor premise. If you can prove that all top-selling auto dealers advertise on TV, and if it is true that those that advertise sell more cars, then your conclusion will be sound.

Reasoning by analogy a special kind of inductive reasoning that draws a comparison between two ideas, things, or situations that share some essential common feature.

Deductive reasoning reasoning from a general statement or principle to reach a specific conclusion.

Syllogism a three-part argument that has a major premise, a minor premise, and a conclusion.

>>> COMMUNICATION AND GLOBALIZATION @ WORK

Effective strategies for developing your persuasive purpose depend on the background and cultural expectations of your listeners. Most of the logical, rational methods of reasoning we've presented evolved from Greek and Roman traditions of developing arguments. Rhetoricians from the United States typically use a straightforward factual-inductive method of supporting ideas and reaching conclusions. First, they identify facts and link them together to support a specific proposition or conclusion. North Americans also like debates involving a direct clash of ideas and opinions. Our low-context culture encourages people to be more forthright in dealing with issues and disagreement than do high-context cultures.

Not all cultures assume a direct, linear, methodical approach to supporting ideas and proving a point.[10] People from high-context cultures, for example, may expect that participants in a debate will establish a personal relationship before debating issues. People from some cultures, such as those of Eastern Europe, use a deductive pattern of

reasoning rather than an inductive pattern. They begin with a general premise and then link it to a specific situation when they attempt to persuade listeners.

People in Middle Eastern cultures usually do not use standard inductive or deductive structures. They are more likely to use narrative methods to persuade an audience. They tell stories that evoke feelings and emotions, allowing their listeners to draw their own conclusions by inductive association.

Although we've emphasized the kind of inductive reasoning that will be persuasive to most North Americans, you may need to use alternative strategies if your audience is from another cultural tradition. If you are uncertain about which approach will be most effective, consider using a variety of methods and strategies to make your point. Use facts supported by analysis, but also make sure you provide illustrative stories and examples. Also, try to observe and talk with other speakers who have experience addressing your target audience.

You use **causal reasoning** when you relate two or more events in such a way as to conclude that one or more of the events caused the others. For example, you might argue that public inoculation programs during the twentieth century eradicated smallpox.

As we noted when we discussed cause and effect as a persuasive organizational strategy, there are two ways to structure a causal argument. One is by reasoning from cause to effect, or predicting a result from a known fact. You know that you have had an inch of rain over the last few days, so you predict that the aquifer level will rise. The inch of rain is the cause; the rising aquifer is the effect. The other way to structure an argument is by reasoning from a known effect to the cause. National Transportation Safety Board accident investigators reason from effect to cause when they reconstruct airplane wreckage to find clues to the cause of an air disaster.

The key to developing any causal argument is to be certain that a causal relationship actually exists between the two factors you are investigating. A few summers ago, one of your authors' sons participated in a project that involved counting chimney swifts in a given area just before sunset. He counted the most swifts on July 4. However, it would not have been valid to argue that fireworks (or watermelon or hot dogs or anything else connected with Fourth of July celebrations) caused an increase in the number of chimney swifts in the area. The Fourth of July holiday and the bird count were not related by cause and effect, but most likely by coincidence.

Trying to establish a causal link where none exists is one type of **logical fallacy.** Unfortunately, not all people who try to persuade you will use sound evidence and reasoning. Some will try to develop arguments in ways that are irrelevant or inappropriate. To be a better informed listener, as well as a more ethical persuasive speaker, you should be aware of some of the following common logical fallacies.

Trying to link the Fourth of July with the chimney swift count is an example of a **causal fallacy,** or to use the Latin phrase, *post hoc, ergo propter hoc* ("after this; therefore, because of this"). Simply because one event follows another does not mean that the two are related causally.

"Jumping on the bandwagon" is a colloquial expression for thinking or doing something because everybody else is. Someone who argues that "everybody thinks that, so you should too" is falling prey to the **bandwagon fallacy.** Speakers using the bandwagon fallacy often use the word *everybody*:

> Everybody knows that the product is defective.
>
> Everybody agrees that the customer is really difficult.

"Either we float the bond issue, or we'll have to bus our students to another school district!" shouts Lupe in a moment of heated debate among the members of the school board. This **either-or fallacy** ignores the fact that there may be other solutions to the district's problem of dilapidated buildings, for example, purchasing portable classroom buildings or drawing new attendance zones within the district.

A person who tries to draw a conclusion from too little evidence or nonexistent evidence is making a **hasty generalization.** For example, one person's getting a raw deal under the company's new sales commission policy doesn't necessarily mean the policy is unfair.

Also known as an *ad hominem* argument, a Latin phrase that means "to the man," a **personal attack** that substitutes for a refutation of issues is a logical fallacy. "The HMO bill is a bad idea because it was proposed by that crazy senator" is an example of a personal attack. Don't dismiss an idea solely because you are against the person who presents it.

Someone is using a **red herring** when he or she attacks an issue by bringing up irrelevant facts or arguments. This fallacy takes its name from the old trick of dragging a red herring across a trail to distract dogs who are following a scent. Speakers use a red herring when they want to distract an audience from certain issues. For example, a congressional representative who has been indicted for misuse of federal funds calls a press conference and spends most of the time talking about a colleague's sexual indiscretions.

Ads in which baseball players endorse breakfast cereal and movie stars pitch credit cards are using an **appeal to misplaced authority.** Although baseball players may know a great deal about the game of baseball, they are no more expert than most of us about cereal. Movie stars may be experts at acting but probably not in personal finance.

If you argue that students should give blood because it is nearly time for final exams, you are guilty of a ***non sequitur*** (Latin for "it does not follow"). Your reason has nothing to do with your argument.

Causal reasoning reasoning that relates two or more events in such a way as to conclude that one or more of the events caused the others.

Logical fallacy false reasoning that occurs when someone attempts to persuade without adequate evidence or with arguments that are irrelevant or inappropriate.

Causal fallacy a faulty cause-and-effect connection between two things or events.

Bandwagon fallacy the argument that because everyone believes something or does something, the belief or behavior must be valid, accurate, or effective.

Either-or fallacy the oversimplification of an issue into a choice between only two outcomes or possibilities.

Hasty generalization reaching a conclusion from too little evidence or nonexistent evidence.

Personal attack attacking personal characteristics of someone connected with an idea, rather than addressing the idea itself.

Red herring irrelevant facts or arguments used to distract someone from the issue under discussion.

Appeal to misplaced authority using someone without the appropriate credentials or expertise to endorse an idea or product.

Non sequitur Latin for "it does not follow"; an idea or conclusion that does not logically follow a previous idea or conclusion.

RECAP: Inductive, Deductive, and Causal Reasoning

Type of Reasoning	Reasoning begins with . . .	Reasoning ends with . . .	Conclusion is . . .	Example
Inductive	specific examples	a general conclusion	probable	Dell, Gateway, and IBM computers are all reliable. Therefore, PCs are reliable.
Deductive	a general statement	a specific conclusion	certain	All financial officers at this company have advanced degrees. Tom Bryson is the chief financial officer at this company. Therefore, Tom Bryson has an advanced degree.
Causal	something known	a speculation about causes or effects of what is known	likely	The number of people with undergraduate degrees has risen steadily since 1960. This increasing number has caused a glut in the job market for people with degrees.

Persuasive speakers who provide logical proof (evidence and reasoning) for their arguments and who avoid logical fallacies heighten their chances for success with their audience. But good speakers know that evidence and reasoning are not their only tools. Emotion is another powerful way to move an audience to support a persuasive proposition.

Using emotion to persuade. People often make decisions based not on logic, but on emotion. Advertisers know this. Think of the soft-drink commercials you see on television. There is little rational reason that people should spend any part of their food budget on soft drinks; they are "empty calories." So soft-drink advertisers turn instead to emotional appeals, striving to connect their product with feelings of pleasure. Smiling people, upbeat music, and good times are usually part of the formula for selling soda pop.

One way to make an emotional appeal is with emotion-arousing verbal messages. Words with positive connotations, such as *mother, flag,* and *freedom,* and those with negative connotations, such as *slavery, the Holocaust,* and *terrorism,* trigger emotional responses in listeners. Patriotic slogans, such as "Remember 9/11" and "Give me liberty, or give me death," are examples of phrases that have successfully aroused emotions in their listeners. McDonald's "I'm lovin' it" and Nike's "Just do it" are short phrases that appeal to positive feelings and the satisfaction of accomplishment.

Another way to appeal to emotions is through concrete illustrations and descriptions. Although illustrations and descriptions are themselves types of evidence or supporting material, their impact is often emotional. When trying to convince her listeners to purchase high-quality child safety seats, a speaker used this example to evoke an emotional response in support of her goal:

> Michelle Hutchinson carefully placed her three-year-old daughter into her child safety seat. She was certain that Dana was secure. Within minutes Michelle was involved in a minor accident and the seat belt that was never designed to hold a child safety seat allowed the seat to lunge forward, crushing the three-year-old's skull on the dash. Dana died three days later.[11]

Effective use of nonverbal messages can also appeal to an audience's emotions. Visual aids can provide emotion-arousing images. A photograph of a dirty, ragged child alone in a big city can evoke sadness and pain. A video clip of an airplane crash can arouse fear and horror. A picture of a smiling baby makes most of us smile, too. As a speaker, you can use visual aids to evoke both positive and negative emotions.

When you use emotional appeals, you do have an obligation to be ethical and forthright. Making false claims, misusing evidence or images, or relying exclusively on emotion without any evidence or reasoning violates standards of ethical public speaking.

Organizing your persuasive message. Most persuasive speeches are organized according to one of four strategies: problem and solution, cause and effect, refutation, and the motivated sequence—a special variation of the problem-solution format that lends itself well to sales presentations.

Even though we discussed **problem-and-solution organization** in Chapter 12, we mention it again here as the most basic organizational pattern for a persuasive speech. The problem-and-solution strategy works best when a problem can be clearly documented and a solution or solutions proposed to deal with the problem. When describing the problem, your goal is to create dissonance or to identify an unmet need.

When you use problem-and-solution organization, apply the principle of appropriately adapting messages to others. If you are speaking to an apathetic audience or one that is not even aware that a problem exists, you can emphasize the problem portion of the speech. Your fellow members of the Chamber of Commerce, for example, who don't see how a new shopping mall in a nearby community will affect retail sales in the downtown area, may need to be jolted from apathy: You can point out that the presence of malls has resulted in drastically declining retail sales in other communities. If your audience is already aware of the problem, you can emphasize your proposed solution or solutions (perhaps to try to stop the mall from being built or to aggressively promote your community as the best destination for shopping). In either case, your challenge will be to provide ample evidence that your perception of the problem is accurate and reasonable. For example, you would need to find statistics that document how a mall can lower sales. You'll also need to convince your listeners that the solution or solutions you advocate are the most appropriate ones to solve the problem. Again, evidence in the form of statistics or examples are needed. As another example, note the problem-solution structure in the example below. The president of a Chamber of Commerce is trying to convince the local school board to address the public perception that the school district is inferior compared to nearby school districts. The community is not attracting new businesses because of perceptions of academic mediocrity. The Chamber of Commerce president analyzes the problem and proposes a solution:

I. PROBLEM: Students in public schools in our community are not learning as well as students in other nearby communities.

   A. Our student test scores are down.

   B. Our teachers are paid less than teachers in nearby school districts.

   C. Parents are not volunteering in our schools.

II. SOLUTION: We should slightly increase property taxes to increase revenues to finance improvements in our schools.

   A. We could hire additional teachers to help improve test scores.

   B. We could increase compensation for our best teachers.

   C. We could hire a volunteer coordinator to increase parent volunteers in our school.

Problem-and-solution organization a strategy for organizing a persuasive speech that works best when a clearly evident problem can be documented and a solution or solutions proposed to deal with the problem.

Cause-and-effect organization a strategy for identifying a situation and then discussing the resulting effects (cause-effect), or presenting a situation and then exploring its causes (effect-cause).

Like the problem-and-solution strategy, the **cause-and-effect organization** pattern was introduced in Chapter 12. We noted that a speaker could either identify a situation and then discuss the resulting effects (cause-effect) or present a situation and then explore its causes (effect-cause).

Regardless of which variation you choose, you should once again apply the principle of being aware of your communication with yourself and others. Specifically, you must analyze the problem and determine the critical causal link and then convince your listeners that the link is valid. An effect may have more than one cause. For example, sales at your company are 10 percent behind sales figures at this time last year. As sales manager, you are responsible for analyzing the issues and presenting your analysis to the company CEO. Here's a way you could organize your message:

I. CAUSE: The design of our product line is out of date.

  A. We have not hired any new engineers in the past five years.

  B. Our engineers are using outdated computer equipment.

  C. Our engineers are relying on outdated software to design our product.

II. EFFECT: Our sales are down.

  A. Our customers find our competitor's product more up-to-date.

  B. Our customers are replacing the products they have purchased from us with products from our competitor.

  C. Our customers have indicated that they do not intend to purchase our product in the future.

When using a cause-and-effect organizational strategy, it's not enough just to assert your causes and probable effects. You need to provide evidence to provide the link between the causes and effects.

A variation on cause and effect is organizing a presentation from effect to cause. For example:

I. EFFECT: The emergency room is too crowded for physicians and nurses to effectively treat the patients who arrive there.

II. CAUSE: Too many people in our county do not have medical insurance and have no place to go for medical care other than the emergency room.

A third way to organize your efforts to persuade an audience is especially useful when you are facing an unreceptive audience—one that does not agree with your point of view or your specific proposition. **Refutation** is an organizational strategy by which you identify objections to your proposition and then refute those objections with arguments and evidence. It is better to present both sides of an issue rather than just your own position if you are certain that your audience is skeptical of your position.

You will be most likely to organize a persuasive speech by refutation if you know your listeners' chief objections to your proposition. In fact, if you do not acknowledge such objections, the audience will probably think about them during your speech anyway. Credible facts and statistics will generally be more effective than emotional arguments in supporting your points of refutation.

Adapt

Suppose you represent a large hotel chain that wants to build a new luxury hotel in a southwestern city. The hotel chain has purchased most of the property it needs to start construction, except for one prime piece of property owned by two sisters who have a tamale stand on their property. You have approached the sisters, but they don't want to sell. They have agreed to meet with you to hear your final offer, so you'll need to be especially effective in refuting their concerns. You understand that the price you're offering is not the reason they are balking at selling. Rather, they promised their mother, who passed away last year, that they would always maintain the family business on the same location where their mother started the business. Here's an outline for a presentation to the two sisters based on the refutation organizational strategy.

I. We would like to build a hotel on this property and we will honor your mother by naming our exclusive roof-top restaurant after her.

II. In addition to purchasing your property, we would like to purchase your mother's recipe for tamales and feature them in our new restaurant.

III. We would like to hire both of you as consultants to the hotel to work in the restaurant and be in charge of quality control of all food served in the hotel.

The presentation to the sisters consists of major points offered to directly refute their objections. When you use a refutation strategy, you address the specific concerns and offer solutions to the objections you know you will encounter.

Like refutation, the fourth organizational strategy is unique to persuasive speaking. The **motivated sequence**, devised by Alan Monroe, is a five-step organizational strategy for a persuasive presentation.[12] This simple yet effective strategy integrates the problem-and-solution organizational method with principles that have been confirmed by research and practical experience. The five steps involved are attention, need, satisfaction, visualization, and action.

Refutation an organizational strategy by which you identify objections to your proposition and then refute those objections with arguments and evidence.

Motivated sequence a five-step plan for organizing a persuasive message: attention, need, satisfaction, visualization, and action.

1. Attention. Your first task, and the first stage in appropriately adapting your message to others, is to get your listeners' attention. Using a rhetorical question, illustration, startling fact or statistic, quotation, humorous story, or a reference to historical or recent events are ways of starting a speech to gain favorable attention. The attention step is, in essence, your application of one of these strategies.

Business executive Raymond Kotcher used this attention-catching opener to begin a speech in which his goal was to encourage recent graduates with communication degrees to become involved in the global marketplace:

> Now, I have a request. I want you graduates to consider what I have to say to you this afternoon not as a commencement address. Rather, think of my remarks—and I'll keep them brief—as an email, written just to you. An email written to you, an emerging communicator. And as with most personal notes that are written to mark milestones in our great and privileged society—setting off for college; yes, graduating from college; that first job; committing to that someone special; the first child—the email offers advice, encouragement, warnings about and hope for the future. Don't hit delete just yet![13]

2. Need. After getting your audience's attention, establish why your topic, problem, or issue should concern them. Tell your audience about the problem. Adapt your message to them by convincing them that the problem affects them directly. Argue that there is a need for change. During the need step (which corresponds with the problem step in a problem-and-solution speech), you should develop logical arguments backed by evidence. It's during the need step that you create dissonance or use a credible fear appeal to motivate listeners to respond to your solution.

In trying to convince his audience that the world is changing and that they ought to be contributing to the global conversation, Kotcher points out that in order to be contemporary, they need to be up-to-date on cyberworld applications:

> The audience of widely read blogs . . . rivals the size of the audiences of the online versions of major newspapers. Each day, 200 million Google searches are conducted, and half aren't in the English language. There are two billion cell phone subscribers in the world today. . . . And while I don't want to overburden this email with statistics, have you, like the estimated twenty million people around the world, played and worked in the cyberworlds created by Entropia or Second Life? Second Life is an online society where you can explore, or socialize, or buy goods and services or even build, rent, and sell real estate—using your credit card! Earlier this month, *Business Week* reported on this 3-D world, and estimates in the article put the size of this virtual economy at $1.5 BILLION—that's in real U. S. dollars—and growing.[14]

3. Satisfaction. After you explain and document a need or problem, you identify your plan (or solution) and explain how it will satisfy the need. You need not go into painstaking detail at this point in your talk. Present enough information so that your listeners have a general understanding of how the problem may be solved. You'll provide the specific action you want them to take later (in the action step). For now, identify in general terms what the solution to the problem is—satisfy the need you have identified. Here's the satisfaction step in Raymond Kotcher's message:

> Relish the idea of joining the conversation. Today's media are participatory—integrating people with people to build community. Gone are the days of command and control. And this new networked world requires a new generation of communication leaders and leadership. Apply what you've learned at [college] and in your life so far. Already, one in five college-age students has traveled abroad in the past three years. More than one in three of you speaks at least two languages. And your generation truly wants to help build this global community.[15]

Visualization using words to create an image in audience members' minds.

4. Visualization. Now you need to give your audience a sense of what it would be like if your solution were adopted or, conversely, if it were not adopted. **Visualization**—using words to create an image in audience members' minds—applies the principle of effectively using verbal messages. With a **positive visualization** approach, you paint a rosy picture of how wonderful the future will be if your satisfaction step is implemented. With a **negative visualization** approach, you paint a bleak picture of how terrible the future will be if nothing is done; you use a fear appeal to motivate your listeners to do what you suggest to avoid further problems. In either case, you use **word pictures**—lively descriptions that appeal to listeners' senses (sight, taste, smell, sound, and touch). Or you might combine both approaches: The problem will be solved if your solution is adopted, but things will get increasingly worse if it is not.

Here's how Kotcher helped his listeners visualize how the world is changing and how some previous college graduates have capitalized on being globally aware and active:

> Justin Lane, for instance, a 1995 . . . graduate, is the New York bureau chief for the European Pressphoto Agency. He won the Pulitzer in 2002 for breaking news photography for his freelance contributions to *The New York Times*' coverage of the September 11 attacks. A year later, he traveled to Iraq to document cultural looting, the crisis facing Iraqi women, and the uncovering of mass graves. His photographs from Iraq garnered two gallery shows in New York and appearances in numerous newspapers, magazines, and books.
>
> Then there's Chris McKee, also class of 1995. . . . He made an award-winning documentary that has opened up the little-known world of Mongolian nomads to the rest of the world. And Tyler Hicks, class of 1992, named by *American Photo* magazine as one of the twenty-five most important photographers, in large part because of his compelling images from war-torn places like Kosovo, Iraq, and Afghanistan.
>
> And Michael Williams. . . . This Academy Award–winning producer is a pioneer in delivering some of the most original content to be seen in theaters and on television. He won an Oscar in 2004 for producing *The Fog of War*, a film that delivered a riveting look at former Defense Secretary Robert S. McNamara and his controversial role in the Vietnam War.[16]

The implication of these positive examples is that if you join the global technology revolution, you too will be successful.

5. Action. The action step is your speech's conclusion. You remind your audience of the problem (outlined in the need step), give them the solution (the satisfaction step), remind them of the great things that will happen if they follow your advice (positive visualization) or the bad things that will happen if they don't (negative visualization). Finally, you tell them what they need to do next (the action step).

To finish his presentation, Raymond Kotcher made this specific recommendation to his listeners:

> So, this email to you is just about finished. Yet I can't close without giving you some personal advice—about what I have gleaned in my career and life since those impossibly cold mornings walking to class at 640 Comm Ave. Here goes:
> ENGAGE YOUR CURIOSITY. Be indefatigable in ferreting out the answers to questions that will inform a world, assist a client, uncover an injustice, right a wrong.
> NEVER FORGET YOUR INTEGRITY AND CREDIBILITY.
> DEVELOP YOUR VOICE. You're a skilled communicator. Always strive to improve and develop your communication skills and apply them atop a deep understanding for all that has preceded you. Combine that with your personal experiences and what is important to you. And be willing to listen and to be taught, because learning NEVER ends.
> FOSTER YOUR CREATIVITY. Oh, how the world, especially the business world, seeks creative and innovative thinkers who can communicate their imaginative ideas.[17]

You can adapt the motivated sequence to the needs of your topic and your audience. For example, if you are speaking to a knowledgeable, receptive audience, you do not need

Positive visualization a rosy word picture of how wonderful the future will be if your solution is implemented.

Negative visualization a bleak picture of how terrible the future will be if nothing is done; a fear appeal used to motivate listeners to adopt a particular solution to a problem.

Word picture lively descriptions that help listeners form a mental image by appealing to their senses (sight, taste, smell, sound, and touch).

Adapt

to spend a great deal of time on the need step. The audience already knows that the need is serious. They may, however, feel helpless to do anything about it. Therefore, you would want to emphasize the satisfaction and action steps.

On the other hand, if you are speaking to a neutral or apathetic audience, you will need to spend time getting their attention and proving that a problem exists, that it is significant, and that it affects them personally. You will emphasize the attention, need, and visualization steps. And if you are speaking to a hostile audience, you should spend considerable time on the need step. Convince your audience that the problem is significant and that they should be concerned about it. You would probably not propose a lengthy, detailed action. In the final section of this chapter, we will offer additional strategies for persuading receptive, unreceptive, and neutral audiences.

Is there one best way to organize a persuasive speech? The answer is no. The organizational strategy you select must depend on your audience, your message, and your desired objective. What is important is to remember that your decision can have a major effect on your listeners' response to your message.

RECAP: Organizational Patterns for Persuasive Speeches

Organizational Pattern	Definition	Example
Problem and Solution	Organization by discussing a problem and then various possible solutions	I. Problem: The company's sales revenues dropped in the last quarter. II. Solution: The company should beef up advertising efforts to bolster sales.
Cause and Effect	Organization by discussing a situation and its causes, or a situation and its effects	I. Cause: Most HMOs refuse to pay for treatment they deem "experimental." II. Effect: Patients die who might have been saved by "experimental" treatment.
Refutation	Organization according to objections your listeners may have to your ideas and arguments	I. Although you may think that our new, higher-premium insurance policy will reduce your standard of living, its comprehensive coverage will save you money over time. II. Although you may think that the high cost of insurance may cost the organization more money and place your jobs in jeopardy, it will actually help us attract and retain higher quality workers.
Motivated Sequence	Alan H. Monroe's five-step plan for organizing a persuasive speech: attention, need, satisfaction, visualization, and action	I. Attention: "An apple a day keeps the doctor busy." What has happened to the old adage? Why has it changed? II. Need: Pesticides are poisoning our fresh fruits and vegetables. III. Satisfaction: Those of you who purchase food for hotels and restaurants should purchase organic fruits and vegetables for your guests. IV. Visualization: Remember the apple poisoned by Snow White's wicked stepmother? You may be feeding such apples to your own guests if you don't buy organic fruits and vegatables. V. Action: Buy fruits and vegetables raised organically.

How to adjust ideas to people and people to ideas. Rhetoric scholar Donald C. Bryant's definition of rhetoric emphasizes the principle of appropriately adapting a message to an audience: "Rhetoric," he said, "is the process of adjusting ideas to people and people to ideas."[18] And with this thought we've come full circle in the process of developing a message for an audience. As we have emphasized throughout our discussion of presentational speaking, analyzing your audience and adapting to them is at the heart of the speech-making process; adapting is one of the fundamental communication principles for a lifetime. In a persuasive speech, that adaptation begins with identifying your specific purpose and understanding whether you are trying to change or reinforce attitudes, beliefs, or values. It continues with your selection of an organizational strategy. For example, if your audience members are not receptive to your ideas, you might choose to organize your speech by refutation, addressing the audience's objections head on. Both research studies and experienced speakers can offer other useful suggestions to help you adapt to your listeners, including receptive, neutral, and unreceptive audiences.

It is usually a pleasure to address an audience that already supports you and your message. You can explore your ideas in depth and can be fairly certain of a successful appeal to action if your audience is receptive.

One suggestion that may help you make the most of such a speaking opportunity is to identify with your audience. Emphasize your similarities and common interests. The introduction of your speech may be a good place in which to do this.

Another suggestion is to be overt in stating your speaking objective, telling your audience exactly what you want them to do, and asking them for an immediate show of support. If, for example, your audience is already receptive to the idea that your company and theirs should merge, you need not worry that being overt will antagonize them. Rather, it will give you more time to rouse them to passionate commitment and action to support the planned merger.

A third suggestion for persuading a receptive audience is to use emotional appeals. If your audience already supports your position, you need not spend a great deal of time providing evidence. Rather, you can focus on moving your receptive audience to action with strong, ethical emotional appeals.

Many audiences fall somewhere between being wildly enthusiastic and being hostile. They are simply neutral. For example, a group of stockholders may have no strong opinions about whether employees should be given discounts at the company's outlet stores. Their neutrality may take the form of indifference: They know about the topic or issue, but they don't see how it affects them, or they can't make up their minds about it. Or, their neutrality may take the form of ignorance: They just don't know much about the topic. Regardless of whether your neutral audience is indifferent or ignorant, your challenge is to get them interested in your message.

One way to get a neutral audience interested is to "hook" them with an especially engaging introduction or attention step.

Another strategy for persuading neutral audiences is to refer to universal beliefs and concerns. These could include such common interests as protecting the environment and having access to good health care.

A third strategy for neutral audiences is to show how the topic affects not only them, but people they care about. For example, real estate agents will be interested in issues and policies that affect the growth of their communities.

Finally, be realistic about what you can accomplish. People who are neutral at the beginning of your speech are unlikely to become enthusiastic after only a few minutes. They are unlikely to be persuaded all at once or after a first hearing of arguments and issues.

One of your biggest challenges as a speaker is to persuade audience members who are not receptive to you or your message. If they are unreceptive to you personally, your job is to seek ways to enhance your credibility and persuade them to listen to you. If they are unreceptive to your point of view, several strategies may help.

First, don't immediately announce your persuasive purpose. Immediately and overtly telling your listeners that you plan to change their minds can make them defensive. Focus instead on areas of agreement. As you would with a neutral audience, refer to universal beliefs and concerns. Instead of saying to an unreceptive audience, "I'm here this morning to convince you that we should increase your employee contributions to your health insurance," you might say, "I think we can agree that we have an important common goal: the best quality of health care that benefits the most people in a fair way."

Second, if you think your audience may be unreceptive, advance your strongest arguments first. This is the principle of primacy, which we discussed in Chapter 12. If you save your best argument for last (the recency principle), your audience may already have stopped listening.

Third, acknowledge audience members' opposing points of view. Summarize the reasons they may oppose your point of view; then cite evidence and use arguments to refute the opposition and support your conclusion. In speaking to students seeking to hold down tuition costs, a dean might say, "I am aware that many of you struggle to pay for your education. You work nights, take out loans, and live frugally." Then the dean could go on to identify how the university could provide additional financial assistance to students to help them cope with an unavoidable tuition increase.

Finally, as with a neutral audience, don't expect a major shift in attitude from an unreceptive audience. Set a realistic goal. It may be enough for an eight- to ten-minute speech just to get listeners to hear you out and at least think about some of your arguments.

RECAP: Adjusting Ideas to People and People to Ideas

Persuading the Receptive Audience

- Identify with your audience.
- Emphasize common interests.
- Provide a clear objective; tell your listeners what you want them to do.
- Appropriately use emotional appeals.

Persuading the Neutral Audience

- Gain and maintain their attention.
- Refer to beliefs and concerns that are important to listeners.
- Show how the topic affects people your listeners care about.
- Be realistic about what you can accomplish.

Persuading the Unreceptive Audience

- Don't tell listeners you are going to try to convince them to support your position.
- Make sure you present your strongest arguments first.
- Acknowledge opposing points of view.
- Don't expect a major shift in attitudes or behavior.

Presenting to Sell

Dietrich Mateschitz, a former toothpaste salesman, had an idea. He thought the world might just be ready to buy a fizzy energy drink, even though there didn't appear to be a market for such a product. When he was on a trip to Thailand as a marketing executive for Procter and Gamble, Mateschitz tasted a drink called Krating Daeng, which is Thai for "red water buffalo." He thought it might have possibilities as a beverage that could be sold to people who needed an energy boost. After considerable marketing research and product development, Mateschitz debuted his product in 1987 in Europe. It sold well, and he launched it in the United States in 2001. Chances are you've sampled his creation—Red Bull.[19]

Dietrich Mateschitz figured out how to sell a product even before people had expressed a need for the product. Now that's a good salesman. What did Mateschitz know that could help you be a top-notch salesperson? We're about to tell you.

Between billboards, posters, TV, the Internet, and radio commercials, you experience hundreds of sales messages every day. Perhaps wherever you are reading this book there is a radio jingle or TV commercial in the background, a billboard attempting to get your attention to sell you something, or a poster on a wall enticing you to spend your spring break in Colorado. If your computer is connected to the Internet, there may be sales messages bouncing around on your computer screen. Sales and marketing experts spend billions of dollars crafting messages to get you to buy or use what they are selling.

To sell is to persuade someone to buy or use a product or service. You can also sell an idea, a proposal, or a policy rather than a tangible object. Since selling is persuading, the principles of and skills for persuasion that we've already discussed are the key strategies that you will use when selling someone something. To maximize your sales potential, we suggest that you first, analyze the sales situation, and second, plan your persuasive sales message using time-tested strategies that, to paraphrase Donald C. Bryant, help you adjust products and services to people and people to products and services.

Sales skills are important leadership skills. We've noted that to lead is to influence others through communication, and often leaders need to sell ideas and methods. So, as we discuss the principles and strategies of sales, keep in mind that leaders sell ideas—whether informally and one on one, in groups and teams, or when speaking to many people. Sales involves more than simply selling a product.

Developing Your Sales Message

We've discussed several strategies for organizing presentations. Some organizational strategies, such as topical or chronological organization, are best suited for informative messages. Most sales presentations are organized using the problem-and-solution pattern. The five-step motivated sequence (which, as we noted, is a form of the problem-and-solution approach) is a good overarching organizational strategy to consider for sales presentations. Catching attention, establishing need, satisfying the need by offering a solution, visualizing the benefits of the solution or describing how the need will not be met if the solution is not adopted, and identifying a specific action to take is a good formula for structuring a sales presentation. The suggestions for organizing a sales presentation we describe below are based on the motivated sequence.[20]

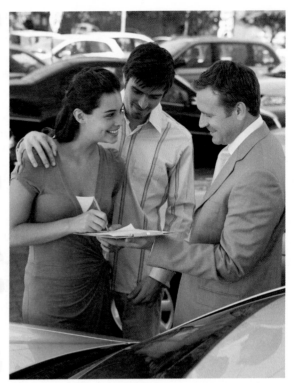

The five-step motivated sequence provides a good way to organize an effective sales presentation that will close the deal.

Hook your listener. A good salesperson does more than merely get a customer's attention; a good salesperson is able to "hook" the customer to gain and keep the person's focus. How do you do that? You must know your customer's interests, needs, and hopes and adapt your message to address them. And, in most cases, you have to grab your listeners quickly. To hook them, ask them an opening question that is based on what you suspect they may need ("Are you interested in a car that costs less yet looks expensive?") or addresses a fear they may have ("Would you like a car that will protect your family if you have an accident?"). Television, radio, and Internet sales pitches spend considerable time simply trying to hook you to get and keep your attention. Unless you hook your customers, they will undoubtedly get away.

Identify the customer's key issue. After hooking the customer, you need to address what he or she needs or wants. Knowing your customer's interests, needs, desires, fears, and hopes is essential for making a sale. How do you find out what your customer likes and needs? Ask. After you ask, you have one more task: Listen. An effective sales message doesn't begin with the salesperson immediately extolling the virtues of the product. First, ask questions that qualify your customer. To **qualify** a customer is to identify whether the customer can afford the product or service you are selling and to learn how to best approach the customer. Does the customer have a family? If so, would he or she be motivated by appealing to concerns for their safety? Is the customer most interested in a low price? Knowing what the customer wants can help you customize your message to your customer. If you already suspect what the customer's needs are, then you can directly identify how what you are selling meets the needs, solves a problem, or addresses an issue that concerns the customer. Your knowledge of what your competitor has to offer and what the customer needs and your ability to briefly and quickly get to the heart of what the customer wants will increase your chances of making the sale.

To identify the customer's needs or issues, you may need to ask specific questions (unless the customer explicitly tells you what he or she wants). Here are some possible questions to ask to help identify a customer's need:

- What do you like best about what you are currently using?
- What would an ideal product look like?
- What do like least about what you are currently using?
- What is missing from what you're currently using?
- How many of these do you use each week?
- What are the key things you're looking for in a new . . . ?

Qualify to identify whether a customer can afford a product or service and to learn how to best approach the customer.

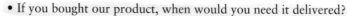

- If you bought our product, when would you need it delivered?
- What could we do to get your business?

Make the recommendation. After you have analyzed, or qualified, the customer, you'll want to note how your product or service addresses the issue you've identified. Although you don't need to ask for the sale quite yet, you need to describe what you're selling and link your product or service to the the customer's needs. Especially if you're selling several models or versions of the same product (such as a car, a computer, or an insurance benefit package), you'll need to direct the customer to a specific recommendation. If you have over a dozen different models, select one or two that you think are best aligned with your customer's needs. Having too many options can be overwhelming for both you and the customer. If you've understood what your customer's concerns are, you'll be in a good position to begin to steer your customer to a recommendation that is best for him or her.

When making your recommendation, explain and demonstrate how the product works. Provide a step-by-step overview of what the product does. If appropriate, let the customer try the product. Most grocery stores know that one way to sell cheese is to give away free samples. Letting your customer use the product to experience the benefits may be your most important sales tool.

Stress benefits, not features. All customers are interested in the benefits of what you're selling to them. This next point is essential: *You must stress the benefits of what you're selling, not just list the features.* What's the difference between a feature and a benefit? A feature is simply a characteristic of whatever the product or service is. For example, if you say, "This computer screen is very bright," you're describing a feature of the product. A benefit is a good result or something that creates a positive response in a customer. Rather than simply noting that the computer screen is bright, you could describe a benefit of the bright screen: "This means that you won't experience eye strain or headaches, and you can get your work done more quickly." Describing a benefit is a customer-centered way of helping the customer visualize the positive things that will happen to him or her if he or she buys what you are selling. Table 14.1 provides additional examples of features and their corresponding benefits.

A skilled salesperson can quickly assess how to describe a product or service in terms of the benefits the customer will receive. Stressing benefits helps the customer have a positive feeling about what he or she is buying. To help the customer experience the good things that will happen if he or she makes the purchase, it's not enough to just state a benefit—you'll need to provide evidence. Testimonials from satisfied customers, demonstrations, and evidence from unbiased sources such as *Consumer Reports* are helpful in documenting the truth of your claims. You have an ethical responsibility not to promise too much or make a claim you can't support. By realistically identifying the benefits, you'll increase your credibility and have the best type of customer—a repeat customer.

Make the close. Every good salesperson knows the most critical part of making a sale is the close. The close is when you ask for (and ideally get) the sale. Most closes involve

Table 14.1	Features and Benefits
Customer Features	**Customer Benefits**
This floor is a no-wax floor.	Because this is a no-wax floor, you will never again have to get down on your hands and knees to scrub another floor.
If you sponsor this concert, your company name and logo will be listed in the program.	Sponsoring this event promotes your company and lets everyone in the community know how much you care about supporting the arts. People will view your company in a positive light, which will increase your sales and maintain the goodwill of your customers.
This ergonomically designed chair will keep your back straight.	This ergonomically designed chair will eliminate backaches, increase your productivity, and give you more time to spend on more pleasurable tasks.

summarizing how the product or service solves a problem or meets a need, cogently listing the benefits, and then asking for the sale.

Some closes use the "yes technique." A salesperson using the yes technique asks the customer a series of questions to which the answer is always yes. If, for example, the customer has already disclosed that he likes a particular model of car, the color of the car, and the features of the car, the salesperson asks a series of questions to which the answer is yes:

Salesperson: "So, Mr. Affolter, you like the Oxford model the best?"

Customer: "Yes."

Salesperson: "And you like the cobalt blue?"

Customer: "Yes."

Salesperson: "You also like the cruise control, satellite radio, and GPS system, right?"

Customer: "Yes, I do."

Salesperson: "So if I can get the Oxford model, in blue, with the features you like, and we can agree on a price, will you buy the car today?"

Customer: "OK, yes."

The yes technique is based on the principle that "It's better to get a message out of someone than to put one in him or her." Get the customer to state what he or she likes and to reach no other conclusion when asked to make the purchase than that the correct answer is yes.

Respond to objections. Textbooks have a way of presenting models or specific strategies that make it seem as though all you need to do is follow the suggested sequence of steps or specific prescriptions and you'll be successful. When attempting to sell something to someone, you'll soon discover that it's usually not quite that easy. In most sales situations, the customer is not likely to simply say yes or "I'll take it" after you've hooked the person, identified the issue, made the recommendation, stressed the benefits, and provided a closing. Customers will likely have questions, concerns, and objections to the claims you've made. How you respond to those will often determine whether you get the sale or not. Consider the following suggestions.

Some customers may not explicitly state what is bothering them. For example, they may not say, "I don't have enough money to buy what you're selling." So, you need to "listen between the lines" if the customer says something like "I'm not sure I'm prepared to buy this product now" or "Buying this product doesn't fit into my plans right now." If price appears to be the objection, suggesting a payment plan spread over a period of time, directing the customer to a less expensive option, or reconfiguring the product so it costs less may be what you need to do to respond to the unspoken issue of price. The more you can remove hidden agendas, the more likely you are to be able to address the specific concern. Open-ended questions such as "What questions do you have about this product?" or "Is there something that I could do today that would help you make a commitment?" can help you find a customer's underlying objection. The closer you can get to a customer's real objection, the more likely it will be that you can address it and get the sale.

How do you determine a customer's real objections? You listen, observe, ask good questions, and listen some more. If you can find the true objection and then successfully address that objection, you've got the sale.

If a customer says no, or "I'll need to think about this," or "I'm not sure I'm ready to decide today," do your best to listen and see if you can identify what it is that is keeping the customer from saying yes. Keep the conversation going. By asking

"If they don't like our proposal I'll show them the kittens. Everybody likes kittens."

follow-up questions, exploring objections, listening for clues, and observing nonverbal behavior, you may be able to successfully respond to a rejection. Once the customer has left or hung up the phone, it's less likely that the person will return (although some customers simply need more time to ponder the options). You're more likely to get the sale if the customer is physically present or if you are in contact with the customer. We don't encourage such high-pressure tactics as "This is a one-time offer, only good in the next hour" or "You must decide today." It's also unethical to claim that the product is the last one left when there are more in the back room.

A customer may ask you something about what you're selling that you don't know. *If you don't know the answer to a question, say so, and find the answer quickly.* Promise to get back to the customer with the answer by a specific time or date. Be sure to keep your promise.

One maxim that has served salespeople well is "Underpromise and overdeliver." Don't promise more than you know your product or service can offer, and work to provide even more than the customer expects. Although customers generally do not like surprises, they are usually delighted when what they've purchased surprises them with more than what was promised.

One of the biggest sales mistakes new salespeople make is talking too much after they have made a sale. Once the customer has made the decision to buy a product or service, don't keep describing additional benefits.

Informing and Persuading as a Team

Very likely in business and professional settings, you'll not only present solo talks but also participate in team presentations. Working as a team takes a coordinated effort. If you are used to developing reports and presentations on your own, it may be a challenge to work with others on a team assignment. Consider these suggestions to enhance teamwork.

Take a few moments to verbalize the team goal. Don't immediately plunge in and try to start dividing up the work just so you can hurry off to your next responsibility. Working as a team, develop a written, specific purpose statement. Remember to state the purpose in terms of what you want your listeners to be able to do.

> Effective specific purpose statement: At the end of our presentation, the McMann and Tate Agency will purchase our company's new electronic widget.

> Less effective specific purpose statement: We want to describe and identify the benefits and features of our new product.

Give group members individual assignments. After you decide on your group's presentation objective, divide up the tasks involved in achieving the goal. Also, devise a plan for keeping in touch with one another frequently to share information and ideas. As you learned in Chapter 9, teams work best when they establish a clear, results-driven structure. This means spelling out who will do what by when. Make a written record of team member assignments and responsibilities.

Develop a team presentation outline. After team members have researched key issues, begin drafting an outline of your team presentation. If you're solving a problem, you could use the reflective thinking steps we presented in Chapter 10 to develop your outline (define the problem, analyze the problem, list possible solutions, choose the best solution, implement the plan). Alternatively, you can outline your presentation according to the motivated sequence (attention, need, satisfaction, visualization, action).

Decide on your presentation format. Unless the format for your presentation has been specified, your group will need to determine whether you will use a symposium, a forum, a panel presentation, or some combination of these approaches. A **symposium presentation** format consists of individual presentations with no audience interaction or conversation. Each person on the team simply presents a portion of the presentation; the presentation is like a series of individual speeches. A **panel presentation** is much more interactive. Team members have a conversation with a moderator or a facilitator who manages the interaction. A **forum presentation** is one in which the team invites questions

Symposium presentation a presentation format that consists of a series of individual presentations without interaction or conversation; each person on the team gives a portion of the presentation.

Panel presentation a presentation in which team members have a conversation with a moderator or a facilitator who manages the interaction.

Forum presentation a question-and-answer session that usually follows a presentation or a symposium.

and conversation from the audience following a presentation. Make decisions about who will present which portions of your outline and how to integrate them. Your presentation should have an introduction and a definite ending that reflect your group's work as a problem-solving team.

Rehearse the presentation. Just as you would an individual speech, rehearse the team presentation. If you are using visual aids, be sure to incorporate them in your rehearsal. Also, be sure to time your presentation when you rehearse.

Be audience-centered. Adapt to your listeners. Although you will want to rehearse your presentation, effective speakers, even those contributing to a team presentation, monitor the nonverbal cues they are receiving from the audience to help them modify their message for maximum clarity and effect.

Clarify your purpose for your listeners. Just as with an individual speech, it's important for listeners to know what your speaking goal is and to understand why you are presenting the information to them; it's also important for each group member to be reminded of the overarching goal of the presentation. It is useful for the first speaker to ensure that the audience has a good understanding of the group's purpose. If your group is responding to a specific discussion question, it may be useful to write the question or purpose of the presentation on a chalkboard, whiteboard, flipchart, or overhead transparency.

Coordinate your use of presentation aids. If your group is using PowerPoint slides, consider having each group member use the same template and font style to give your presentation a coordinated look and feel. It's also best to have one person operate the presentation equipment. You can use presentation aids not only to clarify your purpose, but also to summarize key findings and recommendations. Visual aids can serve the important function of unifying your group presentation.

Choose someone to serve as coordinator or moderator. Teams need a balance between structure (following the outline) and interaction (conversation). Without adequate structure, conversation can bounce from person to person and the presentation will not have a clear focus. A moderator can help provide needed structure for a group presentation by introducing both the topic and the group members. A moderator can also help keep track of time and ensure that no one dominates the discussion or speaks too little.

Following the presentation, be ready to answer questions. Communication, as we've emphasized, is more than just giving people information; it also includes responding to feedback and questions from listeners. Group presentations often include a question-and-answer session (forum) following the presentation. Besides being informed about your topic, it's wise to have thoroughly read any written report the team has distributed.

If it looks like a questioner is using the question-and-answer period to give a oration, gently ask, "And what is your question?" or "How can we help you?" This approach should elicit a question that you can then address and return the communication process back to the control of the group.

Making Special Presentations

Besides informing and persuading others, you may be called on simply to introduce a speaker, present an award, receive an award (because you're such a good leader and communicator), or make a toast. In these special presentation situations, the audience has certain expectations of what you may say. When introducing someone, for example, it's assumed you will extol the virtues and credentials of the person you're introducing. Toasts are expected to be brief yet interesting.

Introducing Others

The ultimate purpose of an introduction is to arouse interest in a speaker and his or her topic and establish the speaker's credibility. When you are asked to give a speech of introduction for a featured speaker or honored guest, your purposes are similar to those of a good opening to a speech: You need to get the attention of the audience, build the speaker's credibility, and introduce the speaker's general subject. You also need to make the speaker feel welcome while revealing some of the speaker's personal qualities so that the audience can feel they know the speaker more intimately. There are two cardinal rules for giving introductory speeches: Be brief and be accurate.

- Be brief. The audience has come to hear the main speaker or honor the guest, not to listen to you.

- Be accurate. Nothing so disturbs a speaker as having to begin by correcting the introducer. If you are going to introduce someone at a meeting or dinner, ask that person to supply you with biographical data beforehand. If someone else provides you with the speaker's background, make sure the information is accurate. Be certain that you know how to pronounce the speaker's name and any other names or terms you will need to use.

The following short speech of introduction adheres to the two criteria we have just suggested: It's brief and it's accurate.

> This evening, friends, we have the opportunity to hear one of the most innovative mayors in the history of our community. Mary Norris's experience running her own real estate business gave her an opportunity to pilot a new approach to attracting new businesses to our community, even before she was elected mayor in last year's landslide victory. The Good Government League recently recognized her as the most successful mayor in our state. Not only is she a skilled manager and spokesperson for our city, but she is also a warm and caring person. I am pleased to introduce my friend Mary Norris.

Finally, keep the needs of your audience in mind at all times. If the person you are introducing truly needs no introduction, do not give one! Just welcome the speaker and step aside. (Note that the President of the United States is always introduced simply, "Ladies and gentlemen, the President of the United States.")

Presenting an Award

Presenting an award is somewhat like introducing a speaker or guest: Remember that the audience did not come to hear you but to see and hear the winner of the award. Nevertheless, delivering a presentation speech is an important responsibility, one that has several distinct components.

First, when presenting an award, you should refer to the occasion of the presentation. Awards are often given to mark the anniversary of a special event, the completion of a long-range task, the accomplishments of a lifetime, or extraordinary achievements.

Next, you should talk about the history and significance of the award. This section of the speech may be fairly long if the audience knows little about the award; it will be brief if the audience is already familiar with the history and purpose of the award. Whatever the award, a discussion of its significance will add to its meaning for the person who receives it.

In the final section of an award presentation, you name the person to whom the award is given. The longest part of this segment is the description of the achievements that elicited the award. That description should be given in glowing terms. Hyperbole is appropriate here. If the name of the person getting the award has already been made public, you may refer to the person by name throughout your description. If you are going to announce the individual's name for the first time, you will probably want to recite the achievements first and leave the person's name for last. Even though some members of the audience may recognize the recipient from your description, you should still save the drama of the actual announcement until the last moment.

Accepting an Award

Anyone who receives an award or nomination usually responds with a brief acceptance speech. Acceptance speeches have received something of a bad reputation because of the lengthy, emotional, rambling, and generally boring speeches delivered annually on prime-time TV by the winners of the film industry's Oscars.

The same audience who may resent a lengthy oration will readily appreciate a brief, heartfelt expression of thanks. In fact, brief acceptance speeches can actually be quite insightful, even inspiring, and can leave the audience feeling no doubt that the right person won the award. Two months before he died in 1979, John Wayne accepted an honorary Oscar with these touching words:

> Thank you, ladies and gentlemen. Your applause is just about the only medicine a fella would ever need. I'm mighty pleased I can amble here tonight. Oscar and I have something in common. Oscar first came on the Hollywood scene in 1928. So did I. We're both a little weatherbeaten, but we're still here and plan to be around a whole lot longer.[21]

If you have the good fortune to receive an award, your acceptance speech may be impromptu, because you may not know that you have won until the award is presented. A fairly simple formula should help you compose a good acceptance speech on the spur of the moment.

First, thank the person making the presentation and the organization that he or she represents. It is also gracious to thank a few people who have contributed to your success—but resist thanking a long list of everyone you have ever known, down to the family dog.

Next, comment on the meaning or significance of the award to you. You may also wish to reflect on the larger significance of the award to the people and ideals it honors.

Finally, find some meaning in the award for your audience—people who respect your accomplishments and who may themselves aspire to similar achievements. In what has become one of the most often quoted acceptance speeches ever made, William Faulkner dedicated his 1950 Nobel Peace Prize for Literature to

Acceptance speeches have a reputation for being boring. If you keep your speech brief and behave graciously, your audience will agree that the right person received the award.

> the young men and women already dedicated to the same anguish and travail, among whom is already that one who will some day stand here where I am standing.[22]

Making a Toast

Most people are asked at some time or another to offer a toast on some momentous occasion—a wedding, a celebration of the birth of a new baby, a reunion of friends, or a successful business venture. A **toast** is a brief salute to such an occasion, usually accompanied by a round of drinks and immediately followed by the raising or clinking together of glasses or goblets. The custom is said to have taken its name from the old custom of tossing a bit of bread or a crouton into a beverage for flavoring.[23] "Drinking the toast" was somewhat like enjoying a dunked doughnut.

The modern toast is usually quite short—only a few sentences at most. Some toasts are very personal, as, for example, one given by a wedding guest who is close friend of both the bride and groom:

> I would like to say a few words about this couple. You see, I knew Rachel and Ben before they were a couple—when they were friends. I first met Rachel when we were freshmen in high school. Her sarcastic sense of humor has kept me laughing ever since.[24]

If you are asked to make an impromptu toast, let your audience and the occasion dictate what you say. Sincerity is more important than wit. At a dinner one of your authors attended in Moscow a few years ago, all the guests were asked to stand at some point during the meal and offer a toast. Although this Russian custom took all of us by surprise, one of our friends gave a heartfelt and well-received toast that went something like this:

> We have spent the past week enjoying both the natural beauty and the many marvels of your country. We have visited the exquisite palaces of the czars and stood in amazement before some of the world's great art treasures. But

Toast a brief speech saluting a momentous occasion.

we have also discovered that the most important resource of Russia is the warmth of her people. Here's to new and lasting friendships.

Our Russian hosts were most appreciative. The rest of us were impressed. Mary's toast was a resounding success because she spoke sincerely about her audience and the occasion.

Communication Principles and Skills for Leadership

Principle One: Be aware of your communication with yourself and others.

- Be consciously aware of using strategies that will make your informative messages clear, interesting, and memorable.
- When you use cause-and-effect organization, you must be aware of and then convince your listeners of the critical causal link.
- To be a better-informed consumer of persuasive messages, as well as a more ethical persuasive speaker, be aware of and avoid using common logical fallacies.

Principle Two: Effectively use and interpret verbal messages.

- Pace the flow of the information you present to enhance message clarity.
- Relate new information you present to information the audience already knows to increase clarity and retention.
- Use simple ideas rather than complex ideas to make your message clear.
- Build message redundancy to enhance message retention.
- To use negative visualization, describe in detail how bleak the future will be if your solution is not implemented.
- To use positive visualization, describe in detail how wonderful the future will be if your solution is implemented.
- To enhance your audience's perception of your competence, cite evidence to support your ideas.
- Prepare a thoughtful conclusion to enhance your terminal credibility.
- Provide logical proof (evidence and reasoning) for your arguments and avoid logical fallacies to heighten your chance for success with your audience.
- Use emotion-arousing words and concrete illustrations and descriptions to appeal to an audience's emotions.

Principle Three: Effectively use and interpret nonverbal messages.

- Observe the nonverbal behavior of your audience to help you determine whether your message has been communicated clearly.
- Nonverbally reinforce ideas to make your message memorable.
- Use presentation aids to help evoke both positive and negative emotions and to reinforce positive and negative visualizations.

Principle Four: Listen and respond thoughtfully to others.

- Before you deliver your presentation to an audience, talk and listen to audience members to help you customize your message for them.
- Be prepared to answer questions after your presentation, regardless of whether there is a planned question-and-answer period.

Principle Five: Appropriately adapt message to others.

Adapt

- Adapt the structure of your presentation to your listeners to enhance message clarity; adapt your examples and illustrations to help you gain and maintain listeners' interest and attention.

- Consider the background and cultural expectations of your listeneers as you develop your persuasive presentation.

- Develop a reason for your audience to listen to you with an appeal to their basic needs.

- In the need step of a motivated sequence presentation, establish that the topic, problem, or issue affects listeners directly and thus should concern them.

- In the action step of a motivated sequence presentation, offer audience members specific action(s) they can take to solve the problem you have discussed.

- If you are speaking to a neutral or apathetic audience, or one that is not aware that a problem exists, emphasize the problem portion of a problem-and-solution presentation; emphasize the attention, need, and visualization steps of the motivated sequence; appeal to universal beliefs and values; or show the audience how your topic affects them and those they love; and be realistic about what you can accomplish.

- If you are speaking to a knowledgeable, receptive audience, state your speaking objective overtly; tell them exactly what you want them to do; ask audience members for an immediate show of support; identify with the audience; use emotional appeals; and emphasize the satisfaction and action steps of the motivated sequence or the solution in your problem-and-solution presentation.

- If you are speaking to an unreceptive audience, acknowledge and then refute their opposing point of view, focus on areas of agreement, and advance your strongest arguments first.

Discussion Questions

1. What are the differences between speaking to inform and speaking to persuade?

2. Identify and describe at least four strategies for making an informative presentation clear, memorable, and interesting.

3. What are the key strategies for developing a briefing, a report, a public relations presentation, and a training presentation?

4. What are four ways to motivate a listener to respond to a persuasive message?

5. Compare and contrast inductive reasoning, deductive reasoning, reasoning by analogy, and causal reasoning.

6. What are four ways to organize a persuasive message?

7. Describe how to prepare for a sales presentation.

8. What are the steps in presenting a sales presentation?

9. What are suggestions for developing and presenting a team presentation?

10. Give some tips for introducing others, presenting and receiving an award, and giving a toast.

Building Your Skills

1. Based on the suggestions in this chapter, write a word picture—a vivid, colorful description that appeals to the senses—describing one of the following:

   - Your first day on a new job
   - Visiting your father or mother at work

- A holiday when you were six years old
- A visit to your grandparents' house
- Your most frightening experience
- Your most memorable birthday celebration

2. Identify the logical fallacy in each of the following arguments:

- We must raise taxes to finance the construction of new schools in our community. Otherwise, we will have to close the schools because our students won't be able to pass state tests.
- Everybody knows that you can't find a decent job in our small town.
- My dentist recommends that we vote in favor of the proposition to reduce immigration, so you should vote for it too.
- The reason our children don't do well in math and science is that the stock market went down 300 points last week.
- Sarah grew up in a state that spends less money on education than any state in the country. She could not possibly have any useful ideas about how to improve our children's scores on standardized tests.

3. To test your ability to identify the persuasive strategies presented in this chapter, save four or five pieces of "junk" email that attempts to persuade you or sell you something. Analyze the persuasive strategies in each one. Look for evidence, reasoning, emotional appeals, applications of cognitive dissonance. Consider the following questions:

- Did any email contain positive or negative motivational appeals?
- Could you identify any elements of the motivated sequence? Explain how any advertisements got your attention, established a need, satisfied the need, helped you visualize how wonderful it would be to have the product or service, and told you what action you needed to take.
- Which persuasive principles do you see used most often these emails?
- Are the persuasive strategies ethical? Did any advertisements make claims not supported with evidence or include any logical fallacies?
- Save the emails to discuss and share in class.

4. Prepare a toast of no more than three or four sentences that you might offer on one of the following occasions:

- The wedding of a good friend
- A retirement party for one of your co-workers
- A party to celebrate reaching a company sales goal
- A dinner hosted by good friends to celebrate their recent adoption of a child

5. Watch an awards show on television. Listen to the thank-you speeches and evaluate their effectiveness, based on the suggestions for accepting an award discussed in this chapter.

Appendix A
Writing for Business

In addition to developing and maintaining relationships, collaborating with teams, and developing and delivering business presentations, leaders must know how to write in an effective manner.[1] In fact, approximately 10 percent of your communication time on the job will be invested in writing.[2] The lack of adequate writing skills among U.S. businesspeople is well documented.[3] A study published in *Management Review* noted that poor writing skills among business leaders were putting companies at risk. Another study published in the *International Journal of Training and Development* reported that executives have identified a lack of writing skills among job candidates interviewing for jobs.[4] The study found that employers were beginning to place greater emphasis on writing and that job offers were going to those who can write.[5] To address this concern, many employers have adopted policies requiring job candidates either to submit a brief written report as part of the screening process or to complete a writing exam as a part of the interview process.[6]

The purpose of this appendix is to introduce you to some of the more important skills for business writing and the preparation of business reports. Thus, the appendix focuses primarily on Principle Two, *Effectively use and interpret verbal messages*. We examine the general rules and styles used for business documents and stress the benefits of clear and effective writing. The appendix examines the customary format of business reports and the tone, content, and purpose of their component parts. Samples of various business documents are provided to give you the opportunity to develop and sharpen your written communication skills.

> "*Put it before them briefly so they will read it, clearly so they will appreciate it, picturesquely so they will remember it, and above all, accurately so they will be guided by its light.*"
>
> — JOSEPH PULITZER

Verbal

appendix outline

After reading this appendix, you should be able to

■ Discuss different methods for organizing a business document.

■ Describe business writing style and explain what is meant by tone and unbiased messages.

■ Describe ways to prepare clear written messages.

■ Define business correspondence and give four examples of common business correspondence.

■ Identify the elements of an interoffice memo.

■ Differentiate between progress reports and activity reports.

■ List and discuss three strategies for effective use of technology in business writing.

■ Discuss what should be taken into consideration before composing any business document.

Business Writing Skills

Certain business writing skills apply to a number of different types of business documents. Writers must be able to organize and develop paragraphs. They must be able to write in a style that reflects appropriate tone and use vocabulary that is adapted to the organization. They must be able to write clearly using appropriate terminology while being concise. Finally, writers must be sure to use correct spelling and grammar. All these skills require planning and preparation before the writing process begins.

Organizing and Developing Paragraphs

Maintaining a clear organizational pattern that flows naturally and is easy for the reader to understand will increase the effectiveness of your written communication. Making the document pleasing to look at and easy to read means "chunking" the information into visually distinct sections, using paragraphs.

Organize the document. Appropriately organizing a document is the first step a business writer can take to make sure the reader understands the message. There are several methods for organizing a document, depending, of course, on the type of document, its content, and the audience. The following paragraphs discuss some options for organizing a business document:

Problem-solution development begins with a description of a problem and moves on to discuss possible solutions or a proposed solution to the problem. A variation on this method is the *cause-and-effect* style of development, which outlines a cause and its possible effects. For example, if you were writing a report on employee turnover, you would start by describing the problem of turnover and its magnitude, then move on to discuss some possible ways to retain employees and minimize turnover. You would then outline the proposed best solution and offer reasons for selecting this solution.

The *chronological* or *sequential* organizational pattern begins with the first in a series of events or steps and moves on to the second, third, and so on. This organization pattern allows you to report on events or steps in the order in which they occurred or will occur. Using sequential development is helpful when writing a training manual, for example. When training someone in how to perform a skill, it is important that the steps be enacted in a particular order. A team leader overseeing fifteen service agents at a customer service call center may need to develop a short training program on how to process a call. The training manual would likely include a step-by-step description of each behavior involved in processing a call effectively and successfully.

Priority development focuses on the most urgent or important information first, then moves on to less important or urgent information. This style would work well when developing an agenda for a business meeting. An agenda lists the items to be discussed in the meeting, in the order they will be discussed. If, for example, an increase in customer complaints were an important priority item to discuss in a meeting, then that would be listed first on the agenda.

General-to-specific development is a format that allows you to begin with the big picture and move on to specific details. When preparing a sales proposal, for example, you may want to start by discussing the overall goals and move on toward the specifics of the product or service you are offering. Another way to use this method is to go from specific to general. For example, a restaurant chain marketing agent might describe a recent drop in sales at one store location and move on to outline the larger, global effects of this decline on the entire organization.[7]

Although this list of organizational patterns is not exhaustive, it can give you an idea of the various methods used to organize information. While organizing your document, you need to be aware of the reader and to select a method that best fits with the subject matter. An effective way to determine a method that works well for your message is to first develop an outline, or a basic skeleton of the information you want to write about. You can review the format to ensure that it fits with your message and makes sense to the reader before you fully develop the document.

Develop paragraphs. The paragraphs in your document are important tools that you can use to divide your information into logical sections. Paragraphs also provide visual breaks on the page, making the message easier to read. Three factors to consider when developing a paragraph are the topic sentence, length, and coherence.

The **topic sentence** of a paragraph is generally the first sentence, and it states the main idea. In other words, the topic sentence informs the reader about the content of the paragraph. The sentences that follow the topic sentence support the idea asserted in the topic sentence. For example, when writing in support of a proposed travel budget increase, you could start with the following sentence: "As a result of the rising cost of fuel, transportation costs have nearly tripled in the last quarter." The sentences following the topic sentence in the paragraph describe and offer evidence of the increased cost.

The second factor to consider in developing a paragraph is length, which again is dependent on your subject matter, reader, and the type of document. A memo, for instance, may have short paragraphs. In a letter or report, making the paragraphs too short could result in an underdeveloped message and information that is not clear to the reader. Paragraphs that are too long are not visually appealing and can be difficult to read if they fail to chunk information into manageable sections for the reader.

The third factor to consider when constructing paragraphs is coherence. **Coherence** refers to unity created by common underlying concepts, logical organization, and clear, natural development of the content.[8] Coherence can be created by, for example, writing in one tense or from one point of view. For example, suppose a manager writes the following in a memo: "The employee training sessions *are being conducted* on Wednesday afternoons. We *trained* six employees in these sessions." The switch from present tense in the first sentence to past tense in the second sentence undermines coherence and makes little sense. Transitions can be used within and between paragraphs to help the paragraphs flow smoothly. Also, to make the information easier to read, headers can be used when separating paragraphs or main ideas. Headers also help to break the page up into visually distinct and easy-to-read sections.

Using Appropriate Writing Style

When writing for business it is important to consider both style and clarity. **Writing style** refers to the tone, language, voice, and overall viewpoint of the sentences. Compared to other forms of writing, business writing style is generally more precise, brief, and direct. Also, the style of business writing has evolved from a previously formal and elaborate style to one that is more personal, although this may vary depending on the organization. The business writer also needs to take into consideration the tone and bias of the language used.

Use appropriate tone and vocabulary. Whatever the type of document they are preparing, writers should consider the tone of their message. **Tone** refers to the attitude of the writer toward both the reader and the subject matter. In many ways the tone of a written document has an effect similar to that of the tone of voice in face-to-face communication—the tone of a document (courteous, brusque, demanding, deferential, or whatever it may be) complements the words used in the document. The following questions will help you to determine the appropriate tone for your message.

- Why am I writing this document?
- Who am I writing to and what do I want them to understand?
- What kind of tone will complement and reinforce my written message?

Fortunately, you can use the same tone for most business messages. Remember that the main goal is to adapt your message to your reader. Using difficult vocabulary or phrases that demonstrate a lack of confidence, such as "I think you will find our product to be useful and beneficial to your organization," may not effectively communicate to your reader that you are convinced of the benefits of your product. Here are some general guidelines to keep in mind when considering what kind of tone to use in your letters and how to present information in that tone:

- Be confident.
- Be courteous and sincere.
- Adapt to the reader by stressing benefits.
- Write at an appropriate level of difficulty.

Use unbiased language. One of the ways you can make your business writing effective is to avoid biased messages. **Biased messages** include words and expressions that offend because they make inappropriate assumptions or repeat stereotypes about gender, ethnicity, physical

Topic sentence generally, the first sentence of a paragraph that states the main idea.

Coherence unity in writing created by common underlying concepts, logical organization, and clear, natural development of the content.

Writing style the tone, language, voice, and overall viewpoint of the sentences in a piece of writing.

Tone the attitude of the writer toward both the reader and the subject matter that is communicated in a written document.

Biased messages messages that include words or expressions that offend because they make inappropriate assumptions or repeat stereotypes about gender, ethnicity, physical or mental disability, age, or sexual orientation.

or mental disability, age, or sexual orientation. Although some people dismiss the notion that they should use unbiased messages as mere "political correctness," in reality, it is what most parents have been teaching their children for years—to be considerate of others. Here are a few ways to use unbiased verbal messages:

Avoid use of the generic *he*. Generic verbal messages include words that may apply to only one sex, race, or other group, as though that group represents everyone. For example, using the word *he* to include both men and women is no longer appropriate in the diverse professional workplace. Some people argue that the use of *he* automatically includes both men and women. But research does not confirm this widely held belief.[9] The use of *he* is exclusionary; it leaves women out.[10] Using *he/she* is awkward in many situations; it's best to use plural pronouns. Rather than writing "A manager is effective because *he* is a competent communicator," write "Managers are effective because *they* are competent communicators."

Contrary to popular belief, when writers use the generic *man* to refer to both men and women (as in the word *mailman*), women feel excluded.[11] In fact, research suggests that people usually visualize men when they hear that label. Additionally, when job titles end in "man," individuals in those positions are assumed to have stereotypically masculine personality traits. Rather than using the generic word *man*, try using the following to make your business writing style more effective and appropriate:

Instead of . . .	*Use . . .*
Chairman	Chair
Freshman	First-year student
Fireman	Firefighter
Salesman	Sales representative
Mailman	Mail carrier

Parallel verbal phrases use language and phrases that are symmetrical. Nonparallel verbal messages treat groups differently and therefore are perceived negatively, as biased. Here are a few examples to clarify the difference between parallel and nonparallel verbal messages.

Nonparallel Phrases	*Parallel Phrases*
Ladies and men	Ladies and gentlemen
Men and girls	Men and women
Boys and women	Boys and girls

Writing Clearly

Clarity refers to the specificity of a message and how easily the reader can comprehend the information. Many of the ideas discussed in this section were also discussed in Chapter 3, which examined how to use and interpret verbal messages. However, Chapter 3 discussed clarity as it pertains to oral, or spoken, messages. In this section, we discuss clarity as it relates to the written word.

When writing for business, as opposed to other forms of writing (such as creative writing), clarity of message and thought is very important. Ambiguous messages or unclear sentences can prevent your writing from communicating to the reader. A clear paragraph is coherent; it has a logical sequence and smooth transitions between the sentences.

Another consideration in achieving clarity is the choice of words. Abstract phrases, such as "use a bright color palette" will not communicate as much or as clearly as concrete phrases, such as "use bright oranges, yellows, and reds." The business writer should also be cautious about jargon. As defined in Chapter 3, **jargon** is language used by a particular group, profession, or culture that may not be understood or used by other people. Jargon is common in the workplace, and it tends to become overused.[12] Phrases such as "Let's dialogue" (instead of "Let's discuss this") can become cliché and can seem inappropriate to a reader outside of the organization. Jargon can be appropriate if readers are familiar with the terms. When writing for an outside audience, however, jargon should be avoided.

A final consideration when writing for clarity is to be concise. **Concise writing** avoids unnecessary words and phrases but does not sacrifice clarity or necessary detail. A report

Clarity the specificity of a message and how easily the reader can comprehend the information.

Jargon language used by a particular group, profession, or culture that may not be understood or used by other people.

Concise writing writing that avoids unnecessary words and phrases.

need not be brief to be concise, and making something shorter is not appropriate if clarity is sacrificed. Here are some suggestions for writing concisely.[13]

Use subordination. Instead of writing "We received the sales report this afternoon. It was five pages. The report clearly illustrated a drop in sales marketwide," subordinate, using conjunctions to combine the ideas from these sentences to make one, coherent, concise sentence: "This afternoon we received the five-page sales report, which clearly illustrates a marketwide drop in sales."

Avoid redundancy. Even if you are not repeating whole phrases and sentences, a report can still be redundant. Eliminate qualifying terms that are not necessary, such as "first and foremost" or "basic and fundamental."

Do not overuse intensifiers. It is not necessary to write "The report was perfectly clear and completely accurate." Instead, just say "The report was clear and accurate."

Avoid telegraphic language. One pitfall in attempting to write concisely is the tendency to oversimplify. **Telegraphic style** is a writing style that condenses a message by eliminating articles, pronouns, conjunctions, and transitions. Although telegraphic style may make a document brief, the document may not necessarily remain clear. Consider the following examples:

> Telegraphic style: Per May 5 memo, meeting agenda attached. Supervisor wants report by Houston office. Meeting as soon as report received. August almost full, please advise to set date.

> Clear message: As I mentioned in my May 5th memo, I have attached the next meeting agenda. The supervisor wants the report to be completed by the Houston office. As soon as we get the report we can schedule a meeting. Our August calendar is almost full, so please suggest a date soon.

Using Correct Spelling and Grammar

Readers often view how you communicate in written messages as a measure of your effectiveness.[14] Paying close attention to spelling and grammar will help you develop credibility with your readers. A document that contains spelling or grammatical errors can be difficult to read and may fail to communicate the message completely. Mistakes will generally reflect poorly on the writer and often on the organization as well.

The spell-check tool on most word-processing programs is a good place to start when you want to identify spelling errors. Spell-checkers are not foolproof, however, and relying solely on a spell-check tool may not give effective results.[15] It is always a good idea to go over a hard copy of any document yourself and then pass it on to a friend or a colleague to proofread before delivering it to readers. Re-read your notes to confirm the spelling of names and places; a proofreader often cannot catch such mistakes. For example, Mr. Schmitt may not appreciate receiving a letter addressed to Mr. Schmidt, but since the latter is a more common spelling, it will likely not be identified as an error by a spell-check program or a proofreader. Examine the following sentences to see if you can identify the mistakes that a spell-checker would miss.[16]

- Of all the perspective employees we have interviewed, you have the most impressive resume and work experience. (*prospective*)
- A background in education training has proven to be a real compliment to my experience as a trainer. (*complement*)
- . . . identified potential roadblocks to ensure that project operations preceded smoothly. (*proceeded*)
- . . . organized and lead a fifteen-member customer service team who processed all the calls in the customer retention department. (*led*)

All the words in these four sentences are spelled correctly and would not be caught by a spell checker. However, the indicated words are not appropriate for the context. Although helpful, a spell-check program is no replacement for editing and proofreading.

Equally important in business writing is proper usage of grammar. **Grammar** refers to the functions of words and the way they work together to form coherent language. Standard English grammatical rules apply in business writing, and being familiar with

Telegraphic style a writing style that condenses the message by eliminating articles, pronouns, conjunctions, and transitions.

Grammar the study of the functions of words and the way they work together to form coherent language.

these rules will help in the writing process. Many word-processing programs have grammar check tools, but be aware these programs may not correct all mistakes. Once again, proofreading a hard copy of your document for grammatical errors is always a good idea.

The skills discussed in this section apply to all forms of business writing. They help make your writing clear, precise, effective, logical, and accurate. The first skill is to clearly develop and organize your document, using structure and clear paragraphs. The second skill is to use the appropriate writing style for your document, audience, and subject. A third skill is to write clearly, using concise, effective messages to enhance communication. The fourth skill we discussed is to make sure your spelling and grammar are correct. This can develop your credibility with the reader and ensure you have effectively communicated your message. Use these skills when developing any business document.

Using Email

Email messaging now exceeds telephoning as the dominant form of business communication.[17] Many people claim that handling their emails can consume half of their day. One *Wall Street Journal* report predicted that employees would soon spend three to four hours a day on email.[18] With the increased use of email as an accepted form of business communication, some basic etiquette rules are being established to keep email usage both effective and professional. Here are some tips for composing professional email messages, either in the workplace or in an academic context:[19]

- *Be concise.* Keep messages brief and to the point. Correct writing doesn't have to be lengthy. Make your writing as concise as possible; it can be frustrating for a reader to have to wade through an email twice as long as needed.

- *Use proper letter case.* Letter case indicates whether words are written using capital (uppercase) letters or lowercase letters. Using all capital letters gives the impression you're shouting; using all lowercase letters gives the impression you're either whispering or lazy.

- *Use blind copy (BCC) and courtesy copy (CC) appropriately.* Use courtesy copy to keep others informed. Use blind copy only when you prefer to keep recipients from seeing who else received a copy of your email message. You would do this if your email involved issues of confidentiality or if the information in it might damage a relationship. For example, suppose you want to let your district manager know how you're handling an employee problem. You email the employee himself to notify him of your plan, and you send a blind copy of the email to the district manager. This way, the district manager knows the problem is being managed, but the employee doesn't know the district manager has been informed. If the problem employee were to know this, his relationship with the district manager might be compromised. Also use BCC when sending to a large distribution list, so recipients won't have to scroll through a long list of names in order to get to the message.

- *Use the subject line.* When sending a new email, always include the important and pertinent information in the subject line. The subject line can be anything relevant—an ID number, a claim number, a meeting date, a project name—or it can be a descriptive subject line that reveals to the reader the nature of your email.

- *Use correct grammar and punctuation.* The advent of text messaging devices has led to a decline in the formality of electronic communication. When sending email, use proper grammar and punctuation. Just because the channel is less formal does not mean the writing can be sloppy.

- *Consider the appropriateness of your content.* Employees have been fired for using email inappropriately (for example, forwarding items with sexual or off-color content) or for personal use. Never put in an email message anything you wouldn't put on a postcard. Remember that email can be forwarded, so unintended audiences may see what you've written.

- *Don't use email as an excuse for not communicating through more appropriate channels of communication.* Don't forget the value of face-to-face or voice-to-voice communication. Email communication isn't appropriate for sending confusing or emotional messages. Don't use email to avoid an uncomfortable situation or to cover up a mistake.

Writing Business Letters

Business letters are standard communication formats that are important and common in the workplace. As a leader, you will likely need to communicate with those outside of your organization—for example, with clients or those in other organizations. Being able to apply the skills discussed earlier to business letters is important and valuable.

Correspondence

Correspondence refers to business letters sent to customers, co-workers, superiors, and subordinates. Because business correspondence often is more personal than formal proposals and reports, it should generally be written in a conversational style. Here are some suggestions for writing effective correspondence.

Develop goodwill. **Goodwill** is a positive perception of the author on the part of the audience. A good way to build goodwill is to keep correspondence audience-focused. Put simply, adapt to your reader. Rather than saying, "*We* need to see a receipt before *we* can process a return or exchange of the merchandise," say, "*You* may receive a full refund or exchange of the merchandise if *you* mail or fax a receipt." The two sentences say essentially the same thing, but the focus in the second sentence is on the needs of the customer. In this case you could build even more goodwill by sending an acknowledgment letter letting the person know the receipt arrived and thanking the person for being prompt.

Adapt

Include standard elements of correspondence. Although the general appearance and format of correspondence may vary, following is a list of elements present in most business correspondence. Use this list as a guideline when deciding what to include in your business letter. Figure A.1 illustrates a sample business letter.

- *Return address.* The return address contains the sender's address and the date the letter was written. If the letter appears on letterhead that includes an address, a date is enough for the return address.

- *Inside address.* Include the name and address of the recipient of the letter before a salutation.

- *Salutation.* A salutation should address the recipient of the letter directly and appropriately. A letter intended to be social and friendly can have a comma after the salutation; a more formal letter should include a colon. Avoid "Dear Sir" unless you are certain the recipient is male. The overused "To Whom It May Concern" is too impersonal. Take the time to determine exactly to whom the letter should be addressed.

- *Body.* The body contains the content of the letter. It should be written in paragraph form. Including a non–task-related message at the beginning of the letter can help to build rapport, for example, "Thank you for expressing interest in exploring the employment options offered at our institution." Then enter into the main message.

- *Closing.* The end of the letter should include a closing expression before your signature. This can be the common and effective "Sincerely," "Cordially," or something more personal such as "Best," or "Respectfully yours." The letter should include both a handwritten signature and a typed signature block. The block usually contains your name, as well as your title and the name of your organization (unless your letter appears on letterhead).[20]

Deliver bad news tactfully. Occasionally correspondence must contain bad news. This must be handled tactfully. A general rule for handling bad news is to deliver it gently and courteously. Here are some suggestions for presenting bad news in correspondence:

- *Open with a description of the context, to provide a buffer.* For example, you might begin a letter with "Thank you for applying for the position of service manager at TRH, Inc."

Correspondence business letters sent to customers, co-workers, superiors, and subordinates.

Goodwill a positive perception of an author on the part of the audience.

| **Figure A.1** | **Sample Business Letter** |

1532 1st Lane
Edinburg, Texas 78541
July 5, 20XX

Mr. Joseph Castillo
InnoTech Associates
817 Freddy Gonzalez Drive
Edinburg, TX 78539

Dear Mr. Castillo:

We appreciated the customer service training program you provided to our company last month. This letter is intended as a follow-up to that training and to thank you for your time and attention to detail.

The training was effective and productive. Our customer service agents have greatly increased morale and motivation when interacting with customers. We have seen great results from your training just in the last month.

We are considering a telephone etiquette course as a follow-up to the customer service training you provided. We were impressed with your demeanor, training style, and attention to detail, and would like InnoTech Associates to conduct the training program. If you are interested in providing us with a training program in customer service telephone etiquette, please contact me.

Once again, thank you for your interest in helping our employees work to improve their customer service skills. You have taught us some invaluable lessons and our company and workers are grateful.

Sincerely,

Sylvia Rodriguez

Sylvia Rodriguez
Training Department Supervisor
PemCo Inc., West Call Center
Phone: (956) 989-3347
Fax: (956) 989-3300
srodriguez@pemcowest.org

- *Explain the bad news rather than simply stating it.* For example, an explanation of a hiring decision might be "Because of the extensive pool of applicants, we have chosen to place someone in the position with ten years of experience, who will need minimum training to begin."
- *Close with a goodwill message that reinforces a positive relationship with the recipient.* For example, you might close with a statement such as "With your excellent academic record and ability to put others at ease, we have no doubt you will be successful in finding a position with another organization."

Use a standard format. When developing a business letter, you also need to consider the format. A common format for correspondence is the full-block, or standard letter style shown in Figure A.1. Although organizations may have their own preferred correspondence format, this format is standard for any letter. Many word-processing programs contain templates for correspondence. If you are using letterhead paper, consider the bottom of the letterhead to be the top of the page when creating margins. Though the length of the letter may vary, it is a good idea to center the letter on the page. A short one- or two-sentence correspondence may be better sent by email. The main consideration with format is that once an organization has developed a standard for outside correspondence, you should be consistent in following the standard in all your correspondence.

Complaint Letters

There will be times when you are not satisfied with a product or service, and you believe some restitution is in order. A **complaint letter** is a letter that expresses dissatisfaction with a product or service. A letter of complaint can be an effective method for resolving a dispute, if it is written with the appropriate tone and does not sound as though you are being accusatory or whining. You might even get more than you expected. Many businesses appreciate knowing when something is going wrong, and they will do what they can to create goodwill with a dissatisfied customer.

The following suggestions will help you write a letter of complaint that's likely to be read and acted on.[21]

- *Complain only when appropriate.* Sending numerous, frivolous letters of complaint will get you nowhere. Send your letters only for genuine problems and only after initial communication with company representatives has failed. In other words, if the widget you bought didn't work as expected, ask the salesperson or the customer service department to correct the problem before you fire off a letter of complaint to the head office.

- *Address the letter to the correct person.* You need to reach the person who has the authority to correct the problem. If your complaint is with a local business, address the letter to the owner or manager. If you're dealing with a local branch of a large corporation, you'll need to find out whether your complaint should be sent to the local branch or if the problem was created by policies set by a corporate office. It might take some detective work to find out who should receive your letter. If you can't find out by asking, try the company website, annual reports, or business directories in your local library.

- *Be courteous and professional.* Avoid sarcasm. No matter how angry you are, sending a rude, discourteous, inflammatory letter will not help you get the problem corrected.

- *Keep it short.* One page is all you need. A recipient is more likely to read and act on your letter if you keep it brief and to the point. No one has time or patience to wade through a six-page tome.

- *Be factual.* Identify the problem and outline the efforts you have made to correct the problem. Remember the questions journalists typically try to cover in their writing: Who, What, When, Where, and How.

- *Identify what you want.* You have a complaint. What will it take to make things right? Do you want your money refunded? The product exchanged? A service contract extended? An apology? Stipulate what you want.

- *Remember to date your letter and include full contact information*, including an email address and account numbers or any other information that the recipient might need to trace your problem.

- *State consequences only if previous letters have failed to get the problem corrected.* It is both unnecessary and ineffective to start out with threats of punitive action. Remember, other people dislike receiving threats as much as you do. But, when previous attempts have failed, it's time to state what you are prepared to do, and when.

Leaders regularly communicate through written correspondence to those outside of the organization. Equally important as writing letters to those outside the organization or team is learning effective strategies for writing other types of business documents.

Writing Business Documents

As a leader, you will be responsible for organizing and developing a number of business documents, including memorandums (more commonly known as memos), progress and

Complaint letter a letter that expresses dissatisfaction with a product or service.

activity reports, sales proposals, and formal reports. This section outlines the basic components of each type of document, as well as considerations for their appropriate use. The sample documents provided are only guidelines; organizations may have their own procedures and formats for the various types of business documents.

Memos

A **memo** is a short and usually informal written communication to others within an organization. Memos are used as reminders or to pass along information. Memos can be as simple as a sentence written on a sticky note but are usually printed on company letterhead. An example of a memo appears in Figure A.2. Although there is no standard format for memos, they should generally contain at least some form of each of the following elements.[22]

Heading. The heading should note the sender and the recipient, the date, and the subject. Ensure that all names of individuals who need to receive the memo are included following the word *TO*. If the subject of the memo is relevant to only one person, do not send the memo to the entire office. Also, be certain that material is not too sensitive to put in a memo; sometimes a face-to-face conversation or a phone call is preferable. For example, a memo is an inappropriate way to notify employees of a layoff. Memos are most effective when they communicate company or job objectives such as a change in a standard procedure.

Memo a short, informal written communication within an organization.

Body. Although a memo's length can vary, depending on the content, a good rule is to keep it under one page. Many organizations have standard memo formats, so it's best to check with your organization first and follow established standards.

Figure A.2	Sample Memo

TRH Incorporated

TO: Kay Marquez, Service Manager
FROM: Stephanie Ramos, Local Store Marketer
DATE: May 17, 20XX
SUBJECT: Opportunity for local ad campaign

TRH has been offered an opportunity to participate in a local advertising campaign in conjunction with the Chamber of Commerce's "Local Tastes" program.

"Local Tastes" is an annual program featuring community restaurants and other businesses, including a two-week mailer campaign and events at local stores. This campaign culminates in a well-attended day-long event at the convention center featuring products from each participating business.

Participating businesses will be featured on a front page of the mailer, get a 30-second spot with a local news outlet, and be given a booth with banner at the "Local Tastes" event on July 3.

I think this would be an excellent opportunity to get the company recognized in the community and interact with the Chamber of Commerce as well as work with other businesses in the area.

Please respond by May 25 with a decision regarding participating in this event. I need to respond to the Chamber of Commerce and turn in a deposit by June 1.

cc: Juan Brown, Managing Partner

Closing. Most memos don't require the standard signature you would find in a letter or other correspondence. It is helpful, however, to include notation of any attachments and a list of people who received copies of the memo. When considering who within the organization should receive copies of your memo, keep in mind that in most companies this can be a highly political issue. Send copies only to those who need the information.

Progress and Activity Reports

A **progress report** gives updates on the status of a project. Figure A.3 shows an example of a progress report. Most project reports are generated by a company that has been contracted to do a particular job or provide a service. In such cases, it is appropriate to submit project reports at regular intervals to communicate the project's status and keep all personnel on task.[23] Although the format for project reports varies depending on the project, the policies of the organization providing the report, and the requirements of the client or customer, all reports should maintain the same format for any particular project. Progress reports may contain information about whether a project is within budget. If you anticipate going over budget, mention that and discuss some possible reasons and solutions. A progress report should also include information about how the work is progressing—what has been completed as well as what is anticipated. If you expect you may not complete the work on schedule, discuss this in the progress report and explain what arrangements need to be made to complete the project.

When communicating the status of a project within an organization, an activity report is most appropriate. An **activity report** is a document that communicates progress and achievements to others within an organization or on a team. Most activity reports give information on the status of one or several ongoing projects. If several departments are working on the same project, a manager may combine all the activity reports; the combined reports could be the basis for a progress report to send to a client. Activity reports are typically issued regularly (bi-weekly or monthly in most organizations) and normally do not require a formal structure because the material is familiar to the readers. Though progress reports and activity reports contain similar content, they differ in audience and

Progress report a report that outlines for a customer or a client the status of a project.

Activity report a document that communicates progress on a project or achievements to others in an organization or on a team.

Figure A.3	Sample Progress Report

Date: August 17, 20XX
To: Juan Brown, Managing Partner, TRH Inc.
From: Mike Caro, NuSheen Services
Subject: Progress Report for July 1–29, 20XX

Dear Mr. Brown,

I am happy to say the parking lot and building refinishing project is on schedule. At this point we are somewhat over budget in terms of materials, but I am confident we will finish early enough to save you money in labor costs.

Costs: The truck rental went over cost by approximately $1700 because of two extra days' rental. The other materials are costing out at the price originally quoted to you.

Work Completed: The building has now been completely refinished. Work on the outside work area and parking lot still needs to be completed.

Work Schedule: With the addition of two crew members, we should be able to complete the work by August 30.

If you have any questions, please contact me.

often in tone. Progress reports are most often written to clients or an audience outside the organization, and are more formal; an activity report is commonly an internal document, with a less formal structure and tone.

Sales Proposals

A **sales proposal** is a document intended to persuade a possible client of his or her need for your product or service. An effective sales proposal demonstrates to the prospective client that he or she has a problem and that your product or service will help to solve that problem. The writer of a sales proposal must first determine the selling points, or the most attractive features of the product or service, and then construct a document that clearly illustrates these points. The proposal should highlight the specific benefits that the customer will receive from the use of the product or service. For example, the owner of a landscaping business might notice that a local restaurant is surrounded by dry, dead grass and overgrown shrubbery. In a proposal offering landscaping services, the business owner would try to persuade the restaurant manager of the appeal of a well-kept, lush, green exterior, and convince him that landscaping could increase his bottom line.

Keep in mind that in many states, sales proposals are **legally binding documents**, which means that any incentives or benefits offered in the sales proposal must be reasonable and must be delivered as promised.[24] It is not uncommon for organizations to be sued over failing to deliver on the promises offered in a persuasive sales proposal.[25]

If you choose to use a former client's testimony or image in a sales proposal, make sure you have permission to do so and that you have not fabricated the testimony. For example, if the landscaping business owner wanted to include comments from current or former customers about the quality of her company's landscaping work in her sales proposal, she would first need to get the customers' permission in writing to use the testimony or pictures of the work in the proposal. Following are some guidelines for creating an effective sales proposal that is adapted to the needs of the client:

Adapt

Outline the problem. Although you may have already discussed the problem with the client, a good sales proposal reminds the potential client of the problem and a need for some solution. Include any requirements the client has mentioned, such as for cost or procedure. Keep your message client focused, aligning yourself with the client's needs.

Discuss your approach. Your sales proposal should discuss exactly what you suggest as an effective solution to the problem. Discuss what particularly needs to be done and how those actions will address the problem. Discuss as well why you and your organization are the best choice for implementing this solution. Mention any support and training you will provide (if necessary) and guarantees on your work or products. The landscaping company owner, for example, could discuss what type of vegetation she proposes to plant around the restaurant, how the plants might be combined and arranged, and possibly a contract for continuing maintenance to keep the outside looking well cared for.

Describe the benefits.   Although they may seem obvious, it is a good idea to identify for the client the biggest benefits of your proposal. Indirect outcomes such as an increase in customer base or employee morale should be outlined. The landscaping business owner could describe what a well-maintained exterior communicates to customers and other business owners about the restaurant. Keep in mind, however, that this section should not promise anything that may not be within your the power to fulfill. You can expose yourself and your organization to legal consequences if promised benefits are not realized.

Mention schedule and costs.   A sales proposal should outline a proposed schedule and cost estimate. These things will later be detailed more formally in a contract but should be discussed in a sales proposal so there will be no surprises later. The restaurant manager may expect the job to start tomorrow and be completed in two days; the landscaping company owner needs to communicate clearly about whether that timeline fits with her schedule. Most clients will not be willing to move on to the contract stage of the process without a clear outline of proposed costs and schedule.

Formal Reports

A **formal report** is a highly detailed and comprehensive report on an ongoing project or a completed project that is often co-authored by several writers. For example, if you were

Sales proposal a document intended to persuade a possible client of his or her need for your product or service.

Legally binding documents documents that record an exchange of promises and that are enforceable by law.

Formal report a highly detailed and comprehensive report on an ongoing project or a completed project, often co-authored by several writers.

implementing new procedures in your organization over a twelve-month period, you might send out a status report midway through the implementation process to those affected by the changes. Once the implementation process was completed, you would send out a final report detailing the process and the effectiveness of the implementation. Reports are more strictly formatted than most other forms of business correspondence, and the format varies according to company policies. Reports are divided into three main parts: the front matter, the body, and the back matter. Each part contains several elements, the order and length of which vary according to company recommendations. Following are basic descriptions of the components of a formal report.[26]

Front matter. **Front matter** consists of those aspects of a report that come at the beginning and serve to prepare the reader for the main information. The report title, the authors' names, lists of the report's contents, and a brief summary should all be a part of the front matter.

- *Title page.* A title page contains the full title of the report, a list of the writers' or researchers' names, date(s) of the report, the organizational affiliations of the writers, and the organization to which the report is being submitted.
- *Abstract.* An abstract is a summary (two or three paragraphs) that highlights the major points of the report.
- *Table of contents.* This should list all the major sections of the report along with page numbers.
- *List of figures and tables.*
- *Foreword or preface.* A foreword is an optional introductory statement about the report written by someone other than the authors; a preface is an introduction written by an author.

Body. The body of a formal report contains the main information in the report, including the reasons for researching the topic, how it was researched, and what was discovered.

- *Executive summary.* This summary provides a more complete overview than the abstract.
- *Introduction.* The introduction provides readers with the report's purpose and scope.
- *Text.* The text presents details on how the topic was researched.
- *Conclusions and recommendations.* This section discusses the findings of the research and consequent recommendations that are offered. Conclusions may be discussed in a separate section from recommendations.

Back matter. **Back matter** refers to those components of a report that traditionally come at the end of the report, after the main body, and that provide further detail and references.

- *Appendixes.* Any appendixes clarify or supplement information in the body of the report with information that is detailed or lengthy and is not necessarily relevant to all audiences.
- *Bibliography.* This is an alphabetical list of all the sources that were cited and consulted in researching the report.
- *Glossary.* This is an alphabetical list of terms and their definitions.
- *Index.* An index is an alphabetical list of all the major topics and subtopics discussed in a report, citing page numbers in the report where the reader can find those discussions.

    If you work for an organization that requires you to write regular formal reports, it is a good idea to use a word-processing program style sheet to create a format for the report. You can then save it as a template and create future reports with the same format. You won't have to refigure font styles and sizes, margins, and the like.

    Leaders have many opportunities to write various kinds of business documents. Letters are generally more formal and addressed to those outside the organization. Memos and activity reports are common interoffice communication forms. Progress reports, sales proposals, and formal reports are common business documents that most leaders will frequently compose or help to compose.

Front matter the components of a report that come at the beginning and prepare the reader for the main information.

Back matter the components of a report that traditionally come at the end, after the main body, and provide further detail and references.

Learning When and How To Use Technology

Although perfecting business writing skills is challenging, what might be more challenging for new leaders is learning when and how to use technology to communicate. Many times the question that confronts a leader is "Should I communicate to others in writing or should I communicate in person?" Leaders need to be aware of when writing a document is more appropriate and when speaking in person is preferable. If a leader decides to communicate through writing, then which format is best? Is an email appropriate, or should a letter be sent? If a leader decides to communicate orally, is a voice-mail message appropriate, or should he or she schedule a face-to-face meeting? These questions are important, especially since *Business Week* writer Michael Mandel reported that 25 percent of 7,800 leaders who were surveyed reported that voice mail, email, and meetings were completely ineffective in the workplace; nearly 40 percent of the leaders spent a half to full day per week on communication activities that were ineffective.[27]

In order to use technology effectively when writing and speaking, it's important to understand what communication researchers refer to as **media richness**, or how closely a technology simulates face-to-face communication.[28] As we noted in Chapter 9, according to media richness theory, a method or channel of communication is rich if it offers the possibility of instant feedback; allows both verbal and nonverbal cues to be processed by senders and receivers; allows the use of natural, informal language rather than formal language; and customizes messages to individuals rather than communicating to a mass of people. Management and marketing researchers Robert Lengel and Richard Daft describe how the channel (face-to-face conversation, email, text message, or whatever it may be) influences how messages are received. Lengel and Daft assert that different media have different degrees of richness; some channels are rich, others are lean. For example, flyers or posters advertising a meeting are considered a lean medium, because they convey messages using a single channel (the visual channel) and because readers of a poster have no interaction with the creator of the poster. On the other hand, face-to-face meetings are considered a rich medium, since they convey messages using multiple channels (sight, sound, smell, touch) and allow people to interact. Figure A.4 illustrates the media richness continuum.[29]

As you can see from Figure A.4, as the number of channels through which messages are conveyed increases, communication becomes more interactive and personal. As the number of channels decreases, communication becomes less interactive and more impersonal. The following sections offer guidelines to help you become aware of media richness and how to apply this model in business and professional settings.

Considering the Qualities of the Message

Messages have certain qualities that will help you decide which channels or media are most appropriate to use to convey them. If your message is routine—meaning that it is simple, straightforward, contains no surprises, and is task related—then lean media such as flyers, letters, and memos are probably most appropriate. If your message is nonroutine—meaning that it is complex, confusing, contains surprise, or is time sensitive—then rich media such as face-to-face meetings or video or web conferences are probably better.[30] When

© 1999 Ted Goff

"Can't talk now. I'm in a seminar about improving communication with technology."

| Figure A.4 | **Media Richness Continuum** |

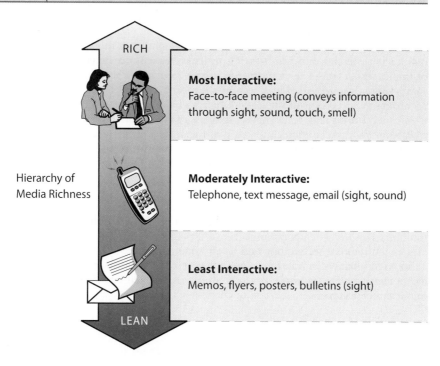

Hierarchy of
Media Richness

RICH

Most Interactive:
Face-to-face meeting (conveys information
through sight, sound, touch, smell)

Moderately Interactive:
Telephone, text message, email (sight, sound)

Least Interactive:
Memos, flyers, posters, bulletins (sight)

LEAN

information is complex and confusing, you want to make sure you receive immediate feedback from your team members so you can clarify and correct any misunderstandings.[31] A rich medium allows such feedback.

Considering the Emotional Impact of the Message

If you've ever been notified by a text message that you were fired, you know how important it is to match the communication channel to the emotional impact of the message. What hurt was not only the message, but also the way the message was delivered. Although both sending and receiving emotionally sensitive information are difficult, the channel—the way the message is transmitted—makes a big difference. For example, if you're laying someone off, the ideal way to do this is face to face (a rich medium) rather than with a text message (a lean medium). A face-to-face discussion allows you to effectively interpret and use nonverbal communication while explaining the layoff and to answer any questions. Taking the time to meet face to face conveys respect for the person being laid off.

Nonverbal

Some organizational communication researchers suggest that it may be more effective to use leaner media (for example, email or text messages) in some emotionally charged situations. Researcher Phil Salem suggests that leaner media may be more effective in some conflict situations.[32] According to Salem, leaner media don't allow for immediate feedback and interaction. This lack of feedback provides a "cooling off" period that may be helpful in emotionally charged situations.

Following Communication Norms of the Organization

When deciding what channel is best to use to convey your message, it's always important to be aware of the communication norms of the workplace. As we noted in Chapter 9, **norms** are general standards that determine what is appropriate and inappropriate behavior in an organization. For example, in some offices you would violate a norm if you were

Media richness the degree to which a channel of communication offers the possibility of immediate feedback; provides both verbal and nonverbal cues; allows the use of natural, informal language; and customizes messages to recipients.

Norms general standards within an organization that determine what is appropriate and inappropriate behavior.

to phone someone in the office next to you or even someone on the same floor; the norm is to phone only people who are not in your immediate location. In other organizations, the norm may be sending email rather than using the phone or talking to the person face to face. One study of over 150 senior executives at the nation's 1,000 largest companies found that only 13 percent of leaders used the telephone as their primary means of communication, which was down from 48 percent five years previously. Also, just 14 percent of the leaders reported relying on face-to-face meetings, compared with 24 percent five years before. Instead, email had become the most common channel for dialogue at work, according to 71 percent of the leaders surveyed.[33] This research data suggests that communication norms may be changing, moving away from rich communication media and toward more lean communication media. Regardless of the research data, it's important to carefully observe the communication norms in your office and work unit and follow the norms already established.

Using Multiple Channels

Organizational communication researcher Keri Stephens recommends that leaders use multiple channels when communicating with employees and team members.[34] Stephens argues that employees are not tied to any one communication technology and that in order to be effective in your communication, it's important to communicate using a variety of channels. For example, if you're preparing to facilitate a meeting next week, you might do the following:

- Send out an email, voice mail, and a text message asking for team members' input on what they would like to discuss at the meeting.
- Send out a paper memo outlining the agenda for the meeting in addition to attaching the memo to an email message.
- Send a text message on the day of the meeting reminding team members of the meeting time and location.
- Communicate face to face at the meeting.

Stephens mentions that by using multiple channels to communicate with team members, you are more likely to reach more of your audience members than if you relied solely on a single technology.

Communication Principles and Skills for Leadership

Principle One: Be aware of your communication with yourself and others.

- When writing business letters and memos, be aware of who will be reading the message and the level of detail and amount of background information that may be needed or expected.
- Be aware of the intended reader's expectations regarding the length, format, and style of the message.

Principle Two: Effectively use and interpret verbal messages.

- Use an appropriate written style (including tone and vocabulary) for memos or letters.
- Write clearly: Be concise, use appropriate subordination, avoid jargon and redundancy, and use appropriate grammar and accurate spelling.
- Express ideas briefly yet clearly; business and professional writing should get to the point yet provide enough detail to help the reader understand if any follow-up action is needed.

Principle Three: Effectively use and interpret nonverbal messages.

- The type of font used, placement of margins, and the number and style of headings and subheadings provide nonverbal information to complement the ideas you are communicating in writing.

- When appropriate, use images, color, or other visual information to make your written message clear, accurate, and interesting.

Principle Four: Listen and respond thoughtfully to others.

- Accurately listening for details and major ideas is important when you need to summarize spoken messages in writing.

- If you are uncertain about expectations regarding format or other aspects of written correspondence, ask others and then listen to their responses, which will guide you in preparing written messages.

Principle Five: Appropriately adapt messages to others.

- Adapt the format, structure, word choice, and style of a written message depending on the recipient and the function of the message.

- When composing a response to an email message, pay attention to cues in the original email and adapt your response accordingly. If your correspondent's email message was short, he or she may only expect a brief response; a longer, more detailed message may signal that he or she expects a more comprehensive response.

Discussion Questions

1. Describe two methods for organizing a business document, and give an example of why you would use each.

2. Explain what is meant by biased messages. Give some examples of biased messages, and explain how to express the same thoughts using unbiased language.

3. List and explain three techniques for writing clear messages.

4. Define business correspondence and give four examples of common business correspondence.

5. Differentiate between progress reports and activity reports.

6. Discuss what should be taken into consideration before composing any business document.

7. Discuss three considerations in determining effective use of communication technology.

Building Your Skills

1. Print out several emails that you have sent to an instructor (or to a supervisor or manager, if you are working). Together with several classmates, critique the emails for effectiveness. Then rewrite them to make them more effective.

2. Rewrite each of the following phrases using concrete words:

   a. Sometime this summer

   b. A substantial saving

   c. A large number of people in attendance

   d. Increase efficiency

3. Rewrite the following messages so that they are more concise:

   a. We wanted to invite you to our Kids' Night special this Tuesday night. The kids will have a lot of fun as we will be having face-painting, kids' games, and the kids can color. The kids eat free as well!

b. We are sending this mailer to let you know that we are giving a free gift and music CD with every $50 you spend on gas at our gas station. The promotion is going on this weekend, July 18–20.

c. The supervisor plans to go to the meeting that will be held on Monday evening at a little bit after 7 p.m. at night.

d. Welcome. We are happy to have in this afternoon's meeting a guest, Mr. Paul Emerson. Mr. Emerson works at the local Chamber of Commerce and he is here to tell us a little bit about the "Local Tastes" program. If after this afternoon's meeting you still have more questions regarding the "Local Tastes" program, feel free to call Mr. Emerson at his office.

4. Think of a time when you were dissatisfied with either a service or a product. Draft a complaint letter, focusing on the suggestions for complaint letters mentioned in this appendix. Exchange letters with a classmate and critique each other's letters.

5. Practice writing a letter expressing bad news, such as a refusal to make restitution after a complaint or a decision to discontinue a project. Exchange letters with a classmate and critique each other's letters.

Appendix B
Managing Time: Managing Communication

It was Mark Twain who wrote "Never put off until tomorrow what you can do the day after tomorrow." Based on the number of projects that many of us postpone and the piles of work that sometimes accumulate on our desks, many of us seem to agree with Mr. Twain. Few people in business and organizational settings claim to be underworked or to have too much time on their hands. Just the opposite is true. There never seems to be enough time to accomplish all of the tasks on our "to do" lists—that is, assuming we make "to do" lists. This chapter is about not only techniques for managing our "to do" lists but also some broad principles to help us manage our time. Time, it appears, is a precious commodity—there never seems to be enough of it.

> *I like work: it fascinates me. I can sit and look at it for hours."*
>
> — JEROME K. JEROME

Some people appear to accomplish more work than others. What is it they know that helps them enhance their efficiency and effectiveness? They understand how to manage time—or so it would appear. But is time really something that can be managed? We all have the same number of seconds, minutes, and hours in a day. Time is a fixed commodity. We believe that it's not *time* that needs to be managed, but something else. It probably won't surprise you that that "something else" is *communication*. As we noted in the early pages of this book, you spend more time communicating with others each day than you do in any other activity. We believe that the best way to enhance your work productivity is through a careful examination of how you communicate with others. How you manage incoming and outgoing messages is central to increasing work efficiency. Although this appendix draws on principles and practices of time management experts, it emphasizes the role of communication in overall work efficiency.

Time management is the use of techniques for analyzing and prioritizing goals and objectives in order to increase efficiency and productivity. By efficiently managing what you spend most of your time doing (communicating), you'll increase your

appendix outline

After reading this appendix, you should be able to

- Write appropriately worded goals and objectives that are specific, measurable, attainable, and observable.

- Make a master list of work tasks and projects.

- Identify and implement strategies for prioritizing work.

- Develop strategies for managing work obstacles to achieve work goals and objectives.

- Take appropriate action to increase work efficiency on team projects.

productivity. And by increasing your productivity you will enhance your ability to lead others. Leaders who manage their time well are also better able to manage their communication with others. It takes time to manage the myriad of messages that leaders manage.

What are the essential time management/communication management competencies? Here's a preview of the essential strategies that we will discuss:

- First, it's vital to identify your goals and objectives. Without a clear sense of what you wish to accomplish, it will be challenging to develop strategies to accomplish what you want to achieve.

- Second, it's important to make a master list of the tasks that you need to accomplish to achieve your goals.

- Third, it's not enough to compile a comprehensive list of your tasks; you need to develop priorities. Determining what you need to do first, second, third, and so on is a key element in effectively managing your time and your communication.

- Fourth, life is punctuated with interruptions. Someone who effectively manages time anticipates potential interruptions and has developed a strategy for working through or around them.

- Finally, you can have goals, make lists, prioritize, and even anticipate interruptions, but unless you take action—turn your plans into behavior—you'll likely see little benefit. So the final task in effectively managing your time is to turn plans into action.

To emphasize the link between managing time and managing communication, we will draw on the five principles of communication to frame our discussion of specific strategies that can enhance your efficiency. Our familiar five communication principles serve as a foundation for our recommendations to enhance your communication efficiency.

Being aware of your communication with yourself and others is an anchoring principle for increasing communication efficiency. Ineffective workers are oblivious to the problems of getting off task, getting distracted, or other causes of reduced efficiency. By identifying strategies to help you identify when you're off task and to increase awareness of your communication strengths, you can improve your ability to manage your time.

Principles two and three, effectively using and interpreting verbal and nonverbal messages, are also important in managing your time wisely. Your ability to make lists and to prioritize the items on those lists are key verbal competencies that, if used wisely, can increase your productivity. Managing interruptions involves using several nonverbal communication behaviors so as to increase efficiency.

The fourth principle, being able to listen and thoughtfully respond, is critical to increasing your efficiency. There are many times when hearing a message accurately in the first place would have saved time, energy, and expense of redoing a project or task. Accurately interpreting what others say is directly linked with increased efficiency and goal achievement.

Finally, the fifth principle of appropriately adapting messages to others is key to managing time. Being able to assess situations and appropriately customize messages and behaviors to accomplish tasks are essential to both effective communication and achievement of goals.

Even without reading this appendix, you probably have a good sense of what a good time manager does as well as what people who are less skilled in efficiently managing their time do. Table B.1 lists the results of a survey that identified the top ten time wasters. To help you get a sense of the time management issues that confront you, make a note of the behaviors on the list that you have found yourself doing. Note how many of the time wasters relate to how we communicate with others. Whether it's the phone, email, text messages, visitors, meetings, socializing, or explicitly poor communication, directly or indirectly most of those factors recognized as time wasters are linked to how we communicate with others. A first step to improving your response to those obstacles is being aware of those behaviors that decrease productivity.

Besides noting time wasters that you may be guilty of from time to time, another way to increase your awareness of your time management competence is to conduct a time audit. Take a moment to complete the time audit form in Rating Scale B.1. After each

Aware
Verbal
Nonverbal
Listen
Adapt

Aware

Time management the use of techniques for analyzing and prioritizing goals and objectives in order to increase efficiency and productivity.

Table B.1	The Ten Biggest Time Wasters[1]

1. Management by crisis

2. Telephone/email interruptions

3. Inadequate planning

4. Attempting too much

5. Drop-in visitors

6. Ineffective delegation

7. Personal disorganization

8. Lack of self-discipline

9. Inability to say no

10. Procrastination

activity listed, estimate how much time (rounded off to quarter and half hours) you spend in a 24-hour period doing each activity. The scale indicates a target amount, which you may or may not agree with, but which gives you something to compare your own time estimates to. Once you've estimated how much time you spend performing each activity, review your estimates to determine if you're comfortable with the time you currently spend on these tasks. If you'd like to spend more time doing an activity (such as sleeping or pursuing a hobby) draw an arrow pointing up next to that activity. If you want to spend less time performing an activity (such as traveling or commuting to and from work or school), draw an arrow pointing down to indicate you'd rather spend less time doing this task. Your time management audit can begin to reveal how you'd like to spend more or less time on a typical day.

Rating Scale B.1   Where Your Time Goes[2]

Daily Activity (Monday–Friday)	Number of Hours Target	Actual
Utility Time		
Sleeping	8	_____
Bathing, Dressing	$\frac{1}{2}$	_____
Eating	$1\frac{1}{2}$	_____
Traveling	$1\frac{1}{2}$	_____
Total Utility Time	$11\frac{1}{2}$	_____
Employment Time/Academic Time		
Working/Studying/Attending Classes/Teaching	8	_____
Breaks	$\frac{1}{2}$	_____
Waiting	$\frac{1}{4}$	_____
Socializing	$\frac{1}{4}$	_____
Total Employment Time	9	_____
Discretionary (Leisure) Time		
Watching TV	1	_____
Athletic and Health Activities	$\frac{1}{2}$	_____
Hobbies, Housework	1	_____
Family and Social Activities	1	_____
Total Discretionary Time	$3\frac{1}{2}$	_____
Total	**24**	**24**

Develop Written Goals and Objectives

Without a map, directions, or a GPS system, it's difficult to navigate from one city to another or to find an unfamiliar address. Just as you need a map or a GPS to help you get where you're going, you also need a map of your work destinations. To manage your time well (and manage your communication, too), you need to establish goals and objectives to clearly identify where you want to go. Being able to develop clear and well-written goals and objectives is the first step in working and communicating more efficiently.[3]

Develop Goals

A **goal** is a clear statement that identifies what you'd like to accomplish in the future. Achieving a goal typically involves accomplishing several short-term tasks. Some time-management experts recommend that you develop a personal goal statement of your mission in life.[4] A personal goal statement prescribes outcomes you'd like to accomplish, such as earning a college degree, becoming more philanthropic, or becoming the chief executive officer of your company. Here are some examples of goal statements:

- Within the next two years I would like to complete my Master's degree.
- Within the next four years I would like to have a major leadership job at a Fortune 500 company on the west coast.
- By the end of the year, our department should have completed transferring our records from the old electronic filing system to the new Internet-based filing system.

Each of these goals articulates long-term outcomes that involve multiple steps and processes. Although it can be a challenge to clearly identify your long-term goals, it's worth the effort and thought. Taking time to become aware of your goals is one of your most important time/communication management tools.

Develop Objectives

An **objective**, like a goal, identifies what you'd like to achieve, but an objective is more immediate than a goal. Completing a specific task by the end of the day or week, making a purchase, and writing a report for your boss are examples of objectives.

A well-worded objective meets four criteria: it is specific, measurable, attainable, and observable.[5]

- *Specific:* An objective should precisely and clearly identify what you'd like to achieve.
- *Measurable:* Your objective should be able to be assessed or measured; you need to be able to determine whether the objective has been accomplished.
- *Attainable:* Appropriate objectives are realistic; they can be accomplished given the resources that you have or can obtain.
- *Observable:* A well-written objective should be stated in terms of an observable behavior.

A key to developing well-worded objectives is to ensure that you use action verbs (*write, read, complete*) that clearly indicate what action you must take to accomplish your objective. Also, it helps to specify a time frame to indicate when you'd like to have the objective completed. Note the following examples:

- By the end of the week, I will finish writing the report about the proposed merger project.
- By the end of the month, I will make fifteen cold sales calls and follow up on each call with a letter to each potential customer.
- By the end of the year, I will complete sixty hours of required training to maintain my general education equivalent requirements.

Goal a clear statement identifying something to be accomplished in the long term.

Objective a statement of something specific, measurable, attainable, and observable to be achieved in the short term.

Each of these objectives meets our four criteria (each is specific, measurable, attainable, and observable) and includes verbs that specify action steps (*write* a report, *make* sales calls, *complete* training).

Time management expert David Allen believes that the best way to begin accomplishing goals and objectives is to identify the next specific action step that you could take to implement the outcome you'd like to achieve.[6] For example, if you want to complete a report by the end of the week, what is the next, precise action step you should take? Perhaps that action step is as simple as going to your computer, turning it on, and beginning to write. Or, perhaps you need to make a phone call to a colleague to get data that you will include in the report. Whatever the next action step is, that is the precise task you should identify. Making a written note of that next step may be just the prompt you need to take action.

Make a Master List

Once you have identified what you need to accomplish, it's important to combine all of your objectives into a comprehensive master list. If you only had one goal or objective to achieve you wouldn't need to make a list. But most of us have many tasks and projects to juggle. A written list helps you remain aware of what needs to be done.

Time management experts suggest a variety of ways to make and keep lists. Your list of action steps to achieve your goals and objectives can be as simple as a handwritten list on a piece of notebook paper. Some time management experts suggest using a day calendar that incorporates space to make lists as you keep your daily appointments.[7] We believe there is no single best system for making a list that works for everyone. Whether you make your list on sticky notes, store it in your computer, or write it on notebook paper, here's the key: *Have some system of tracking the various tasks and projects in an easy-to-use, easy-to-read format that you regularly review.* Develop a system that you will use. Here are other suggestions to help you make a master list of your tasks and projects.

- *Write it down.* What all time management experts seem to agree on is this: Your list of objectives and tasks should be a written list. It's not enough just to think about what you need to do. Again, the list needs to be in a format and system that works for you, whether you write it on paper or enter it into your computer or your personal digital assistant (PDA). Many cell phones permit you to make notes and lists and remind you of the projects and tasks on your "to do" list. The format doesn't matter as long as you have some system of tracking the various tasks on your list. Some suggest developing a list and then making a detailed analysis of each task by noting its overall importance, urgency, potential for delegation, and the key people you need to communicate with to accomplish each task.

- *Cross it off.* Whatever system you use for listing your tasks, it's important to be able to cross a task off the list once you've completed it.

- *Consolidate items when appropriate.* If you can bundle several related tasks together, you're more likely to tackle them. For example, if you have several phone calls to make, your list entry could read "Phone calls," followed by the names and numbers of those you need to call and a note on when to call them. The goal is not to make your master list as long as possible, but to make it manageable. One way to make your list less daunting is to consolidate items. Make your list realistic.

- *Review your list.* It does no good to have a master list of your projects and tasks unless you look at it. One good habit is to look at your list at least twice: as you begin your workday and at the conclusion of your day. At the beginning of your day, note the projects and tasks that you want to make sure you achieve *that day.* Your "in basket" (whether it's in cyberspace or on your desk) is a good place to keep your master list. You are more likely to use your list if you keep it someplace where you can look at it frequently throughout the day.

- *Don't use your calendar as a substitute for your master list.* Since we've just suggested that you should keep your master list in or near your "in basket," you may think it's OK to keep several "to do" lists in your calendar. We don't recommend that option. Although you may use your calendar to remind yourself of important deadlines, some time management experts suggest it's better to keep your master list separate from your daily appointment calendar and to keep a single master list. An old Chinese proverb says, "A person who has two watches never knows the correct time." If you have more than one calendar or more than one list, you may lose track of something. The key to lists and calendars is having a consolidated, single place to show you when you need to be where (your calendar) and a single, comprehensive list of what needs to be done (your master list). You could make subcategories in your master list, but we don't recommend having multiple lists in multiple places. One list, one place.

- *Schedule tasks on your list at your best times.* Are you a "morning person"? A morning person views the first half of the day as the best half and is at his or her best then. Or, maybe you work best late at night. Regardless of when your peak working hours are, schedule your work to correspond to those times to the extent possible.

Prioritize Your Work

Now that you have identified both your larger goals and your immediate objectives and you have a system for keeping track of your tasks by making a master list, you need to determine your work priorities. Several time management experts suggest that one of the best ways to establish your priorities is to analyze the tasks on your list by asking yourself two questions:

Aware

1. How urgent is this task?
2. How important is this task?[8]

Is it urgent? Urgency is about time. Something is urgent if it is time sensitive. Urgent messages or urgent tasks are things that someone believes need to be accomplished sooner rather than later. One problem is that what other people may perceive as urgent may actually not be urgent to you. So your challenge as you review the many ways you could spend your time, is to decide how urgent a task is. Similarly, there are some things that others may ask you to do that are urgent but not important to you. That leads to the next key question.

Is it important? What makes something important? A task is important if it helps you accomplish your goals and objectives. If you have not thought about your goals and objectives, then it will be difficult to determine what is important and what is not.

As shown in Figure B.1, you can sort any work task according to its urgency and importance. Is the task I'm planning to do (or being asked to do) urgent or not urgent? Is the task important or not important? Increasing your awareness of the tasks on your list as important or urgent can help you determine your work and communication priorities.

The use of technology to increase the speed at which we receive and send messages can create "unimportant urgency." This is not to say that technology can't help us increase our productivity—of course it can. But modern technology—email, cell phones, fax machines, BlackBerrys—can increase the speed and thus the *perceived* urgency of some messages that may not be urgent at all. Another factor that increases a sense of urgency is being overbooked and making too many commitments to others that we can't keep. Overscheduling can make a small task seem daunting. We need to make some room in our schedules for those unexpected tasks that are simply part of our everyday life experiences. But if we've unwisely constructed a daily schedule that is chock full of tasks, projects, and mandatory events, we have no room for those things that emerge during the course of the day. That "one more thing" may not be all that time-consuming, but it may be the task that induces greater stress and perceived urgency because we just can't fit it in.

Urgent and important. You probably don't have to worry about whether you will accomplish something that is both urgent and important. If you get an emergency call from your boss who asks you to help with an important project, you don't need to check a master list to determine if this task is something that you'll do. Given that the task is both time sensitive and important (because it comes from your immediate supervisor), you'll no doubt give it immediate attention.

Important and not urgent. Most of us also have a tendency to avoid important but not urgent tasks because there is no immediate need to complete the task. So one of the ways

| **Figure B.1** | **Identifying What Is Urgent and Important** |

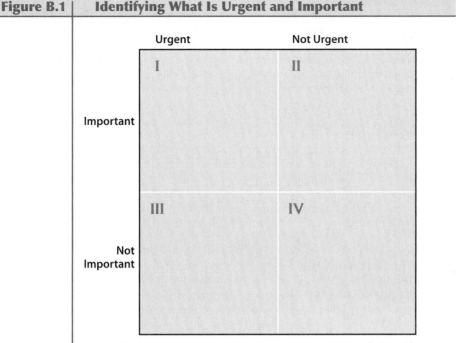

Source: Stephen Covey, A. Roger Merrill, and Rebecca R. Merrill, *First Things First* (New York: Fireside, 1996).

to increase your performance and work quality is to make a conscious effort to spend time on the important and not urgent tasks. Developing your goals and objectives and making a master list of your projects and tasks are examples of important yet not urgent tasks. What effective, productive leaders and managers know that unproductive people don't know is that you *must* spend time on important but nonurgent work. How do you do that? One way is to schedule time for it. Some important but nonurgent tasks not only affect your work, they also affect your health. Getting exercise, for example, is an example of an important but nonurgent task. To be more productive in the long run, identify those activities on your master list that are important but may not have an immediate deadline and budget time for them. Recreation activities and vacations are other examples of important yet nonurgent activities that we may postpone yet shouldn't.

Urgent and not important. The tricky part of managing your time and your communication comes when someone who is not your immediate supervisor views a task as urgent, but it's not important to you. Having a sense of what is important (based on your own goals and objectives rather than someone else's) will help you sort through whether you should take action on the task or not. You'll no doubt receive phone calls and email messages relating to tasks that someone else views as urgent and that must be accomplished soon, but that may not be all that important to you. A key in setting priorities is to sort through what is really important and what is really urgent, given all of the tasks on your master list.

DILBERT: ©Scott Adams/Dist. by United Feature Syndicate, Inc.

Not urgent and not important. Finally, there are some things you do that are neither urgent nor important. These time wasters can include things like watching YouTube, mindlessly surfing the Internet, or playing computer Solitaire. We're not suggesting that you eliminate these activities—if they truly help you relax and recharge your mental and physical batteries, then by all means, enjoy them. The problem comes when we find ourselves engaging in activities that aren't, in the long run, edifying or helpful—they just waste time; those are the activities to remove from our daily routines.

Manage Interruptions

We've extolled the virtues of having goals and objectives, making a master list, and then prioritizing your tasks. The next logical part of managing your time is simply to start accomplishing the high priority items at the top of your list. But before you begin whittling down the tasks and projects on your master list, it's important to plan for the interruptions that are a normal part of our work and personal lives.

Stuff happens. As John Lennon noted in the lyrics to one of his songs, "Life is what happens to you when you're making other plans." Interruptions can range from a phone call, to a text message that you feel you need to check, to someone poking her head in your door to ask if you've got "a minute" to talk. In the daily course of doing your work these are normal and expected. The problem comes when you have not developed a plan to manage these interruptions. Unless your job is to answer the phone, you may not need to immediately take every phone call you receive. Unless your job is to serve as a receptionist, you may not need to accommodate everyone who stops by for information. Even the paperwork that streams across your desk can interrupt your work productivity.

People who are less productive have not developed a plan for managing the data, information, and messages that come their way. As we noted earlier, it's not time that we manage, but communication. Developing a system for managing the routine interruptions and distractions you encounter can help boost your productivity.

Manage Messages: Time Management Principles

Before we suggest tips for managing specific distractions and interruptions, we'll consider some general time management principles that can help you process the volume of verbal and nonverbal messages that will come to your attention.

Batch your work. To batch your work is to group your tasks so that you budget time to do one kind of thing at a time. For example, it's more efficient to respond to several email messages at a time—in one batch—than to respond to each email message as it arrives. Similarly, schedule a period in your workday to return phone calls rather than hopping from one task to another. Of course, if a phone call or email is both urgent and important (a call from your boss, for example) you should respond immediately. But many routine messages can wait and can be batched to be more efficiently managed.

Do your work once. There are really only three options for handling any given task:

- *Do it*: Respond to the request for action or information.
- *Delegate it*: If you are a supervisor or have staff support, you could assign the task to others.
- *Delete it*: Some messages, such as email messages, may not need a response.[9]

The most common but least efficient response to incoming work is to just stack it in a pile and assume that you'll get to it someday. Before you know it, you'll have a stack of "stuff" that can clutter up your work life. "Stuff," according to time management expert David Allen, is anything that is not related to any specific goal or action step.[10] It's best to make a decision about each work chore when it hits your in basket: do it, delegate it, or delete it.

Organize your workspace. Another way to increase your efficiency is to have everything you need to do your work at hand. The tools, supplies, sources of information, and anything else you need to do your work should be within easy grasp. If you have to hunt for paperclips, tape, notepads, a pen, or other resources that you typically use, you lose time.

Use a reminder file. Instead of missing deadlines and being surprised by due dates, develop a reminder file or a system for tracking project due dates. One recommended system is to get a large file with multiple pockets, either five pockets for each day of the week, or (better yet), one with thirty pockets, one for each day of the month. If a task is routinely due on the 15th of each month, you simply look in the pocket marked "15th" for reminders you've placed in that pocket. Or, if you need to pay bills on a certain date each month, place the bills as they arrive in the file pocket corresponding the day they are due (or the day when checks must be mailed or payment posted online). Just check the file each day to remind yourself of what needs to be accomplished that day. Another way to remind yourself is to make a note on your calendar of the due dates of major projects. In addition, most computers, cell phones, BlackBerrys, and other electronic tools can be programmed to remind you of deadlines. If a project is large and complex, you may want to provide update reminders several days or weeks before the project is due to remind yourself of what you should have accomplished by those dates in order to remain on schedule.

Manage Email

Verbal

Email can dramatically increase your efficiency because it makes sending information, documents, or files to people who need them so easy and quick. But many people can find themselves buried by the avalanche of text messages and email messages that pour into their electronic in-boxes each day. If you miss a day of work, the next day you may find yourself overwhelmed by the email that you need to respond to.

Set aside a specific time of the day to check email. Unless it's part of your job to immediately respond to email messages, use the principle of batching tasks that we mentioned earlier. For example, check your email first thing in the morning, at noon, and an hour before the end of your work day; or find some time frame for checking email that is compatible with the work cycle where you're employed. We don't recommend setting your email program to notify you every time you receive an email; you may be tempted to see who just sent you a message rather than more efficiently processing your email in batches.

Use the two-minute rule. The email two minute rule is this: If you can't respond to an email message in two minutes or less, wait to respond to it when you're responding to several email messages at the same time.[11] You can work more efficiently if you are working on the same kind of task (such as responding to email) than if you're checking email, deleting some messages, and then spending more than two minutes responding to others.

Create action files. If it takes more than two minutes to respond to or make a decision about what to do with an email message, create action files—files in your email system where you store messages to review later. At first it may sound as though we're encouraging procrastination, but what we're actually encouraging is more efficient management of your responses to messages. The simplest files to create are for action, for waiting, and for lengthy messages that simply need to be read. The action file can include all email messages that need more than two minutes in which to write a response. The waiting file is for email messages that don't need an immediate response but that you don't want to delete. Finally, the read file is for email that will take you longer than two minutes to read. By filing and batching your email, you'll work more efficiently.

Manage Paperwork

Email was supposed to eliminate paper and paperwork, and there are some organizations that have succeeded in stemming the rising tide of paper, but most workers still shuffle an ample amount of paper.

Some of the most common paperwork problems include indecision about what to do with incoming paperwork (so it gets handled more than once), procrastination, failure to delegate work to others, keeping or filing documents that you really don't need, or the complete lack of a system for managing the paper parade. Here are several strategies that can help overcome these problems.

Read something once and handle it once. After you read a document, decide what you want to do with it. Keeping it on your desk or carrying it around in your briefcase only means you'll eventually have to figure out what to do with the document. Make the decision to file it, throw it away, or delegate it to someone else the first time you read it.

Dispose of what you don't need again after you read it. One time management expert estimates that 80 percent of the daily flow of paperwork can be read and thrown away, yet the typical reader disposes of about 20 percent.[12] Decide whether you really need to keep what hits your in basket.

Develop a strategy for filing what you need. A reason some people are clogged with paperwork is because they file things they really don't need. Don't over-file—avoid placing things in a permanent, long-term file that don't need to be there. If you do develop a short-term holding file, make sure documents don't stack up there. Purge the file of outdated and unneeded documents periodically.

Don't paper hop. Not only should you read something just once, you should also avoid starting to read one document, then stopping and switching to a different document so that you're hopping from one document to the other. You'll waste time. You work more efficiently if you stick to one task until you finish it. You may be praised for multi-tasking, but the more focused you are on one task, the more efficiently you'll work.

Manage the Telephone

A phone call is a classic example of an urgent but not important interruption. Obviously, some phone calls *are* important, and if your job requires you to answer the phone whenever you get a call, you should do so. But if your responsibilities give you some flexibility and freedom in responding to phone calls, you'll need to give careful thought to how you will manage incoming telephone calls. And you often have a choice of when you return phone calls; some return calls can be made at your convenience.

Among the most common telephone interruption problems are the lack of a system to screen calls, missing phone calls, and playing telephone tag. You may also find that you spend too much time on the phone, either in off-task conversation or because either you or the other person has difficulty ending the call. All of these problems are less about managing time and more about managing verbal and nonverbal communication.

Here are several strategies to help you manage telephone calls.[13]

Return nonurgent calls in batches. Rather than intermittently returning calls throughout the day, you'll work more efficiently if you set aside a time of the day to return phone calls.

Communicate your phone availability to others. When you've called someone and the person you want to speak with is not available, in addition to leaving your name and phone number, indicate when it would be best for the person to call you. If someone takes phone messages for you, have that person find out the best time for you to return the call. Similarly, if you have voice mail or use an answering machine, make sure that the message callers hear asks them to indicate when it's best for you to return their call. You'll spend less time playing phone tag if you have information about when it's best to connect.

Know how to tactfully end a phone call. It may seem to happen when you're at your busiest: Callers want to chat or prolong a phone call. You don't want to be rude, so you listen. And listening is both a virtue and a vital communication skill that we've emphasized throughout this book. But an equally important skill is to know how to politely and tactfully end a phone call that's neither important nor urgent. We can suggest three termination strategies:

- Identify your time limits when you begin the call. For example, say, "Frank, it's good to hear from you. I have about ten minutes right now, is that enough time for our conversation?" If the time frame you suggest isn't enough, you may need to schedule the call at another time.
- Signal that you'd like to end the call soon. You might say, "Roberta, before we end our visit I have one more thing to say" or, "Before we conclude, do you have any more suggestions?"
- Be honest about your need to end the call. "Steve, I'm sorry, but I do have a meeting in a few minutes that I need to attend."

Develop a phone call screening system. This advice won't apply to you if your job is to be the phone screener (if you're a receptionist, for example), but if you don't have a way of screening your calls, develop one; you need some way of knowing who is calling so that you can make it your choice to answer the phone. If you have a receptionist, tell him or her when you're available for calls and when you're not. Many, if not most, phone systems include caller ID; use this information to decide whether to take a call or let your voice message system take it for you. If you're involved in writing a report, or in the middle of drafting a lengthy email message that needs your sustained concentration, you'll be more productive if you continue with your task rather than switching from your writing task to answer the phone. You may find it helpful to designate a "quiet hour" during part of each day in which you don't take calls (unless they are from your boss or customers). Of course, you'll have to customize our suggestions to fit your job and work culture, but the key to managing incoming calls is to be aware of the need to do so and then develop a system that works for you and your situation.

Manage Unscheduled Visitors

"Do you have a minute?" The person who pokes his head in your office or cubical probably needs more than a minute. These "minute" conversations can sap your time and energy and reduce your work productivity. Yet most jobs involve being available to respond to people who need your help. Rather than email or phone calls, it may be people who interrupt your work rhythm most frequently. People stop by because they need to see you in person. But if you always have an open door, you may find that it's difficult to balance responding to the immediate presence of someone who needs to speak with you and attending to the volume of work stacked on your desk or waiting for you in cyberspace.

One of the primary reasons drop-by visitors erode work efficiency is because no system has been developed for managing when or how to respond to visitors. Most of us like to be available to our colleagues and certainly to our customers and clients, yet if we set no limits on our availability it may be difficult to work efficiently and accomplish other tasks that are also important to our jobs. It may be also difficult to manage the flow of people who want to see you if

- You're the boss and the people who report to you need access to you.
- You pride yourself on an open door policy.
- You work in a cubical and have no door to open or close to signal when you're available.
- You have a boss or a colleague who frequently needs (or just wants) to visit.
- Your office is in a high traffic area of the building; many people see you and stop to chat.

Again, it's not that you need to manage time, it's that you need to develop a system to manage communication. Here are some communication management strategies to help you balance the need for separateness and the need for connection that are integral to most jobs.

Find a quiet place to work on tasks that need your full concentration. Rather than doing all of your work at your desk, consider finding a place where you can work independently, even if it's only for half an hour or an hour. Taking your laptop to a quiet corner in the company cafeteria, or finding an empty conference room where you can work undisturbed may let you reclaim the solitude that you need to accomplish a task that needs your uninterrupted concentration.

Verbally communicate your availability to others. Let your colleagues and customers know the best times for you to meet with them. Set specific time frames for communicating in person.

Use nonverbal cues to signal your availability to others. If your office has a door, you may need to close it from time to time to express your desire not to be interrupted. If you work in a cubicle and have no door, if possible face away from the opening to your workspace. The more readily colleagues can establish eye contact with you, the more likely it is they will stop to visit. Some people without doors have posted signs to indicate when they are available and when they may not be available even though they are present in their workspace. (However, before implementing this strategy, consider the organizational culture of your workplace.) The key is to make sure that you are in control of communication regulatory cues. Since it's often nonverbal cues that indicate whether or not we are available to communicate, monitor the nonverbal messages you and your office arrangement signal to others.

Politely but assertively end conversations or let others know that you are busy. When someone wants to see you, it can be hard not to be seen. A person's physical presence is a nonverbal cue of immediacy or urgency. But there are times when you may need to politely end a conversation or redirect your visitor to someone else. Here are some strategies to help limit or end conversations:

- When someone comes into your workspace, stand to greet the person. By remaining standing you signal that you're not inviting the person in for a long chat. Not everyone will pick up on this subtle cue, but by standing rather than sitting, you are indicating nonverbally that you expect the conversation to be short.

- Meet people in their office or workspace rather than yours. If you are in someone else's office, you are less likely to get involved in a long conversation from which you can't escape. When the meeting is in your office, you have nowhere else to go; if you're visiting in a colleague's office you can keep the meeting short.

- Verbally communicate how much time you have for a visit. Let others know what your time limits are. You might say, "Janice, I'm due at a meeting in ten minutes, can we discuss this issue in that time?" We're not suggesting that you lie about meetings or other appointments to avoid conversations. But do honestly let others know of your time parameters.

- If you have an administrative assistant, ask him or her to announce when your next appointment is, which will help you signal the need to end a meeting.

- Verbally signal that your time is up. By saying, "Do you have any final observations before we conclude our visit?" you send a clear message that your time is limited. With some people you may need to be even more explicit: "Ken, I'm sorry, but I have to conclude our meeting."

Take Action

Having goals and objectives, making a master list, prioritizing your work, and managing interruptions won't be enough to achieve increased productivity unless you act. The final element in managing your time and managing communication in order to increase your efficiency is to turn your plans into action. One strategy that can help you take appropriate action to accomplish your goals and objectives is to use the power of reflection.

One of your most powerful time management/communication management tools is the power of reflection. When you reflect, you take time for an important but not urgent task: to review what you need to do next. As we emphasized at the beginning of this appendix, becoming aware of what keeps you from achieving your work goals and having clear goals and objectives is the starting place for taking concrete steps to working more efficiently.

The worksheet in Rating Scale B.2 lists common time/communication management problems. Review the list and identify the problems you need to address most immediately. Once you have distilled what you perceive as the biggest obstacles to your success, review the material in this appendix and identify specific action steps that you can take to address the problems you identify.

Rating Scale B.2   Classifying Time Problems[14]

Study the list of time problems carefully. Place a check mark in the blank beside each one that is applicable to you.

Personal Habits and Attitudes

_____ Personal disorganization
_____ Lack of personal goals
_____ Lack of personal priorities
_____ Lack of personal deadlines
_____ Inability to delegate
_____ Over-commitment
_____ Procrastination
_____ Indecision
_____ Inability to say no
_____ Fatigue
_____ Lack of planning
_____ Perfectionism
_____ Other _____
        _____

General Organizational Environment

_____ Too many meetings
_____ Too many classes
_____ Long meetings
_____ Lack of organizational goals
_____ Lack of organizational priorities
_____ Lack of organizational deadlines
_____ Unclear lines of responsibility or authority
_____ Poor information
_____ Lack of clear standards or expectations
_____ Poor records or filing system
_____ Red tape
_____ Poor communication
_____ Too much email
_____ Management by crisis
_____ Unwieldy paper flow

Types of Interruptions

_____ Telephone
_____ Social drop-ins, clients, and other outsiders
_____ "Putting out fires"
_____ Questions from colleagues
_____ Questions from superiors
_____ Other _____

Look back over the items that you checked and circle each check mark that indicates a problem you could remedy—or at least markedly improve—by a change in your personal attitudes or behavior, given necessary knowledge and adequate motivation.

Now list below, in rank order, several of your most pressing time management problems. Then devise one action you can take this week that will contribute to the solution of these problems. Remember that time management is a continuing activity; one action will not magically change your whole environment. But one action makes a start.

My Biggest Problems

1. _____
2. _____
3. _____
4. _____
5. _____

Action Needed

1. _____
2. _____
3. _____
4. _____
5. _____

Work Efficiently on Team Projects

You can apply the principles and strategies we've noted in this chapter to group and team projects. Although the only person you can really change is you, using the principles and strategies we've offered in this chapter can help you develop a blueprint for working efficiently with others. To apply the time management principles to the work of a team, consider the following strategies:

- Make sure your team has clearly written, measurable, attainable, and specific work objectives.
- Before plunging in on a team task, make a master list of the key steps that the team needs to accomplish. Without a comprehensive list of the steps needed to

do the work, it will be more difficult to develop clear team member roles and more challenging to divide and conquer the work objectives.

- Assess what the team priorities are. What is truly urgent and important? What needs to be accomplished first, second, and so on?

- Note obstacles that may keep the team from working efficiently. But do more than describe the obstacles—develop a plan to address the potential barriers that you identify.

- Take action by implementing the collaborative plan that the team has developed. Periodically take the time to assess how well the team is meeting its goals.

RECAP: Applying Communication Management Principles to Team Projects

	How To Improve Individual Performance	**How To Improve Team Performance**
1. Set Goals	Write clear, measurable, attainable, and specific goals.	As a team, identify and discuss the team goals.
2. Make a Master List	Make a master list of all that you have to do.	As a team, list and describe the steps that need to be accomplished to achieve the team or project goals.
3. Prioritize	Identify the high-priority tasks. Determine what should be done first, second, and so on.	As a team, determine the priority of the steps or tasks and decide who should take responsibility for each task.
4. Manage Distractions	Identify what may keep you from accomplishing your goal and develop strategies to manage or eliminate the distractions (phone calls, interruptions, and the like).	As a team, identify the obstacles that may keep the team from achieving its goals. Identify strategies to overcome the obstacles.
5. Take Action	Identify what you need to do and then do it.	As a team, take action to achieve the goals of the project. Periodically meet to evaluate the plan and assess whether you are meeting your objectives.

Communication Principles and Skills for Leadership

Principle One: Be aware of your communication with yourself and others.

- Increase your efficiency by first becoming aware of how you currently use your time.
- Be cognizant of the goals and objectives you want to accomplish.
- Use the power of reflection to mindfully identify strategies for taking action.

Principle Two: Effectively use and interpret verbal messages.

- Develop written goals and objectives to significantly increase the likelihood that you will accomplish what you want to achieve.
- Make a written master list of all of your tasks, projects, and objectives to help increase both effectiveness and efficiency.

Principle Three: Effectively use and interpret nonverbal messages.

- Make sure that everything you need is within easy reach in your workspace to increase your efficiency.
- Minimize eye contact with people passing by your workspace to stay focused on your work and increase work efficiency.
- Develop nonverbal symbols, such as a closed door, to signal when you are not available to visit.

Principle Four: Listen and respond thoughtfully to others.

- Respond to the messages and responses of others to help you manage them with greater accuracy and effectiveness.

Principle Five: Appropriately adapt messages to others.

- Adapt your method of communicating to others (email, phone, in person) to help you work more effectively and efficiently; there may be no need to visit a colleague's office when a short email message will be just as effective in communicating a message.

Discussion Questions

1. What are the differences between goals and objectives?

2. What are the advantages of making a master list of your tasks, objectives, and projects?

3. How will being able to identify work tasks that are urgent and important help you manage your work priorities?

4. What are tips and strategies for managing the volume of email, paperwork, phone messages, and visitors that you receive?

5. Identify how the principles of time management can be applied to team projects.

Building Your Skills

1. Use the following list to help you identify important yet nonurgent tasks that you should spend more time on. (Examples: spend more time planning, reading, studying, preparing for class, building relationships with others)

   A.

   B.

   C.

   D.

   E.

   What will you do to re-order your life to make time for these important but nonurgent tasks? (Examples: schedule time in my appointment book, develop a personal goal statement, make a master list).

   A.

   B.

   C.

   D.

   E.

Glossary

A

Accommodator   someone who manages conflict by giving in rather than engaging in the conflict.

Activity report   a document that communicates progress on a project or achievements to others in an organization or on a team.

Adaptive skills   self-management skills that allow you to adjust to a variety of social situations.

Adult learners   people who prefer to be given information they can use immediately, to be actively involved in the learning process, to connect their life experiences with the new information they learn, to know how the new information is relevant to their busy lives, to know how the information will solve a problem, and to receive information that is relevant to their needs.

Affirming message   a message that reveals that you value and support another person.

Agenda   a written list of issues, questions, information, or topics to be discussed or tasks to be completed in a meeting.

Amiable   a social style characterized by high responsiveness and low assertiveness. People with this style are considered relationship specialists; they enjoy working in supportive and helpful roles.

Analogy   a comparison between an unfamiliar idea, thing, or situation and something the audience already understands.

Analytical   a social style characterized by low responsiveness and assertiveness. Individuals with this social style are considered technical specialists; they enjoy working in technical positions.

Appeal to misplaced authority   using someone without the appropriate credentials or expertise to endorse an idea or product.

Appraisal interview   an interview in which a supervisor shares information with an employee about his or her job performance; also known as a *performance review.*

Argumentativeness   a tendency to advocate strongly for one's own position on an issue and criticize the positions of other people.

Articulation   the enunciation of speech sounds.

Artifact   a personal object used to communicate some part of one's identity.

Assertiveness   an individual's capacity to make requests, actively disagree, express positive and negative personal feelings, and stand up for himself or herself without attacking another.

Asynchronous   communication in which there is a time delay between when a message is sent and when it is received.

Attend   to focus on a specific message.

Authoritarian leaders   leaders who influence by giving orders and seeking to control others.

Avoider   someone who manages conflict by steering clear of it.

B

Back channel cues   nonverbal cues that signal to the other person that we are listening and wish for them to continue talking.

Back matter   the components of a report that traditionally come at the end, after the main body, and provide further detail and references.

Bandwagon fallacy   the argument that because everyone believes something or does something, the belief or behavior must be valid, accurate, or effective.

Bar graph   a graph that uses bars of different lengths to represent statistical data.

Biased messages   messages that include words or expressions that offend because they make inappropriate assumptions or repeat stereotypes about gender, ethnicity, physical or mental disability, age, or sexual orientation.

Boolean search   an advanced web-searching technique that allows a user to narrow a key word search by specifying certain parameters.

Briefing   a short talk that provides information to an audience.

C

Career-search information interview   an interview in which you gather information about careers, jobs, and organizations and network with others so that you will have a job when you are ready for one.

Causal fallacy   a faulty cause-and-effect connection between two things or events.

Causal reasoning   reasoning that relates two or more events in such a way as to conclude that one or more of the events caused the others.

Cause-and-effect organization   a strategy for identifying a situation and then discussing the resulting effects (cause-effect), or presenting a situation and then exploring its causes (effect-cause).

Central idea   a one-sentence summary of your presentation; sometimes called a thesis sentence.

Centralized power cultures   cultures that value a more concentrated or narrow distribution of power; power is held by one person or a select few.

Channel   the means by which a message is expressed to the receiver.

Charisma   a form of dynamism; a charismatic speaker possesses charm, talent, magnetism, and other qualities that make the person attractive.

Chronemics   the study of how people use and structure time.

Chronological organization   organization by sequential order, according to when each step or event occurred or should occur.

Clarity   the specificity of a message and how easily the reader can comprehend the information.

Classical leadership   a leadership style that assumes that there is one best way to perform a specific task within an organization with maximum efficiency, and that a leader's job is to influence workers to behave in this way.

Classification   defining something by placing it in a group or category based on its qualities or characteristics.

Clique   a smaller group of people within a larger group who form a common bond among themselves.

Closed question   an interview question that limits the range of possible responses and requires a simple, direct, and brief answer.

Closure   a sense of being complete or "sounding finished" provided in the conclusion of a speech by finishing a story, answering a rhetorical question, or reminding the audience of a statistic presented in the introduction.

Coercive power   power stemming from the ability to punish others.

Cognitive dissonance   psychological discomfort experienced when a person is presented with information that is inconsistent with his or her current thinking or feelings.

Coherence   unity in writing created by common underlying concepts, logical organization, and clear, natural development of the content.

Cohesiveness   the degree of attraction that members of a group feel toward one another and the group.

Collaborator   someone who manages conflict by being willing to work with others to solve problems and make decisions.

Collectivistic cultures   cultures whose members value group or community interests over individual interests.

Communibiological perspective   an interdisciplinary approach to the study of human communication that makes connections between the fields of neurology, psychology, and communication.

Communication   the process of acting on information.

Communication apprehension (CA)   fear or anxiety associated with ongoing or anticipated communication with another person or persons.

Communication interaction pattern   communication pattern that emerges based on who talks to whom.

Communication trait   a label used to describe a person's communication behaviors.

Competence   the perception that a person is skilled, knowledgeable, and informed about the subject he or she is discussing.

Competitor   someone who manages conflict by being competitive and pushing ideas and solutions on others.

Complaint letter   a letter that expresses dissatisfaction with a product or service.

Complexity   arrangement of speech ideas from simple to complex.

Compromiser   someone who manages conflict by giving up part of what he or she wants in exchange for the other person's giving up part of he or she wants.

Concise writing   writing that avoids unnecessary words and phrases.

Conclusion   the closing sentences of a speech, intended to summarize the speech, to reemphasize the main idea in a memorable way, to motivate the audience to respond, and to provide closure.

Concrete   referring to something you can experience with your senses.

Conditional statements   statements that qualify what is being said; they leave room for interpretation.

Confidentiality   the ethical principle that requires interviewers to keep information disclosed during an interview private.

Conflict phase   the second phase of group interaction, in which group members experience some disagreement about social issues and group tasks.

Conflict style   the way people are perceived to express and manage conflict.

Connotative meaning   the interpretation of a word based on personal experiences.

Consensus   group agreement that occurs when all group members support and are committed to a collective decision.

Content   the new information, ideas, or suggested actions that a speaker wishes to express.

Content dimension   the communication dimension that focuses on what is said; the verbal message.

Context   the physical, historical, and psychological environment in which communication occurs.

Conversational rituals   learned, routine scripts that people use when talking and responding to others.

Corrective feedback   communication feedback whose goal is to alter negative or inappropriate behavior.

Correspondence   business letters sent to customers, co-workers, superiors, and subordinates.

Cover letter   a document that accompanies a resume; a sales pitch that argues why you are the best candidate for a position.

Credibility   a listener's perception of a speaker as competent, trustworthy, and dynamic.

Cube   a small, modular office unit with no door and no floor-to-ceiling walls.

Cultural context   the nonverbal cues related to culture that surround and give meaning to messages.

Culture   a learned system of knowledge, behavior, attitudes, beliefs, values, and norms that is shared by a group of people.

D

Decentralized power cultures   cultures in which people value a broad distribution of power; the power belongs to the people, or the many, not to one person or group.

Decision making   the process of making a choice from among several alternatives.

Declarative statements   statements expressed as truths that leave no room for interpretation.

Decoding   the process of interpreting ideas, feelings, and thoughts that have been translated into a code.

Decorative font   a font designed to convey a feeling or tone.

Deductive reasoning   reasoning from a general statement or principle to reach a specific conclusion.

Definition   a brief explanation that identifies and clarifies what something is by classifying it or describing how it works.

Delegation   a manager's assignment of a specific task or project to an employee.

Delivery cues   notes a speaker uses to remind himself or herself of nonverbal behaviors to use while making a presentation.

Delivery outline   a condensed, abbreviated outline that provides the notes a speaker uses when presenting a speech.

Democratic leaders   leaders who consult with the group before issuing edicts.

Demographic information   statistics about audience characteristics such as age, gender, and cultural background.

Denotative meaning   the literal or dictionary definition of a word.

Derived credibility   the perception of a speaker's credibility that the audience forms as he or she presents a speech.

Description   a word picture; a detailed image that allows an audience to mentally see, hear, smell, touch, or taste whatever a speaker is describing.

Descriptive approach   an approach to team development that seeks to identify the typical ways teams behave in solving problems.

Devil's advocate   someone who criticizes or opposes something in order to provoke a discussion or an argument.

Dialect   a consistent style of pronunciation and articulation that is common to an ethnic group or a geographic region.

Downward communication   communication that flows from superiors to subordinates.

Driver   a social style characterized by high assertiveness and low responsiveness. Persons with this social style are considered control specialists; they often enjoy working in leadership and management positions.

Dynamism   an aspect of a speaker's credibility that reflects whether the speaker is perceived as energetic.

E

Either-or fallacy   the oversimplification of an issue into a choice between only two outcomes or possibilities.

Elaboration strategies   mental processing strategies that give information new meaning by organizing the information.

Emblem   a gesture that has a direct verbal translation and may substitute for a word or phrase.

Emergence phase   the third phase of group interaction, in which conflict or disagreement is managed and decisions are made.

Empathy   the emotion experienced by someone who feels what another is feeling.

Encoding   the process of translating ideas, feelings, and thoughts into a code.

Ethics   the beliefs, values, and moral principles by which we determine what is right and wrong.

Ethos   the credibility or ethical character of a speaker.

Evidence   the illustrations, definitions, statistics, and opinions presented as supporting material in persuasive speaking.

Exit interview   an interview in which an employer gathers information from an employee who is leaving the organization about his or her work experiences.

Expert power   power derived from having knowledge and expertise.

Expert testimony   an opinion offered by someone who is an authority on the subject under discussion.

Explanation   a statement of how something is done or why it exists in its present form or existed in its past form.

Expressive   a social style characterized by high assertiveness and responsiveness. Individuals with this social style are considered social specialists; they are able to use their communication skills to gain recognition and attention, and enjoy being noticed by others.

Extemporaneous speaking   speaking from a written or memorized speech outline without having memorized the exact wording of the speech.

F

Feed-forward messages   messages that inform others of how to process information from you.

Feedback   the response to a message.

Feminine cultures   cultures in which people have more of a social orientation and tend to value caring, sensitivity, and enhancing quality of life.

Figurative analogy   a comparison between two essentially unlike things or events that nevertheless share some feature.

Final summary   the final part of a speech, which restates a speaker's most important ideas.

Force field analysis   a tool that structures the analysis of a problem by identifying the driving forces that increase the probability that a goal will be achieved and the restraining forces that decrease that probability.

Formal report   a highly researched report on an ongoing project, often co-authored by several writers.

Forum presentation   a question-and-answer session that usually follows a presentation or a symposium.

Front matter   the components of a report that come at the beginning and prepare the reader for the main information.

Functional approach   an approach to leadership that suggests that leaders perform essential functions, tasks, and processes that help an organization or team achieve goals; an approach to team development that suggests that in order for a team to be effective, certain communication functions must occur.

Funnel sequence   a questioning sequence that begins with broad, open questions and proceeds toward more closed questions.

G

Gaps analysis   an analysis conducted by a supervisor of an identified gap between a performance standard and an employee's actual performance.

Gatekeeper   a person who controls the flow of communication within an organization.

Gender   the cultural and psychological characteristics that are associated with biological sex.

Goal   a clear statement identifying something to be accomplished in the long term.

Goodwill   a positive perception of an author on the part of the audience.

Grammar   the study of the functions of words and the way they work together to form coherent language.

Group communication   verbal and nonverbal message transaction that occurs among from three to about fifteen people who share a common purpose or goal.

Group deviate   a team member who holds an opinion different from the rest of the group; group members may spend considerable talk time trying to change this person's opinion.

Grouphate   the loathing many people have for collaborating with others in groups and teams.

Groupthink   a faulty sense of agreement that occurs when team members seemingly agree but they primarily want to avoid conflict.

H

Haptics   the study of how we communicate through touch.

Hasty generalization   reaching a conclusion from too little evidence or nonexistent evidence.

Hearing   the physiological process of decoding sounds.

Hierarchy of needs   Abraham Maslow's classic theory that humans have five levels of needs and that lower-level needs must be met before people can be concerned about higher-level needs.

High-contact culture   a culture in which touching is seen as commonplace and appropriate.

High-context cultures   cultures in which nonverbal cues are extremely important in interpreting messages.

Horizontal communication   communication between peers.

Hostile environment sexual harassment   unwelcome conduct of a sexual nature that interferes with a person's ability to perform a job or gain an education and that creates a hostile or intimidating environment at the workplace.

Human communication   the process of making sense out of the world and sharing that sense with others by creating meaning through the use of verbal and nonverbal messages.

Human resources   an approach to leadership that views workers as resources who can be full partners in enhancing a team or organization.

Hygiene factors   basic aspects of a job that have to be there for a worker to feel satisfied about the work, including salary, working conditions, and supervision.

Hypothetical illustration   a description of something that has not actually occurred but that could happen.

Hypothetical question   a question that asks for an interviewee's reaction to an imaginary emotion-arousing or value-laden situation in order to gauge the person's likely response in a real situation.

I

Illustration   a story or anecdote about an idea, issue, or problem a speaker is discussing.

Illustrator   a gesture that illustrates or complements a verbal message.

Immediacy   a perception of psychological and physical closeness.

Impersonal communication   communication that occurs when people are treated as objects, or when others respond to people's roles rather than to who they are as unique people.

Impromptu speaking   delivering a speech without advance preparation.

Individual roles   behaviors that focus attention on an individual rather than the group.

Individualistic cultures   cultures whose members value individual interests over group interests.

Inductive reasoning   reasoning that arrives at a general conclusion from specific instances or examples.

Inflection   variation in vocal pitch.

Inform   to share information with others to enhance their knowledge or understanding of the information, concepts, or ideas presented.

Information-gathering interview   a focused, structured conversation whose goal is to seek out information from another person.

Information overload   the inability to effectively process information because there is too much of it.

Initial credibility   the impression of a speaker's credibility that listeners have before a speech begins.

Initial preview   the first statement of the main ideas of a presentation, usually presented in conjunction with or as part of the central idea.

Interaction   the give-and-take conversation that occurs when people collaborate.

Interest   a desire, need, concern, or fear that motivates one to take a particular position.

Internal previews   previews that introduce and outline ideas that will be developed as a speech progresses.

Internal summaries   summaries that occur within and throughout a speech to help listeners keep ideas in mind as the speech progresses.

Interpersonal communication   communication that occurs when two people interact to mutually influence each other, usually for the purpose of managing relationships.

Interview   a form of oral interaction structured to achieve a goal; it often includes just two people (but can include more) who take turns speaking and listening.

Interview schedule   a guide that lists all of the questions and follow-up probes to be used in an interview so that the interviewer can sequence questions.

Interview topic   a standard theme that is explored with a particular category of questions that are asked during an interview.

Introduction   the opening sentences of a speech, intended to get the audience's attention, introduce the topic, give the audience a reason to listen, establish the speaker's credibility, and preview the main ideas.

Inverted funnel sequence   a questioning sequence that begins with closed questions and proceeds to more open questions.

J

Jargon   language used by a particular group, profession, or culture that may not be understood or used by other people.

Job description   a document outlining the specific skills required for and basic duties of a particular position.

Job interview   a structured interview in which an interviewer assesses an interviewee's qualifications and skills for employment.

Job-related skills   skills that are specific to a particular occupation.

K

Kinesics   the study of gestures, posture, and body movement.

L

Laissez-faire leaders   leaders who take a hands-off, laid-back approach to influencing others.

Language   a system of symbols (words) common to a community of people and structured by grammar (rules and standards) and syntax (patterns in the arrangement of words) that make it possible for people to understand and communicate with one another.

Lay testimony   an opinion or a description offered by a non-expert who has firsthand experience.

Leadership   the process of influencing others to achieve goals through verbal and nonverbal messages.

Leading question   a question that suggests either explicitly or implicitly the answer expected.

Legally binding documents   documents that record an exchange of promises and that are enforceable by law.

Legitimate power   power that stems from being elected or appointed to a specific position or office.

Line graph   a graph that shows trends over time and relationships among variables.

Listening   the process of receiving, constructing meaning from, and responding to verbal and nonverbal messages.

Literal analogy   a comparison between two similar things.

Literary quotation   an opinion or description by a writer, expressed in a memorable and often poetic way.

Logical fallacy   false reasoning that occurs when someone attempts to persuade without adequate evidence or with arguments that are irrelevant or inappropriate.

Logos   the use of logical arguments.

Low-contact culture   a culture in which touching is uncommon.

Low-context cultures   cultures in which people rely more on explicit language and words and use fewer contextual cues to send and interpret information.

M

Manager   someone who has been appointed to coordinate and facilitate, to keep things organized and accomplish a task.

Manuscript speaking   reading a speech from a written text.

Masculine cultures   cultures in which people have a task orientation and tend to value achievement, heroism, material wealth, and more traditional roles for men and women.

Media richness the degree to which a channel of communication offers the possibility of immediate feedback; provides both verbal and nonverbal cues; allows the use of natural, informal language; and customizes messages to recipients.

Media richness theory theory that a communication medium is rich if it has (1) potential for instant feedback, (2) verbal and nonverbal cues that can be processed by senders and receivers, (3) natural language, and (4) a focus on individuals.

Meeting a structured conversation among a small group of people who gather to accomplish a specific task.

Memo a short, informal written communication within an organization.

Memorized speaking delivering a speech word for word from memory without using notes.

Message written, spoken, and unspoken elements of communication to which people assign meaning.

Message directness an indication of the extent to which a message expresses details clearly and leaves no doubt as to the intended meaning.

Metadiscussion discussion about discussion; comments that describe the discussion process rather than the topic under consideration.

Mindfulness awareness of your own and others' thoughts, actions, and motivations.

Mnemonic device a short rhyme, phrase, or other mental technique that makes information easier to memorize.

Moderately structured interview an interview that includes some scripted questions but allows the interviewer the flexibility to deviate from the script.

Monochronic cultures cultures that stress a high degree of scheduling, concentration on one thing at a time, and promptness.

Motivated sequence a five-step plan for organizing a persuasive message: attention, need, satisfaction, visualization, and action.

Motivation factors aspects of a person's job that motivate the person to do better.

N

Negative visualization a bleak picture of how terrible the future will be if nothing is done; a fear appeal used to motivate listeners to adopt a particular solution to a problem.

Negotiating strategy the overall approach taken in an exchange of proposals and counterproposals during negotiation of a settlement to a conflict.

Negotiation an exchange of proposals and counterproposals as a means of reaching a satisfactory settlement to a conflict.

Noise interference, either literal or psychological, that hinders the accurate encoding or decoding of a message.

Nominal-group technique a brainstorming method in which members work individually on ideas, rank suggested solutions, and then report their findings in a group discussion.

Non sequitur Latin for "it does not follow"; an idea or conclusion that does not logically follow a previous idea or conclusion.

Nonverbal communication any communication, other than written or spoken language, that creates meaning for someone.

Nonverbal messages visual and audible symbols that do not rely on words but create meaning for the receiver.

Nonverbal transitions nonverbal behaviors (facial expressions, pauses, changes in vocal pitch or speaking rate, or movement) that are used either alone or in combination with verbal transitions to show relationships among ideas in a speech.

Norms general standards within an organization or a group that determine what is appropriate and inappropriate behavior.

O

Objective a statement of something specific, measurable, attainable, and observable to be achieved in the short term.

Offshoring sending work to be done in other countries with lower labor costs.

Open question an interview question that is broad and unstructured and allows the respondent considerable freedom to determine the amount and kind of information she or he will provide.

Operational definition an explanation of how an item being defined works or what it does.

Oral citation an oral statement of the source of information used in a speech.

Organizational culture the learned pattern of beliefs, values, assumptions, rules, and norms that are shared by the people in an organization.

Orientation phase the first phase of group interaction, in which members become adjusted to one another and to the group's task.

Other-oriented focused on the needs, motives, desires, and goals of others in one's communication.

Outward communication communication between a service provider and a customer.

P

Panel presentation a presentation in which team members have a conversation with a moderator or a facilitator who manages the interaction.

Paradigm a worldview; a way of thinking or a set of attitudes that guide your communication and behavior.

Paraphrasing   restating in your own words what you think another person is saying.

Parliamentary procedure   a comprehensive set of rules that prescribe how to take action on specific issues that come before a group. For a complete guide to parliamentary procedure, see *Robert's Rules of Order*.

Part-whole learning style   the style of a learner who prefers learning details first, before the big picture.

Pathos   the use of emotional appeals to move an audience.

Person-focused leader   a leader who places value on and makes a priority of getting to know people on a personal level.

Personal attack   attacking personal characteristics of someone connected with an idea, rather than addressing the idea itself.

Personality trait   any distinguishable, relatively enduring way in which one individual differs from another.

Persuade   to change or reinforce a person's attitudes, beliefs, values, or behavior.

Persuasive interview   a structured conversation intended to influence a person's attitudes, beliefs, or behaviors.

Physical attraction   the attraction we have toward others because of their appearance.

Pie graph   a circular graph that shows the distribution of data as a proportion of a total.

Pitch   how high or low a speaker's voice is.

Polychronic cultures   cultures in which human relations and interactions are valued over arbitrary schedules or appointments.

Position   in a conflict, what each person wants to see in a negotiated outcome.

Positive visualization   a rosy word picture of how wonderful the future will be if your solution is implemented.

Power   the ability to influence others' behavior.

Powerful language   language that is stereotypically masculine: direct, assertive, task-oriented, and focused more on the content of a message.

Powerless language   language that is stereotypically feminine: indirect and focused more on the quality of a relationship than on the information being exchanged.

Preparation outline   a detailed outline of the central idea, main ideas, and supporting material for a speech; may also include the specific purpose, introduction, and conclusion.

Prescriptive approach   an approach to team development that assumes that team members need a specific sequence of steps and techniques in order to stay on task and be productive.

Presentation aid   any tangible item or image used to help communicate ideas to an audience.

Preview   a statement of what is to come in a speech.

Primacy   arrangement of ideas from most important or convincing to least important.

Primary tension   the tension that results from the uncertainty and discomfort people experience when they meet in a group for the first time.

Probing question   an interview question that encourages the interviewee to clarify or elaborate on partial or superficial responses and that usually directs the discussion in a particular direction.

Problem solving   a process of overcoming obstacles to achieve a goal.

Problem-and-solution organization   a strategy for organizing a persuasive speech that works best when a clearly evident problem can be documented and a solution or solutions proposed to deal with the problem.

Process functions   functions performed by leaders that help maintain a harmonious climate by encouraging amiable relationships among others.

Progress report   a report that outlines for a customer or a client the status of a project.

Proof   evidence and the conclusions you draw from it.

Proximity   the physical space and distance that we maintain in our communication with others.

Psychological information   listener attributes such as attitudes, beliefs, and values.

Public communication   communication that occurs when a speaker addresses a gathering of people with the intent to inform, persuade, or entertain them.

Public relations presentation   a presentation in which the speaker is specifically providing information to promote a positive public image for the person or organization the speaker is representing.

Q

Qualify   to learn as much as possible about a customer or an audience, such as backgrounds, likes, dislikes, interests, needs, and goals; to identify whether a customer can afford a product or service and to learn how to best approach the customer.

Quid pro quo sexual harassment   actual or threatened use of rewards or punishments to gain sexual compliance from a subordinate.

R

Rapport talk   talk focused on sharing information about relationships.

Reasoning   the process of drawing conclusions from evidence.

Reasoning by analogy   a special kind of inductive reasoning that draws a comparison between two ideas, things, or situations that share some essential common feature.

Receiver   the person who interprets a message.

Recency   arrangement of ideas from least to most important, based on the principle that audiences remember best what they hear last.

Red herring   irrelevant facts or arguments used to distract someone from the issue under discussion.

Referent power   power that stems from being liked.

Refutation   an organizational strategy by which you identify objections to your proposition and then refute those objections with arguments and evidence.

Regulator   a nonverbal cue that helps control the interaction and flow of communication between two people.

Reinforcement phase   the fourth phase of group interaction, in which group members express positive feelings toward each other and toward the group.

Reiterating   restating information using different words.

Relational conflict   an expressed struggle between at least two interdependent individuals, each of whom perceives incompatible goals, scarce rewards and resources, and interference from the other person in achieving his or her goals.

Relational dimension   the dimension of communication that offers cues about the emotions, attitudes, and amount of power and control a speaker feels in relation to listeners; the communication dimension that focuses on how a message is said; the nonverbal message.

Relational goals   in an interview, using interpersonal skills so as to be perceived as attractive and credible.

Relational messages   messages that build rapport and are aimed at establishing relationships.

Relationship   an ongoing connection developed with another person through interpersonal communication.

Relevant messages   messages that others perceive to satisfy their own needs and goals.

Remember   to recall information from memory.

Repeating   restating information using the same words in the same order.

Report   a summary of what has been accomplished in the past or an update on a project.

Report talk   talk focused on sharing practical or statistical information.

Respond   to let another person know whether you understood a message or to validate the other person.

Responsiveness   an individual's capacity to be sensitive to the communication of others, be seen as a good listener, and to make others comfortable in communicating.

Resume   a concise, well-organized, written description of your background, training, and qualifications for a job.

Reward power   power arising from the ability to grant favors, money, or other rewards.

Rhetoric   the process of discovering the available means of persuasion in a given communication situation.

Role   the consistent way someone communicates with others in a team, based on the person's own expectations and what others on the team expect of the person.

S

Sales proposal   a document intended to persuade a possible client of his or her need for your product or service.

Sans serif font   a font without lines (serifs) at the tops and bottoms of letters and with letters of uniform thickness.

Schema   a mental representation of knowledge.

Script font   a font that imitates handwriting, but is precise and uniform.

Select   to focus on one sound among all the sounds competing for attention.

Serif font   a font that has lines (serifs) at the tops and bottoms of the letters.

Servant leadership   a style of leadership in which the leader explicitly views himself or herself as being of service to the group or team.

Sex   biological characteristics present from birth that identify an individual as male or female.

Sexual harassment   deliberate and/or repeated sexual or sex-based behavior that is not welcome, not asked for, and not returned.

Signpost   a verbal or nonverbal signal that a speaker is moving from one idea to another.

Situational leadership   an approach that views leadership as an interactive process that links a particular style of leadership with such factors as culture, time limitations, group member personalities, and the work the group needs to do.

Small group   a collection of from three to fifteen people who share a common purpose, feel a sense of belonging to the group, and exert influence on each other.

Small group communication   the transactive process of creating meaning among from three to fifteen people who share a common purpose, feel a sense of belonging to the group, and exert influence on each other.

Social decentering   the process of stepping away from your own thoughts and attempting to experience the feelings of another person.

Social roles   behaviors that manage relationships and affect group climate; these roles help resolve conflict and enhance the flow of communication.

Social style   a pattern of communication behaviors that others observe when you interact with them.

Source   the originator of a thought or emotion, who puts it into a code that can be understood by a receiver.

Spatial organization   organization based on location, position, or direction.

Specific purpose   a concise statement of precisely what you want your listeners to be able to do, remember, or feel when you finish your speech. Your specific purpose statement indicates the *audience response* you seek.

Standard outline format   numbered and lettered headings and subheadings arranged hierarchically to indicate relationships among main ideas, subpoints, and supporting material in a speech.

Statistics   numerical data that summarize several examples.

Status   an individual's importance and prestige.

Strategically ambiguous messages   messages that may not convey all available information or may be unclear and are used purposely by the source to reach some goal.

Structure   the way a group or team discussion is organized; provided by the agenda and by techniques that help a group stay focused on the task at hand.

Structured interview   a scripted interview that uses a set of standard questions that are asked of every person who is interviewed.

Style flexing   the process of adapting your communication to how others communicate.

Supporting material   illustrations, explanations, descriptions, definitions, analogies, statistics, and opinions that clarify, amplify, and provide evidence to support the main ideas and the thesis of a presentation.

Supportive feedback   communication feedback whose goal is to encourage desirable behavior.

Syllogism   a three-part argument that has a major premise, a minor premise, and a conclusion.

Symbol   a word, sound, visual image, gesture, or object that represents a thought, a concept, another object, or an experience.

Symposium presentation   a presentation format that consists of a series of individual presentations without interaction or conversation; each person on the team gives a portion of the presentation.

System   any entity (such as an organization, a group, or a team) that is made up of many interconnected and interdependent pieces.

Systems approach   an approach to leadership that views organizations and teams as complex interconnected sets of elements that are not easily influenced by simple techniques and tools.

T

Target audience   a specific segment of your audience that you most want to influence.

Task analysis   a detailed, step-by-step description of precisely what a trainee should do and know in order to perform a particular skill.

Task-focused leader   a leader who believes that work takes priority over personal relationships.

Task functions   behaviors that help a team or organization get work done.

Task goals   in an interview, asking and answering questions in a clear, concise, and thoughtful manner in order to convey appropriate information.

Task messages   messages that focus on the content of an interview.

Task roles   behaviors that help a group achieve its goal and accomplish its work.

Team   a coordinated group of individuals who collaborate to achieve a specific common goal; usually more structured and organized than a group.

Team-based organization   an organization that has a flat structure rather than a hierarchical structure (one with many layers and levels of supervisors).

Team ground rules   explicit, agreed-on prescriptions for acceptable and appropriate behavior, which help the team organize routine tasks and procedures.

Team mission statement   a concise description of a team's goals or desired outcomes.

Telecommuting   working from somewhere other than an office using mobile technology.

Telegraphic style   a writing style that condenses the message by eliminating articles, pronouns, conjunctions, and transitions.

Terminal credibility   the perception of a speaker's credibility listeners have at the conclusion of a speech.

Theory X   a view of leadership that assumes that workers are generally lazy and that a leader's job is to reward good work and punish bad work.

Theory Y   a view of leadership that assumes that workers are self-motivated and inherently want to do a good job. If a leader treats people well and builds good relationships with them, they will work hard.

Theory Z   an approach to leadership that assumes that people have a long-term relationship with an organization and that the relationship is based on trust, collaboration, and a common organizational goal.

Time management   the use of techniques for analyzing and prioritizing goals and objectives in order to increase efficiency and productivity.

Time orientation   how members of a culture structure, organize, and use time.

Toast   a brief speech saluting a momentous occasion.

Tone   the attitude of the writer toward both the reader and the subject matter that is communicated in a written document.

Topic sentence   generally, the first sentence of a paragraph that states the main idea.

Topical organization   organization by natural divisions of a central idea presented according to primacy, recency, or complexity, or arbitrary arrangement of ideas that are equal in importance.

Touch avoidant   the tendency to avoid touch in interpersonal interactions.

Training   a type of informative speaking in which a trainer seeks to develop specific skills in listeners to help them perform a specific job or task more effectively.

Trait approach   an approach to leadership that focuses on the psychological and physical attributes or traits that make leaders effective.

Transactional   occurring simultaneously.

Transferable skills   skills that are useful in a variety of jobs and positions.

Transformational leadership   the process of influencing people to see the future in new ways.

Trustworthiness   the aspect of credibility that reflects whether a speaker is perceived as believable and honest.

Tunnel sequence   a questioning sequence that uses a combination of open and closed questions to gather a large amount of information in a short amount of time.

U

Uncertainty avoidance   a measure of how accepting a culture is of a lack of predictability.

Understand   to assign meaning to the verbal and nonverbal messages received.

Unstructured interview   an unscripted interview that is unique to the individual being questioned; it does not include a standard set of questions.

Upward communication   communication that flows from subordinate to superior.

V

Verbal messages   messages that use words to create meaning.

Verbal transitions   words or phrases that show relationships between ideas in a speech.

Vigilant thinkers   people who pay attention to the process of how work is done in teams rather than focusing only on techniques used to achieve a goal.

Virtual team   a team that interacts via a channel other than face-to-face communication but rather uses email, video conferences, or other technological tools.

Visualization   using words to create an image in audience members' minds.

Vocalics   the nonverbal aspects of the voice, including pitch, rate, and volume.

W

Whole-part learning style   the style of a learner who prefers learning the big picture first, then the details.

Willingness to communicate (WTC)   an individual's natural tendency to initiate communication with others.

Word pictures   lively descriptions that help listeners form a mental image by appealing to their senses (sight, taste, smell, sound, and touch).

Writing style   the tone, language, voice, and overall viewpoint of the sentences in a piece of writing.

Endnotes

Chapter 1

1. S. S. Smith, "Coffee Talk with Starbucks CEO Howard Schultz," *Entrepreneur*, n.d. Retrieved February 9, 2008, from http://findarticles.com/p/articles/mi_m0DTI/is_n5_v26/ai_20923860.

2. H. Schultz, *Pour Your Heart Into It* (New York: Hyperion, 1997).

3. Schultz, *Pour Your Heart Into It*, 116; B. Ardoin, "A Diffusion Analysis of H. Schultz's Pour Your Heart Into It." April 15, 2000. Retrieved February 9, 2008, from http://www.start-at-zero.com/papers/schultz.htm.

4. See "Can Communicators Help Improve Business Performance?" *Business Communicator* 6 (December 2005/January 2006): 1–2; R. E. Riggio and S. J. Taylor, "Personality and Communication Skills as Predictors of Hospice Nurse Performance," *Journal of Business and Psychology* 15 (Winter 2000): 351–359; S. Jo and S. W. Shim, "Paradigm Shift of Employee Communication: The Effect of Management Communication on Trusting Relationships," *Public Relations Review* 31 (2005): 277–280; F. DiMeglio, "New Role for Business School Research," *Business Week Online* 14 (August 2007); B. Palmer, M. Walls, Z. Burgess, and C. Stough, "Emotional Intelligence and Effective Leadership," *Leadership and Organizational Development Journal* 22 (2000): 5–10.

5. The five fundemental principles are taken from our "sister" book: S. A. Beebe, S. J. Beebe, and D. K. Ivy, *Communication: Principles for a Lifetime* (Boston: Allyn & Bacon, 2010).

6. Associated Press, "JetBlue Didn't Break Any Guidelines by Keeping Passengers on Plane for Hours." February 16, 2007. Retrieved February 24, 2008, from http://www.foxnews.com/story/0,2933,252381,00.html; JetBlue's apology on YouTube. February 19, 2007. Retrieved February 24, 2008, from http://www.youtube.com/watch?v=-r_PIg7EAUw.

7. F. E. X. Dance and C. Larson, *Speech Communication: Concepts and Behavior* (New York: Holt, Rinehart and Winston, 1972).

8. Beebe, Beebe and Ivy, *Communication: Principles for a Lifetime*.

9. P. Watzlawick, J. B. Bavelas, and D. D. Jackson, *Pragmatics of Human Communication* (New York: W.W. Norton & Company, 1967).

10. Watzlawick, Bavelas, and Jackson, *Pragmatics of Human Communication*.

11. F. DiMeglio, "New Role for Business School Research."

12. F. DiMeglio, "New Role For Business School Research."

13. J. Casner-Lotto and L. Barrington, "Are They Really Ready to Work? Employers' Perspectives on the Basic Knowledge and Applied Skills of New Entrants to the 21st Century U.S. Workforce," *The Conference Board, Partnership for 21st Century Skills, Corporate Voices for Working Families, and Society for Human Resource Management*. October 2006. Retrieved February 9, 2008, from http://www. conference-board.org/publications/describe.cfm?id=1218.

14. J. Casner-Lotto and L. Barrington, "Are They Really Ready to Work?"

15. B. Goodwin, "Develop Business Skills to Survive Offshoring Challenge, IT Staff Urged," *Computer Weekly* (February 27, 2007): 17; also refer to "Improve Those Tech Skills," *Wall Street and Technology* (July 2007): 14–16.

16. L. Alexander and S. Campbell, "Degrees and Skills Make for a Profitable Package," *The London Times* (June 29, 2006): 8; see also K. N. Kinnick and S. R. Parton, "Workplace Communication," *Business Communication Quarterly* 4 (2005): 429–456.

17. E. T. Klemmer and F. W. Snyder, "Measurements of Time Spent Communicating," *Journal of Communication* 20 (June 1972): 142.

18. W. Schutz, *FIRO: A Three-Dimensional Theory of Interpersonal Behavior* (New York: Rinehart, 1958); W. Schutz, *The Interpersonal Underworld* (Palo Alto, CA: Science and Behavior Books, 1966).

19. S. R. Covey, *The 7 Habits of Highly Effective People* (New York: Simon & Schuster, 1989); S. R. Covey, *The 8th Habit: From Effectiveness to Greatness* (New York: Free Press, 2004).

20. Our definition of "relationship" and our discussion of relating skills is based on information from S. A. Beebe, S. J. Beebe, and M. V. Redmond, *Interpersonal Communication: Relating to Others* (Boston: Allyn & Bacon, 2010).

21. For an excellent discussion of the power of dialogue to enrich the quality of communication, see D. Yankelovich, *The Magic of Dialogue: Transforming Conflict into Cooperation* (New York: Simon & Schuster, 1999).

22. S. A. Beebe and J. T. Masterson, *Communicating in Small Groups: Principles and Practices* (Boston: Allyn & Bacon, 2009).

23. E. Ross and A. Holland, *100 Great Businesses and the Minds Behind Them* (Naperville, IL: Sourcebooks, Inc. 2006), 24–26.

24. A. Keith, as cited by J. Kouzes and B. Posner, *The Leadership Challenge* (San Francisco: Jossey-Bass, 2002).

25. A. Raes, U. Glunt, M. Heijltjes, and R. Roe, "Top Management Team and Middle Managers—Making Sense of Leadership," *Small Group Research* 38, no. 3 (2007): 360–386.

26. C. Mason and M. Griffin, "Group Task Satisfaction—The Group's Shared Attitude to Its Task and Work Environment," *Group & Organization Management* 30, no. 6 (2005): 625–652.

27. B. A. Fisher and D. G. Ellis, *Small Group Decision Making* (New York: McGraw-Hill, 1990).

28. W. Bennis and B. Nanus, *Leaders: The Strategies for Taking Charge* (New York: Harper and Row, 1985).

29. R. E. Kelly, *The Power of Followership: How to Create Leaders That People Want to Follow and Followers Who Lead Themselves* (New York: Doubleday/Currency, 1992).

30. Kouzes and Posner, *The Leadership Challenge*, 25.

31. M. S. Limon and B. La France, "Communication Traits and Leadership Emergence: Examining the Impact of Argumentativeness, Communication Apprehension, and Verbal Aggressiveness in Work Groups," *Southern Communication Journal* 70, no. 2 (2005): 123–133.

32. R. M. Smith, "A Business Champion," *Newsweek*, October 20, 2008: 20.

33. D. K. Goodwin, "The Secrets of America's Great Presidents," *Austin American-Statesman Parade*, September 14, 2008: 4.

34. R. M. Stogdill, "Personal Factors Associated with Leadership: A Survey of the Literature," *Journal of Psychology* 25 (1948):

35–71; R. M. Stogdill, *Handbook of Leadership* (New York: The Free Press, 1974).

35. R. White and R. Lippitt, "Leader Behavior and Member Reaction in Three Social Climates," in *Group Dynamics*, 3rd ed., edited by D. Cartwright and A. Zander (New York: Harper & Row, 1968), 319.

36. For a description of situational leadership approaches, see F. Fiedler, *A Theory of Leadership Effectiveness* (New York: McGraw-Hill, 1967), 144; P. Hersey, K. H. Blanchard, and D. E. Johnson, *Management of Organizational Behavior: Leading Human Resources* (New Delhi: Prentice-Hall of India, 2004), 175.

37. B. M. Bass and M. J. Avolio. "Transformational Leadership and Organizational Culture," *International Journal of Public Administration 17* (1994): 541–554. Also see F. J. Yammarino and A. J. Dubinsky, "Transformational Leadership Theory: Using Levels of Analysis to Determine Boundary Conditions," *Personnel Psychology 47* (1994): 787–809.

38. R. Piccolo and J. Colquitt, "Transformational Leadership and Job Behaviors: The Mediating Role of Core Job Characteristics," *Academy of Management Journal 49*, no. 2 (2006): 327–340; R. K. Greenleaf, *The Servant as a Leader* (Indianapolis, IN: Greenleaf Center), 4.

39. P. M. Senge, "The Leader's New Role: Building Learning Organizations," *Sloan Management Review 32*, no. 1 (1990).

40. For an excellent review of transformational leadership and its applications to cultural contexts, see A. Ergeneli, R. Gohar, and Z. Temirbekova, "Transformational Leadership: Its Relationship to Culture Value Dimensions," *International Journal of Intercultural Relations 31* (2007): 703–724.

41. J. Barbuto, Jr. and D. Wheeler, "Scale Development and Construct Clarification of Servant Leadership," *Group & Organization Management 31*, no. 3 (2006): 300–326.

42. R. Piccolo and J. Colquitt, "Transformational Leadership and Job Behaviors"; R. K. Greenleaf, *The Servant as a Leader*, 4.

43. J. R. Hackman and R. Wageman, "A Theory of Team Coaching," *Academy of Management Review 30*, no. 2 (2005): 269–287; P. Scholtes, B. Joiner, and B. Streibel, *The Team Handbook*, 3rd ed. (Madison, WI: Oriel Incorporated, 2003), p. A-1.

44. Hackman and Wageman, "A Theory of Team Coaching," 269.

45. J. Carson, P. Tesluk, and J. Marrone, "Shared Leadership in Teams: An Investigation of Antecedent Conditions and Performance," *Academy of Management Journal 50*, no. 5 (2007): 1217–1234.

46. Hackman and Wageman, "A Theory of Team Coaching," 269.

47. M. F. R. Kets de Vries, "Leadership Group Coaching in Action: The Zen of Creating High Performance Teams," *Academy of Management Executive 19*, no. 1 (2005): 61–76.

48. R. Rubin, D. Munz, and W. Bommer, "Leading from Within: The Effects of Emotion Recognition and Personality on Transformational Leadership Behavior," *Academy of Management Journal 48*, no. 5 (2005): 845–858; L. C. Spears, *Reflections on Leadership: How Robert K. Greenleaf's Theory of Servant-Leadership Influenced Today's Management Thinkers* (New York: John Wiley).

49. Kelly, *The Power of Followership*, 89–97.

Chapter 2

1. E. J. Langer, *The Power of Mindful Learning* (Reading, MA: Perseus Books, 1997); E. Ju-Lee, "When Placebic Information Differs from Real Information: Cognitive and Motivation Bases of Mindful Reactions to Information Social Influence," *Communication Research 32* (2005): 615–645.

2. D. W. Merrill & R. H. Reid, *Personal Styles and Effective Performance* (Radnor, PA: Chilton, 1981); R. Norton, *Communicator Style: Theory, Applications, and Measures* (Beverly Hills, CA: Sage, 1993); G. L. May and L. E. Gueldenzoph,

"The Effect of Social Style on Peer Evaluation Ratings in Project Teams," *Journal of Business Communication 43* (2006): 4–20.

3. V. P. Richmond and J. C. McCroskey, *Communication: Apprehension, Avoidance, and Effectiveness* 5th ed. (Boston: Allyn and Bacon, 1998); J. J. Teven, J. C. McCroskey, and V. P. Richmond, "Communication Correlates of Perceived Machiavellianism of Supervisors: Communication Orientations and Outcomes," *Communication Quarterly 54* (2006): 127–142.

4. Richmond and McCroskey, *Communication: Apprehension, Avoidance, and Effectiveness*; Teven, McCroskey, and Richmond, "Communication Correlates of Perceived Machiavellianism of Supervisors."

5. V. P. Richmond and J. C. McCroskey, *Organizational Communication for Survival* (Boston: Allyn & Bacon, 2008); K. W. Thomas, *Thomas-Kilmann Conflict Mode Instrument* (Mountain View, CA: CPP, Inc., 2002).

6. Richmond and McCroskey, *Organizational Communication for Survival*; Thomas, *Thomas-Kilmann Conflict Mode Instrument*.

7. From Richmond and McCroskey, *Communication: Apprehension, Avoidance, and Effectiveness*; Teven, McCroskey, and Richmond, "Communication Correlates of Perceived Machiavellianism of Supervisors."

8. R. Bolton and D. G. Bolton, *People Styles at Work: Making Bad Relationships Good and Good Relationships Better* (New York: American Management Association, 1996); G. L. May and L. E. Gueldenzoph, "The Effect of Social Style on Peer Evaluation Ratings in Project Teams," *Journal of Business Communication 43* (2006): 4–20.

9. Adapted from R. Bolton and D. G. Bolton, *People Styles at Work*; May and Gueldenzoph, "The Effect of Social Style on Peer Evaluation Ratings in Project Teams."

10. Fredrick Taylor, *The Principles of Scientific Management* (New York: Harper & Row, 1911).

11. Max Weber, *Max Weber: The Theory of Social and Economic Organization*, translated by T. Parsons and A. Henderson (New York: Free Press, 1947).

12. Abraham H. Maslow, "A Theory of Human Motivation," in *Motivation and Personality* (New York: Harper & Row, 1954), Chapter 5.

13. F. J. Roethlisberger and W. J. Dickson, *Management and the Worker* (Cambridge, MA: Harvard University Press, 1939); E. Mayo, *The Social Problems of an Industrial Civilization* (Cambridge, MA: Harvard University Press, 1945).

14. F. Herzberg, *Work and the Nature of Man* (Cleveland, OH: World, 1966).

15. D. McGregor, *The Human Side of Enterprise* (New York: McGraw-Hill, 1960).

16. Dennis Romig, *Side-by-Side Leadership* (Marietta, GA: Bard Press, 2001).

17. Robert Blake and Jane Mouton, *The New Managerial Grid* (London: Chartered Management Institute, 2005).

18. William G. Ouchi, *Theory Z* (New York: Avon Books, 1981).

19. Adapted from B. Nussbaum, "The Power of Design," *Business Week*, May 17, 2004. Retrieved June 27, 2008, from http://www.businessweek.com/pdf/240512BWePrint2.pdf.

20. Aparna Joshi, "The Influence of Organizational Demography on the External Networking Behavior of Teams," *Academy of Management Review 31*, no. 3 (2006): 583–595.

21. For excellent discussions of organizational culture, see K. Miller, *Organizational Communication: Approaches and Processes* (Belmont, CA: Thompson/Wadsworth, 2006); G. W. Driskil and A. L. Brenton, *Organizational Culture in Action: A Cultural Analysis Workbook* (Thousand Oaks, CA: Sage, 2005); J. Keyton, *Communication and Organizational Culture: A Key to Understanding Work Experiences* (Thousand Oaks, CA: Sage, 2005).

22. C. Geertz, *The Interpretation of Cultures* (New York: Basic Books, 1973), p. 5.

23. T. J. Peters and R. H. Waterman, Jr., *In Search of Excellence: Lessons from America's Best-Run Companies* (New York: Collins, 1982). An updated edition of Peters and Waterman's book was published in 2004.)

24. See F. M. Jablin, "Organizational Entry, Assimilation, and Exit," in *The New Handbook of Organizational Communication*, edited by F. M. Jablin and L. L. Putnam (Thousand Oaks, CA: Sage, 2001): 732–881.

25. J. Martin, *Organizational Culture: Mapping the Terrain* (Thousand Oaks, CA: Sage, 2002), 120.

26. E. Schein, *Organizational Culture and Leadership* (San Francisco: Jossey-Bass, 1992).

27. S. M. Davis, *Managing Corporate Culture* (Cambridge, MA: Ballinger, 1984), 7–8.

28. H. Wee, "Corporate Ethics: Right Makes Might," *Business Week*, April 11, 2002. Retrieved January 17, 2008, from http://www.businessweek.com/bwdaily/dnflash/apr2002/nf20020411_6350.htm?chan=search.

29. For a brief review of these headlines, please refer to the *Washington Post* website, http://www.washingtonpost.com/wp-dyn/business/specials/corporateethics/.

30. T. Leoni, "I Survived Enron," *Business Week*, February 6, 2006. Retrieved January 17, 2008, from http://www.businessweek.com/magazine/content/06_06/b3970081.htm?chan=search.

31. N. Byrnes, "Tyco's Kozlowski Confronts His Peers," *Business Week*, September 30, 2003. Retrieved January 16, 2008, from http://www.businessweek.com/bwdaily/dnflash/sep2003/nf20030930_0548_db017.htm?chan=search.

32. Leoni, "I Survived Enron."

33. B. McLean and P. Elkind, *The Smartest Guys in the Room: The Amazing Rise and Scandalous Fall of Enron* (New York: Penguin, 2003).

34. The ideas on ethical challenges were adapted from M. Z. Hackman and C. E. Johnson, *Leadership: A Communication Perspective 4th ed.* (Long Grove, IL: Waveland Press, 2004); C. E. Johnson, *Meeting the Ethical Challenges of Leadership: Casting Light or Shadow* (Thousand Oaks, CA: Sage, 2001).

35. This information was adapted from the George S. May International Company. Retrieved January 17, 2008, from http://ethics.georgesmay.com/check_yourself.htm.

36. McLean and Elkind, *The Smartest Guys in the Room.*

Chapter 3

1. Refer to http://www.starbucks.com/aboutus/jobcenter.asp.

2. E. M. Eisenberg, "Ambiguity as Strategy in Organizational Communication," *Communication Monographs 51* (1984): 227–242.

3. J. H. Fielder, "The Vioxx Debacle," *Engineering in Medicine and Biology, 24* (2005): 101–109.

4. B. H. Spitzberg, "Methods of Interpersonal Skill Assessment," in *Handbook of Communication and Social Interaction Skills*, edited by J. O. Greene and B. R. Burleson (Mahwah, NJ: Lawrence Erlbaum, 2003), 93–134.

5. D. R. Siebold, S. Kudsi, and M. Rude, "Does Communication Training Make a Difference? Evidence for the Effectiveness of a Presentation Skills Program," *Journal of Applied Communication Research 21* (1993): 111–129.

6. Adapted from P. Kedrosky, "Why We Don't Don't Get the (Text) Message" *Business 2.0 Magazine*, October 6, 2006. Retrieved February 20, 2008, from http://money.cnn.com/magazines/business2/business2_archive/2006/08/01/8382255/index.htm.

7. J. M. Keller, "Motivational Design of Instruction," in *Instructional Design Theories: An Overview of Their Current Status*, edited by C. M. Reigeluth (Hillsdale, NJ: Lawrence Erlbaum, 1983), 383–434.

8. J. Chesebro and M. Wanzer, "Instructional Message Variables," in *The Handbook of Instructional Communication: Rhetorical and Relational Perspectives*, edited by T. Mottet, V. P. Richmond, and J. C. McCroskey (Needham Heights, MA: Allyn & Bacon, 2006), 89–116.

9. Adapted from Steven Covey's 7 Habits of Highly Effective People Signature Program, http://www.FranklinCovey.com.

10. S. Lohr, "Market Place; A Growing Group of Disgruntled Relatives May Seal the Fate of Hewlett-Packard and Compaq." *New York Times*, November 8, 2001. Retrieved August 13, 2008, from http://query.nytimes.com/gst/fullpage.html?res=9900E6DD1E39F93BA35752C1A9679C8B63.

11. R. M. Guzley, "Organizational Climate and Communication Climate: Predictors of Commitment to the Organization," *Management Communication Quarterly 5* (1992): 379–402.

12. J. R. Gibb, "Defensive Communication," *Journal of Communication 11* (1961): 141–148.

13. K. K. Sereno, M. Welch, and D. Braaten, "Interpersonal Conflict: Effects of Variations in Manner of Expressing Anger and Justifications for Anger upon Perceptions of Appropriateness, Competence, and Satisfaction," *Journal of Applied Communication Research 15* (1987): 128–143.

14. A. M. Bippus and S. L. Young, "Owning your Emotions: Reactions to Expressions of Self- versus Other- Attributed Positive and Negative Emotions," *Journal of Applied Communication Research 33* (2005): 26–45.

15. J. J. Teven, J. C. McCroskey, and V. P. Richmond, "Communication Correlates of Perceived Machiavellianism of Supervisors: Communication Orientations and Outcomes," *Communication Quarterly 54* (2006): 127–142.

16. N. Ambady and R. Rosenthal, "Half a Minute: Predicting Teacher Evaluations from Thin Slices of Nonverbal Behavior and Physical Attractiveness," *Journal of Personality and Social Psychology 64* (1993): 431–441.

17. A. Mehrabian, *Nonverbal Communication* (Chicago: Aldine Atherton, 1972), 108.

18. D. Lapakko, "Three Cheers for Language: A Closer Examination of a Widely Cited Study of Nonverbal Communication," *Communication Education 46* (1997): 63–67.

19. J. K. Burgoon and A. E. Bacue, "Nonverbal Communication Skills," in *Handbook of Communication and Social Interaction Skills*, edited by J. O. Greene and B. R. Burleson (Mahwah, NJ: Lawrence Erlbaum, 2003), 179–219; B. H. LaFrance, A. D. Heisel, and M. J. Beatty, "Is There Empirical Evidence for a Nonverbal Profile of Extraversion? A Meta-Analysis and Critique of the Literature," *Communication Monographs 71* (2004): 28–48.

20. P. Watzlawick, J. B. Bavelas, and D. D. Jackson, *Pragmatics of Human Communication* (New York: W. W. Norton & Company, 1967).

21. Adapted from the transcript of "Building to Extremes," PBS, February 10, 2004. Retrieved February 21, 2008, from http://www.pbs.org/wnet/innovation/transcript_episode1.html.

22. M. L. Knapp, J. M. Wiemann, and J. A. Daly, "Nonverbal Communication: Issues and Appraisals," *Human Communication Research 4* (1978): 271–280; J. K. Burgoon, "Nonverbal Signals," in *Handbook of Interpersonal Communication*, edited by M. L. Knapp and J. Daly (Thousand Oaks, CA: Sage, 2002), 240–299.

23. M. L. Knapp and J. A. Hall, *Nonverbal Communication in Human Interaction* 6e (Belmont, CA: Wadsworth, 2005).

24. I. H. Frieze, J. E. Olson, and J. Russell, "Attractiveness and Income for Men and Women in Management," *Journal of Applied Social Psychology 21* (1991): 1039–1057. See also J. Ross and K. R. Ferris, "Interpersonal Attraction and Organizational Outcomes: A Field Examination," *Administrative Science Quarterly 26* (1981): 617–632.

25. Frieze, Olson, and Russell, "Attractiveness and Income."

26. M. Lynn and T. Simons, "Predictors of Male and Female Servers' Average Tip Earnings," *Journal of Applied Social Psychology 30* (2000): 241–252.

27. Quoted in J. Kita, "All To Be Tall," *Men's Health* (January-February 2004): 131–135. See also D. Elman, "Physical Characteristics and the Perception of Masculine Traits," *Journal of Social Psychology* 103 (1977): 157–158.

28. J. Kita, "All To Be Tall."

29. K. J. Gross and J. Stone, *Chic Simple Dress Smart for Women: Wardrobes that Win in the Workplace* (New York: Warner Books, 2002). K. J. Gross and J. Stone, *Chic Simple Dress Smart for Men: Wardrobes that Win in the Workplace* (New York: Warner Books, 2002).

30. R. E. Bassett, A. Q. Stanton-Spicer, and J. L. Whitehead, "Effects of Attire and Judgments of Credibility," *Central States Speech Journal* 30 (1979): 282–285. See also S. G. Lawrence and M. Watson, "Getting Others to Help: The Effectiveness of Professional Uniforms in Charitable Fundraising," *Journal of Applied Communication Research* 19 (1991): 170–185; T. L. Morris, J. Gorham, S. H. Cohen, and D. Huffman, "Fashion in the Classroom: Effects of Attire on Student Perceptions of Instructors in College Classes," *Communication Education* 45 (1996): 135–148.

31. S. Arnoult, "Dressed for Success," *Air Transport World* (June 2005): 58–60. See also K. Lovegrove, *Airline: Identity, Design, and Culture* (New York: teNeues, 2000); J. Schmeltzer, "McDonald's Lovin' Idea of Cool, New Threads," *Austin American Statesman* (July 6 2005): D6.

32. Bassett, Stanton-Spicer, and Whitehead, "Effects of Attire and Judgments of Credibility." See also Lawrence and Watson "Getting Others to Help"; Morris, Gorham, Cohen, and Huffman, "Fashion in the Classroom."

33. Per T. Mottet, former in-flight service manager for Northwest Airlines.

34. A. Entzminger, "Dress Down or Up? Banking Dress Codes Continue to Evolve," *ABA Banking Journal* (2005): 7–10. Also see K. K. P. Johnson and S. J. Lennon, "Introduction: Appearance and Social Power," in *Appearance and Power*, edited by K. K. P. Johnson and S. J. Lennon (New York: Berg, 1999), 1–10; M. Rucker, E. Anderson, and A. Kangas, "Clothing, Power, and the Workplace," in *Appearance and Power*, edited by K. K. P. Johnson and S. J. Lennon (New York: Berg, 1999), 59–78.

35. Entzminger, "Dress Down or Up?

36. W. McPherson, "Dress Down in the Business Communication Curriculum," *Business Communication Quarterly* 60 (1997): 134–146.

37. M. C. Jenkins and T. V. Atkins, "Perceptions of Acceptable Dress by Corporate and Noncorporate Recruiters," *Journal of Human Behavior and Learning* 7 (1990): 38–46.

38. J. S. Seiter and A. Sandry, "Pierced for Success? The Effects of Ear and Nose Piercing on Perceptions of Job Candidates' Credibility, Attractiveness, and Hirability," *Communication Research Reports* 20 (2003): 287–298.

39. A. A. Acor, "Employers' Perceptions of Persons with Body Art and an Experimental Test Regarding Eyebrow Piercing," *Dissertation Abstracts International: Section B: The Sciences and Engineering*, Vol. 61 (7-B), (February 2001): 3885.

40. For a review of the research, see J. K. Burgoon, T. Birk, and M. Pfau, "Nonverbal Behaviors, Persuasion, and Credibility," *Human Communication Research* 17 (1990): 140–169. Also see W. B. Pearce and F. Conklin, "Nonverbal Vocalic Communication and Perception of Speaker," *Speech Monographs* 38 (1971): 235–241; R. L. Street, Jr. and R. M. Brady, "Speech Rate Acceptance Ranges as a Function of Evaluative Domain, Listener Speech Rate, and Communication Context," *Communication Monographs* 49 (1982): 290–308.

41. L. L. Hinkle, "Perceptions of Supervisor Nonverbal Immediacy, Vocalics, and Subordinate Liking," *Communication Research Reports* 18 (2001): 128–136. Also see Burgoon, Birk, and Pfau, "Nonverbal Behaviors, Persuasion, and Credibility."

42. Mehrabian, *Nonverbal Communication.*

43. W. G. Woodall and J. P. Folger, "Nonverbal Cue Context and Episodic Memory: On the Availability and Endurance of Nonverbal Behaviors as Retrieval Cues," *Communication Monographs* 52 (1985): 320–333; A. A. Cohen and R. P. Harrison, "Intentionality in the Use of Hand Illustrators in Face-to-Face Communication Situations," *Journal of Personality and Social Psychology* 28 (1973): 276–279; Knapp and Hall, *Nonverbal Communication in Human Interaction.*

44. S. Goldin-Meadow, H. Nussbaum, S. D. Kelly, and S. Wagner, "Gesture: Psychological Aspects," *Psychological Science* 12 (2001): 516–522.

45. S. Duncan, "Some Signals and Rules for Turn Taking in Conversations," *Journal of Personality and Social Psychology* 23 (1972): 283–292.

46. P. Ekman and W. V. Friesen, *Unmasking the Face* (Englewood Cliffs, NJ: Prentice-Hall, 1975).

47. A. R. Hochschild, *The Managed Heart: Commercialization of Human Feelings.* 20th anniversary edition (Los Angeles: University of California Press, 2003).

48. J. Timmick, "How You Can Learn to Be Likeable, Confident, Socially Successful for Only the Cost of Your Present Education," *Psychology Today* 16 (1982): 42–49.

49. M. Hickson III, D. W. Stacks, and N. J. Moore, *Nonverbal Communication: Studies and Applications* 4e (New York: Oxford University Press, 2004), 394.

50. S. A. Beebe, "Eye Contact: A Nonverbal Determinant of Speaker Credibility," *Speech Teacher* 23 (1974): 21–25; J. M. Droney and C. I. Brooks, "Attributions of Self-Esteem as a Function of Duration of Eye Contact," *The Journal of Social Psychology* 133 (1993): 715–722; L. P. Napieralski, C. I. Brooks, and J. M. Droney, "The Effect of Duration of Eye Contact on American College Students' Attributions of State, Trait, and Test Anxiety," *The Journal of Social Psychology* 135 (1995): 273–280.

51. N. Gueguen and C. Jacob, "Direct Look versus Evasive Glance and Compliance with a Request," *The Journal of Social Psychology* 142 (2002): 393–396.

52. C. I. Brooks, M. A. Church, and L. Fraser, "Effects of Duration of Eye Contact on Judgments of Personality Characteristics," *The Journal of Social Psychology* 126 (1986): 71–78; G. Amalfitano and N. C. Kalt, "Effects of Eye Contact on Evaluation of Job Applicants," *Journal of Employment Counseling* 14 (1977): 46–48; Burgoon, Birk, and Pfau, "Nonverbal Behaviors, Persuasion, and Credibility."

53. E. T. Hall, *The Hidden Dimension* (Garden City, NY: Anchor Books, 1966).

54. J. K. Burgoon and J. L. Hale, "Nonverbal Expectancy Violations: Model Elaboration and Application to Immediacy Behaviors," *Communication Monographs* 55 (1988): 58–79.

55. J. K. Burgoon, "A Communication Model of Personal Space Violations: Explication and an Initial Test," *Human Communication Research* 4 (1978): 129–142; J. K. Burgoon and S. B. Jones, "Toward a Theory of Personal Space Expectations and Their Violations," *Human Communication Research* 2 (1976): 131–146.

56. N. M. Sussman and H. M. Rosenfeld, "Influence of Culture, Language, and Sex on Conversational Distance," *Journal of Personality and Social Psychology* 42 (1982): 66–74; Hall, *The Hidden Dimension.*

57. L. Baxter and J. Ward, "Newsline," *Psychology Today* 8 (1975): 28.

58. Hickson, Stacks, and Moore, *Nonverbal Communication.*

59. E. T. Hall, *The Dance of Life: The Other Dimension of Time* (New York: Anchor Books, 1984); E. T. Hall, *The Silent Language* (Garden City, NY: Anchor/Doubleday, 1959).

60. J. K. Burgoon, J. B. Walther, and E. J. Baesler, "Interpretations, Evaluations, and Consequences of Interpersonal Touch," *Human Communication Research* 19 (1992): 237–263.

61. Hickson, Stacks, and Moore, *Nonverbal Communication*; P. A. Andersen, "Researching Sex Differences within Sex Similarities: The Evolutionary Consequences of Reproductive Differences," in *Sex Differences and Similarities in Communication*, edited by D. J. Canary and K. Dindia (Mahwah, NJ: Lawrence Erlbaum, 1998), 83–100.

62. P. A. Andersen and K. Leibowitz, "The Development and Nature of the Construct Touch Avoidance," *Environmental Psychology and Nonverbal Behavior 3* (1978): 89–106.

63. M. S. Remland, T. S. Jones, and H. Brinkman, "Proxemics and Haptic Behavior in Three European Countries," *Journal of Nonverbal Behavior 15* (1991): 215–231; M. S. Remland, T. S. Jones, and H. Brinkman, "Interpersonal Distance, Body Orientation and Touch: Effect of Culture, Gender, and Age," *Journal of Social Psychology 135* (1995): 281–295.

64. Remland, Jones, and Brinkman, "Proxemics and Haptic Behavior in Three European Countries"; Remland, Jones, and Brinkman, "Interpersonal Distance, Body Orientation and Touch."

65. Hickson, Stacks, and Moore, *Nonverbal communication*.

66. A. Mehrabian, *Silent Messages: Implicit Communication of Emotions and Attitudes* 2e (Belmont, CA: Wadsworth, 1981).

67. Mehrabian, *Silent Messages*; V. P. Richmond, J. C. McCroskey, and A. Johnson, "Development of the Nonverbal Immediacy Scale (NIS): Measures of Self- and Other-Perceived Nonverbal Immediacy," *Communication Quarterly 51* (2003): 504–517.

68. W. F. Chaplin, J. B. Phillips, J. D. Brown, N. R. Clanton, and J. L. Stein, "Handshaking, Gender, Personality, and First Impressions," *Journal of Personality and Social Psychology 79* (2000): 110–117.

69. Gueguen and Jacob, "Direct Look versus Evasive Glance and Compliance with a Request."

70. For a review of the research, see Burgoon, Birk, and Pfau, "Nonverbal Behaviors, Persuasion, and Credibility." Also see W. B. Pearce and F. Conklin, "Nonverbal Vocalic Communication and Perception of Speaker," *Speech Monographs 38* (1971): 235–241; R. L. Street, Jr. and R. M. Brady, "Speech Rate Acceptance Ranges as a Function of Evaluative Domain, Listener Speech Rate, and Communication Context."

71. D. G. Leathers, "Impression Management Training: Conceptualization and Application to Personal Selling," *Journal of Applied Communication Research 16* (1988): 126–145.

72. M. Reiss and P. Rosenfeld, "Seating Preferences as Nonverbal Communication: A Self-Presentational Analysis," *Journal of Applied Communication Research 8* (1980): 22–30.

73. C. Ward, "Seating Arrangement and Leadership Emergence in Small Discussion Groups," *Journal of Social Psychology 74* (1968): 83–90; L. T. Howels and S. W. Becker, "Seating Arrangement and Leadership Emergence," *Journal of Abnormal and Social Psychology 64* (1962): 148–150.

74. T. P. Mottet, S. A. Beebe, P. C. Raffeld, and M. L. Paulsel, "The Effects of Student Responsiveness on Teachers' Granting Power to Students and Essay Evaluation," *Communication Quarterly 53(4)* (2005): 421–436; T. P. Mottet, S. A. Beebe, P. C. Raffeld, and M. L. Paulsel, "The Effects of Student Verbal and Nonverbal Responsiveness on Teachers' Liking of Students and Willingness to Comply with Student Requests," *Communication Quarterly 52(1)* (2004): 27–38; T. P. Mottet and S. A. Beebe, "The Relationship Between Student Responsive Behaviors, Student Socio-Communicative Style, and Instructors' Subjective and Objective Assessments of Student Work," *Communication Education* (in press).

75. S. L. Webb, "Sexual Harassment Should Be Defined Broadly," in *What Is Sexual Harassment?* edited by K. L. Swisher (San Diego, CA: Greenhaven Press, 1995), 10–18.

76. Webb, "Sexual Harassment Should Be Defined Broadly."

77. Webb, "Sexual Harassment Should Be Defined Broadly."

78. Webb, "Sexual Harassment Should Be Defined Broadly."

79. R. Paetzold and A. O'Leary-Kelly, "The Legal Context of Sexual Harassment," in *Sexual Harassment: Communication Implications*, edited by G. L. Kreps (Cresskill, NJ: Hampton Press, 1993), 63–77.

80. K. L. Scheppele, as quoted in E. Goodman, "The 'Reasonable Woman' Definition of Sexual Harassment Makes Sense," in *What Is Sexual Harassment?* edited by K. L. Swisher (San Diego, CA: Greenhaven Press, 1995), 25–27.

81. D. S. Dougherty, "Dialogue Through Standpoint: Understanding Women's and Men's Standpoints of Sexual Harassment," *Management Communication Quarterly 12* (1999): 436–468. Also see D. S. Dougherty, "Sexual Harassment as [Dys]functional Process: A Feminist Standpoint Analysis," *Journal of Applied Communication Research 29* (2001): 372–402; J. Keyton and S. C. Rhodes, "Organizational Sexual Harassment: Translating Research into Application," *Journal of Applied Communication Research 27* (1999): 158–173; B. A. Gutek, A. G. Cohen, and A. M. Konrad, "Predicting Social-Sexual Behaviors at Work: A Contact Hypothesis," *Academy of Management Journal 33* (1990): 560–577; J. W. Lee and L. K. Guerrero, "Types of Touch in Cross-Sex Relationships Between Co-Workers: Perceptions of Relational and Emotional Messages, Inappropriateness, and Sexual Harassment," *Journal of Applied Communication Research 29* (2001): 197–220.

Chapter 4

1. S. R. Covey, *The 7 Habits of Highly Effective People* (New York: Simon & Schuster, 1989); S. R. Covey, *The 8th Habit: From Effectiveness to Greatness* (New York: Free Press, 2004).

2. A. D. Wolvin and C. G. Coakley, "Listening Education in the 21st Century," *International Journal of Listening 14* (2000): 143–152.

3. J. D. Weinrauch and R. Swanda, Jr., "Examining the Significance of Listening: An Exploratory Study of Contemporary Management," *The Journal of Business Communication 13* (1975): 25–32; see also L. A. Janusik and A. D. Wolvin, "24 Hours in a Day: A Listening Update to the Time Studies," paper presented at the 2006 meeting of the International Listening Association, Salem, OR.

4. L. A. Janusik and A. D. Wolvin. "Listening Treatment in the Basic Communication Course Text," in *Basic Communication Course Annual*, edited by D. Sellnow (Boston: Academic Press, 2002).

5. J. Grau and C. Grau, "New Communication Demands of the 21st Century Workplace," *Listening Professional 2* (Summer 2003): 3, 19.

6. AICPA, "Highlighted Responses from the Association for Accounting Marketing Survey. Creating the Future Agenda for the Profession—Managing Partner Perspective." Retrieved April 8, 2005, from http://www.aicpa.org/pubs/tpcpa/feb2001/hilight.htm; V. P. Goby and J. H. Lewis, "The Key Role of Listening in Business: A Study of the Singapore Insurance Industry," *Business Communication Quarterly 63* (June 2000): 41–51.

7. S. A. Beebe, "What Do Communication Trainers Do?" *Communication Education 56* (2007): 249–254; Wolvin and Coakley, "Listening Education in the 21st Century" J. Brownwell, "Developing Receiver-Centered Communication in Diverse Organizations," *Listening Professional 2* (2003): 5–25.

8. A. L Darling and D. P. Dannels, "Practicing Engineers Talk About the Importance of Talk: A Report on the Role of Oral Communication in the Workplace," *Communication Education 52* (2003): 1–16.

9. D. A. Schwartz, "Listening Out of the Box: New Perspectives for the Workplace," *International Journal of Listening 18* (2004): 44–55.

10. International Listening Association, "An ILA Definition of Listening," *ILA Listening Post 53* (April 1995): 1, 4.

11. E. Raudsepp, "Listen Lessons: Poor Listening Habits Cost Qualified MBAs Job Offers and Promotions," *Minority MBA*

(1993–94): 36–39; A. K. Robertson, *Listen for Success: A Guide to Effective Listening* (Burr Ridge, IL: Irwin Professional Publishing, 1994); R. Weiner, "Seven Rules for Effective Communication," *Public Relations Quarterly 52* (2007): 9–11.

12. G. M. Goldhaber and C. H. Weaver, "Listener Comprehension of Compressed Speech When the Difficulty, Rate of Presentation, and Sex of Listener Are Varied," *Speech Monographs 35* (1968): 20–25; T. G. Sticht, "Learning by Listening," in *Language Comprehension and the Acquisition of Knowledge*, edited by V. H. Winston (New York: Wiley, 1972), 285–314.

13. D. Tannen, "How Men and Women Use Language Differently in Their Lives and in the Classroom," *Education Digest 57* (1992): 3.

14. R. W. Preiss and B. M. Gayle, "Exploring the Relationship Between Listening Comprehension and Rate of Speech," in *Classroom Communication and Instructional Processes: Advances Through Metaanalysis*, edited by B. M. Gayle, R. W. Preiss, N. Burrell, and M. Allen (Mahwah, NJ: Lawrence Erlbaum, 2006), 315–327.

15. Preiss and Gayle, "Exploring the Relationship Between Listening Comprehension and Rate of Speech."

16. B. Quirke and A. Lamb, "Get Your Internal Communication Match Fit," *Strategic Communication Management* (June-July 1999): 24–29; M. Thatcher, "Dealing with Information Overload—What Is the Communicator's Role?" *Strategic Communication Management* (September-October 2007): 4–6.

17. The Radicati Group, Inc. Retrieved August 24, 2008, from http://www.radicati.com.

18. Ferris Research. Retrieved August 24, 2008, from http://www.ferris.com/research-library/industry-statistics/.

19. L. R. Wheeless, "An Investigation of Receiver Apprehension and Social Context Dimensions of Communication Apprehension," *The Speech Teacher 24* (1975): 263.

20. G. D. Bodie, "Aspects of Receiving Information: The Relationship Between Listening Preferences, Communication Apprehension, Receiver Apprehension, and Communicator Style," *International Journal of Listening 17* (2003): 47–67.

21. K. L. Winiecki and J. Ayres, "Communication Apprehension and Receiver Apprehension in the Workplace," *Communication Quarterly 47* (1999): 430–440; J. L. Chesebro, "Effects of Teacher Clarity and Nonverbal Immediacy on Student Learning, Receiver Apprehension, and Affect," *Communication Education 52* (2003): 135–147; J. L. Chesebro and J. C. McCroskey, "The Relationship Between Teacher Clarity and Immediacy on Students' Experiences with Receiver Apprehension When Listening to Teachers," *Communication Quarterly 46* (1998): 446–456; C. V. Roberts, "A Validation of the Watson-Barker Listening Test," *Communication Research Reports 3* (1986): 115–119.

22. J. L. Hayhurst, *The Big Three as Related to Receiver Apprehension and Listening Behaviors*. Unpublished master's thesis. West Virginia University, Morgantown, WV, 2002.

23. J. Levy, H. Pashler, and E. Boer, "Central Interference in Driving: Is There Any Stopping the Psychological Refractory Period?" *Psychological Science 17* (2006): 228–235; K. Woznicki, "Multi-Tasking Creates Health Problems," United Press International, August 6, 2001. Retrieved April 21, 2009, from http://www.umich.edu/~bcalab/articles/UPIArticle2001.html.

24. Woznicki, "Multi-Tasking Creates Health Problems."

25. K. Watson, L. Barker, and J. Weaver, "The Listening Styles Profile (LSP16): Development and Validation of an Instrument to Assess Four Listening Styles," *International Journal of Listening 9* (1995): 1–13.

26. J. L. Cloudsley-Thompson, "Time-Sense of Animals," in *The Voice of Time* 2e, edited by J. T. Fraser (Amherst, MA: University of Massachusetts Press, 1981), 296–311; K. C. Hammer, "Experimental Evidence for the Biological Clock," in Fraser, *The Voice of Time*, 281–295; C. M. Ciarleglio, K. K. Ryckman, S. V.

Servick, A. Hida, S. Robbins, N. Wells, J. Hicks, S. A. Larson, J. P. Wiedermann, K. Carver, N. Hamilton, K. K. Kidd, J. R. Kidd, J. R. Smith, J. Friedlaender, D. G. McMahon, S. M. Williams, M. L. Summar, and D. H. Johnson, "Genetic Differences in Human Circadian Clock Genes Among Worldwide Populations," *Journal of Biological Rhythms 23* (2008): 330–340.

27. "Why Some of Us Are Early Risers," The BBC News. Retrieved April 13, 2006, from http://news.bbc.co.uk/2/hi/health/2996364.stm.

28. J. Sandberg, "Morning People vs. Late Risers: The Workplace Battle Continues," *The Wall Street Journal*. Retrieved April 13, 2006, from http://www.careerjournal.com/columnists/cubicleculture/20040514-cubicle.html.

29. P. Watzlawick, J. B. Bavelas, and D. D. Jackson, *Pragmatics of Human Communication* (New York: W.W. Norton, 1967).

30. Schwartz, "Listening Out of the Box."

31. Schwartz, "Listening Out of the Box."

32. I. W. Johnson, C. G. Pearce, T. L. Tuten, and L. Sinclair, "Self-Imposed Silence and Perceived Listening Effectiveness," *Business Communication Quarterly 66* (2003): 23–45.

33. M. V. Redmond, "The Functions of Empathy (Decentering) in Human Relations," *Human Relations 42* (1993): 593–606; K. I. Miller, "Compassionate Communication in the Workplace: Exploring Processes of Noticing, Connecting, and Responding," *Journal of Applied Communication Research 35* (2007): 223–245.

34. These ideas were adapted from M. Booth-Butterfield, *Interpersonal Essentials* (Boston: Allyn & Bacon, 2002), 163.

35. R. Bierck, "How to Listen: Listening Is an Integral Part of Good Business Communication," *Harvard Management Communication Letter* (January 2001): 4–5.

36. Bierck, "How to Listen."

37. A. Sueyoshi and D. M. Hardison, "The Role of Gestures and Facial Cues in Second Language Listening Comprehension," *Language Learning 55* (2005): 661–699; G. A. Mueller, "Visual Contextual Cues and Listening Comprehension: An Experiment," *Modern Language Journal 64* (1980): 355–360.

38. T. P. Mottet, "Interactive Television Instructors' Perceptions of Students' Nonverbal Responsiveness and Their Influence on Distance Teaching," *Communication Education 49* (2000): 146–164; Sueyoshi and Hardison, "The Role of Gestures and Facial Cues in Second Language Listening Comprehension."

39. A. Mehrabian, *Nonverbal Communication* (Chicago: Aldine-Transaction, 2007).

40. A. Mehrabian, *Silent Messages: Implicit Communication of Emotions and Attitudes* 2e (Belmont, CA: Wadsworth Publishing Company, 1981), 2.

41. M. Gladwell, *Blink: The Power of Thinking Without Thinking* (New York: Little, Brown, 2005).

42. Gladwell, *Blink*; A. Damasio, *The Feeling of What Happens: Body and Emotion in the Making of Consciousness* (New York: Harcourt, 1999); J. K. Burgoon, "Nonverbal Signals," in *Handbook of Interpersonal Communication*, edited by M. L. Knapp and G. R. Miller (Thousand Oaks, CA: Sage, 1994), 229–285.

43. Mehrabian, *Silent Messages*; J. A. Russell and L. F. Barrett, "Core Affect, Prototypical Emotional Episodes, and Other Things Called Emotion: Dissecting the Elephant," *Journal of Personality and Social Psychology 76* (1999): 805–819; J. A. Russell and A. Mehrabian, "Distinguishing Anger and Anxiety in Terms of Emotional Response Factors," *Journal of Consulting and Clinical Psychology 42* (1974): 79–83.

44. Mehrabian, *Silent Messages*; V. P. Richmond, J. C. McCroskey, and A. Johnson, "Development of the Nonverbal Immediacy Scale (NIS): Measures of Self- and Other-Perceived Nonverbal Immediacy," *Communication Quarterly 51* (2003): 504–517.

45. P. Andersen, *Nonverbal Communication: Forms and Functions* (Long Grove, IL: Waveland Press, 2007).

46. M. S. Mast and J. A. Hall, "Who Is the Boss and Who Is Not? Accuracy of Judging Status," *Journal of Nonverbal Behavior 28* (2004): 145–165; M. Helweg-Larsen, S. J. Cunningham, A. Carrico, and A. M. Pergram, "To Nod or Not to Nod: An Observational Study of Nonverbal Communication and Status in Female and Male College Students," *Psychology of Women Quarterly 28* (2004): 358–361; L. Z. Tiedens and A. R. Fragale, "Power Moves: Complementarity in Dominant and Submissive Nonverbal Behavior," *Journal of Personality and Social Psychology 84* (2003): 558–568; Mehrabian, *Silent Messages*.

47. L. B. Resnick, "Cognition and Instruction: Recent Theories of Human Competence," in *Psychology and Learning: The Master Lecture Series*, Vol. 4, edited by B. L. Hammonds (Washington, DC: American Psychological Association, 1985), 127–186.

48. Resnick, "Cognition and Instruction."

49. R. G. Nichols and L. A. Stevens, "Listening to People," *Harvard Business Review 35* (September–October 1957): 85–92.

50. A. King, "Autonomy and Question Asking: The Role of Personal Control in Guided Student-Generated Questioning," *Learning and Individual Differences 6* (1994): 163–185.

51. M. Imhof, "How to Listen More Efficiently: Self-Monitoring Strategies in Listening," *International Journal of Listening 15* (2001): 2–20.

52. King, "Autonomy and Question Asking."

53. R. E. Mayer, "Elaboration Techniques That Increase Meaningfulness of Technical Text. An Experimental Test of the Learning Strategy Hypothesis," *Journal of Educational Psychology 72* (1980): 770–784; Imhof, "How to Listen More Efficiently."

54. C. G. Pearce, I. W. Johnson, and R. T. Barker, "Assessment of the Listening Styles Inventory," *Journal of Business & Technical Communication 17* (2003): 84–113.

55. K. K. Halone and L. L. Pecchioni, "Relational Listening: A Grounded Theoretical Model," *Communication Reports 14* (2001): 59–71.

56. Pearce, Johnson, and Barker, "Assessment of the Listening Styles Inventory."

57. Pearce, Johnson, and Barker, "Assessment of the Listening Styles Inventory."

58. Pearce, Johnson, and Barker, "Assessment of the Listening Styles Inventory."

59. M. Imhof, "What Makes a Good Listener? Listening Behavior in Instructional Settings," *International Journal of Listening 12* (1998): 81–105; T. P. Mottet, S. A. Beebe, P. C. Raffeld, and A. L. Medlock, "The Effects of Student Verbal and Nonverbal Responsiveness on Teacher Self-Efficacy and Job Satisfaction," *Communication Education 53* (2004): 150–163.

60. Adapted from Mottet, "Interactive Television Instructors' Perceptions of Students' Nonverbal Responsiveness."

61. K. Miller, "The Experience of Emotion in the Workplace: Professing in the Midst of Tragedy," *Management Communication Quarterly 15* (2002): 571–600; V. R. Waldron, "Once More, with Feeling: Reconsidering the Role of Emotion in Work," *Communication Yearbook 17* (1994): 388–416; A. S. King, "Capacity for Empathy: Confronting Discrimination in Managing Multicultural Work Force Diversity," *Business Communication Quarterly 58* (1995): 46–50.

62. O. Hargie, ed., *A Handbook of Communication Skills* (New York: Routledge, 2003); J. Authier, "Showing Warmth and Empathy," in *A Handbook of Communication Skills*, edited by O. Hargie (New York: New York University Press, 1986), 441–464.

63. Many of the ideas discussed in this section were adapted from J. C. McCroskey and V. P. Richmond, eds., *Fundamentals of Human Communication: An Interpersonal Perspective* (Prospect Heights, IL: Waveland Press, 1996), 142–156; J. Chesebro, "Student Listening Behavior," in *Communication for Teachers*, edited by J. L. Chesebro & J. C. McCroskey (Boston: Allyn & Bacon, 2002), 8–18.

64. J. H. Gittell, *The Southwest Airlines Way: Using the Power of Relationships to Achieve High Performance* (New York: McGraw Hill, 2003).

65. C. I. Hovland, I. L. Janis, and H. H. Kelley, *Communication and Persuasion* (New Haven, CT: Yale University Press, 1953).

66. T. P. Mottet, S. A. Beebe, and C. Fleuriet, "Students Influence Messages," in *Handbook of Instructional Communication: Rhetorical and Relational Perspectives*, edited by T. P. Mottet, V. P. Richmond, & J. C. McCroskey (Boston: Allyn & Bacon, 2006), 143–166.

67. To learn more about how to use nonverbal responses to enhance receiver understanding, refer to T. P. Mottet and V. P. Richmond, "Student Nonverbal Communication and Its Influence on Teachers and Teaching," in *Communication for Teachers*, edited by J. L. Chesebro & J. C. McCroskey (Boston: Allyn & Bacon, 2002), 47–61.

68. R. C. Atkinson and R. M. Shiffrin, "Human Memory: A Proposed System and Its Control," in *The Psychology of Learning and Motivation: Advances in Research and Theory*, Vol. 2, edited by K. W. Spence (New York: Academic Press, 1968), 89–195; F. I. M. Craik and R. S. Lockhart, "Levels of Processing: A Framework for Memory Research," *Journal of Verbal Learning and Verbal Behavior 11* (1972): 671–684.

69. L. Wheeless, "An Investigation of Receiver Apprehension and Social Context Dimensions of Communication Apprehension," *The Speech Teacher, 24* (1975): 261–268.

Chapter 5

1. For the most comprehensive review of this research, see M. J. Beatty, J. C. McCroskey, and K. M. Valencic, *The Biology of Communication: A Communibiological Perspective* (Cresskill, NJ: Hampton Press, 2001).

2. C. M. Condit, "Culture and Biology in Human Communication: Toward a Multi-Causal Model," *Communication Education 49* (2000): 7–24; M. J. Beatty and J. C. McCroskey, "A Few Comments About Communibiology and the Nature/Nurture Question," *Communication Education 49* (2000): 25–28.

3. J. A. Daly and A. M. Bippus, "Personality and Interpersonal Communication: Issues and Directions," in *Communication and Personality: Trait Perspectives*, edited by J. C. McCroskey, J. A. Daly, M. M. Martin, and M. J. Beatty (Cresskill, NJ: Hampton Press, 1998), 1–40.

4. Beatty, McCroskey, and Valencic, *The Biology of Communication*.

5. J. C. McCroskey, J. A. Daly, M. Martin, and M. J. Beatty eds. *Communication and Personality: Trait Perspectives* (Cresskill, NJ: Hampton Press, 1998).

6. M. J. Beatty, A. Heisel, A. Hall, T. Levine, and B. LaFrance, "What Can We Learn from the Study of Twins About Genetic and Environmental Influences on Interpersonal Affiliation, Aggressiveness, and Social Anxiety? A Meta-Analytic Study," *Communication Monographs 69* (2002): 1–18; M. J. Beatty, J. C. McCroskey, and A. Heisel, "Communication Apprehension as Temperamental Expression: A Communibiological Paradigm," *Communication Monographs 65* (1998): 197–219.

7. Beatty, McCroskey, and Valencic, *The Biology of Communication*.

8. A. G. Smith, ed. *Communication and Culture* (New York: Rinehart & Winston, 1966).

9. Condit, "Culture and Biology in Human Communication."

10. J. P. Guilford, *Personality* (New York: McGraw-Hill, 1959); D. C. Funder, *The Personality Puzzle* (New York: W. W. Norton, 1997).

11. D. A. Infante, A. S. Rancer, and D. F. Womack, eds. *Building Communication Theory* 4e (Prospect Heights, IL: Waveland Press, 2003).

12. J. C. McCroskey and V. P. Richmond, "Willingness to Communicate," *Communication and Personality: Trait Perspectives*, edited by J. C. McCroskey, J. A. Daly, M. M. Martin, and M. J.

Beatty (Cresskill, NJ: Hampton Press, 1998), 119–131; K. B. Wright, L. Frey, and P. Sopory, "Willingness to Communicate About Health as an Underlying Trait of Patient Self-Advocacy," *Communication Studies* 58 (2007): 35–51.

13. V. P. Richmond and K. D. Roach, "Willingness to Communicate and Employee Success in U.S. Organizations," *Journal of Applied Communication Research* (1992): 95–115.

14. V. P. Richmond and J. C. McCroskey, *Organizational Communication for Survival: Making Work, Work* 4e (Boston: Allyn and Bacon, 2008); V. P. Richmond, "Implications for Quietness: Some Facts and Speculations," in *Avoiding Communication: Shyness, Reticence, and Communication Apprehension*, edited by J. A. Daly and J. C. McCroskey (Beverly Hills, CA: Sage, 1984), 145–156; V. P. Richmond and J. C. McCroskey, "Willingness to Communicate and Dysfunctional Communication Processes," in *Intrapersonal Communication Processes*, edited by C. V. Roberts and K. W. Watson (Scottsdale, AZ: Gorisuch Scarisbrick, 1989), 292–318.

15. B. Horwitz, *Communication Apprehension: Origins and Management* (New York: Singular, 2001).

16. J. C. McCroskey and V. A. Richmond, "Communication Apprehension and Small Group Communication," in *Small Group Communication: A Reader* 5e, edited by R. S. Cathcart and L. A. Samovar (Dubuque, IA: William C. Brown, 1988), 405–420.

17. V. P. Richmond and J. C. McCroskey, *Communication: Apprehension, Avoidance, and Effectiveness* 5e (Boston: Allyn and Bacon, 1998).

18. J. C. McCroskey, "Validity of the PRCA as an Index of Oral Communication Apprehension," *Communication Monographs* 45 (1978):192–203.

19. J. C. McCroskey and M. J. Beatty, "Communication Apprehension," *Communication and Personality: Trait Perspectives*, edited by J. C. McCroskey, J. A. Daly, M. M. Martin, & M. J. Beatty (Cresskill, NJ: Hampton Press, 1998), 215–231.

20. Richmond and McCroskey, *Communication: Apprehension, Avoidance, and Effectiveness*, 67–78; J. J. Teven, "Effects of Supervisor Social Influence, Nonverbal Immediacy, and Biological Sex on Subordinates' Perceptions of Job Satisfaction, Liking, and Supervisor Credibility," *Communication Quarterly* 55 (2007): 155–177.

21. Richmond and McCroskey, *Communication: Apprehension, Avoidance, and Effectiveness*; C. B. Crawford and C. S. Strohkirch, "The Critical Role of Communication in Knowledge Organizations: Communication Apprehension as a Predictor of Knowledge Management," *Journal of Knowledge Management Practice* 7. Retrieved August 16, 2008, from http://www.tlainc.com/articl122.htm.

22. Richmond and McCroskey, *Communication: Apprehension, Avoidance, and Effectiveness*; see also M. Booth-Butterfield and S. Booth-Butterfield, *Communication Apprehension and Avoidance in the Classroom* (Edina, MN: Burgess Publishing, 1992); L. Kelly, "Skills Training as a Treatment for Communication Problems," in *Avoiding Communication: Shyness, Reticence, and Communication Apprehension*, edited by J. A. Daly, J. C. McCroskey, J. Ayres, T. Hopf, and D. M. Ayres (Cresskill, NJ: Hampton Press, 1997), 331–365; L. Kelly and J. A. Keaten, "Treating Communication Anxiety: Implications of the Communibiological Paradigm," *Communication Education*, 49 (2000): 45–57.

23. D. A. Infante and A. S. Rancer, "A Conceptualization and Measure of Argumentativeness," *Journal of Personality Assessment* 46 (1982): 72–80.

24. A. S. Rancer, "Argumentativeness," in *Communication and Personality: Trait Perspectives*, edited by J. C. McCroskey, J. A. Daly, M. M. Martin, and M. J. Beatty (Cresskill, NJ: Hampton Press, 1998), 149–170.

25. D. A. Infante and W. I. Gorden, "Superior and Subordinate Communication Profiles: Implications for Independent-Mindedness and Upward Effectiveness," *Central States Speech Journal* 38 (1987): 73–80; D. A. Infante and W. I. Gorden "Argumenta-

tiveness and Affirming Communicator Style as Predictors of Satisfaction/Dissatisfaction with Subordinates," *Communication Quarterly* 37 (1989): 81–89; D. A. Infante and W. I. Gorden, "How Employees See the Boss: Test of an Argumentative and Affirming Model of Superiors' Communicative Behavior," *Western Journal of Speech Communication* 55 (1991): 294–304.

26. A. S. Rancer and T. A. Avtgis, *Argumentative and Aggressive Communication: Theory, Research, and Applications* (Thousand Oaks, CA: Sage, 2006).

27. Infante and Rancer, "A Conceptualization and Measure of Argumentativeness"; Rancer and Avtgis, *Argumentative and Aggressive Communication*.

28. Rancer and Avtgis, *Argumentative and Aggressive Communication*; Beatty, McCroskey, and Valencic, *The Biology of Communication*; Rancer, "Argumentativeness."

29. Smith, *Communication and Culture*.

30. E. T. Hall, *Beyond Culture* (Garden City, NY: Doubleday, 1976).

31. For example, see A. V. Matveeve and P. E. Nelson, "Cross Cultural Competence and Multicultural Team Performance: Perceptions of American and Russian Managers," *International Journal of Cross Cultural Management* 4 (2004): 253–270.

32. G. Hofstede, *Culture's Consequences: International Differences in Work-Related Values* (Beverly Hills, CA: Sage, 1980); G. Hofstede, *Cultures and Organizations: Software of the Mind* (London: McGraw-Hill, 1991).

33. Hofstede, *Culture's Consequences*.

34. S. Ohlemacher, "White Americans No Longer a Majority by 2042." Retrieved August 14, 2008, from http://abcnews.go.com/Politics/wireStory?id=5575766.

35. Hall, *Beyond Culture*.

36. L. A. Samovar, R. E. Porter, and L. A. Stefani, *Communication Between Cultures* (Belmont, CA: Wadsworth, 1998).

37. E. T. Hall and M. R. Hall, *Understanding Cultural Differences* (Yarmouth, ME: Intercultural Press, 1990).

38. D. I. Ballard and D. R. Seibold, "Time Orientation and Temporal Variation Across Work Groups: Implications for Group and Organizational Communication," *Western Journal of Communication* 64 (2000): 218–242.

39. Ballard and Seibold, "Time Orientation and Temporal Variation Across Work Groups."

40. See also an excellent review of conflict and culture research in W. B. Gudykunst, *Bridging Difference: Effective Intergroup Communication* (Newbury Park, CA: Sage, 1994).

41. S. Ting-Toomey, "A Face Negotiation Theory," in *Theories in Intercultural Communication*, edited by Y. Kim and W. Gudykunst (Newbury Park, CA: Sage, 1988).

42. C. Christians and M. Taber, *Communication Ethics and Universal Values* (Beverly Hills, CA: Sage, 1997).

43. G. Hofstede and G. J. Hofstede, *Cultures and Organizations: Software of the Mind*, Revised and Expanded 2nd Edition (New York: McGraw-Hill USA, 2005).

44. S. Ting-Toomey, "Toward a Theory of Conflict and Culture," in *Communication, Culture, and Organizational Processes*, edited by W. Gudykunst, L. Stewart, and S. Ting-Toomey (Beverly Hills, CA: Sage, 1985).

45. Ting-Toomey, "A Face Negotiation Theory."

46. Hofstede, *Culture's Consequences*; Hofstede, *Cultures and Organizations*.

47. P. Salem, ed. *Organizational Communication and Change* (Cresskill, NJ: Hampton Press, 1999).

48. Hofstede, *Culture's Consequences*; Hofstede, *Cultures and Organizations*.

49. Hofstede, *Culture's Consequences*; Hofstede, *Cultures and Organizations*.

50. G. Hofstede, *Culture's Consequences: Comparing Values, Behaviors, Institutions and Organizations Across Nations* 2e. (Thousand Oaks, CA: Sage, 2001).

51. Hofstede, *Culture's Consequences: Comparing Values, Behaviors, Institutions and Organizations Across Nations.*

52. G. Hofstede, "Cultural Dimensions in Management and Planning," *Asia Pacific Journal of Management* (January, 1984): 81–98; Hofstede, *Cultures and Organizations.*

53. Hofstede, *Culture's Consequences: Comparing Values, Behaviors, Institutions and Organizations Across Nations.*

54. J. L. Chin, B. Lott, J. Rice, and J. Sanchez-Huckles, eds. *Women and Leadership: Transforming Visions and Diverse Voices* (Malden, MA: Blackwell); see also "Women in Leadership Roles: Report of Online Discussion," Division for the Advancement of Women, United Nations Department of Economic and Social Affairs, and Women Watch. Retrieved March 17, 2009, from www.un.org/womenwatch/feature/women_leadership_on-line _discussion_report_Women_in_Leadership_Roles.pdf.

55. Adapted from N. Payne, "Intercultural Communication Tips." Retrieved March 17, 2009, from http://ezinearticles.com/? Intercultural-Communication-Tips&id=254094.

56. H. Sirkin, J. Hemerling, and A. Bhattacharya, *Globality: Competing with Everyone from Everywhere for Everything* (New York: Business Plus, 2008).

57. D. Tannen, *You Just Don't Understand: Women and Men in Conversation* (New York: Morrow, 1990); D. Tannen, *Talking from 9 to 5: How Women's and Men's Conversational Styles Affect Who Gets Heard, Who Gets Credit, and What Gets Done at Work* (New York: Morrow, 1994).

58. D. J. Canary and K. Dindia, eds. *Sex Differences and Similarities in Communication: Critical Essays and Empirical Investigations of Sex and Gender in Interaction* (Mahwah, NJ: Lawrence Erlbaum, 1998).

59. R. Lakoff, "Language and Woman's Place," *Language in Society* 2 (1975): 45–80; R. Lakoff, *Language and Woman's Place* (New York: Harper & Row, 1975).

60. J. Wood, *Gendered Lives: Communication, Gender, and Culture* 8e. (Belmont, CA: Wadsworth, 2008).

61. L. M. Timmerman, "Comparing the Production of Power in Language on the Basis of Sex," in *Interpersonal Communication Research: Advances Through Meta-Analysis*, edited by M. Allen, R. W. Preiss, B. M. Qayle, and N. Burrell (Mahwah, NJ: Lawrence Erlbaum, 2002), 73–88.

62. K. Quina, J. A. Wingard, and H. G. Bates, "Language Style and Gender Stereotypes in Person Perception," *Psychology of Women Quarterly 11* (1987): 111–122; L. L. Haleta, "Student Perceptions of Teachers' Use of Language: The Effect of Powerful and Powerless Language on Impression Formation and Uncertainty," *Communication Education 45* (1996): 16–28.

63. M. Z. Hackman, M. J. Hills, T. J. Paterson, and A. H. Furniss, "Leaders' Gender-Role as a Correlate of Subordinates' Perceptions of Effectiveness and Satisfaction," *Perceptual and Motor Skills 77* (1993): 671–674; B. Q. Griffin, *Perceptions of Managers: Effects of Leadership Style and Gender.* Paper presented at the annual meeting of the Southeastern Psychological Association, Knoxville, TN, March, 1992.

64. N. A. Burrell and R. J. Koper, "The Efficacy of Powerful/Powerless Language on Attitudes and Source Credibility," in *Persuasion: Advances Through Meta-Analysis*, edited by M. Allen and R. Preiss (Cresskill, NJ: Hampton, 1998), 203–216.

65. D. Tannen, "The Power of Talk: Who Gets Heard and Why," *Harvard Business Review 73* (September–October 1995): 138–148.

66. Tannen, "The Power of Talk"; Tannen, *Talking from 9 to 5.*

67. Tannen, "The Power of Talk."

68. Tannen, *Talking from 9 to 5.*

69. Tannen, *Talking from 9 to 5*; see also H. T. Reis, "Gender Differences in Intimacy and Related Behaviors: Context and Process," in *Sex Differences and Similarities in Communication*, edited by D. J. Canary and K. Dindia (Mahwah, NJ: Lawrence Erlbaum, 1998), 203–231.

70. D. Geddes, "Sex Roles in Management: The Impact of Varying Power of Speech Style on Union Members' Perception of Satisfaction and Effectiveness," *The Journal of Psychology 126* (1992): 589–607; Tannen, *Talking from 9 to 5*; Wood, *Gendered Lives*; K. Patterson, J. Grenny, R. McMillan, and A. Switzler, *Crucial Conversations: Tools for Talking When Stakes Are High* (New York: McGraw Hill, 2002).

71. Geddes, "Sex Roles in Management."

72. D. Tannen, *Talking from 9 to 5.*

Chapter 6

1. P. M. Sias, *Organizing Relationships: Traditional and Emerging Perspectives on Workplace Relationships* (Los Angeles: Sage, 2009); B. Fix and P. M. Sias, "Person-Centered Communication, Leader-Member Exchange, and Employee Satisfaction," *Communication Research Reports 23* (2006): 35–44.

2. R. Badowksi and R. Gittines, *Managing Up: How to Forge an Effective Relationship with Those Above You* (New York: Doubleday Business, 2004).

3. V. P. Richmond and J. C. McCroskey, "The Impact of Supervisor and Subordinate Immediacy on Relational and Organizational Outcomes," *Communication Monographs 67* (2000): 85–95.

4. L. K. Lewis, "Employee Perspectives on Implementation Communication as Predictors of Perceptions of Success," *Western Journal of Communication 70* (2006): 23–46; B. Kay and D. M. Christophel, "The Relationships Among Manager Communication Openness, Nonverbal Immediacy, and Subordinate Motivation," *Communication Research Reports 12* (1995): 200–205; H. L. Walter, C. M. Anderson, and M. M. Martin, "How Subordinates' Machiavellianism and Motives Relate to Satisfaction with Superiors," *Communication Quarterly 53* (2005): 57–70; P. M. Sias, "Workplace Relationship Quality and Employee Information Experiences, *Communication Studies 56* (2005): 375–395.

5. T. B. Green and J. T. Knippen, *Breaking the Barrier to Upward Communication* (Westport, CT: Quorum Books, 1999); M. Dobson and D. S. Dobson, *Managing Up* (New York: Amacom, 2000); J. Owen, "Managing Your Boss," *Industrial and Commercial Training 39* (2007): 79–84; D. T. McAlister and J. R. Darling, "Upward Influence in Academic Organizations: A Behavioral Style Perspective," *Leadership and Organizational Development Journal 26* (2005): 558–573.

6. J. W. Koehler and G. Huber, *Effects of Upward Communication on Managerial Decision-Making.* Paper presented at the annual meeting of the International Communication Association, New Orleans, LA, May, 1974.

7. Green and Knippen, *Breaking the Barrier to Upward Communication.*

8. As cited in L. Hawkins, "Facing the Future: Global Job Shifts Have Just Begun," *Austin American-Statesman* (September 12, 2004): J1, J4.

9. "Smashing the Clock: No Schedules, No Mandatory Meetings. Inside Best Buy's Radical Reshaping of the Workplace," *Business Week*, December 11, 2006. Retrieved February 21, 2008, from http://www .businessweek.com/magazine/content/06_50/ b4013001. htm.

10. C. Sandlund "Telecommuting: A Legal Primer," *Business Week Online*, March, 2000. Retrieved May 18, 2009, from www. businessweek.com; J. Welch and S. Welch, "The Importance of Being There," *Business Week Online*, April, 2007. Retrieved May 18, 2009, from http://www.businessweek.com/@@z6ai6 GQQES15Th0A/perm/content/07_16/b4030109.htm?chan=search; "Smashing the Clock."

11. Welch and Welch, "The Importance of Being There."

12. Sandlund "Telecommuting: A Legal Primer"; Welch and Welch, "The Importance of Being There."

13. These reasons are reviewed in S. A. Myers and A. D. Johnson, "Perceived Solidarity, Self-Disclosure, and Trust in Organizational and Peer Relationships," *Communication Research*

Reports 21 (2004): 75–83; T. H. Feeley, J. Hwang, and G. A. Barnett, "Predicting Employee Turnover from Friendship Networks," *Journal of Applied Communication Research* 36 (2008): 56–73.

14. B. Rose, "For Folks Like Us, It's Not a 9-to-5 World Anymore," *Austin American-Statesman* (June 2, 2005): C1, C3.

15. Bureau of Labor Statistics, United States Department of Labor, USDL 08-0859, June 25, 2008. Retrieved August 20, 2008, from http://www.bls.gov/news.release/atus.nr0.htm.

16. K. A. Jehn and P. P. Shah, "Interpersonal Relationships and Task Performance: An Examination of Mediating Processes in Friendship and Acquaintance Groups," *Journal of Personal and Social Psychology* 72 (1997): 775–790; C. M. Riordan and R. W. Griffeth, "The Opportunity for Friendship in the Workplace: An Underexplored Construct," *Journal of Business and Psychology* 10 (1995): 141–154; B. A. Winstead, V. J. Derlega, M. J. Montgomery, and C. Pilkington, "The Quality of Friendships at Work and Job Satisfaction," *Journal of Social and Personal Relationships* 12 (1995): 199–215; Myers and Johnson, "Perceived Solidarity, Self-Disclosure, and Trust in Organizational and Peer Relationships."

17. B. Carey, "Didya Hear the Latest? Gossip Has a Purpose," *Austin American-Statesman*, (August 16, 2005): A1, A5.

18. Myers and Johnson, "Perceived Solidarity, Self-Disclosure, and Trust in Organizational and Peer Relationships."

19. Myers and Johnson, "Perceived Solidarity, Self-Disclosure, and Trust in Organizational and Peer Relationships."

20. M. Thatcher, "The Grapevine: Communication Tool or Thorn in Your Side?" *Strategic Communication Management* 7 (2003): 30.

21. Carey, "Didya Hear the Latest?"

22. Carey, "Didya Hear the Latest?"

23. Thatcher, "The Grapevine."

24. K. Davis, "Care and Cultivation of the Corporate Grapevine," *Dun's Review* 102 (1973): 46.

25. A. L. Darling and D. P. Dannels, "Practicing Engineers Talk About the Importance of Talk: A Report on the Role of Oral Communication in the Workplace," *Communication Education* 52 (2003): 1–16; A. Vangelisti and J. A. Daly, "Correlates of Speaking Skills in the United States: A National Assessment," *Communication Education* 38 (1989): 132–143.

26. V. P. Richmond, "The Impact of Supervisor and Subordinate Immediacy on Relational and Organizational Outcomes," *Communication Monographs* 67 (2000): 85–95; J. W. Kassing, "Investigating the Relationship Between Superior-Subordinate Relationship Quality and Employee Dissent," *Communication Research Reports* 17 (2000): 58–70; K. Ellis and P. Shockley-Zalabak, "Trust in Top Management and Immediate Supervisor: The Relationship to Satisfaction, Perceived Organizational Effectiveness, and Information Receiving," *Communication Quarterly* 49 (2001): 382–398.

27. K. G. Lamude, J. Scudder, D. Simmons, and P. Torres, "Organizational Newcomers: Temporary and Regular Employees, Same-Sex and Mixed-Sex Superior-Subordinate Dyads, Supervisor Influence Techniques, Subordinate Communication Satisfaction, and Leader-Member Exchange," *Communication Research Reports* 21 (2004): 60–67; V. P. Richmond and J. C. McCroskey, *Organizational Communication for Survival: Making Work, Work* 4e (Boston: Allyn & Bacon, 2008); V. P. Richmond, J. C. McCroskey, and L. M. Davis, "The Relationship of Supervisor Use of Power and Affinity-Seeking Strategies with Subordinate Satisfaction," *Communication Quarterly* 34 (1986): 178–193.

28. Lamude, Scudder, Simmons, and Torres, "Organizational Newcomers"; Richmond and McCroskey, *Organizational Communication for Survival.*

29. A. Bernstein, *Grounded: Frank Lorenzo and the Destruction of Eastern Airlines* (New York: Simon Schuster, 1991).

30. D. Katz and R. Kahn, *The Social Psychology of Organizations* (New York: Wiley, 1966).

31. Google Corporate Information. Retrieved August 16, 2008, from http://www.google.com/corporate/facts.html.

32. *Manager's Toolkit: The 13 Skills Managers Need to Succeed* (Boston: Harvard Business School Press, 2004).

33. Adapted from FranklinCovey, The 7 Habits of Highly Effective People Signature Program, Workbook, Version 3.0 (2005) p. 96; see also S. R. Covey, The 7 Habits of Highly Effective People (New York: Simon & Schuster, 1989); S. R. Covey, *The 8th Habit: From Effectiveness to Greatness* (New York: Free Press, 2004); *Manager's Toolkit.*

34. A. Marken, "Skills Training Is Becoming a Neverending Process," Office World News, June 1, 2001. Retrieved May 14, 2009, from http://yellowbrix.netbusiness.com.

35. W. S. Z. Ford, "Communication Practices of Professional Service Providers: Predicting Customer Satisfaction and Loyalty," *Journal of Applied Communication Research* 31 (2003): 189–211.

36. Ford, "Communication Practices of Professional Service Providers"; W. S. Z. Ford, "Evaluation of the Indirect Influence of Courteous Service on Customer Discretionary Behavior," *Human Communication Research* 22 (1998): 65–89; W. S. Z. Ford, *Communicating with Customers: Service Approaches, Ethics, and Impact* (Cresskill, NJ: Hampton, 1998); W. S. Z. Ford, "Customer Expectations for Interactions with Service Providers: Relationship Versus Encounter Orientation and Personalized Service Communication," *Journal of Applied Communication Research* 29 (2001): 1–29; W. S. Z. Ford and C. N. Etiennne, "Can I Help You? A Framework for the Interdisciplinary Literature on Customer Service Encounters," *Management Communication Quarterly* 7 (1994): 413–441.

37. W. S. Z. Ford, "Communication and Customer Service," in *Communication Yearbook 22*, edited by M. E. Roloff (Thousand Oaks, CA: Sage, 1999), 341–375.

38. Sias, *Organizing Relationships.*

39. The following list of customer service communication skills was adapted from a document prepared by the Northwest Regional Educational Laboratory. Retrieved November 26, 2008, from www.nwrel.org/assessment/pdfRubrics/csr.PDF.

40. C. D. Koermer and L. McCroskey, "Sociality Communication: Its Influence on Customer Loyalty with the Service Provider and Service Organization," *Communication Quarterly* 54 (2006): 53–65.

41. F. Carroll, "The Rudeness Revolution," *Austin American-Statesman* (July 29, 2005): E1, E3.

42. P. Blackshaw, *Satisfied Customers Tell Three Friends, Angry Customers Tell 3,000* (New York: Doubleday, 2008).

43. Blackshaw, *Satisfied Customers Tell Three Friends, Angry Customers Tell 3,000.*

44. J. L. Hocker and W. W. Wilmot, *Interpersonal Conflict* 7e (New York: McGraw Hill, 2005).

45. Covey, *The 7 Habits of Highly Effective People*; R. Fisher and W. Ury, *Getting to Yes: Negotiating Agreement Without Giving In* (New York: Penguin Books, 1991); K. Patterson, J. Grenny, R. McMillan, and A. Switzler, *Crucial Conversations: Tools for Talking When Stakes Are High* (New York: McGraw-Hill, 2002).

46. K. Dobbs, "Knowing How to Keep Your Best and Brightest," *Workforce* (April 2001), 57–60.

47. R. Kilmann and K. Thomas, "Interpersonal Conflict-Handling Behavior as Reflections of Jungian Personality Dimensions," *Psychological Reports* 37 (1975): 971–980; K. W. Thomas and R. H. Kilmann, *Thomas-Kilmann Conflict Mode Instrument* (Tuxedo, NY: XICOM, 1974); K. W. Thomas, "Conflict and Conflict Management: Reflections and Update," *Journal of Organizational Behavior* 13 (1992): 265–274.

48. K. W. Thomas, "Toward Multi-Dimensional Values in Teaching: The Example of Conflict Behaviors," *Academy of Management Review 3* (1987): 487. R. S. Lulofs and D. D. Cahn, *Conflict: From Theory to Action* 2e (Boston: Allyn and Bacon, 2000).

49. These strategies were adapted from J. C. McCroskey, V. P. Richmond, and L. L. McCroskey, *An Introduction to Communication in the Classroom: The Role of Communication in Teaching and Training* (Boston: Allyn & Bacon, 2006).

50. J. Collins, *Good to Great: Why Some Companies Make the Leap . . . and Others Don't* (New York: HarperCollins, 2006).

51. E. Hatfield, J. T. Cacioppo, and R. L. Rapson, *Emotional Contagion* (New York: Cambridge University Press, 1994).

52. Hatfield, Cacioppo, and Rapson, *Emotional Contagion.*

53. A. Mehrabian, *Nonverbal Communication* (Chicago: Aldine-Atherton, 1972); A. Mehrabian, *Silent Messages* (Belmont, CA: Wadsworth Publishing, 1990).

54. P. Ekman and W. V. Friesen, "Nonverbal Leakage and Clues to Deception," *Psychiatry 32* (1969): 88–105.

55. Mehrabian, *Silent Messages*; T. P. Mottet, J. Parker-Raley, C. Cunningham, S. A. Beebe, and P. C. Raffeld, "Testing the Neutralizing Effect of Instructor Immediacy on Student Course Workload Expectancy Violations and Tolerance for Instructor Unavailability," *Communication Education 55* (2006): 147–166; D. J. Canary, "Managing Interpersonal Conflict: A Model of Events Related to Strategic Choices," in *Handbook of Communication and Social Skill Interaction*, edited by J. O. Greene and B. R. Burleson (Mahwah, NJ: Lawrence Erlbaum, 2003), 515–549.

56. M. Booth-Butterfield, *Interpersonal Essentials* (Boston: Allyn & Bacon, 2002).

57. Booth-Butterfield, *Interpersonal Essentials.*

58. The idea for this model originated with the work of F. F. Fournies, *Coaching for Improved Work Performance* (New York: McGraw Hill, 1995).

59. L. L. Putnam, "Bargaining as Organizational Communication," in *Organizational Communication: Traditional Themes and New Directions*, edited by R. D. McPhee and P. K. Tompkins (Newbury Park, CA: Sage, 1985), 129.

60. A. Wrzesniewski and J. E. Dutton, "Crafting a Job: Revisioning Employees as Active Crafters of Their Work," *Academy of Management Review 26* (2001): 179–201.

61. Covey, *The 7 Habits of Highly Effective People*; S. R. Covey, *Principle-Centered Leadership* (New York: Simon & Schuster, 1991).

62. Adapted from FranklinCovey, The 7 Habits of Highly Effective People Signature Program, participant training guide, Version 3.0 (2005).

63. Covey, *The 7 Habits of Highly Effective People.*

64. Fisher and Ury, *Getting to Yes*; M. E. Roloff, L. L. Putnam, and L. Anastasiou, "Negotiation Skills," in *Handbook of Communication and Social Skill Interaction*, edited by J. O. Greene and B. R. Burleson (Mahwah, NJ: Lawrence Erlbaum, 2003), 801–833.

65. Fisher and Ury, *Getting to Yes*, 41.

Chapter 7

1. C. J. Stewart and W. B. Cash, Jr., *Interviewing: Principles and Practices* 12e (New York: McGraw Hill, 2007).

2. M. Bolch, "Lights, Camera . . . Interview!" *HR Magazine* (March 2007): 99–102; K. Stephens and T. P. Mottet, "Interactivity in a Web-Conferencing Learning Environment: Effects on Trainers and Trainees," *Communication Education 57* (2008): 88–104.

3. Bolch, "Lights, Camera . . . Interview!"

4. B. Karsh, "How Can I Kick Some Butt in a Phone Interview?" *Advertising Age 78* (2007): 18.

5. Stewart and Cash, *Interviewing: Principles and Practices.*

6. T. W. Dougherty, D. B. Turban, and J. C. Callender, "Confirmatory First Impressions in the Employment Interview: A Field Study of Interviewer Behavior," *Journal of Applied Psychology 79* (1994): 659–665.

7. W. F. Chaplin, J. B. Phillips, J. D. Brown, N. R. Clanton, and J. L. Stein, "Handshaking, Gender, Personality, and First Impressions," *Journal of Personality and Social Psychology 79* (2000): 110–117.

8. Chaplin, Phillips, Brown, Clanton, and Stein, "Handshaking, Gender, Personality, and First Impressions."

9. D. Tannen, *You Just Don't Understand: Women and Men in Conversation* (New York: Morrow, 1990); D. Tannen, *Talking From 9 to 5: How Women's and Men's Conversational Styles Affect Who Gets Heard, Who Gets Credit, and What Gets Done at Work* (New York: Morrow, 1994).

10. C. McKerney and S. Rimer, "Dean at MIT Resigns, Ending a 28-Year Lie," *The New York Times* (April 30, 2007).

11. P. Rosenfeld, "Impression Management, Fairness, and the Employment Interview," *Journal of Business Ethics 16* (1997): 801–808; R. Gifford, C. F. Ng, and M. Wilkinson, "Nonverbal Cues in the Employment Interview: Links Between Applicant Qualities and Interviewer Judgments," *Journal of Applied Psychology 70* (1985): 729–736.

12. M. Mino, "The Relative Effects of Content and Vocal Delivery During a Simulated Employment Interview," *Communication Research Reports 13* (1996): 225–238.

13. Stewart and Cash, *Interviewing: Principles and Practices*; D. B. Goodall and H. L. Goodall, "The Employment Interview: A Selective Review of the Literature with Implications for Communications Research," *Communication Quarterly 30* (1982): 116–123.

14. L. K. Thaler and R. Koval, *The Power of Nice: How to Conquer the Business World with Kindness* (New York: Currency, 2006).

15. T. P. Mottet and S. A. Beebe, "The Relationship Between Student Responsive Behaviors, Student Socio-Communicative Style, and Instructors' Subjective and Objective Assessments of Student Work," *Communication Education 55* (2006): 295–312.

16. M. McLoughlin, J. L. Sheler, and G. Witkin, "A Nation of Liars?" *U.S. News and World Report* (February 23, 1987): 54–61, See also J. S. O'Rourke, "The Ethics of Resumes and Recommendations: When Do Filler and Fluff Become Deception and Lies?" *Business Communication Quarterly 58* (1995): 54–56.

17. S. M. Ralston and W. G. Kirkwood, "Overcoming Managerial Bias in Employment Interviewing," *Journal of Applied Communication Research 23* (1995): 75–92.

18. R. L. Kahn and C. F. Cannell, *The Dynamics of Interviewing* (New York: John Wiley & Sons, 1964), 205.

19. "Manager's Toolkit: The 13 Skills Managers Need to Succeed," *Harvard Business Essential Series* (Boston: Harvard Business School Press, 2004), 295–298.

20. M. Mattson, M. Allen, D. J. Ryan, and V. Miller, "Considering Organizations as a Unique Interpersonal Context for Deception Detection: A Meta-Analytic Review," *Communication Research Reports 17* (2000): 148–160.

21. M. Z. Sincoff and R. S. Goyer, *Interviewing* (New York: Macmillan, 1984), 80; T. Washington, *Interview Power: Selling Yourself Face to Face in the New Millennium* (Bellevue, WA: Mount Vernon Press, 2000.)

Chapter 8

1. M. Farr, *Next Day Job Interview* (Indianapolis, IN: JIST Publishing, 2005).

2. M. S. Granovetter, "The Strength of Weak Ties," *American Journal of Sociology 78* (1973): 1360–1380.

3. Granovetter, "The Strength of Weak Ties."

4. D. R. McKay, "Informational Interviews." Retrieved March 18, 2008, from About.com: Career Planning, http://careerplanning.about.com/cs/occupations/a/info_interviews.htm.

5. Farr, *Next Day Job Interview*.
6. R. N. Bolles, *What Color Is Your Parachute?* (Berkeley, CA: Ten Speed Press, 2007).
7. Farr, *Next Day Job Interview*.
8. Farr, *Next Day Job Interview*.
9. The sample resume and our suggestions for developing a resume are based on information in the *2005 Texas State University Career Services Manual* (San Marcos, TX: Office of Career Services, 2005).
10. Bolles, *What Color Is Your Parachute?*
11. Farr, *Next Day Job Interview*; also see G. Crispin and M. Mehler, "Careerxroads 5th Annual Sources of Hire Survey," February 23, 2006. Retrieved May 14, 2009, from http://www.careerxroads.com/news/sourcesofhire05.pdf.
12. Crispin and Mehler, *Careerxroads 5th Annual Sources of Hire Survey*.
13. Farr, *Next Day Job Interview*.
14. Farr, *Next Day Job Interview*.
15. D. Waters, "Digital Citizens, Another Blogger Dooced," *BBC News UK*, July 20, 2005.
16. M. Conlin, "You Are What You Post," *Business Week* (March 27, 2006).
17. J. Flesher, "How to Clean Up Your Digital Dirt Before It Trashes Your Job Search," *The Wall Street Journal* (January 12, 2006): 4A.
18. Bolles, *What Color Is Your Parachute?*
19. M. Gladwell, *Blink: The Power of Thinking Without Thinking* (New York: Little, Brown, and Company, 2005).
20. R. Gifford, C. F. Ng, and M. Wilkinson, "Nonverbal Cues in the Employment Interview: Links Between Applicant Qualities and Interviewer Judgments," *Journal of Applied Psychology 70* (1985): 729–736.
21. D. Jones, "CEOs Say How You Treat a Waiter Can Predict a Lot About Character," *USA Today*, April 17, 2006. Retrieved May 14, 2009, from http://www.usatoday.com/money/companies/management/2006-04-14-ceos-waiter-rule_x.hym.
22. R. E. Riggio and B. Throckmorton, "The Relative Effects of Verbal and Nonverbal Behavior, Appearance, and Social Skills on Evaluations Made in Hiring Interviews," *Journal of Applied Social Psychology 18* (1988): 331–348; L. M. Watkins and L. Johnston, "Screening Job Applicants: The Impact of Physical Attractiveness and Application Quality," *International Journal of Selection and Assessment 8* (2000): 76–84.
23. C. J. Stewart and W. B. Cash, Jr., *Interviewing: Principles and Practices* 12e (New York: McGraw Hill, 2007).
24. J. S. Seiter and A. Sandry, "Pierced for Success? The Effects of Ear and Nose Piercing on Perceptions of Job Candidates' Credibility, Attractiveness, and Hirability," *Communication Research Reports 20* (2003): 287–298.
25. K. Rodriguez, "Kids Can Find What Principals Can't on a Prospective Teacher's Character," *San Antonio Express-News* (February 4, 2007): B-1, B-3; see also T. Ferguson, "Want a Job? Clean up your Web Act," March 28, 2007. Retrieved March 30, 2007, from http://news.cnet.com/2100-1025-3-6171187.html; M. Goodman, "The Dumbest Online Job Hunt Blunders," July 31, 2008. Retrieved July 31, 2008, from http://abcnews.go.com/business/CareerManagement/story?id=5483048&page=1.
26. J. Hopkins, "Job Seekers Show Rather Than Tell," *USA Today* (April 25, 2007): 3B.
27. J. Hopkins, "Job Seekers Show Rather Than Tell."
28. "Do's and Don'ts of Video Resumes." Retrieved March 25, 2009, from http://www.careerbuilder.com/JobSeeker/VideoResumes/DosDonts.aspx. For additional information see Hopkins, "Job Seekers Show Rather Than Tell."
29. J. Ayres, T. Keereetaweep, P. Chen, and P. A. Edwards, "Communication Apprehension and Employment Interviews," *Communication Education 47* (1998): 1–17.
30. Farr, *Next Day Job Interview*; see also Stewart and Cash, *Interviewing: Principles and Practices* 12e; Bolles, *What Color Is Your Parachute?*
31. T. DeGroot and S. J. Motowidlo, "Why Visual and Vocal Interview Cues Can Affect Interviewers' Judgments and Predict Job Performance," *Journal of Applied Psychology 84* (1999): 986–993.
32. Farr, *Next Day Job Interview*.
33. A. Desjanun, "Video Adds Heft, Hurtles to Resumes," ABC News, May 1, 2007. Retrieved May 14, 2009, from www.abcnews.go.com/Business/Wirestory3106228.
34. A. Desjanun, "Video Adds Heft, Hurtles to Resumes."
35. P. Butler, "A Review of the Literature on Portfolios and Electronic Portfolios," *Canadian Journal of Learning and Technology 31* (2005): 261–268.
36. Dan Macsai, ". . . And I Invented Velcro," *Business Week* (August 4, 2008): 15.
37. J. Perkins, "Questions Can Lead to Perfect-Fit Job," *Austin American Statesman* (October 29, 2006): D1; Bolles, *What Color Is Your Parachute?*, 87–88.
38. C. I. Hovland, I. L. Janis, and H. H. Kelley, *Communication and Persuasion* (New Haven, CT: Yale University Press, 1953).
39. Farr *Next Day Job Interview*, 127–128.
40. S. E. Needleman, "Thx for the IView! I Wud ♥ to Work 4 U!!" *Wall Street Journal* (July 29, 2008): D1, D4.
41. H. Karp, "The Lost Art of Feedback," in *1987 Annual: Developing Human Resources*, edited by J. W. Pfeiffer (San Diego, CA: University Associates, 1987), 14–24.
42. N. R. F. Maier, *The Appraisal Interview* (New York: John Wiley and Sons, 1958).
43. H. H. Meyer, "A Solution to the Performance Appraisal Feedback Enigma," *Academy of Management Executive 5* (1991): 68–76; J. L. Pearce and L. W. Porter, "Employee Responses to Formal Performance Appraisal Feedback," *Journal of Applied Psychology 71* (1986): 211–218.
44. Meyer, "A Solution to the Performance Appraisal Feedback Enigma"; F. F. Fournies, *Coaching for Improved Performance* 3e (New York: McGraw-Hill, 1999).
45. D. Fandray, "The New Thinking in Performance Appraisals," *Workforce 80* (2001): 36–40, retrieved March 27, 2009, from http://findarticles.com/p/articles/mi_mOFXS/is_5_80/ai_74886392; Meyer, "A Solution to the Performance Appraisal Feedback Enigma."
46. G. Thornton, "Psychometric Properties of Self-Appraisals of Job Performance," *Personnel Psychology 33* (1980): 263–271.
47. "Manager's Toolkit: The 13 Skills Managers Need to Succeed," *Harvard Business Essentials Series* (Boston: Harvard Business School Press, 2004); also refer to G. Shepard, *How To Make Performance Evaluations Really Work* (Hoboken, NJ: John Wiley & Sons, 2005).
48. F. F. Fournies, *Why Employees Don't Do What They're Supposed To Do and What You Can Do About It* (New York: McGraw-Hill, 2007).
49. Meyer, "A Solution to the Performance Appraisal Feedback Enigma," 68–76; J. L. Pearce and L. W. Porter, "Employee Responses to Formal Performance Appraisal Feedback," *Journal of Applied Psychology 71* (1986): 211–218; Shepard, *How To Make Performance Evaluations Really Work*.
50. G. T. Fairhurst, "Dualism in Leadership Research," in *The New Handbook of Organizational Communication: Advances in |Theory, Research, and Methods*, edited by F. M. Jablin and L. L. Putnam (Thousand Oaks, CA: Sage, 2001), 379–439; L. P. Cusella, "Feedback, Motivation, and Performance," in *Handbook of Organizational Communication: An Interdisciplinary Perspective*, edited by F. M. Jablin, L. L. Putnam, K. H. Roberts, and L. W. Porter (Newbury Park, CA: Sage, 1987), 624–678.

51. FranklinCovey, *Latest FranklinCovey Research Reports Major Gaps in U.S. Workers' Focus and Execution on Top Organizational Priorities*. Retrieved March 27, 2009, from http://franklincovey.bg/news, 2003, 2, en.

52. A. N. Kluger and A. DeNisi, "Effects of Feedback Intervention on Performance: A Historical Review, a Meta-Analysis, and a Preliminary Feedback Intervention Theory," *Psychological Bulletin* 119 (1996): 254–284.

53. B. Feng and E. L. MacGeorge, "Predicting Receptiveness to Advice: Characteristics of the Problem, the Advice-Giver, and the Recipient," *Southern Communication Journal* 71 (2006): 67–85.

54. Meyer, "A Solution to the Performance Appraisal Feedback Enigma"; Pearce and Porter, "Employee Responses to Formal Performance Appraisal Feedback"; Shepard, *How To Make Performance Evaluations Really Work*.

55. Fournies, *Coaching for Improved Performance*.

56. E. Hatfield, J. T. Cacioppo, and R. L. Rapson, *Emotional Contagion* (New York: Cambridge University Press, 1994).

57. J. K. Burgoon, L. A. Stern, and L. Dillman, *Interaction Adaptation: Dyadic Interaction Patterns* (New York: Cambridge University Press, 1995).

58. K. Anderson, *Resolving Conflict Sooner: The Powerfully Simple 4-Step Method for Reaching Better Agreements More Easily in Everyday Life* (Berkeley, CA: Ten Speed Press, 1999); see also K. Anderson, "Handling Criticism with Honesty and Grace," *Public Management* 82 (2000): 30–34.

59. Fournies, *Coaching for Improved Performance*.

60. B. F. Skinner, "The Science of Learning and the Art of Teaching," *Harvard Educational Journal* 24 (1954): 86–97; see also B. F. Skinner, *Science and Human Behavior* (New York: Free Press, 1953).

61. Skinner, "The Science of Learning and the Art of Teaching."

62. Fairhurst, "Dualism in Leadership Research"; Cusella, "Feedback, Motivation, and Performance."

Chapter 9

1. The origins of Tupperware are described in E. Ross and A. Holland, *100 Great Businesses and the Minds Behind Them* (Naperville, IL: Sourcebooks, Inc., 2006), 308.

2. S. Sorensen, "Grouphate." Paper presented at the annual meeting of the International Communication Association, Minneapolis, Minnesota, May 1981.

3. R. K. Mosvick and R. B. Nelson, *We've Got to Start Meeting Like This!* (Glenview, IL: Scott, Foresman, 1987); R. Y. Hirokawa, "Communication and Group Decision-Making Efficacy," in *Small Group Communication Theory and Practice: An Anthology*, edited by R. Y. Hirokawa, R. S. Cathcart, L. A. Samovar, and L. D. Henmann (New York: Oxford University Press, 2007), 125.

4. B. Harrington and G. A. Fine, "Where the Action Is," *Small Group Research* 37, no. 1 (2006): 4–19.

5. M. A. Hackman and C. E. Johnson. *Leadership: A Communication Perspective* (Prospect Heights, IL: Waveland Press, 2000).

6. T. Rapp and J. Mathieu, "Evaluating an Individually Self-Administered Generic Teamwork Skills Training Program Across Time and Levels," *Small Group Research* 38, no. 4 (2007): 532–552; E. Sales and J. A. Cannon-Bowers, "The Science of Training: A Decade of Progress," *Annual Review of Psychology* 52 (2001): 471–499.

7. R. Rico, M. Sanchez-Manzanares, F. Gil, and C. Gibson, "Team Implicit Coordination Processes: A Team Knowledge-Based Approach," *Academy of Management Review* 33, no. 1 (2008): 163–184.

8. D. Strubler and K. York, "An Explanatory Study of the Team Characteristics Model Using Organizational Teams," *Small Group Research* 38, no. 6 (2007): 670–695.

9. See N. R. F. Maier, "Assets and Liabilities in Group Problem Solving: The Need for a Integrative Function," *Psychological Review* 74 (1967): 239–249; M. Argyle, *Cooperation: The Basics of Sociability* (London: Routledge, 1991); H. A. M. Wilke and R. W. Meertens, *Group Performance* (London: Routledge, 1994).

10. E. Stark, J. Shaw, and M. Duffy, "Preference for Group Work, Winning Orientation, and Social Loafing Behavior in Groups," *Group & Organization Management* 32, no. 6 (2007): 699–723.

11. Maier, "Assets and Liabilities in Group Problem Solving"; Argyle, *Cooperation*; Wilke and Meertens, *Group Performance*.

12. S. A. Beebe and J. T. Masterson, *Communicating in Small Groups: Principles and Practices* 9e (Boston: Allyn and Bacon, 2009).

13. N. Katz and G. Koenig, "Sports Teams as a Model for Workplace Teams: Lessons and Liabilities," *Academy of Management Executive* 15 (2001): 56–67.

14. Our discussion of teams and teamwork is from Beebe and Masterson, *Communicating in Small Groups*; for an excellent review of teamwork theoretical models, see V. Rousseau, C. Aube, and A. Savoie, "Teamwork Behaviors—A Review and an Integration of Frameworks," *Small Group Research* 37, no. 5 (2006): 540–570.

15. A. G. Sheard and A. P. Kakabadse, "From Loose Groups to Effective Teams: The Nine Key Factors of the Team Landscape," *Journal of Management Development* 21 (2002): 133–151.

16. See F. C. Broadbeck and T. Breitermeyer, "Effects of Individual Versus Mixed Individual and Group Experience in Rule Induction on Group Member Learning and Group Performance," *Journal of Experimental Social Psychology* 36 (2002): 621–648.

17. S. B. Shimanoff, *Communication Rules: Theory and Research* (Beverly Hills, CA: Sage, 1980).

18. M. Hoegl and K. P. Parboteeah, "Goal Setting and Team Performance in Innovative Projects: On the Moderating Role of Teamwork Quality," *Small Group Research* 34 (2003): 3–19.

19. H. Van Mierlo, C. Rutte, M. Kompier, and H. Kompier, "Self-Managing Teamwork and Psychological Well-Being: Review of a Multilevel Research Domain," *Group Organization Management* 30, no. 2 (2005): 211–235.

20. L. Erbert, G. Mearns, and S. Dean, "Perceptions of Turning Points and Dialectical Interpretations in Organizational Team Development," *Small Group Research* 36, no. 1 (2005): 21–58.

21. R. Y. Hirokawa and J. Keyton, "Perceived Facilitators and Inhibitors of Effectiveness in Organizational Work Teams," *Management Communication Quarterly* 8 (1995): 424–426.

22. D. J. Devine and J. L. Philips, "Do Smarter Teams Do Better? A Meta-Analysis of Cognitive Ability and Team Performance," *Small Group Research* 32 (2001): 507–535.

23. C. E. Larson and F. M. J. LaFasto, *Teamwork: What Must Go Right/What Can Go Wrong* (Beverly Hills, CA: Sage, 1989).

24. Hoegl and Parboteeah, "Goal Setting and Team Performance in Innovative Projects."

25. D. Crown, "The Use of Group and Groupcentric Individual Goals for Culturally Heterogeneous and Homogeneous Task Groups," *Small Group Research* 38, no. 4 (2007): 489–508.

26. M. A. Marks, J. E. Mathieu, and S. J. Zaccaro, "A Temporally Based Framework and Taxonomy of Team Processes," *Academy of Management Review* 26 (2001): 356–376.

27. Devine and Philips, "Do Smarter Teams Do Better?"

28. F. LaFasto and C. Larson, *When Teams Work Best* (Thousand Oaks, CA: Sage, 2001). Our discussion of the six characteristics of effective team members is based on information presented in Chapter 1, pages 4–25.

29. M. S. Limon and F. J. Boster, "The Effects of Performance Feedback on Group Members' Perceptions of Prestige, Task Competencies, Group Belonging, and Loafing," *Communication Research Reports* 20 (Winter 2003): 13–23.

30. P. Balkundi and D. Harrison, "Ties, Leaders, and Time in Teams: Strong Inference about Network Structure's Effects on Team Viability and Performance," *Academy of Management Journal 49*, no. 1 (2006): 49–68.

31. D. A. Romig, *Breakthrough Teamwork: Outstanding Results Using Structured Teamwork* (Chicago: Irwin, 1996), 41–42.

32. M. Irvine, "E-Mail's No Longer Fast Enough." *Austin American-Statesman* (July 24, 2006): D3.

33. C. M. McGrath, "The Pleasures of Text," *The New York Times Magazine* (January 22, 2006): 15.

34. Y. Amichai-Hamburger, ed., *The Social Net: Human Behavior in Cyberspace* (New York: Oxford University Press, 2005), v.

35. M. Adkins and D. E. Brashers, "The Power of Language in Computer-Mediated Groups," *Management Communication Quarterly 8* (1995): 289–322.

36. V. J. Dubrovsky, S. Kiesler, and B. N. Sethna, "The Equalization Phenomenon: Status Effects on Computer-Mediated and Face-to-Face Decision-Making Groups," *Human Computer Interaction 6* (1991): 119–146.

37. A. I. Shirani, M. H. A. Tafti, and J. F. Affisco, "Task and Technology Fit: A Comparison of Two Technologies for Synchronous and Asynchronous Group Communication," *Information & Management 36* (1999): 139–150.

38. J. Walsh and N. Maloney, "Collaboration Structure, Communication Media, and Problems in Scientific Work Teams," *Journal of Computer-Mediated Communication 12* (2007): 712–732.

39. See the excellent review of the effect of technology on group decision making in M. S. Poole and G. DeSanctis, "Micro Level Structuration in Computer-Supported Group Decision Making," *Human Communication Research 19* (1992): 5–49.

40. R. E. Rice and G. Love, "Electronic Emotion: Socioemotional Context in a Computer-Mediated Communication Network," *Communication Research 14* (February 1987): 85–108.

41. See J. B Walter, "Computer-Mediated Communication: Impersonal, Interpersonal, and Hyperpersonal Interaction," *Communication Research 23* (1990): 3–43.

42. See R. Johansen, J. Vallee, and K. Spangler, *Electronic Meetings: Technical Alternatives and Social Choices* (Reading, MA: Addison-Wesley, 1979).

43. P. L. McLeon and J. K. Liker, "Electronic Meeting Systems: Evidence from a Low Structure Environment," *Information Systems Research 3* (1992): 195–223.

44. M. Finley, "Welcome to the Electronic Meeting," *Training* (July 1991): 29–32. See also Poole and DeSanctis, "Micro Level Structuration."

45. T. Fletcher and D. Major, "The Effects of Communication Modality on Performance and Self-Ratings of Teamwork Components," *Journal of Computer-Mediated Communication 11* (2006): 557–576.

46. C. Erik Timmerman and C. Scott, "Virtually Working: Communicative and Structural Predictors on Media Use and Key Outcomes in Virtual Work Teams," *Communication Monographs 73*, no. 1 (2006): 108–136.

47. T. Halfhill, E. Sundstrom, J. Lahner, W. Calderone, and T. Nielsen, "Group Personality Composition and Group Effectiveness—An Integrative Review of Empirical Research," *Small Group Research 36*, no. 1 (2005): 83–105.

48. K. D. Benne and P. Sheats. "Functional Roles of Group Members," *Journal of Social Issues 4* (1948): 41–49. For a good review of role development in groups, see A. P. Hare, "Types of Roles in Small Groups: A Bit of History and a Current Perspective," *Small Group Research 25* (1994): 433–438; A. J. Salazar, "An Analysis of the Development and Evolution of Roles in the Small Group," *Small Group Research 27* (1996): 475–503.

49. R. F. Bales, *Interaction Process Analysis* (Chicago: University of Chicago Press, 1976).

50. A. Aritzeta, B. Senior, and S. Swailes, "Team Role Preference and Cognitive Styles—A Convergent Validity Study," *Small Group Research 36*, no. 4 (2005): 404–436.

51. B. Hindo, "The Empire Strikes at Silos," *BusinessWeek* (August 20, 2007): 63.

52. M. Hogg and S. Reid, "Social Identity, Self-Categorization, and the Communication of Group Norms," *Communication Theory 16* (2006): 7–30.

53. M. Shaw, *Group Dynamics: The Psychology of Small Group Behavior* (New York: McGraw Hill, 1981), 281.

54. N. Katz, D. Lazer, H. Arrow, and N. Contractor, "Network Theory and Small Groups," *Small Group Research 35* (2004): 307–332.

55. See D. A. Romig, *Side-by-Side Leadership* (Chicago: Irwin, 1997).

56. P. R. Scholtes, B. L. Joiner, and B. J. Streibel, *The Team Handbook* 2e (Madison, WI: Joiner, 1996); J. R. Katzenbach and D. K. Smith, *The Wisdom of Teams: Creating the High-Performance Organization* (New York: HarperCollins, 1993).

57. C. Anderson, J. Beer, J. Chatman, S. Spataro, and S. Srivastava, "Knowing Your Place: Self-Perceptions of Status in Face-to-Face Groups," *Journal of Personality and Social Psychology 91*, no. 6 (2006): 1094–1110.

58. J. I. Hurwitz, A. F. Zander, and B. Hymovitch, "Some Effects of Power on the Relations Among Group Members," in *Group Dynamics: Research and Theory*, edited by D. Cartwright and A. Zander (New York: Harper & Row, 1953), 483–492; D. C. Barnlund and C. Harland, "Propinquity and Prestige as Determinants of Communication Networks," *Sociometry 26* (1963): 467–479; G. C. Homans, *The Human Group* (New York: Harcourt Brace and World, 1992); H. H. Kelly, "Communication in Experimentally Created Hierarchies," *Human Relations 4* (1951): 36–56.

59. M. R. Singer, *Intercultural Communication: A Perceptual Approach* (Englewood Cliffs, NJ: Prentice-Hall, 1987), 118.

60. J. R. P. French and B. H. Raven, "The Bases of Social Power," in *Group Dynamics*, edited by D. Cartwright and A. Zander (Evanston, IL: Row, Peterson, 1962), 607–623.

61. Adapted from E. G. Bormann and N. C. Bormann, *Effective Small Group Communication* (Minneapolis: Burgess Publishing Company, 1980), 70–72.

62. K. Jonas, P. Brazy, K. Sassenberg, and J. Shah, "Why Some Groups Just Feel Better: The Regulatory Fit of Group Power," *Journal of Personality and Social Psychology 92*, no. 2 (2007): 249–267; D. Mackie, E. Smith, and C. Seger, "Can Emotions Be Truly Group Level? Evidence Regarding Four Conceptual Criteria," *Journal of Personality and Social Psychology 93*, no. 3 (2007): 431–446.

63. M. Barrick, B. Bradley, and A. Colbert, "The Moderating Role of Top Management Team Interdependence: Implications for Real Teams and Working Groups," *Academy of Management Journal 50*, no. 3 (2007): 544–557.

64. J. Wellen and M. Neale, "Deviance, Self-Typicality, and Group Cohesion—The Corrosive Effects of the Bad Apples and the Barrel," *Small Group Research 37*, no. 2 (2006): 165–186.

65. S. Wheelan, B. Davidson, and E. Tilin, "Group Development Across Time: Reality or Illusion?" *Small Group Research 334* (2003): 223–245; S. Furst, M. Reeves, B. Rosen, and R. S. Blackburn, "Managing the Life Cycle of Virtual Teams," *Academy of Management Executive 18* (2004): 6–22.

66. B. A. Fisher, "Decision Emergence: Phases in Group Decision-Making," *Speech Monographs 37* (1970): 60.

67. For a discussion of primary tension and group phases, see E. Bormann, *Discussion and Group Methods* (New York: Harper & Row, 1975).

68. T. M. Sheidel and L. Crowell, "Idea Development in Small Discussion Groups," *Quarterly Journal of Speech 50* (1994): 140–145; C. J. Gersick, "Time and Transition in Work Teams:

Toward a New Model of Group Development," *Academy of Management Journal 32* (1989): 274–309; C. J. Gersick and J. R. Hackman, "Habitual Routines in Task-Performing Groups," *Organizational Behavior and Human Decision Processes 47* (1990): 65–97; A. Chang, P. Bordia, and J. Duck, "Punctuated Equilibrium and Linear Progression: Toward a New Understanding of Group Development," *Academy of Management Journal 46* (2003): 106–117; M. S. Poole, "A Multisequence Model of Group Decision Development," *Communication Monographs 50* (December 1983): 321–341.

69. R. Y. Hirokawa, "Discussion Procedures and Decision-Making Performance: A Test of a Functional Perspective," *Human Communication Research 12* (1985): 203–224.

70. R. Y. Hirokawa, "Why Informed Groups Make Faulty Decisions: An Investigation of Possible Interaction-Based Explanations," *Small Group Research 18* (1987): 3–29.

71. R. Y. Hirokawa and K. Rost, "Effective Group Decision-Making in Organizations: Field Test of the Vigilant Interaction Theory," *Management Communication Quarterly 5* (1992): 267–288; Hirokawa, "Why Informed Groups Make Faulty Decisions"; R. Y. Hirokawa, "Group Communication and Decision-Making Performance: A Continued Test of the Functional Perspective," *Human Communication Research 14* (1988): 487–515; M. O. Orlitzky and R. Y. Hirokawa, "To Err Is Human, to Correct for It Divine: A Meta-Analysis of Research Testing the Functional Theory of Group Decision-Making Effectiveness." Paper presented at the meeting of the National Communication Association. Chicago, IL, November 1997.

72. Hirokawa, "Discussion Procedures and Decision-Making Performance."

73. We thank Dennis Romig, president of Side-by-Side and author of *Side-by-Side Leadership: Achieving Outstanding Results Together* (Marietta, GA: Bard Press, 2001) for this idea.

74. See R. Y. Hirokawa and R. Pace, "A Descriptive Investigation of the Possible Communication-Based Reasons for Effective and Ineffective Group Decision Making," *Communication Monographs 50* (December 1983): 363–379. The authors also wish to acknowledge D. A. Romig of Performance Resources, Inc., in Austin, Texas for his contribution to the discussion.

75. D. G. Leathers, "Quality of Group Communication as a Determinant of Group Product," *Speech Monographs 39* (1972): 166–173; R. Y. Hirokawa and D. S. Gouran, "Facilitation of Group Communication: A Critique of Prior Research and an Agenda for Future Research," *Management Communication Quarterly 3* (August 1989): 71–92.

76. See F. J. Sabatine, "Rediscovering Creativity: Unlearning Old Habits," *Mid-American Journal of Business 4* (1989): 11–13.

77. Orlitzky and Hirokawa, "To Err is Human, to Correct for It Divine."

78. Beebe and Masterson, *Communicating in Small Groups.*

Chapter 10

1. D. Barry, *Dave Barry's Guide to Life* (New York: Wings Books, 1991), 311.

2. "Survive Meetings with High-Tech Tools," *USA Today Online*, January 22, 1999. http://www.usatoday.com.

3. T. Hopthrow and L. Hulbert, "The Effect of Group Decision Making on Cooperation in Social Dilemmas," *Group Processes & Intergroup Relations 8*, no. 1 (2005): 89–100; J. Bonito, "A Longitudinal Social Relation Analysis of Participation in Small Groups," *Human Communication Research 32* (2006): 302–321.

4. R. K. Mosvick and R. B. Nelson, *We've Got to Start Meeting Like This!* (Glenview, IL: Scott, Foresman, 1987).

5. D. M. Berg, "A Descriptive Analysis of the Distribution and Duration of Themes Discussed by Task-Oriented Small Groups," *Speech Monographs 34* (1967): 172–175; E. G. Bormann and N. C. Bormann, *Effective Small Group Communication* 2e. (Min-

neapolis: Burgess, 1976), 132; M. S. Poole, "Decision Development in Small Groups III: A Multiple Sequence Model of Group Decision Development," *Communication Monographs 50* (1983): 321–341.

6. Mosvick and Nelson, *We've Got to Start Meeting Like This!*; R. Y. Hirokawa, "Communication and Group Decision Making Efficacy," in *Small Group Communication Theory and Practice: An Anthology*, edited by R. Y. Hirokawa, R. S. Cathcart, L. A. Samovar, and L. D. Henmann (New York: Oxford University Press, 2007), 125.

7. The discussion of the advantages and disadvantages of working in small groups is based in part on N. R. F. Maier, "Assets and Liabilities in Group Problem Solving: The Need for an Integrative Function," *Psychological Review 74* (1967): 239–249; see also M. Argyle, *Cooperation: The Basis of Sociability* (London: Routledge, 1991).

8. F. Brodbeck, R. Kerschreiter, A. Mojzisch, and S. Schulz-Hardt, "Group Decision Making Under Conditions of Distributed Knowledge: The Information Asymmetries Model," *Academy of Management Review 32*, no. 2 (2007): 459–479; T. Reimer, S. Kuendig, U. Hoffrage, E. Park, and V. Hinz, "Effects of the Information Environment on Group Discussions and Decisions in the Hidden-Profile Paradigm," *Communication Monographs 74*, no. 1 (2007): 1–28; R. de Vries, B. van den Hooff, and J. de Ridder, "Explaining Knowledge Sharing—The Role of Team Communication Styles, Job Satisfaction, and Performance Beliefs," *Communication Research 33*, no. 2 (2006): 115–135; D. Henningsen and M. Henningsen, "Do Groups Know What They Don't Know? Dealing with Missing Information in Decision-Making Groups," *Communication Research 34*, no. 5 (2007): 507–525; E. Dane and M. Pratt, "Exploring Intuition and Its Role in Managerial Decision Making," *Academy of Management Review 32*, no. 1 (2007): 33–54.

9. J. E. Tropman and G. C. Morningstar, *Meetings: How to Make Them Work for You* (New York: Van Nostrand Reinhold, 1985), 56; J. E Tropman, *Making Meetings Work* (Thousand Oaks, CA: Sage, 1996).

10. See D. A. Romig, *Breakthrough Teamwork* (Chicago: Irwin, 1996); T. A. Kayser, *Mining Group Gold* (El Segundo, CA: Serif Publishing, 1990).

11. J. Campbell and G. Stasser, "The Influence of Time and Task Demonstrability on Decision-Making in Computer-Mediated and Face-to-Face Groups," *Small Group Research 37*, no. 3 (2006): 271–294.

12. A. Parker and B. Fischhoff, "Decision-Making Competence: External Validation Through an Individual-Difference Approach," *Journal of Behavioral Decision Making 18* (2005): 1–27.

13. D. S. Gouran and R. Y. Hirokawa, "Functional Theory and Communication in Decision-Making and Problem-Solving Groups: An Expanded View," in *Communication and Group Decision Making*, edited by R. Y. Hirokawa and M. S. Poole (Thousand Oaks, CA: Sage, 1996), 55–80; D. S. Gouran, R. Y. Hirokawa, K. M. Julian, and G. B. Leatham, "The Evolution and Current Status of the Functional Perspective on Communication in Decision-Making and Problem-Solving Groups," in *Communication Yearbook 16*, edited by S. A. Deetz (Newbury Park, CA: Sage, 1993), 573–600; E. E. Graham, M. J. Papa, and M. B. McPherson, "An Applied Test of the Functional Communication Perspective of Small Group Decision Making," *The Southern Communication Journal 62* (1997): 169–279.

14. Gouran and Hirokawa, "Functional Theory and Communication," 69.

15. K. Tasa and G. Whyte, "Collective Efficacy and Vigilant Problem Solving in Group Decision Making: A Non-Linear Model," *Organizational Behavior and Human Decision Processes 96* (2005): 119–129.

16. See K. Adams and G. Galanes, *Communicating in Groups: Applications and Skills* (New York: McGraw-Hill, 2007), 256;

D. W. Johnson and F. P. Johnson, *Joining Together: Group Theory and Group Skills* (Englewood Cliffs, NJ: Pearson, 2006), 99–104.

17. G. Schrah, R. Dalal, and J. Sniezek, "No Decision-Maker Is an Island: Integrating Expert Advice with Information Acquisition," *Journal of Behavioral Decision Making* 19 (2006): 43–60.

18. R. Prislin, W. M. Limbert, and E. Bauer, "From Majority to Minority and Vice Versa: The Asymmetrical Effects of Losing and Gaining Majority Position Within a Group," *Journal of Personality and Social Psychology* 79, no. 3 (2000): 385–397.

19. C. H. Kepner and B. B. Tregoe, *The Rational Manager* (New York: McGraw-Hill, 1965); see also G. Galanes and K. Adams, *Effective Group Discussion: Theory and Practice* (New York: McGraw-Hill, 2009).

20. We thank D. Romig for this observation. For additional information about structuring problem solving in teams, see D. A. Romig, *Breakthrough Teamwork: Outstanding Results Using Structured Teamwork* (New York: Irwin, 1996).

21. B. J. Broome and L. Fulbright, "A Multistage Influence Model of Barriers to Group Problem Solving: A Participant-Generated Agenda for Small Group Research," *Small Group Research* 26 (February 1995): 24–55.

22. See A. B. VanGundy, *Techniques of Structured Problem Solving* (New York: Van Nostrand Reinhold Company, 1981), 4.

23. VanGundy, *Techniques of Structured Problem Solving*, 4.

24. J. Dewey, *How We Think* (Boston: D. C. Heath, 1910).

25. This discussion of the Journalists' Six Questions is based on a discussion by J. E. Eitington, *The Winning Trainer* (Houston: Gulf Publishing, 1989), 157; also see R. Schwarz, *The Skilled Facilitator* (San Francisco, CA: Jossey-Bass, 2002).

26. Based on the research of K. Lewin, "Frontiers in Group Dynamics," *Human Relations 1* (1947): 5–42.

27. Adapted from J. E. Eitington, *The Winning Trainer*. Used with permission. All rights reserved.

28. E. Ross and A. Holland, *100 Great Businesses and the Minds Behind Them* (Naperville, IL: Sourcebooks, Inc. 2006), 112–115.

29. L. Gilson, C. Shalley, and T. Ruddy, "Creativity and Standardization: Complementary or Conflicting Drivers of Team Effectiveness?" *Academy of Management Journal* 48, no. 3 (2005): 521–531.

30. Ross and Holland, *100 Great Businesses and the Minds Behind Them*.

31. C. C. Miller and R. D. Ireland, "Intuition in Strategic Decision Making: Friend or Foe in the Fast-Paced 21st Century?" *Academy of Management Executive* 19, no. 1 (2005): 19–29; Brodbeck, Kerschreiter, Mojzisch, and Schulz-Hardt, "Group Decision Making Under Conditions of Distributed Knowledge."

32. S. Taggar, "Individual Creativity and Group Ability to Utilize Individual Creative Resources: A Multi-Level Model," *Academy of Management Journal* 45 (April 2002): 315–330.

33. T. J. Kramer, G. P. Fleming, and S. M. Mannis, "Improving Face-to-Face Brainstorming Through Modeling and Facilitation," *Small Group Research* 32, no. 5 (2001): 533–557.

34. A. F. Osborn, *Applied Imagination* (New York: Scribner's, 1962).

35. A. L. Delbecq, A. H. Van de Ven, and D. H. Gustafson, *Group Techniques for Program Planning: A Guide to Nominal-Group and Delphi Processes* (Glenview, IL. Scott, Foresman, 1975) 7–16.

36. B. L. Smith, "Interpersonal Behaviors That Damage the Productivity of Creative Problem-Solving Groups," *The Journal of Creative Behavior* 27, no. 3 (1993): 171–187.

37. J. J. Sosik, B. J. Avolio, and S. S. Kahai, "Inspiring Group Creativity: Comparing Anonymous and Identified Electronic Brainstorming," *Small Group Research* 29 (1998): 3–31.

38. G. Philipsen, M. Mulac, and D. Dietrich, "The Effects of Social Interaction on Group Generation of Ideas," *Communication Monographs* 46 (June 1979): 119–125; F. M. Jablin, "Cultivating Imagination: Factors That Enhance and Inhibit Creativity in Brainstorming Groups," *Human Communication Research* 7, no. 3 (Spring 1981): 245–258; S. Jarboe, "A Comparison of Input-Output, Process-Output, and Input-Process Output Models of Small Group Problem-Solving Effectiveness," *Communication Monographs* 55 (June 1988): 121–142. The idea of incorporating individual or silent brainstorming into the traditional brainstorming approach emerges from the nominal-group technique suggested by Delbecq, Van de Ven, and Gustafson, *Group Techniques for Program Planning*, 7–16; see also S. Jarboe, "Enhancing Creativity in Groups: Theoretical Boundaries and Pragmatic Limitations." Paper presented at the annual meeting of the Speech Communication Association, Atlanta, Georgia, November 1, 1991; F. M. Jablin and D. R. Seibold, "Implications for Problem-Solving Groups of Empirical Research on 'Brainstorming': A Critical Review of the Literature," *Southern Speech Communication Journal,* 43 (1978): 324–356; Philipsen, Mulac, and Dietrich, "The Effects of Social Interaction"; VanGundy, *Techniques of Structured Problem Solving*; J. A. Goncalo and B. M. Staw, "Individualism-Collectivism and Group Creativity," *Organizational Behavior and Human Decision Processes* 100 (2006): 96–109.

39. D. Stewart, C. Stewart, and J. Walden, "Self-Reference Effect and the Group-Reference Effect in the Recall of Shared and Unshared Information in Nominal Groups and Interacting Groups," *Group Processes & Intergroup Relations* 10, no. 3 (2007): 323–339.

40. E. Rietzschel, B. Nijstad, and W. Stroebe, "Productivity Is Not Enough: A Comparison of Interactive and Nominal Brainstorming Groups on Idea Generation and Selection," *Journal of Experimental Social Psychology* 42 (2006): 244–251.

41. H. Barki and A. Pinsonneault, "Small Group Brainstorming and Idea Quality: Is Electronic Brainstorming the Most Effective Approach?" *Small Group Research* 32, no. 2 (2001): 158–205.

42. D. H. Gustafson, R. K. Shukla, A. Delbecq, and G. W. Walster, "A Comparative Study of Differences in Subjective Likelihood Estimates Made by Individuals, Interacting Groups, Delphi Groups and Nominal Groups," *Organizational Behavior and Human Performance* 9 (1973): 280–291; VanGundy, *Techniques of Structural Problem Solving*; see also S. Beebe and J. Masterson, *Communicating in Small Groups: Principles and Practices* 9e (Boston: Allyn & Bacon, 2009).

43. Jarboe, "A Comparison of Input-Output, Process-Output, and Input-Process-Output Models"; Rietzschel, Nijstad, and Stroebe, "Productivity Is Not Enough."

44. Delbecq, Van de Ven, and Gustafson, *Group Techniques for Program Planning*.

45. K. L. Dugosh, P. B. Paulus, E. J. Roland, and H. C. Yang, "Cognitive Stimulation in Brainstorming," *Journal of Personality and Social Psychology* 79, no. 5 (2000): 722–735.

46. M. C. Roy, S. Gauvin, and M. Limayam, "Electronic Group Brainstorming: The Role of Feedback on Productivity," *Small Group Research* 27 (1996): 215–247.

47. Sosik, Avolio, and Kahai, "Inspiring Group Creativity"; W. H. Cooper, R. B. Gallupe, S. Pollard, and J. Cadsby, "Some Liberating Effects of Anonymous Electronic Brainstorming," *Small Group Research* 29 (1998): 147–177.

48. M. C. Roy, S. Gauvin, and M. Limayam, "Electronic Group Brainstorming: The Role of Feedback on Productivity," *Small Group Research* 27 (1996): 215–247; also see C. E. Timmerman and C. R. Scott, "Virtually Working: Communicative and Structural Predicators of Media Use and Key Outcomes in Virtual Work Teams," *Communication Monographs* 73 (2006): 108–136.

49. Erich Witte, "Toward a Group Facilitation Technique for Project Teams," *Group Processes & Intergroup Relations* 10, no. 3 (2007): 299–309.

50. F. Niederman and R. J. Volkema, "The Effects of Facilitator Characteristics on Meeting Preparation, Set Up, and Implementation," *Small Group Research* 30 (1990): 330–360.

51. Material in this box adapted from L. Schloff and M. Yudkin, *Smart Speaking: Sixty-Second Strategies for More Than 100 Speaking Problems and Fears* (New York: Plume, 1992).

52. U. Klocke, "How to Improve Decision Making in Small Groups—Effects of Dissent and Training Interventions," *Small Group Research* 38, no. 3 (2007): 437–468.

53. D. Matz and W. Wood, "Cognitive Dissonance in Groups: The Consequences of Disagreement," *Journal of Personality and Social Psychology* 88, no. 1 (2005): 22–37.

54. J. F. Veiga, "The Frequency of Self-Limiting Behavior in Groups: A Measure and an Explanation," *Human Relations* 44 (1991): 877–895; S. Shulz-Hardt, F. C. Brodbeck, A. Mojzisch, R. Kerschreiter, and D. Frey, "Group Decision Making in Hidden Profile Situations: Dissent as a Facilitator for Decision Quality,' *Journal of Personality and Social Psychology* 91, no. 6 (2006): 1080–1093.

55. R. Y. Hirokawa, D. S. Gouran, and A. Martz, "Understanding the Sources of Faulty Group Decision Making: A Lesson from the *Challenger* Disaster," *Small Group Research* 19, no. 4 (November 1988): 411–433.

56. I. L. Janis, "Groupthink," *Psychology Today* 5 (November 1971): 43–46, 74–76.

57. D. Seibold and R. Meyers, "Group Argument—A Structuration Perspective and Research Program," *Small Group Research* 38, no. 3 (2007): 312–336.

58. A. Gurtner, F. Tschan, N. Semmer, and C. Nagele, "Getting Groups to Develop Good Strategies: Effects of Reflexivity Interventions on Team Process, Team Performance, and Shared Mental Models," *Organizational Behavior and Human Decision Processes* 102 (2007): 127–142.

59. K. Sager and J. Gastil, "The Origins and Consequences of Consensus Decision Making: A Test of the Social Consensus Model," *Southern Communication Journal* 71, no. 1 (2006): 1–24.

60. M. C. Roy, S. Gauvin, and M. Limayem, "Electronic Group Brainstorming: The Role of Feedback on Productivity," *Small Group Research* 27 (1996): 21–47.

61. Mosvick and Nelson, *We've Got to Start Meeting Like This!*

62. A. Weitzel and P. Geist, "Parliamentary Procedure in a Community Group: Communication and Vigilant Decision Making," *Communication Monographs* 65 (1998): 244–259.

63. K. W. Hawkins and B. P. Fillion, "Perceived Communication Skill Needs for Work Groups," *Communication Research Reports* 16 (1999): 467–474.

Chapter 11

1. E. Ross and A. Holland, "eBay," *100 Great Businesses and the Minds Behind Them* (Naperville, IL: Sourcebooks, 2006), 248–250.

2. T. Jeary, *Life Is a Series of Presentations* (New York: Simon and Schuster, 2004).

3. D. C. Bryant, "Rhetoric: Its Functions and Its Scope," *Quarterly Journal of Speech* 39 (December 1953): 26.

4. Survey conducted by R. H. Bruskin and Associates, *Spectra* 9 (December 1973): 4; D. Wallechinsky, I. Wallace, and A. Wallace, *The People's Almanac Presents the Books of Lists* (New York: Morrow, 1977).

5. S. B. Butterfield, "Instructional Interventions for Situational Anxiety and Avoidance," *Communication Education* 37 (1988): 214–223; also see M. Motley, *Overcoming Your Fear of Public Speaking: A Proven Method* (New York: McGraw-Hill, 1995).

6. J. Ayres and T. S. Hopf, "The Long-Term Effect of Visualization in the Classroom: A Brief Research Report," *Communication Education* 39 (1990): 75–78; J. Ayres and T. K. Wongprasert, "Measuring the Impact of Visualization on Mental Imagery: Comparing Prepared Versus Original Drawings," *Communication Research Reports* 20 (Winter 2003): 45–53.

7. J. Burk, "Communication Apprehension Among Master's of Business Administration Students: Investigating a Gap in Communication Education," *Communication Education* 50 (January 2001): 51–58; L. Kelly and J. A. Keaten, "Treating Communication Anxiety: Implications of the Communibiological Paradigm," *Communication Education* 49 (January 2000): 45–57; A. N. Finn, C. R. Sawyer, and R. R. Behnke, "Audience-Perceived Anxiety Patterns of Public Speakers," *Communication Education* 51 (Fall 2003): 470–481.

8. M. Porhola, "Orientation Styles in a Public-Speaking Context," paper presented at the National Communication Association convention, Seattle, Washington, November 2000; R. R. Behnke and M. J. Beatty, "A Cognitive-Physiological Model of Speech Anxiety," *Communication Monographs* 48 (1981): 158–163; P. Addison, E. Clay, S. Xie, C. R. Sawyer, and R. R. Rehnke, "Worry as a Function of Public Speaking State Anxiety Type," *Communication Reports* 16 (Summer 2003): 125–131.

9. A. M. Bippus and J. A. Daly, "What Do People Think Causes Stage Fright? Naïve Attribution About the Reasons for Public-Speaking Anxiety," *Communication Education* 48 (1999): 63–72; also see D. C. Duff, T. R. Levine, M. J. Beatty, J. Woolbright, and H. Sun Park, "Testing Public Anxiety Treatments Against a Credible Placebo Control," *Communication Education* 56 (January 2007): 72–88.

10. L. Fletcher, *How to Design & Deliver Speeches* (New York: Longman, 2001): 3.

11. R. R. Behnke and Chris R. Sawyer, "Public-Speaking Procrastination as a Correlate of Public-Speaking Communication Apprehension and Self-Perceived Public-Speaking Competence," *Communication Research Reports* 16 (1999): 40–47.

12. P. D. MacIntyre and J. R. MacDonald, "Public-Speaking Anxiety: Perceived Competence and Audience Congeniality," *Communication Education* 47 (October 1998): 359–365.

13. J. Ayers and T. S. Hopf, "Visualization: A Means of Reducing Speech Anxiety," *Communication Education* 34 (1985): 318–323; J. Ayres and B. L. Heuett, "An Examination of the Impact of Performance Visualization," *Communication Research Reports* 16 (1999): 29–39.

14. Addison, Clay, Xie, Sawyer, and Behnke, "Worry as a Function of Public Speaking State Anxiety Type."

15. MacIntyre and MacDonald, "Public-Speaking Anxiety"; P. D. MacIntyre and K. A. Thivierge, "The Effects of Audience Pleasantness, Audience Familiarity, and Speaking Contexts on Public-Speaking Anxiety and Willingness to Speak," *Communication Quarterly* 43 (1995): 456–466; P. D. MacIntyre, K. A. Thivierge, and J. Renee MacDonald, "The Effects of Audience Interest, Responsiveness, and Evaluation on Public-Speaking Anxiety and Related Variables," *Communication Research Reports* 14 (1997): 457–468.

16. MacIntyre and MacDonald, "Public-Speaking Anxiety"; R. B. Rubin, A. M. Rubin, and F. F. Jordan, "Effects of Instruction on Communication Apprehension and Communication Competence," *Communication Education* 46 (1997): 104–114.

17. The late W. Braden, long-time professor of speech communication at Louisiana State University, presented a memorable speech at the 1982 Florida Speech Communication Association in which he emphasized "the audience writes the speech" to indicate the importance and centrality of being an audience-centered speaker.

18. D. P. Boman, *Presentations: Proven Techniques for Creating Presentations That Get Results* (Avon, MA: Adams Media Corporation, 1998).

19. For an excellent discussion of how to adapt to specific audience situations, see J. Sprague and D. Stuart, *The Speaker's Handbook* (Belmont, CA: Thompson, 2007), 345.

20. See D. A. Lieberman, *Public Speaking in the Multicultural Environment* (Boston: Allyn and Bacon, 1997).

21. D. P. Starr, "Writing for the Web," *Vital Speeches of the Day* 73, no. 6 (2007): 269–270.

Chapter 12

1. T. Jeary, *Life Is a Series of Presentations* (New York: Simon and Schuster, 2004), 149.
2. F. E. X. Dance, *Speaking Your Mind: Private Thinking and Public Speaking* (Dubuque, IA: Kendall/Hunt Publishing Company, 1994).
3. These criteria for evaluating web resources are adapted from J. Alexander and M. A. Tate, "How to Recognize an Informational Web Page," 1996–2005, Wolfgram Memorial Library, Widener University. Retrieved March 25, 2009, from http:www3.widener.edu/Academics/Libraries/Wolfgram_Memorial_Library/Evaluate_Web_Pages/Checklist_for_an_Information_Web_Page/5720.
4. T. Longaberger, "Leading," *Vital Speeches of the Day* 73, no. 8 (2007): 347–348.
5. A. W. Herbert, "Your Part in History," *Vital Speeches of the Day* 72, no. 12 (2006): 376–378.
6. S. Trujillo, "Now That the Dog Has Caught the Bus—What Next?" *Vital Speeches of the Day* 72, no. 20/21 (2006): 589–590.
7. J. C. Humes, *The Sir Winston Method: The Five Secrets of Speaking the Language of Leadership* (New York: William Morrow and Company, Inc., 1991), 137.
8. M. Blakey, "The Unexpected," *Vital Speeches of the Day* 72, no. 10 (2006): 318–320.
9. N. Volkow, "Drug Addiction," *Vital Speeches of the Day* 72, no. 16/17 (2006): 505–508.
10. W. B. Harrison, Jr., "Challenges and Opportunities in a Globalizing World," *Vital Speeches of the Day* 72, no. 13 (2006): 400–404.
11. Adapted from M. Klepper and R. Gunther, *I'd Rather Die Than Give a Speech* (New York: Carol Publishing Group, 1995).
12. E. Wolff, *Winning Orations 1994* (Mankato, MN: Interstate Oratorical Association, 1994), 67.
13. R. L. Weaver II, "Sticky Ideas," *Vital Speeches of the Day* 73, no. 8 (2007): 353–356.
14. F. Karakas, "Noah's Pudding," *Vital Speeches of the Day* 72, no. 12 (2006): 369–373.
15. D. Gallagher, "Understanding World Is Key," *Austin American-Statesman* (July 24 1996), Letter to the Editor.
16. K.C. Jones, "Social Networking Site Hi5 Nearly Doubles Monthly Visitors," *Information Week* (August 15, 2008). Retrieved March 25, 2009, from http://www.informationweek.com/news/internet/social_network/showArticle.jhtml?articleID=210100252.
17. As cited by G. Kolata, "Study Shows Why the Flu Likes Winter," *The New York Times* (December 5, 2007): 1.
18. M. F. Curtin, "Media and the Degradation of Language," *Vital Speeches of the Day* 72, no. 20/21 (2006): 578–580.
19. M. Kushner, *Successful Presentations for Dummies: A Reference for the Rest of Us* (Foster City, CA: IDG Books, 1997), 66.
20. D. A. Lieberman, *Public Speaking in the Multicultural Environment* 2e (Boston: Allyn and Bacon, 1997), 23.
21. Lieberman, *Public Speaking in the Multicultural Environment*, 23.
22. Harrison, "Challenges and Opportunities in a Globalizing World"
23. A. Lincoln, "Gettysburg Address," delivered at Gettysburg, PA, November 19, 1863. Douglass Archives of American Public Address. Retrieved July 12, 1999, from http://www.gettysburg.com/bog/address.htm.
24. D. MacArthur, "Farewell to the Cadets," address delivered at West Point, May 12, 1962. Reprinted in *Contemporary American Speeches* 7e, edited by R. L. Johannesen, R. R. Allen, and W. A. Linkugel (Dubuque, IA: Kendall/Hunt, 1992), 393.
25. M. L. King, Jr., "I Have a Dream," delivered in Washington, DC, August 28, 1963. Reprinted in *Contemporary American Speeches*, edited by R. L. Johannesen, R. R. Allen, and W. A. Linkugel (Dubuque, IA: Kendall/Hunt, 1992), 369.
26. J. McNerney, "Secrets of High-Performing Executive Teams," *Vital Speeches of the Day* 72, no. 11 (2006): 349–352.

Chapter 13

1. A. H. Monroe, "Measurement and Analysis of Audience Reaction to Student Speakers' Studies in Attitude Changes," *Bulletin of Purdue University Studies in Higher Education* 22 (1937). For an excellent discussion of the importance of speaker delivery as discussed by both classical and contemporary rhetoricians, see J. Fredal, "The Language of Delivery and the Presentation of Character: Rhetorical Action in Demosthenes' 'Against Medias,'" *Rhetoric Review* 20 (2001): 251–267.
2. P. Heinbert, "Relationship of Content and Delivery to General Effectiveness," *Speech Monographs* 30 (1963): 105–107.
3. A. Mehrabian, *Nonverbal Communication* (Hawthorne, NY: Aldine, 1972).
4. J. C. Humes, *The Sir Winston Method: The Five Secrets of Speaking the Language of Leadership* (New York: William Morrow, 1991), 160.
5. Adapted from R. Ailes, *You Are the Message* (New York: Doubleday, 1989), 37–38.
6. Humes, *The Sir Winston Method*.
7. Humes, *The Sir Winston Method*.
8. S. A. Beebe, "Eye Contact: A Nonverbal Determinant of Speaker Credibility," *Speech Teacher* 23 (1974): 21–25; S. A. Beebe, "Effects of Eye Contact, Posture, and Vocal Inflection Upon Credibility and Comprehension," *Australian Scan Journal of Nonverbal Communication* 7–8 (1979–1980): 57–70; M. Cobin, "Response to Eye Contact," *Quarterly Journal of Speech* 48 (1963): 415–419.
9. Beebe, "Eye Contact."
10. Beebe, "Eye Contact."
11. M. J. Beatty, "Some Effects of Posture on Speaker Credibility," library paper, Central Missouri State University, 1973.
12. P. Ekman, W. V. Friesen, and S. S. Tomkins, "Facial Affect Scoring Technique: A First Validity Study," *Semiotica* 3 (1971).
13. P. Ekman and W. Friesen, *Unmasking the Face* (Englewood Cliffs, NJ: Prentice-Hall, Inc., 1975).
14. Ekman and Friesen, *Unmasking the Face*.
15. Adapted from S. A. Beebe and S. J. Beebe, *Public Speaking: An Audience-Centered Approach* 7e (Boston: Allyn & Bacon, 2008).
16. M. M. Gill, "Accent and Stereotypes: Their Effect on Perceptions of Teachers and Lecture Comprehension," *Journal of Applied Communication* 22 (1994): 348–361.
17. K. K. Sereno and G. J. Hawkins, "The Effects of Variations in Speakers' Nonfluency upon Audience Ratings of Attitude toward the Speech Topic and Speakers' Credibility," *Speech Monographs* 34 (1967): 58–74; G. R. Miller and M. A. Hewgill, "The Effect of Variations in Nonfluency on Audience Ratings of Source Credibility," *Quarterly Journal of Speech* 50 (1964): 36–44; A. Mehrabian and M. Williams, "Nonverbal Concomitants of Perceived and Intended Persuasiveness," *Journal of Personality and Social Psychology,* 13 (1969): 37–58.
18. J. W. Neuliep, *Intercultural Communication: A Contextual Approach* (Boston: Houghton Mifflin, 2000), 247.
19. As reported by M. Kushner, *Successful Presentations for Dummies: A Reference for the Rest of Us* (Foster City, CA: IDG Books, 1997), 261.
20. B. Filson, *Executive Speeches: Tips on How to Write and Deliver Speeches from 51 CEOs* (New York: John Wiley & Sons, Inc., 1994).
21. Filson, *Executive Speeches*.
22. E. Ross and A. Holland, "Subway," *100 Greatest Businesses and the Minds Behind Them.* (Naperville, IL: Sourcebooks, Inc., 2006): 388–391.
23. E. Bohn and D. Jabusch, "The Effect of Four Methods of Instruction on the Use of Visual Aids in Speeches," *The Western Journal of Speech Communication* 46 (Summer 1982): 253–265.
24. M. E. Patterson, D. F. Dansereau, and D. Newbern, "Effects of Communication Aids and Strategies on Cooperative Teaching," *Journal of Educational Psychology* 84 (1992): 453–461.

25. S. Roberts, *Who We Are Now* (New York: Times Books, 2004), 50.

26. "One Day in America," *Time* (November 2007): 44.

27. Roberts, *Who We Are Now*, 42.

28. Roberts, *Who We Are Now*, 244.

29. For a good discussion of how to develop and use PowerPoint visuals, see J. Weissman, *Presenting to Win: The Art of Telling Your Story* (Upper Saddle River, NJ: Financial Times/Prentice-Hall, 2003).

30. B. M. Gayle, R. W. Preiss, N. Burrell, and M. Allen, *Classroom Communication and Instructional Processes* (Mahwah, NJ: Lawrence Erlbaum, 2006), 62–74.

31. See D. Cyphert, "The Problem of PowerPoint: Visual Aid or Visual Rhetoric?" *Business Communication Quarterly* (March 2004): 80–84; R. E. Mayer and V. K. Sims, "For Whom Is a Picture Worth a Thousand Words? Extensions of a Dual-Coding Theory of Multimedia Learning" *Journal of Educational Psychology* 86 (1994): 389–401.

32. We acknowledge D. Cavanaugh's excellent supplement *Preparing Visual Aids for Presentations* (Boston: Allyn and Bacon/Longman, 2001) as a source for many of our tips and suggestions.

Chapter 14

1. J. C. Humes, *The Sir Winston Method: The Five Secrets of Speaking the Language of Leadership* (New York: William Morrow, 1991), 58.

2. M. Knowles, *Self-Directed Learning* (Chicago: Follett Publishing, 1975).

3. R. E. Flax, "A Manner of Speaking," *Ambassador* (May-June 1991): 37.

4. R. J. Rivera and H. Paradise, "2006 State of the Industry Report," *American Society for Training & Development* (2007).

5. S. A. Beebe, T. P. Mottet, and K. D. Roach, *Training and Development: Enhancing Communication and Leadership Skills* (Boston: Allyn & Bacon, 2004).

6. Beebe, Mottet, and Roach. *Training and Development*.

7. A. Maslow, "A Theory of Human Motivation," in *Motivation and Personality* (New York: Harper & Row, 1954), Chapter 5.

8. See I. L. Janis and S. Feshback, "Effects of Fear Arousing Communications," *Journal of Abnormal and Social Psychology* 48 (January 1953): 78–92; F. A. Powell and G. R. Miller, "Social Approval and Disapproval Cues in Anxiety Arousing Situations," *Speech Monographs* 34 (June 1967): 152–159; K. L. Higbee, "Fifteen Years of Fear Arousal: Research on Threat Appeals, 1953–1968," *Psychological Bulletin* 72 (December 1969): 426–444.

9. Aristotle, *The Art of Rhetoric*.

10. D. A. Lieberman, *Public Speaking in the Multicultural Environment* 2e (Boston: Allyn & Bacon, 1997), 23.

11. A. Bogeajis, "The Danger of Child Safety Seats: Why Aren't They Safe?" *Winning Orations 1996* (Mankato, MN: Interstate Oratorical Association, 1996), 10.

12. D. Ehninger, B. E. Gonbeck, R. E. McKerrow, and A. H. Monroe, *Principles and Types of Speech Communication* (Glenview, IL: Scott, Foresman, 1986), 15.

13. R. L. Kotcher, "Join the Conversation." *Vital Speeches of the Day* 72, no. 18/19 (2006): 541–543.

14. Kotcher, "Join the Conversation."

15. Kotcher, "Join the Conversation."

16. Kotcher, "Join the Conversation."

17. Kotcher, "Join the Conversation."

18. D. C. Bryant, "Rhetoric: Its Functions and Its Scope," *Quarterly Journal of Speech* 39, no. 4 (December 1953): 26.

19. E. Ross and A. Holland, "Red Bull: Taste Doesn't Always Matter," *100 Greatest Businesses and the Minds Behind Them* (Naperville, IL: Sourcebooks, Inc., 2006), 28–29.

20. In addition to using the motivated sequence, our suggestions for organizing a sales presentation are based on strategies discussed in D. DiResta, *Knockout Presentations: How to Deliver Your Message with Power, Punch, and Pizzazz* (Worcester, MA: Chandler House Press, 1998), 166–171.

21. C. Pearlman, "Oscar Speeches: Statues in Their Hands, Feet in Their Mouths," *Austin American-Statesman* 24 (March 1997): E8.

22. W. Faulkner, acceptance of the Nobel Prize for Literature, December 10, 1950, in *A Treasury of the World's Great Speeches*, edited by H. Peterson (New York: Simon & Schuster, 1965), 815.

23. "Slainte! Toasts, Blessings, and Sayings." Retrieved June 28, 1998, from http://zinnia.umfacad.maine.edu/~donaghue/toasts07.html.

24. S. Husberg, "A Wedding Toast," in *Allyn & Bacon Video II User's Guide*, edited by T. Van Horn, L. Charron, and M. Charron. (Boston: Allyn & Bacon, 2002).

Appendix A

1. This appendix was written by Katrina D. Newell, under the direction of Timothy Mottet. Ms. Newell teaches in the Department of Communication at the University of Texas–Pan American, Edinburg, Texas.

2. L. Barker, R. Edwards, C. Gaines, K. Gladney, and F. Holley, "An Investigation of Proportional Time Spent in Various Communication Activities by College Students," *Journal of Applied Communication* 8 (1980): 101–110.

3. F. Tortorici, "Most Young People Entering the US Workforce Lack Critical Skills for Success," press release, The Conference Board, October 2, 2006. Retrieved June 12, 2008 from http://www.conference-board.org/utilities/pressDetail.cfm?press_ID=2971.

4. J. Sturges, R. Simpson, and Y. Altman, "Capitalising on Learning: An Exploration of the MBA as a Vehicle for Developing Career Competencies," *International Journal of Training and Development* 7 (2003): 53–66.

5. R. Ettison and J. Knowles, "Speaking in Tongues," *MIT Sloan Management Review* 47 (2006): 99–108.

6. J. Gordon, "Best (Hiring) Practices," *Business Week Online*, August 10, 2006. Retrieved June 12, 2008 from http://www.businessweek.com/careers/content/aug2006/ca20060810_662254.htm.

7. G. J. Alred, C. T. Brusaw, and W. E. Oliu, *The Business Writer's Companion* 4e (Boston: Bedford/St. Martin's, 2005).

8. *Webster's New Collegiate Dictionary* (Springfield, MA: Merriam, 1979), 216.

9. J. Gastil, "Generic Pronouns and Sexist Language: The Oxymoronic Character of Masculine Generics," *Sex Roles* 23 (1990): 629–643; M. C. Hamilton, "Masculine Bias in the Attribution of Personhood: People = Male, Male = People," *Psychology of Women Quarterly* 15 (1991): 393–402; J. Y. Switzer, "The Impact of Generic Word Choices: An Empirical Investigation of Age- and Sex-Related Differences," *Sex Roles* 22 (1990): 69–82; W. Todd-Mancillas, "Masculine Generics—Sexist Language: A Review of Literature and Implications for Speech Communication Professionals," *Communication Quarterly* 29 (1981): 107–115.

10. J. Wood, *Gendered Lives: Communication, Gender, and Culture*. 8e. (Belmont, CA: Wadsworth, 2008).

11. S. B. Gmelch, *Gender on Campus: Issues for College Women* (New Brunswick, NJ: Rutgers University Press, 1998); Wood, *Gendered Lives*.

12. I. Selvarajah, "Overusing Business Buzzwords," GenerationY Consultant, March 31, 2008. Retrieved April 7, 2009 from http://genyconsultant.com/2008/03/overusing-business-buzzwords.html.

13. Alred, Brusaw, and Oliu, *The Business Writer's Companion*.

14. J. H. Siess, "The Most Common Spelling Errors," Ezine Articles, October 22, 2007. Retrieved June 10, 2008 from http://ezinearticles.com/?The-Most-Common-Spelling-Errors&id=794024.

15. Alred, Brusaw, and Oliu, *The Business Writer's Companion.*

16. J. O'Malley, "Quiz—Are You Smarter Than a Spell-Checker?" Pongo Resume Online, April 29, 2008. Retrieved June 30, 2008 from http://www.pongoresume.com/blogPosts/146/quiz-are-you-smarter-than-a-spell-checker.

17. S. A. Hewlett, "Is Your Blackberry Lowering Your IQ?" Harvard Business Online, September 20, 2007. Retrieved February 13, 2008 from http://www.businessweek.com/managing/content/sep2007/ca20070920_461254.htm?chan=search.

18. L. Stack, "Use Proper Email Netiquette to Avoid Wasting Others' Time," ArticleCity, December 15, 2005. Retrieved February 15, 2008 from http://www.articlecity.com/articles/computers_and_internet/article_2117.shtml.

19. Stack, "Use Proper Email Netiquette to Avoid Wasting Others' Time."

20. Alred, Brusaw, and Oliv, *The Business Writer's Companion.*

21. J. Bear and M. Bear, *Complaint Letters for Busy People* (Boston: Career Press, 2000).

22. Alred, Brusaw, and Oliu, *The Business Writer's Companion.*

23. C. Bovee, J. Thill, and B. Schatzman, *Business Communication Today* 7e (Upper Saddle River, NJ: Prentice Hall, 2003).

24. D. Seibert, "Legal Precautions When Writing Proposals," The Siebert Group, December 17, 2007. Retrieved May 29, 2008 from http://www.persuasionselling.com/LegalPrecautions.htm.

25. Bovee, Thill, and Schatzman, *Business Communication Today.*

26. Alred, Brusaw, and Oliu, *The Business Writer's Companion.*

27. M. Mandel, "The Real Reason You're Working So Hard . . . and What You Can Do About It." *Business Week*, October 3, 2005. Retrieved February 5, 2008 from http://www.businessweek.com/magazine/content/05_40/b3953601.htm?chan=search.

28. R. H. Lengel and R. L. Daft, "The Selection of Communication Media as an Executive Skill," *Academy of Management Executive 2* (1988): 225–232.

29. Adapted from Lengel and Daft, "The Selection of Communication Media as an Executive Skill."

30. Lengel and Daft, "The Selection of Communication Media as an Executive Skill"; see also K. Stephens and T. P. Mottet, "Interactivity in a Web-Conferencing Learning Environment: Effects on Trainers and Trainees," *Communication Education 57* (2008): 88–104.

31. For more about how to match the message to the communication channel, see P. G. Clampitt, L. Berk, and M. L. Williams, "Leaders as Strategic Communicators," *Ivey Business Journal 66* (2002): 51–55; P. G. Clampitt and M. L. Williams, "Decision Downloading," *MIT Sloan Management Review 48* (2007): 77–82.

32. These ideas were taken from personal conversations with organizational communication scholar Phil Salem, Texas State University–San Marcos, January 17, 2008; see also P. Salem, *Organizational Communication and Change* (Cresskill, NJ: Hampton Press, 1996).

33. "We Don't Talk Anymore," press release, January 18, 2006. Retrieved February 7, 2008 from http://www.officeteam.com/PressRoom?id=1601.

34. K. Stephens, "The Successive Use of Information and Communication Technologies at Work," *Communication Theory 17* (2007): 486–507.

Appendix B

1. S. Winston, *The Organized Executive: The Classic Program for Productivity: New Ways to Manage Time, Paper, People, and the Digital Office* (New York: Warner Books, 2001).

2. A. McGee-Cooper, *Time Management for Unmanageable People* (New York: Bantam Books, 1994).

3. G. P. Latham and L. M. Saari, "The Importance of Union Acceptance for Productivity Improvement through Goal Setting," *Personnel Psychology 35*, no. 4 (1982): 781–787; G. P. Latham, T. R. Mitchell, and D. L. Dossett, "The Importance of Participative Goal Setting and Anticipated Rewards on Goal Difficulty and Job Performance," *Journal of Applied Psychology 62*, no. 2 (1978): 163–171; A. Tziner and R. Kopelman, "Effects of Rating Format on Goal-Setting Dimensions: A Field Experiment," *Journal of Applied Psychology 73*, no. 2 (1988): 323–326; A. Tziner and G. P. Latham, "The Effects of Appraisal Instrument, Feedback and Goal Setting on Worker Satisfaction and Commitment," *Journal of Organizational Behaviour 10*, no. 2 (1989): 145–153.

4. S. R. Covey, *The 7 Habits of Highly Effective People* (New York: Simon & Schuster, 1989).

5. S. Beebe, T. Mottet, and K. D. Roach, *Training and Development: Enhancing Communication and Leadership Skills* (Boston: Allyn & Bacon, 2004).

6. D. Allen, *Getting Things Done: The Art of Stress-Free Productivity* (New York: Viking, 2001).

7. S. Covey, A. R. Merrill, and R. R. Merrill, *First Things First* (New York: Fireside, 1996).

8. Covey, Merrill, and Merrill, *First Things First.*

9. Allen, *Getting Things Done.*

10. Allen, *Getting Things Done.*

11. Allen, *Getting Things Done.*

12. Allen, *Getting Things Done.*

13. M. J. Cook, *Time Management: Proven Techniques for Making the Most of Your Valuable Time* (Holbrook, MA: Adams Media, 1998); R. Alexander, *Commonsense Time Management* (New York: AMACOM, 1992).

14. Alexander, *Commonsense Time Management.*

Index

Photo Credits

Page 2, © Elaine Thompson/AP Images; 6, © Rubberball/Getty Images; 12, © Rob Lewine/Corbis; 14, © JupiterImages Royalty-Free/AP Images; 19, © Stan Honda/AFP/Getty Images; 25, © Ronaldo Schemidt/AFP/Getty Images; 28, © Corbis RF/JupiterImages; 32, © David Levenson/Alamy; 40, © John Giustina/Getty Images; 46, David Butow/Saba/Corbis; 51, © iStockphoto International; 53, © David Roth/Getty Images; 57, © Imaginechina/AP Images; 64, © Greg Nikas/Corbis; 69, © Jon Feingersh/Getty Images; 74, © Image Source/SuperStock; 85, Image Source/AP Images; 90, © Javier Larrea/AGE Fotostock; 93, © Mark Lennihan/AP Images; 103, © Helen King/Corbis; 110, © Reza Estakhrian/Getty Images; 117, © Eric Audras/AGE Fotostock; 127, © VEER Florian Franke/Getty Images; 136, © Purestock/Alamy; 142, © ONOKY RF/Getty Images; 149, © Simon Watson/Getty Images; 155, © Image Source/AGE Fotostock; 160, © Jeff Greenberg/PhotoEdit; 166, © Topic Photo Agency/AGE Fotostock; 178, © Jon Feingersh/zefa/Corbis; 181, © Lisette Le Bon/SuperStock; 185, © Creatas Images/JupiterImages; 191, © Stockbyte/Getty Images; 198, © Blend Images/SuperStock; 205, © Corbis RF/SuperStock; 213, © NASA; 218, © Bananastock/JupiterImages; 226, © Blend Images/Getty Images; 236, © Jim West/The Image Works; 240, © Topham/The Image Works; 248, © EyeWire Collection/Getty Images; 255, © Stewart Cohen/Getty Images; 263, © Fahad Shadeed/Reuters/Landov; 274, © Polka Dot Images/SuperStock; 277, © Stock Connection; 284, © Michael Rosenfeld/Getty Images; 287, © PictureNet/Corbis; 294, © Michael Newman/PhotoEdit; 302, © Christoph Dernbach/dpa/Landov; 309, © JupiterImages Royalty-Free/AP Images; 312, © David Paul Morris/Getty Images; 322, © Mario Tama/Getty Images; 331, © Ableimages/Getty Images; 334, © Pixland/AGE Fotostock; 337, © Bambu Productions/Getty Images; 340, © Jose Luis Pelaez/Corbis; 351, © Pixland/SuperStock; 357, © Jose Luis Pelaez/Corbis.